Art, Education, & African-American Culture

ALBERT BARNES
AND THE SCIENCE
OF PHILANTHROPY

Art, Education, &
African-American
Culture

MARY ANN MEYERS

WITH A NEW INTRODUCTION
BY THE AUTHOR

TRANSACTION PUBLISHERS
NEW BRUNSWICK (U.S.A.) AND LONDON (U.K.)

Third paperback printing 2009

Copyright © 2004 by Transaction Publishers, New Brunswick, New Jersey.

Library of Congress Catalog Number: 2003066263
ISBN: 978-1-4128-0563-6
Printed in the United States of America

Library of Congress Cataloging-in-Publication Data

Art, education, and African-American culture : Albert Barnes and the science
    of philanthropy / Mary Ann Meyers.
        p. cm.
    Includes bibliographical references and index.
    ISBN 0-7658-0214-7 (alk. paper)
        1. Barnes, Albert C. (Albert Coombs), 1872-1951. 2. Art—Collectors
    and collecting—Pennsylvania—Biography. 3. Barnes, Albert C. (Albert
    Coombs), 1872-1951—Knowledge—African American arts. I. Title.

N5220.B28M49 2003
709'.2—dc22
[B]   2003066263

For
Clarice Mildred Daniel Dye
1908-1999
and
Her Great-Granddaughter
Sydney Morgan Kasmer

Contents

Illusrations follow page 172

Introduction to the Paperback Edition

The future of the Barnes Foundation is no longer in the hands of its creator. Through an exceedingly detailed Indenture of Trust, Albert Coombs Barnes exercised significant control over its operations for more than a half-century after his death. But a long-awaited judicial decision approving the petition of the Foundation's board to relocate the world-class art collection eliminated the strictures that, for good or ill, had long been in place. The paintings can be moved to Philadelphia from Merion, Pennsylvania, the Main Line suburb where they have resided since Barnes assembled them. The sky hasn't fallen, but Judge Stanley Ott's December 2004 ruling, which gave public interest precedence over the stipulations of the Foundation's governing documents, will have consequences cascading down the decades.[1]

It has been met with a few howls and a chorus of loud hosannas.[2] Let me put my own assessment bluntly. From the perspective of years of close attention to Barnes affairs, I applaud Judge Ott's decision on grounds of access, but lament its *weightlessness*, that is, the court's failure to seize the opportunity to re-enforce the idea that education is central to the Foundation's mission in language that could guide present and future Barnes trustees. The charter of the institution remains unchanged, but an opinion that underlined the pedagogical nature of Albert Barnes's grand experiment would have been welcomed by those, like me, who would be loath to see the Foundation morph into just another, albeit spectacular, museum. It is puzzling, moreover, that Judge Ott cited no Pennsylvania case law, including earlier judicial opinions related to the Foundation, in handing down his verdict on the lawfulness of relocation.[3] While he had previously taken a more conservative approach, this time around, he granted the petition of the Barnes trustees to make monumental modifications in the collector's Indenture on the basis of a permissive interpretation of the legal doctrine of deviation. The doctrine holds that a variation from the terms of a will or trust is allowed to avoid defeating the document's purpose. Judge Ott was persuaded that the philanthropic rescue tied, as it was, to a move to center city was the Foundation's best shot at avoiding financial collapse. But why he didn't attempt to anchor his ruling by tying it to legal reasoning in applicable cases, nor offer a fuller explanation of how it serves the public good, is a mystery.

Nearly a year earlier, the Pennsylvania jurist had agreed to an increase in the Barnes board to fifteen members. With permission to pull up stakes now the centerpiece of the bouquet he has presented to the Foundation's trustees, I believe change can be anticipated in both the experience of viewing the collection of masterworks and in the Barnes educational program. Whether they will be debased, as critics fear, or enhanced, as supporters hope, depends upon the vision of the Barnes leadership and of the three foundations that are financing the relocation of the Barnes treasures.

It also depends upon their understanding of and faithfulness to the aesthetic and pedagogical purposes that infused the long-running clinical trial undertaken by Barnes, a physician-scientist before he was an art collector. The story told here is about those intentions and the alliances and collaborations that flowed from them. Having written a narrative of the collector's life and offered an analysis of the events that coalesced to bring his Foundation to the brink of bankruptcy, my task in this brief introduction to the paperback edition of *Art, Education, and African-American Culture* is to recount and interpret the denouement of the drama.

From the bench in Montgomery County Orphans' Court, Judge Ott ruled in January 2004 that the Barnes could triple its five-member board, which during the subsequent year was reduced through the death of a trustee to four members. It was surely necessary for new trustees to understand the nature of the challenges facing them, so the delay in their election until after Jude Ott announced his decision on the petition to move the Foundation was reasonable even though the expanded board will have to face momentous decisions with little time to establish the trust in one another that might ease their burden.[4]

As so often in Barnes matters, however, the difficulty was in some measure self-imposed. At a four-day hearing in December 2003 on its petition deviate from the guidelines set down in Albert Barnes's Indenture of Trust, the Foundation provided so little evidence of how a move might work financially that the Orphans' Court judge admonished the petitioners to come back only when they had hard numbers. He agreed with them that the collector "could have foreseen neither the complicated, competitive, and sophisticated world in which nonprofits now operate, nor the range of expertise and influence that members of their governing bodies must now possess."[5] That the Barnes faced a financial crisis, he allowed had been proven beyond any doubt. But he also said the Foundation had produced insufficient evidence for him to rule on the central question of relocation. He directed the trustees and Kimberly Camp, the Barnes executive director, to ascertain whether a $50 million endowment could be raised by the sale of non-gallery artwork and/or Ker-Feal, property owned by the Foundation in Chester County. Judge Ott also insisted that they produce a detailed feasibility study and business plan, including projections for earned revenue, to enable him to assess whether $100 million to build a new facility and $50 million to replenish the endowment, monies pledged by three philanthropic foundations on the condition of a move to downtown Philadelphia, were enough to give the beleaguered Barnes a reasonable chance for survival.

The Pew Charitable Trusts and the Lenfest and Annenberg foundations paid for the requested studies and continued to foot the Barnes's legal bills during the next year, as well as contributing operating funds. For six days in late September of 2004, the Foundation was back in court along with three Barnes students to whom Judge Ott had granted the right to participate in the case on a limited basis as *amicus curiae* or "friends of the court." He had initially denied standing to another group of students, but reversed himself when Lincoln University dropped its objections to a Barnes plan for expanding the board and the Pennsylvania Attorney General said he supported the Foundation's petition (see chapter 17). The students' witnesses and their attorneys, who were allowed to cross-examine Foundation witnesses, were the only voices raised in the courtroom to oppose the moving of the Barnes collection. They challenged as lowball the Foundation's estimates of the likely sale price of its Chester County property and of certain paintings and pieces of sculpture not on display in the Merion gallery, notably *The Shepherdess* (*La Bergère*) by Gustave Courbet. They tried to show that a move and the Foundation's intention to operate three campuses would increase the precariousness of the Barnes's financial position. But at the heart of their concern was the conviction that transforming the Foundation into a museum by the act of relocation would have the effect, intended or not, of downgrading its educational mission to the point of extinction.

Witnesses for the Foundation sought to show that for $100 million, the Barnes gallery could be recreated inside a larger facility that would have additional space for classrooms and temporary exhibitions, as well as an auditorium and a gift shop. Estimates of the annual number of visitors (200,270 general visitors and 20,000 student visitors) and corresponding changes in income from admissions, licensing, merchandising, and gallery shop sales were presented along with projections for income from development efforts (membership fees, special events, and an aggressive annual giving campaign totaling $4.25 million a year) and investments ($2.5 million annually). With an annual operating budget of $12,275,000 for the opening year and $11.3 million for the two years thereafter, the bottom line, according to the Barnes, was that it could maintain: one, a downtown gallery where most teaching would take place; two, the original Merion campus, which in addition to the arboretum would house administrative offices and archives and provide a place to view art not now on display; and three, Ker-Feal, which would become a living history center. All this—and still have a modest surplus each year.

The testimony of the Foundation's key witnesses, Camp and Watson, was critical. In response to questions from Judge Ott, the executive director emphasized her commitment to exactly replicating the Merion gallery, that is, the ensemble arrangement of paintings and decorative art objects created by Barnes to highlight thematic affinities. She said a Philadelphia gallery would be open seven days a week, including several evenings, to allow forty-two hours for public visitation and twenty-seven hours for exclusive use by students. Watson reiterated an earlier statement to the court about the Mayor of Philadelphia's promise to provide a site on the Benjamin Franklin Parkway on which a new facility could be built. He stressed the board's conviction that relocation of the gallery was the least drastic alternative available to ensure the Foundation's survival.

Judge Ott was convinced. He accepted the Barnes's estimate of the yield from liquidating non-gallery art and selling Ker-Feal and concluded that the proceeds of some $20 million "would not halt the Foundation's downward financial spiral."[6] He ruled, moreover, that the Barnes had met the burden of proof on the cost of constructing a new facility and the feasibility of operating on three sites. Acknowledging that, "by many interested observers, permitting the gallery to move to Philadelphia will be viewed as an outrageous violation of the donor's trust," he cited a 1923 letter by the collector to his lawyer that he said led him to think otherwise. In the document, which was introduced into the court record by the Foundation, Barnes expressed concern about a statement in an affidavit prepared for the Internal Revenue Service that described the Barnes Foundation as "an art gallery for the education of the public." He agreed that "the education of the masses in art" would be its purpose after he was gone, but was loath to declare his hand. "I am building for the future," the collector wrote; "I want to guarantee my privacy, and I want to prepare the way for the gallery to be a public one after my death."[7] Judge Ott seized upon this single clue to the donor's intent (ignoring arguably contradictory ones), combined it with what he said was the Foundation's "absolute guarantee" that its formal education programs would be "preserved and, indeed, enhanced" as the result of relocation, and decided he "could sanction this bold new adventure with a clear conscience."[8]

But while granting every request of the Barnes board, including, in a later clarification of his decision, the right to hold fund-raising events for the Foundation and others in the proposed new building, sell any Barnes art that does not hang in the Merion gallery, mount special exhibitions of art not owned by the Foundation, and open any days and times the board chooses, Judge Ott expressed some skepticism about the Foundation's ability to meet its ambitious goals for raising money. Will what a witness for the Barnes characterized as "alpha donors" be there after the excitement wanes or should the economic climate worsen? Much depends on the cohesiveness and hard work of the Barnes board.

A day after Judge Ott announced his decision, Philadelphia Mayor John Street made good on his promise of land. The city will move the residents of a juvenile detention center, oddly situated on the Parkway between 20th and 21st Streets, and demolish the building so that the Barnes could conceivably start construction by early in 2008. The new gallery will be next door to the Rodin Museum, across the street from a proposed Calder Museum and from the Franklin Institute, and just over a half mile from the Philadelphia Museum of Art at the apex of the Parkway. All of these institutions will eventually compete with the Barnes for contributions. But public trust in the stability of the Foundation will certainly enhance its fund-raising potential.

Pew intends to collect, pool, and hold the $100 million pledged for the construction of the Barnes's new home. Its staff will scrutinize and pay invoices as they are submitted by the Foundation. With its philanthropic partners, Pew will take the lead in helping the new Barnes board to raise the $50 million or more sought for the Foundation's endowment. But the donor base need not be local given the international interest in the fabled collection generated by the world tour of selections from its masterworks in the mid-1990s. Nor is the dominant role in Barnes affairs of the Pew, Lenfest, and Annenberg foundations meant to be more than interim. It would be naïve, however, not to follow the money, and that trail suggests that its benefactors will have the power to shape the twenty-first-century Barnes Foundation.

If the journey undertaken on the following pages to try to understand the exceedingly complex Albert Barnes leads anywhere, it is to the conclusion that his overriding purpose was to carry out an educational experiment. He created not a museum but a school dedicated to furthering a particular aesthetic philosophy, one grounded in the pragmatism of his friend John Dewey. It was not art appreciation in any conventional sense, but its goal was to teach people to see how artists solved problems by analyzing certain formal qualities of paintings. The laboratory to which his students repaired to hone the skills they were learning happened to be a gallery housing a stunning installation of Impressionist, post-Impressionist, and early modern art along with rare African sculpture. The preservation of Barnes's legacy requires the preservation of his educational mission. Judge Ott could have, but did not, appoint someone or some group to try to monitor the Foundation's fidelity to it. So the task falls to the Barnes board, and it may, in the long run, dwarf the trustees' other challenges.

The importance of "getting it right" has been acknowledged by the Foundation and its philanthropic partners. But what exactly do they mean by *it*? To begin with, Pew played a major role in the selection of the new Barnes board. Under terms of the revised bylaws approved by the court, the Trusts exercised, on a one-time basis only, the right of reviewing nominations with the power to reject any that did not pass muster—and certainly they helped to identify most of the new trustees elected in 2005. Attentiveness by the Barnes and its backers to the selection of an architect for the center city facility can be taken for granted. "Designing museums has become a major, and perhaps the most prominent, concern of architecture during the last twenty-five years," Charles Rosen and Henri Zerner wrote in an essay on the re-creation of New York's Museum of Modern Art.[9] But to suit the Parkway setting, where a neighbor, the Free Library of Philadelphia, will have new wing designed by Moshe Safdie, and to successfully situate a replica of the Merion gallery within the new building will be immensely difficult. So, too, the hanging of the art in rooms of a different scale. Barnes determined the principles of presentation in the densely hung Merion gallery. They will be honored (although some critics of the move have suggested that decision be re-thought[10]), but retaining the original proportionality—the, to some eyes, exquisite relationship of one thing to another—in a larger space is daunting. A good starting point in designing the downtown home of the Barnes collection would be an honest facing up to what will be lost in the move: intimacy, historical context, and the exceeding complement the arboretum pays to the art.

What will be gained, at least potentially, besides a boost for Philadelphia's tourist industry, can be best evaluated by returning to the collector's purposes. The "plain people," who Barnes favored over the rich and famous, and to whom he reached out in the criteria he set for admission to his gallery, never lived in Merion. Nor do they live in Philadelphia's revitalized museum area. But they have a better chance of seeing his pictures in a building that is opened at night and can be reached by city bus than in Paul Cret's graceful château in the suburbs. The students to whom Barnes wanted so much to convey his ideas about art were youth of college age or men and women teaching in the public school system. St. Joseph's University has always been a block from the Foundation and several other colleges are only a short train ride distant. But despite a brief flirtation with Haverford and a three-decade-long, off-again on-again romance with his alma mater, the University of Pennsylvania in West Philadelphia, college students never took Barnes courses in substantial numbers. A Parkway site, however, means two art schools, Moore College of Art and Design and the Pennsylvania Academy of Fine Arts, are just blocks away; a bit further but still close is the University of the Arts; Penn and Drexel University are within two miles; and somewhat more distant are Temple and LaSalle universities. The Foundation has received American Council of Education approval of its courses as worthy of college credit. Teachers enrolled in them are able to count them toward continuing education requirements. Whatever the motivation of future students for taking classes at the Barnes, it is up to the board to ensure that they have suitable gallery time for study since Judge Ott approved the excising of a section of the original bylaws that mandated that the gallery be open five days a week exclusively for educational purposes. It is with the Barnes trustees and administrators, moreover, that responsibility rests for the rigor and authenticity of the curriculum. They alone can prove unwarranted the fears of former students that relocation will doom the educational enterprise to token status.

Judge Ott has ruled that the quirky genius, who had put together the collection of art that hung in Merion for more than fifty after his death, could not forever control all aspects of what he assembled with growing passion and rare discernment. But he acted in the belief that the changes he allowed, which are *radical* in both the political sense of "extreme" and the medical sense of "innovative," were consistent with the Indenture of Trust in law and in spirit. It is the burden of this book to illuminate the animating principles that set Albert Barnes on the bold course he held to with courage and tenacity.

November 2005

Notes

1. Judge Ott's decision did not go unchallenged. In an unusual exercise of its "King's Bench" powers, the Supreme Court of Pennsylvania agreed to consider an appeal of his ruling made by former Barnes student Jay Raymond who had been denied standing in the case by the Montgomery County Orphans' Court in 2003. Raymond made his appeal to the Superior Court in January 2005. Refusing a request of the Barnes Foundation to dismiss it, a three-judge panel agreed in March to rule not only on the issue of standing but, if it found in Raymond's favor, also on the merits of the December 2004 opinion that permitted relocation and a change in governing rules. The Foundation, later joined by Raymond, asked the Supreme Court for an expedited review. Its petition warned of a cash crisis by the end of the year because the appeal had delayed donors' payment of pledges and prompted the Pew Charitable Trusts and the Lenfest and Annenberg foundations to cut off the contributions they had been making to the Foundation's operating budget since the autumn of 2002. The Foundation said it anticipated that an intermediate review by the Superior Court would inevitably result in an appeal to the Commonwealth's highest court. But the legal uncertainty was soon over. In April, the Supreme Court dismissed Raymond's appeal after review of the record because it said he had waited too long to appeal Judge Ott's decision against him. Just before then, in an attempt to ease its financial situation in a period of transition, the Foundation decided to double its general admission ticket prices from $5 to $10, a price bringing it in line with other institutions displaying art. The three charities supporting its move to Philadelphia subsequently resumed their "bridge" funding.
2. See, for example, "The Barnes Foundation, RIP," *New Criterion*, January 2005, pp. 1-3 and Roberta Smith, "Does It Matter Where This Painting Hangs?," *New York Times*, December 15, 2004, Section E, pp. 1 and 7. Opponents of a move stress that permission to relocate isn't a mandate, and proclaiming their eagerness to have the Barnes Foundation stay in Merion, some neighbors of the Foundation, along with the Merion Civic Association, even proposed zoning changes to the Lower Merion Township Commission that would allow the Barnes to increase the number of visitors to the gallery on Latch's Lane.
3. See Jonathan Scott Goldman, "Just What the Doctor Ordered? The Doctrine of Deviation, the Case of Dr. Barnes's Trust and the Future Location of the Barnes Foundation," *Real Property, Probate and Trust Journal*, Winter 2005, pp. 711-764.
4. The term of Barnes President Bernard C. Watson expired at the end of 2004. Lincoln University, which under the new bylaws approved by Judge Ott, has the right to nominate five of the fifteen board members, declined to re-nominate him. It nominated Harold E. Doley, Jr., CEO of the investment firm Doley Securities, Inc., and

Andre V. Duggin, chairman and CEO of AV International, Inc., with the intention that they would take Watson's place and that of Jeff Donaldson who had died earlier in the year. Instead, the Barnes board, consisting of Stephen J. Harmelin, the managing partner of Dilworth Paxon, Jacqueline F. Allen, a judge in the Court of Common Pleas in Philadelphia, and Stephanie Bell-Rose, president of the Goldman Sachs Foundation, re-elected Watson and named him chairman once again. In January, the four-member board elected Doley and Duggin as well as Joseph Neubauer, CEO of ARAMARK Corp., Aileen Kennedy Roberts, the wife of Comcast CEO Brian L. Roberts and president of the Aileen and Brian Roberts Foundation, and Neil L. Rudenstine, the former president of Harvard University and chairman of the board of ARTstor. The nine-member board then elected Agnes Gund, president emerita of New York's Museum of Modern Art and a trustee of the J. Paul Getty Trust. Sheldon Bonovitz, chair and CEO of the Philadelphia law firm Duane Morris and a noted collector of "outsider" art, and Gwendolyn King, president of Podium Prose, a Washington speakers bureau and speechwriting service, were subsequently nominated by Lincoln and elected this past June. The now twelve-member Barnes board will choose three other members. On a one-time basis only, as previously agreed to by the Foundation and Montgomery County Orphans' Court, the Pew Charitable Trusts gave its blessing to Watson and the new trustees *before* votes were cast by the Barnes board.

5.   Memorandum Opinion and Order Sur Second Amended Petition to Amend Charter and Bylaws, Judge Stanley R. Ott, Montgomery County Court of Common Pleas, Orphans' Court Division, January 29, 2004, p. 24.
6.   Ibid., p. 26.
7.   Albert C. Barnes to Owen J. Roberts, 1923. Quoted in ibid, p. 18.
8.   Ibid., p. 28f.
9.   Charles Rosen and Henri Zerner, "Red-Hot MoMA," *New York Review of Books*, January 13, 2005, p. 18.
10.   See especially Edward J. Sozanski, "Perfect copy may not be perfect," *Philadelphia Inquirer*, December 19, 2004, Section H, pp. 1 and 8f.

Acknowledgements

My debts are greater than I can properly acknowledge, but it is my pleasure to list here at least some of the people who contributed so variously and immensely to this book. In the beginning, there were librarians and archivists. My research was launched in their lairs—at once places of refuge, which welcomed a writer needing to start somewhere and uncertain when or how her project would end, and treasure troves, which provided maps for the continuing journey. I thank Paul H. Mosher, former vice provost and director of libraries at the University of Pennsylvania, and the exceptional Penn library staff, particularly Nancy Shawcross, Lee Pugh, and Edward Deegan. Penn's archivist, Mark Frazier Lloyd, and his assistants were able guides through more than a quarter-century of records and correspondence. At the Langston Hughes Memorial Library at Lincoln University, Emery Wimbish, Jr., the librarian, and Khalil Mahmud, the former archivist, could not have been more helpful. I am also grateful to the directors and staff of various other repositories where I worked, or with which I corresponded, including: Anne Slater and Lorett Treese at the Canady Library, Bryn Mawr College; Robert Sanders at Central High School; Leo B. Slater at the Chemical Heritage Foundation; the College of Physicians of Philadelphia; Linnea M. Anderson at the Columbia University Archives; the Free Library of Philadelphia; Diane Peterson at the Magill Library, Haverford College; Joellen El Bashir at the Moorland-Spingarn Research Center, Howard University; Marcia Bass at the Ludington Library in Bryn Mawr, Pennsylvania; the Nantucket Atheneum; Cheryl A. Leibold at the Pennsylvania Academy of the Fine Arts; Louise Rossmasler at the Philadelphia Museum of Art; the Pierre Matisse Archives at the Pierpont Morgan Library; Elizabeth E. Fuller at the Rosenbach Museum and Library; Patricia F. Owen at the Esther Raushenbush Library and Archives, Sarah Lawrence College; the Archives of American Art at The Smithsonian Institution; David V. Koch at the Special Collections Research Center, Morris Library, Southern Illinois University, Carbondale; Margaret Jerrido at the Urban Archives, Temple University; Linda Seidman at the W. H. B. Du Bois Library, University of Massachusetts, Amherst; and the Beinecke Library, Yale University.

Many individuals contributed to my study by sharing with me memories and/or materials, particularly letters, related to the lives of Albert Barnes, Laura Barnes, and Violette de Mazia or to the Foundation that has so far survived them all. Jon D. Longaker entrusted me with the contents of an attic that he meticulously preserved for half a century. I am abidingly grateful to him. I also thank Roger Abrahams, Josephine Bachman, Marilyn Bauman, Julia Bond and her son, Julian Bond, the late J. Carter Brown, Elizabeth Cowitz, the late Roderick Chisholm, Joyce de Botton, Tony de Mazia, Anne d'Harnoncourt, Celeste Devereux, Marlene Dubin, James Ettelson, Richard Feigen, Selma Fishman, Charles Frank III, Nancy and Walter Herman, Gilbert High, Martin Kilson, Joseph Manko, Frances McCarthy, Irving Nahan, Richard Nenneman, David Rawson, Bea Robinson, Henrietta Rogers, the late Joanna Reed, Wendy Samat, Richard Segal, the late Harold Stassen, Niara Sudarkasa, Richard C. Torbert, the late Esther Van Zant, Robert Venturi, William Webster, and William Wixon.

Frederick S. Osborne, Nick Tinari, and Cuyler H. Walker not only shared their stories but also were kind enough to read portions of my manuscript and provide corrections, leads, and sources for further information. Other readers to whom I am especially indebted are Elijah Anderson, Renée C. Fox, Martin Meyerson, Franklyn Rodgers, and David Weinstein. Two people who read every word, and without whose help the manuscript would never have become a book, are Miki Mahoney and Irving Louis Horowitz. I am grateful to them—and also to Marilyn Allen, Nancy Grace, Coleen O'Shea, and Sarah Slavin for their indispensable encouragement. My thanks to Alexander Rementer for his consultation on computer matters, to Laurence Mintz, my editor at Transaction, and to two generous financial supporters: Patricia Murphy Gruber and the Maple Hill Foundation. Two other people to whom I owe and offer thanks, but in doing so must make explicit that I imply no endorsement on their parts of my book, are, first of all, Richard H. Glanton, the former president of the Barnes Foundation, and, second, Bernard C. Watson, the president as I bring my tale to a close.

Finally to my family—my children, Andrew and Kate, my son-in-law, Gary, and my husband, John—thank you for your good will, your tolerance, and your patience through the long years I spent researching and writing *Art, Education, and African-American Culture*. I take responsibility for any errors that have crept into these pages despite my best efforts and those of my editors. Learning to see takes a lifetime, and from my study of Albert Barnes and his Foundation, I have come to deeply appreciate that perception is situational—we all look at pictures from our own perspective.

Mary Ann Meyers
Wynnewood, Pennsylvania
September 2003

Introduction

Memories of the stirring melodies stayed with him. More than half a century after the eight-year-old white boy from Philadelphia first heard black men and women sing at a camp meeting in Merchantville, New Jersey, he spoke of the experience as mystical. Not only their songs but also their "movements as they wandered to and fro, their shouting, [the] waving of their arms, [the] dancing" held him enthralled.[1] The powerful drama he witnessed fifteen years after the Emancipation was rooted in the brutal transplantation of West Africans to America and chronicled the transition of slaves to freedmen.[2] Albert Coombs Barnes, who put together the finest privately formed collection of early modern paintings in the world, said the impression the performance made on him was "so vivid and so deep" that it "influenced [his] whole life, not only in learning much about the Negro, but in extending the esthetic phase of that experience to an extensive study of art."[3]

Can we take him at his word? Pursuing the question can lead us, I believe, to a more subtle understanding of Barnes than we have had before. The "compelling charm"[4] he found in African-American art forms, particularly music, helps explain his way of looking at paintings, some of the emphases in his collection, and the series of choices he made about who would control the Barnes Foundation after he was gone. Together with his later scientific training, which gave him an approach to learning he would never abandon, his emotional response to the spirituals sung by black worshippers influenced him to the end of his days.

Barnes was a more complicated character than has been acknowledged by either his contemporary or later detractors. But it is not necessary to excuse his notorious irascibility, his well-documented rudeness, nor his infamous penchant for vulgarity to admire the insight and passion he brought to collecting art. Barnes was an outsized character and a man of extreme contradiction. Brilliant, energetic, strong, forceful, and persistent, he was also uncommonly defensive, kept grievances brightly intact for decades, and allowed volcanic anger to cloud his normally clear judgment. So shifty a material as human nature makes reaching any kind of "truth" about one's subject highly problematic. But it is time, nevertheless, to begin to come to terms with the crusty, combative collector.

I have looked closely at the environment in which he was born and nurtured, the education, formal and informal, he pursued in schools and in galleries and museums, the career he undertook in applied science and business at a singular moment for both, the development and growth of his enthusiasm for collecting pictures and sculpture, his pragmatic aesthetic theories, the educational experiment he undertook in a consuming effort to foster an appreciation of art in painting and the rest of life, his role as a patron, his enduring friendships, his relationships with his wife of fifty years and with his muse and literary collaborator, the institutional links he sought and those he disparaged, and the one cause he consistently supported and promoted: public recognition of the unique and significant cultural contributions of black Americans to the nation.

Far-reaching philosophic and legal issues have been raised by a succession of lawsuits initiated to force and facilitate, resist and block the transformation of the unique picture-viewing experience in the Barnes galleries. During the period of my research, I have had an opportunity to observe and analyze an institution in transition. A sea change has taken place in Merion since Lincoln University, the first college in the United States founded to provide a higher education for young men of African descent, gained effective control of the Barnes Foundation. Under terms of the Foundation's bylaws, as amended nine months before the collector's accidental death, Lincoln was empowered to nominate trustees as vacancies arose due to the resignation or death of four out of the five board members chosen by Barnes or his widow. The university, once known as the black Princeton, named its third trustee in 1989. The following year, the Barnes board elected a black partner in a prestigious Philadelphia law firm as its first African-American president.

Inheriting a building in need of renovation and a restricted endowment, Richard H. Glanton began his tenure by making a controversial proposal, which he quickly abandoned, to sell some of the Barnes pictures. The museum establishment, a group the collector loved to hate, was as horrified by the idea of deaccession as it was receptive to the Glanton idea that superseded it: a world tour of masterpieces from the Barnes Collection. The unprecedented traveling exhibition raised some $17 million, which paid for gallery renovations.

But none of the efforts of the Glanton-led board to increase the assets of the Foundation and improve access to its holdings were accomplished without a battle. The trustees' tragic misreading of the devotion of alumni and students to the instructional core of the institution as obstructionism denied them a natural, crucial body of supporters. A failure to address promptly the concerns of neighbors and a protracted squabble with a local zoning board over the right to build a parking lot escalated into charges of racism and slander that echoed the long-ago quarrels Barnes himself had with township government. The cost of the dispute, in terms of dollars spent, energy diverted, and ill will generated was monumental. The Barnes endowment is now gone, and support from the philanthropic community has been promised on the sole condition that the Foundation move its renowned collection to a new site in Philadelphia, expand its governing board to fifteen members, and eliminate provisions in its bylaws restricting board discretion. But Lincoln University was initially reluctant to acquiesce in the dilution of its power—and any change in the Foundation's governing documents requires the approval of the court. The case remains in litigation. However it is finally decided, the years just ahead will be the most momentous in the history of a shrewd entrepreneur's remarkable creation.

At the dedication of the Barnes Foundation in 1925, John Dewey said "art is not something apart, not something for the few, but something which should give . . . meaning . . . to all the activities of life."[5] Barnes agreed with the philosopher, his sometime teacher, sometime pupil, with all his heart, but he also imagined for art a more specific role. He thought it could help foster "a working alliance"[6] between black and white people, based on cultural not racial identity, and the unfolding promise of his legacy is that his magnificent collection can. On the creativity and strength of their partnership rests the future of a unique institution that has yet to realize its potential either as a school or a museum with holdings of a quality and value that no one will ever be able to assemble again.

1

The Early Years

The service had begun with a bugle call at dusk. Candles in the trees and cooking fires provided illumination. The tall tapers on a raised platform in the tabernacle flickered in the summer breeze, and the boy seated beside his mother on the women's benches strained to see and hear the preacher. The revivalist's closing prayer, delivered at a fever pitch, was drowned out by shouted responses—a chorus of "Glory, Hallelujahs!" At the final "Amen," black men and women, who had been gathered behind the speaker's stand, moved, one by one, in front of the white congregation and formed a hollow circle facing inward. The ring of dancers moved counter-clockwise in single file, slapping their thighs, clicking their heels, and singing:

> Brudder Joshua fit de battle of Jericho,
> Jericho, Jericho,
> Brudder Joshua fit de battle of Jericho
> And the walls come tumblin' down.

The tempo built up gradually until it reached an ecstatic breaking point. "Under the inspiration of sentiments like these," one contemporary observer wrote, "what wonder if the suddenly unfettered spirit signaled the glad occasion by walking, and leaping, and praising the Lord."[1]

By general consent, the camp meeting rules requiring quiet after the congregation returned to their sleeping tents were suspended on the last night for African Americans. It was said that "great billows of sound . . . rolled over the encampment, and was (sic) echoed back from hill and wood for miles away, until the morrow's dawning."[2] With the blows of hammer and axe, "the plank partition walls separating the white and colored precincts" were knocked down, according to a Methodist minister and historian who witnessed such revivals throughout the mid-Atlantic region. "After the order of David before the arc," he wrote, the dancers inaugurated a grand march around the encampment.

Come, childering, storm ole Jericho's walls;
Yes, blow an' shout, an' down dey falls!

O come an' jine de army,
An' we'll keep de arc a movin',
As we goes shoutin' home!

When we gits dere we'll all be free;
An' oh, how joyous we shall be!

O come an' jine de army,
An' we'll keep de arc a movin',
As we goes shoutin' home!

It is not hard to imagine the excitement of young Albert Barnes as he peered out of the parted curtains of his tent at the spectacle. For him, going home meant crossing from the New Jersey to the Pennsylvania side of the Delaware River by ferry. He would take with him lasting memories of the music he had heard—the sorrow songs, which told of the black worshippers' past and present trials, as well as the jubilees, which expressed their joyful anticipation of a better future.

Psychologists have demonstrated not only that children are likely to recall with accuracy emotional events that are personally meaningful but also that such events can have an impact on their goals.[3] The African-American spirituals Barnes heard at a religious revival awash in feeling led him years later to another art form—the construction of a collection of magnificent paintings and sculpture. The religious as well as the social and economic environment in which he grew up shaped the man he became no matter how quickly and far he distanced himself from it. Geographically speaking, of course, he barely even left his hometown since Merion, Pennsylvania, the suburban community where he lived the last forty-five years of his life, was only six miles from Kensington, a blue-collar section of Philadelphia where, on January 2, 1872, Barnes was born. The City of Brotherly Love was aptly described shortly thereafter as "a village which ha[d] swallowed a metropolis."[4] Although its consolidation with outlying boroughs had given Philadelphia the tax base a growing industrial center needed for survival, neighborhoods still retained their own peculiar characteristics. The poorer ones contained deteriorating older homes and harbored street gangs, young hoodlums like the Moyamensing Killers, the Bleeders, the Smashers, and the Tormenters, who fought each other over territorial rights. Within walking distance of many places like Kensington, however, Walnut Street formed the backbone of a distinctively fashionable precinct. Inside the red brick houses with marble trimmings that lined the thoroughfare, as well as in the brownstone palazzos around Rittenhouse Square, a late nineteenth-century observer found "somewhat of the warmth of Southern hospitality and of the Southern zest for friendly assemblings."[5]

During the Civil War, Philadelphia was, in fact, a border city. In 1860, its black population of 22,000, while only 4 percent of the total population and small by later standards, was the largest of any northern city at the time and second only to Baltimore.[6] At best, white residents were suspicious and disdainful of African Americans. Since 1838, they had denied them the vote, which property-owning free black citizens of Pennsylvania had previously enjoyed, and not only did employment in the city's new factories remain generally closed to blacks, African-American men lost out to Irish and German immigrants in their bid for semiskilled and unskilled jobs, though once they had found work as hod carriers and stevedores. Well-to-do black families existed in Philadelphia, but they were an exception; not only were most of the brothers and sisters poor, their prospects of economic progress were steadily deteriorating. Residential segregation had long been the rule, and a state law enacted in 1854 required separate schools for black children in districts where there were more than twenty African-American pupils.[7] The city's new, horse-drawn street railways accepted only white passengers. Lecture halls were rented with the express understanding that no blacks should be allowed to enter them. Writing ten years before Barnes's birth, Frederick Douglass said "there is not perhaps anywhere to be found a city in which prejudice against color is more rampant than in Philadelphia."[8] Even churches were segregated, and it was in the city's twenty-five black congregations that free men and women of African descent found community and solace. The majority of these were Methodist.[9]

Methodism was the evangelical faith embraced by Albert Barnes's mother. We don't know what Lydia Schaffer[10] looked like, but we have her son's word for her "keen and penetrating intelligence."[11] She was twenty-one when she was married to John J. Barnes on April 4, 1867 by the Rev. William Cooper, a Methodist minister, in a parsonage at Fifth and Oxford streets. Of German descent, Lydia was the daughter of Charles and Catherine Schaffer and had been born in Philadelphia on June 29, 1846. It is likely that her husband's family was originally Quaker. Barnes told the daughter of a friend that his paternal ancestors came to Philadelphia with or soon after William Penn in 1682.[12] Whatever the family's circumstances during the next century and a half, the collector's father was born in Philadelphia on October 27, 1844. Interment records at the Odd Fellows Cemetery in Burlington, New Jersey indicate that John was the son of Albert Coombs Barnes, listed in Philadelphia city directories in the mid-nineteenth century as an ice dealer, and his wife Susanna.

John Barnes was a butcher when, at nineteen, he was enlisted as a private to serve three years with Company D of the 82nd Regiment of Pennsylvania Volunteers. Nothing survives to indicate whether he was a substitute for a shirker of means who paid him to serve in his stead or a bored boy seeking a reprieve from slicing liver. As a new recruit, he would have joined veteran members of the infantry regiment in guarding Confederate officers confined on Johnson's Island in Lake Erie during the early months of 1864. When the ice broke in May, the 82nd was dispatched to Washington and then to Fredericksburg, Maryland, where it was detailed to guard a train to the front. John Barnes participated in brief skirmishes with rebel forces in northern Virginia, but it was not until June 3 on a barren, dusty crossroads near the Chickohominy River and close to Richmond that he was engaged in a major battle. At Cold Harbor, General Ulysses S. Grant ordered a frontal assault on the Confederate line. The attack was to begin at dawn on June 2, but high-command blundering forced its postponement for twenty-four hours. General Robert E. Lee used his day of grace well. The Southern entrenchments were expertly sited, and 7,000 Union officers and men fell within thirty minutes. A rebel colonel noted that "the dead covered more than five acres of ground about as thickly as they could be laid."[13] Admitting defeat, Grant temporarily called off further effort, and federal doctors labored through the night to salvage what they could from the human wreckage. Among the wounded was the young butcher from Philadelphia. A crude field amputation of his right arm above the elbow probably saved his life. After spending the next year in military hospitals, Barnes was honorably discharged on June 26, 1865 with a disability pension of eight dollars a month. A year later he received an artificial arm, which he could not wear with ease and found of little use. But within two years, the short (five foot three and a half inches tall, according to his Army discharge certificate), dark-eyed young man obtained a government job as a letter carrier and found himself a wife.

The young couple had six different addresses and three sons during their first five years of marriage. The eldest, Charles, was born in 1868. John, Jr. was born two years later and in an all-too-common tragedy died of diphtheria before his first birthday. The Barneses lived in a four-room house at 1466 Cook (subsequently called Wilt) Street when Lydia, attended by a midwife, gave birth to Albert. The baby was named for his paternal grandfather, and his birth certificate lists his father's occupation as mechanic. The family moved five more times within the next decade. All their homes were small, rented dwellings near one another and close to the Kensington cemetery. John worked as an inspector, a laborer, and a watchman. The 1870s were depression years, and many men without skills were unemployed. The couple's fourth son, George, was born in 1880 and died in 1882. Lydia had some help caring for her boys from a younger sister, Hannah, who was employed in a knitwear mill and lived with the Barneses from time to time. The cemetery, a grassy plot with headstones dating back to the late eighteenth century, was the only open space, besides the streets, for children to play in the densely populated area. Albert went to the neighborhood public school, but by 1880, Charley was done with formal education and listed in the census as an errand boy. Methodism had taken root in Kensington at a very early period, and the family may have attended the Cohocksink Chapel or one of several other smaller meeting-houses. "I was brought up in the Methodist Church," Albert Barnes reminded a friend when he was more than seventy; and, ever ready to test himself, he gleefully added: "I'd like to compete with the best equipped ecclesiastic son-of-a-bitch . . . in the number of Methodist hymns to be howled with gusto."[14] It is certainly true that Methodists liked to sing, but the songs Barnes heard at the camp meeting across the Delaware in Merchantville were not the familiar lyric poems of Isaac Watts and Charles Wesley. They were new songs with repetitive phrases and catchy tunes. Often composed on the spot, the texts consisted of isolated lines from prayers, from the Scriptures, and from every-day experience strung together and made longer by the addition of choruses or the interjection of refrains between verses.[15] Invariably the dual subjects of the songs were the realities of slavery and the possibility of freedom. They were based as firmly on the bitter experience of black people in America as on the sweet promises of Christian faith. W. E. B. DuBois would call them the "singu-lar spiritual heritage of the nation and the greatest gift of the Negro people."[16] After his initial exposure to the songs of African Americans, Barnes, by his own account, sought out other "camp meetings, baptizings, [and] revivals" where he might hear them.[17] His unusual interest—he called it an "addiction"—must surely have set him apart from other boys in working-class Kensington and in "The Neck," an even poorer part of Philadelphia, situated on low-lying land near its southern edge, where his family moved when he was eleven. But the proximity of The Neck to the Seventh Ward, the section of the city with the largest black population, would have allowed him to visit African-American congregations by simply taking a five-cent horse car or walking to their meet-ing places. Four of the city's seventeen black Methodist churches were within twenty-five blocks of the three houses on South 12th and South 13th streets that the Barneses occupied in the mid-1880s. Throughout the summer of 1883, moreover, revival meetings were held in a huge tent in the heart of Philadel-phia at Broad and Spring Garden streets. Erected and initially used by an Australian circus, it was acquired by a Methodist evangelist, the Rev. Andrew Manship, for thrice-daily religious services. Attendance grew from fifty per-sons to assemblies of more than a thousand.[18] The congregation was biracial, and the featured speakers included black preachers whose "soul-winning" sermons attracted the attention of local newspapers and won Manship's praise for their powerful effect on worshippers.[19] As "barefoot children, women with-out bonnets on their heads, and men in their shirt sleeves" responded to exhor-tations from the makeshift pulpit with volleys of "Yes, Lords,"[20] the homilist's voice became part of the surging chorus. An eleven-year-old Albert Barnes could well have been present as a participant or an observer. If so, the merging of spoken or shouted word into group song must have thrilled the sensitive boy who responded with such empathy to what he would describe years later as the innate "feelings for rhythm, poetry and music" of African Americans that "constitute the universal language of emotion."[21]

Contemporary analysts of the vernacular tradition of black expression have described "the much needed psyche escape from the workaday world" that spirituals offered African Americans.[22] It may be that black church songs also provided young Albert with a temporary respite from a hard childhood. As an adult, he recalled being hungry as a boy. He also remembered neighborhood toughs stealing his treasured tops, toys he had paid for with money earned as the result of his own enterprise--perhaps by loading clover-mixed sods into a wheelbarrow and selling them to brickyards. When he protested the theft, the ruffians beat him up, which prompted him to work for more pennies, buy boxing gloves with them, and practice with his brother Charley in the cellar. They picked up pointers by slipping into local boxing matches. It was an activity that an elderly Barnes would cite as an attempt to adjust himself to his environment and as his first contact with science.[23] He learned to use his fists and whatever else might be handy. "When I was kid down in The Neck, Bill Vare came at me with a shovel and I knocked him cold with a bottle—so you can see that early habits crop up later in life," he told a friend.[24] More than one slugfest was broken up by the police, and Barnes boasted that he had been "arrested several times, and spent twenty-four hours in Moyamensing Prison . . . for being better able to use my hands than the fellow who started something."[25]

Barnes would also speak late in life about an early interest in art. One of the houses occupied by his family was near at fire station. The gracefully moving horses pulling a shiny red wagon inspired him to make a drawing with chalk.[26] Art had a prominent place in the curriculum of Philadelphia public schools in the 1870s and 1880s, and Albert would have studied drawing and a subject concerned with colors and the qualities of objects at the William Welch School at Thirteenth and Jackson streets. At a time when schooling was not compulsory in Pennsylvania nor child labor prohibited, he must have shown an aptitude in other courses as well to have continued beyond the primary level. As a twelve-year-old eighth-grade student, Barnes was one of only two boys at Welch who took and passed the examination that would admit them to the all-male Central High School, the crowning stone in the arch of the city's public education system.[27]

When Barnes entered in the fall term of 1885, sciences and modern languages were stressed over the classics, and the high school's mission was to prepare boys for "the pursuits of commerce, manufacturer, and the useful arts."[28] Barnes's instructors, all men, were addressed as "Professor." A majority had attended college and/or professional schools, and four of the fourteen with advanced degrees held degrees in medicine. Central students were selected on the basis of superior intelligence. Only those who had demonstrated their ability were admitted, and the roster included some of the most academically gifted boys in the city. But if Barnes shared a high I.Q. and proven diligence with his 124 classmates, he did not share their decidedly middle-class origins. Two-thirds of their fathers were professionals, proprietors, self-employed craftsmen, or other workers who wore stiff white collars. School records note that his father then delivered newspapers. The legend and likely truth is that Barnes arose before dawn to help him. Albert, who would one day describe his mother as a "marvelous" woman of great "courage" and, "best of all . . . poise and balance," said his father had a "good intelligence" and "tremendous energy" but lacked "the composite we call character." John, it seems from later observation, spent his leisure time with the bottle. "Unfortunately, I needed a father," Barnes dryly observed when he was nearly fifty.[29]

It must have been tough for a thirteen-year-old boy from The Neck to make friends, at least initially, at Central. Although his classmates traveled to school from neighborhoods all over the city, no others returned home to a landscape dotted with stagnant pools and refuse dumps through which pigs, raised for slaughter, ran freely. Clothes, then as now, set teenagers apart, and years later Barnes dredged up the painful memory of sitting through lectures in frayed pants.[30] Nevertheless, at a time when only about 20 percent of an entering class graduated from Central, young Albert persisted. He worked hard at his studies and made his mark politically.[31] A sports enthusiast as an adult, he may well have played in an intramural baseball league. He became a close chum of a ball player named S. William James Glackens, who was also a skilled draftsman, and, probably through Glackens, got to know another aspiring artist among his schoolmates, John Sloan.[32] Barnes apparently showed some drawings he had made to Glackens who gently disparaged his talent. But if his friend's criticism was a momentary blow, Barnes seems to have moved on quickly. As he later recalled, he had already embraced the credo of "living by experimenting."[33] His most spectacular high school accomplishment was surely being elected vice president of his senior class in December of 1888. The other officers were the sons of a cattle broker, an insurance agent, and a clergyman. Barnes counted the class president, Jacob (Jay) Schamberg, among his best buddies. A student's background mattered at Central but less than at most other educational institutions. Boys were rewarded for merit alone, and they learned early to expect a great deal of themselves.

During the spring of Albert's junior year, his family moved into a row house at 1331 Tasker Street. It was a brick, three-story dwelling, still standing, that Lydia Barnes had purchased for $3,500. Money for the first house the Barneses had owned in twenty-one years of marriage may have come from a small inheritance or, when Lydia could get her hands on the money, savings from her husband's wages. Two years earlier, his Army pension had been raised to thirty-six dollars a month. Her elder son, then twenty, was still living at home but steadily employed as a plumber. The family's prospects were looking up, and those of the second son were bright. At commencement ceremonies, held on

June 27, 1889 at the Chestnut Street Opera House, he received the academic A.B. degree, which the state legislature had given Central the right to confer in recognition of the rigor of the curriculum. Its graduates were prepared to take their places in the new entrepreneurial and corporate economy on the rise in America. Since they had not studied Greek, French, and the advanced Latin courses required for admission to most colleges and universities, however, only a fifth then entered the professions.[34] But according to Henry Hart, a protégé of Barnes who wrote an early biography of him, Lydia Barnes encouraged her gifted son to study medicine.[35] He applied and was accepted at the University of Pennsylvania School of Medicine, an easy commute from Tasker Street and the oldest and among the finest medical schools in the nation. Because Central students had been encouraged to work things out for themselves with a variety of instruments, models, charts, samples, and organs— known as philosophical apparatus, Barnes was not only well positioned to make the most of the next phase of his academic career, but also for a life devoted to experiment—in business, education, and the acquisition of art.

Just before he began his professional studies, medical teaching burst the bounds of the lecture hall as leading medical schools adopted a more complex system of laboratory instruction. Barnes's very first class at Penn was general chemistry. Because of his proficiency in the subject, he was one of thirteen medical students appointed as assistants in the Chemical Laboratory—and the only one of them not to have previously studied at a college or university. The stipend surely helped with his $150 annual tuition, but the position apparently didn't last beyond his first year. As he told the story a half century later, he was "fired" after one of the undergraduates in his charge combined two chemicals in a way that caused a minor explosion.[36] Whatever the circumstances leading to the loss of his assistantship, Barnes was soon earning money by tutoring and playing semipro baseball in a city that was a mecca for this version of the national pastime. Despite the necessity of working, however, he maintained good grades, and, on the basis of them, won a Philadelphia Board of Education Scholarship for the 1890-91 academic year.[37] But the scrappy scholar's competitiveness was not confined to the classroom. According to fellow student Jay Schamberg, Barnes thought he had killed a man on one occasion when an opponent he had challenged to a fistfight was felled by his punch, struck his head on a curb, and momentarily lost consciousness.[38] Spared expulsion as a felon or even a reprimand for roughhousing, he made a bid for some measure of social life in his senior year by joining a newly reorganized fraternity, Phi Gamma Delta, which then seemed to attract mostly students studying for professional degrees. It wasn't a fashionable house; on the Greek scene at Penn, family still mattered.

Barnes's own, especially his mother, Lydia, must have felt enormous pride when twenty-year-old Albert was awarded his M.D. on May 6, 1892 at the Medical Department's commencement. He was the sixth of 154 newly minted physicians to walk across the stage of Philadelphia's Academy of Music and shake the hand of the august Provost William Pepper. The details of how Barnes spent the next eight years remain cloudy. But it is clear that he did not long retain any interest in becoming a healer. By his own account, he "took up professional gambling as a post-graduate course." He told the philosopher John Dewey, who became his closest friend, that for a year after earning his medical degree, he "was a bookmaker on the racetracks at Saratoga and Washington and . . . played baccarat, roulette or poker" every night. He didn't mention how his Methodist parents regarded his activities, if they knew of them, or whether they were more profitable than semipro baseball, but he says that one of the most valuable things he learned "was to recognize the 'come-ons' [and] the 'sure-thing' counterfeits."[39]

When he wasn't gambling, Barnes may have worked in the wards and dispensaries at the Philadelphia Polyclinic, a hospital and medical postgraduate school, under the tutelage of a senior physician. He may also have spent a short time at Mercy Hospital in Pittsburgh.[40] He told Henry Hart that he "interned" at the State Hospital for the Insane in upstate Warren, Pennsylvania.[41] While internships were not required for medical licensure at the time, graduates of Penn's School of Medicine were encouraged to try for hospital residencies or assistant residencies, which major institutions customarily filled by a competitive examination of candidates. General hospitals did not admit psychiatric patients to their wards, so for Barnes to pursue an interest in the emerging discipline of psychiatry, his only choice for further clinical study was an asylum. The famed Pennsylvania Hospital for the Insane, founded by Benjamin Rush, was a few blocks from the University Hospital in West Philadelphia, but perhaps Barnes's selection of Warren was dictated by a desire to leave home for the first substantial period in his life.

He told Hart that his experience with the patients there convinced him that "wrong beliefs and habits can cause sane people to 'lose their minds.'" He came to believe, moreover, that sanity could be restored if the mentally ill, whose disease had no organic nor chemical base, "could be led to accept valid ideas and acquire new attitudes and habits."[42] It is likely that Barnes continued his observations of psychiatric patients on a visit to hospitals in London and Paris during the summer of 1893. It was his first trip abroad, and one wonders if he paid for his ship's passage with his winnings at gaming tables. For years thereafter, he was given to quoting from Bernard Hart's *The Psychology of Insanity*, and he may well have met the respected theorist and clinician at University College Hospital, London where Dr. Hart was a physician in psychological medicine. Barnes also may have observed the demonstrations of hysteria that the French neurologist Jean-Martin Charcot induced by hypnosis before audiences in the lecture hall at Salpêtrière, then an asylum cum teaching hospital, in Paris. But while he continued to read widely in the fields of psychology and psychiatry throughout most of his life, his career interests lay elsewhere.

According to information that Barnes provided for the tenth reunion of his Penn Medical School Class, he "took up the study of experimental therapeutics (pharmacology) and chemistry" in Berlin in 1895 after doing work there in clinical medicine and experimental physiology the previous year.[43] Some of the world's greatest research chemists could be found in the German capital then, and their presence attracted many junior scientists with whom Barnes could have made special arrangements. Speaking before the Rhode Island Philosophical Society in 1943, he told his audience he also studied philosophy and pursued his interests in music and in painting.[44] Giving English lessons would have been the usual way for an American student to earn money for fees and living expenses, and since Barnes had a strong background in the German language from his classes at Central High School, he undoubtedly supported himself as a tutor. Hart said he also sold stoves for an American manufacturer.[45] Two different journalists who interviewed him about his education and early career reported that Barnes told them he had sung spirituals in German beer gardens.[46] But coins from the patrons couldn't have amounted to much, and Barnes's money soon ran out. He earned his passage home by working as a deckhand on an oil tanker. Back in Philadelphia, and taking up residence again with his family on Tasker Street, he further demonstrated his ambition by finding two jobs: as an advertising copywriter for Gray's Glycerin Tonic and as a consulting chemist to H. K. Mulford and Company, a small manufacturing pharmacy that had been incorporated in 1891, quickly acquired a reputation for high-quality medicines, and eventually was absorbed by Merck.

The 1890s was a yeasty decade in industrial chemistry. The idea that chemical compounds could be visualized as groups of real atoms united by real bonds led young chemists to undertake synthetic studies in an attempt to find the utmost limits of chemical affinity and molecular stability. In Germany, Felix Hoffmann synthesized a shelf-stable form of acetylsalicylic acid and his company, Bayer, began marketing the drug it christened aspirin. In the United States, Mulford pioneered in the development of a commercial form of diphtheria antitoxin and soon added a tetanus antitoxin, a smallpox vaccine, and a pneumoccic antibody serum to its product line.[47] One of the first American pharmaceutical firms to develop therapeutic agents through laboratory science, Mulford was an early proponent of hospital-based drug trials and maintained close ties to the mainstream medical community. The young scientists on its staff worked in a modern laboratory complex on a forty-acre campus in suburban Glenolden. Barnes was not, however, a company man. By temperament, he was an entrepreneur, and he would soon join the ranks of the phenomenally successful.

But at twenty-eight, in the first year of the new century, he decided to return to Germany for further academic training at the University of Heidelberg. During the summer semester of 1900, he studied pharmaceutics with Professor

Rudolf Gottlieb and worked in Gottlieb's pharmaceutical institute where he probably conducted experiments. He also enrolled in a class in experimental toxicology and attended a philosophy seminar taught by Professor Kuno Fischer.[48] Barnes rented a room near the university, and he would later tell of putting his knowledge of psychology to use in counseling a gun-wielding visitor, another American student who was distraught over a ruined love affair to the point of threatening suicide. "From midnight to five the next morning, we walked the streets, drank beer, and talked," Barnes wrote. "When he left, I had [his] revolver in my pocket and a promise from him to forget the girl."[49]

Barnes published the results of his research at Heidelberg in a respected German medical journal, *Archiv fur Experimentelle Pathologie und Pharmakologie*. His paper described the effects of two morphine derivatives on frogs and rabbits. One is benign; the other induces severe spasms leading to death. Barnes attempted to locate the physiological site of the chemical's attack. His work was certainly adequate to earn him a German medical degree, which was then awarded solely on the basis of publishing some original (but not necessarily more than minimal) research, and it is likely his studies toward a second M.D. to which he referred when, on several occasions, he wrote of "making" or "doing" his "Docktor's Arbeit."[50] Whatever credential he was seeking, it was toward the end of his German university studies that he requested the assistance of the head of the Heidelberg chemistry department in finding a chemist to join the Mulford research staff. Professor Theodor Curtius recommended a Ph.D. student named Hermann Hille.[51] A few months older than Barnes, Hille was born in Moelln in the far north of Germany. He was state-licensed pharmacist who had studied at the universities of Kiel and Würzburg and worked in the laboratory of the physicist Wilhelm Roentgen, at the time Roentgen developed the x-ray, before taking up chemistry at Heidelberg. When Barnes met him, he was defending his dissertation, a successful endeavor that earned him a doctor of natural philosophy degree in August of 1900. Hille spoke several languages, including English, and with his research published, he seems to have been ready for a new adventure. On a walk along the Neckar River, Barnes persuaded him to come to America. He then returned to his own job at Mulford. With the promise of a research appointment, Hille sailed in September and, according to the plan they had no doubt launched in Heidelberg, the two young scientists joined forces in the search for a medicine with a good benefit-to-risk and benefit-to-cost ratio that would "put [them]," as Barnes wrote later, "on easy street."[52]

The aspiring entrepreneur had the wit to recognize that he was in the right place at precisely the right time. At the turn of the last century, heroin, morphine, quinine, and aspirin, then three-years-old and the first mass-produced and mass-marketed drug in the world, were the only major medicines available to relieve pain and treat disease. But some other chemicals, notably silver compounds, were recognized as effective against bacteria and used for therapeutic purposes. Barnes would have known of the discovery made in 1884 by Karl S. F. Crede, a German obstetrician, who found that a few drops of silver nitrate placed in the eyes of new-born babies prevented blindness from gonorrheal infection passed *in utero* from mother to child. But he also would have been aware that the antiseptic action of silver, both in its free form and in the form of salts, was complicated by undesirable side effects, principally irritation and pain, and, in some applications, astringency and corrosion. Since the application of silver nitrate to mucous membranes caused them to become viscous before the compound could penetrate deeper cellular structures, moreover, its therapeutic benefit was limited to surface tissue. In the competition that was then underway among chemists to find a substitute for silver nitrate, pharmacologists working in Europe were intrigued by the possibility that combining silver with proteins might have therapeutic value. But before any of them could bring a product to market, Albert Barnes and Hermann Hille described the development of what they would soon call Argyrol. They presented their findings in a paper read in New York at the third annual meeting of the American Therapeutic Society on May 14, 1902. It was printed ten days later in the *Medical Record*.[53]

Their active search had taken two years, and Barnes appears to have been considering the problem for even longer. He told Dewey that "the idea of Argyrol, in its form that made good, sauntered" into his head on "a hot day in August 1900" while he was conducting his research on morphine derivatives.[54] Before leaving for his second stay in Germany, he may have performed some early experiments using silver nitrate in the laboratory he had rigged up in the basement of his family's home on Tasker Street. In any case, when Hille arrived in Philadelphia in the autumn of 1900, Barnes rented a stable on Thirteenth Street near Spruce Street, which provided living quarters for his partner and space for another makeshift laboratory where the two worked after finishing their day jobs at Mulford. Their focus was on combinations that could be formed from native and derived proteins, and their first joint venture was the development of a synthetic iron compound that they tested for assimilability on puppies.[55] Next they produced a synthetic tannin compound that was resistant to the attenuating effects of digestion. They gave it to calves suffering from intractable diarrhea and were so encouraged by the results that they persuaded two hospitals in Philadelphia and one in New York to test it on patients with diseases of the intestines.[56]

In addition to his driving scientific interest, Barnes also had, for the first time in his life, a serious romantic one. Upon his return from Germany in the late summer of 1900, he had visited a cousin, a family physician in practice in Milford, a Delaware River resort town in northeastern Pennsylvania close to the New York State border. One day a petite young woman, blonde with blue eyes, came to the door with a fox terrier in her arms. It had recently been spayed and the reopened wound needed attention. At the behest of the dog's owner, her sister Edith, Laura Leighton Leggett was seeking medical help. The Leggett sisters and their mother were staying in a Milford hotel on a summer holiday. Laura, then twenty-five, was the fifth of the six children of Richard Lee and Clara Cox Leggett of Brooklyn. Her father was a successful wholesale grocer. A captain with New York City's Seventh Regiment during the Civil War, he had married in 1862 and, after his discharge, bought a large brownstone in a genteel neighborhood. Originally from Essex, England, his ancestors had immigrated to Barbados, B.W.I. and then to New York's Westchester County in the seventeenth century; his wife's father had been a silversmith in Birmingham, England and her mother's people had fled two revolutions, first in France and then in Santo Domingo, before settling in the United States in the first decade of the nineteenth century.

The contrasts in their backgrounds did not turn out to be a stumbling block in Albert Barnes's courtship of Laura Leggett. She was clearly a "catch," and he pursued her with the fierce determination and expectation of success that would mark all his ventures. At twenty-eight, he was just under six-feet tall, broad-shouldered, square-jawed, with a brush mustache, light brown hair combed back from his high forehead, and piercing blue eyes behind rimless glasses. He was plenty rough around the edges and keenly ambitious. Laura was demure and soft-spoken. Her gentle demeanor did not, however, mask her intelligence, and her self-discipline matched Barnes's own. They also shared a love of music. Although the circumstances are no longer recoverable, he had at some point learned to play the violin, and it is not beyond the realm of possibility that on those sultry August evenings, he serenaded his sweetheart. In any case, he returned to Philadelphia with permission to call upon her in Brooklyn, and by October, she had agreed to marry him. The wedding took place on June 4, 1901 in St. James Protestant Episcopal Church, her parents' Brooklyn parish. The couple spent a few days in Atlantic City and then went to Europe on a honeymoon that was probably a gift from the Leggetts. Sailing from Philadelphia, they debarked at Bremerhaven and traveled on to Heidelberg, where Professor Gottlieb, Barnes's former teacher, entertained them and permitted the bridegroom to conduct some experiments in his laboratory. The couple then traveled through the Black Forest, toured Switzerland, and visited Rome before sailing home from Genoa. Back in Philadelphia, they spent a few days on Tasker Street then moved to a hotel until they found an attractive white stucco house to rent at 6374 Drexel Road in Overbrook on the city's affluent western edge.

Barnes was still holding down two jobs. The combined salaries enabled him to finance the chemical experiments he and Hille were conducting in the converted Thirteenth Street stable. Impatient with the pace of their research, however, he engaged Daniel L. Wallace, a Penn instructor in analytical chemistry whom he had known when he was a medical student, to assist in the bench work.[57] Their diligence soon paid off. The young investigators created a new compound in which the more disagreeable and dysfunctional effects of silver ions were mitigated by the presence of a substance that served as a protective colloid and soothed abraded mucous membranes. Barnes and his colleagues extracted gliadin, a protein found in wheat and rye, and, through a process involving evaporation, dehydration, drying, and heating, converted it into a vitellin, a protein occurring naturally in egg yolks and in certain plants. To a salt solution of vitellin, they gradually added a concentrated (30 percent) solution of silver nitrate. The surface fluid was poured off and the crystalline solid, filtered and dried in a vacuum, appeared as a dark brown powder. It was cheap to produce and highly portable. Barnes had a product that could be economically packaged and sold to druggists who would dissolve it in water or, in some cases, glycerin, and dispense it as an antiseptic.

But he wanted the endorsement of the medical community, and so decades before the era of government-mandated clinical trials, he asked one of his former medical school teachers for advice about testing the substance he had named after the Greek word for silver. Dr. Edward Martin, then Penn's clinical professor of genitourinary surgery, suggested immersing a strand of ordinary catgut (a tough cord usually made from the intestines of sheep) in a solution of the new silver salt to determine Argyrol's penetrative action. The researchers found that the catgut became "impregnated through and through with the silver," and they deduced that Argyrol would "exert [its] antiseptic effects . . .in the deep submucous structures" where pathogens lurked "in spite of energetic measures to eradicate them."[58] Barnes then persuaded Martin and other physicians to test his silver salt on patients.

Their accolades helped him make a fortune. Rather than approaching druggists directly, Barnes created a demand for his product by sending circulars containing doctors' endorsements of Argyrol to other doctors. Martin called it the "best silver preparation I have ever used . . . remarkably efficient and absolutely non-irritating." His colleague, Dr. Hiliary M. Christian, chief surgeon at the genitourinary dispensary of the Hospital of the University of Pennsylvania and a professor of genitourinary diseases at the Philadelphia Polyclinic, said Argyrol was "the best silver compound ever offered to the [medical] profession for the treatment of gonorrhea." Their opinion was echoed by scores of other physicians in the United States and abroad. Dr. S. Bond, professor of genitourinary surgery at the University of Maryland, wrote that in long-standing cases of cystitis, he had "obtained extremely good—even brilliant results" from Argyrol. In an address to the Paris Ophthalmological Society, Dr. A. Darier, a lecturer on ocular therapeutics at the University of Paris, said "Argyrol marks a long step forward in the treatment of diseases of the eye because it is absolutely painless and yields better and quicker results than we have yet been able to obtain with any other silver salt." With great prescience, Dr. Frank Gray, professor of ophthalmology and otology at Fort Worth University, wrote that it "should find a place in every obstetrical bag and application of it to the infant's eyes should be as much a matter of routine as tying the umbilical cord." Dr. Charles H. Knight, professor of laryngology at Cornell Medical College and a surgeon at Manhattan Eye and Ear College, reported that he had used Argyrol to treat "various conditions of the larynx and pharynx instead of silver nitrate" and found it "quite as effective and far more agreeable." Dr. M. D. Lederman, professor of laryngology and rhinology at New York Polyclinic, found Argyrol effective in treating "cases of so-called 'Hay Fever.'"[59]

It sounded like a magic bullet. But Barnes did not attempt to patent the new silver salt. Acquiring a patent would have required him to publish the exact chemical composition of Argyrol. His exclusive rights to the product would have expired in seventeen years, and under the law of trade secrets, anyone able to replicate the mild silver protein would then have been free to manufacture it. On November 18, 1902, Barnes did register the name Argyrol as a trademark, which gave him protection against unfair competition exceeding that which he could claim under common law.[60] The petition to register he filed four months earlier contained a hand-drawn shield bearing in its center the monogram "B-H" and between its outside lines the German words *Enigkeit Macht Stark* ("United Strong Power"), the motto of Hille's fraternity (Landsmannshaft Teutonial), that presumably sought to advertise the silver vitellin's medicinal characteristics. The young entrepreneur's next task was to capitalize his venture. He may have secured a loan of $1,000 from his mother-in-law;[61] it is certainly not beyond the realm of possibility that he could have saved $1,600, the sum Hart said he put up to start his company.[62]

Resigning their positions at Mulford, Albert Barnes and Hermann Hille began to manufacture Argyrol in the summer of 1902 in the laboratory they had built in the stable on Thirteenth Street. Barnes later said the start-up capital would only have lasted three months if luck had gone against them.[63] But tight as money was, the partners realized they needed more space if the business was to grow, and they rented eight rooms in a rundown building at 24 North Fortieth Street, which had once been a hotel. On April 30, 1903, some eleven months after they had begun to make medicines for sale, the two men entered into a formal, five-year partnership agreement. The firm would be called Barnes & Hille Company. The partners would have "joint equal right and ownership in and to . . . the products of the business." In addition to Argyrol, the agreement listed Ovoferrin, an iron-based tonic to stimulate appetite that had met with some success, and two products they ultimately dropped from their lines, Interim, an intestinal astringent, and Biodol, a dusting powder.[64]

The document went on to specify the partners' respective duties. Hille was identified as the bench scientist who would devote his time and attention to experimentation in a search for new "chemical preparations, formulae and commodities." Barnes was the front-office partner. His job was to promote and market company products. With the help of his wife, who addressed sales materials in their Drexel Road home, he sent Barnes & Hille pamphlets, which soon contained the enthusiastic endorsements of more than thirty physicians, to other doctors and to drug jobbers and wholesalers throughout the United States and abroad. The intensity of his focus can be judged by the tale he told Dewey of boarding a train for California in the middle of the night after he had "awakened from a dream" with an idea for marketing Ovoferrin.[65] From the first, Barnes's target audience was international. He traveled to the British Isles and to Paris and Berlin to distribute one-ounce bottles of Argyrol and collect yet other endorsements and orders. By 1904, the company was turning a profit and had opened sales offices in London and in Sydney, Australia.

Barnes invested heavily in research and new product development for several years. In 1906, he went to Germany to discuss two mercury-based antiseptics with his former teacher, Rudolf Gottlieb, and one of the most enthusiastic and productive scientists in the field of chemotherapeutics, Paul Ehrlich. Then head of the State Serum Institute at Frankfort-am-Main, Ehrlich was working on the synthesis of a new arsenic compound that he would later market as Salvarsan and Neosalvarsan, the standard treatment for syphilis until the age of antibiotics. But apparently the future Nobel laureate disabused the young American of the idea that products he had seen as "world beaters" were worth any further attention. Barnes came home, as he later wrote to a former classmate, "with a wholesome respect for sound special knowledge and experience."[66]

The company he had started in a stable never had more than about twenty people on its payroll. The tiny initial staff included Barnes's father who, in the 1904 *Philadelphia City Directory*, is listed as a manager and then, successively through 1907, as a packer, superintendent, and druggist! Hille's daughter told William Schack that her father said he was employed as a caretaker and was frequently found in the factory basement "stiff drunk."[67] Whatever the case, the successful son took care of both his parents and never forgot where he came from, though those whom he scorned would say that the memory haunted him. Barnes's only living sibling, Charley, appears to have played almost no role in his adult life. The first non-relative he employed was Nelle E. Mullen, who came to work for Barnes & Hille as a bookkeeper at eighteen and remained with the Barnes Foundation until her death, at eighty-three, in 1967. She was a stocky blonde, able and tireless, who served her employer with total dedication and absolute fidelity. In turn, he trusted her as he trusted few other people and gave her an increasingly large measure of administrative responsibility. In time, she ran the business, never a large or complex enterprise, and handled all of Barnes's investments.

Nelle's older sister, dark-haired, slender Mary, who was just two years younger than Barnes himself, joined the company several years after its inception to help with advertising and promotion. She, too, remained in Barnes's employ until she died in 1957. The sisters, who had been born in the small, south central Pennsylvania town of Columbia and had moved to Philadelphia with their family before the turn of the century, were high school graduates.

But it was Mary, a woman with an intellectual turn of mind and a gift for cogent expository writing, who proved to be the better pupil when, a decade later, Barnes attempted to impart to the sisters his knowledge of psychology and philosophy and his growing understanding of painting. She would take charge of his factory school, write a book about art education, and become a teacher at the Barnes Foundation.

But one of her first responsibilities, as a new employee of Barnes & Hille, was to gather evidence against wholesale and retail druggists who sold imitations of Argyrol, under the trademark name, at less than the market price. She would buy the silver nitrate solution from suspected counterfeiters and turn over the products acquired to Barnes for analysis. Not surprisingly, he enjoyed playing detective himself, and, on at least one occasion, raided a competitor's establishment without a search warrant. The New York judge hearing the case reprimanded Barnes, but, as he related the incident to Dewey, the jurist went on to rule that his business had been injured by unfair competition and sentenced the offenders to six-month terms in prison.[68] Another time, his request for an injunction to restrain a rival reached the Circuit Court of Appeals where Barnes won again in a case that set a legal precedent.[69]

The aggressive pursuit of potential infringers on the Argyrol trademark paid off in spades. Barnes & Hille reportedly netted $100,000 in profits in 1903.[70] But even as the business succeeded, the personal chemistry between the two scientists was becoming explosive. In 1907 Hille brought suit to dissolve the partnership. Barnes countered with a Bill in Equity entered against Hille in Philadelphia's Court of Common Pleas. His lawyer was the best that money could buy—fellow Central alumnus John G. Johnson. A big man of gentle disposition with a passion for art, who since the late 1880s had become an important client of picture dealers in Philadelphia, New York, London, Paris, and Berlin, Johnson owned the finest collection in America of fifteenth- and sixteenth-century Flemish primitives, superb early Spanish and French paintings, and single masterpieces of Italian Renaissance and Dutch seventeenth-century art.[71] He had turned down the requests of two presidents to serve on the Supreme Court and declined the offer of a third to serve as U.S. attorney general by the time Barnes engaged him to protect his business interests. In addition to representing the newly rich manufacturing chemist with his customary skill, Johnson may well have shared with his young friend the joy he found in intelligent collecting.

Barnes's need of wise counsel may be judged in relation to the considerable assets at stake and the seriousness of his complaints against his partner. He claimed Hille had "divulged secrets of the firm to its prejudice," neglected his duties by leaving "important phases of production in the hands of irresponsible employees" with the result that the business was "injured by abnormal products," taken firm property from the laboratory, refused to furnish Barnes with the records of his research, and even threatened his life. The Bill in Equity asserted that "personal communications between the partners have become impossible owing to the threats and conduct of the defendant." In a hand-written insertion, Johnson added "the relations have become so hostile and inharmonious that the complainant cannot continue them consistently with his self respect."[72]

Barnes sought a dissolution of the partnership just as Hille did, and in 1908, the court gave its consent. It was not convinced, however, that Hille had improperly disclosed any of the firm's "discoveries, inventions, formulae, methods, or processes," a violation of contract that would have caused him to forfeit his financial rights. The judge ruled that, in accordance with the agreement the two men had struck in 1903, they should bid against each other for the business. The purchaser was to pay over to his former partner half of the purchasing price. Barnes said years later that exclusive rights to Argyrol, Ovoferrin, and other company products cost him "several hundreds of thousands of dollars."[73] Before Hille left for Chicago, where he established his own successful laboratory, he made, at the insistence of the court, all of the company's medicines in Barnes's presence.[74] Satisfied that he could oversee their technical production himself, Barnes incorporated the A. C. Barnes Company within days of the dissolution of Barnes & Hille and hired all his old employees.

By then the stable core of his work force included a dozen African-American men. It was a time when little more than one percent of the black population of Philadelphia was employed in industry.[75] Prejudice in employment was rife, and many whites refused to work with black people. African Americans who found jobs tended to be employed in outdoor occupations such as street cleaning and garbage collecting or as laborers handling grease and tallow, materials shunned by those with greater options.[76] At his West Philadelphia chemical factory, located in the building he purchased for $8,000 after the break-up of his partnership, Barnes offered clean, indoor work. And more. He offered his black along with his white employees respect, an unusual measure of freedom in carrying out their workplace responsibilities, and access to information with the power to transform their lives.

2

Experiments in Education and Living

Between 1908 and 1912, the A. C. Barnes Company was reorganized "on a cooperative basis worked out," as the owner would later explain, "on lines that were merely adaptations of the principles of psychology." Barnes said that "a good part of those four years was consumed in efforts to unify to a common purpose the diverging temperaments" of all involved in the manufacture and distribution of the firm's product line. He identified a shared "spirit of adventure" and a "common respect for the personality of each individual" as the critical ingredients in the company's success. In an era in which a new progressive spirit was streaked with paternalism, Barnes was discovering a high correlation between workplace democracy and enhanced productivity. "The business never had a boss and . . . never needed one," he said, "for each participant had evolved his or her own method of doing a particular job in a way that fitted into the common needs."[1] But he not only empowered his workers to help organize their toil, he sought to improve their minds. With an evangelical zeal, sometimes tempered but more often inflamed by his faith in science, Barnes embarked on a grand experiment. His goal was not simply to produce better employees. It was to produce happier people, that is, people with more options and more resources, by providing his employees with something quite like a liberal education.

By the turn of the twentieth century, company-owned schools could be found across the United States from southern textile towns to western mining communities. Mostly segregated along racial lines, their main purpose was to facilitate the assimilation of immigrants.[2] But whereas workers in the Boston Woven Hose and Rubber Company studied English and those enrolled in the Ford Company's factory classes were instructed about hygiene and the routine of naturalization, the black men and white women employed by A. C. Barnes were introduced to far more challenging fare. They studied on company time, moreover, because their boss had decided that orders for Argyrol could be filled in six hours. Since the "tradition that eight hours at the place of business were necessary" was not one Barnes was willing to buck, he saw to it that the

19

extra two hours were devoted to reading and discussing the works of philosophers, psychologists, historians, novelists, and playwrights.[3] Barnes said he got the idea for his factory seminars from William James, John Dewey, and George Santayana. Largely an autodidact in the humanities, his reading was eclectic. He "shopped," a hungry boy in a market who suddenly finds his pockets filled with coins, and he took what he liked from authors without worrying about how precisely their ideas fit together. Barnes never claimed that his pedagogical methods were original, but "it was that experience," he said referring to the Argyrol plant classes, "that caused me to start the Foundation."[4] The trinity of classic American philosophers should be considered, therefore, not only as the sources of Barnes's inspiration for his workplace experiment in education but also for the experiment in art education he made in Merion.

For all their differences, a biological view of intelligence derived from Darwin's theory of evolution united the three thinkers. They located the mind in nature and regarded consciousness as part of nature's warp and woof. Their pragmatism, which rapidly became the dominant American philosophy, was rooted in a belief that men and women could manipulate their environment. It was a fundamentally optimistic worldview that broke the grip of Herbert Spencer's gradualistic fatalism, an early reaction to Darwinism, by insisting on the efficacy of ideas. William James, trained at Harvard's Lawrence Scientific School and its School of Medicine, was a physiologist before turning to psychology and, later still, philosophy. His *Principles of Psychology* (1890), which deeply influenced John Dewey, presented the mind as the crucial instrument of humankind's adaptation and survival. Dewey, who took a Ph.D. at Johns Hopkins where he studied with the pioneer child psychologist G. Stanley Hall, taught that a general application of scientific methods, to every possible field of inquiry, was the only way to improve the lot of working people in an industrial democracy. In education, he insisted on combining instruction with doing and linked the development of an individual's cultural interests with the development of his or her problem-solving skills. George Santayana, who studied at Harvard with James, said the central challenge facing men and women, as creatures of nature, was to live rationally in an irrational world. The thesis of his five-volume work, *The Life of Reason* (1905-6), is that "the progressive organization of irrational impulses makes a rational life."[5] He argued that all good art is "fine" that springs from spontaneous expression and that its value "lies in making people happy, first in practicing the art and then in possessing its product."[6]

It was Mary Mullen's job to unpack the complex ideas in the writings of James, Dewey, and Santayana and present them to the factory class of minimally educated workers. With instinctive fidelity to one of the core meanings of pragmatism, she used concepts from the philosophers' works to help her students cope with conditions of the rapidly changing world in which they found themselves. The course was carried on by discussion that Mullen described as "informal but not haphazard or desultory." Attendance was always voluntary. She said the purpose of the seminar was "to cultivate intelligence by showing the possibilities of which every-day life is full, and to make intelligence effective by setting it to work to realize those possibilities." She resisted the impulse "to impose solutions or lay down rules dogmatically." As Barnes had long before recognized the beauty of black song, the woman he had handpicked to carry out his pedagogical experiment recognized the beauty of black speech. "Grammatical blunders [were] passed over without notice," she wrote, "and the men encouraged to express themselves in the way most natural to them."[7]

According to Barnes, the first two years of the factory seminar were devoted to the works of William James. He said the class progressed with relative ease from *Talks to Teachers* (1900) through the *Principles of Psychology, Pragmatism* (1907), and *The Varieties of Religious Experience* (1902), but "foundered" on *Essays in Radical Empiricism* (1912), the series of articles in which the philosopher presented his theory of mind and matter.[8] It was Dewey's *How We Think* (1910) that enabled these adult students to adapt what they had been reading to their own experiences, he claimed. Written in a simple, non-technical style, and making extensive use of illustrations from everyday life, the little book contains a wonderfully lucid five-step analysis of an act of reflective thought. But if, indeed, Mary Mullen's pupils found their lessons useful, it was undoubtedly because she worked hard at presenting ideas from the new science of psychology "stripped of academic trappings." Much discussion appears to have been focused on the nature and organization of impulses. "The legitimacy of every human instinct was insisted on," she said, "together with the limitation imposed by due consideration for every other instinct. In the same way, both the advantages and disadvantages of habit were made clear—the value of habit in giving stability to character, and the danger that habit may harden into fixation and inertia. . . .The function of intelligence in . . . remolding the environment" was a recurring theme.[9]

People outside of the A. C. Barnes Company, probably friends and neighbors of employees, heard about the Argyrol seminars and, according to Barnes, their interest led Mary Mullen, who then lived with her sister Nelle in the Germantown section of Philadelphia, to conduct additional classes in her home. For the plant workers, Barnes established a circulating library to which he continued to add volumes well into the 1920s. His selections are further evidence of his enthusiastic embrace of modernism. They reflect a keen interest in writers who explored the possibilities of individual liberation, celebrated experience, and experimented with form. Employees could find on the factory shelves Bertrand Russell's widely quoted and reprinted essay, *Free Man's Worship* (1903), a reflection upon human vulnerability in which the philosopher concludes that only the products of the most creative imaginations merit reverence in an unfathomable and hostile universe. Along side the eloquent "skeptic's manifesto" was the author's *Why Men Fight* (1915), an analysis of the reasons human beings so often act in a destructive fashion. Russell, whom Barnes would one day hire and subsequently fire, goes on to suggest that people might be persuaded to behave in more constructive ways if they were given more control over their lives in the workplace as well as in the realm of politics.

The Argyrol library also contained some of the works of Russell's godfather, John Stuart Mill, the English philosopher and economist who wrote on an extraordinary number of topics, including sensations of color. In addition, Barnes chose to share with his employees Friedrich Nietzsche's *The Birth of Tragedy* (1872) in which the brooding German metaphysician, who was stylistically a pioneer of discontinuity, affirms art not as a luxury but as a necessity, which helps men and women, particularly the poor, to find consolation and even freedom in a world he judged immoral and irrational. Borrowers of Tolstoy's "What Is Art?" (1898) would have read a pioneering essay on formalist aesthetic criticism wherein the Russian novelist and philosopher says the artist's task is to render visible the emotions resulting from his perceptions of the beauty existing in nature.

Another book in the collection was *The Dance of Life* (1923) by English psychologist Havelock Ellis in which the author argued that aesthetics was the essence of morality and prophesied that the leisure conferred on workers by shorter days of toil would set in motion an aesthetic revolution. There were also works by the Harvard-based psychologist William McDougall, who investigated the influence of emotional perception on internal neurological events and external behavior. Barnes made available the pungent critical essays of H. L. Mencken, inverter of conventional prejudices, Ibsen's plays about people who rebelled against conventional society, and the novels of Sherwood Anderson, one of America's first writers to break the rules of structure to embody moment and to explore the subconscious instincts of individuals in his dark and brooding tales. No writer represented in the factory library drew more fervent praise from Barnes than the then popular English novelist Dorothy Richardson who in her twelve-volume series, *Pilgrimage* (1915-1938), tried to find a pattern in her own psychic history. The collector called her a "star of unique magnitude." He admired her skill in constructing the stream of images that ran through the mind of her heroine and told John Dewey that she "related and explained the mind of woman better than anyone else ha[d] ever done."[10]

All these books were subject to discussion in Mary Mullen's classes. But she also engaged her students in some consideration of the day's most powerful scientific idea, evolution, and in at least a tentative exploration of the scientific method itself. Particular attention was paid to race issues. "The social and economic handicaps under which the Negro suffers . . . were naturally in the center of the men's consciousness," Mullen said, "and the coordination of particular facts with general principles was easiest in this field." The thirty-something teacher of African-American students, both older and younger than herself, did not wholly avoid a maternalistic attitude. There is no evidence, moreover, that she understood that the principal cause of the "handicaps" born by blacks lay in the pervasive racism of the times and not, as she once suggested, "in the Negro himself." Nevertheless, she recognized that the African-American men in her classes possessed the "resources" to raise themselves up. Giving voice to the ethic of objective setting and delayed gratification, she taught her adult pupils that "the Negro's spontaneity, his impulsiveness, his delight in imagination were valuable only if kept within limits, and that a resolute, self-denying effort to reach a distant goal was often, under existing conditions, more important than enjoyment of the pleasures nearest at hand." Through discussion not exhortation, she tried to "overcome the timidity, the self-distrust of the Negro by showing him the achievements of his race, the things of which it is capable. To overcome his tendency to live in the moment, to shirk the practical difficulties of organization," she attempted to convince him "that persistent effort through times of distraction and discouragement is essential if advance on his part is to be anything more than a pious hope."[11]

Barnes was reluctant to claim too much for the factory classes, and, on at least one occasion, he expressed a considerable degree of frustration. He wrote to Dewey in 1920 of the students' failure to show "a spark of response" and attributed it to their not wanting "anything different" despite efforts to give them "a glimpse of a life better than the[ir] drab . . . routine."[12] Three years later, however, he spoke with measured pride of success "to a certain extent, at least, in developing an environment which attracted . . . a number of people whose time out of business hours had been a desolate waste."[13] Mullen wrote that the men in her class "came increasingly to rely on their intelligence." She said "their ability to view a situation dispassionately, to seek and to find the information needed to solve a practical or personal problem was amply vindicated, and this increasing display of rationality was not accompanied by any falling off in the dramatic quality of the discussions."[14] Mullen and her employer embraced what was for James and Dewey the essence of pragmatism: the belief that there are no foregone conclusions in life. Destiny isn't written in the stars—or proscribed by class or race. People are the agents of their own fate.

Indeed, Barnes liked to tell the story of Johnny White, a black employee who had some talent as a professional fighter. White never took time off from his job to train, and his boss appreciated his loyalty and sense of responsibility. But he was concerned about the punishment Johnny took on weekends in the "battle royal" at Bailey's Broadway Athletic Club. It was a slugfest in which four men fought an unlimited number of two- or three-minute rounds until the only one left standing was declared the winner. The fighters were paid fifty cents, and Barnes suggested to Johnny that he could do better financially, with less chance of serious injury, if he competed in the regulated eight-round boxing bouts. Taking up Johnny's training himself, Barnes said he "put William James and John Dewey into his boxing."[15] But whatever Johnny learned from the philosophers, it wasn't sufficient to take him all the way to the championship of his class, for he lost to the title-holder. Still, Barnes took some satisfaction in knowing that his protégé now earned more for one night in the ring than for a week's labor in the Argyrol factory.

What pleased Mullen most was the receptivity of Johnny and his co-workers to her art appreciation lessons. She marveled at "the temperamental affinity" she found "between the Negro and art in all its forms. What was colorful, what was picturesque, what was rhythmic, impressed him instantly," she said. "His initiation into the world of art seemed as natural as his initiation into breathing, and just as natural was his assimilation of art into his own life. Spontaneous, even automatic, as the manifestation of his aesthetic interest was, it was intelligent as well: he not only enjoyed, he was able to learn why he enjoyed."[16]

Heading the reading list for Mullen's classes were Santayana's *The Sense of Beauty* (1896) and his *Reason in Art* (1905). Students also were introduced to Percy Moore Turner's *Appreciation of Painting* (1922) and the articles and essays of the English apostle of modern art, Roger Fry, notably those collected and published in 1920 as *Vision and Design*, a work that greatly influenced Barnes himself. He had begun to buy paintings in significant quantity and hung on the factory walls those of his favorite American artists, William Glackens, Ernest Lawson, and Maurice Prendergast. By the early twenties, the Argyrol plant regularly had on exhibit about a hundred pictures. Barnes sold individual canvases at cost to employees who expressed a desire to own them. The purchasers included the Mullen sisters who, between the two of them, put together eclectic personal collections of more than a hundred American and French early modern paintings. Always careful to avoid conveying the impression that the factory classes had created "art connoisseurs," Barnes nevertheless took credit for having "stirred an intelligent interest in spiritual things created by living people" among his workers.[17]

His own interest in collecting began about the same time he and Laura built their first house on the Philadelphia Main Line. The quick success of Barnes's pharmaceutical business enabled him to purchase property in Merion, Pennsylvania, less than a mile from the house he had rented for his bride in pleasant, middle-class Overbrook, but rather more distant in terms of social status—and a world away from the neighborhoods in which he had lived as a boy. On January 16, 1905, the Barneses bought two and three-quarters acres of land on Rose Hill Road, for $30,600, from Deborah Cresswell, the widow of a man whose family owned a huge iron foundry. Earlier known as Union Avenue and later as Latch's Lane, Rose Hill was then, as now, a "good address" in a decidedly well-to-do neighborhood.[18] The large estates along the dirt-packed road all had names, and Barnes followed the custom by calling his new house rising next to "Red-Slates," the fifteen-acre arboretum owned by Colonel Joseph

Lapsley Wilson, "Lauraston."[19] The name was an affectionate tribute to his wife who supervised the construction of the twelve-room, English-style dwelling built of granite. Even late in life, Laura recalled the great pleasure she had derived from the project, especially her role in overseeing the exterior planting. Although the marketing of Argyrol and Ovoferrin must have consumed most of his time, her husband took considerable interest in the interior decoration of their home, which would be filled with furniture custom-made by the highly regarded local firm of Hale and Kilburn. One of Barnes's first major art purchases was a Corot landscape for "Lauraston."

He also bought horses and, with his wife, took riding lessons. They joined the Rose Tree Hunt, the oldest fox-hunting club in the Philadelphia area, and in scarlet (traditionally known as "pink") coat, white breeches, black and mahogany boots, and black top hat, Barnes rode to hounds in rural Delaware County. Among participants in the rigorous sport, who set a premium on courage, he was known for his doggedness, resolutely remounting after his frequent falls. For a while he also rode with a group that became the Pickering Hunt. He met a young painter who liked to jump horses, and for a brief period, he and the well-connected George Biddle pursued their equestrian hobby together. But Barnes eventually concluded that spending weekends in the saddle was not the best use of his time. Within a few years, he gave up riding and contented himself with walking for exercise and watching Connie Mack's Philadelphia Athletics play baseball for excitement. He no doubt felt freer to indulge his penchant for blunt and bawdy language in Shibe Park than at Rose Tree where the use of ancient cries, such as "yonder, he goes," when a member sighted a fox, was prescribed by tradition. Although he had become a connoisseur of whiskey, taking the entire annual output of a small distillery in Scotland, and of the wines of Burgundy and Bordeaux, club life was not for him. Nor did he and Laura ever become part of a conventional social set. Barnes's neighbors did not become his friends.

With his income increasing, however, he took advantage of their changing circumstances to buy additional real estate on Latch's Lane as properties went on the market.[20] In the years 1912 and 1913, he spent more than $100,000. Barnes was not speculating; he made no significant profit on his real estate transactions. His motive appears to have been keeping up the tone of the neighborhood once the descendants of the original or long-time owners decided to convert their inheritance into hard currency. But it occasionally took some juggling to finance land purchases and housing construction at the same time he was feeding a growing appetite for art.

3

The Collector and His Tutors

Barnes's lawyer, John G. Johnson, was one of the most discriminating collectors in America. His legal acumen had made him rich, but just as he always refused to accept an exaggerated fee for his services as an attorney, he declined to pay inflated prices for art. He studied books on painting and poured over catalogues of exhibitions. As Aileen Saarinen has written, Johnson "learned to evaluate the advice he was given, to see through the schemes of the dealers, to appraise the petulant bickering of the experts, and, in the final analysis, he depended on his own good judgment of the intrinsic quality of the work itself."[1] Barnes could not have had a better model for his own first forays into the art market. Since he admired his friend's scholarship, if not Johnson's emphasis on what he viewed as "antiquity and depressing piety,"[2] it is probable that he consciously adopted aspects of Johnson's approach to acquiring pictures.

Barnes had likely bought his first few, small paintings when he was a student in Germany. The profits from Argyrol enabled him to become a big-time collector, but the quality of his collection is a reflection of growing discernment—a willingness to work hard at learning to see. As his assets grew, Barnes visited galleries in New York and Philadelphia, on the whole unwaveringly conservative establishments, where he purchased the rural landscapes and depictions of peasant life favored by the masters of the Barbizon School. Johnson, too, had bought the canvasses of these mid-nineteenth century French painters, and his young client followed in his footsteps, acquiring works by Millet and Narcisse Diaz in addition to portraits by Jean-Jacques Henner and another Corot.[3] But Barnes was nothing if not an independent thinker, and he soon developed an eye for the paintings of artists whom he described as "men that make up the greatest movement in the history of art—the Frenchmen of about 1860 and later, whose work is so richly expressive of life that means most to the normal man alive today."[4] He would also buy the works of Americans influenced by the Impressionists and Post-Impressionists, and one of them, his Central High School classmate William Glackens, provided what

Barnes acknowledged as "the most valuable single . . . factor" in his art education.[5] More than the books of art historians, critics, and connoisseurs, his "association with a life-long friend who combines greatness as an artist with a big man's mind" helped him develop critical insight into the ways and work of painters.[6]

Barnes wrote to "Butts," as he always called Glackens, seeking to renew their friendship in 1910 or 1911. The artist had become one of America's best-known illustrators and was gaining an increasingly solid reputation as a painter associated with a group of rebel realists, most originally from Philadelphia, called The Eight. While Barnes had studied medicine, Glackens had attended the Pennsylvania Academy of the Fine Arts intermittently and worked as an artist-journalist for several Philadelphia newspapers. In 1895, he went to Paris where, at first, his work reflected, in its muted tones, the influence of Whistler then, in its dark palette and robust manner, the early Manet. On returning to the United States, after more than a year abroad, Glackens settled in New York and continued his career as an illustrator. He was sent to Cuba to cover the Spanish-American War for *McClure's* and produced a series of memorable action sketches showing the carnage of the battles for Santiago and San Juan. In 1904, he married a spirited woman, Edith Dimock, the artist daughter of a silk tycoon. Within a few years he began to devote himself almost entirely to painting, and after spending more time Europe, first in Madrid and then in Paris, he started to work with brighter colors and increasingly capture, as a contemporary critic observed, "the quickness of the rhythm of modern life."[7]

Glackens and his artist friends, Robert Henri, John Sloan, George Luks, Everett Shinn, Arthur B. Davies, Maurice Prendergast, and Ernest Lawson, were thrust into the limelight when they exhibited at the Macbeth Gallery in 1908. But Barnes was preoccupied with the demands of his newly solo business venture at the time, so he may have paid little attention to press accounts of the "ash-can school," an epithet reflecting conservative scorn for the artists' choice of commonplace subjects. In any case, Glackens was a busy and successful artist when he heard from his high school chum, and Barnes had to write several more letters and, finally, send a telegram before Butts finally answered him.[8]

The painter was an amiable man, endowed with an unflappable serenity, and he seems to have been pleased to reestablish a relationship with the classmate he had not seen for some twenty years. But their adult friendship would be based on more than shared memories. Barnes sought out Glackens because of his growing interest in art, particularly as it related to education. He found an unexpected joy in collecting and wanted to test his first, tentative ideas about what to look for in paintings with someone he respected and felt he could trust. A combination of instinct and luck led him to an artist who was delighted by the color of the world, had an eye for the comedy in life, and whose opinions about art making were straightforward and unpretentious.

Glackens's consistent failure "to indulge in blah," as an admiring editor once noted, undoubtedly endeared him to his classmate.[9]

William and Edith and Albert and Laura were soon spending occasional weekends together. The summer of 1911 found them both on the south shore of Long Island, where the Glackenses had rented a cottage in the artists' colony of Bellport and the Barneses visited Laura's mother at her summer place in nearby Blue Point. It was at Bellport that William Glackens introduced Barnes to his friend Maurice Prendergast, the only other American painter whose work Barnes would come to value as highly as that of his pal from Central High School. In Merion, Butts and Edith would be introduced to musicians and treated, on occasion, to intimate performances by members of the Philadelphia Orchestra, including piano solos by its new conductor, Leopold Stokowski, who came to Philadelphia from England in 1912. It was not unusual during the years before and after World War I for wealthy men and women to engage prominent classical musicians to give private concerts at their homes, but Barnes seems to have particularly admired Stokowski for his willingness to premier the work of contemporary composers and his bold experiments with new technology.

For his part, Glackens had rejected the fashionable salon-painting manner that took its cue from John Singer Sargent and moved beyond his fascination with the early Impressionists. His work shared a brightness and vibrancy with the work of Renoir, the painter whom, according to Barnes's later observation, he resembled "psychologically" above all others.[10] The approach of each to his visual environment was joyful. What Barnes valued most in Glackens's paintings were human values—"things," he said, "which move us in life most deeply."[11] Ira Glackens tells us that his father was not impressed with his friend's nascent collection of Barbizon pictures. But his appraisal was undoubtedly made with the same gentleness and good humor that he once displayed in assessing his classmate's artistic talent. He suggested Barnes had paid too much for "safe" pictures and told him about painters that he thought more deserving of his attention.[12]

The tyro collector took Glackens's advice seriously. He must have turned initially to a handful of art journals and little magazines, such as *American Art News*, the *Arts*, *Burlington Magazine*, *Camera Work*, and the *Dial*, for information about modern French painters, and he would have had a chance to see their work at "291," Alfred Stieglitz's pioneering gallery on Fifth Avenue in New York City. In addition to Henri and Prendergast, Glackens introduced him to such American artists as Charles Demuth and Alfred Maurer, and Barnes began to buy their work. Driving "a very hard bargain," he purchased a reclining nude from John Sloan,[13] the first painting his fellow Central alumnus had ever sold. He also acquired six pictures by Henri for $5,500 and some fifty works by Glackens himself, including *Race Track* and *The Float*, which he considered among his friend's finest paintings.[14]

By early 1912, Barnes was ready to add modern European art to his collection. He sent Glackens to Paris with a $20,000 line of credit to buy a selection of designated pictures and to seek other works for his approval. Not only did Glackens know the city well, his traveling companion, "Alfy" Maurer, one of the first American painters to embrace sophisticated European styles, had made Paris his home for more than a decade. Sailing aboard the *du Rocheanbeau,* the two American artists landed in Le Havre on February 12, and an account of their activities on behalf of Barnes is provided in letters Glackens wrote to his wife over the next several weeks. He mentioned, in particular, that shortly after their arrival in Paris, Maurer introduced him to the American collector Leo Stein, who was then living in the French capital with his sister Gertrude. But Glackens had little time for socializing. Within four days of making the rounds of the galleries, he bought his first picture. From Joseph and Georges Durand-Ruel, who specialized in works by Impressionists, he "got a fine little Renoir" oil of "a little girl reading a book." He wrote his "dearest Teed" that he "paid seven thousand francs for it ($1,400)," and since the dealers were asking eight and the painting was from Renoir's "best period," he considered *Child Reading* "a bargain." But he also noted that "Barnes will not get as much for his money as he expects. You can't touch a Cézanne under $3000," he wrote, "and that for a little landscape. His portraits and important pictures range from $7,000 to $30,000."[15]

Glackens bought two more small paintings by Renoir from Durand-Ruel.[16] At auction, he acquired Van Gogh's *The Postman.* From Ambroise Vollard, he purchased Picasso's *Women with a Cigarette* for 1,000 francs, and he spent 13,200 francs at Galerie Bernheim-Jeune for one of Cézanne's rich and subtle but not very large Sainte-Victoire landscapes. Having exhausted the funds Barnes made available to him, Glackens located a fine Degas. He cabled his friend, and by return cable, Barnes provided the money for a final purchase. By March 1 Glackens's work was done, and he wrote Teed: "I sail tomorrow. . . . Everything is settled up here and the pictures [are] being boxed. I am mighty glad it is finished and I am sick of looking at pictures and asking prices."[17]

What was Barnes's reaction when his new acquisitions were uncrated in Merion? Ira Glackens said he studied them for weeks. According to the artist's son, he was sure that "there must be some scientific analysis—a sort of laboratory test—to which a painting could be subjected, and which would prove irrefutably whether it was true gold or base metal."[18] He had the pictures' antique French frames removed, reframed the pictures, then restored the original frames. The works they enclosed were fundamentally different, in the look of the art and the techniques employed in creating it, from his feathery Barbizon paintings. Their parts were separable into independent patches of color. Barnes looked at the discrete shapes before him and saw an individualism and vitality that led him to fall in love with early modern art. With the same high intelligence, focus, and discipline that had marked his business career, he embarked on an intense and rigorous program of educating himself about what would become an enduring passion. He never again designated an emissary to buy paintings.

But before he began his forays into the European art market, there were family matters requiring his attention. At the same time that he was letting go of his early affection for an older tradition in painting, his mother became seriously ill. Barnes had no choice but to relinquish what had been an early and likely constant source of encouragement—the woman he saw as "marvelous" and whose "balance" he admired perhaps in some measure because he lacked that very quality. Lydia died of pneumonia on May 2, 1912, a passing that her son, the doctor, must have recognized as a blessing since a contributory factor, according to the death certificate, was a tumor of the brain. She had owned several plots in the Odd Fellows Cemetery in Burlington, New Jersey, and it was there that Barnes laid her to rest. The grieving son then embarked on the defining adventure of his life as he turned his formidable energies to becoming a remarkably discerning collector in the interest of a grand educational experiment.

In the summer of 1912, he went to Paris on his own shopping expedition, the first of many that took him to Left Bank garrets and cafés as well as prominent galleries in search of artistic treasures, which he always hoped to acquire at thrift-shop prices. The chase of pictures energized him far more than the chase of foxes. He approached art inductively, the way he had learned to do science. The starting point was data collection. At first, Barnes turned to the authoritative texts of his day, but while deriving some help from them, he soon concluded there was no substitute for the direct experience of works of art. "That situation makes worthwh[i]le getting a collection that is the owner's personal exponent," he wrote. It was not so much a rich man's indulgence as his "keen pleasure." Barnes's "working formula" was to "to buy a painting . . . to have honest painters in . . . [his] house and talk to them about . . . [his] pictures, to lose no opportunity to look at paintings everywhere, to read books on art and not to be discouraged at how little they give to make an artist's work enjoyable and understandable."[19]

Leo Stein, a vastly knowledgeable and intractably neurotic American who was among the most important publicists and patrons of early modern French painters, shared with Barnes a dislike of "twaddle about art instead of hard-boiled common sense."[20] Alfred Maurer had introduced the two collectors in 1912. Stein and Barnes were the same age. Family money, derived from a prosperous clothing business, provided Stein with the means to live independently if not grandly. Born in Pittsburgh, he had spent part of his childhood in Europe then moved with his family to Oakland, California. He began his undergraduate education at the university in Berkeley. When he was orphaned at nineteen, he transferred to Harvard College as a special student. He went on to study at Harvard Law, but dropped out to travel and pursue his interest in art.

When Barnes was studying pharmacology and chemistry in Berlin, Stein was spending his days in the Louvre. The summer of 1900, when Barnes returned to Germany to work in a laboratory in Heidelberg, Stein, too, came back to Europe, intending to make his home there. He lived first in Florence, then London, and, finally, settled in Paris where he took painting classes at the academies Julian and Colarossi, studied briefly with Matisse, and haunted the galleries for the work of living artists.

With his famous relatives, sister Gertrude and brother and sister-in-law Michael and Sarah, Leo had purchased Matisse's *Woman with a Hat* for the asking price of $100 at the Autumn Salon of 1905. The year before that key exhibition in the history of art, at which Matisse and others acquired the sneering appellation wild beasts (*fauves*), he had bought a Picasso gouache, *Acrobat's Family with a Monkey*, from Clovis Sagot's, and returned with Gertrude to buy the artist's *Young Girl with a Basket of Flowers*.[21] From then until the beginning of World War I, the Steins' Saturday night salons at 27, rue de Fleurus, the apartment Gertrude and Leo shared, attracted everyone connected in any significant way with modern art. In addition to works by the young Spaniard and Matisse's bright pictures, paintings by Cézanne, Renoir, Gauguin, Degas, Bonnard, Vallotton, Manguin, Daumier, Manet, El Greco, and Toulouse-Lautrec hung, crowded together, on the walls. It was a dazzling and unique array, and the upstart collector from Philadelphia came with money to spend and an intuitive understanding that he had much to learn there.

Ira Glackens paints a hilarious word picture, presumably transmitted from Maurer to his father to him, of Barnes chasing Gertrude around her dining table "in pursuit not so much of Gertrude as of a canvas by Picasso that was in her possession," which he "won at a thumping good price."[22] But he hardly endeared himself to the famously inspirational hostess who had studied psychology with William James and medicine with William Osler before dedicating herself to writing "perfect sentences." Though she would later sell him two paintings by Matisse, *View of the Sea, Collioure* for 900 francs and *Still Life with Melon* for 3,100, she dismissed him as a greedy millionaire, waving his checkbook in the air as he tried to buy her pictures. Gertrude's brother, however, found he shared a deep interest in psychology and aesthetics with his guest. Leo Stein and Albert Barnes were forty when they met, and for the next thirty-five years, they maintained a friendship, which was based as much on the understanding of each other's weaknesses as a respect for each other's strengths.

In a letter to a psychologist who had treated him, Stein confessed, "Barnes once objected that I liked to expound my own aesthetics, but was impatient of listening to his expositions. He said: 'This hurts like Hell.'"[23] Barnes wanted Stein to take him seriously as an intellectual though he would come to regard the brilliant expatriate, who had trouble mustering the will to write anything substantial for publication, as a man who had "misspent [his] life."[24] He listened to Stein's analysis of the power of modern art as he held forth on the rue de Fleurus surrounded by some of the best of it. When his friend was willing or needed to sell paintings from his collection, he bought them or helped to arrange for their sale. They quarreled in print on several occasions, and Barnes could not resist using his knowledge of Stein's neurosis to score. But he would write his friend a heartfelt letter of appreciation that was the great comfort and blessing of Leo's final days.

Barnes entreated Stein to introduce him to collectors.[25] Should they ever have to sell paintings, he wanted to have the chance of buying directly from them. But, of course, he had to make most of his purchases through dealers. Just before his mother's death, he had bought Renoir's *Torso* and the painter's *Girl with Jumping Rope* from Durand-Ruel's New York gallery,[26] and on his first solo buying trip that summer of 1912, he acquired a Gauguin, a Delacroix, a Van Gogh, a Vallotton, and three Bonnards from Joseph and Gaston Bernheim-Jeune.[27] Returning to Philadelphia, he negotiated with Ambroise Vollard, through Alfred Maurer, for Cézanne's *Woman in a Red-Striped Dress*, but at the end of October, just after Barnes had cabled shipping instructions, the deal fell through.[28] Barnes lost little time in coming back in Paris to take on the city's dealers in a public arena. What an art magazine of the time called an "epoch-making" sale took place from December 9-11, 1912 when the famous collection of Henri Rouart was presented at auction. The *Burlington Magazine* reported that "when Cézanne's little *Baigneuses* [*Five Bathers* 1877-78], measuring only 16 by 17 inches, was put up by the experts at 8,000 francs and rapidly rose to 18,000 (19,800 including charges), at which point it was bought by Mr. Barnes, an American collector, there was derisive laughter from some of the worthy dealers and others. . . . Who, they evidently thought, are the lunatics let loose among us?"[29] Barnes also purchased two small Cézanne still lifes at the Rouart sale for which he paid 2,000 and 7,000 francs, respectively.[30] On December 10, Ambroise Vollard sold him three additional Cézannes: a portrait of Madame Cézanne for 39,950 francs, a composition of bathers for 14,980 francs, and *Fruits*, 1885 for 4,875 francs.[31] A few days earlier at a private sale in the Hôtel Drouot, he had acquired Renoir's *Women with Bouquet* for 26,400 francs and the painter's *Women Crocheting* for 18,700, as well as two paintings by Daumier and one by Pissarro.[32] It was quite a haul for a week in winter. In a matter of days, Barnes had become a major player in an elite game—the buying and selling of modern art. He arranged for Durand-Ruel to ship his purchases to Philadelphia and was home before Christmas.

The holiday season that year was an especially busy one for his friend Butts Glackens who, with other members of The Eight, was in the midst of last-minute preparations for what had been conceived as another comprehensive exhibition of independent artists and became, under the leadership of the urbane painter Arthur B. Davies, a historic survey of modern European art now known as the Armory Show. Glackens was in charge of the large American section. But he could not persuade Barnes to alter his already established policy of not lending any of his pictures. Displaying the possessiveness of a bridegroom, the new collector wrote to Davies, "If you knew what those paintings meant to me, I am sure you would not put me in the position where I appear selfish or unsympathetic in refusing the loan. They are with me not an incident or pieces of furniture—they are simply my daily life itself and I could no more be without them for a month than I could go without food for a like period."[33] The Armory Show opened on February 17, 1913 with about 1,600 works of art. The French modernists were well represented in the great hall of the New York National Guard's 69th Regiment at Twenty-Sixth Street and Lexington Avenue. The lawyer-collector John Quinn, counsel to the sponsoring committee, bought heavily, spending nearly $6,000.[34] Even the Metropolitan Museum of Art, which owned a single Renoir, *Mme. Charpentier with Her Children*, purchased its first Cézanne. Barnes's acquisitions were limited to one Vlaminck landscape for which he paid $162.[35] He readily acknowledged, however, that the exhibition was "the sensation of the generation."[36] It "had a tremendous influence for good upon live American painters," he said, and, as the years passed, he frequently alluded to its catalytic power.[37]

During the run of the Armory Show, Barnes was negotiating with Durand-Ruel for another Cézanne still life. The picture was owned by Vollard, but Barnes apparently did not want to pay the owner's price of 30,000 francs nor to be known as the buyer. Keeping his identity secret, therefore, Durand-Ruel bargained with Vollard until he sold it for 23,000 francs. As the firm had promised, it then sold the painting to Barnes for the same amount plus a 300-franc commission all the while begging him to keep silent about the transaction. The collector paid the commission but said that he had thought it was to be 5 rather than 10 percent, and, if he was correct, Durand-Ruel should credit him the difference.[38]

The venerable firm recognized the rich Philadelphian as a customer with extraordinary potential. Exasperating, certainly, but the market for modern art was still small, and he had established his bona fides as a serious collector. Indeed, he returned to Paris in June, spent 30,000 francs for Renoir's *The Luncheon*, which he bought from the young dealer Roger Levesque de Blives, acquired a Gauguin, a Delacroix, and a Van Gogh from Bernheim-Jeune,[39] and again engaged Durand-Ruel as an intermediary in making three major purchases from Vollard. But as the art historian John Rewald has shown, it was vastly complicated business.[40] Barnes initially made an arrangement with Durand-Ruel to buy a large number of paintings that he would pay for on a monthly-installment basis. The next day, however, he wrote that the real-estate transactions in which he was engaged made it unwise for him to take on additional financial obligations. He canceled his previously made selection of Renoirs as well as instructions to buy certain pictures at the upcoming Marczell de Nemes sale. He also cancelled the purchase he had made from

Vollard on June 2, including a Cézanne (probably *House among Trees*), two Picassos (*Blue Child* and *Composition: The Peasants*), and *Head of a Child*, another Renoir.[41]

But building a collection was more important to him than building country houses, and he added a postscript to his letter to Durand-Ruel. He said that if the firm could buy the pictures he wanted from Vollard for 35,000 francs and could arrange with Vollard for him to pay for them at the rate of 7,000 francs a month, he would send Durand-Ruel a monthly bank draft for 7,200 francs. Barnes was on his way to visit friends in Heidelberg, and it was there that Durand-Ruel cabled him Vollard's counter offer—50,000 francs cash for the Cézanne, the Picasso, and the Renoir. The collector replied to his agent that he had rearranged his finances to meet the demands of "his Majesty, Vollard, the first," but only if Vollard would meet certain conditions with respect to the framing of the pictures and their packing and transportation to Le Havre.[42] Negotiations continued for several days. Barnes cabled Nelle Mullen from Heidelberg to defer his real estate transactions for a month. He suggested to Durand-Ruel that he visit Vollard and offer him 45,500 francs on the spot. If Vollard accepted, he would take the paintings home with him and send his agent 50,000 francs within a few days to cover the advance. At last a deal was struck. Barnes wrote to Durand-Ruel on June 23 from Philadelphia to say he had sent a check for $11,067.96 to the firm's New York branch. He had his pictures—a few months too early to avoid stiff import duties. Another collector, attorney John Quinn, had persuaded Congress to change the 1909 tariff law to exempt the work of living as well as long-dead artists, but it was September before the Senate had finished its intensive scrutiny of the House measure and October before President Wilson signed the bill that permitted the free entry of original paintings and sculpture.

Barnes returned to Europe again in April of 1914 on an extended trip that took him to galleries and museums from Paris to Madrid to Florence. By then, Leo and Gertrude Stein had come to a parting of the ways. Not only had their household included Alice B. Toklas for the past several years, but Leo had met a beautiful former artist's model, Nina Auzias, whom he would finally marry in 1921. In February, when the collector had learned of the Steins' impending separation, he wrote Leo asking to buy Renoir's "mother with child, & the little nude standing in water."[43] But *Standing Nude* had been sold already, and Leo wanted to keep the creamy image of maternal affection.[44] Barnes wrote again offering to show him how to finance writing about art: "Things you can say better than anyone else I know."[45] In the spring, to help pay for a move to the Tuscan village of Settignano, Leo sold Barnes another Renoir (Barnes already had a dozen) and a Cézanne landscape, *Spring-House*, the latter for 15,000 francs.[46]

Barnes also bought five small cubist Picassos from Kahnweiler and a Courbet and a Charles Conder from Bernheim-Jeune.[47] But once again he would make his major purchases through Durand-Ruel. He bought eight Renoirs, a Cézanne, and El Greco's *St. Francis of Assisi* directly from the dealer, and Durand-Ruel acted as his agent at a public auction where he acquired Renoir's large *Nude in Brook*.[48] Later he sought to return the El Greco, writing to Durand-Ruel on June 26, that another American collector, whom he did not name, had questioned its authenticity. He also complained that several frames in the latest shipment of his purchases had been damaged in transit. But the letter did not reach Paris until after the assassinations of the Archduke Ferdinand and his wife in Sarajevo. Durand-Ruel replied that the El Greco came from a highly respected collection whose owner had purchased it some forty or fifty years earlier on the advice of Degas, and then added, "As you may suppose, business is entirely at a standstill. The question of claiming any damage for the broken frames will have to be taken up later on, after the war is over."[49]

The Great War put a temporary stop to Barnes's twice-yearly trips to Europe. But his art collection was already a superb one. In February of 1914, he had written to Leo Stein that it contained twenty-five Renoirs and a dozen Cézannes.[50] Four months later, the editor of *Arts and Decoration*, painter Guy Pène DuBois, declared that Barnes had assembled "the most consistently modern collection in America."[51] The clash of armies slowed his pace of acquisition, but he kept on buying. "Good paintings," he wrote, "are more satisfying companions than the best of books and infinitely more so than most very nice people."[52] Glackens was the exception Barnes undoubtedly had in mind, and in October of 1914, he demonstrated his affection for his friend by faithfully attending him during an appendectomy. Ira Glackens said he "donned a surgeon's white coat" and stood by during "the operation to count the sponges."[53] Butts wrote to his wife from Philadelphia's Jefferson Hospital that Barnes had brought him homemade soup and that he would spend the first five days or so of his recuperation under his friend's watchful eye in Merion.[54]

But Barnes's gaze never strayed for long from the art market. On October 19, 1914, he acquired Renoir's *Sailor Boy* from Durand-Ruel, and a month later, he bought the artist's *Girl with Parasol*.[55] When word reached him that Renoir had entrusted a self-portrait to Durand-Ruel for safekeeping, he wrote to the dealer expressing interest in the picture. In a letter dated January 25, 1915, he asked Durand-Ruel to tell the artist that he owned fifty of his paintings, regarded him as the greatest living painter, and intended to give the collection he was assembling to the city of Philadelphia.[56] But his entreaty fell on deaf ears. Renoir did not wish to sell. In the spring, however, Durand-Ruel was able to obtain another picture Barnes had asked his agent to try to buy for him. It was a portrait of Madame Cézanne, now entitled *The Artist's Wife in a Green Hat*, which was owned by Vollard. Barnes offered 35,000 francs in a letter dated January 15, but it was not until March 29 that Vollard accepted Durand-Ruel's offer of 33,000 francs and Durand-Ruel, on the same day, sold it to Barnes for 40,000.[57] The firm's commission was more than twice what it had received in the past from its Philadelphia client, but the war had changed many things.

Barnes used the time he had previously spent traveling abroad on a program of study at home. He had begun his self-education almost as soon as he began to commit large sums to his growing passion. In July of 1914, he wrote to Leo Stein:

> I have been reading and thinking so damn much about art during the past three years that it has become almost an obsession. . . . I have lived with my own two hundred paintings as constant companions and objects of study from two o'clock every day until ten o'clock at night. . . . I find I am constantly changing: paintings which interested me and which I fairly loved a year or even six months ago now leave me cold. I have in the store-room of my house probably twenty paintings, many of which cost me considerable money and which were discarded because I think the personal message of the painter was either insincere or his presentation so bungling that it is not to be considered a work of art.[58]

The collector told John Johnson, "I've given more time and effort to trying to find out what is a good painting than I've ever given to any other subject in my life."[59] When Barnes decided he needed formal, systematic instruction of a broad nature to aid him in his search for understanding, he selected Lawrence Ladd Buermeyer, a University of Pennsylvania graduate student, as a tutor. Buermeyer had taken his A.B. at Penn in 1912 and held the University's distinguished Harrison Fellowship in Philosophy. The young scholar's new assignment was to examine and discuss with the collector the "psychology of aesthetics and the practical application of those principles to paintings."[60] At the time, Barnes was considering the publication of an illustrated book on the works in his collection,[61] and he may have wanted someone to help him with the project. Whatever the range of his duties, Buermeyer took the train from West Philadelphia to Merion three afternoons a week. He and Barnes read William James together for three to four hours each session. The collector was already familiar with a number of the philosopher's books, which he had introduced into his factory classroom, but now he had a guide to lead him through a systematic review and further exploration of the nuances of James's pragmatism. Starting with *The Principles of Psychology*, they proceeded through all his works until, as Barnes later told John Dewey, "James crystallized for me into a beautiful gem."[62] The focus on facts and action of the psychologist/philosopher was enormously appealing to him. It validated his own inclination to give priority to method over belief and reinforced his scientific approach to life wherein the highest value was placed on verification. But Barnes's work with his tutor was not limited to a single author. Over the next five years, while Buermeyer was studying for his Ph.D. at Princeton, the two men met on a regular basis and "traveled" together, again in Barnes's words, "from Aristotle to Freud."[63]

The physician who became a chemist then a businessman and finally a collector was at last obtaining the liberal arts education he had missed as a poor boy scrambling to prepare himself for a practical profession. Barnes almost certainly discussed the materials he and Buermeyer perused with Mary Mullen, and, in a remarkably swift intellectual transfer, Mullen took them up in bare-bones fashion with her worker students. Barnes's study sessions with Buermeyer also gave him the confidence to write his first article on art for publication. "How To Judge A Painting" was published as the lead essay in the April 1915 issue of *Arts and Decoration*. Noting that the author's home contained "the most comprehensive collection of modern pictures in America," the editor suggested to his readers that Barnes's "opinion should be of exceptional interest."[64] He also may have counted on photographs of five works from the collection (a Cézanne, three Renoirs, and a Glackens) to attract attention to his magazine.

Barnes never answers the title question of his essay in the text. He has yet to develop his formalistic analysis of paintings, and he only knows that, at their best, books about art pale before direct experience of an artwork. But his initial bid to become a public intellectual is interesting as a prototype of the Barnesian approach. The author exhibits familiarity with the literature. He analyzes the strengths and weaknesses of given writers, indulges in caustic criticism of those whose ideas he finds wanting, and turns to medicine for images to use in delivering what he regards as a verbal knockout punch. The power of plain speaking is diluted by ostentatious riffs. But there is, overall, an emotional honesty that suggests Barnes is attempting, in a significant regard, to hold himself to the same high standards he holds painters—and, indeed, most other people.

He acknowledges that a recent book by the English critic Clive Bell, which he found "most helpful" in 1915, "would have been so much Greek" to him five years earlier. Credited for a "stimulating" enthusiasm that a novice collector once found useful, the German art historian Julius Meier-Graefe is also ridiculed for his "verbosity and froth." George Moore, the Irish writer, critic, and painter, is lauded for his "insight into art essence." Leo Stein's neighbor in Settignano, the art historian and connoisseur Bernard Berenson, is praised for his skillful detective work and his ability to write "concisely and precisely." The American academic painter and writer Kenyon Cox, a harsh critic of modernism, is lambasted as an "artistic cripple, hobbling through the present on the tottering crutches of the dead artistic past." Barnes celebrates the work of Picasso ("a great artist and a great painter"), Matisse ("a greater artist than a painter"), and Renoir ("who, for me, breathes the spirit of perpetual youth in a garden of perennial June loveliness"), as well as his friends Lawson (a "clear manly voice") and Glackens (whose "painting, drawing, color, composition evidence . . . joy in creating"). He defines great artists as "men who saw extraordinarily well or felt deeply and told what they saw or felt simply, directly, honestly and in the spirit of their age."

In evaluating other, private American collections, Barnes observes, with apparent approval, that most "are to be freely seen by applicants." He writes that the collection of John G. Johnson's clients, the Havemeyer, "is the best and wisest . . . in America" and considers it the place where "one could study art and its relations to life to better advantage . . . than in any single gallery in the world." In discussing the education of collectors, he says "every collector who studies his paintings soon learns to accept his own discarded pictures as . . . necessary milestones on [the] way to his destination. Sooner or later," he adds, "one gets a collection that is quite as personal as its owner's face." Barnes rhapsodizes about living with pictures "as friends, children, objects of worship, diversions, serious mental occupations, whichever role . . . fit[s] the mood of the moment." For him, the least of the pleasures of collecting "is the mere possession." One of the enduring joys is related to the power of paintings to "stretch . . . the beholder's personal vision." With ringing confidence in his hard-won discernment, he concludes: "If Mr. Widener would offer to give his seven hundred thousand dollar Raphael Madonna for my Renoir bust, I would refuse to be cheated. That great Altman Rembrandt, woman cutting her nails, would be an inadequate swap for my greater Cézanne portrait of his wife."

The same month that Barnes's essay appeared in *Arts and Decoration*, Leo Stein sailed from Genoa to New York. Nina had returned to Paris, and the war made it impossible for him to get money out of France. He had been spending the principle from his estate for several years. Now he had the expense of living in America, which included sessions with two psychoanalysts, as well as paying rent for the house in Settignano and providing for Nina. In an effort to relieve his financial distress, he sold another painting, Cézanne's small *Group of Bathers*, to Barnes for $5,000 in December of 1915.[65] He accepted an invitation to lecture to an art history class at Bryn Mawr College and took on some writing assignments for Herbert Croly's new magazine of ideas, the *New Republic*.

Stein's first article, entitled "Cézanne," appeared in the January 22, 1916 issue. Evidencing a vague disappointment with modern art, it criticizes the painter's work for expressing a narrow range of life experience. Stein suggested that Cézanne, "tormented, agitated, a prey to endless fears, with nothing in the world around him to sustain him, created for himself the thing he most needed." He used color "to render matter stable and organic form substantial," and for that, the author conceded, he is "perhaps the most important figure in the history of modern painting."[66] Barnes immediately fired off a letter to the editor. He called the article "illuminating" but rebuked his friend for misapplying the Freudian theory that aesthetic feeling is "a product of frustrated action."[67] Stein had written that "the action aroused in us by what we see is contradicted by an impulse to sit quietly and look," and the consequent emotions elicited by these opposing tendencies "are experienced as a quality of the thing beheld."[68] Barnes claimed that Freud's theory of sublimation would be a better guide in any quest for the elusive origin of feelings associated with the experiencing of art. Quoting other psychologists and art critics, Stein defended himself in the next issue: "What I have stated in my own way is, *pace*, Mr. Barnes, essentially orthodox."[69] But the Philadelphia collector was clearly enjoying the exchange, and his second letter, published the following month, argued that there was scant empirical data for any "psychological explanation of aesthetic experience."[70] Michael Stein described the disagreement for sister Gertrude as "an old fashioned epistolary vituperative quarrel."[71] Had Barnes known of Stein's characterization, he would have loved it.

4

Mr. Dewey

Gertrude Stein's disdain for Barnes stemmed from their first meeting at 27, rue de Fleurus when he inquired, with characteristic directness, how much she had paid Picasso for her portrait—and seemed astonished that it had been a gift.[1] The picture, completed in 1906 at the end of the artist's Rose Period of harlequins and circus clowns, anticipated Cubism in its sharp and angular characterization of the sitter. Picasso gave full expression to the radical new style a year later in *Les Demoiselles d'Avignon*. The revolutionary painting, his sardonic commemoration of five prostitutes, would become a landmark in the development of modern art. In part, its innovation lay in Picasso's application of flesh tones as large quadrangular patches of color—the planes of Cézanne reinterpreted in a stunningly original work. But Leo Stein, who had bought sketches related to the *Demoiselles*, considered the finished painting a "horrible mess."[2]

Barnes shared his tutor's contempt. In his second published essay, a premature and, as it happened, mistaken judgment on the influence and development of the new style of picture making, entitled "Cubism: Requiescat in Pace," he wrote, "Cubism is academic, repetitive, banal, dead." Citing William James and Henri Bergson as his authorities, the collector pronounced the cubists' claim that "planes are the essentials of the forms of objects" faulty psychology and faulty metaphysics. "Experience is continuous," he said. "When we . . . isolate its aspects, break it into strata, we destroy its . . . character." Denying that emotion, an inherently subjective phenomenon, could be conveyed "in the terms of geometry, the most objective of sciences," he found Cubist painters guilty of carrying "expression to the extreme" and noted, wryly but not wrongly, "Gertrude Stein is the only analogue in letters, or, let us say, words."[3]

Pictures in the Cubist style failed to pass the most important test Barnes employed in judging a work of art: they did not evoke an aesthetic response in him. He would spend his money only on paintings that enriched his experience. He valued Renoirs above all others. The collector told Leo Stein that in looking at Renoir's pictures he never felt "the enui [sic] or disgust with the platitudinous, emptiness and general damn rot" that he had sometimes felt when looking at "the work of practically every man represented in [his] collection. . . . I would sooner live with Renoir[s] than Rubens," he said, and even as German Zeppelins dropped the first bombs ever to fall on Paris, Durand-Ruel managed to procure them for its American client.[4] Barnes acquired *After the Bath* and three other works by the artist in December of 1915 and, sometime in 1916, both *Noirmoutiers* and *Garden Scene in Brittany*.[5]

The most enriching experience he had during the war years, however, was meeting John Dewey. The "common sense" philosopher became a public intellectual of enormous influence with the publication of his *Democracy and Education* in 1916. In the fullest exposition he had yet made of his philosophy, Dewey turned to evolutionary biology and functional psychology to support his view of the kind of education required by a modern democratic society. The assumption underlying his pedagogical theory, like that underlying Barnes's rejection of Cubism, was the continuity of experience. For him, authentic learning grew out of living and doing.

Despite a labored prose style, *Democracy and Education* was received with high praise—one reviewer ranked it with Plato's *Republic* and Rousseau's *Émile* as a third testament in the philosophy of education[6]—and quickly became a best seller. Barnes found in its pages an official sanction for what he was trying to accomplish in his factory school. Dewey wrote that far from being confined to "technical and merely physical matters," the experimental method "holds equally to the forming and testing of ideas in social and moral matters."[7] *Democracy and Education* inspired Barnes, at age forty-five, to study with the author. In the academic year of 1917-18, he enrolled as a special student in Dewey's Columbia University seminar in social and political philosophy. With a secretary in tow, he took the train from Philadelphia to New York once each week to attend the great man's lectures. But as he later told Dewey, "I worshipped at your shrine long, long before I knew you."[8]

Barnes's idol was not an engaging speaker. He would sit at his desk fumbling with the notes he had made on sheets of yellow paper and crumple them into balls as he addressed his students. They sometimes felt he was unaware of their presence. Dewey had been born in Vermont in 1859, the year Darwin published his *Origin of the Species*, and at fifty-eight, he spoke slowly, with little emphasis, and often with long pauses between sentences, his eyes seemingly focused on something outside the classroom window. Recalling his former professor's lectures, the philosopher Irwin Edman said he came to understand that he "had been listening to a man actually thinking" in the presence of his students.[9] "Dewey's greatest gift as a teacher," Edman concluded, was "that of initiating inquiry rather than that of disseminating doctrine."[10] Although a shy man, the philosopher was instinctively courteous and insatiably curious, and he readily gave sympathetic consideration to the ideas and opinions of all who approached him.

It is little wonder that Barnes considered the days he spent on the Columbia campus some of the happiest of his life.[11] Dewey's seminar met after lunch on Tuesdays, and his pupil from Philadelphia—a stocky, dark-browed man dressed in an elegantly-tailored pin-striped suit — sat in the front of the room and was known to doze—sometimes sleeping through the closing bell as Dewey gathered up his books, cast a bemused smile in his direction, and shuffled out the door.[12] Barnes's classmates, mostly graduate students in their twenties, included, in addition to Edman, Brand Blanchard, who would later head the philosophy department at Yale University, his twin brother, Paul Blanchard, an ordained Congregational minister who became a prominent editor and author, and Margaret Frances Bradshaw, who married Brand the next year and would write a well-received book on aesthetics. There was also, in addition to a number of other young men in pursuit of Ph.Ds, a somewhat older woman enrolled, like Barnes, as a special student.

Her name was Anzia Yezierska. About thirty-five at the time, she listened with rapt attention to everything said in the seminar but rarely offered a comment or opinion. Red-haired and rebellious, "a wildly independent" woman, according to her niece, the writer Shana Alexander,[13] Yezierska had immigrated with her large family from Polish Russia in 1893. By her late teens, she had fled a strict and pious home where her father studied Talmud, but escaping the poverty of New York's Lower East Side took longer. She ironed shirts in a laundry for ten hours a day and dreamed of a literary career; at night, she took classes at the Educational Alliance, a school for immigrants, and, struggling to express herself in English, wrote poetry. A measure of her creativity was her ability to persuade the New York society women on the board of the Clara de Hirsch Home for Working Girls that she wanted to teach domestic science. In an unusual gesture for the times, they paid her tuition to Teachers College, newly part of Columbia University.

Although "notoriously uninterested and ungifted in any of the household arts," as Alexander has observed,[14] Yezierska graduated in 1904 and found a job as a substitute cooking teacher. By the time she met Dewey in 1917, she had studied acting, married and left two husbands, given birth to a daughter who she had decided to let the child's father raise, and published her first short story. Her ferocious will led her to seek the assistance of America's leading authority on education when she took up teaching once again and sought a permanent position in the New York City school system. The kindly Yankee philosopher was persuaded to observe Yezierska in front of her class and read the manuscripts about teeming tenement life she left with him. Attracted by her vibrancy, he invited her to audit his seminar and, as fall turned into winter, love blossomed. Their affair was brief; their relationship, tender and, although probably physically unconsummated, deeply felt.[15] Albert Barnes abetted it.

He and Dewey had become friends during the course of the academic year. Their relationship, characterized by growing intimacy, mutual respect, and complete trust, is documented in hundreds of letters exchanged over more than three decades. Dewey, among the first members of a new occupational class of higher education professionals, had chaired philosophy departments at the University of Michigan and the University of Chicago before joining the Columbia faculty in 1904. The author of more than a dozen books and hundreds of articles, he was famous outside of academic circles as a social critic and reformer. Without giving up his interest in educational experiments, like the Laboratory School he and his brilliant, activist wife, Alice Chipman Dewey, had founded in Chicago, or in the settlement house movement in which he had first become involved as a friend and supporter of Jane Addams, Dewey enlarged his focus, after America's entry into Word War I, to include President Woodrow Wilson's new internationalism. His support for joining the fight for democracy in the muddy trenches of France caused disenchantment with his intellectual leadership among more pacifistically inclined progressives. But he found understanding in the classroom.

Barnes wrote to Dewey in early November of 1917 to say that on his way home from the seminar, he had heard of his professor's "plan to organize enlightened liberal thought for intelligent prosecution of the war." He expressed sympathy with the idea and suggested that he "might possibly be instrumental in helping by some of the means which college professors do not always have at their disposal—money, business organization, and the assistance of practical men of affairs." He invited Dewey to visit him in Merion over the weekend to discuss the matter, promising, with local pride that would vanish soon enough, "a very good symphony orchestra concert" on Saturday night, as well as "theaters and a boxing match, and on Sunday afternoon . . . music at my house with an audience of four people."[16] The letter was address to "Mr. Dewey," and the philosopher replied the next day, advising "Mr. Barnes" that other engagements prevented him from accepting the kind invitation.[17] But a lecture at Swarthmore College would bring Dewey to the Philadelphia area in early January, and it was then that he paid his first visit to Merion. Barnes had provided his unlisted number (470) so his prospective guest could telephone from the local train station, and he assured him: "There are enough interesting things here to see and for us to talk about that the time will not seem long."[18]

It was true. Dewey wrote his host from New York to thank him "for the extraordinary experience which you gave me. I have been conscious of living in a medium of color ever since Friday—almost swimming in it," he said, and, more psychologist than connoisseur, added: "I can but feel that it is a mark of the quality of your paintings that there has been no nervous exasperation or fatigue accompanying this sensation."[19] Since Dewey did not extend his thanks to Laura Barnes nor mention Alice, it seems likely that the mistress of "Lauraston" was away that weekend, perhaps visiting her family in New York, and that Mrs. Dewey, whose health had begun to decline, did not accompany her husband. Barnes would surely have cherished the opportunity to have the philosopher's undivided attention. There was a cook to prepare the elegantly simple meals Barnes preferred, maids to serve them, Havana cigars, and good whiskey. The new friends walked about looking at pictures. Barnes discussed them in deep, slow tones that descended like gravel. For the first time in a relationship that would be marked by frequent role reversals, his teacher became his pupil. But in addition to art, we can be certain their conversation, as the host had intended, included the war.

Barnes was eager "to find a niche in the universal doings that might compensate [him] for the comparative inertia entailed by [his] age and lack of specific qualifications for active participation."[20] The American Expeditionary Forces had been fighting in France since June. Twenty-four of his Penn classmates were serving in the United States Army Medical Corps. But since he had not practiced medicine for years, he wrote to the Gas Defense Division of the Army to volunteer his services in some aspect of the research then underway on protection against poison gas. Barnes was the son of a casualty of the Civil War. He knew the cost to men and their families of battle wounds. He would one day display an amputation saw from the Civil War in his Merion gallery. Now he showed Dewey his earnest letter. The philosopher had lost two boys, one to diphtheria, the other to typhoid fever, and his only surviving son, Frederick Archibald, was an Army major working on gas defense in a unit commanded by a cousin, Lt. Colonel Bradley Dewey. John Dewey promised to be of whatever assistance he could to Barnes if Washington officials should contact him.[21]

The collector's bid for an active role in his country's defense was never realized, though he eventually provided financial backing to a group of scientists in Cleveland, Ohio who helped develop a type of gas mask that was more comfortable and effective than older models.[22] But Dewey's favorable reaction to his pictures gave him a more immediate mission: the education in art of America's philosopher. "Come over soon for a weekend," he wrote, "and we can look at the [paintings] in the light of . . . Santayana's *Reason in Art*." He invited Dewey to bring his daughter, Evelyn, to hear a Russian violinist and a Danish pianist who regularly gave concerts at his house. "Select your date," he said, "because I devote every Saturday and Sunday to the fairy world as I get it from pictures and music."[23]

Making the acquaintance of artists had been a critical step in Barnes's own art education, and he intended that Dewey should have the same opportunity. It must have been with considerable pride that he introduced him in early 1918 to his friends, William Glackens and Maurice Prendergast, in their New York studios. Barnes was careful not to neglect Alice as he shared the world of brush and canvas he had come to know so well with her husband. She was grateful to him for a chance to meet John Sloan and for a letter of introduction to Durand-Ruel's New York gallery.[24] In turn, Alice invited Barnes to dinner at the Deweys' New York apartment, where she introduced him to her friend, Mrs.

Winifred Rieber, an occasional artist who had painted a group portrait of three Harvard philosophers. The next day he visited Mrs. Rieber in her Gramercy Park studio to look at the picture. What he thought of it is not known, but Barnes did give Alice an unsolicited psychological evaluation of her friend. It was a practice he seemed unable to resist, and over and over again through the years, he would make similar assessments of people based on his reading of Freud, Adler, and Jung, and their various followers and interpreters. Here, he felt certain, was a case of split personality.[25]

Alice Dewey took Barnes's diagnosis of Mrs. Rieber with more than a grain of salt, but she did not take offense. The collector was kind to her family; he readily acceded to her request that another friend, Mabel Weeks, who was also an intimate of Leo Stein's, be permitted to visit his collection; and, most importantly, he was providing her husband with new interests when, though he was at the height of his career, she recognized he needed them. At the time Barnes met Dewey, the philosopher had begun consulting an Australian practitioner, F. Matthais Alexander, who had come to New York to promote a type of therapy based on the idea that the way the muscles and, indeed, the whole body are used affects an individual's physical and psychological well-being. Dewey told friends that he suffered from a stiff neck and eye trouble, but in his biography of Dewey, Steven C. Rockefeller suggests that the philosopher was close to a nervous "breakdown."[26] Alexander's physiological approach to psychological problems appealed to him, and he recommended the therapist to Barnes who visited him on several occasions. Dewey believed Alexander had demonstrated scientifically "the existence of a central control in the organism" that could be consciously directed by intelligence.[27] But when he introduced Barnes to the therapist's 1910 book, *Man's Supreme Inheritance*, Barnes's reaction was a typically incisive analysis. He demonstrated such familiarity with the psychological literature of the day that he could site the derivation of Alexander's not wholly original ideas in a dozen works. He suggested to Dewey that were Alexander to write a book on his own system giving the scientific bases of his theories, the therapist would be guaranteed a wider and more respectful audience.[28] But whatever Dewey's reaction, another project, closer to the philosopher's heart, notwithstanding his gratitude to Alexander, got in the way.

It, too, was proposed by Barnes as a means, at least in part, of continuing his association with his teacher over the summer. The philosopher was constantly stressing the link between shared experience and a vibrant democracy. In an increasingly pluralistic society, the ability to communicate across barriers of class, race, religion, and national origin was more important than ever. His concern that cultural isolation could preclude the kind of amicable cooperation essential to a democratic civilization fed a long-standing interest in the assimilation of immigrants. Barnes capitalized on it in suggesting a field study of the Polish-American community in Philadelphia. He would provide munificent stipends of $100 a month to four members of Dewey's seminar, Irwin Edman, Brand and Paul Blanchard, and Frances Bradshaw,[29] to investigate why the first- and even second-generation Poles living on the edge of Kensington retained their own language and customs to a greater degree than had other newcomers and remained more or less separate from the rest of the city.

Barnes envisioned the project as producing data "for a series of illuminating articles" and as "a mighty good test" of the investigators' ability to apply "scientific methods" in "practical" situations.[30] He considered it an experiment that might help unpack the reasons for Polish resistance to Americanization and, if attitudes could be changed, show whether Dewey's philosophy, as stated in *Democracy and Education*, could be made "dynamic in its democratizing possibilities."[31] The philosopher was intrigued. He was then involved in plans to establish the New School for Social Research, and he told Barnes that something like the undertaking he had proposed for "the summer might well be[come] a normal part of graduate instruction."[32] He thought that besides shedding light on the impediments to ethnic integration, it might be possible to discover why many Polish Americans appeared to support a conservative faction of imperialistic Poles. The clique, which was based in Paris, sought to establish a new monarchy in a redefined Poland that President Wilson had given Poles everywhere reason to hope the Allies would carve out of Germany, Austria, and Russia after the war. Dewey wanted to encourage a more liberal faction, which favored a democratic, moderately socialistic government in a united, free, and independent nation. Why were the largely Catholic right-wingers, represented in the United States by the pianist-politician Ignace Jan Paderewski and his wife, making so much headway? The fieldwork in Philadelphia could provide an answer. Dewey agreed to supervise the project.

But the novice researchers would need a translator. Dewey suggested to Barnes that "Mrs. Levitas" be considered for the position and sent him a typescript of one of her stories. Barnes read it and wrote that he would like to meet her to "try to form an opinion as to whether the "abnormalities she manifests . . . would be against her as one of the workers."[33] The philosopher must have moved quickly and effectively to allay his concerns. In a letter to Alice Dewey, dated the day after his letter to her husband expressing his reservations, Barnes asked her to "please tell Mr. Dewey that what he has written me about the Polish-Jew makes me think that we most certainly do want her to work here in Philadelphia and that I hope to see the woman . . . at his office in Columbia."[34] The interview in early May was only a formality. John Dewey and Anzia Yezierska would be together, ninety miles from New York and its attendant memories and obligations, during at least some of the long, hot summer days ahead.

Yezierska traveled to Philadelphia in advance of the other investigators to find housing for them. But she encountered difficulties, suspicion on the part of residents in the Polish neighborhoods and opposition from local politicians, so Barnes "settled the question by buying outright a very desirable house" at 3007 Richmond Street.[35] Though he had described his former classmate to Alice Dewey in language that sounds anti-Semitic to our ears, he was not about to let the religious prejudice of others spoil his plans for bringing his teacher to Philadelphia, and he soon wrote to him that "the ferret and the bee have nothing on Mrs. Levitas. . . . There are so many threads visible already," he continued, "I can hardly wait until the men get here in June to follow them up, and I am impatient to get you on the job to guide us in interpreting an extremely interesting sociological condition. . . . If you have any time between now and when you arrive, I wish you would think over the general tendency of the Catholic church to hold in . . . intellectual and physical serfdom [a] large part of the population. We have encountered it here, but shall make no fight until you arrive and have sized up the situation." He did not refrain, however, from telling "the Grand Mogul" of Philadelphia politics to call off "the three bastards who are opposing us."[36]

Dewey had gone to California to deliver a month-long series of lectures at Stanford University at the end of the spring term. Before he left, he bought Yezierska her first typewriter. The gesture was typical of the generosity he showed his protégés, but he did more. Having just been paid for an article, he emptied his pockets and gave her all the money he had with him so she could do "real work" before she earned her first paycheck from Barnes. "Tell me how I can work calmly?" she asked in her letter of thanks. "I have this aching sense of being in debt. . . . And yet—I can think of no deeper happiness on earth than to be indebted to you." Dewey replied: "Dear Love of God . . . Since you have begun to ask you will soon find the answer yourself. In time your body will discover what your soul already knows, that it is free, that you are not just having a reprieve from prison, but are out, once and forever."[37]

In addition to serving as translator for her colleagues, Yezierska was to investigate conditions affecting family life and women. Edman was to study the influence of the Polish-language press, Brand Blanchard was to examine the influence of the Catholic Church, and Bradshaw was to observe the education of children in both public and parish schools. Paul Blanchard, whom Barnes considered "more or less of a staller," returned to New York before even receiving a special assignment.[38] The others "are pulling well together," their patron told Dewey. Barnes noted in particular that "Anzia, like the true artist she is, keeps aloof from the science which she detests, and spends considerable time in her room building phantasies, some of which she is putting into stories and a novel, and some into my private ear, in the form of beliefs that she is not appreciated by the others; but her compensation is . . . that you will appreciate the kind of work she is doing, and in that hope, she is living contentedly. There is no friction." Not among the researchers. But Barnes went on to confess to Dewey that for two days he had been "a guest of the city" for "fighting and resisting an officer."[39] Hart says he sometimes took Edman and Brand Blanchard to saloons where Polish laborers congregated after finishing work in the nearby shipyards.[40] Had whiskey contributed to a run in with the law? Were neighborhood cops trying to tell him to lay off his sociological investigation?

Political intrigue titillated Barnes all his life, and what he considered the international ramifications of the Polish study fascinated and excited him. He visited his research team at least twice a week, eager to hear the latest discoveries and observations of each member, and passed along to Dewey a frank assessment of their capabilities. Except those of Yezierska. She "is an artist, " he told Dewey, "and, as Santayana says, to criticize her would be the same degree of irrationality as to criticize the color of a child's eyes." He considered Edman "far and away the best of the lot" and recommended that he be put in charge in Dewey's absence.[41] Dewey appreciated both his analysis and his advice. "Your letters . . . gave just the steers needed and certainly saved me time and quite likely mistakes," he told Barnes when he arrived on the scene in early July.[42]

The discoveries of the research team galvanized the thinker into action. Edman presented evidence of what he described as "flagrant autocratic interference with the affairs of a large domestic population."[43] The reactionaries had organized a convention, to be held in Detroit in late August, which would ostensibly represent all of the 4,000 Poles living in the United States. It appeared, however, that the Paderewski group would not only pack the meeting with sympathetic delegates, carefully excluding Jewish Polish Americans, but also control the agenda and thereby solidify their power. Edman reported that the imperialist faction was gaining support in Washington, so it seemed essential to Dewey to try to counter their propaganda efforts. With Barnes's enthusiastic support, he attempted to bring his analysis of the situation to the attention of the public and the Wilson administration. But memoranda Dewey sent to the Commission of Inquiry, a federal body that had been established to prepare for the future peace conference, evoked scant interest. A meeting he and Barnes had with Colonel Edward M. House, President Wilson's chief political adviser, was more productive. It led to an invitation for Dewey to visit the Office of U.S. Military Intelligence in Washington and prepare a full report on his findings.[44] To supplement the data gathered in Philadelphia, he assigned Edman to attend the Detroit convention. In an article for the *New Republic*, the philosopher set out what he had learned so far. His sharp analysis of the data assembled by his researchers was given an emotional depth by a sensitivity to the plight of immigrants that had been sharpened in association with one who had struggled to find a place for herself in an alien country.[45]

By the time Dewey's article appeared, Barnes had concluded that the "international phase" of their work was "the most interesting and the most promising in results."[46] He advised his friend that the Richmond Street house should be closed and all the investigators except Edman dropped from the payroll by the first of September.[47] Dewey, then working night and day on his report for the Intelligence Office, had no objections. He wrote to Barnes that he had visited with Justice Louis Brandeis to apprise him of the Polish situation and asked Barnes's advice about lawyers in face of a threatened suit for libel by Paderewski's supporters.[48] The press agent for the group was soon accusing Barnes of a connection with German dye interests. Barnes unequivocally denied any tie and demanded an immediate retraction of the charge. Dewey wrote to Justice Brandeis seeking contacts from whom he might obtain the low down on the publicist,[49] and Barnes, his engine fully revved, counseled Dewey to ask the justice if they had grounds for initiating a libel action against Paderewski. "The moral advantage of the first blow is enormous," the former boxer told the philosopher.[50] It was a conviction he held to with a zealot's fiery passion all his life.

He suggested to Dewey that he give up teaching to work full time in Washington "on the problem of smaller subject nations. . . . It would be research worthy of your mettle, and there would be opportunity to exercise all your active, latent, and unsuspected qualities," Barnes argued. "That your work would get the prompt attention of the President, I have no doubt. . . . It would be an entering wedge to get official approval and practical support for a plan of national education where you could give full swing to all your frustrated desires. It is not my purpose to urge you to do anything against your wishes," Barnes continued, "but the chance to serve your country in a manner worthy of your power is certainly there; so, please think it over and make the decision firmly so there'll be no hangovers."[51] What he apparently had in mind, and thought he could help the philosopher obtain, was a Cabinet-level post focusing on American education.[52]

Dewey was not swept up in Barnes's enthusiasm for a new career for him. He was eager for a change of scene, and he had accepted an invitation to give a series of lectures at Berkeley. But his "frustrated desires" involved only a single immigrant. After finishing his report for the Military Intelligence Office at his summer cottage in Huntington, Long Island, he went into the city to meet with Anzia Yezierska. Alice Dewey was already in California. Yezierska reconstructed the scene in her 1932 novel, *All I Could Never Be*, and eighteen years later in *Red Ribbon on a White Horse*, an even more explicitly autobiographical conflation of fact and fiction.

> For a long moment we stood silent. Then I was in his arms and he was kissing me. His hand touched my breast. The natural delight of his touch was checked by a wild alarm that stiffened me with fear. . . . His overwhelming nearness, the tense body closing in on me was pushing us apart instead of fusing us. A dark river of distrust rose between us. I had not dreamed that God could become flesh.[53]

The dark side of what Yezierska had called elsewhere an "irresistible force" that "flared up between Jew and Gentile" was this Slav's momentary, atavistic suspicion of an Anglo-Saxon.[54] She had dreamed of his embrace while he exhibited a poignant restraint. When he yielded to impulse, setting aside the "day's unilluminated duties" and slipping through the "silken web in which [he felt] bound," Dewey saw an aging fool reflected in his sweet love's frightened eyes.[55] The image repelled him. He took Yezierska home and, the next day and the day after that, when she went to his office seeking a reconciliation:

> Harsh lines rose between his brows. "You want love but you do not want me. You do not love me. You only dramatize your want of love."

> "You're all that I want in life. You've given me myself."

> His eyes softened and he bent toward [her]. "Some day when you're older, you'll see I have nothing more to give you; I've given you everything I had."[56]

The affair was over. Dewey asked Barnes to consider paying Yezierska's salary for a year so the leader of the liberal Polish faction could take her on as an assistant, but she spurned the philosopher's offer of help.[57] Dewey then turned his attention to Barnes's efforts to counter the serious charges of trafficking with an enemy that had been falsely made against him by the reactionary Poles. His Philadelphia friend had been disappointed that he would not give up his plans to spend three months in California for a possible appointment in Washington, but he was soon on his way to the nation's capital himself, intent on defending his good name. When the Justice Department sought to question him about alleged subversive activities, he apparently sent a blistering telegram to the chief of the Military Intelligence Office, and Dewey cautioned him: "I don't wonder you hit back about the attack upon you, but don't make the mistake of underestimating the strength of your own position. I mean its strength just as it stands without any reinforcement from further statements. Give 'em rope and let them hang themselves—you should worry. Let them walk the floor. They can't touch you and the further you let them go in attacking you before you hit back, the stronger you can hit them."[58] The next day he urged Barnes again to "sit tight," and, in early October, perhaps worried that his pugnacious friend would do real harm, Dewey, who had just accepted an invitation to lecture at a Japanese university, suggested that Barnes and his wife "consider a trip, too." The wounds to his spirit caused by his parting from Yezierska were raw, and it would help him heal to have his friend's company. He sweetened his appeal: "We . . . could eschew politics and devote ourselves to the scenery and art."[59]

Barnes must have been pleased by the invitation, but it was not possible to leave a business swamped by wartime orders even if the Argyrol factory did not need his day-to-day supervision. His generous response was to offer Dewey a loan of $2,000 to help him meet the expenses of living abroad. The philosopher declined for Mrs. Dewey and himself but requested that Barnes make up to half the amount available to their daughter Evelyn should she need it while he was gone.[60] Barnes was glad to oblige his friend. "I hope," he wrote to Dewey in Berkeley, "it is no more annoying to you to receive my almost daily letters than it is for me to write them."[61] He told him of sending off by night letter a preemptive challenge to Gilbert Hitchcock, chairman of the Senate Foreign Relations Committee, who had introduced a bill requiring recognition of the Paderewski group as official representatives of free and independent Poland. Barnes recommended Senator Hitchcock read Dewey's *Confidential Report on the Condition of Poles in the United States* and called on him "to debate the democratic and educational principles [therein] embodied."[62] He was gleeful when he learned, less than a month after the Armistice, that at a gathering of representatives of all factions in Poland, the Paris-based reactionaries had been denounced. "It gave me all the feelings that come with a third cocktail," he told Dewey.[63] In a momentary state of euphoria, he even agreed to take on the pro tem presidency of a local European Relief Committee. When an editor at the *Dial* asked him for an article on the Polish situation, he was happy to oblige her.

The essay, entitled "Democracy, Watch Your Step!," began with the observation that Wilson's Fourteen Points reflected a "striking feature" of the President's psychology: his "unerring sense of the popular will." Barnes went on to denounce the "gullibility" of high officials at the State and War Departments who, having been taken in by the Paderewski faction, could not be persuaded by "disinterested parties" to abandon their foolish faith in the reactionaries. But Barnes could not resist, as he would prove time and time again, undercutting his cogent analysis with ill-tempered complaints that his advice had been ignored when he proffered it. Bounding back from bathos, he ended with an implicit and, in this case, altogether reasonable challenge to the President, then attending the Paris Peace Conference, "to tell the exploiters their sun has set."[64] But as it happened, when an exhausted Wilson was confronted with the Poles' open disavowal of his principles of self-determination, their forceful-incorporation of non-Polish territories, and their persecution of minorities within their own borders, he did not have "the greatness of soul" Barnes had hoped he would exhibit, or perhaps any longer the energy, to "appeal over the heads of the rulers to the people themselves."[65] On January 22, 1919, the United States gave de jure recognition to the Paderewski government.

But Barnes had wearied of the struggle to free captives, too. Hurt and angered when the *Dial* asked him to discuss revisions to a review article he had submitted for the editor's consideration and when, on taking it back and sending it off to the *New Republic*, Herbert Croly rejected his work outright, Barnes nursed his wounds. He declined a request "to go to Poland with a commission appointed by the American Jewish Congress to make a study of alleged pogroms."[66] As Dewey sailed for Japan on a trip that would end in China and keep him out of the country for three years, Barnes turned the "savagery," as Dr.

Alexander had described one aspect of his character, on an easier target than ethnocentric nationalists five thousand miles from Philadelphia.[67]

The only Central High School classmate, besides William Glackens, with whom he maintained a friendship through the years was Jay Schamberg. After graduating with Barnes from Penn medical school, Schamberg had spent a year of postgraduate study in Vienna, Paris, and Berlin, then returned to Philadelphia to practice dermatology. Among his patients was the art collector Peter A. B. Widener, who suffered from psoriasis. Widener provided funds for Schamberg and two colleagues to found the Dermatological Research Laboratories. It was there Schamberg and George Raiziss synthesized Salvarsan and Neosalvarsan, Paul Ehrlich's famed treatments for syphilis, at the outbreak of World War I. In addition to research and teaching, Schamberg carried on a busy practice, and in 1917 he treated both Barnes and his father for skin problems.

During one visit, the dermatologist told Barnes about his development of Mercurophen, a local antiseptic used initially to treat gonorrhea and thus a potential competitor for some of the Argyrol market. His confidence provoked the chemist/collector to write him a series of increasingly vituperative letters. Barnes said Ehrlich had discouraged him from developing his own version of the germicide (Mercurial compounds can be extremely toxic, and excessive doses can lead to systematic and chronic poisoning.) and suggested to Schamberg that he was in need of "psychoanalysis . . . to banish [his] phantasies."[68] The dermatologist ignored him, which prompted Barnes to send his erstwhile friend, known for his elegant attire and widely respected for the papers he published in medical journals, the following diatribe:

> One of my side-interests of late years has been in studying abnormal psychology which in your case takes the form of an identification-neurosis. It manifests itself pathognomonically [sic] in the exhibition-bottle of Mercurophen on your desk, your constant chatter about chimiotherapy, your writings, your manner, and even the adornments of your person. The difference between you and the asylum Napoleons is not one of kind but only of degree. It is responsible for the inveterate four-flushing which has amused me since our boyhood days, and for the way in which you take the obvious, touch it up with your complexes and turn out potboilers which you believe are masterpieces.[69]

When Barnes still could not provoke a response, he replied to a form letter of invitation, which had been sent under Schamberg's name to members of University of Pennsylvania School of Medicine's Class of 1892, proposing a debate on Mercurophen as a "sporting event" in connection with their Twenty-Fifth Reunion. He called Schamberg a "quasi-scientist who exhibits the signs and symptoms of Freudian neurosis in need of treatment" and offered to deposit $10,000 with their classmate, the distinguished Dr. David Riesman, as security if Schamberg would do the same. The winner would have his certified check returned and the loser's deposit would be given to the Red Cross Section of the Overbrook Branch of the Needlework Guild of America for war relief.[70] The ploy was one Barnes would repeat in his eagerness to take on others he perceived as opponents. But receiving no response to his hot-tempered challenge from Schamberg, he stopped writing to him. Three years later, however, when he apparently encountered the dermatologist on the street, Schamberg's understandable aloofness produced the following lecture on behavior: "The explosive 'hello Jay' on the street to-day was a spontaneous burst from early pleasant memories. I'd forgotten about the letters I'd written you about mercury—but your cool nod brought them back. . . . I've never been a rival of yours & now that my work lies in other & congenial fields, I'm writing this in the mellower spirit that age has brought to bear on all past experiences tinged with emotion. . . . Life is a much bigger game than warrants pettiness."[71]

Finally, Schamberg, whose mercurial compound would soon be manufactured and marketed by Barnes's former employer, H. K. Mulford, answered his intemperate correspondent.

> You say that you had forgotten the letters that you had written to me, but my cool nod recalled the memory of them. I declined at the time to make reply to the letters in question because their extravagant verbiage and audacious insolence gave me serious doubt as to the sanity of the writer at the time. The only condonation for the writing thereof would have been a temporary aberration.

The dermatologist then detailed his development of Mercurophen, and concluded: "It is perhaps strange that my associates and myself should cling to the opinion that this compound is a valuable one in the face of the statement 'of a specialist of twenty years experience' that it should be cast into the 'junk pile.'"[72]

The letter evoked a full-court press from the recipient. Barnes wrote:

> You have only yourself to blame for those letters. You strutted in front of me with wild assertions about a product which I had known as an abandoned one for twelve years, and then after I had told you the truth about yourself which everybody with discernment knows, you violate scientific respectability with frothy blather in the *Journal A. M. A.* about a "new and superior mercurial," or some such characteristic bunk. You ought to be damned thankful that I didn't publish the obituary of Mercurophen in the next issue of the same journal. . . . Get . . . Adler's *The Neurotic Constitution* and you'll see that I'm just as right about my diagnosis of your personal over-compensations as I was about the scientific cripple you paraded in public on the crutches of your neurosis. . . . As a scientist, you're a piker. . . . With your path through life nicely paved by others, you've had very little stimulus to get the necessary training in science that would enable you to refuse to cash in, in the form of tufts, struts, brass, and the like, the contributions of real scientists. . . . That you consider your work scientific is merely a confusion of values or, in other words, plain delusions. . . . As I said before, I have nothing against you personally—in fact when you used to stop four-flushing and patronizing long enough to be human, I had—and still have—a friendly affection . . . .[73]

The next day Barnes sent Schamberg cigarettes. When they were returned by messenger, he declared: "So be it—my hat is in the ring,—if that's your attitude!"[74] The mean persistence with which the collector stalked his prey, coupled with his appeals for friendship while ignoring common rules governing the conduct of people seeking amicable relations with others, raises questions about his own psychological profile. He played rough and gave no quarter. Dewey warned him about the disadvantages "of pinning . . . butterflies to the pages of books."[75] He told him that he didn't "really gain anything by knocking [people] down and out."[76] But despite Barnes's admiration and respect for the philosopher, his counsel fell on deaf ears.

5

"The Temple" in Merion

Dewey's good influence on his friend—his sincere appreciation of his genius, his steadfast support for his dreams, his gentle chiding about his most serious faults—is surely linked to Barnes's extraordinary achievements in the decade between the end of World War I and the beginning of the Great Depression. During the 1920s, he took on an increasingly public role as a champion of modern art. He bought a great many fine paintings. He wrote articles for avant-garde journals, which led to an important book, mounted spirited defenses of major museum exhibitions of late nineteenth- and early twentieth-century paintings, and, for the first and last time, lent a significant selection of works from his own collection. The fulcrum around which his activity swirled was the most entrepreneurial venture he had yet undertaken—the creation of the Barnes Foundation in Merion. But the period began with a frustrating defeat for the collector.

When Renoir died in December of 1919, his sons decided to give the painting that the artist considered the culmination of his life's work to the Louvre. They offered *Women Bathers* to the Paris museum, but the Louvre "considered the colors too 'loud'" and turned down the donation.[1] Barnes learned of the starchy rebuff and cabled Jean Renoir with an offer to buy the picture. To own the painting, which its creator rated above all his other works, would be a coup, and he could promise it would hang in good company. Barnes uncharacteristically held his breath. But while members of the artist's family were considering his proffer sympathetically, the Louvre had a change of heart. National pride may well have prompted the museum's reversal of its initial decision. Whatever the reason, the collector was deeply disappointed; he hated to lose even one picture.

He must, however, have found considerable satisfaction in his first Renoir purchase of the new decade. Barnes acquired the artist's compelling evocation of Raphael, *Mother and Child*, from Durand-Ruel sometime in 1920. He paid $31,500 for the picture that had been owned in the early 1890s by the pioneering Chicago collector Mrs. Potter Palmer.[2] He would later write that he considered it one of the artist's finest paintings from the early 1880s.[3] The opportunity to acquire in a fell swoop additional pictures by the artist directly from a contemporary collection came about quite unexpectedly. Barnes wrote to Dewey in February of 1920 that he had just received a letter from Leo Stein asking him to make an offer for his sixteen Renoirs. Stein "bought them very cheap years ago," he told the philosopher, "and now, after raving over them in and out of season, is ready to pass the joy on to others." Then reaching for a familiar medical phrase to make a sexual pun, Barnes added: "I wonder what he'd do with a wife after the acute stage had subsided."[4]

Stein had given Barnes a chance to buy paintings before when he required ready cash, although never so many. But upon returning to Italy from the United States, where he had been grounded until after the 1918 Armistice,[5] he may have had another motive. Barnes's erstwhile mentor and friend once said that the most important Renoir collectors were "men who were lonely, who were socially isolated, who felt the dearth of warm human companionship."[6] And Leo, after a long and trying courtship, was prepared at last to marry Nina Auzias, a step he finally took in early March of 1921. Letters on the proffered sale crisscrossed the Atlantic for somewhat more than a year. The collector's enthusiasm for Renoir, which he expressed yet again in a tribute to the artist published (after rejection by the *New Republic*) in the *Dial* in February 1920, led Stein to believe he had a buyer for his treasures. But an extended bout of sickness kept him from following up his initial letter on the matter even though his financial reserves had been severely diminished by the war,

In the meantime, Barnes made his first postwar trip to France and, according to Hart, visited Renoir's studio in Cagnes where he bought "quite a few" pictures.[7] It may have been some months before he replied to Leo. In any case, Stein wrote at the end of December to say he had several unfinished letters to him lying about. He reported that his "analysis had been substantially successful," and that he could be "more cheerful in the midst of desolation than [he] used to be in the midst of comparative plenty. Of course, desolation can be overdone." he added, "so I want to ask you for advice." Stein then gave a gloomy rationale for his hoped-for divestment:

Apart from a painfully small property which has been enjoying some shrinks lately, my principal possession is my Renoirs. My own conviction in 1917-18 was that I ought to have sold them, but I had too many resistances. Since then, Renoirs are constantly going up in price and the franc is coming down. You know more about the Renoir market in America than anyone else I know, so I am asking you . . . what I had better do. My moral health has been too long a coming back and my physical health, on the other hand, has been declining, so I can't look forward to being much of a money earner in the future. I may do a little writing which will be better than what I used to do, but none the less it will be more likely rather scanty and financially a moderate resource. So I don't want to do anything foolish with those Renoirs. I don't know where to strike the balance between the rise in Renoir prices and the fall in francs. If you don't mind giving me some counsel in the matter as to whether there is a practicable market now or whether one had better wait; whether selling at auction gives a fair return or whether some other method were more judicious. . . . I still have my doubts whether painting has a serious future. Paintings undoubtedly have, and in fifty years old paintings may come to have fabulous values if there are in fifty years still fabulously rich men to buy them.[8]

Barnes was well aware of the rising market for Renoirs. "Since Renoir's death," he had written Dewey ten months earlier, "his paintings have soared."[9] He also relished the role of financial advisor and readily agreed to evaluate Stein's pictures. Just days after his marriage, Leo wrote to express his gratitude. He had previously shipped most of his collection to New York where a cousin had made arrangements for storage. "Do about them whatever you think advisable," he told Barnes. "I'm afraid you think of them as more important than they are. Most of them are small and slight, and one very lovely nude I cracked by foolish handling in the old days of my pathological impatience." He added that "besides the Renoirs, there are some other things, a Delacroix, Cézanne water colors, a Daumier, a Cézanne painting, and a bronze of Matisse."[10] As an agent, Barnes worked quickly. Within two months, he wrote to Dewey that he had been able to turn over some $30,0000 to Stein. "Hard times made it rather difficult," he said, referring to the postwar slump. "Of course I bought the most important Renoirs and Matisses for myself at prices which [Stein] said were very satisfactory to him. Since you left [for the Far East]," he added, "I've blown myself in strengthening the collection, and it is now in a class by itself. In the last two years, I must have bought a score or more of Renoirs (one at $80,000.00) and now have over a hundred of his works, and over 30 Cézannes."[11]

Barnes acquired nearly half of the latter in the summer of 1920 from a collection assembled by the Dutchman Cornelis Hoogendijk who had died in 1911. When his family sold his Cézannes to a syndicate of Paris dealers, the Durand-Ruels cabled their American client about the availability of thirteen paintings. Barnes's offer was at first refused, but his dealers sacrificed part of their commission to facilitate the transaction. The pictures, all still lifes and landscapes, included one of the artist's best renderings of his famous mountain, *Sainte-Victoire* (V.457). "Barnes now saw his collection overtaking numerically the group of Cézannes owned by Mrs. [Henry O.] Havemeyer," John Rewald writes. His latest acquisition put him in "possession of some of Cézanne's finest works."[12] Barnes knew it even then. He wrote to Dewey that he was "terribly excited" about what he described as "a windfall." He called the thirteen pictures "masterpieces of rare power."[13] He said they enabled him to trace Cézanne's "psychological and technical development from the time he was working with Pissarro, Monet and Renoir in the seventies down to the final period when he was his pure, unique self."[14] The Amsterdam pictures cost Barnes 1,557,325 francs. To Durand-Ruel's annoyance, he took advantage of fluctuations in the international currency market to reduce his dollar expenditure.[15]

Nevertheless, the purchases, as he told Dewey, "dug some hole" in his resources. Still, he had the funds, and his investment enabled him to boast that the Cézannes, "with a dozen or so Renoirs of the best quality that I've got since the war, make my collection easily the most important in the world of modern art."[16]

Although John Sloan resented Barnes's relative lack of attention to contemporary American artists once he started collecting Renoirs and Cézannes,[17] Sloan's former schoolmate did not altogether neglect them after his first purchases from Glackens, Maurice Prendergast, Demuth, Maurer, and Sloan himself. With Laura and Laurence Buermeyer, he visited the vibrant art colony at Woodstock, New York one September weekend in 1920. He dictated copious notes to Buermeyer but made no commitments during his tour of the artists' studios. A few days later, letters from Philadelphia brought offers to Andrew Dasburg for a small oil and to Paul Rohland for five monotypes. The next spring Barnes also bought four works by Marsden Hartley at auction in New York.[18] In a letter from China, Alice Dewey had urged him to write about American painters, but he claimed he could not muster the necessary emotional distance.[19]

He was struggling, however, to sort out his thoughts about Renoir and Cézanne. He told Alice he "had never been able to decide" which of them "was the biggest man of the last century in art. Cézanne," he said, "was intense, passionate, almost cruel in his insight into reality; Renoir . . . charming, human, lyric—sheer beauty and feeling. I have made an analysis of their contrasting greatnesses," he added, "and if I can put it into words, I'll publish it."[20] The article he wrote was rejected by *The Dial*, but appeared in the November 1920 issue of *Arts & Decoration*. In his recently published essay on Renoir, Barnes had written that the viewer of the artist's work "feels that color sings harmoniously and richly but never stridently; that the composition is made up of . . . sensuous elements [made] dramatically meaningful; that the picture soon ceases to be drawing, color, composition; that it becomes a repose saturated with spirit of place, where self is no more, where all is peace and harmony . . . ."[21] Now he focused on Cézanne, but at one point, he directly compared the two painters. Cézanne's "constant pursuit of physical reality, to grasp it and portray it in its essence, was akin to the zeal and thoroughness of the investigator in science," he said. "Where Renoir found poetry and charm in everything, Cézanne saw weight, mass, volume, texture, tactile qualities. He was critical and analytical, with a high intensity of mind and spirit in his search of facts to attain to the secret springs of form and structure. It was a passion," Barnes wrote, that made some of his paintings "seem cold and stern and hard." But the work of few painters, the collector concluded, "survives on a wall with Cézanne's."[22]

Barnes did not, of course, restrict his purchases to pictures by the two artists who intrigued him above all others. In late January of 1921, he added to his

French paintings by acquiring eight Degas—four oils and four pastels—at a sale, in New York's Plaza Hotel, of the collection of Jacques Seligman. He hastened to tell Dewey that the pictures "did not bring one-third of their value." Noting that the works he purchased would "normally" have cost him "about one hundred thousand dollars," he said he had paid "just a trifle under thirty thousand dollars" for them, and acknowledged: "They make an important addition to my collection."[23]

Barnes's acquisitions, together with his attempts to write seriously about art, captured the attention of the small, tight circle of Philadelphia artists and their patrons. Henry McCarter, a well-known illustrator who had studied at the Pennsylvania Academy of the Fine Arts with Eakins and in Paris with Puvis de Chavannes, probably was introduced to the collector through their mutual friend, Butts Glackens. McCarter had been teaching at the Academy since 1902 and was an intimate of another artist and teacher, his own former student Arthur B. Carles, who had also studied with Matisse. Their crowd included the gentlemen painters Carroll S. Tyson, Jr. (himself an important collector) and Adolphe Boire, and one of the city's most energetic patrons of the arts, attorney R. Sturgis Ingersoll. Under Carles's leadership, McCarter, Tyson, and Borie had helped mount an ambitious Academy exhibition entitled "Paintings and Drawings by Representative Modern Masters." The 254 borrowed pictures, mostly by European artists, spanned the nineteenth century from Daumier to Degas to Toulouse-Lautrec, as well as that of the twentieth-century avant-garde, Matisse, Picasso, and Braque. Philadelphia-born artist Mary Cassatt, an Academy alumna who lived in France, was represented by nineteen paintings and an extensive series of etchings, and there were works by her late ex-patriot countryman, James McNeill Whistler, and by the young American Stanton Macdonald-Wright, whose brilliant chromatic experiments were known as synchromism. Barnes lent nothing to the show, the first museum exhibition of modern art in America, but he developed friendly relations with the organizers and invited them, along with Ingersoll, to see his pictures. Visitors recalled that they covered the walls of every room of his house, including the bathroom, and that two Cézannes hung over twin beds in the master bedroom.[24] They were stunned by the quantity and the quality.

When Carles again helped organize a bold Academy exhibition, the April 1921 all-American show entitled "Exhibition of Paintings and Drawings Showing the Later Tendencies in Art," Barnes paid his friend the compliment of choosing, from among the 280 assembled works, eight for his own collection. His purchases included two paintings by Thomas Hart Benton, *The Beach* and *Study for Decoration*, Alfy Maurer's *Head: Number Three*, and *Landscape* by Andrew Dasburg plus works by several now largely forgotten painters.[25] In a letter to Carles, which he shared with a local newspaper, Barnes said the Academy's selection of a diverse group of eight-eighty contemporary American artists was "the first real move to shake Philadelphia out of the lethargy which has been the reproach to us from artists and collectors of other cities."[26] A dozen years earlier, Henry James had observed that Philadelphia had "no pretext for bristling,"[27] and now, courtesy of one of its most conservative institutions, it did.

Intellectual journals and art magazines bestowed high praise on the show. The popular press, however, had a field day at the Academy's expense. They were aided by a group of local alienists, as psychiatrists and neurologists were then known, who delivered a series of lectures at the Philadelphia Art Alliance in a grotesque attempt to apply their medical judgments to modern art and its makers. The instant experts sought to demonstrate that the pictures on exhibition were the products of sick minds. Charles W. Burr, a prominent professor of mental diseases at the University of Pennsylvania School of Medicine, diagnosed as "degenerate" a great many works that he said created, or were intended to create, "unhealthy feelings of pleasure in the diseased onlooker, and which a healthy-souled artist would not have painted." Francis X. Decrum, the alienist who was called as a consultant when President Wilson suffered his breakdown, said he could "only infer that, in large degree, the pathological element enters into these paintings and drawings, both in the representation of colors and of forms. . . . I believe also," he added, "that a certain number of people who paint these curious pictures are merely shallow tricksters, who try to achieve prominence by coming in on a wave and floating into the public eye, getting some sort of reputation which they could not get by legitimate hard work. . . . I think the main feature, however, is the disease of the color sense, and the disease of a great many other mental faculties." W. B. Wadsworth, a well-known pathologist, found the modernists' works "represented those ghastly lesions of the mind and body which usually land people in the hospitals and in the asylums," but sometimes permit them to "walk around, feed themselves, avoid a commission in lunacy, and paint."[28]

When a reporter for the *Arts* queried Barnes about his reaction, the collector was ready with his own diagnosis. He told the magazine:

I believe it is the general opinion of those who specialize in psychology that the doctors mentioned are not qualified to speak. I believe that Drs. Decrum, Burr and Wadsworth come within the category of what is known as 'old hats,' that is, men who have arrived at positions of eminence by conforming to the traditions of a bygone age, standing pat on somebody else's thinking and vociferously denouncing the work of men who have devoted their lives to research work in art and science. To such men as the doctors mentioned the monumental work done by Freud, Jung and Adler is a closed book. . . . In short, I think that when Drs. Decrum, Burr and Wadsworth make public statements concerning matters about which they have no scientific knowledge, they can be classed as ignoramuses with a penchant for limelighting. . . .The Art Alliance is composed largely of what may be classed as 'social climbers,' who look upon art as a step in the ladder that leads to the kind of prominence that everyone is familiar with [who] reads the society columns of the daily press. Among the members of the Art Alliance may be found that group of Philadelphia painters who exploit everything available to find a market for their substitute for art. . . . I think if you put the background and speaker-doctors together you will see . . . a typical example of the unfortunate situation so prevalent in Philadelphia as regards intelligence and art.[29]

Unchastened by these observations of a fellow physician, at least one of the self-anointed art clinicians, Francis Decrum, attacked a loan exhibition of French modernism at the Metropolitan Museum of Art a few months later. The new charge of degeneracy by the alienist, whom Barnes first knew as a Penn instructor in nervous diseases when he was in medical school, prompted the collector to say he would give his own paintings, and a gallery to house them, to the city of Philadelphia if "Dr. Decrum could prove himself qualified in the science of normal and abnormal psychology." When his opponent ignored his challenge, he upped the ante by offering to build a gallery big enough to house, in addition, the art collection left to Philadelphia by the late John G. Johnson. "I have no sympathy with the painters of futuristic and cubistic pictures," Barnes said, "but I believe the spirit of fair play should be extended to the group of honest, intelligent, and capable artists whom Dr. Decrum holds up to ridicule and misrepresentation."[30] Though there is no evidence that he ever seriously contemplated fleeing Philadelphia like his artist friends Glackens, Sloan, and Demuth, the rant of the alienists against the groundbreaking exhibition made Barnes's hometown seem increasingly foreign to him.

But there was a city in which he felt at home. Paris had long ago cast its spell upon him, and now he was once again able to visit for several weeks at a time at least once, and usually twice, a year. "The Louvre, the streets, cafes, artists' studios, galleries of dealers, the people have weaved into the fabric of my life a strand which, if broken, would leave me impoverished," Barnes said. "I know of no material possession that can compare with [Paris] in yield of spiritual richness." Within the City of Lights, moreover, there was one place that drew him like a moth to a flame. "I have named it 'The Temple,'" he wrote in 1924, "because in no other rendezvous have I witnessed so much devotion by so many of the painters, sculptors, composers, writers, connoisseurs, who have made up the art history of our epoch; and they are there to worship works of art and to commune with kindred spirits. The high priest . . . is Paul Guillaume, a creator in the greatest of arts, life itself."[31]

Guillaume was a young French art dealer. The brilliant son of a bank messenger, he was just over thirty in 1922-23 when Barnes made him his principal Parisian art supplier. Around 1911, before opening his first gallery, Guillaume began to collect and sell African sculpture. Wholly self-taught, his researches on tribal art were pioneering. As Barnes would write, he "rescued [it] from its mere ethnological significance."[32] Paul Guillaume's appreciation of the aesthetic qualities of ancient wood carvings and bronzes from Gabon and the Congo was shared by the renowned poet and critic Guillaume Apollinaire, who provided the amiable and ambitious youth with important contacts in the art community. He opened a small gallery on the rue Miromesnil, and later on the fashionable rue la Boetie, which became one of the best-known commercial outlets for modern art in Paris. For Barnes, it was a kind of Mecca. As he had returned again and again to camp meetings and black houses of worship in his youth to hear the sorrow songs of former slaves, he came back to Guillaume's gallery for an experience that was at once aesthetic and spiritual.

"I have visited the temple a hundred times," Barnes wrote.

> I have seen six chiefs of African tribes there at the same time with four principals of the Russian ballet. Like a stream of worshippers all nationalities flow into . . . Paul Guillaume's, English, Japanese, Norwegian, German, American, Italian artists—painters, sculptors, composers, poets, critics—whom I had known only by name. I have heard there criticism more penetrating and more comprehensive than I had ever heard or read elsewhere, for a glance of the eye, a quality of voice add much to the transfer of what we mean. . . . One summer afternoon when the heat was intolerable outdoors, I called at the temple and found Roger Fry and Paul Guillaume discussing Negro art. I listened for a while and then took possession of Roger Fry and had a talk on Renoir and Cézanne which I shall remember for the rest of my life. The atmosphere of the place is imperturbably peaceful, for no matter how keen the discussion it is never desecrated by a personal quarrel between artists of even widely diverging opinions. One instinctively and always respects a sanctuary.[33]

In describing the temple-gallery of the suave Parisian art dealer, Barnes provides an intimation of the psychological impetus for the plan that he had formulated over a period of several years. "No psychologist," he wrote, "would deny that what we like, we must share with others to obtain its full savor. The truth of that is never so completely shown as in our enjoyments of the great spiritual forces that have always constituted the most important phases of the life of man. In this communal participation, the soul, the intellect, the whole personality unfold."[34] Barnes had witnessed the phenomenon at humble camp meetings and in chic salons. Not only did he get a huge kick out of talking about and showing off his art, the process reinforced his sense of accomplishment; and it stimulated him to think about the works themselves in new ways. Since he first began collecting, he had welcomed visitors, in his fashion, to his Merion home where paintings hung in every nook and cranny. To artists and others knowledgeable about art, it was becoming a place of pilgrimage. During the Pennsylvania Academy exhibition of "Later Tendencies," New-Yorkers, who had traveled to Philadelphia to see the modernist show, stopped by Latch's Lane from morning to night.[35]

Barnes 's rapid acquisition of pictures after the war ended soon presented him with a dilemma. "I wonder if their possession will put you under the necessity of having a great place to keep them in, and of all the care and obligations to them and to the art seeker which you have said you wanted to avoid," a perceptive Alice Dewey had written from China. "Never mind," she added, "your whole life shows you do not really shirk that chore."[36] Indeed, as

Leo Stein had observed, Barnes had a "great capacity for action."[37] It was a product of his pragmatism, as was his persistence, which paid off spectacularly in May of 1922 when, after several years of effort, the collector purchased from his neighbor, Colonel Joseph Lapsley Wilson, a beautifully-planted twelve-acre parcel of land on the same side of Latch's Lane as "Lauraston." The elderly Wilson agreed to the sale on the condition that the new owners would preserve the arboretum, which he had nurtured for more than forty years. Laura was a serious horticulturist, and her husband's commitment to Wilson not only to maintain but also expand the arboretum gave her a project that became a calling and brought her joy to the end of her days. Barnes also agreed to build and lease to his neighbor a small house on the property. He then turned his attention to the construction of a gallery, his Temple in Merion.

The architect he selected was the French-born Paul Philippe Cret, a professor of architectural design at the University of Pennsylvania. Cret proposed the construction of linked French Renaissance chateau-style buildings, one for the collection and the other for the Barneses. His intention in the former was "to secure those conditions that the painter would wish for the display of his work."[38] Instead of a typical top-lit gallery, his plan called for small rooms, varying in dimension to avoid monotony, and studio lighting provided by windows placed high on the walls under vaulted ceilings. There would be no useless corridors; rather, on each of the gallery's two floors, traffic would be expected to flow through rooms starting from and leading to a central hallway. The exterior would be built of specially selected buff-colored limestone.

The interior would be devoted to a special kind of education designed to develop art appreciation. Barnes had decided to expand his factory-school experiment. In late 1919, he had written to John Dewey suggesting the philosopher give a seminar on aesthetics when he returned to Columbia, but Dewey, who was then in China, declined on the grounds that he wished to reserve one aspect of experience from "devastating analysis."[39] Later he wrote Barnes: "Why the devil don't you do it? Why should the responsibility fall on me? . . . The thing you want to see done—and which I fully agree needs doing very badly—can only be done in 'art,' not in philosophy."[40] Barnes was initially reluctant. "Your question is easily answered," he said. "I haven't got the endowment. . . . I don't see how I can do anything but continue either to spend big sums on art, or let it pile up and then be an idiot in my will or do the conventional charity stunts."[41] Near the end of his life he stated plainly, "I never intended to start a foundation until Dewey urged me to after he saw for himself our experiment with a group of mixed white and black people."[42] But having made a decision, he moved swiftly.

With the advice and help not only of Dewey but also of his friend and attorney Owen J. Roberts, who was later appointed to the United States Supreme Court, the collector drew up a plan for a free-standing educational institution. The Barnes Foundation was granted a charter by the Commonwealth of

Pennsylvania on December 4, 1922. Under terms of an Indenture of Trust, Barnes provided it with an endowment, which was estimated to be worth $6 million and included his works of art, the Wilson land, and the gallery under construction in addition to 900 shares of A. C. Barnes Company common and capital stock. As stated in its bylaws, the mission of the newly created Foundation was twofold: "to promote the advancement of education and the appreciation of the fine arts; and for this purpose to erect, found and maintain . . . an art gallery and other necessary buildings for the exhibition of works of ancient and modern art, and the maintenance in connection therewith of an arboretum, wherein shall be cultivated and maintained trees and shrubs for the study and for the encouragement of arboriculture and forestry." The bylaws proclaimed the art gallery would be "an educational experiment under the principles of modern psychology," and among the provisions for governing the Foundation after the death of Barnes and his wife was one requiring the trustees to "ensure that it is the plain people . . . men and women who gain their livelihood by daily toil in shops, factories, schools, stores and similar places, who shall have free access to the art gallery upon those days when the gallery is to be open to the public."

Philadelphia newspapers reported that it was Barnes's intention that his "museum eventually become public property."[43] But he wasn't in town to read the speculation. His long-term objective was less than clear; his immediate one was to buy more art, and he went off to Paris on a major shopping expedition. Six months earlier, he had purchased Renoir's *The Embroiderers* and Cézanne's *Woman in a Red-Stripped Dress, Peasant Standing* from Vollard for a total of 575,000 francs.[44] He also had acquired Renoir's *Children on the Seashore* from Barbazanges Hodebert & Cie. for 180,000 francs, and just before sailing for Europe, he bought, through Durand-Ruel, Matisse's celebrated *The Joy of Life* for 45,000 francs from the Danish collector Christian Tetzen-Lund.[45] When Barnes arrived in the French capital, he picked up a "choice Greco and an extraordinary Claude Lorraine." According to his letter to William Glackens, the paintings were in a private collection where they had been for years and "so dirty that nobody at a casual glance would recognize their values." He bought them "on the spot," and also acquired some forty Greek and Egyptian sculptures, as well as three fifteenth-century primitives—one Dutch and two Italian. He called the trip "the most successful I have ever had."[46] But it was so, in part, because he made several startling new discoveries.

Upon the recommendation of Guillaume, he sought out the sculptor Jacques Lipchitz who had come to Paris from Lithuania in 1909. As Lipchitz tells the story, the dealer knocked on his door in December of 1922 in the company of a stranger.[47] Guillaume's companion was a middle-aged, solidly built American with penetrating eyes, beetle brows, a squarish face, and an incisive, abrupt manner. He spoke little French, and the dealer acted as an interpreter. Somewhat reluctantly, since he had recently quarreled with Guillaume, Lipchitz showed the unexpected visitors the sculpture in his house atelier and, at Barnes's request, more works in a nearby studio. Disregarding Guillaume's services as a translator when he discovered that the Yiddish-speaking Lipchitz understood German, Barnes began asking prices. At first, the sculptor quoted very low figures, but realizing the potential for financial disaster if Barnes should buy many works, he quickly raised them. Eventually Barnes chose eight sculptures, added up the prices, and offered Lipchitz 10 percent less than the total. When the sculptor gratefully accepted the collector's proposal, Barnes asked him to ship his purchases collect and said he would send his check after the works arrived in Philadelphia. Making a leap of faith, Lipchitz agreed to the collector's terms, and Barnes left. A few moments later, he returned and invited the sculptor to join him and Guillaume for a drink at a favorite watering hole for artists, the Café Rotonde.

The next day Barnes asked the sculptor to meet with him at Guillaume's gallery, and when Lipchitz arrived, he found his new American patron studying architectural drawings and sipping cognac. Barnes looked up, reached in his pocket, and presented the sculptor with a bank draft in full payment of his purchases. He then explained that there were five niches for sculpture on the facade of the museum Paul Cret was building for him in the United States. Barnes asked Lipchitz if he could fill them. On the condition that he would be free to design whatever he chose, Lipchitz accepted the commission. Barnes took him to dinner, and the following day, as the collector had insisted, Lipchitz presented him with a detailed estimate of the cost of creating the requested bas-reliefs. Without a moment's hesitation, Barnes accepted it and told him to ship each sculpture to Philadelphia as soon as it was done. Other commissions followed, including a garden sculpture for Mrs. Barnes. For several years, the collector and the artist enjoyed a warm friendship, based upon mutual regard. It ended, as would so many relationships in the course of Barnes's life, when the collector, displaying an extreme sensitivity to being used by others, discovered Lipchitz was unable to resist the all too human impulse to seek a favor for a needy friend. With great apprehension, and only after they had dined well and shared several bottles of wine, the sculptor asked his patron to look at the work of a fellow artist, who had begged for an introduction in hopes of selling a painting to pay for surgery for his wife. Barnes resisted but then came around to Lipchitz's studio, where the pictures were on display, and bought two of them. The sculptor saw him only once again. On his next trip to Paris, Barnes failed to call Lipchitz in advance, as had become his custom, but one day appeared in his doorway, a hard-eyed, scowling visage, and informed him of his unpardonable sin: he had caused the collector to confound philanthropy with art.

Despite his disappointment that a good deed should be so punished, Lipchitz would always remember with a sense of wonder the heady winter weeks of their first meeting. On the day they concluded arrangements for the bas-reliefs, Barnes had been captivated by an extravagantly colored portrait of a seated adolescent with a monstrous ear displayed in Guillaume's gallery window. The artist who had created *The Little Pastry Cook* was unknown to him, but Guillaume was eager to capitalize on his interest. Lipchitz soon found himself accompanying Barnes and Guillaume to the home of the Polish poet turned art dealer, Léopold Zborowski, the kindly protector of Chaim Soutine, to whom the artist had consigned his paintings. The sculptor knew the thirty-year-old painter as a member of the cosmopolitan community of Eastern European Jewish artists pursuing their dreams in Montparnasse.

Born near Minsk in Belorussia, Soutine had studied art in the Lithuanian city of Vilna before making his way to Paris. He enrolled in the Ecole des Beaux-Arts, but his most important school was the Louvre where he was deeply influenced by the work of Courbet and, especially, Rembrandt. After the war, he settled for a number of years in the south of France and painted with feverish haste. From ruthless portraits, he turned to distorted still lifes and landscapes. Soutine returned to Paris in 1922 with some two hundred works, but he had sold almost none of them when Barnes arrived at Zborowski's. The collector recognized the painter's dark, tormented genius and also the possibility of snapping up the powerful, violent pictures before him at bargain prices. He bought a great many—somewhere between sixty and seventy-five—for $3,000.[48] Soutine, who would meet Barnes the next day, immediately spent a chunk of the money to hire a taxi to take him to Nice. It was a ride of at least fifteen hours, but the young painter had reason to celebrate for the American collector's purchase brought about a spectacular rise in the prices of his work and propelled him from a life of near poverty to one of considerable financial security. It seems, however, that Soutine took an instant dislike to Barnes, and Barnes was hardly more gracious. He boasted of his coup to the press almost immediately and, in later years, would recall with perverse pleasure how he acquired the paintings of a hungry sot, albeit a virtuoso, for a mere pittance.

Barnes also bought a number of works by Soutine's former studio partner, the Italian-Jewish artist Amedeo Modigliani, who had lived most of his short life in poverty and died of tubercular meningitis in 1920. Modigliani's gracefully erotic nudes and sculptural, silky flat portraits captivated the American collector. The purchases he made in January 1923 launched the posthumous career of a painter whose superb draftsmanship was at the time barely acknowledged outside his own small circle. Barnes also acquired several pictures by the Italian artist Giorgio de Chirico. Born in Greece, de Chirico studied art in Athens and Munich before coming to Paris in 1911. Several years later, he painted a portrait of Apollinaire, and at the poet's suggestion, Paul Guillaume became his first dealer. Guillaume gave him a one-man show in 1922 and, again, in 1926, the year he made two portraits of Barnes, a drawing and an oil. The collector wrote the preface to the show's catalogue.

Another artist from whom Barnes made a substantial number of purchases on his winter 1922-23 trip to Paris was the gifted, troubled Jules Pascin. A

Sephardic Jew, who had been born in Bulgaria of Spanish parents, Pascin first became known for the satirical illustrations he created for the infamous Munich publication *Simplicissimus*. The artist was spending the war years in the United States when Barnes had first reviewed his portfolio of often grotesque, sometimes humorous drawings. He had declined to make any purchases then, but now, meeting the artist through Lipchitz, he found much to admire in Pascin's sensitively drawn, delicately painted, always sensuous nudes and reached out in friendship to their creator. Pascin subsequently visited Barnes in Merion, and the collector gave a dinner in his honor at which he poured his best wines. When the table was cleared, according to George Biddle's account of the evening, guests were offered champagne. Pascin noticed that instead of withdrawing, the servers, joined by other members of the household staff, stood around the room in silence. Addressing them, Barnes praised the artist's work and announced that he would say a few words. Pascin struggled to his feet, made the first and only speech of his career, and soon felt the faces of his audience melt away before him. He was jolted awake when Barnes asked "Mr. Sam" what he thought of a Pascin watercolor. The black employee identified it as hanging between a Picasso and a Matisse in the hallway and said he loved the drawing.[49] But despite the approbation of common folk and connoisseurs alike, Pascin soon became a tragic suicide. Barnes was in Paris at the time, and he joined the large throng of people that accompanied the artist's body to the cemetery. As a rabbi in the traditional tricornered hat and robes of the French synagogue spoke words of blessing, the collector was observed weeping openly at the graveside.

Barnes may have felt freer to express genuine emotion publicly in Paris than in Philadelphia, where he would increasingly play a role that involved exaggerated displays of outrage and ill temper. Certainly the winter he first met Lipchitz, Soutine, and Pascin in the French capital, he did not try to disguise his surging delight in life. Paul Guillaume easily won his permission to exhibit seventy-five of the purchases he made on his feverish buying spree. Reports of the show reached the Philadelphia press, if not directly from Barnes through Guillaume with the collector's ready approval. He had a sophisticated understanding of the uses of publicity from his early days of promoting Argyrol. Before returning home in mid-January 1923, he authorized the first public announcement of the creation of the Barnes Foundation. It appeared in that month's issue of the *Arts*. Photographs of sixteen works from the Barnes collection accompanied the article in which the magazine's new editor, Forbes Watson, proclaimed: "We are to have, at last, a public museum of . . . the most vital art that has been produced since 1870 to the present day." He speculated upon Barnes's impact on the market: "Old established collectors, who thought they had done the last thing in collecting by gathering expensive if not always interesting 'old masters,' began to question themselves. . . . Dr. Barnes' collection began to be more talked about than the collections of some of the safe

investors. . . . Painters themselves . . . were just begging for a chance to see [it].
. . . And today people all over the world are interested, and will be glad to hear
that this great collection of modern art is getting a permanent setting, and
being opened to the general public."[50]

The Philadelphia papers immediately picked up the story. They repeated
Watson's estimate that the Foundation contained more than 400 paintings,
and noted that while most of them were the works of modern French artists,
about a third of the canvases were by Americans. When the Philadelphia *Evening
Bulletin* sought out Joseph Lapsley Wilson for his views, he confirmed that his
residence, stables, and tenant houses would be "torn down to make way for the
museum."[51] The editor of the *Arts* had quoted a letter from Barnes in which he
addressed, in rather clumsy language, the purpose of the Foundation: "Primarily the hope is that every person, of whatever station in life, will be allowed to
get his own reactions to whatever the Foundation has to offer; that means that
academism, conformity to out-worn conditions, counterfeits in art, living and
thinking can have no place in the intended scope of the Foundation."[52] The
local papers highlighted the collector's clue to his populist intentions. They
eagerly delineated the extent of his holdings: 150 works of Renoir, fifty
Cézannes, and paintings by Matisse, Degas, Picasso, Manet, Puvis de
Chavannes, and Van Gogh, as well as such old masters as the "fine portrait of a
man by the Spaniard Goya," and among American artists, the works of Glackens,
Prendergast, Eakins, Davies, Lawson, and Demuth. They also quoted Barnes
as saying he had the finest collection of African sculpture in existence.[53] The
collector wanted the world, and particularly Philadelphians, to know that the
thirty-seven pieces he had acquired over several years excelled work in the
Congo Museum in Brussels and in the British Museum. [54]

It seems safe to say that readers of the *Public Ledger* were more interested in
the announcement that John Dewey would be the education director of the
Foundation. The paper also reported that his associate would be Laurence
Buermeyer, who had resigned his position at Princeton, effective at the end of
the academic year, to assume his new duties. In fact, Buermeyer's three-year
teaching contract would be up then, and he would be out of a job. So home
from his travels, Barnes concocted other uses for what he considered Buermeyer's
"rare talents."[55] They would be made available, on loan, in support of the
collector's goals. Barnes told the press that "the educational work of the Barnes
Foundation [would] be conducted in connection with the departments of fine
arts and aesthetics on the campuses of several universities and colleges."[56] But
he had yet to approach any academic institution about a possible affiliation.

His friends on the faculty of the Pennsylvania Academy of the Fine Arts,
however, put an intriguing proposition to him. Arthur Carles and Henry McCarter
asked Barnes to let them bring the pictures and European sculpture from the
Guillaume Gallery show to the Academy. Was Philadelphia ready? In the January issue of his magazine, *Les Arts à Paris*, Guillaume had assured the "Painters

of the Rotonde" that the American collector, "this distinguished ambassador of French art, will fight for you . . . against those who laugh, the imbeciles, the ignorant, the impotent of the New World."[57] And so he would. Barnes agreed to let Carles and McCarter organize an exhibition. He even wrote to John Frederick Lewis proposing that the Academy include his primitive African sculpture if it could secure locked cases in which to display the priceless works. "Paris went wild over this exhibition," the collector told the Academy president, "and the critics were unanimous that it was the best and most representative exhibition of modern painting ever assembled in Paris. Certainly nothing equal to it has ever been held in this country," he continued, "and I think you can bank on a full measure of praise from the moderns and of condemnation from the conservatives."[58]

The Academy passed on the primitive African sculpture, but it opened a four-week exhibition of the most recent additions to Barnes's collection on April 11, 1923. The seventy-five works, representing the then radical edge of European modernism, included nineteen of the collector's Soutine and seven of his Modigliani pictures as well as seven Lipchitz sculptures, five works each by Matisse and the leading French exponent of Fauvism, André Derain (Barnes would later refer to him as "André *de rien*"), four each by Pascin and the Polish-born painter Moise Kisling, two each by Picasso and Utrillo, and single paintings by de Chirico, and, among less well-known artists, two women, Helene Perdriat and Marie Laurencin. The Barnes selections were part of an odd triple bill that included historical portraits by the Peale family and a group of contemporary paintings by Japanese artists. Although he initially told Lewis that he did not wish his name to appear in any announcement of the show, Barnes soon prepared an essay that he proposed the Academy use as an introduction to the exhibition catalogue. He gave three reasons, revealing festering wounds and reflecting entangled emotions of fear, pride, and hope:

(1) No critic, connoisseur or professor can puncture its logic or psychology, without a push from me that will put him in a grave already prepared—figuratively.

(2) It can't help but be educational to the crowds who will visit the show eager for some word of explanation. . . .

(3) That introduction will be used in much the same form as a text book in every college near Philadelphia within three years from now. The colleges don't know yet that they will use it—but I know it, and will bet we succeed. We have the necessary men, paintings, and, best of all, we've got more money to use in the fight than all the colleges put together could beg, borrow or steal.

"Oh, boy!" he exclaimed after mentioning two London critics whom he had heard would write articles about the Barnes Foundation. "Was the time ripe to take the world by the ears in the cause of modern art?"[59]

The Pennsylvania Academy agreed to use Barnes's essay—and to accept his subsequent offer to pay for the printing of 3,000 catalogues. He provided fifteen photographs of pictures included in the exhibition, which carried, undoubtedly by design, the simple, non-provocative title "Contemporary European Paintings and Sculpture." The collector proffered advice on the height of pedestals for the sculpture and on dealing with the press. "Pull several proofs of my article," he told Academy officials, "and give it to each one of the representatives of the Philadelphia daily papers. Newspaper writers know nothing of art, but they have to turn in copy, and it is our job to see that their copy is at least fairly representative of what the show stands for."[60] Barnes thought he could, to a degree at least, control reaction to his prized pictures.

His catalogue essay provided a competent introduction to the artists represented in the show. He explained that while most lived in Paris, they were born and grew up in countries other than France, a phenomenon illustrating, he suggested, the "influence of French environment upon cultures and endowments racially and radically foreign to France." He commented upon the youth of the vast majority of the painters and sculptors. Reminding viewers of William James's observation that people like what is familiar to them and condemn what is strange, he pointed out that when Leopold Stokowski had introduced Arnold Schoenberg's *Kammersymphonie* to Philadelphia audiences in 1915, the composer's "effrontery of strange contrasts and explosive dissonances was resented with snickers, jeers and scoffs. Eight years after," he said, "that same conductor played that same piece to practically that same audience [and was] listened to with respect and rapt attention." The work in the Academy show would "probably seem strange to most people," Barnes admitted. But a painter or sculptor, he said, "should be judged on his ability to express himself in a work of art" not on his conformity to "'forms' we associate with [works] we know and like." With rising passion, he concluded:

> These young artists speak a language which has come to them from the reaction between their own traits, the circumstances of the world we live in, and the experience[s] they themselves have had. . . . To quarrel with them for being different from the great masters is about as rational as to find fault with the size of a person's shoes or the shape of his ears. If one will accord to these artists the simple justice of educated and unbiased attention, one will see the truth of what experienced students of painting all assert: that old art and new art are the same in fundamental principles. The difference lies only in the degrees of greatness, and time alone can gauge that.[61]

Alas, the collector's commentary failed to forestall a barrage of criticism. Although young American artists flocked to the exhibition, the reaction of the press ranged from ridicule to outrage. C. H. Bonte wrote in the *Inquirer* that the show was filled with "frequently indescribable curiosities." He found Soutine's landscapes "incomprehensible masses of paint" and said it required "an exercise of vivid imagination" to find in his portraits likenesses "to plausible human beings."[62] The Soutines also upset Edith Powell of the *Public Ledger*. Before Barnes's most recent trip to Europe, she had seen his collection on numerous occasions, but nothing had prepared her for the new pictures. Seizing the obvious device of wondering what Charles Wilson Peale, his son, Rembrandt, and his brother, James, might have thought of Soutine's portraits "of the dregs of humanity" hanging so near their literal transcriptions of historical figures, she made their imagined response her own: "the creations of a disintegrating mind." Soutine "may be mad," she wrote, "he may be an outcast, and being a Russian he may be morbid, emotional and unilateral, but," she conceded, "he presents life as he sees it. . . . The question is: Are we willing to look at the world with his eyes? Are we willing to give careful attention to what actually exists for him even if it seems to us diseased and degenerate? Is it a good thing to visit morgues, insane asylums and jails?"[63] Writing for the *Record*, Francis J. Ziegler, declared the "pictures . . . most unpleasant to contemplate." He described them as "debased art in which the attempt for a new form of expression results in the degradation of the old formulas. . . . It is hard to see," he concluded, "why the Academy should sponsor this sort of trash."[64] In her articulation of the journalistic consensus, Dorothy Grafly, art critic for the *North American* and sister of the conservative sculptor Charles Grafly who taught at the Pennsylvania Academy, proclaimed the leper's ancient warning: "Unclean!"[65]

Twenty-five years after Barnes opened the Sunday papers to read the response of Philadelphia critics to the treasures he loaned the Academy for the enjoyment and enlightenment of his fellow citizens, the journalists' words still stung. He recalled, accurately if not precisely, being labeled a "perverter of public morals."[66] His immediate reaction had been to fire off angry letters. Edith Powell, whom he had considered a friend, received an especially vile and insulting missive. Barnes suggested that the cure for her inadequacies as a critic was to have relations with the iceman, the fellow with bulging biceps wielding tongs who was then a symbol of male virility.[67] It was if the collector's own masculinity had been challenged by the disparagement of the pictures he had so carefully assembled and loved with a passion that would be unbearable in a father for his children.

But retrenchment, which was the Academy's reaction to the critical storm, was not even within the realm of psychological possibility for a man who, as a boy, had learned to box for self protection and saw life as a daily struggle to stamp out ignorance and beat back bullies. "After I hit hard, it is a complete release of emotion and there are no hangovers," the great admirer of Freud wrote to Dewey.[68] Only the first part of his self-analysis was correct. But it is true that following the delivery of his epistolary rebukes and rebuttals to those who derided his pictures, he set off for Paris in search of more art, and the whole furious fracas strengthened his convictions about the importance of a systematic approach to teaching art appreciation.

Barnes had attempted to explain his educational objectives in an article published in the *New Republic* on March 14, 1923. He described his collection, emphasized that the choices were his own not those of a dealer or similar expert, and stated his belief that the Foundation's "most valuable asset" was not the pictures but his "twenty years' experience in the working out of a community plan" for the "growth" and "personal development" of his Argyrol factory employees. He called it, frankly, "an experiment" in which "nothing [w]as definitely proved," but he declared the results "sufficiently encouraging to justify the attempt to continue the experiment on a larger scale through the medium of the Foundation. The resources we have are of vital importance to many people," Barnes wrote, if he was to judge by the number of those, "with or without college affiliations, who [had] visited [his] collection . . . for the past ten years." He said he had seen "aesthetic capacity developed in many people in whom it was latent" and "become a factor operative in their daily lives. The difficulty," he continued, "has been to persuade teachers and students, who have been drilled in the traditions that only old art is worthy of study," to approach modern art "with an open mind." The collector thought he knew how to engender an appreciative approach to new works, but he was under no illusion that he could accomplish it single handedly. In a key statement of his intentions, Barnes said:

> We believe . . . paintings, trees or any objects representing genuine human values can be made more interesting, more vital, more valuable if they are studied according to methods which it has been the great achievement of a few educators to put into such shape that they can be used by teaching organizations. We hope to effect some working plan with colleges and universities in which the scientific approach to the study of our resources shall be made part of the curriculum. In that way what has been a vital experience to a few may . . . be repeated and amplified in connection with educational genius and equipment not possessed by our small organization.[69]

Courses in the history and appreciation of art were taught in barely more than one hundred American colleges and universities in the early 1920s.[70] The best departments were at Princeton, under the distinguished leadership of Frank Jewett Mather, Jr., Harvard, where Paul Sachs had developed a renowned program of study, Columbia, and New York University. Penn's courses were offered in the School of Fine Arts, which had been organized in 1921 upon a nucleus of existing departments. To architecture and music, the university had added a four-year program in fine arts leading to the BFA degree. The lone art history professor, Harvard-educated sculptor Herbert E. Everett, taught general histories of both painting and sculpture, a history of Italian painting and sculpture between the fourteenth and seventeenth centuries, and a course in early American painting. His classes attracted a small number of students from the College and public school teachers seeking certification as art teachers through the School of Education or baccalaureate degrees through the university's collateral course program, as well as Fine Arts students. But there were only a handful of majors in the new BFA program, and art history courses were regarded by the professionally oriented architecture students as little more than a hurdle on the way to a coveted degree. The School of Fine Arts valued them for providing a theoretical basis for understanding styles of design, and it hoped that with the rapid growth of art museums in the United States, Penn might supply a projected demand for trained curators. Its catalogues emphasized that the University Museum afforded students opportunities for studying excellent examples of ancient and Oriental art and that the prospective opening of the Johnson collection of paintings, at the Pennsylvania (subsequently Philadelphia) Museum of Art, would provide facilities for study previously available only in the great museums and galleries of Europe.

But Barnes was aware of the limitations of Penn's art program, even if he was largely ignorant of how Penn or other universities operated, and his loyalty to his alma mater was sufficient to propel him to make an extraordinary proposal to President Josiah Penniman. On January 27, 1924 he wrote to Penniman offering to endow a chair in modern art. With little understanding of the fierceness with which institutions of higher learning guarded their prerogatives for appointing faculty, he said that Laurence Buermeyer should be the occupant with the rank of full professor. Barnes even prescribed his teaching duties: "two lectures a week at the University and two practical talks each week at the Foundation." The collector informed Penniman of Buermeyer's educational achievements and experience and noted that the Penn alumnus had a book on aesthetics ready for press. Pointing out that Princeton, Harvard, and Columbia, unlike Penn, already gave courses in modern art, Barnes said those who taught them "bewail[ed] the absence of available modern paintings which are indispensable to make the subject a living reality." He told the president that in addition to its collection of late nineteenth and early twentieth century art, the Barnes Foundation had "sufficient . . . primitive . . . art— ancient Greek, Egyptian, Negro, etc.— in choice and representative pieces to show the origins of the forms clearly apparent in the best of the moderns. In short," he concluded, "I think we could make the proposed course unique, beyond comparison with anything available in the world."[72]

With his letter, Barnes included a copy of Professor Cret's sketch of the Foundation buildings then under construction. He observed that while the gallery would not be ready for purposes of instruction for about a year, the didactic part of Buermeyer's course should be started the following fall. He asked Penniman to put his proposition to the board of trustees and let him have an answer within a few weeks. The president, a scholar of English literature, turned at once to Warren P. Laird, an architect trained at Cornell and the Ecole des Beaux Arts in Paris, who had come to Penn in 1891 as dean and professor of architecture. A man of continental sophistication with strong mid-Western roots,

Laird had created a model for America architectural education at the University. As dean of the newly crafted School of Fine Arts, he provided Penniman with a cogent analysis of the unexpected proposal from the Medical School alumnus and recommended accepting it on its merits while retaining firm administrative control over faculty appointments.

In a confidential report to the president, Laird wrote: "As an institution dedicated to the search for truth and its dissemination, the University should welcome an opportunity to include in its curriculum the teaching of the principles of modern art. The fact that its manifestations in painting have failed of understanding and acceptance by the public and created violent controversy among the cognoscenti cannot be accepted as a reason for refusal. The modernist and his doctrines have created storm centers in each succeeding age, but if sound in essence, the new thought has emerged to lead for its time. And this aspect of art has received enough thoughtful attention by serious students to fully warrant its inclusion among University courses." But then the dean cautioned: "The University should not establish a chair whose incumbent is designated by another institution even though salary charges be borne by the latter. . . . The suitable way to carry the proposition into effect would be for the chair . . . to be endowed in the University by the Barnes Foundation, which then should have the right of nomination of the incumbent. . . . The incumbent . . . should have the same relation to the Trustees as have other members of faculties. And as the University makes it a rule to require of candidates for full professorships a prior tentative service in rank not less than that of assistant professor so the candidate here proposed should be elected to an assistant professorship and promoted in due course under usual conditions. . . . The proposed course should be cordially welcomed but its nature and condition is such that the University should have complete administrative control over its presentation."[72]

On the strength of Laird's recommendation and within a week of receiving it, Penniman presented Barnes's proposition, with accompanying administrative reservations, to the Penn trustees. The board referred the matter to the president with power to act on its behalf. Before replying to Barnes, Penniman sought the advice of a trustee who had been unable to attend the board meeting, Joseph Early Widener, son and heir of the collector Peter A. B. Widener who had died in 1915. With Widener's approval, and after further consultation with the full board, the president then wrote to the university's potential benefactor that Penn would be "happy to cooperate in carrying forward to realization" a proposition of significance in advancing "understanding of the nature and purpose of art." He said the trustees were willing to accept and administer "an endowment in amount sufficient to assure the income required permanently to maintain a professorship in modern art and to meet other costs incident to its work," but that the university "must control the selection of the teaching staff." He assured Barnes that an instructor as well prepared as

Buermeyer would not fail of election, but that it "would be wise to adhere to established practice" of electing him to "an initial three-year period of service as assistant professor."[73]

Two days later, Barnes replied in a cordial, cagey letter that was itself a work of art. He begged Penniman to thank the board for its "very kind consideration" of his proposal. He then supplied information, which he said he had wrongly assumed was in the trustees' possession and bore upon the essential points covered in the president's letter. The "missing" data had to do with the identity and purpose of the Barnes Foundation, its endowment ("securities of the highest class which any conservative banking house with sufficient capital would buy on the spot for a sum exceeding five million dollars"), additional resources ("paintings accumulated during nearly twenty years for which I paid in excess of two million dollars"), method of instruction used in the Argyrol factory classes and its comparative value, and the attention accorded his work and plans abroad. The collector assured the president that the Foundation shared with Penn a commitment to the "advancement of knowledge, but I feel," he said, "that we could make that desideratum more sure of attainment by the preservation of our own identity than by becoming the appendage of the University . . . which the conditions stated in your letter of March 18th would bring about. We have been a going concern for more than ten years and we ask nothing but the right to stand upon our own feet."

Barnes added that aside from the matter of Buermeyer's prestige, he thought an assistant professorship in modern art would be "rather incongruous" inasmuch as there did not exist a full professorship in the field. He then proposed "a simple experiment": establish a chair in modern art with Buermeyer as professor, funded by the Foundation, and see "if within a reasonable time any student who wished to study . . . art from the period of the Renaissance to the present would not perforce ignore Harvard, Columbia, and Princeton and enroll in the University of Pennsylvania." Let the trustees judge if what "I have written" is of sufficient appeal to move them "to modify the conditions stated in your letter," Barnes said. And, oh by the way, "a minor consideration, at present . . . [according to] the deed which Mr. Roberts drew up, the University of Pennsylvania is one of three who control the entire resources of the Barnes Foundation after my death. Naturally that would have to be changed if some other educational institution should accept the proposal which up to the present has been made to the University of Pennsylvania only."[74]

No such golden apple had ever before been dangled in front of Barnes's modestly endowed alma mater. Several years earlier, the trustees had committed themselves to a $10 million-fund drive and the goal was still distant. The contemplative Penniman, a man with little aptitude for finance, pondered the collector's audacious letter. The worldly Laird suggested a compromise. The university could not modify the principle of administrative control over faculty appointments, but it could and did accept visiting lecturers from other institutions and accept for credit the work done by its students under such visitors.[75] The president wrote to Barnes that Penn would gladly "receive the Professor of Modern Art of the Barnes Foundation," give him every facility accorded to its own faculty members, open his courses to its students, and accept for credit toward its degree in Fine Arts the work certified by the Barnes Foundation to have been satisfactorily completed by such students, "as is done with all institutions of acceptable grade." He suggested that an arrangement between the university and the Foundation be made for a trial period and "made subject to termination thereafter by either party under reasonable provisions." His alternative to Barnes's initial proposal, Penniman said, was "intended fully to respect and even emphasize the identity of the Barnes Foundation."[76]

The collector was delighted by the university's response, especially in light of a monkey wrench that Laurence Buermeyer, his designated link to academic respectability, had thrown, inadvertently, into his carefully laid plans. Barnes thanked Penniman "both for the tribute your decision pays to us and for the fine spirit of cooperation which cannot help but result in a positive advance for American culture. I believe the details you mention will offer no difficulties to completing a liaison mutually satisfactory," he said. "But a serious breakdown in Mr. Buermeyer's health has complicated the situation somewhat." At thirty-six, the collector's mentor/protégé had apparently gone into a debilitating depression on finishing his book. Barnes assured the president that he and Dewey were making a "survey of the field of suitable men." He hinted that Irwin Edman might be spared by Columbia for a year though there would be "a howl" if he were "taken away." Edman, he revealed, "is the very man who asked me to make with Columbia the arrangement which I proposed with you."[77] Penniman replied the same day: "I think with you that the plan suggested by me will solve our problem." He added that Edman seemed certainly "able to do the work that we both desire so earnestly to have done."[78]

With Dewey's intercession, it seemed for a brief moment likely that the star of the Polish field study might give up New York for the latest opportunities awaiting him in Philadelphia. But according to Barnes, the dean of Columbia's Graduate Faculties and the executive officer of its philosophy department "reared up and pawed the air."[79] Edman's aesthetics course attracted more than two hundred students a year, and the young professor's classroom efforts had been praised in the *New Republic* as heralding "a renaissance of grace and clear, cool sense."[80] The collector, however, had a back-up candidate. He was Thomas W. Munro, a man, Barnes assured Penniman, with an even "better practical knowledge of . . . art and psychological aesthetics than Mr. Edman" and highly regarded by all his colleagues.[81] A graduate of Columbia College, Munro had earned his Ph.D. in philosophy at Columbia in 1920 and subsequently taught the subject there in the adult education program and summer sessions. Barnes wrote Penn's president that Munro would accept a university position "as the representative of the Barnes Foundation."[82] He suggested a two-year renewable contract and urged Penniman to reach a decision as soon as possible, as Munro would be joining him and the ailing Buermeyer on a trip to Europe within weeks. The university trustees met that day and passed a resolution empowering Penniman, Laird, and Widener to arrange the details of a plan whereby Penn would receive as a visiting lecturer or exchange professor during the 1924-25 and 1925-26 academic years a teacher provided by the Foundation to give a course in modern art.

Penniman wrote to Barnes on May 2, 1924 offering to enter into an agreement with the Foundation. He spelled out the terms covering the title of the visiting lecturer, course structure, credit units, duration of the contract, and said Penn found either Buermeyer or Munro acceptable.[83] Barnes returned the Foundation's ratification of the agreement the next day. With soaring hope for what might be accomplished by the new alliance, he told Penniman: "You and I have started on something which it would be difficult to imagine the importance of for American culture. One thing is sure that no human power can stop Philadelphia from becoming the only place in the world where . . . art can be adequately studied objectively and scientifically." He said Munro was "up on his toes about his new job" and suggested a press release, conveniently supplying a three-page draft.[84] Penniman referred it to Laird for review, and he then sent Barnes a somewhat modified version clarifying the fact that the University was "giving audience to the teaching work of another institution."[85]

When negotiations on the wording of a public announcement were finally completed to both parties' satisfaction, a statement was given to the press. The reaction of local art educators was captured in a headline in the *North American*: "Art Circles Flay Barnes Foundation." In high dudgeon, Theodore M. Dillaway, director of art in the city's public schools, said: "It is all very well for arrived men to experiment with modernistic theories, but when it comes to teaching them to students, it is an entirely different matter, and a pernicious one. . . . It would not be long before we should note anarchistic tendencies, as a result." Harriet Sartain, dean of the School of Design for Women (now Moore College of Art and Design), protested that she was "not a conservative in art matters" and had "always been open to new ideas," but then said she was "aghast" at the alliance between Penn and the Barnes Foundation. "From what appeared as part of the Barnes Foundation collection at the Pennsylvania Academy last spring, I cannot appreciate the present stand of the University in instituting a course with such art as source material. It is a bad thing to put any such ideas before susceptible minds." Huger Elliott, principal of the School of Industrial Art, detected "Bolshevist" influences in the proposed courses. But no one expressed greater angst than the sculptor Charles Grafly, the Pennsylvania Academy teacher whose sister, Dorothy Grafly, had been among the several Philadelphia journalists to receive torrid letters from Barnes in response to their criticism of the Academy's 1923 exhibition of works from his collection. He called Barnes's pictures "rot," claimed students using his collection for research could "acquire only an appreciation for the abnormal," and said he could not "imagine a greater calamity, either in the world of art or of education" than transporting Penn students to the Merion gallery to study them.[86]

Perhaps not surprisingly, Penniman and Laird received letters from alumni who questioned the wisdom of a university alliance with the Barnes Foundation and the character of the man with whom they had made the deal. But the president politely dismissed his critics and warmly welcomed Munro in a meeting held on campus before the young instructor left for Europe. The dean rushed to put a prominent announcement of his course in the 1924-25 Fine Arts catalogue.[87] Then this cosmopolitan academic made a serious error in judgment. In a morning telephone conversation with Barnes in late October, he asked permission to bring some visitors from out of town to the Foundation. The collector called back in the afternoon to say "no." His anger at the presumption made upon a professional relationship was under tight control, and the next mail brought a letter in which he patiently laid out his reasons. In addition to Munro's class, the Foundation had instituted a second class "intended to reach the kind of people who do not go to colleges but have a genuine interest in art." He described it as a "continuation and amplification" of his Argyrol factory class designed to attract school teachers through whom he hoped to revolutionize the teaching of art in Philadelphia's public schools. "In order to carry out the whole system as planned, our resources of time, energy, and personnel will be taxed to the utmost," Barnes said. "Unless we stick to the plan, the results hoped for cannot materialize; consequently," he added with a rapid rapier thrust, "it will probably be necessary to offend a great many people who would like to go themselves and take their out-of-town friends to see the Collection."[88] Laird took the negative decision with good grace, and wrote to Barnes that his reasons were "logically determined and must," in his opinion, "satisfy reasonable people. If I am right," he concluded, "you will pay a much more negligible price than you anticipate for carrying out your plan."[89]

Although he didn't mention it to Laird, the collector continued to include Pennsylvania Academy students in his grand experiment in part, perhaps, because the institution's insurgent modernist, Arthur Carles, had bravely spoken out in support of his efforts when the city's most prominent art educators were publicly attacking the Penn-Barnes connection the previous spring. While Academy officials had remained silent following Charles Grafly's gratuitous condemnation of the alliance, Carles had said: "Philadelphia does not appreciate, as it should, what Dr. Barnes is trying to do. I dislike the distinction constantly made between so-called 'modern' paintings and the old, conservative masterpieces. There are only two kinds of painting, good and bad, and those of Dr. Barnes happen to be good. It is a representative collection, recognized in Europe as one of the best in the world."[90]

Acceding to Carles's subsequent request to suggest a plan whereby the Foundation's resources could be made available to Academy students, Barnes invited them and at least some of their teachers to visit his gallery when the building was completed at the beginning of 1925. While they were there, he observed them, and disturbed by what he regarded as their inability to see what was before them, he engaged Carles's sister Sara, who had been trained by Mary Mullen, to hold a weekly class for the young artists-in-training in which they read and discussed the psychology underlying artistic expression and then re-visited his pictures. The indomitable Miss Mullen offered a class for men and women aspiring to become art teachers.[91] "They are crazy to have entree to our collection," Barnes told Dewey. "I make the price attendance at our classes, and it work[s]."[92] Barnes himself began giving gallery talks on Friday and Sunday mornings to large numbers of invited guests. Making the list not only guaranteed a memorable experience but also held the promise of future delights.

When the fall term came to an end in December, Barnes was off again for Europe in search of more pictures. From Vollard, he acquired a Cézanne, a Renoir, and a Picasso, and using Guillaume as an agent, he bought Picasso's large *Acrobat and Young Harlequin* and major works by Matisse, including *Blue Still Life*, *Red Madras Headdress*, and *Seated Ruffian*, from Lund in Copenhagen.[93] Returning home, he conferred with Dewey, the apparently recovered Buermeyer, and Munro about ways to increase the educational value of the Foundation. They approached Columbia, and Munro's alma mater agreed to his offering a course in applied aesthetics using the resources of the Metropolitan Museum of Art.

Barnes then wrote to Penniman that Munro believed that he could make more progress in his Penn classes if his students had a general knowledge of the fundamental principles of philosophy and psychology. He proposed that Buermeyer offer such a course at the university drawing on materials from his new book, *The Aesthetic Experience*, which had just been published under the aegis of the Barnes Foundation.[93] Munro subsequently called upon the president to discuss the matter. Penniman then reviewed the collector's latest proposal with Laird and instructed him to take it up with the department of philosophy and psychology. Since Buermeyer was a product of the department and two members of its senior faculty, Edgar A. Singer, Jr. and Louis W. Flaccus, were well known to Barnes, sympathetic consideration of his idea was practically certain.

Flaccus had introduced aesthetics to the university curriculum when he joined the faculty in 1905 after taking his Ph.D. with William James at Harvard. He was in Europe on sabbatical during 1924-25 to finish research for his own book on the subject. Singer, who had studied civil engineering as a Penn undergraduate before going on to earn his Ph.D. in philosophy, had been a post-doctoral assistant to James in the mid-1890s. His central interest was in the theory of evidence. He held that philosophical questions should be so phrased that answers could be found through an empirical or experimental method. Singer had attended Central High School during Barnes's freshman year there, and his brother had graduated as the valedictorian of Barnes's class, so the Penn philosopher's acquaintance with the collector went back nearly forty years. They shared a profound belief in science as a tool that enables human beings to make progress toward a better life.

When Singer heard from Laird that Barnes was eager to fund a visiting professor in his department, he wrote a warm note to his potential benefactor suggesting a meeting. Barnes replied with an invitation to visit him in Merion. He said he would send a car to fetch Singer and promised him lunch, a sip of 1840 sherry and a tour of the new buildings. The collector added that the purpose of the Foundation was "to serve as a bridge between fellows like yourself, Dewey, Santayana, Russell, etc. and the well-meaning, well-endowed human beings who have never taken you seriously." He told Singer about his factory-school experiment, and said: "All I want to do at Penn is to have that experience tried out further by people better trained than I was and to give the method a meaning by something concrete, like the intelligent study of paintings. After that, a fair inference is that habit will take hold of the job and people will see that it really pays, by yields of new kinds of satisfaction, to take more seriously what the 'strange' people—philosophers, painters, musicians—say and do." Barnes said he couldn't imagine "Flaccus having any objection for the course would merely reinforce much of what he says and, no doubt, would offer if he had the time. I shall have no finger in the pie. I have nothing up my sleeve," he assured Singer. "All I want is to bring home what you and your colleagues are doing. *C'est tout—et c'est assez.*"[95]

The meeting persuaded Singer of the wisdom of accepting Barnes's offer. The collector told him that he would eventually like to finance the establishment of a fine arts department in the College, headed by Flaccus, and with Buermeyer and Munro as faculty. But the key to the larger benefaction was Penn's acceptance of Buermeyer as a visiting lecturer to teach a course in aesthetic experience. Singer told Barnes that there were rumors about his candidate's lackluster performance at Princeton. Barnes convinced him that Buermeyer was more than ready for a new challenge, and Singer conveyed his enthusiasm for the appointment to the president.[96] The collector's handwritten note, "Thanks, big!," expressed his delight.[97] He also wrote to Penniman to invite him to Merion and said, "I think you will be surprised to see how far advanced are the material preparations to carry out the educational plan that, when you and I are in Heaven, our successors will find better to their liking than anything their predecessors had . . . ."[98] The president accepted his invitation and told Barnes: "The plan that you have, as I understand it, is a great one. The future alone will demonstrate how great, but I believe that you have started something, which will have permanent and far-reaching results."[99] Although the collector had once told Dewey that Penniman had "the imagination of a goat,"[100] the flattery pleased him. He became nearly giddy when he learned that more than thirty students had enrolled in his protégée's second-semester Penn class. There had been only six the first semester, and Barnes had personally sent out thousands of circulars advertising the next iteration. In early March, the students visited the Merion gallery for the first time, and Barnes not only greeted them himself but also arranged for Penniman, Laird, Singer, and Cret to make brief remarks of welcome.

It was a prelude to another, grander ceremony. Barnes was determined to dedicate his foundation in style. He worked like "the very devil" to bring the speakers he wanted together in Merion.[101] In the end, he was forced to choose a date when Penniman would be out of town, but it was the only one suitable to both Dewey and Leopold Stokowski, who agreed to represent the artists of America. Mrs. Gifford Pinchot, the wife of the governor of Pennsylvania did not favor him with a reply to his invitation to represent the Commonwealth, but Barnes produced a state senator, a judge representing Montgomery County, and a Lower Merion Township official. Along with Stokowski, Singer, who represented Penn, and Columbia's representative, John J. Coss, the executive officer of its philosophy department, they "accepted" the Barnes Foundation after Dewey, the keynote speaker, dedicated it to the cause of education.

Dewey had previously asked Barnes if there were any particular points he wanted him to include in his remarks, and the collector had reminded him that his interest in painting and sculpture grew out of his "discovery that doing everyday things, for the sake of the things themselves, was an artistic experience. . . . Negroes helped us," he said, "because everything they do—their walk, speech, glance—is shot through and through with natural-born artistic expression." It was an acknowledgement of how his admiration of African American culture shaped his boldest entrepreneurial venture. Barnes's emotional response to the rhythm and melody of black life was a key factor in his creation of his Foundation. The collector wanted America's philosopher to avow that debt. He also suggested that Dewey take his "hat off to the score of people, without previous schooling, who had the natural brains and intelligence to grasp what you thinkers have done. A little bow to Nelle Mullen and to Mary Mullen" for their contributions to the enterprise was in order, he said. Then he told Dewey what, of course, his friend knew but others, who were eager to see his pictures, would have to learn: "The Foundation is an educational institution and not an entertainment bureau for 'aesthetes.' Anybody serious can link up with us, but nobody is rich enough or prominent enough to get in with us on those qualities [alone]."[102]

March 19, 1925 was an unseasonably warm day. The temperature had reached the low seventies by early afternoon. For more than an hour, thunder and lightening lashed much of the area, but by three o'clock the skies had cleared and the last guests arriving at the Barnes Foundation could roll up their umbrellas.

Peering over his glasses, Dewey addressed his audience with atypical eloquence. He began with a reference to two telegrams from Europe, which called
the educational work of the Foundation "monumental" and "epoch-making,"
and said they indicated that "sometimes people at a distance see things in a
truer perspective than [those] who are nearer. . . .We are . . . celebrating today,"
Dewey declared, "one of the most significant steps taken in this country for
freedom of pictorial or plastic art, for art education, and also for what is genuine and forward-moving throughout the whole field of education." He observed that the Argyrol factory school had been "the source of the ideas, the
experience, ideals, expectations and plans, which are incarnate here and which
are, to a very large extent, a memorial to the past work of the people who have
been engaged in the enterprise." In a gracious nod to Laura Barnes, Dewey said
that "under her direction, the beauty of the surroundings will be a worthy
setting for the beauty within [and] will also become part of the educational
resources of the Foundation."

Then he spoke, as Barnes had requested, of art and black people:

It is . . . significant that you will find in this gallery one of the finest collections in the
world of African art, which records the aesthetic activities of individuals whose names
are not known, probably have not been known for centuries. For it suggests that
members of the negro race . . . people of African culture have also taken a large part in
the building up of the activity which has culminated in this beautiful and significant
enterprise. I know of no more significant, symbolic contribution than that which the
work of members of this institution have made to the solution of what sometimes
seems to be not merely a perplexing but a hopeless problem—that of race relations.
The demonstration that two races may work together successfully and cooperatively,
that the work has the capacity to draw out from our negro friends something of that
artistic interest and taste in making the contribution which their own native temperament so well fits them to make, is something to be dwelt upon in a celebration like this.
We may well rejoice at every demonstration of the artistic capacity of any race which
has been in any way repressed or looked upon as inferior. It is the demonstration of
this capacity for doing beautiful and significant work which gives the best proof of
the fundamental quality, and equality, of all people.

Dewey echoed Barnes in his conclusion that "art is not something apart,
not something for the few, but something which should give . . . meaning . . . to
all the activities of life. . . . I feel confident," he said, "we can open our eyes and
look into the years ahead, to see radiating from this institution, from the work
of this Foundation, influences which are going to effect education in the
largest sense of the word: development of the thoughts and emotions of boys
and girls, youths, men and women all over the country, and to an extent and
range and depth which makes this . . . one of the most important educational
acts, one of the most profound educational deeds, of the age in which we are
living."[103]

The dedication ceremony was followed by a dinner, which Albert and Laura
Barnes gave for the Deweys and other invited guests. The next day the local

papers reported on the death toll from a tornado that had swept through Illinois and Indiana, on a fire that destroyed the famous Breakers Hotel in Palm Beach, on an admiral who admitted hiding data from Congress about the leasing of Teapot Dome, on local police raids in search of home stills, on the record crowds that attended the Philadelphia Flower Show, on the Philadelphia Athletics' triumph over the New York Giants in training camp games, and on a late rally in the stock market. But there was no mention of the Barnes Foundation. The *Public Ledger* noted that Madame Maria Jonnesco, artist, author, and lady in waiting to the Queen of Rumania, had been entertained at tea by Mrs. George Horace Lorimer, the wife of the editor of the *Saturday Evening Post*. The foreign visitor was quoted as saying: "The time will come when America is renown for turning out the cleverest artists in the world as well as the world's cleverest businessmen." She predicted that the country would experience "a great renaissance of art."[104]

6

The Art in Painting

Barnes understood the power of words to bring about change. His overriding ambition was to engender a revival. Not a spiritual rebirth in any conventional sense, but a renewal of vigorous artistic and intellectual interest and activity that would surpass any previous high-water mark in terms of the numbers of ordinary people able to appreciate painting and sculpture. Walt Whitman's impassioned cry—"To have great poets there must be great audiences too!"—was also Barnes's watchword. "He took his museum awfully seriously," activist educator Alvin Johnson, a founder and president of the New School for Social Research, recalled. "He thought it could be the beginning of a Renaissance."[1]

Barnes saw literary magazines like the *Dial* and progressive journals like the *New Republic*, where Johnson was as an editor from 1917 to 1923, as natural allies. He was crushed whenever they declined to publish his essays. The rejection notices shook his confidence in his literary skills even as they hurt his pride, and he was moved to reach out to one of Johnson's colleagues, the rising journalistic star Francis Hackett, for assistance in bringing his ideas to the attention of a wider audience. An Irish-born newspaperman, Hackett had written about literature for the *Chicago Evening Post* before coming to New York. In December of 1919, Barnes invited him for a weekend to see pictures and discuss a proposition for more remunerative employment than writing for the *New Republic*. Hackett accepted the invitation, and when he arrived, the collector offered to pay him a generous salary for several years while he studied psychology and art, under his direction, in preparation for helping him with a book. It would describe paintings as observable phenomena in relation to other facts and events of human experience. Hackett was intrigued by the opportunity. But his lively wife, the writer Signe Toksvig who had accompanied him to Merion, didn't like any part of it. Barnes had ignored Toksvig, leaving her to forge a bond with Laura, which she did not, and according to the collector, Signe "queered" the deal.[2] Hackett "was as fine as he could be," Barnes told Dewey. "It was his tabby that misbehaved and she has him . . . completely under the thumb."[3]

The journalist's refusal to take a job with the collector sent him into what Johnson called one of his "epic rages." He threatened to loose detectives, whom he employed to investigate trademark infringements, on the *New Republic* and produce evidence of wrongdoing that could blow it "sky high."[4] But the magazine, which could count on the affection of liberal friends throughout the country, ignored his menacing letters, and he never acted on his angry impulse. "You'll size the matter up as . . . thoroughly disreputable, which it is," Barnes admitted to Dewey. His lame self-defense was that "until the idealists learn the technique of 'rough-house', their efforts will continue to be amiable intellectual gymnastics. . . . They are one and all a parasitic growth on decency in intelligent society," he groused.[5]

It was to a writer for the *Dial* that the collector next turned in his effort to hire a pen. Thomas Craven, a free-lance journalist originally from Kansas, wrote its art reviews, and Barnes invited him and the artist Thomas Hart Benton, with whom Craven was then sharing a New York apartment, to Merion for a series of weekend art discussions. The collector paid their train fare from Manhattan, and beginning sometime in the late spring of 1921, they made the 180-mile round trip journey several times a month to talk about paintings with him. In the course of their conversations, Barnes shared with the young men his hopes for the Foundation and told them he needed a writer for a book about judging and enjoying art. Craven must have hesitated as he sensed, before Barnes did, that their respective views were fundamentally incompatible. While they shared an interest in the technical development of individual artists, Barnes's focus was on the picture. The critic looked at individual works in search of springboards the artist had used or might employee for further development. He would stay on at the *Dial* and soon publish a two-part series, entitled "The Progress in Painting," a concise survey of modern art in which he linked it to the great tradition in Western painting, took a firm stand against Impressionism as producing "nothing more vital than a number of very real and convincing representations of sunlight," and hailed the early modernists for their creative thought and vigor.[6]

Unlike Craven, Benton had no steady source of income and was eager for paid employment. Barnes had just purchased two of his pictures at the April Pennsylvania Academy of the Fine Arts exhibition, and he offered to hire the painter, who had studied in Paris and had once been a member of the American vanguard, to make formal drawings of the pictures in his collection for the purpose of compositional analysis. Initially, Barnes was intrigued by Benton's theories about form. The artist held that it was a "function of meaning," that is, determined in some measure by subject matter.[7] Their discussions probably helped the collector shape his own ideas, but, according to Benton and for reasons he never understood, Barnes broke off their relationship in the late summer of 1922. Although Barnes would later single out Benton for praise in the introductory essay he wrote for the Academy exhibition of the latest French additions to his collection, he sent him an insulting letter from Paris, which the artist saw as an expression of a lot of pent-up anger.[8] Looking back on his visits to Merion from the vantage point of more than thirty years, he described Barnes as "ahead of all the critics" in his understanding of modern psychology and philosophy.[9] Benton valued highly the opportunity he had to test his ideas in debate with Barnes and, summarizing his feelings in a memorable assessment, said: "He was friendly, kindly, hospitable and, at the same time, a ruthless, underhanded . . . magnificent son-of-a-bitch."[10]

Despite the publication of his essays on Renoir and Cézanne in influential journals, Barnes continued to brood over each rejection slip. He looked for scapegoats. An expert reviewer he had described as a "mental hobo with fringe around [his] trousers" to the startled diners in a New York restaurant was retaliating five years after the incident by turning thumbs down on a submission![11] When both the *New Republic* and the *Dial* turned down a book review he wrote in late 1921 on Percy Moore Turner's *Appreciation of Painting*, a kind of student's guide to European painting that discussed modern works sympathetically, he complained to Dewey: "Nobody wants my stuff, no matter what I write about."[12] Both the philosopher and his wife tried to restore their friend's confidence. When he confided in them joyfully laid but utterly screwball plans for retaliation, Dewey urged him to have some perspective and not to let others have the satisfaction of getting his goat. Alice praised his literary efforts lavishly. "Do put down more about what you think about art and people," she told him.[13] "Getting the real emotions into words, shape, form, is too hard work for the most part. . . . So I hope you will do it for us."[14]

In January 1923, Forbes Watson finally published his essay on Turner's guide not "as a timely review" but to "revive . . . interest in a useful book." The editor said it was valuable because it illuminated "the beliefs and ideas of the donor of the Barnes Foundation."[15] Barnes's only quarrel with the author was over his failure to discuss the contributions of Picasso and Matisse. The little book's main thesis, that anyone willing to persevere may attain an intelligent appreciation and enjoyment of the painting of any age, was a concept he wholeheartedly endorsed. It was the proposition on which he was basing his own experiment. What was needed was a systematic approach that reduced to a minimum the role of merely personal preference. He thought he had one. He had been unable to find a professional writer to help him convey his ideas about aesthetics, but he had Buermeyer to help him organize his thoughts and as a resource in analyzing concepts used in discourse about art. Why not write his own book?

Even as he turned to the daunting project, the Barnes Foundation published its first title. Mary Mullen, who along with Buermeyer was an associate director of education, had written a wholly credible primer, with fifty reproductions from the Barnes collection, entitled *An Approach to Art*. It drew on the experiences of her students in the factory school as well as on the works of the various authors she introduced to them. Mullen's style was straightforward, and she illustrated her points with examples from a workingwoman's everyday life—watching Tom Mix on the silver screen, operating a bottle-corking machine in a factory, selecting material for a dress, learning stenography. In a scant twenty-five pages, she sketched the psychology of creating and enjoying art. Her intention was to enable her readers to liberate an aesthetic sense, which had been suppressed by practical concerns, and further refine it. "A person with a highly developed sense of beauty, but unable to express himself by means of paint and canvas, will experience feelings as deep and satisfying as those of an artist when an object stimulates him to expression," she wrote. Mullen then turned to a model close at hand to drive the message home. Consider, she told her readers, the "connoisseur [who] acquires paintings and sculpture which he knows are expressions of the artists' true feelings . . . arranges the pictures and sculpture . . . in such a way that each individual work contributes its share to the making of a perfect whole. The result is a wonderful creation, comparable in unity and loveliness with the separate paintings; in that case the collector is the artist."[16]

Mullen's little book was probably a synopsis of her classroom talks, and Barnes promoted *An Approach to Art* as part of the Foundation's general educational program. Its second title, *The Aesthetic Experience*, was the book by Laurence Buermeyer Barnes had touted to Penn's Provost Penniman. Buermeyer sought to provide readers with an understanding of the role the fine arts play in human experience, the human impulses out of which they arise, and the conditions necessary for their full enjoyment and appreciation.[17] The slender treatise attracted the attention of more than a score of colleges and universities, which purchased it and may have used it in their philosophy and/or art history courses. But *The Aesthetic Experience* made few claims to originality, and it was not going to revolutionize the teaching of art appreciation.

The book that Barnes began writing sometime in early 1924 had the potential to change radically the way schools and institutions of higher learning approached the subject. *The Art in Painting*, which the collector told a reporter he had completed in six months,[18] presents a method for the rigorous objective scrutiny of pictures. It was initially published by the Barnes Foundation in 1925, and a trade edition was issued by Harcourt Brace and Company the next year. The collector hoped his book could provide the basis for a comprehensive science of aesthetics. His goal was to promote a more penetrating understanding and a richer enjoyment of works of art. Although there are clearly antecedents in nineteenth- and early twentieth-century writing about art for some of the book's key concepts, Barnes amplifies, extends, and applies ideas implicit in the work of others in wholly new ways. As he must have known from his contacts with the faculties at Penn and Columbia, the area of study in which he threw himself was not yet glamorous or even academically respected, which is to say that his energy demonstrated a personal passion. Even with Buermeyer's assistance, and even if, as is more than likely, he exaggerated the swiftness with which he prepared his manuscript, writing *The Art in Painting* required an extraordinary effort.

Barnes made it, in a fundamental sense, on behalf of the inexperienced observer. He sought the pleasure of sharing what he had learned over the past dozen years from visiting museums and galleries and contemplating his own collection. He believed that art is intrinsically educative. He was convinced that painting and sculpture, in particular, could lead people to an understanding of the distinctive elements in the natural world and the world of human relationships that give life value and meaning. The key to extracting the individual from the generic, so as to savor the richness and variety of everyday experience, was, in Barnes's view, learning to see. "To draw out and make clear the true character of anything is the task of the artist," he wrote. "The artist gives us satisfaction by seeing for us more clearly than we could see for ourselves, and showing us what an experience more sensitive and profound than our own has shown him."[19] The "penetrating eye" of the painter or sculptor "sees to the core of the structure of things" and his "skilled hand . . . reproduces [these essential aspects]so that they awaken [in the observer] the intellectual content of the perceptions" and the emotions associated with them.[20] The picture on the canvas and the form shaped in clay recall "hushed reverberations,"[21] in the words of George Santayana frequently quoted by Barnes, that are at once the source and measure of our common humanity. The collector wrote his book to give students, who were willing to expend sufficient time and energy to learn his method, the ability to apprehend the individual and social experience preserved, transmitted, and intensified in works of art and partake thereby, if only momentarily, in "deeper harmonies."[22]

The heart of *The Art in Painting* is an analysis of form. It was a way of looking at art that had much in common with the way Barnes listened to the music of African Americans: for fundamental aesthetic qualities without reliance on historical context and without regard for the biographical facts of the artist's life. As a disciplined and voracious reader, Barnes was familiar with the concept of form, as opposed to subject, that had been developed by Walter Pater, the English critic. The year the collector was born, Pater had published *Studies in the History of the Renaissance* to which he would later add a new essay, "The School of Giorgione," where he suggested that the form of a painting is not simply a means of telling a story but the chief factor in determining the painting's value. His ideas were seized by critics chafing at the Victorian notion that the value of art lay in its moral lessons to support their self-indulgent claims of "art for art's sake." Seeking to free art from so restricted a meaning, Tolstoy maintained in his 1898 essay, *What is Art?* that the artist's challenge is to render visible the powerful emotions resulting from his perceptions. For the Russian writer, what was even more important than transmission of feeling by the painter was the observer's reaction to it. In 1914, Clive Bell, an early champion of the Post-Impressionists, wrote in his little book *Art* that "significant form" is the one essential quality shared by all works of art that stir our "aesthetic emotions." But he left the term largely undefined except to say that it included "combinations of lines and colors."[23] Bell's Bloomsbury mentor (and his wife's erstwhile lover), Roger Fry, also promoted a formalistic analysis that encouraged appreciation of modern art. In the essays collected in his influential 1920 book, *Vision and Design*, he returned again and again to the question of how a painting was put together. Form was for Fry the vector the artist used to transmit his message to the viewer.

But Barnes went further than any of his intellectual predecessors in testing his ideas about aesthetic objects by application to the objects themselves. He distinguished between *matter*, the distinctive aspect of reality in which the artist is interested, *form*, by which he meant the structural design resulting from the artist's selection and emphasis of certain visual qualities from among the many residing in things, and *technique*, the technical means used by the artist to render various forms. In contradistinction to Bell, who asserted that "the representative element in a work of art . . . is irrelevant,"[24] he argued that there can be so close a link between form and matter that the two are fused into a single value. For Barnes, the recognition of subject and the perception of design become united in the observer's experience of them. He provided a theoretical basis for a middle way between art historians, like Princeton's Frank Jewett Mather, who discussed art preponderantly in terms of subject matter, and critics, taking their cue from Bell, who said subject matter had no part whatsoever to play in aesthetic effect. Differentiating, moreover, between what he considered the legitimate from the illegitimate use of subject matter, Barnes gave viewers a definite, if somewhat general, criterion for judgment. By applying his principle to the work of specific artists, moreover, he sought to substantiate its value as a guidepost in critical analysis:

> In an ordinary magazine illustration, the familiar devices are shuffled and recombined . . . but there is [an] absence of any individual perception. . . . Even great artists . . . sometimes . . . resort to the illegitimate use of subject matter. Delacroix . . . was . . . highly romantic and liked to portray fervid emotions. . . . What he felt as heroism and romance, and depicted by exotic subject matter and exaggerated gestures, seems to us now not sublime but overdramatic, if not bombastic. . . . Tintoretto also painted subjects of a highly dramatic nature, but he gave us the equivalent of the human values intrinsic to the situation, so that while in Delacroix we see flamboyance and melodrama, in Tintoretto we find peace that aesthetic satisfaction always yields.[25]

Barnes used the word "plastic" throughout his writing about art. Odd to our ears, the term is one reason his books are difficult to read today. But what he meant was that because a painter could work line, color, and space into various forms, they were his "plastic means." Barnes considered color the most important because it "comes nearest being the raw material of painting." The effect produced by color, he said, depends on "its intrinsic quality, independent of all relation to the other constituents in the aesthetic ensemble of the picture." Describing that "intrinsic quality" was a formidable task probably doomed to failure. As reviewer of David Batchelor's *Chromophobia*, has pointed out, "color has always remained beyond the powerful, organizing grip of language."[26] But Barnes made a heroic effort. The color in Raphael, he found "ordinarily . . . either indifferent or displeasing . . . like . . . a cheap rug or fabric—either dull or over brilliant." In "Giorgione, Cézanne or Renoir," he said, "we see quite the reverse in the immediate sensuous charm that pervades and heightens all the more complicated effects . . . not unlike that which simple physical charm gives to personality, in making moral and intellectual qualities more vivid and appealing, more intensely *felt*, as well as judged favorably." Barnes considered the Venetian painter and the two French modernists, along with Giotto, Titian, and Rubens, to be the "great colorists" of Western art. In their work, he wrote, "there seems to be no limit to the multiplicity of hues and tints introduced into the simplest object, an orange, a cup, a hand, a lock of hair; yet there color-chords are invariably units in themselves. . . . The picture . . . seems a symphony of color, in which the . . . appeal is enormously heightened by the sense of the relations between the colors . . . with each color setting off and being itself set off by all the others."[27]

Not only did Barnes differentiate richness of pigment, "the subtly modified dark tones" of Rembrandt that "suggest a great variety of color," from mere brightness, colors used, as Kisling sometimes employed them, in ways that give "no sense of glow or splendor," but he also suggested another, quite original distinction. "Juiciness," he said, was always present in the work of the master colorists, though he did not consider its opposite, "dryness," a term of "unqualified reproach. There are aesthetic effects to which dry color is a positive reinforcement," Barnes explained and, as an example, pointed to Poussin, whose color he found "almost invariably dry" but whom he ranked highly for his "fine feeling for the sensuous nuances of different colors and a rare power to make color function harmoniously in composing his canvases." The collector went on to consider the relation of color to light in creating atmosphere, its structural role in rendering solidity, and how it is used to make a design. "By far the most important characteristic of color," he said, "is its capacity for actually contributing a part of the relations that make up plastic form, instead of merely being the material of the picture."[28]

The best part of the discussion of line and composition, like that of color, in *The Art in Painting* lies in illustrations from the works of individual painters. "When the linear motive is dominant, as in Ingres," Barnes said, "line . . . functions as enrichment, both by its individual expressiveness and by its relation" to other elements in a picture. "In Titian," he pointed out, "the objects often seem to melt into one another, and this represents the expressive function of drawing achieved with the minimum of means." Turning to the arrangement of objects in space, Barnes pointed to Giotto's early frescoes at Assisi as examples of constructions in which central mass is discarded entirely and "elements are kept from falling apart by subtle relationships" that express the artist's "feeling for groupings." He argued that by his mastery of the constituent elements of form, Giotto "compels us to enter that union with the world which is the basis of religion, whether Pagan or Christian." His possession of "that power in the highest degree" made the Florentine painter, in Barnes's view, "perhaps the greatest of all artists."[29]

The collector understood that color, line, and space contributed to a picture's decorative quality, and he hailed decoration as providing the viewer pleasure comparable to the satisfaction he or she might take in physical health. "In it there is nothing so momentous that it thrills or exalts us acutely, but it is a necessary background to our intense experiences, if these are to be satisfactory," he wrote. His view was that the best paintings and sculpture were "ones in which the decorative forms . . . merge[d] with the structural ones." In Michelangelo's *Moses*, he felt ostentatious ornamental details of the tomb figure detracted from the solid, structural character of the work while, in the finest Egyptian sculpture from 2500 B.C., the restraint with which they were employed contributed to "unalloyed satisfaction." But in the work of his artistic archangels, Giotto, Giorgione, Titian, Tintoretto, Rembrandt, Cézanne, and Renoir, he found the decorative and structural forms "so completely fused that the[ir] paintings function as perfect unities." They possess "a pervasive and subtle quality which defies analysis," he admitted. Its appreciation depends ultimately upon "the native sensitivity and funded mass of experience" of the viewer. "The forms themselves," Barnes insisted, "will have little significance, except as decorative patterns or as units carrying the values of represented subject matter, unless the spectator has within himself the spark of life which makes those forms living realities capable of setting in vibration feelings akin to those which the artist had when he painted the picture."[30]

The psychology of learning to see received early but not extensive attention in *The Art in Painting*. Barnes stated plainly an idea he took from Tolstoy, which Dewey would later elaborate: "A work of art presents to the spectator an opportunity to live through experience . . . and whatever other value it has depends upon this value. If it lacks this, it is a counterfeit." He believed that responding to art was an active process. "Awakening in ourselves," in whatever degree, "the experience of the artist . . . involves effort and entails fatigue," the collector said.[31] While allowing that "natural aptitude" played some role in a person's ability to appreciate art in the fullest possible sense, he stressed the importance of previous experience both of a general and specialized kind. A fund of the latter could be acquired through systematic study of the traditions of painting. Because he believed that the process of education required constant cross-reference between contemporary art and art of the past, he devoted nearly half of his book to artists working before 1850.

Barnes began with Cimabue, as the first major artist to graft individual expression upon the Byzantine mosaic tradition, then lauded Giotto above every other painter, both for his technical contributions and the beauty of his creations. With considerable originality, he analyzed the work of subsequent Florentines from Masaccio, who took important steps toward naturalism in his depiction of realistic figures, to Raphael, whose pictures Barnes judged "artificial, formalized, devoid of spontaneity." The often-neglected Andrea del Castagno received high marks for his "dignified, balanced, simplified use of line, light, and color." Fra Filippo Lippi won measured praise for his skill in subtly incorporating foreground and background into an organic whole in stereotypical compositions that could nevertheless charm the viewer. Barnes said Fra Angelico's sentimental literary pictures provided "a good example of how technical skill can be combined with lack of . . . ability to use it." He found Piero della Francesca of interest for his distinctive design, particularly "exceedingly rich color-effect" produced by simple means. Botticelli was rated as "mediocre . . . a master of line [who] had no fine discrimination in using it." Barnes considered Leonardo "a scientist more than an artist" whose "researches produced results that have had an enormous influence on painting," but whose "frequent failure to apply paint skillfully" had to be weighed against "his fine sense of composition and his great command over space, light, and line." Recalling a visit to the Sistine Chapel, he described Michelangelo's frescoes as possessing "a unique moving force. . . . No other painter so fully conveys the idea of abstract power," the collector said, but he withheld his highest accolades because he detected "a deliberate striving for effects" in the artist's work that "partake of the nature of illustration."[32]

Barnes judged Venetian painting as "the pictorial high-water mark." The basis of his valuation was the "greater naturalness" in the form characteristic of the best painters in that tradition compared with any of the Florentines. He found "more human feeling" in Venetian figures. He said they were "more completely realized" and fit into the landscape with more ease, and the landscape itself, he found "more rich and convincing." The chief means employed by the Venetians to obtain their extraordinary results was, according to the collector, "the use of color, first, structurally, and then in combination with light" to produce "a pervasive, circumambient atmosphere or glow . . . [that] over and above its function in holding the design together and adding to the glamour or mystery or poetry of the subject, has a direct appeal to the sense." Barnes hailed Giovanni Bellini as the first painter to make color "seem to enter into the solid substance of objects." He considered his use of light "epoch-making" in terms both of his convincing modeling, which achieves "solidity without . . . over accentuation," and his "construction of a complicated but unified pattern" that influenced the work of the greatest Venetians. In the work of Carpaccio, he discovered "expressive handling of spaces" evidenced by "intricate designs in the individual units" of his large narrative paintings that invariably merged into strong overall arrangements of aesthetic details. Carpaccio also won the collector's praise for his use of architectural detail.[33]

But it was Giorgione whom Barnes considered "a serious rival of Giotto for the highest place in the hierarchy of art. . . . The foundation of his form is color," Barnes wrote; "it functions in the design to the greatest extent of which color is capable of functioning. . . . It supplies the maxim sensuous charm and decorative quality, blends with the light, welds together the composition, and contributes to the power and expressiveness of the drawing." Giorgione's expression, lyric, idyllic, Arcadian, "is probably the most poetic in all painting," the collector said, and ever the chemist, he concluded: "The elevation of Giotto, the power of Michelangelo, the drama of Tintoretto, the mystery of Rembrandt are all present in solution." Barnes rated the work of Titian, the most celebrated of all Venetian painters, weaker, but, at its best, exhibiting "greater fluidity of drawing," which "becomes a fusion of line, light, and color, and is the means of some of his best effects, as in *The Man with the Glove*." He considered Titian's religious paintings "among the greatest in existence." The movement in Tintoretto's pictures impressed Barnes profoundly. He felt the artist achieved it through "modification of line tending toward distortion." Tintoretto could so control the movement he depicted "that he could adapt it to a great variety of subjects," Barnes noted, and he praised the painter's use of color and light to produce "intensely dramatic" pictures. The importance of the artist's contribution, he said, can be realized when one considers that "El Greco derived chiefly from Tintoretto and that much of what is best in modern painting comes from El Greco."[34]

Barnes credited El Greco for the creation of "a new and distinctive form that shows a powerful use of the imagination in obtaining richer and more varied decorative designs" than even those of his teacher. His critique of the painter's work, following a discussion of the development of the tradition of Venice in the work of Rubens and Poussin, illustrates as well as anything he ever wrote his own finely honed capacity to see. "Very soon El Greco's line grows finer and more animated," Barnes said.

> The metallic and translucent qualities in the color of Tintoretto become more vivid and lustrous, and the ribbon-like bands of light become broader and enter into more dramatic contrasts with adjacent colors. As his particular form develops, we see these lines, color, and light worked into the most amazingly intricate patterns in all parts of the canvas, and these subsidiary designs enter into an extremely complex design, a rhythmic surge of tremendous aesthetic power.
>   . . . An examination of his work compels admiration for the imaginative scope that onceived plastic forms of such variety that they embody human values in subject matter of the greatest diversity. At times, the plastic elements appear to be reeling in disequilibrium as we note that excitement and anxiety are the dominating emotions of the scene. At other times, the perfect balance of the plastic means, through which the

subject matter is expressed, yields the effect of deep peace. The greatest range of human emotions gets adequate plastic embodiment through marvelous combinations of a really very limited number of plastic means. The line is so fine, so . . . nervous, and so often repeated in a particular unit, that it seems to form almost a tangle. The simple and stark colors— red, green, yellow, blue—take on a series of relationships through their variations by light and become a shimmering mass of variegated tones that insinuate themselves into the serpentine line to form designs that cover the whole gamut of color-contrasts and color-harmonies. . . . Everything is distorted into a pattern, even the shadows, and particularly the contrasts of bright colors against a comparatively dark background are vivified and dramatized by broad streaks of light. We see a design in . . . every part of the canvas and in the canvas as a whole. Each unit . . . glows and flows into a pattern with other units—it is movement itself, but with an eerie, ghastly quality that makes the drama otherworldly. . . . In our materialistic age his subjects have comparatively little appeal; but his design, his plastic forms, are as moving today to the sensitive spectator as his subject matter was to the Christian mystic of the seventeenth century. His distorted figures—with the narrow oval faces, crooked noses, squinting eyes, strange brows, ears of extraordinary angles, elongated fingers, twisted arms, swollen legs—these are things in themselves and their own aesthetic justification. To seek in them representative naturalistic values is to overlook both their intention and the total significance of art. The distortions are necessary to the design and prove that out of the elements of objects an artist can produce something that moves us more than anything we find in nature.[35]

Barnes's enthusiasm for the Spanish tradition naturally embraced Spain's greatest painter, Velázquez, whom he considered in a class by himself because of mastery of painterly means and "his ability to achieve realism of a vivid and particular character. He has never been surpassed in versatility," the collector wrote. He found in his work "a quality of impersonality, a detachment, a freedom from expressed emotion" that made "Velázquez the supreme realist." He said the painter had an eye that saw to a thing's "essential character" and caused him to eliminate everything not intrinsic to it, including himself. "This impersonality of spirit is matched by his complete concealment of his technical means," the collector wrote. "In Velázquez, nothing stands out; color, light, tactual quality, the space, both two-dimensional and three-dimensional, composition and rhythm of line and mass are there, but no one of them is what the picture is made of: it is made of them all, in measure and proportion." Barnes thought it "probable that much of Cézanne's search for essentials in objects . . . came from an unconscious absorption of Velázquez's obvious power to select and generalize by ignoring the adventitious." Manet, Courbet, Monet were all indebted to him. Even Renoir, he said, shared the Spanish painter's "detached realism that moves us aesthetically more than expressed emotion ever does" because it forces "us to see and feel with our own mind . . . what we could not see except through the artist's deeper vision and greater sensibilities."[36]

Barnes found another painter of the first rank in Rembrandt. He placed him among "the greatest of artists" on the basis of his "originality, plastic power, and [the] universality of the emotions his work calls forth." His means, "chiefly light and shadow used in . . . combination," enabled him to depict a whole gamut of powerful feelings, which the collector considered "deeply tinged with mysticism." His "repertoire of actual colors was very limited," Barnes pointed out, but "through the medium of chiaroscuro," these characteristically somber hues "take on a great variety of color-forms that have tremendous power to reveal the significance of things." He praised Rembrandt's line for achieving a "distinctiveness of contour so subtle that it is impossible to say how the work is done." He said the "intervals between masses" in his paintings "are so clean-cut and distinct that each figure moves in its own world of space, but one that relates itself with other spaces and forms designs full of simplicity and charm. No other painter has so combined economy of means with richness and convincingness of effect," he concluded. "In him imaginative interpretation of the real world reaches its greatest height."[37] But after Rembrandt Barnes found little to interest him in Dutch painting. In the first edition of his book, he dismissed Vermeer with a single sentence in which he linked him to Peter de Hooch as the best of the genre painters. In subsequent editions, he discussed his work in some 500 words, calling it "very uneven" but acknowledging that through the painter's "consummate use of color," his best pictures, *View of Delft* and *Street in Delft*, reached "the highest ranges of art."[38]

Of eighteenth-century French painting, Barnes judged only the work of Fragonard, within the Rubens tradition, and Chardin, outside it, as worthy of significant attention. He said Fragonard had a "vigorous and original sense of design" along with an admirable "sprightliness" and "three-dimensional solidity." Chardin, the collector wrote, gave "a French quality and thereby . . . a new form" to Dutch genre-painting, which "many later painters, especially Cézanne, modified to their own ends." In analyzing his pictures, Barnes found everything "done simply and subtly and the degree of attention given to each object . . . exactly proportioned to its importance in the canvas. . . . The general effect is dignity, masterly use of technical means, absence of tawdry or melodramatic effects, reality."[39]

Barnes's assessment of nineteenth-century French painting began with a quick dismissal of David as unoriginal. He thought Ingres more interesting. "The distinctive feature in his design," the collector said, "is the personal and extraordinarily skilful manner of using line in the formation of sharp and clear-cut arabesques and rectangular patterns, which practically always unify in a total form that arrests and holds the attention." Delacroix's drama may have been "offensively romantic," but he considered him "both an important artist and a very important figure in the history of painting . . . because of his use of color. His color is brighter, deeper, richer, stronger than most of his predecessors," Barnes wrote. "It enters into the structure of objects and functions powerfully in composing the picture." The painter Daumier, known best in his lifetime as a political and social cartoonist, was rated by Barnes as the most influential of all the mid-nineteenth-century French artists, both on his contemporaries and successors as a consequence of his emphasis upon design and comparative neglect of subject matter. "Daumier better than any other man except, perhaps, Cézanne knew how to select from the literally innumerable planes that constitute objects in space, and thereby create something which has all the essentials of a naturalistic object, plus an added, forceful convincing reality," the collector said. He gave him high marks for his ability to make color function structurally and for achieving maximum results with an economy of means. He wrote that his skill in employing "space in successful union with line and color has never been excelled." Barnes found Courbet of interest because of the radical break he made with the romanticism of Delacroix by turning "for subjects to the world of everyday objects and events, which he painted with force and in stark reality." He found glamour and poetry in his work and hailed him for advancing "beyond the Barbizon school in eliminating the specious and obvious" in his achievement of "effective design." The collector thought Corot's figures less powerful than Courbet's but "more appealing by virtue of perhaps obvious human values."[40]

The Art in Painting has chapters on portraiture and on landscape as distinct traditions, but while the Impressionists further developed the latter, Barnes concluded that Goya was the last great portrait painter since he said the Impressionists were not interested in making likenesses of particular individuals so much as particular individual creations. He considered Claude Gelée (known as Lorraine or Le Lorrain) the first genuine landscapist and lauded him for evoking a feeling of place that was epic in scope. Barnes said Claude "took the Venetian glow and converted it into a new form, a brilliantly lighted and colorful atmosphere that gives [a] sense of . . . liveliness in nature, a warmth and charm." The artist's strengths were space composition and the "use of diffused color-harmonies, atmosphere, and light." Although he sometimes neglected to solve technical problems, Barnes said his genius lay in an unrelenting focus on his chief objective of "realizing an effective total design." But it was the English landscape painter, Constable, whom the collector considered "the father of Impressionism." His technique of breaking color into "small units, tinged with spots of lighter paint, so that no one spot is all of the same color, but is a mosaic of colors in itself" was adapted for their own purposes by both Delacroix and Monet. In contrast to "Claude's grandeur, majesty, mystery," Barnes wrote, "we have in Constable the charm of simplicity, of the *intime*, the quietly mystical feeling of the countryside; there is an appealing, crude, this-world solidity to Constable. . . .Wagons, houses, trees are rendered with a greater degree of naturalistic detail than in the Impressionists, with more attention to outline, and less to the play of light. . . .The shadows are dark but rich, and the broad painting enhances the general decorative quality of the canvases." In Turner, Barnes found nothing much of interest "except a skillful use of the brush," and Millet he excoriated for the "shoddiness of his technical means matched by the cheapness of his feelings."[41]

The collector recognized that modernism is a moving frontier, and his point in tracing the evolution of painterly form was to show the continuity between apparently diverse artists over the course of more than six centuries. "The chief point of difference between the old and the new," he said, is that "the moderns exhibit greater interest in relatively pure design." Not that the early Italian painters lacked an interest in design, but, as Barnes pointed out, in an age when books were accessible only to a few, they were unable to separate their fascination with form from their desire or obligation to illustrate religious and historical subject matter. He identified the removal of such external constraints on artistic motivation as an important event in the transition to modern painting. But he was at pains to show the methods characteristic of the Impressionists and Post-Impressionists were rooted in the practices of the greatest painters of past periods. In the work of the first modernists he found more liberties taken with the actual coloring of things depicted than in that of early artists. "With the Impressionists, it is the mode of presentation and not the object presented that counts," he wrote. To his eyes, one of their most important innovations was "the distortion of perspective."[42] But just as with their particular methods of using light and color to obtain particular effects, it evolved from the best parts of various traditions.

Barnes believed that Monet developed the Impressionist technique in its most complete form. He said his best pictures, such as *House Boat* and *Madame Monet Embroidering*, reflected "great skill in the use of each of the plastic elements and sensitive adaptation of them to the rendering of the essential quality of the subject matter." But he also thought his color lacked sensual appeal, and that the artist was "only moderately successful" in its structural use. He found Monet often "so preoccupied by the . . . evanescent effects of sunlight upon objects at various hours of the day that the result was . . . a too literal reproduction of the superficial appearance of things." He rated Pissarro "by far the most important purely Impressionistic painter." Barnes said his "ability to make . . . juxtaposed colors more dynamic by the use of brush-strokes gives . . . a rich, deep lustrous glow that endows both the surfaces and the design with strong aesthetic power." But Pissarro's later pointillism he considered "an obvious over accentuation of a plastic means" that Seurat adapted with much greater success. "The combination of a fine sense of composition, the ability to compose with color, to make space dynamic, and to paint with distinction give to Seurat's best work the character of great art," he wrote. In *Models*, Barnes said in a passage he added to later editions of his book after purchasing the magnificent picture, Seurat "achieves a classic form akin to that of the old masters."[43]

Manet was for the collector the principal link between the traditions represented by Rembrandt and Velázquez and Renoir and Cézanne. He considered his influence fundamental on the two French Impressionists whose work formed the heart of his collection. Barnes admired Manet quite simply for "his marvelous ability to apply paint." He rated him a "great colorist" on the basis of his skill in using color compositionally. Manet's early work, *The Dead Christ with Angels*, indicated that he "was perhaps the first of the Impressionists to distribute areas of color and light all over the canvas for the purpose of achieving a design," Barnes said. "Color and light . . . used in broad areas, together with drawing simplified to the point of extreme generalization and the application of paint with obvious brush-strokes, make up his perfected technique." In the collector's carefully formed opinion, "Manet's actual productions and the developments for which he is responsible place him among the very great artists of all time."[44]

Two painters who lived during the same period as the Impressionists, Degas who employed their methods selectively and Puvis de Chavannes who was not at all influenced by them, also intrigued Barnes. Degas is applauded for his individualism and the strength of his design. Barnes wrote that "his varied and highly expressive line has never been excelled." He felt the painter of pensive ballerinas used line to extraordinary advantage in portraying both movement and suspended movement. "His attention was centered upon the events of everyday life," the collector further observed, and he "saw and emphasized the ironic and sardonic." Barnes found the color in Degas's oils "usually dull, drab, dry," but he thought the pastels the artist preferred to work with full of "animation and sparkle." The mural decorations of Puvis de Chavannes he considered "distinctive in pattern, drawing, quality of color," and he praised the painter's ability "to bring compositional units into harmonious relations." There was a "classic, delicate" quality to Puvis's work, which, though it departed from naturalistic representation far more than early frescoes, harked to a long distant era.[45]

The modernists' commandment, apparently coined by Daumier and made a watchword by Manet, "*Il faut être de son temps avant tout*" (It is necessary to be a man of your times.), was embraced by both of the painters whose work summoned Barnes's highest admiration and most enduring attention. Renoir and Cézanne were unquestionably men of their times. In the two longest chapters devoted to individual artists in *The Art in Painting*, the collector analyzed the sources of their inspiration, their natural endowments, their stylistic development, the essence of their appeal, and their central weaknesses. His implied assessment was that Renoir was the greater painter and Cézanne the greater artist. With relatively unlimited funds, he never had to choose between them, but if that had been necessary, his heart almost certainly would have moved him to spend his fortune one way, his head to spend it in another.

Barnes felt that both men were deeply influenced by Delacroix and Courbet. But he found that Renoir had explicit debts to Fragonard and Rubens in terms of his use of color and to Velázquez and Manet in terms of his interest in the things of everyday life. Cézanne's earliest method of applying color, together with his use of light, he traced to Pissarro; his creation of distorted planes showed, he said, El Greco's impact. Barnes wrote that from the beginning, "mastery of color" and an "extraordinary facility in using paint" characterized Renoir's work. He considered Cézanne "deficient in natural facility in the use of the brush." Renoir's earliest paintings had a finished quality, according to Barnes. Cézanne's first efforts were tentative and experimental. From the early 1870s through the early 1890s, he traced four distinct stages in Renoir's development. When he was starting out, before the wide use of divided color tones, he worked somewhat in the manner of Manet, using "broad brush work but with more and richer color." In the late seventies, Barnes noted that Renoir's technique changed as he employed "juxtaposed brush strokes or spots or streaks of contrasting color." In a search for new color forms, he experimented during the eighties with "sharp, incisive line" and "dry," almost acid, colors, which Barnes said "gave a fluid, luminous quality" to his pictures "such as no other painter ever achieved except in water color." By the late eighties, Renoir was focused upon the "development of a technique that would enable him to render the movement of volumes in deep space," and by the nineties, the collector observed, his "drawing, by means of color, ha[d] become extremely fluid. . . . Literalism is completely avoided, and all the ordinary means of rendering solidity, outline, perspective begin to be replaced by obvious distortions. The interest in relatively abstract design comes to be more and more dominant . . . but . . . with no loss of conviction, no degradation of the form to the status of mere pattern." Barnes said his pictures became "as varied and harmonious as a fugue or symphony." He considered him an "artist of the first magnitude," and he wrote that "more than that of any other painter, his work constitutes an epitome and rounding out of the whole history of painting." What Barnes called "incomparable sensuous charm" and a general decorativeness achieved by chords of color was the key element in his pictures' appeal to the collector. The weaknesses in Renoir's work, counterparts of its strengths, he described as a certain impersonality, an absence of restraint, a lack of poignancy. But in Barnes's opinion, Renoir possessed "a greater command of means, greater variety of effect, and certainly a greater decorative quality than any other painter."[46]

The collector's reading of Cézanne's pictures is in some ways even more insightful than his analysis of the work of his beloved Renoir. His attention never strays from the canvas even to reflect on his own response. He writes that the painter's progressive use of "a thinner impasto resulted in an increasing ability to render the effects of solidity in terms free from the sculptural tendency of his earlier thick paint." The effect is "a lightness and delicacy that involves no loss of strength." As Cézanne developed his own characteristic style, Barnes said he honed his "ability to compose in deep space, with great heightening of conviction and moving power. At the same time, there is a softening of contours. His line . . . loses its earlier tendency to hardness and comparative isolation from other elements. . . .The shapes of the objects become less naturalistic and more arbitrarily subordinated to the requirements of design." Barnes believed that Cézanne's genius, expressed in his mature work, was a "feeling for the dynamic relationships between objects and the ability to coordinate the resulting forms into . . . designs," which he found "as original and moving as those of Giotto. . . . Naturalistic considerations in the representation of subject matter were sacrificed to the desire to make lines, perspective, and space so fuse in planes of color that all elements come into equilibrium. . . . In [his] power to give the feeling of the real while avoiding all literal realism, Cézanne vies with Rembrandt and Velázquez," Barnes said. "More than either of these painters, Cézanne stripped away everything not absolutely essential, and through new technical means succeeded in giving that sense of profound fidelity to the deeper aspects of things, which is characteristic of all great art." The painter's shortcomings, in Barnes's view, were his "never wholly perfect command of his medium" and, as a direct result of "his resolute adherence to essentials," his relative lack of "interest in sensuous charm" that accompanied the decorative quality the collector prized in Renoir. But in the last analysis, he considered Cézanne "the equal of the greatest artists in making his forms embody the abstract feelings, the human values, that the objects and events of everyday life communicate" and in rendering the core of those emotions "moving, vital, and beautiful."[47]

Barnes's glance at the European Post-Impressionists is hasty, and he devotes only relatively more space to nineteenth- and early twentieth-century American painters. He exhibited some interest in Van Gogh's modification of the techniques associated with Impressionism, particularly the painter's use of a simplified and distorted "figure or mass against a background contrasting with it in color and usually in manner of treatment." The effect is dramatic, according to Barnes, who saluted Van Gogh for infusing "a spirit of emotional tenseness into themes ordinarily placid or composed and a feverish, almost delirious quality into situations intrinsically dramatic." He judged him to have been especially influential on Matisse and Soutine. Although Barnes credited Gauguin, the key proto-modernist, with the skillful use of broad areas of contrasting color and a good utilization of space, he slighted his paintings as "essentially decorations." He found Maurice Denis's work to reflect a more effective use of line and more varied use color, "made brilliant by floods of intense light," but he felt it, too, was essentially decorative. Bonnard was recognized as an "important, though minor, colorist" who succeeded, in his small pictures of interiors, in conveying a charming and powerful sense of intimacy.[48]

Barnes dismissed the earliest painting done in America by Benjamin West, Gilbert Stuart, the Peales, and Thomas Sully as "utterly uninspired." He said "brilliance in the use of a borrowed technique" characterized the work of John Singer Sargent, Robert Henri, and George Bellows but covered "an aesthetic vacuum." He gave barely a nod to George Inness (pleasing landscapes "in a well-known language") and noted that the "daintiness and grace" of James McNeill Whistler's pictures was "generally used to render poses" not only of the subject but also of the painter who seemed to Barnes always "to be putting his best foot forward to make an impression" rather than a work of art. The collector took Winslow Homer seriously as "an important artist" on the basis of his ability to portray and relate objects effectively in space "upon a background of striking general pattern." But he said Homer had no feel for "the sensuous quality of individual colors" and considered his excessive use of light responsible for converting "drama into melodrama. . . . His artistic conceptions were greater than his power to realize them in paint," Barnes somewhat sadly concluded.[49]

The collector praised Thomas Eakins's portrait of Dr. Agnew as capturing the essential character and dignity of the subject but considered the general run of the artist's work "unfortunately . . . much inferior." He found Albert Ryder's land and seascapes "profoundly moving," apparently responding to what he called their "pagan" mysticism. He said Ryder was a "great colorist," even though he felt his "fusion of light and color in atmosphere" was "comparatively unsatisfactory," and wrote that "his work considered in all its aspects stands high in the ranks of artistic creation." Barnes rated George Luks's paintings "very uneven." He accused the artist of "frequent recourse to cheap sentimentality," and while he said Luks skillfully employed a restricted palette of grays and browns in his genre pictures, he described his attempts to use a wide range of colors "disastrous."[50]

Among American Impressionists, Barnes declared Maurice Prendergast, his old chum Glackens, and Ernest Lawson the most important. He said each contributed something of his own to the tradition. Prendergast, who had died in 1924, was praised for pictures that expressed "the vision of a child-like mind, seeing simply, naively, yet penetratingly, the beautiful things in life, and rejoicing in them." The collector said "no painter ever had a finer feeling for pure color, both in its direct sensuous quality and in the possible variety of its uses." Glackens was hailed for his "expressive drawing, his fine sense for the drama of everyday life, his extraordinary feeling for color, the ability to effect well-organized compositions, and the command of his medium." Barnes commented on his psychological kinship to Renoir ("Both men were born artists and they painted as naturally, as easily, and as inevitably as they breathed.") and noted that, like Velázquez, his work is impersonal in that "he selects the picturesque and significant and renders them without comment of his own." Again, it is a sense of color that sets Lawson apart in Barnes's eyes, and although he found a certain monotony in the painter's landscapes, as the result of his unvarying use of the technique he took from Monet, he praised a "distinctively personal quality" in his design.[51] Barnes had the utmost respect for artists who spoke in their own voices. Although he stopped short of a total embrace of modernism, as it unfolded in purely abstract art, his tolerance for deviations from resemblances to nature was broad, and in *The Art in Painting*, he turned from his affectionate embrace of his three favorite American Impressionists to painters he called simply "contemporary" with notable intellectual relish.

"The art of painting as it emerges from the hands of Renoir and Cézanne has in its possession as never before two all-important principles," Barnes wrote. "First, the principle of pure design, embodying the values of human experience but not tied down to literal reproduction of the situations in which these values are found in ordinary life. Second, the principle of color as the most essential of all the plastic elements, the means most entirely intrinsic to the medium of paint." He acknowledged the specific contributions of Gauguin's "unusual color contrasts" and Van Gogh's "long, narrow, ribbonlike streaks of color" to the development of modern design, and then he paused and singled out for special comment the influence of sculpture created by Africans. He admired its formal organization and expressive power. "Its freedom from anything adventitious or meaningless gives Negro art a sculptural quality purer than that of the best Greek periods and also of Renaissance sculpture," he wrote. Carefully avoiding any suggestion of immediate borrowing, Barnes recognized that it "enriched contemporary painting" by providing "a new source of inspiration." In particular, he noted that "Matisse, Soutine, and Modigliani render the essential feeling, the spirit of Negro art and give it force" in settings of their own.[52] The impact of African sculpture was a theme to which he would return as a missionary to the unenlightened, and often disdainful, public in his own land.

As Arthur Danto has observed, Barnes acquired Matisse's work in the artist's "most difficult and uningratiating period."[53] In *The Art in Painting*, the collector makes the point that in contrast to a Picasso embarked upon "cubistic excursions," Matisse "has always been interested in the real world." He viewed him as continuing in the tradition of Cézanne while departing from the latter's form, and with considerable insight, he traced Matisse's development through an analysis of his evolving technique. Barnes said the artist's early painting was characterized by the "highly successful" application of color "in spots predominantly small but differing in size, shape, and direction, with only vague indications of subject matter." He found these color-relations novel and powerful and heightened by Matisse's use of mass and line and handling of light. As the painter matured, Barnes said he "constantly increas[ed] control over his means. Design becomes more and more paramount," the collector observed. "Color becomes more pleasing sensuously, enters into more daring contrasts, more firmly knits the composition together." He praised Matisse's "distortion of perspective" as an "act of violence to literal reproduction" that enhanced his pictures. "Figures become more and more definitely plastic units: sometimes they resemble Negro masks, sometimes sculptural Hindu figures of the third century," he noted. "The heavy, ragged line is often so freed from its ordinary function of fixing the contours of a body as a whole that the head, hands, breasts, etc. seem to be detached from the trunk." Barnes found "all the possibilities hinted at in the extremely simple" *The Joy of Life,* which was painted in 1910, "realized in the infinitely complex" 1921 work, *The Music Lesson.* He declared Matisse "bold and original in his choice and combination of colors" and "unsurpassed in his single-mindedness and consistency in subordinating all other effects to the realization of forms that are a successful fusion of all the plastic elements through the medium of color." Although he felt the artist paid for his "interest in pure design . . . by a loss of sensuous charm and content" reflecting "deep, universal human values," he concluded his assessment with the daring and unhesitating claim that Matisse "is by far the most important painter of our age."[54]

In his treatment of Picasso, Barnes seemed determined to show that the artist did not stand outside the familiar traditions of painting. He linked his earliest work with that of Degas and Toulouse-Lautrec, and in his "Blue Period," he found echoes of Cézanne, El Greco, and the fourteenth-century Piero della Francesca. "In the less successful pictures" of that time, "the separate influences . . . are more or less perceptible in isolation," the collector said, "but in his best work, as represented by the *Girl with Cigarette,* they are very well fused into a characteristic Picasso form." He considered the paintings done in 1907 and for the next year or so to be "pictorial representations of the plastic values" of African sculpture. It was a transitional phase, Barnes wrote, that "paved the way" for the artist's "later work in which the sculptural forms are more fully assimilated in terms proper to painting." Noting that Picasso's "departure for cubism" began about 1909 when the "sculptural influence began to be paramount," he observed that the painter left behind naturalism to such a degree that "what we see is of little or no assistance in enabling us to recognize the object as it exists in nature. But distortion is consistence with the imaginative purpose of art," he added, to the extent that it is "aesthetically moving." The problem, Barnes believed, was that "many cubist pictures do not sufficiently anchor the[ir] forms to anything in the real world to make possible a transfer to them of the many echoes and reverberations which objects gain by their multiform relationships in ordinary experience." Alas, the collector concluded that when Picasso finally "resumed interest in painting in which the representative element is more in evidence," his pictures showed "a decided retrogression when compared with the . . . best of his earlier work." He lamented what he termed an absence of "deeply purposeful effort toward a style adequate to carry a profoundly personal and original vision." It seemed to him almost willful. Picasso's "veerings," he concluded, "suggest an impulsive temperament, going off in a tangent from the line of maximum advance rather than using every new element of technique to deepen and enrich a fundamentally organic grasp of the world of plastic forms. Picasso's sensitiveness and his power to assimilate are far too great," Barnes wrote, "to allow his unreflectiveness to degenerate into mere imitativeness or superficiality, but his wavering does make him less powerful and original than men of first rank."[55]

In the first edition of *The Art in Painting*, the collector dealt with Soutine, Pascin, and Modigliani in separate chapters just as he had Matisse and Picasso. In later editions, they were classified with a short list of other contemporaries, but stood apart from the rest in terms of the collector's attention. He wrote that Soutine's "design is founded on color of extremely pleasing sensuous quality—deep, rich, juicy, and varied." Noting that his manner of applying paint, in long ribbons, resembled Van Gogh's technique, Barnes wrote that "everywhere there is animation, motion, heightened by variety in the directions in which the streaks run. The color," he noted, "is diversified and intensified by light," and its rhythms "are extremely vivid, intense, and dramatic." Although he criticized the artist for an "absence of deep space required for monumental effects and his inability to organize the plastic units into an ensemble," Barnes said "no contemporary painter has achieved . . . more originality and power than Soutine." He lavished even greater praise upon his friend Pascin. Considering him an "illustrator of first rank," he also said that "in his sense for the compositional relation of masses, both in two and three dimensions, Pascin ranks with the greatest of contemporary painters." He found his ability to represent movement extraordinary. "Everything in his canvas is *alive*," Barnes wrote, "and so, thanks to the pervasive delicate, graceful rhythms, is the canvas as a whole."[56]

The collector described Modigliani's languorous female nudes as "focal masses in a . . . design rather than as in any way interpretive of the human form." He hailed his "incisive and very graceful line," color that was "rich, delicate, and light," his "subtle" command of space, and "harmonious and effective" composition. In quick succession, he tipped his hat to Rousseau's pictures for a "strange, naive, exotic quality of great appeal," to the "rich, glowing delicacy and poetic charm" of Utrillo's best street scenes and landscapes, and to Rouault's effective combination of "decoration and expression" in strong and moving paintings constructed mainly of color and swirling line. He said Demuth's watercolors had "a delicate, fluid charm," but all that could be said for Derain, according to the collector, was that he had the "skill and erudition . . . to paint in the manner of anyone." Barnes thought that the "exotic quality" of de Chirico's color gave a "mystic feeling" to pictures characterized by strong design. Finally, he found that "simplicity, economy of means, deep color, and vigorous painting" endowed the work of the now nearly forgotten André Dunoyer de Segonzac, "with novelty and considerable power."[57]

Included in the appendix to *The Art in Painting* were more than one hundred pages of analysis of individual works of art created by the painters Barnes mentioned in the text plus others he considered interesting or relevant. Initially, he discussed some two hundred and twenty-six paintings by eighty-six artists.[58] His comments were extensive in some cases; in others, he simply called attention to what he judged the more important or less obvious aspects of a picture. But in all his remarks, he tried to evaluate the various elements of paintings in terms of their role in the overall design. He criticized "academicians" for considering plastic qualities, when they considered them at all, almost wholly in isolation. Frank Jewett Mather is singled out for special scorn for making "the most elementary of all mistakes, that of interpreting paintings by their subject matter." Barnes said another kind of confusion was exemplified by Elie Faure whose "four-volume work on the history of art might with propriety be entitled a historical romance in which painters and paintings are extensively mentioned. . . . The long-drawn, almost orgiastic, ecstasy of his manner betrays a total submergence of intelligence in emotion," he gleefully added.[59]

As for the man he acknowledged as "the most influential contemporary writer on art," Bernard Berenson, Barnes wrote that his analyses were based upon an "always untenable, and now obsolete" psychological theory, which maintained "that in perceiving an object we . . . go through a process of internal mimicry of it." The collector quarreled, of course, with Berenson's view that color was less important in judging a painting than other qualities, what the writer called "tactile values" as well as movement, and space-composition. He declared that Berenson ignored "the fundamental principle of art" when he omitted any consideration of a painter's success in adjusting form to expression in his assessment of a picture's quality. In a final harsh rebuke to the famous and respected art historian, he said: "Mr. Berenson's work deals not with the objective facts that enter into an appreciation of art-values, but with a form of antiquarianism made up of historical, social, and sentimental interests entirely adventitious to plastic art. It would be unworthy of serious attention except for the regrettable influence his writings have had in filling our universities with bad teaching on art and our public galleries with bad Italian painting."[60]

John Dewey, who always dealt respectfully and courteously with scholars with whom he disagreed, must have cringed just a little when he read the gratuitous attacks Barnes slipped into the otherwise disciplined exposition and demonstration of a method for studying the aims and accomplishments of artists that the author dedicated to him. The volume's inscription read: "To John Dewey, whose conceptions of experience, of method, of education, inspired the work of which this book is a part." It was an expression of profoundly felt indebtedness and an effort to link *The Art in Painting* to a larger effort. Reviews were generally favorable. The critic for the *New York Herald Tribune*, Raymond Weaver, praised the volume as a tonic. "It offers something scholarly, sound and real to replace the sentimentalism, the antiquarianism, which makes futile the present courses in universities and colleges generally," he declared. "*The Art in Painting* is an original and impressive book. And what is more, it is interesting and clear."[61] Writing in the *Nation*, Joseph Wood Krutch said: "Mr. Barnes's . . . treatment of the development of tradition is particularly illuminating, especially in so far as it deals with the relationship existing between modern and old masters. . . . [His] book seems to me . . . a distinct and important contribution. . . . Mr. Barnes furnishes a method of approach in consequence of which one may talk about a picture and be sure one is, indeed, talking about a picture and not archaeology, literature, the physics or physiology of vision, or merely vague impressionistic reactions."[62] Alfred H. Barr, Jr., who had moved from Vassar to Princeton on his way to the Museum of Modern Art, wrote in the *Saturday Review of Literature*: "This is an important book because it presents a systematic and confident statement of what is central in the 'modern' attitude toward painting. . . . The plastic means of the great Masters are dissected diligently and often with considerable originality. . . . The plastic developments of Renoir and Cézanne are very thoroughly analyzed by the man whose Renoirs and Cézannes should be the envy of every museum in the country—especially the Metropolitan. . . . There is further excellent criticism of Picasso. Soutine, Modigliani, and Pascin . . . are made subordinate only to Matisse and Picasso in the contemporary hierarchy. Certainly Mr. Barnes is right in seeing Pascin a great and very moving draughtsman. Soutine perhaps does not deserve such trumpeting." But then, quite beyond a minor disagreement over ranking, Barr made a subtle, significant, and, to a would-be educator as zealous as Barnes, devastating criticism of the collector's approach to art:

> Mr. Barnes will find many, especially among those whom Aldous Huxley terms "the absurd young," who are more or less in sympathy with his position. Among them is the reviewer who has frequently found himself engaged in a long analysis of a painting without the slightest consciousness of subject matter until some philistine undergraduate brings the discussion to earth by asking why the Madonna has such a funny chin. The undergraduate's impatience is pardonable. His aesthetic illiteracy is shared by all but a few of those who find pictures interesting. . . . Only a few are deeply interested in plastic value. Nor has this few up to our own time included many influential critics . . . [who] have all helped the public lose themselves in what Mr. Barnes would term with good reason irrelevancies. But even if it were possible, would it be wise to emphasize plastic values to the exclusion of subject matter, historical and biographical backgrounds, archaeological problems, stylistic differentiation, literary association, and all the ancillary baggage which is customarily presented in a book on painting or a college art course? So far as education is concerned, some carefully devised compromise is the obvious solution. But extreme as it may appear, Mr. Barnes's position is temporarily very powerful. If by the literary canons of the last century he seems to over-emphasize the rhetoric of painting, by the canons of music he is merely revealing the essentials. In the light of history and experience neither fashion is final, though at present the latter is crescent.[63]

The Art in Painting shared space in the *New York Times Book Review* on June 20, 1926 with Will Durant's *The Story of Philosophy*. It was a privilege for a first-time author to be there. H. I. Brock wrote the prominent essay on Barnes's book, which was accompanied by photographs of a Soutine and a Matisse from his collection and a Degas from the Louvre. The *Times's* reviewer identified the author of *The Art in Painting* as "a gentleman of profitable commercial antecedents who has a notable and controversial art collection" and the "confidence . . . to offer the world a guaranteed, reliable method of analysis for determining the presence of true art on a given expanse of painted surface." He went on to question the absolutism of Barnes's assessments of various individual paintings and the finality of his verdict on works of art "that must stand the test of time" but concludes that "the proof of the pudding is in the eating." With tempered admiration, if ill-disguised snobbery, Brock said: "The reader really ambitious to become a finished product of the great American art connoisseur canning factory might go a long way by following these analyses through. Without doubt the serious student of art for art's sake may also learn something. Perhaps he may learn much."[64] Robert Cortes Holliday, who wrote for the *Bookman*, was not so sure. "Systems for beating the races or anything else," he said, "are always to be looked in the mouth. There is something rule of thumb about this scheme."[65] But in London, the writer for the *Times Literary Supplement*, who parodied Barnes's tendency toward tautology, agreed that the author's analysis of particular paintings had value and found it "more clear than his aesthetic."[66]

The review that mattered most to Barnes was the one Leo Stein wrote for the *New Republic*. It was the first public appraisal of his work, written soon after the publication of the original Barnes Foundation edition of the book. The collector read a copy of Stein's review essay several weeks before it appeared in the magazine. He was not the least bit happy with it. But his friend and erstwhile mentor, "the one man's opinion" he really "cared a damn about,"[67] began his article with measured praise. "The author stresses relations in character as more important than chronology, and shows what similarities and differences there are in the use of plastic means of artists remote from each other in time and space," Stein wrote. "Mr. Barnes's book differs from any other that I know in the systematic thoroughness of these analyses. He . . . seeks effectually to make clear what will be of use to one who likes to look at pictures." But then Stein focused on what he considered a "serious defect" of *The Art in Painting*, which he attributed to the author's interest in education. "Mr. Barnes," he said, "is not satisfied to help the student approach all art intelligently; he also insists on telling the student what of good and bad he ought to find in different works that are studied. . . . Valuations are personal and not systematic," Stein continued. "Mr. Barnes's scale of values points very clearly the direction of his own interest but it would be a great mistake on the part of any student to direct his effort toward a similar vision. . . . His own valuations . . . are always intelligent and genuine, but they have no validity except for the experience of which they are the natural consequences."[68]

Barnes told Dewey the review was "stupid." He said he had pointed out to Stein the passage in his introduction in which he declared: "'It is not assumed that the conclusions reached with respect to particular paintings are the only one compatible with the use of the method: any one of them is of course subject to revision.' It's the old story of psychic deafness and blindness," he complained.[69] Several days later, he boasted to Dewey that his book had "been bought by over sixty American universities and colleges and requested his friend's strategic assistance. "Don't you think that *New Republic* readers . . . might like to hear what you have to say on the point Stein emphasizes?" he asked.[70] Dewey took Barnes's meaning. He agreed to write a response to Stein's review. The collector was delighted. He said the proposed essay would be "the best kind of reply—that is, to show that [Stein's] article is not criticism because it fails to recognize the basic principles of the conception I tried to put over. . . . I think what makes me maddest at Stein," he told Dewey, "is that he never once studied the thesis of my book. . . . Please accept my sincere thanks both for the article and for such a reinforcement of my feeble efforts."[71] Published on February 24, 1926, Dewey's essay posed a rhetorical question: "Is art in painting so foreign to education and education so foreign to art that they must be kept apart, or is art intrinsically educative?" The philosopher wrote that the answer was clear, "but," he added, "paintings do not educate at present till we are educated to enjoy, to realize, their educative potential." Pointing to the general "submergence of aesthetic appreciation by the ruling tendencies of our present culture," he also pointed to the disposition of connoisseurs to put art on a pedestal," an attitude fostered, in its turn, "by the customs of institutionalized museums and the habits of professional critics." The would-be enjoyer of paintings is not only given no directive assistance, he or she is also, Dewey said, subject to "influences which . . . confuse and mislead." Barnes's book and his foundation attempted, he said, "a reversal of this process."[72]

The philosopher's defense of *The Art in Painting* notwithstanding, criticism of the book's implied pedagogy was not far off base. Barnes had neither training nor, aside from his role as "principal" of the Argyrol factory school, experience as an educator, and the danger was real that his zealous approach could engender either rebellion to the point of total rejection of his method or a slavish adoption by less independent students of his evaluations as their own. Indeed, the collector told Dewey that he had given up his advanced classes at the Foundation temporarily in the fall of 1925 because the students, "while full of enthusiasm, were passive, as revealed by behavior tests" he gave them. The pupils included Nelle Mullen, Sara Carles, and Tom Munro, and he told them: "Forget my book and . . . get in front of those paintings and apply that method or any other method in finding out what a particular painting means to you."[73] But the fact remains that Barnes had something important to teach. Almost no historical writing about art, and therefore few if any university courses on art, then dealt with the history of form. The focus had been on a miscellany of associated facts that, in their abundance, could fall as a screen between students and the directly observable qualities of pictures. *The Art in Painting* sought to lift it.

The book remains an amazing feat when considered in the context of its time. The second trade edition, published in 1928, added a discussion of early German, Flemish, Dutch, and French painters, and Harcourt Brace brought out yet a third, revised edition in 1937. Though the writing is often clumsy, the hefty volume reflects a quite astounding erudition. Barnes had taught himself about the history of forms by direct analysis of the data in museums, galleries, and churches throughout Europe. He also had taken advantage of opportunities to acquaint himself with Asian and African art, and he was among the first writers to include samplings of these traditions for purposes of comparison with the Western canon. His familiarity, moreover, with the latest research in experimental psychology enabled him to approach aesthetic form in a new and deeply searching way. He saw, and he wanted others to see, paintings as stimuli to appreciation, which involved, as a mature Munro would later write, "the apprehension of complex configurations of sensory detail and suggested meanings."[74] Barnes knew, however, that those meanings would remain hopelessly inaccessible to most people unless they were given a chance to learn something of the objective characteristics of great art of the past, as well as trained to perceive relations of continuity, resemblance, and contrast among visible things. His deep-rooted conviction and abounding self-confidence in his approach to art, together with his financial independence, enabled him to push on with his educational mission in the face of criticism. But his extreme sensitivity prevented him from doing so without lashing back at his critics.

7

The Art of Polemics

The physician become collector had at hand a balm for psychic wounds as effective as the therapy for sagging shoulders and spirits that Dr. T. Matthias Alexander once provided Dewey. "I can forget everything in looking at pictures and in creating new and more striking harmonies by hanging them in different ensembles," Barnes told Paul Guillaume.[1] Arranging and rearranging paintings as he added to his collection challenged his ingenuity and restored his soul. Now that he had adequate space for his treasures, creating designs by the placement of paintings, according to certain relationships he wished to emphasize, intrigued and delighted him. He hung his pictures, paying no attention to chronology, in a tableaux created to highlight aesthetic, rather than narrative or thematic, affinities. One grouping might illustrate compositional strategies, another color; still others qualities such as power, simplicity, or delicacy that are common to disparate paintings. The pictures might be joined to create an architectural or geometric form on the wall itself. Later, as Barnes began to collect ironwork, he added all manner of locks, keys, joints, latches, and scissors to his displays. But as pleasant a preoccupation as designing "wall pictures" might be, as safe as he might feel in his sanctuary, Barnes had a crusade to carry on. With few foot soldiers under his command, he founded a journal to catapult his ideas and hurl his missiles.

Barnes perceived himself not only as a "voice in the wilderness," but one which "the combined voices of academies, newspapers, [and] art magazines threatened to drown." Reflecting on his editorial efforts, he told Dewey that when he started the *Journal of the Barnes Foundation* in the spring of 1925, he had "the choice of drowning or drowning the other fellows. Of those I went after . . . not one is a living force today," he concluded with satisfaction sixteen years after his little magazine ceased publication.[2] He meant that his method of formal analysis of pictures—and his uncompromising stand against what he considered less rigorous approaches to aesthetic instruction—had won some measure of acceptance in art education. The drug manufacturer who had successfully marketed Argyrol throughout the United States was selling a style of seeing. As an adjunct to his school, his short-lived periodical was a way to promote it, make it desirable, give it cachet. As the editors of the *Nation* observed, "Mr. Barnes and his associates now ha[d] an organ for the free expression of their program." They would use "its pages not only to develop their theories of art and the teaching of art" but also "to criticize their contemporaries in the latter field." Since the publisher's pockets were deep and his acquaintance in the art community wide, the opportunity to generate the kind of conversation he relished at Guillaume's Paris temple was indeed real. "The *Journal* promises to strike a good many sparks from the flint of convention," the *Nation* said; "it may write a new chapter in the history of American education."[3]

The magazine's failure to do so had everything to do with Barnes's personality, the quirks that propelled him toward polemics. Was the rout at Cold Harbor that cost his father an arm a constraint on the son's forbearance if not a cause of his pugnaciousness? The erstwhile chemist described vengeance to Dewey as "a binary compound of anger and positive self-feeling," and what he acknowledged in himself as "vengeful emotion" drove him, at least in part, to write his biting essays.[4] Leo Stein was the subject of one of them. The successful entrepreneur began with a Veblen-like attack on the leisure class that was grounded in Dewey's epistemology. Barnes embraced the notion that knowledge is born of doing—a manifestation of experience. "It is . . . nonsense to suppose that one part of society can take charge of the facts, the moving forces of life, and another look after the ideals," the collector said. "Unless the ideals are practicable ideals, they are moonshine. The 'idealist' who cannot vindicate his claim to the role of prophet and lawgiver by demonstrating his ability to set events moving in the desired direction stands not above but below the despised artisan. . . . To point to an idea, without offering any positive suggestions about means of attaining it, is the very essence of day-dreaming; when to this is added impatience with the only approximations to the ideal which are at present available, the day-dreaming becomes not only idle but petulant and pernicious. Evidence of the precious occupation of the ivory tower is nowhere more clearly presented than in Mr. Leo Stein's recent review . . . of *The Art in Painting*."

Barnes complained that Leo had set up an unattainable "ideal of objectivity" and then attacked "any attempt to approach the relative objectivity which is possible." He characterized, quite gratuitously, his "sublime aloofness" as evidence not of "highly sensitive intellectual conscience, but [of] a dread of accepting the responsibilities of action." He noted that Leo never considered that "errors arising from a subjective bias in the application" of a scientific method could be corrected "by application of the same method in the hands of someone else. . . . The judgments in *The Art of Painting*," he asserted, "are offered not as finalities but as challenges." So they were. But Barnes couldn't leave it at that. With the pugilist's instinct for the solar plexus, he concluded: "Mr. Stein's criticism . . . is hot-house preciosity passing for distinction. . . . It shows that life freed from responsibilities is not richer but more attenuated because it nourishes not thought but reverie. It is inefficacious . . . not because it is too fine for the real world, but because it is too feeble; its sterility is an indication of its inner emptiness. It explains why the book on aesthetics which, fifteen years ago, Mr. Stein announced as forthcoming, has never materialized."[5]

The roughhouse tactics, which were characteristic of the *Journal of the Barnes Foundation* from its first issue, contributed to a growing unease in the relations between Barnes and the University of Pennsylvania. But even before its publication, which occurred a week after Edgar Singer, as a stand-in for President Penniman, "accepted" the Foundation on behalf of American education, there were signs of tension. Two days before the dedication of his grand enterprise, the collector conveyed to the Penn philosophy professor a proposition as bold as the one initially responsible for the fledgling alliance linking the West Philadelphia university to the enterprise in Merion. The previous fall, Penn's School of Fine Arts had established a program in landscape architecture, which suggested to Barnes another possible area of cooperation. In a letter intended for Penniman, he wrote:

> No informed person would question that the new arrangement at Penn puts [it] in the lead for teaching aesthetics and plastic art. Now let's try to do the same thing for a new science and art which is dawning on the horizon with much effulgence and even greater promise. I mean arboriculture and horticulture which, like plastic art, can be studied intelligently only in an objective manner.

The nucleus of his idea was that the university should purchase a property adjacent to the twelve-acre park where the Barneses had started "a little experiment in floriculture." The sale price for the seventeen-and-a-half acre tract, which had just come on the market, was $450,000. Barnes said if Penn bought the land, he would commission Paul Cret to design and build a $300,000 lecture hall and not only give it to the university but also pay the salary of a new professor. He saw his plan as catapulting his alma mater to the top of the field of landscape architecture and promised "the active cooperation" of the Barnes Arboretum staff, including its director, Colonel Wilson, Laura Barnes, and John W. Prince, whom he had just hired away from London's Kew Gardens. "We would try to run the new department as little as I would try to run your Department of Fine Arts under our present agreement," the collector promised, and then added with an enticing flourish: "When I go to Heaven, it will be found that there will be enough money remaining to prove that I was superfluous in carrying out what I induced Penn to take up."[6]

Josiah Penniman was quickly learning how "little" the university's generous benefactor was interested in running its fine arts program. Within two days, he wrote to Singer about the letter from Barnes, which the philosopher had brought at once to his attention. The president said that while "there was no doubt that in a rounded out University, there would be a place for the teaching of landscape gardening and a good many other subjects" for which

Penn did not then have facilities, it wasn't a priority. Barnes had suggested that certain Penn trustees could supply the needed purchase price, but Penniman informed Singer that until other needs were met, "it would not be fair to undertake additional obligations, unless an amount of money sufficient to carry [out] these obligations were in sight, if not actually in hand." Singer was asked to "explain" the situation to Barnes.[7] Without a donation of the land itself, there would be no deal; and there was none.

Poor Singer was also the bearer of the news about Penn's discomfort with the very first issue of the *Journal of the Barnes Foundation*. The collector joyfully predicted that within days of its appearance "all hell will be loose." He told Dewey it contained "bombs,"[8] and, indeed, two articles, one by Buermeyer and one by Barnes himself, caused a major ruckus. Both Columbia and Penn heard from alumni who professed outrage at the collector's jeering attack on a respected member of the educational community and his young colleague's parody of a respected local institution. The educator was Theodore Dillaway, the head of Philadelphia's public school art program, who had pontificated about modern art leading to anarchy at the time of the initial announcement of the alliance between the Barnes Foundation and Penn. The collector had nursed his anger for nearly a year. But when Tom Munro suggested to him that his goal of reforming art teaching could be advanced by working directly with the schools, he wrote to Superintendent Edwin G. Broome offering the Foundation's resources in providing professional development for art teachers. He also pointed out, quite correctly, that Dillaway was likely to be an obstacle to full cooperation.[9] When he received no response, Barnes fired a broadside entitled "The Shame in the Public Schools of Philadelphia," his inaugural contribution to the Foundation's new journal. He called the city's educational system "obsolete." He said the teaching of art was "not guided by any intelligent purpose" and, consequently, was "without order or method." He claimed that "no proper preparation" for their duties was either "required or furnished for teachers." The cause, he suggested, was "partly mere inertia, partly the personality and opinions of Theodore M. Dillaway." He accused the art education director of "demagoguery" and "a disposition to seek the lime-light at the expense of facts and of the reputation of others," which Barnes considered "proof of his incompetence and irresponsibility." He ridiculed Dillaway's methods of classroom instruction and found further evidence of his "determination to make Philadelphia . . . ridiculous [in] his acceptance of ideas from Mr. S.S. Fleisher in the preparation of his new educational policy." Ending with a call to arms, he said, "if teachers prefer our plan and will do their duty to their profession by refusing to carry out further the antiquated, unintelligent system now in operation in the public schools, we shall be pleased to receive them . . . in our classes."[10]

As a companion piece to Barnes's polemic, Buermeyer's contribution to the *Journal* was a direct attack on his boss's perceived rival. S. S. Fleisher was

Samuel Fleisher, a textile manufacturer who provided free art classes for students from all over the city at his Graphic Sketch Club. The Foundation's associate director of education lampooned the building that housed the club, with its attached basilica-style church containing a portrait of the donor hung in a position to "call to mind [an] altar-piece," and mocked Fleisher for "soup-kitchen" charity that fostered "a deferential, subservient, imitative disposition." He criticized the students' work and observed that the club's collection of photographs of historically important paintings and pieces of sculpture were "aimlessly jumbled together" with "no attempt to show the progress of art or the continuity of traditions." The Graphic Sketch Club, Buermeyer wrote, was "a fortress of conventionalism" that had contributed "substantially nothing" to real education.[11] What made Fleisher fair game? Barnes had never met him. But the philanthropist had once stated publicly that he thought teaching students "modernistic theories" of art was dangerous, and the affiliation between his art club and the public-school art program, which Barnes had just read about in the local papers when he wrote to Broome, was interpreted by the collector as a setback to his campaign to radically change the way art appreciation was taught across America. But surely there also was an element of envy. Fleisher's contributions to art education had been recognized the previous year by the city's prestigious Bok (now the Philadelphia) Award.[12] It symbolized a degree of acceptance by the Philadelphia elite that the collector's habit of resorting to verbal fisticuffs when provoked guaranteed he had no chance of winning.

Indeed, within days of the appearance of the first issue of the *Journal of the Barnes Foundation*, Barnes seized another opportunity to continue his assault on Dillaway and those he perceived as aiding and abetting him. Since 1914, Penn had been hosting an annual conference for public school administrators, high school teachers, members of normal school and college education faculties, and school board representatives. With Buermeyer, Munro, and other staff members in tow, the collector showed up at the 1925 gathering and pressed the art education chief and two other speakers to explain the value of the present system. According to observers, their questions were exceedingly ill tempered. But, in fact, Barnes was having a ball. He described his activities to Dewey as "Fourth of July stuff" and said, "The audience liked "vaudeville . . . and I gave it to them in full measure."[13] One of the targets of his scorn was Alon Bement, author of an art textbook and director of the Maryland Art Institute, who wrote to President Penniman that an open meeting was not the place for Barnes to settle differences of opinion with guests of the university and that the "invectives [he] indulged in . . . would have been out of place in any meeting held under academic auspices."[14] In a wise and judicious letter to Munro, Bement pointed out that as a "rank modernist," he had long ago learned the value of "patience and tact" in dealing with those "confused or offended by modernistic art." Bement went on to observe that "intellectual ability and financial power notwithstanding," the public school art teachers could not "be driven; they must be won." Barnes's attack on their "hard-working and very much respected superiors," would only, he said, "cut off the chance of giving the children a chance for enlightenment."[15] In his role as a trustee of Columbia's Teachers College, Superintendent Broome wrote directly to Dewey to complain about the collector's tactics.[16] The philosopher replied that although Barnes was solely responsible for whatever he published under his own name, "it would be a source of lasting regret" to him "if any controversy were to deprive the public schools of Philadelphia of the opportunity to take full advantage of the educational facilities of the Barnes Foundation."[17] Dillaway told Dean Laird that the whole matter should be brought to the attention of the Penn board of trustees.[18]

Singer was given the task of trying to convey to Barnes some sense of why his tactics embarrassed the university. The collector actually apologized—"for the trouble I unwittingly got you into"—and, in a mixture of staged naiveté and real conviction, declared: "I just feel that if everybody has backbone enough at this critical moment we will clinch one of the bigger victories for education that has happened in America."[19] But he failed to understand that Penn was more concerned about his caricature of Fleisher than his quarrel, however counterproductive, with a public school official. When he learned from Buermeyer, who had been called on the carpet by his former professors and intended colleagues in the philosophy department, that the *Journal* article on the Graphic Sketch Club was viewed by university officials as the unscrupulous singling out of a private citizen for scorn, he resorted to a defensive and threatening missive. If university authorities "think we have exceeded the limits of good judgment, decent behavior or what not," he wrote, "it indicates a difference in our respective fundamental concepts which would prevent me from assenting to any new alliance, or indeed a continuation of the one entered into a year ago."[20] Singer replied that while he understood that Barnes had meant to "sew dragons' teeth" with the first issue of the *Journal*, he could not have intended to raise the hackles of people "whose first object of attack would naturally be your ally." The public, he said, would never believe that Penn was ignorant of the Foundation's apparent campaign to "'get' people that d[idn't] agree with it about . . . art. . . . Can you put aside the heat, without which you could not be a crusader in any cause, long enough to think things out with me?" he asked.[21] A direct answer would not be forthcoming, as Barnes told Singer he never received his letter. But after a conversation with his chosen Penn liaison, he wrote to him "as a friend, and not as a plea to have the University forgive the offense," that "if [Penn officials] see it in our light, the sky is the limit to what the University and the Foundation can do together for aesthetics and educational methods and nobody is big enough to delay materially the steady progress to the cerulean haven that fellows like Dewey and yourself have glimpsed and indicated the way."[22]

A few days later he sent Singer another note saying he would "give $5,000 to any person who [could] furnish evidence that [he] ever got into a fight except in defense of attacks upon the liberty of an artist to express himself as he pleases without being publicly maligned by ignorant people."[23] It was a familiar challenge: put up or shut up. But the proximate cause was likely Dewey's reaction to his recent musings that the time had come for the Foundation "to stand on [its] own feet, continue [its] open criticism of fundamental issues, and let the University continue to be ruled by the kind of opinion represented by its alumni" if Singer and his colleagues on the faculty, who approved of what he was trying to accomplish, failed to "win the day."[24] In three prophetic and uniquely stern letters, the man Barnes admired above all others warned him of the serious and unintended consequences of his present course. As a contemporary historian recently observed, Dewey had "a singularly irenic personality." He believed that "antagonism is unnecessary" and "based on misunderstanding of one's own best interests."[25] In writing to his friend, therefore, he pulled no punches.

In the first letter, Dewey told Barnes he thought it "a serious mistake . . . to publish so many negative articles at once [for] it will strike the readers you will most need as out of balance. . . . Even the teachers who . . . are dissatisfied . . . want positive help more than anything else," he said. "If you pursue a too negative policy you will find the Foundation isolated for educational purposes some day."[26] Within twenty-four hours, he reiterated and strengthened his criticism, saying:

> I take it you are not satisfied simply with some classes for individuals who can attend courses . . . but wish to extend the use of certain principles and methods very generally. . . . I think the policy of negative criticism which is being adopted instead of attaining these ends is inconsistent with them, and as I said yesterday, if persisted in will result in the end in rendering the Foundation isolated as an educational influence. A policy of even ten percent vituperation, to say nothing of fifty percent, will gradually and surely alienate, or render access difficult to, the persons whom you are concerned to reach. One group after another will fall away, and you will [be] left with simply a few courses at the Foundation itself attended by a comparatively small number of persons. Now of course if this [is] what you want and are satisfied with, I have nothing more to say, but I suppose that your aims are wider.
>
> Take the University situation as an example. . . . To cut off the promising University connections which were so quickly established would have a disastrous far-reaching tendency to bring about the limitation of the educational influence of the Foundation. I do not think the situation which has arisen is properly viewed as any tendency to muzzle or interfere with [Munro's] actual teaching there. That is not the crucial element in the situation, but . . . resentment at being capitalized in a controversy which you may have with others outside the University entirely [is]. . . . No university in the world would fancy . . . that having Munro give a course was intended as an endorsement of everything the Foundation as an independent institution might get into.

In other words, it seems essential to consider just what the University connection—I mean generically not just one university—stands for and is worth, both intrinsically and representatively. I do not think it was worth your while to get these connections merely for the sake of the immediate and temporary advertising prestige. From this standpoint, if a short connection is of advertising value, a longer one is worth correspondingly more, while quick sundering of the relationship would seem calculated to more than offset the publicity value previously gained. But personally I think this advertising value the least important element in the situation; there are intrinsic substantial values at stake.

. . . Supposing that aside from the University connection you have broken off by controversial methods relations with the state educational people, with the local people, and with Philadelphia . . . what is the outcome to be? With whom and what is the Foundation to cooperate? I don't know how many letters of individual approval you get, nor what are the motives or standing of those who write them, but I have great difficulty in believing that they offset the isolation produced by these alienations.[27]

Later the same day, Dewey wrote yet a third time: "What is need[ed] it seems to me is that you should realize the positive strength of the Foundation and of your position. You are established, not struggling; the Foundation is a going concern; it doesn't need to fight for recognition, much less existence. It can go ahead and do a big constructive work; why then waste time and energy in unnecessary controversies? . . . Even suppose these men are all you say they are, you don't really gain anything by knocking them down and out."[28] Barnes did not resent his friend's admonitions ("You speak frankly and bring home a man's own weaknesses in a way that he sees them intellectually. That's wisdom plus art."), but took them, as they were meant, as an expression of love ("I would sooner die than betray such proof of faith."). At the same time, he simply couldn't kick a life-long habit. "I'm in bad with the bankers, preachers, locomotive-makers and politicians who control the University and the schools," he told Dewey, "but that we have them licked, and that the Foundation plan will win, I would bet every dollar I own."[29] A few days later, when he heard that Dean Laird had publicly defended Penn's connection with the Foundation, he could almost taste victory. "Oh boy!" he said. "It means a liberalizing, a loosening up of the academic tightness termed propriety; in short, intelligent bar-room methods have subjugated parlor manners!"[30] Not that he could let down his guard; still, the second issue of the *Journal* was notably milder in tone than the inaugural publication. Upon Dewey's advice, Barnes had changed the title of his contribution from "Crutches for Artistic Cripples" to "Art Teaching That Obstructs Education." It was a swipe at a method of art instruction then enjoying considerable vogue in public and private schools. Tom Munro took on Bernard Berenson in an essay that extended the criticisms Barnes had made of the famous connoisseur's approach in *The Art in Painting*. He also wrote a thoughtful, constructive article on reforming college art teaching. The ever-practical Mary Mullen, who had described the Argyrol plant experiment in the first issue of the *Journal*, continued a down-to-earth exposition of the Barnesian method as she applied it in Foundation classrooms. Dewey tidied up his dedication address for publication, Singer contributed a parable about the value of patronizing the arts based on the speech he had given at the March ceremony, and Buermeyer offered two essays that dealt with aesthetics generally and so broadened the focus of the little magazine beyond the plastic arts. But what it did not contain was a letter that Penn philosophy professor Louis Flaccus had sent Barnes expressing his enthusiasm for the Foundation and its links with the university but also apparently chastising the collector and Buermeyer for their indecorous treatment of educators with differing views. In a cover note, Flaccus had said that he understood that he was "chancing" Barnes's "personal enmity" by stating his position frankly.[31] But he had no idea the degree of the risk!

Whatever members of the elite academic community might think of his tone and tactics, Barnes was heartened by letters from art teachers who hailed his plain speaking. Besides, with the end of the spring semester classes at the Foundation, he was transferring his educational base to Europe. Munro, Mullen, and Buermeyer would each take a group of students on a three-month study tour through galleries and museums in France, Italy, Spain, and England. The Foundation provided several scholarships; otherwise, there was a modest fee to cover expenses. While in Paris during the early part of the summer, the Deweys attended one of Barnes's lectures to students visiting the Louvre. Renewed, as always, by his travels, the collector returned home ready to continue waging war. In a defiant editorial appearing in the October *Journal*, he drew another line in the sand. Drafted by Buermeyer, "Construction and Controversy," was notable for its reference to alcoholism, an affliction from which Barnes's father suffered and to which the author himself would later succumb, as well as its defense of personal attacks whatever Penn might think of them. The editorial declared:

We believe that the Barnes Foundation's policy of branding as radically false and pernicious what seems to it such, offers the most hopeful method of eliminating the irrational and antiquated practices so strongly entrenched in influential art and educational circles. An attempt to bring into existence something new invariably finds the ground on which it must build already occupied. . . . And since everything fights for life, such a struggle cannot always be kept within the rules of decorum which regulates friendly association between individuals; but to consider decorum the first necessity of debate is often to surrender a cause.

This is especially true when existing institutions are firmly established, and surrounded by prestige which prevents any impartial examination of their right to exist. . . . We all know that deeply rooted habits do not yield to any merely abstract reasoning. . . . Nothing short of severe shock can secure genuine attention to the matter at issue. An individual, for example, addicted to the excessive use of alcohol, will rarely or never give any real thought to what he is doing until the consequences of it are forcibly impressed upon him by such unmistakable danger signals as loss of health or employment. . . .

To attack in terms wholly free of ambiguity may thus be the necessary prelude to any fruitful discussion. Such attacks are frequently said to be "in bad taste." They are in bad taste if they spring from malice, desire for personal aggrandizement or any other motive than desire for the general good. If, however, all discussion that seeks to go to the roots of the matter . . . is in bad taste, then "good taste" is nothing but a weapon by which vested interests may fight any penetrating analysis of their prestige and privileges. Criticism, however destructive in appearance, is always legitimate if it offers an alternative to what is criticized, and if it is free from animus. . . . The harm done by ill-intentioned persons is utterly trivial when compared with that done by those whose consciences approve their every act. The militarist, the religious persecutor, the defender of unintelligent subservience to mere custom and authority—these, who are not considered criminals at all, are the real enemies of humanity. . . . Their guilt is shared by all who in the presence of unmistakable evils take refuge in inertia or invoke prestige to stifle discussion. To refrain from bringing to light the harm done by well-intentioned persons is to resign one's self to futility.[32]

Barnes distributed some 25,000 copies of the *Journal* to individuals and educational institutions. He was in a momentarily ebullient mood. Buermeyer was teaching aesthetics to a Foundation class of fifteen art supervisors and a half dozen art teachers. At Columbia, twenty-eight students were enrolled in Munro's modern art course. Although his class at Penn had attracted just five university students, the young instructor had told Barnes their qualifications were "infinitely superior" to those of the students in his spring class. His mentor was pleased, but he thought the small size indicated a failure on the part of Penn's faculty to coordinate their resources with those of the Foundation. Nevertheless, he expressed appreciation to Laird for his efforts and admitted that, to a certain extent, the small enrollment was "intrinsic to the situation—that is," he said philosophically, "anything new is bound to be considered as strange."[33]

Barnes had a considerable emotional stake nonetheless in a course entitled Aesthetic Experience that Buermeyer finally offered at Penn in the spring term of 1926. The university intended it as a kind of sequel to Flaccus's first-term philosophy course in aesthetic analysis. The collector hoped that exposing students to the psychology of beauty would create a well-prepared core of undergraduates for Munro's modern art classes. But when only six students enrolled in the new course, Barnes told Buermeyer he couldn't continue to be financially responsible for it in light of such a low return on his investment. Nevertheless, he wrote to Flaccus that he was "not going to let die the opportunity for mutual benefit that would result in public good without a final attempt to get the attention of the University teachers and officials to what we have to offer." He pointed out that he was an alumnus who recognized his alma mater's "great power and value" and had a "vision of the future" in which a combination of their resources would create a program "unique in the whole world in education in art." Acknowledging that his own enthusiasm for the project may have obscured its educational value to less than sharp-eyed University administrators, though he doubted they were blind to "the material results that might accrue later from a successful alliance," Barnes passed along a copy of an article on "Art in Education—and Education in Art" written by Dewey for the current issue of the *New Republic* as a "more detached" argument.[34]

The essay declared that "aesthetic appreciation and art . . . are not additions to the real world, much less luxuries. . . . The demand of the soul for joy, or freshness of experience," the philosopher said, could be supplied only "through art." He took issue with Leo Stein's criticism of *The Art in Painting* and praised the book's "conviction that art as displayed in painting is inherently educative. But paintings," he added—and this was the message that Barnes was trying to get across to Penn, "do not educate at present till we are educated to enjoy, to realize, their educative potentialities" because of an array of forces in American culture submerging aesthetic appreciation.[35] The collector asked Flaccus if, in light of Dewey's articulation of the need for the kind of art education provided by the Foundation, he would convene his colleagues and come up with a plan for procuring a sufficient number of upperclassmen or graduate students, who had studied psychology and aesthetics, "to give Munro a fair chance to see what his knowledge and personality working with our resources could produce in the direction of making Penn lead in the field of education in art. I don't want to be a nuisance and I may be asking the impossible," he added; "at any rate it is the best method that occurs to me at this moment to effect a practical working plan by which we could do something for the University and the University could do something for us—that is, give a fair trial to what looks like something entirely new in educational practice."[36]

Recognizing a quid pro quo when he saw one, Penniman, to whom Flaccus had passed on the collector's letter, hastened to reassure Barnes that "only with time" could one expect a response to new elective courses commensurate with their merits.[37] The collector's answer, one part conciliation to three parts threat, was the work of a master chemist. He told the president his letter was "so fair in its presentation of the common sense of the situation that it makes me feel I have been both unfair and impatient." But he also mentioned that he had "stalled" an overture from Princeton for an alliance that would make the Barnes collection available to its students "with the perfectly true statement that our gallery is occupied every day with classes." He didn't want to drop the university's Thursday afternoon class "and let an outsider get away with the leadership in art education that will surely be Penn's in a few years if we can only pass the critical stages. It is true that Rome wasn't built in a day," he added, "but then the foreman on the job wasn't ourselves."[38] To facilitate progress, Barnes suggested Singer confer with Dewey. *Plop.* Penniman returned the ball, telling Barnes that he would act at once on his suggestion and ask the Penn philosopher to request a meeting. "Like yourself, I am anxious that the University of Pennsylvania be a leader and not a follower," he wrote, and added: "I believe that . . . we can look forward confidently to a growing interest in the courses presented by the representatives of the Barnes Foundation."[39]

Singer's call upon Dewey took place in mid-March, and afterwards he, along with Flaccus, two other professors, Laird, and the dean of the College, met with Buermeyer and Munro to discuss what might be done to assure the young instructor in modern art of better-prepared students. It was decided that Laird would appoint a faculty committee to extend "among students the knowledge of the courses now being offered by the visiting lecturers of the Barnes Foundation," and Munro, as well he might, expressed his gratitude and satisfaction.[40] As the end of the 1926 spring semester approached, Penniman sent an official letter to Barnes expressing the university's willingness, if the collector so desired, to renew for another two years the agreement, which would soon expire, between Penn and the Foundation for a course in modern art and also to include Buermeyer's Aesthetic Experience course in the contract. In a second, personal letter, he thanked the collector "most heartily" for the contribution he had made to the School of Fine Arts through the Barnes Foundation lecturers and said, "we shall be very glad indeed, if you are willing to continue the arrangement."[41]

Barnes replied that the Foundation would be happy to renew its agreement with Penn for another two years. He added that he especially appreciated the president's personal note and was convinced that together they could "do something for art education that has never been done before." But then, speaking frankly in a spirit of "true friendship," he raised the ante. Barnes said that during their two-year alliance, "no material progress" had been made "toward the solution of the most important and serious problem in [his] whole life." The troubling question, he continued, was what, after his death, would become "of a twelve acre park and magnificent buildings," whose then worth he set at $1 million, to say nothing of "a collection of paintings that could be sold new for more than $6 million, and which is increasing daily in value," and, in addition, "a yearly income of about $600,000. One object of the experiment . . . with Penn," he said, "was to find out if the University could size up to the job of being made the legatee of both the assets and the determination to take art education out of the chaos it now occupies . . . and put it on the rational basis that governs education in science." Barnes said the results had not been very encouraging, and he expressed doubt they ever would be "under the plan in operation in . . . Fine Arts." From his point of view, the problem was the subservience of the department, then run somewhat left-handedly by Laird, to architecture. He pointed out that the obstacles to a successful working alliance with the Barnes Foundation, which he detailed in a separate three-page memorandum, required "a reorganization," spelled out in yet another addendum, so as to "take into account modern educational principles and practices that are ignored in the present system." Turning from pedagogy to polemics, he defended the militancy of the *Journal*, but he also acknowledged that certain articles could have embarrassed his alma mater and declared: "The *Journal* has accomplished its intended purpose in answering by logical arguments the charges of people who would like to push back the clock. We look upon that stage of our career as finished because the victory for progress has been won." The collector said that henceforth he would be "proceeding in a more conventional, orderly way," and he suggested that before the university took "any decided steps" in appointing a professor of fine arts and undertaking the needed departmental reorganization, Penniman visit, with Penn's attorney, the office of his attorney, Owen J. Roberts, "and scrutinize the parts of a new indenture in which the name of the University figures. Then," Barnes concluded, "if you decide that what you have learned is of value to the University, kindly make an appointment for me to talk with your Board of Trustees at the earliest moment after I return from Europe on August first."[42]

What the president would find was that the collector had amended paragraph 30 of Article IX of the Foundation bylaws on the 11th of May to open the gallery after his and Laura's death "to students and instructors of Penn in connection with University courses in Fine Arts and Aesthetics." It wasn't money in the bank, but it was a step along what Penniman surely knew would be a long and difficult road if there was, indeed, any real hope that Barnes would make good on his implicit promise. But inexplicably, the president did not formally respond to Barnes's letter with his usual promptness and courtesy. He referred it to Laird, who wrote to Munro offering to convene the faculty committee charged with promoting the Foundation courses among Penn students. Munro, however, was in no rush. The semester was nearly over, he was planning to accompany his employer to Europe, and, besides, he, and more importantly Barnes, were miffed that only six university professors had bothered to attend a mid-May meeting in Merion at which the young instructor outlined a plan for improving the working relationship between the Foundation and Penn. Munro suggested postponing the committee meeting until the fall. He then joined Barnes abroad, as did John Dewey later in the summer. The philosopher went along with his friend and the students in Munro's charge to museums in Paris, Rome, Madrid, and Toledo. Their roles now reversed, he listened to Barnes lecture, took notes, and struggled to stay awake as the collector analyzed dozens of paintings. But his interest was genuine, as was his respect for his teacher, and the experience contributed to his work on the nature and function of the aesthetic dimension of experience, which culminated six years later in his William James Memorial Lectures at Harvard.

When classes resumed at Penn in late September of 1926, Munro's modern art seminar, now listed as a full-year course, attracted thirty-one students, and he gave it entirely at the Barnes Foundation. Buermeyer's Aesthetic Experience was again scheduled for the spring semester, but it seemed the visiting lecturer, described in the School of Fine Arts catalogue as the Barnes Foundation Professor of Psychological Aesthetics, would be commuting from Manhattan, since during the summer, he accepted a position as an assistant professor of philosophy at New York University. Within the month, however, it became open to question whether he would be able to teach at either institution for some time. Buermeyer was the victim of what Laird described to Penniman as a "murderous attack."[43] He was hospitalized in New York for several weeks, and Barnes told Singer that he planned to bring him to Merion to recuperate and then take him to Europe in December. Whatever the nature of the assault, it, along with the collector's simmering fury at not receiving a response to his suggestions for reorganizing Penn's fine arts program and a new book by Louis Flaccus, doomed the fragile alliance between the university and the Foundation. On November 2, Barnes wrote to Singer that he had "torn up the plans [he] had dreamed of for a long distance future with Penn."[44] But he also indicated that he intended to live up to the new two-year contractual agreement for providing courses. Then he read *The Spirit and Substance of Art* by Singer's fellow philosophy teacher.

Flaccus had sent Barnes an autographed copy not knowing that the collector already had his hands on a review copy passed along to him by an art critic for a New York magazine. In the preface, the Penn philosopher had expressed his gratitude to the Foundation for the "opportunity to see and study many of the newer masters," which he said widened his appreciation of painting.[45] He expected a note of thanks and, perhaps, even some praise for the guide to appreciating all the arts that he had written for use in college aesthetics courses. Barnes accused him of plagiarism. In what would become a finely honed talent for avoiding libel suits, he ascribed the accusation to the unnamed critic who, he said, termed the thesis of the book a "flagrant steal" from *The Art in Painting*. In words that anticipate George Orwell's description of activity in a police state, the collector told Flaccus: "The small number of your visits to the Foundation is a matter of record in its official files, side by side with psychological data of reactions which is a routine part of our experimental researches in the observation of methods of approach to painting. The plain fact is that no true plastic experience, of the character your book states was yours, ever resulted or could result under the circumstances. The proof of this assertion is furnished by your book itself where it gives specific objective facts as existential in particular paintings in our collection, and which data are demonstrably not present, and which do not fit into the theory to which you twist them. . . . Your child 'pictorial form,' stripped of its padding, seems to be the natural son of 'plastic form,' a term I was the first to publish in the content paraphrased by you." Not only was Flaccus pinching a term from him, in Barnes's view, he was incapable of applying the concept it represented to works of art. "Your net result," the collector wrote, "is just . . . another 'learned' book on a subject of which its author knows nothing by experience. The injustice to the Foundation in quoting its name and in perverting its contributions to what you pretend is experience, and then prove its opposite, is that you place the responsibility for the educational crime upon our ideas and our paintings."[46]

In a note to Singer, Barnes called Flaccus's book "pretentious sage humbuggery" and said "the author . . . is in a bad hole and so is the publisher, from a legal standpoint. The University's plight is worse because, at this moment, I see no way of preventing a public scandal without sacrificing fundamental principles of education and ethics." He went on to say that he was available to talk privately with Singer about the matter and seemed to have no clue about the total impossibility of Singer's accepting his offer. Few more serious charges than plagiarism can be laid against an academic, and the chairman of the Penn philosophy department replied promptly and primly: "Under no circumstances that I can think of would I be tempted to intrude on the affairs of an author and his critic." He suggested that Barnes publish his opinion of the book "in one of the usual journals" thereby giving Flaccus a chance to respond publicly to any criticism. "Only then could one judge," he told Barnes, "whether it was author or critic who was 'in the hole,' as you put it."[47]

In a response, drenched in sarcasm, the collector informed his Penn ally that his "dodging [of the] realities" of the situation was "equivalent to a pleasant drunk as a release from a wearisome job, a nagging woman, or a raging toothache. Let me state the cold facts," he said. "Your apparent indifference to the danger, revealed by your irrelevant reply to my warning, is certainly no funeral of mine. The only resource left is prayer; and I offer all I have that your students and the public never learn why Penn has been kicked out of the Foundation. I am sure that you will pray, too, because your letter bespeaks the contented superiority of faith to works. And part of your faith, I fancy, is in your friend's work and in the practical efficiency of your kind of thinking."[48] Barnes referred to an official letter of dismissal, which, indeed, was hand delivered that same day to the secretary of the university. Signed by Nelle Mullen, the secretary of the Foundation, it said: "We regret to be compelled to inform you that the University of Pennsylvania has been suspended from further participation in our educational program. The suspension takes effect as of this date. The cause for our action may be obtained from sources other than ourselves."[49]

The mails were thick with missives on the matter. Singer wrote to Dewey, as the Foundation's education director, asking him to use his influence as a scholar to insure that Flaccus had an opportunity to answer any charges in a serious journal. Barnes sent Penn an eight-page indictment outlining the deficiency of its art instruction, the history of its relations with the Foundation, what the present alliance might have led to, and the obstacles to effective cooperation. The main problems, according to the collector, were "the inadequate and injurious preparation given to students," which made them unfit "to take advantage of the opportunities offered," and "the inertia" of the university's faculty and administrative officers, "which amounted sometimes to open hostility" towards new ideas. He noted, with an ill-concealed sense of injury, that Penniman had never visited the Foundation.[50]

Within a few days, Singer forwarded to the president a "preliminary statement" that Flaccus had presented in his defense. The Penn author carefully and convincingly refuted the collector's accusations one by one. Apparently, no "final" statement was ever required by the university. Flaccus pointed out that the Barnes method of analysis was not entirely new and that his own term, "pictorial form," was a translation of the German *Bildform*, which could be found in many books in that language on aesthetics. With impressive dignity, he asserted that the few analyses in his book of works cited as examples of the Barnes collection, like his analyses of all the paintings referred to in *The Spirit and Substance of Art*, were entirely his own. "The fact that Barnes . . . states that I see in his pictures what is not there tends to nullify his statement that I have stolen," he said. Finally, echoing Leo Stein, Flaccus declared that while he approved "of going directly to a painting," he objected "to an intolerance which insists that a man has no right to his own eyes and his own interpretation."[51] Dewey wrote to Singer that he agreed that the accused Penn philosopher should be given an opportunity to reply "upon equal terms" to any criticism of his book. But Dewey also expressed a reluctance to intrude on the editorial policies of professional journals, and he pointed out that he had stepped down some time ago as educational director of the Barnes Foundation.[52]

Despite his professed concern for the reputation of one of his departmental colleagues, Singer probably never thought Flaccus's standing in the guild of philosophers was in any real jeopardy. The collector's charge, which spoke volumes about his seemingly limitless capacity to take offense, was absurd. But when Singer discovered, belatedly, that Barnes's proposal for reorganizing the university's fine arts program had never received an official response, he wrote a memorandum to the file saying the "attack upon Flaccus is the next and last episode," and he declared the "situation . . . suddenly . . . hopeless."[53] The Penn administration, however, was catapulted into action. On the fourth of December, Laird sent, after preparing three drafts, a letter asking pardon for his delay in responding to Barnes's May letter, which Penniman had forwarded to him. "Through a mischance," he told Barnes, "you have been shown an unintended discourtesy for which I am solely responsible." He explained that the "fundamental importance" of the collector's criticisms and suggestions "necessitated most careful consideration by members of the University faculties." Laird assured Barnes that a committee was at work on the matter and that he expected a report before the end of the term.[54] Penniman sent an oddly formal, not quite apology several days later expressing his eagerness to confer with Barnes once he had the committee report in hand.[55]

It was all too little too late. Laird received a letter from "A. Reilly," purportedly a Foundation secretary, saying "Dr. Barnes is busy getting ready to leave for Europe and I have charge of the mail. What he said when I showed him your and Dr. Penniman's letters beat anything I ever heard him attempt in picturesque profanity."[56] Several days later, Nelle Mullen wrote to the University secretary declaring that assumptions in Laird's and Penniman's letters were "utterly erroneous" as to the reasons for Penn's "suspension." But she added that "since a de facto enforcement of the suspension in mid-season would work injury to innocent and needy students, our gallery will continue to be open to the regular University class every Thursday afternoon until the end of the present semester."[57] Meanwhile, Dewey had told Barnes of Singer's correspondence with him, and the collector wrote angrily to the Penn philosopher: "What makes you think he is a nurse, that we are in need of one, or that you can 'pass the buck' to him? . . . You chose the issue," he said, "and I challenged you to fair combat and asked no favors." Barnes went on to suggest that if Flaccus wasn't an exploiter of his "ideas and property to base educational ends," he was "so completely deluded as to be adjudged insane." He declared the end of the alliance "a sad finish to a unique opportunity. But who lost?" he asked. "What Penn had offered to her will be making [an impact on] civilization when her present officials will be forgotten except for the shiver of vicarious shame that future Penn alumni feel when they know that her present servants cut Penn's throat in assuming that timidity, inertia, politics or snobbism could inhibit the force of Nature."[58]

Singer replied that the collector was "quite right; it is a public shame," he said, "as well as a personal disappointment that plans which promised so much and so permanent good should have come to shipwreck. . . . Had we succeeded in working together along the lines we planned together," he continued, "I believe the future would have had occasion to bless us a little: that is, you would have received the blessing, and I should have had the fun of helping you earn it. . . . But there is no use wasting regrets on a lost gamble," the Penn philosopher concluded sadly in the last letter he ever wrote to Barnes.[59] But Barnes couldn't quite let go. A bout of grippe that lingered for weeks had forced him to delay his annual winter trip to Europe, and he wrote Singer two days before Christmas recapitulating his complaints against Penn. "What a pity it is," he said, "to make innocent students suffer for the sins of others."[60] On the eve of the holiday, he set down a résumé of the "obstacles" to cooperation with the University. "The Foundation has been . . . degraded to a means of giving credits to students in a mill for bluffs and job-holders masquerading as educators," he said. Penniman was an "exalted *functionarie*," Laird a "politician," Singer "lazy, indifferent, and a dreamer," and Flaccus, "dry and colorless," indulged in "cheap exploitation."[61] So rest ye merry gentlemen.

After the first of the year, Barnes was well enough to re-book a steamer, and Munro was left to tell the students in his class that while they could attend his weekly lectures at the Foundation, no credit would be given for modern art in the second term. The university elected to refund advance payments of tuition. The spring brought solid praise from reviewers for Flaccus's book, which was published in two subsequent enlarged editions. The author continued to teach at Penn until his retirement. Singer was named to the Adam Seybert Chair of Moral and Intellectual Philosophy and enjoyed an increasingly wide reputation for thoughtful books and brilliant lectures. Laird retired as dean of the School of Fine Arts and professor of architecture in 1932 after forty-two years on the faculty. Penniman remained as chief executive officer until 1930, then as chief academic officer for nine more years. Tom Munro learned from Barnes that his contract would not be renewed when it expired in the summer of 1927, but his parting from the Foundation was amicable, and he went on to an academic career at Rutgers, Long Island University, and Western Reserve, later becoming curator of education at the Cleveland Museum of Art. Penn kept in its files a letter to a Fine Arts faculty member from a colleague in the medical school, the infamous Charles Burr, warning that the collector was "a dangerous man to have anything to do with and," the alienist predicted, "he will get more and more dangerous as time goes on."[62]

8

A New Valuation of Black Art

The notion that association with Barnes involved some degree of risk arose from the assessments Philadelphia gentlemen made in the privacy of their clubs about the chances institutions dealing with the collector might have for public embarrassment on account of his combative nature. But it was linked, as well, to another of his predilections that had considerable capacity to shock the local gentry. The mass northward migration of Southern blacks during and after World War I roiled white prejudice. Real estate covenants kept even the black bourgeoisie in segregated neighborhoods; job discrimination effectively excluded African Americans, regardless of their attainments, from more than marginal participation in the economic life of the larger community. Furthermore, as one astute and prominent member of the Philadelphia black middle class noted in 1921, rights, not taken for granted but cherished by her people, to utilize and enjoy "the same social and educational facilities as whites . . . were withdrawn."[1] *Birth of A Nation*, D.W. Griffith's stereotypical portrayal of black folk that had caused race riots after its release in 1915, was still a box office hit. And while the alarmist rhetoric of hate mongers about the so-called "rising tide of color" may not have been taken seriously in Rittenhouse Square or Main Line drawing rooms, neither did their inhabitants regard the activities of blacks as of any real consequence. Barnes not only supported African-American demands for equal opportunity, he admired and valued the intellectual and artistic accomplishments of black men and women. He believed in the existence of a distinctive black aesthetic, and, unlike most of the secular black leadership of the period, he recognized its religious basis. The abiding conviction of the gruff, middle-aged white man that blacks have an innate capacity to respond to auditory and visual stimuli had its roots in the boy's experience of African Americans singing and dancing at the camp meeting he attended with his mother. He wanted people of color to take pride in their artistic gifts. He thought they had something, much perhaps that could not necessarily be specified, to contribute to an emerging modern society.

Not accidentally, the second book published by the Barnes Foundation, in the spring of 1926, was a collaboration between Tom Munro and Paul Guillaume entitled *Primitive Negro Sculpture*. The authors credited Barnes with providing them the "initial impetus toward writing" it, and he may well have contributed much of the stylistic analysis.[2] Illustrated with photographs of forty-one works from the Foundation collection, the 134-page volume reflected Barnes's carefully formed opinion that the creations of the unknown African artists were beautiful. Guillaume had introduced him to their varied works a few years earlier, and under the tutelage of the Parisian picture dealer, he had developed an appreciation for the artistry reflected in the masks and fetish figures carved in wood, and less commonly in ivory, stone, and even metals, in village huts on the West African coast and inland along remote tributaries of the Niger and the Congo. That their provenance was often uncertain mattered little to Barnes. He admired the formal organization of the sculpture and responded to its expressive power. Soon after construction of the Foundation buildings began, he wrote to Guillaume that "the walls of the vestibule in the gallery are to be of especially made multi-colored tiles of which Negro art will be the motif. That shows how much I esteem Negro art," he said.[3] Indeed, the ceramic entrance was modeled on the relief of a granary carving from the Ivory Coast. Inside, some 130 rare figurative sculptures were exhibited side by side with the modern masterworks, whose creators, Barnes believed, drew inspiration from the ancient art brought back to Europe by missionaries and explorers.

Such treasures had usually been tucked into luggage as an afterthought, since nineteenth-century travelers to Africa had not been much interested in tribal art. A disdainful attitude toward primitive peoples, widespread on the Continent and in Britain and America, was reinforced by Darwinism and served colonial ambitions. Early, and still classic, ethnographic studies, while mentioning ornament and design, largely ignored sculpture. The development of art was seen as one aspect of evolution, and the work of indigenous peoples were invariably viewed as a rudimentary expression of the aesthetic impulse. Not until 1893, when German art historian Alois Riegl wrote in praise of African "geometric" style, was any substantial attention given to the forms of art created by native populations.[4] In 1912, the year Barnes sent Glackens to Paris to buy his first Impressionist and Post-Impressionist pictures, another German, Wilhelm Worringer, became among the first scholars to suggest that primitive sculpture was a forerunner of modern art.[5] But in France, although sociologist Emile Durkheim had considered the religious manifestations of aboriginal totems,[6] few were paying any attention to the fetish figures and tribal masks coming out of the nation's West African colonies at the time Guillaume began to study and acquire them. When the picture dealer shared his newfound enthusiasm with his most important client, Barnes quickly grasped the impact the ancient carvings had had on a handful of contemporary artists whose work he was collecting. Accustomed to looking at paintings from the painter's perspective, he saw in African art the same formal solutions that were seized upon by Gauguin, the Brücke artists in Germany, the Fauves, especially Matisse, Lipchitz, Brancusi, Soutine, Modigliani, and, most of all, Picasso.

Guillaume undoubtedly knew and passed on to Barnes the story of Maurice de Vlaminck's purchase of two or three primitive statutes sometime around 1904. The painter was subsequently given several more, along with a large white mask from the Congo, which captivated his artist friend Derain who bought it for himself. It was in Derain's studio, according to Vlaminck, that both Matisse and Picasso first saw and admired African art.[7] Matisse began buying a few sculptures, and he brought one to a Saturday gathering in the apartment of Leo and Gertrude Stein long before Barnes set foot in it.[8] A number of the young artists then working in Paris had visited the Ethnographical Museum at the Trocadéro Palace, and it was there, in 1907, that Picasso, alone one evening, was so struck by the power of African art that he returned to his studio and made more studies for the *Demoiselles*. The faces of the two right-hand figures became masks. His Negroid period lasted only a couple of years, but he found in the work of tribal artists what Guillaume called a "fertilizing germ" that proved to be an extremely important stimulant to his creativity.[9] The inspiration Picasso and his fellow painters and sculptors drew from African art had an abiding impact on their work. "After catching the spell of its vigorous and seductive rhythms, no artist can return to academic banalities," Guillaume and Munro observed. "Negro forms . . . are capable of infinite development and combination with others, and of adaptation to new media."[10]

Barnes's two young colleagues, the foreign secretary of the Foundation and its instructor in modern art, misdated many of the works illustrated in their book. But they were credited at the time by the influential *Saturday Review of Literature* with producing "the first adequate and thorough-going discussion of the important subject of African art."[11] In Germany and England, critics, with whose work they and the collector were familiar, had been effusive in their praise of primitive sculpture. Carl Einstein believed its makers had solved the fundamental problem of representing cubic mass by direct methods.[12] Roger Fry described it as "greater . . . than anything we produced even in the middle ages."[13] But their discussions were fragmentary and brief, commentaries on particular exhibitions or texts accompanying photographic reproductions, and they made no effort to describe the well-marked varieties and traditions in the art coming out of Africa. European eyes, long blind to the aesthetic qualities of primitive sculpture, now tended to view it romantically. Uncritical appreciation was hardly less racist than disregard. The Barnesian approach taken by Guillaume and Munro permitted no eulogizing of the exotic. It did enable the authors to differentiate among the work of tribal artists in Gabon, the Ivory Coast, Sudan, the Congo, Guinea, Dahomey, Benin, and

Cameroon in terms of formal values. They demonstrated, moreover, that the ovoid limbs and conical breasts of the fetish figures were not meant as realistic copies from nature, but were purposeful and systematic exaggerations. "One comes to regard the statue not as a distorted copy of a human body," they wrote, "but as a new creation in itself, recalling the human form in a general way, but independently justified by its own internal logic." Similarly, "a Negro mask is not simply a design, or simply a face: it is a face made into a design," Guillaume and Munro said. It "has a direct aesthetic effect, independent of all associations, by the shapes and combinations of its parts. . . . African sculpture must have had its individual geniuses, for its most powerful creations are unique," they concluded. "It lacked the differentiating force of conscious individualism, but also the crystallizing force of rigid social order. Its inertia was of life itself, instinctively conservative, yet impelled unconsciously into new channels of growth."[14]

In reviewing *Primitive Negro Art* for the *New Republic*, Lewis Mumford noted that the book would undoubtedly appeal "to those who are interested in the contemporary renaissance of the Negro."[15] Barnes's decision to make reproductions of his unrivaled collection of African sculpture available to the young authors was, indeed, driven by his desire to provide black Americans with visual proof of their rich artistic heritage. The collector had become convinced that the descendents of the tribal artists could become agents of America's cultural salvation. "Modern life has forced art into being a mere adherent upon practical affairs," he wrote. But "the Negro has kept nearer to the ideal of man's harmony with nature. . . . His art is so deeply rooted . . . that it has thrived in foreign soil. . . . This mystic whom we have treated as a vagrant has proved his possession of a power to create out of his own soul, and our own America, moving beauty." Although Barnes's taste in music, aside from the spirituals he loved, was classical, he recognized the growing popularity of another black musical form, jazz, which had begun reaching the public through phonograph records, the radio, and talking pictures—and would soon give the era its name. He hoped, in his liberal heart, that acknowledgment of black contributions to popular culture would be the beginning of the end of discrimination. The "white race owes to the soul-expressions of its black brother too many moments of happiness not to acknowledge ungrudgingly the significant fact that what the Negro has achieved is of tremendous civilizing value," he said. "When we take to heart the obvious fact that what our prosaic civilization needs most is precisely the poetry which the average Negro actually lives, it is incredible that we should not offer the consideration which we have consistently denied to him."[16]

Barnes provided financial support to black organizations and enjoyed cordial, albeit complex, relationships with several of the leading figures of the Harlem Renaissance. The most straightforward was with the sociologist Charles S. Johnson, the founder and editor of the National Urban League's journal *Oppor-*

tunity, a publication for which Barnes had written a laudatory endorsement as part of its campaign for subscriptions. Both men were action-oriented pragmatists who embraced, earlier than most liberal supporters of integration, what was later known as cultural pluralism—the idea, as Langston Hughes would articulate it, that "Negro artists . . . express [their] dark-skinned selves."[17] Johnson had come to New York from Chicago in 1921 to be the Urban League's director of research, and a grant from the Carnegie Corporation allowed him to launch Harlem's finest monthly magazine two years later. The brilliant, entrepreneurial social scientist played a pivotal role in black cultural awakening not only by making the pages of *Opportunity* available to young African American writers and artists but also by bringing the writers and artists together with white editors, publishers, and other patrons.

On the publication of the first novel by the Cornell-educated daughter of one of Philadelphia's most distinguished black-bourgeoisie families, Jessie Redmon Fauset, Johnson organized a gala dinner to facilitate Uptown-Downtown networking. His key advisor on cultural matters, essayist and critic Alain Locke, sent an invitation to Barnes, whom he had met in Paris, through Paul Guillaume, a few months earlier. Although the collector joked that recent letters he had mailed to the editor of the *Dial* put him at risk of arrest by the New York City police ("I don't mind the nabbing but I prefer to fight on my home grounds."[18]), he happily joined one hundred guests gathered at the Civic Club on March 21, 1924 to honor Fauset, who was then literary editor of the *Crisis*, the official organ of the National Association for the Advancement of Colored People (NAACP). The young literati in attendance were members of an informal writers' guild. But the shrewd editor of *Opportunity* also produced an impressive number of cultural lions. In addition to Locke, whose day job was chairman of the philosophy department at Howard University, there was W. E. B. Du Bois, the long-time editor of the *Crisis* who made his first public address since his return from a mission to Liberia as American plenipotentiary, the poet, editor, and composer James Weldon Johnson, then serving as the NAACP's first African American field secretary, and Carl Van Doren, the editor of *Century* magazine, as well as several heads of publishing companies. Fauset's book, *There Is Confusion*, was hailed as the first novel of the "Negro Renaissance," and two poets in their early twenties, Gwendolyn Bennett and Countee Cullen, read their poems.

It was a moment of high expectation. Intellectual patriarch Du Bois predicted an end to the literature of accommodation in which style had been largely imposed by barriers against publication of creative writing about black people. The cosmopolitan James Johnson, who had edited a landmark anthology of poetry by African Americans two years earlier, was honored for giving a new generation access to an important part of their cultural history. The dapper and erudite Locke talked of the "spiritual wealth" that, if properly expounded, would force a "new judgment and reappraisal of the race."[19] Van Doren professed "a genuine faith in the future of imaginative writing among Negroes in the United States. . . . The Negroes of the country are in a remarkable strategic position with reference to the new literary age," he said. "What American literature decidedly needs at the moment is color, music, gusto, the free expression of gay or desperate moods. If the Negroes are not in a position to contribute these items, I do not know what Americans are."[20] The atmosphere was incandescent when Barnes rose to speak to the exuberant guests about primitive African art and its influence on the work of modern painters and sculptors. He, too, wanted the gifted black young people in the audience to take an enabling satisfaction in their cultural roots.

The talent of these men and women in their twenties impressed him mightily, and he sought out Bennett, who had studied fine arts at Columbia and was then a student at the Pratt Institute, to attend the new courses at the Barnes Foundation on a full scholarship that would cover her living expenses while attending the free classes. Though it would be several years before she was able to accept his offer, the interracial banquet produced a number of more immediate opportunities for the artists and writers in attendance. Even before the high-toned evening ended, Paul Kellogg, the editor of *Survey Graphic*, told Charles Johnson he would devote an entire issue of his magazine, which had all but ignored black Americans, to the progressive spirit celebrated at the Civic Club. The theme would be black literature and art. Locke was enlisted to assemble and edit materials for the "Harlem project." A slight, effete figure, like Fauset a member of an OP (Old Philadelphia) black family, Locke had graduated from Central High School and gone on to Harvard and then to Oxford, as the first African American Rhodes Scholar. He studied philosophy at the University of Berlin fifteen years after Barnes had studied chemistry there, returning to the United States to teach at Howard, the country's leading black university, in 1912 just as his fellow Central alumnus was launching his career as a collector of modern European and American paintings.

The almost comically contrasting characters, the large-framed white businessman and the wispy black scholar (Locke was barely five feet tall and weighed just under 100 pounds), shared more than two alma maters and an appreciation of fine tailoring. In contrast to elitists of both races, they believed the common man and woman had a role to play in the cultural life of the nation. Carrying forward the spirit of his Argyrol factory experiment, Barnes had singled out "plain people" for special mention in the charter of his Foundation when discussing the question of public admission to the gallery in Merion. Locke located the fundamental inspiration for the Harlem Renaissance among "the rank and file." He wrote that "it is the 'man farthest down' who is most active in getting up." Observing the great northward migration, the historic trek from farm to city, he saw "the clergyman following his errant flock, the physician or lawyer trailing his clients." Turning to Albert Barnes for a contribution to the Harlem issue of *Survey Graphic*, he found a collaborator who also believed "a transformed and transforming psychology permeate[d] the masses."[21]

Their friendship, for a time mutually beneficial, began in December of 1923. Barnes subsequently sought information from Locke about contemporary black writers in connection with an article he was preparing for *Ex Libris*, the journal of the American Library in Paris. He explained, not altogether clearly, that he wanted to show the relation of the contributions of the "best-known Negro artists . . . to what the ordinary, unknown Negro lives every day in spiritual things."[22] His intention was to stimulate racial pride, an objective Locke had already identified as a crucial step in overcoming social divisiveness. The Howard philosopher recommended several books, and Barnes was soon writing to him about the personal pleasure he derived from reading black authors whose work he had not previously known. He called poet Angelina Weld Grimke "a star of the first magnitude" and said Jean Toomer's novel *Cane* was "a peach."[23] When he sent Locke his completed manuscript, "Contribution to the Study of Negro Art in America," Barnes noted that it would appear in Guillaume's *Les Arts à Paris*, as well as *Ex Libris*, and encouraged Locke to send the essay, if he thought it worthy, to an American magazine where it might reach a sympathetic audience.[24] Agreeing to act as agent, Locke invited Barnes to several informal gatherings of race leaders in New York. The collector accepted with enthusiasm, and, in turn, invited Locke to Merion to study his African sculpture, which he was eager to bring to the attention of black intellectuals.

Barnes already had made one particularly significant effort. On the day following the Civic Club dinner, he wrote directly to Charles Johnson to see if the editor of *Opportunity* might be interested in publishing an article he had written on Guillaume's Paris gallery and to suggest that he dedicate an upcoming issue to primitive art. His letter also proposed that a "fine Negro mind trained to the point, say, of going up for his Ph.D. at Harvard" be identified to undertake advanced work at the Foundation. "Nobody competent has ever studied Negro art according to the modern conceptions of the psychology of aesthetics," Barnes wrote. "If the right man takes it up, he ought to land . . . the world distinction that scholarly research in a new field always assures for investigators with brains, character and energy. It is no job for a piker, and it needs the best Negro brains of today to select that man strictly on his qualifications and with a clear conception of what a successful outcome would mean in prestige for the race."[25]

Johnson responded enthusiastically to all of Barnes's proposals. "How you got in ahead of most of the rest of the world in appreciating and collecting these specimens [of African sculpture] is incomprehensible," he wrote. "There is unquestionably an opportunity for a young Negro to take up the study of this art and begin researches. It would mean a great deal more than world distinction for him. It would restore stature to Negroes and more. . . . This suggestion of yours should bear fruit and you may depend upon me to push it to the limit."[26] Within the editor's immediate and certain power were the pages of *Opportunity*, and he quickly solicited essays from Locke and Guillaume to accompany Barnes's piece on the French dealer's "temple" that had become a meeting place for Africanists. Even as the two men prepared their contributions, the collector was doing his best to recreate the heady atmosphere of the rue la Boétie in Merion. With much care, he arranged to bring Locke and the two Johnsons, Charles and James, for an April evening that began with good whiskey, was followed by a fine dinner, and ended with talk of art and race into the early hours of the morning. One can imagine a conversation that dealt not only with the plasticity of form but, more significantly, of group identity.

The editorial introducing the May *Opportunity* was entitled "Dr. Barnes." Charles Johnson, enterprising social scientist and grateful guest, wrote:

> Those who know Dr. Albert C. Barnes treat him as a valuable secret. . . . He was the first and is distinctly the last word in Primitive African Art and his pieces, the rarest of their kind—exquisite, exotic, distinctive,—once casually valued at fifty thousand dollars, are becoming invaluable. . . . And there are yet Philadelphians who ask "Who is Dr. Barnes?" . . . It is perhaps pardonable if this ritual of silence is broken, if only for a moment, on one who has known the native art of Negroes longer and who still knows it better than anyone in the United States, and who ranks close to Paul Guillaume as one of the foremost authorities on it in the world.
>
> Primitive Negro art is a new note—firm, refreshing, and irresistibly stimulating. . . . It was prophetic vision, uncanny in its sureness, that prompted this connoisseur to encourage . . . modern painters by buying their pictures before they felt the glimmer of a promise of prominence and recognition. . . . It was the same uncanny foresight that drew into his possession many of the best pieces of this African art—the inspiration of these modern artists. The whole modern art movement thus owes an immense debt to him, and it is not improbable that his foresight was in some measure trained by an interest of longer standing in certain native qualities of the Negro which held for him a fascination, and which lend color and the tone of genuine sincerity to his amazing industrial experiment.
>
> He recognizes in the Negro a natural rhythm—a self-propelling thing, capable of insinuating into business the unoppressive [sic], competent strides that come from spiritual "pulling together". With the individuals included in his community plan— whites and Negroes, this rhythm has been intellectualized. . . . The workers, none of whom have university degrees, in their daily seminars . . . have by assimilable bits mastered the teachings of many of the world's best minds. A Negro, scarcely literate a few years ago, is leading the seminar in discussions of Well's [sic] "Outline of History". Such is the practical application of a theory developed . . . years ago with much the same community and with little capital. . . .
>
> With the same resoluteness which characterizes the application of a conviction to business—but one of his interests, he has recorded with finality his instinctive appreciation of merit in new art. A bas-relief by Lipchitz is set in the imported French stone of the $600,000 Barnes Foundation Building now in course of erection, and a design in primitive African art taken from a native Temple door is being set into the entrance to the building. Behind each conviction is a long, tireless, searching interest.
>
> Soon primitive Negro art will invade this country as it has invaded Europe. . . . And there will come with it a new valuation of the contribution of Negroes, past and yet possible, to American life and culture. It is on this certainty that Dr. Barnes has quietly combed Europe for the choicest of the specimens brought from Africa, and is even

now urging serious study and exclusive research into the field, still uncharted, by competent and interested Negro students.[27]

Johnson's words were surely sweetest balm to a collector whose painstaking and discriminating assembly of modern to say nothing of primitive art had rarely won praise from the white media. Guillaume predicted that Barnes's "act of artistic audacity" in placing "African sculpture on the same plane as incontestable masterpieces of contemporaneous art" would "have a world-wide significance." To an article describing the Foundation's primitive holdings, he added a ringing coda: "Negro art has a spiritual mission; it has the great honor to develop the taste, to stir the depths of the soul, to refine the spirit, to enrich the imagination of this very Twentieth Century, which will be ashamed, perhaps, because it thought that it had nothing more to learn, when so numerous were the discoveries yet to be made in the domain of beauty."[28]

While Barnes described to *Opportunity* readers the thrill of lingering in Guillaume's "little gallery and museum of ancient Negro sculpture," which had become a "mecca" to artists "from all parts of the world," Locke paid tribute to the collector in an essay in which he warned that "having passed . . . through a period of neglect and disesteem . . . African art [wa]s . . . in danger of another sort of misconstruction, that of being taken up as an exotic fad and a fashionable amateurish interest. Its chief need," he said, was "to be allowed to speak for itself, to be studied and interpreted rather than to be praised or exploited." Observing that "one of the purposes and definite projects of the Barnes Foundation" was to study African art "organically, and to correlate it with the general body of human art," Locke predicted that African art would serve "not merely the purpose of a strange new artistic ferment," but also "have its share in the construction of a new broadly comparative and scientific aesthetics." After a nuanced analysis of the impact of the "dusty trophies of imperialism" on modern painting and sculpture, of the idiom and rhythm of African languages on contemporary French poetry, and of African folk songs and American Negro spirituals on French music, the self-described "philosophical midwife" to the younger generation of black writers and artists considered what effect African art might have "on the life of the American Negro." He said black Americans "must believe that there still slumbers in the blood something which once stirred will react with peculiar emotional intensity. . . . Nothing is more galvanizing than the sense of a cultural past," he concluded. "This at least the intelligent presentation of African art will supply to us."[29]

The African art issue of *Opportunity* was handsomely illustrated with photographic reproductions of sculptures and masks from the Barnes Foundation. The collector made even more available to Locke for his special issue of *Survey Graphic*. They conferred about the project when they met in Paris in July of 1924. Barnes was there with the newly hired Munro on his usual summer visit to the city's museums and galleries. Locke, on his way to a

German spa, had come to Paris in pursuit of an immensely talented twenty-two-year-old black American poet named Langston Hughes who was working as a night dishwasher at a cabaret on the rue Pigalle. A poem Hughes wrote about Africa, which he had visited the year before on a merchant steamer, had followed Locke's essay in the May issue of *Opportunity*, and Jessie Fauset also had published Hughes's work in the *Crisis*. The Howard philosopher had started a correspondence with him eighteen months earlier, and he awakened Hughes in his stifling attic room at noon on the 31st of July with an offer of lunch. At their first face to face meeting, Locke, undoubtedly carrying his signature rolled umbrella and, according to Hughes, wearing spats, talked excitedly about his plans for what he was calling "The New Negro" issue of *Survey Graphic* and asked the young poet to contribute new work to it. Flattered, Hughes readily agreed; he copied off some poems and took them to Locke's hotel near the Madeleine. The special editor was pleased with the verses—and with their handsome author. He took Hughes to see *Manon* at the Opéra Comique and arranged for him to visit Guillaume's African treasures. He then won the young man's promise to join him in Italy after the cabaret closed for the season and, mission accomplished, left town.

Soon afterwards, Hughes received a *pneumatique* asking him to lunch at the Café Royale. The signature on the note was "Albert C. Barnes." Locke had talked with his young friend about the collector, so intrigued by the invitation, Hughes hurried along to the designated restaurant. When he arrived, he found Barnes and Tom Munro already eating. They had not been able to wait for him, Barnes explained, because the day was to be devoted to studying paintings in the Louvre, and they were short of time. Urged to sit down, the poet ordered strawberries and listened, not very attentively, to Barnes talk about modern art, which sounded, he would recall, "like my father talking about business."[30] Did Hughes mean Barnes was more engrossed in his subject than his audience? Whatever the case, some of the collector's rapid-fire erudition may have made an impression on the poet, for the next year he would write a poem describing "Harlem, like a Picasso painting in his cubistic period."[31]

The brightness and many-faceted nature of the new race capital was what Locke tried to capture in the ninety pages of prose, verse, and graphic art that would made up the March 1925 *Survey Graphic*. There were twenty-three contributors; all but five were black. In addition to articles on African-American workers in the cities of the North, settlement patterns in Harlem, and West Indian migration, Locke presented the short fiction and poetry of the best young African-American writers of the postwar generation. His focus was on their rich legacy and even richer promise. His stated aim was to give the mostly white, upper middle-class readers of the magazine a "glimpse" of "the New Negro." But not for the sake of satisfying idle curiosity; rather that they might come to know him—"for precisely what he is," as the Howard philosopher put it, and "for that reason," he said, the New Negro "welcomes the new scientific rather than the old sentimental interest."[32] Locke was convinced, as he had stated a decade earlier in a series of public lectures, that modern societies "require social assimilation."[33]

He wasn't writing, of course, only, or perhaps even mainly, for whites. By defining its culture, he was attempting to empower a race that was no longer enslaved but still widely denigrated in a nation that sanctioned apartheid. A reassessment of the black American's African past was essential to his task. Among the four essays he contributed to *Survey Graphic* was a short piece entitled "The Art of the Ancestors," which was accompanied by photographs of four African objects in the Barnes collection. Photographs of four more objects served as illustrations for Countee Cullen's haunting poem, "Heritage." It began with the question: "What is Africa to me?" Albert Barnes's fine masks and sculptured figures offered one answer. As Locke had written: "Surely this art, once known and appreciated, can scarcely have less influence upon the blood descendants than upon those who inherit by tradition only. And at the very least, even for those not especially interested in art, it should definitely establish the enlightening fact that the Negro is not a cultural foundling without an inheritance."[34]

The collector's literary contribution to the magazine was the essay originally published in *Ex Libris* and *Les Arts à Paris*. When H.L. Mencken turned it down for the *American Mercury*, Locke decided to use it himself. In "Negro Art and America," Barnes gave his view of the nature and value of the contributions of black Americans to the culture of their adopted land. Beginning, as he so often did, with an attempt to describe the psychological complexion of his subject, he wrote that the outstanding characteristic of the African American was his "tremendous emotional endowment, his luxuriant and free imagination and truly great power of individual expression. He has in superlative measure that fire and light which, coming from within, bathes his whole world," Barnes said. "The Negro is a poet by birth." Recalling the camp meeting that had so quickened his boyish heart, he wrote:

> [Among] the masses . . . poetry expresses itself in religion which acquires a distinction by extraordinary fervor. . . . The outburst may be started by any unlettered person provided with the average Negro's normal endowment of eloquence and vivid imagery. It begins with a song or a wail which spreads like fire and soon becomes a . . . of harmony of rhythmic movement and rhythmic sound unequalled in the ceremonies of any other race. Poetry is religion brought down to earth and it is of the essence of the Negro soul. He carries it with him always and everywhere; he lives it in the field, the shop, the factory. His daily habits of thought, speech and movement are flavored with the picturesque. . . . Adversity has always been his lot but he converted it into a thing of beauty in his songs which constitute America's only great music—the spirituals. . . . In their mighty roll is a nobility truly superb. Idea and emotion are fused in an art which ranks with the psalms and songs of Zion in their compelling, universal appeal.

... Today [the Negro] has not yet found a place of equality in the social, educational or industrial world of the white man. But he has the same singing soul as the ancestors who created the single form of great art that American can claim as her own. . . . Through the compelling powers of his poetry and music the American Negro is revealing to the rest of the world the essential oneness of all human beings. . . . We have to acknowledge not only that our civilization has done practically nothing to help the Negro create his art but that our unjust oppression has been powerless to prevent the black man from realizing in a rich measure the expression of his own rare gifts. We have begun to imagine that a better education and a greater social and economic equality for the Negro might produce something of true importance for a richer and fuller American life. The unlettered black singers have taught us to live music that rakes our souls and gives us moments of exquisite joy. The later Negro has . . . shown us that the events of our every-day American life contain for him a poetry, rhythm and charm which we ourselves never discovered. . . . He has taught us to respect the sheer manly greatness of the fiber which has kept his inward light burning with an effulgence that shines through the darkness in which we have tried to keep him. . . . He may consent to form a working alliance with us for the development of a richer American civilization to which he will contribute his full share.[35]

The degree of eloquence Barnes mustered was a measure of his conviction. His words reflected his long-standing and profound admiration for people of African descent. It is striking, however, that the lover of paintings did not refer to any contemporary black painters. The reason appears to be that he had not yet seen the work of any he considered promising. Locke himself had commissioned Winold Reiss, a German-born artist working in New York, to make portraits of the New Negro for *Survey Graphic* because he thought Reiss was better than any black artist he knew in portraying African Americans. Both he and Barnes then believed that most black artists were "victims of the academy tradition" and "shared the blindness of the Caucasian eye."[36] Reiss's cover portrait of the tenor Roland Hayes, who had made his American concert debut just two years earlier, together with his drawings of representative African Americans throughout the magazine, captured what Locke described as "the folk character back of the individual, the psychology behind the physiognomy."[37] Readers were fascinated, and *Survey Graphic* had to go back on press to meet the demand for copies of the special issue. It had the largest circulation of any in the history of the magazine. Two printings sold out thanks, in part, to Barnes who purchased a thousand copies and distributed them widely in Philadelphia. As he had used his flyers containing physicians' endorsements of Argyrol to win customers, he used *Survey Graphic*, a testimony to black talent, to recruit supporters for the New Negro movement.

Albert and Charles Boni published an expanded and polished version of the Harlem issue in November of 1925. The path-breaking anthology, entitled *The New Negro*, used most of the material in the magazine and supplemented it with commissioned work, as well as the prize-winning entries in the first of a series of annual *Opportunity* literary contests launched in 1924 by Charles Johnson. But apparently Locke hesitated to include Barnes's essay. He initially sought a substitute from the writer and critic Carl Van Vechten, and only used the collector's article, which he considered "kindly but vague," when Van Vechten said he was too busy to prepare anything.[38] Locke was eager, however, to again use photographs of African sculpture from the Barnes collection to illustrate the book. He turned once more to Reiss for portraits and type sketches, and, in addition, he included work by one of Reiss's students, the only black artist represented in the book that heralded a great cultural awakening in black America.

Aaron Douglas was then twenty-four years old and had been persuaded to come to New York from Kansas City the year before by Charles Johnson. The savvy editor not only helped his protégé find a place to live in Harlem and bought his drawings for *Opportunity*, he provided him with a coveted introduction to Barnes. The collector soon invited Douglas to spend a day in Merion and sent him train fare for the journey. The Midwesterner had never before had access to African sculpture, let alone such superb examples, or, indeed, to modern European painting. He was strongly influenced by the experience. The stark, black-and-white drawings with African motifs he made for *The New Negro* came to be regarded as the archetypal visual expression of the Harlem Renaissance. Douglas's work responded to Locke's exhortation to return to the ancestral arts for inspiration and to Reiss's counsel to incorporate his roots into his own art. But the young artist also heeded Barnes's advise to look to the rhythms of everyday life, and he made the work and play of black people—as well as their history, religion, and myths—the subject matter of his work. Douglas's first mural commission, executed in 1927 for Harlem's Club Ebony, contained pastel panels of dancers and musicians in both jungle and urban settings. Attending the unveiling, Barnes told him to do it over in color. While he found the work pleasing, the collector thought it lacked richness and depth, and the artist would expend "an enormous amount of sweat and labor" to incorporate Barnes's suggestions in his future art.[39]

The "pioneering Africanist," as Locke described Douglas, had a material as well as a spiritual debt to the collector. Barnes provided him with a scholarship to study at the Barnes Foundation in 1927-28, and in 1931, as America was sinking into the Depression, he enabled him to spend a year in Paris. Shortly after the invitation to take classes in Merion arrived, Douglas became acquainted with another white patron, Park Avenue dowager Charlotte Van der Veer Quick Mason. She gave the artist the then princely sum of $125 for one of his drawings and tried to persuade him to turn down the Barnes award. When he accepted it anyway, she had her chauffeur drive her to Philadelphia, where Douglas had a room in a black neighborhood, and spent an hour trying to talk him into coming back to Harlem.[40] "Godmother" (as Mason liked to be known in hopes of protecting her anonymity) was seeking to save another African-American artist from the commercialism of white society as a means of feeding her fantasies about the nobility of primitives. But Douglas stayed put from

Tuesday through Friday each week for a year. He wanted to educate himself about the techniques and styles of modern masters, and his fellowship paid him a generous $125 a month for "looking at pictures." Although he was awed by the Barnes collection, admired his benefactor as a writer and a critic, and would remember with pleasure all his life the time he shook hands with Bertrand Russell and John Dewey in Merion, Douglas didn't find the Foundation classes entirely pleasant, once describing them as "cramped" and "pressured." [41] He also may have felt somewhat isolated and lonely. His only black classmate was Gwendolyn Bennett, the gifted young writer-artist who had read her poem at the Civic Club dinner.

Bennett had taught art at Howard and then studied art in Paris on a sorority scholarship after graduating from Pratt. Upon returning to the United States, she took a job as an assistant editor of *Opportunity*. She wrote a literary chit-chat and arts-news column called "Ebony Flute" and drew cover illustrations. By January of 1928, she had taken on the additional position as art critic for the *Crisis*, and it was Du Bois's magazine that announced that Douglas and Bennett had won Barnes scholarships and were enrolled in a "specialized course in picture analysis."[42] While pursuing their studies in Merion, the two never met personally with Barnes until near the end of the academic year. As Douglas recalled the conversation nearly a half century after it took place, the collector asked them to attack Locke in some kind of written statement. Had he got wind of *The New Negro* editor's attitude toward his essay? It's possible, but what Douglas remembers him saying is that Locke took material for his own essay, "The Legacy of the Ancestral Arts," from conversations with Barnes without acknowledging his debt.[43] The collector was probably referring to passages on the influence of African art on French and German modernists, and once again his highly proprietary attitude about ideas resulted in a bogus charge of plagiarism. But with what must have been considerable skill, the scholarship students were able to turn aside his suggestion, if not his anger, and go back to their course work. When they had finished, Bennett returned to Howard University and Douglas renewed his relationship with Mason. He soon began murals for the Fisk University Library in Nashville and for the Sherman Hotel in Chicago that celebrated the spiritual triumph of black people able to sing and dance in the face of myriad adversities.

Douglas called it his "Hallelujah period," and although Barnes was rarely given to shouting for joy, his response to the New Negro's call for understanding was a foursquare endorsement of the artistic endowments and cultural contributions of black people. Harlem was not for him a cheap safari. Nor did he embrace it as a vehicle of rebellion since his purchase of modern art had shock value to spare, at least in Philadelphia. He sought no alternative to Western technological civilization. Alleged black sensuality was not a myth he bought. Trendy "slumming" was not his style; he didn't attend the house-rent parties of the African-American working class or the legendary do's given by A'Lelia Walker, heiress of the Madam Walker hair-straightening fortune. Barnes allied himself with black men whom he perceived as race leaders, and his annoyance with Locke did not adversely affect his relationship with Charles Johnson. Six months after the publication of *The New Negro*, the editor of *Opportunity* devoted another issue to black art—and the contributors included, in addition to Barnes, his retinue: Buermeyer, Munro, Guillaume, Mary Mullen, who described the ongoing Agyrol factory experiment, and a new instructor, Violette de Mazia, who translated into English the French writer Blaise Cendrars's African folk tale, "The Legend of Ngurangurane."

In his editorial introducing the May 1926 issue, Johnson paid tribute to the collector and his dealer for their roles in fostering appreciation of African art in Europe and America. *Opportunity*, he said, was "fortunate in having the guidance and collaboration of the Barnes Foundation." On the subject of "Negro art," he declared yet again, "there is no greater authority."[44] The lead article by Paul Guillaume was taken from an address the picture dealer had delivered to the students enrolled in Barnes's classes when he visited the Foundation the previous month. He declared that the African statues, which twenty years earlier had been of interest only to anthropologists and antiquarians, had since then "played a role no less important for [the modern] age than was the role of classic art in inspiring the Renaissance."[45] Munro's essay, "Primitive Negro Sculpture," was excerpted from his and Guillaume's book. Laurence Buermeyer, the Lutheran pastor's son, contributed a probing, original analysis of the spiritual as the finest flower of African American religion, which "expressed the whole personality of the Negroes" as no element of "orthodox Christianity" ever "expressed the whole personality of the whites." The long delayed recognition of the importance of the spiritual "as a distinctive and authentic art form" could be attributed, Buermeyer said, to both an intellectual and moral deficiency on the part of white critics—a failure to recognize the primacy of a rich and complex rhythmic organization and pattern in black music, to which melody and harmony are secondary, and, no less significantly, to outright "race prejudice." Following Barnes, he declared the spiritual as the sole "important indigenous art" in the United States. "The only approach to it," Buermeyer said, was "the poetry of Walt Whitman, but while "Whitman's vogue was among the over civilized," the spiritual "appealed to and was enjoyed by those whose lives it celebrated." Commenting upon the contrapuntal effects, which were due in part to the African-American gift for improvisation and largely lost in the printed versions of spirituals, the Foundation's associate director of education concluded that the spiritual as sung "by the chorus of the Bordentown Manual Training and Industrial School for Negroes," a group Barnes often brought to Merion, "reveal[ed] reaches and depth of musical and human experience unexplored by the art of any other race."[46]

Barnes's contribution to the second African art issue of *Opportunity* was taken from an address he delivered to the Women's Faculty Club at Columbia

University on March 26, 1926. It built upon and extended Guillaume's, Munro's, and, especially, Buermeyer's articles. The essay's significance lay not in its political correctness, though it reflected liberal sentiments held by white supporters of the New Negro movement whom the African-American novelist Zora Neale Hurston dubbed "Negrotarians," but in its encapsulation of Barnes's remarkably comprehensive knowledge of the art of black people, past and present. It should not have been surprising that "the failing powers of European art [were] revived by the art of the Negro," he wrote, since "Ptolemaic sculpture had been enriched by the influence of Greek art," which, in turn, influenced the "best Gabon, Sudan and Ivory Coast work. . . . The place of the Negro in modern art [w]as not that of a parvenu or an intruder, but of one who belong[ed] there by natural right and artistic inheritance." Barnes went on to talk about the "natural gifts" of blacks as they had been "stifled or developed" by colonialism and slavery. Reflecting familiarity with the then recent writing on the sociology of religion by the German social scientist Max Weber, the collector suggested that African Americans initially embraced Christianity chiefly as "a means of consolation." He speculated that "what interested them . . . was its assurance to the lowly of their intrinsic importance and value and its promise to the disinherited and the outcast that a happier existence was in store for him." Barnes said "religion is always a search for harmony, for an environment which shall meet and satisfy our desires, and in which we can feel at home."[47]

It was a telling description that suggests what art was to him: a replacement for the stirring faith of his childhood. He pointed out that Methodism was among the first denominations to attract the slave because, like the Baptists, "Methodists . . . provided a highly emotional ritual . . . in which all could share . . . frequent camp meetings." He further observed that through the years, "religion remained the point about which all common activities [of black people] were focused. Even today, in the South," he said, "the church is not only a house of worship, but a place where societies and lodges meet, suppers are held, entertainments and lectures are given, charity distributed, and views exchanged. It is a community center—much as the Roman Catholic Church was in the Middle Ages. And just as the great achievements of the Middle Ages, the building of the cathedrals, was an outgrowth of community life inspired by religion, so the greatest artistic achievements of the Negroes, and, indeed, of America, were the 'spirituals' in which the sufferings, the griefs and hopes of the slaves were given an embodiment at once religious and aesthetic." Barnes again noted that "nominal emancipation" had been "by no means a real liberation." Genuine freedom, he argued, "was out of the question until economic security was established and full self-respect achieved. Of the two, the latter was probably the more important," he said, "since an intelligent, resolute effort toward material improvement is impossible in the absence of independence of mind and self-confidence." Barnes applauded the role of the

Fisk Jubilee Singers in introducing spirituals to a wider audience in the 1870s, and he called attention to Dvorak's use of some of them in his *Symphony No. 9* ("*From the New World*"). But he ascribed, quite properly, credit for appreciation of their "true importance" to the "pioneering" efforts of John and Frederick Work, the African-American brothers who collected, edited, and published black American folk music. "Recognition of his musical accomplishment" laid the foundations of the "Negro's pride in his race," Barnes claimed, and he said that pride was "powerfully fortified by the rediscovery of ancient Negro sculpture and by acknowledgment, on the part of the most important contemporary artists, of the magnitude of their debt to it." Naming the European painters, sculptors, musicians, poets, and even dress designers and decorators, who had been inspired by primitive art, and praising the work of contemporary African-American poets and novelists, Barnes predicted that when consciousness of his "spiritual stature" is "fully spread through his own race and the race of his oppressors, the Negro will be assured of the high place he deserves" in the life of the nation.[48]

For awhile, the collector thought Jessie Fauset's cousin, Arthur Huff Fauset, might be just the young black man to undertake a pioneering study of African art at the Barnes Foundation.[49] But Fauset, a Central graduate who went on to earn a Ph.D. from the University of Pennsylvania, had more interest in social science and religion than in art, and the Philadelphia schoolteacher became a pioneering African-American anthropologist instead. Barnes then considered repeating some variant of the Polish field investigation in the black community. Buermeyer announced in the *Nation* that a study was underway of the living conditions of African Americans, the manner in which their interests and activities were molded by their environment, and the means by which the latter could be made "more free, more intelligent, more humane."[50] But evidently this iteration involved no Columbia post-docs, and little headway was made with the project. Under the direction of a sociologist of Charles Johnson's distinction, the research might have produced data with the potential to affect the nascent public policy debate over civil rights. When the Carnegie Corporation failed to renew its support for *Opportunity* in 1927, however, Johnson began negotiations with the president of Fisk University for a faculty position he would take up in the fall of 1928.

About the same time, Barnes quarreled with Lower Merion Township Commissioners over a change in zoning regulations that would permit a local contractor to erect what he called a "row of small houses" on Old Lancaster Road, a short distance from the Foundation. As a ploy, but with the faintest undertone of real intention, he publicly announced contingency plans to move his collection to New York and establish, in its place, "a world center for the education and artistic development of the colored races." He told the press that "if the people decide to let politicians make a city block out of my side yard," his pictures and classes in art appreciation would be transferred to the Metropolitan

Museum of Art. Barnes said that under the guidance of the Urban League, he would create a "center for development, by scientific educational methods, of the rare artistic and mental endowments of the Negro." Observing that Leopold Stokowski had taken a leave from his post as director of the Philadelphia Orchestra, he declared that "no creative and far-seeing movement [wa]s permitted to thrive in Philadelphia."[51] Was the boy boxer, at a vigorous fifty-five, stepping out of the ring?

While Barnes might regret the conservative tastes of his fellow citizens, their hostility toward modern art and music was more stimulant than depressant. There is little evidence, moreover, that he entertained for long the possibility of substituting a program primarily concerned with educating African-American students from Southern colleges for a program of art appreciation for local students and teachers. Barnes believed that the Lower Merion Commissioners' amendment of long-standing zoning regulations threatened to decrease the value of his suburban property. Enraged, he showed that he was not above capitalizing on racial prejudice for his own ends since he could predict the reaction—though not, happily the uniform reaction—of his neighbors to the possibility of a black education center in their midst.[52] At the same time, Barnes did not view his pipe dream as pure retaliation.

As early as 1924, he had talked with Alain Locke, Charles Johnson, and others about his interest in improving educational opportunities for African Americans. Under the name of Paul Hogans, one of the black employees in his Argyrol factory, he published *A New Plan for Negro Education* that he said leaders of the Harlem Renaissance had endorsed at a meeting in Philadelphia. The document was notable for its emphasis on different styles of learning, as well as for putting the implementation of the ideas it sketched "exclusively" in black hands. There can be little doubt that Barnes believed with all his heart that an extension of the pedagogy he had applied in his factory school would lead increasing numbers of African Americans "to share . . . in the higher intellectual and artistic activities of [the] nation."[53] He had once taken the stage of Philadelphia's segregated Dunbar Theater to enjoin a crowd of black youth to finish high school and go on to college—a speech that moved one observer to report to a friend, "Dr. Barnes has a passion for our cause."[54] But by 1927, the collector had lived in Merion for twenty-two years. There was little chance that he would move and even less chance that he would separate himself from his treasures. Certainly, many residents of the township had developed a sixth sense for what one Latch's Lane neighbor characterized as his penchant for "idle threat."[55]

For several weeks, Barnes honed what was becoming his classic rhetorical response to any situation he perceived as frustrating his ends—charges of misuse of political power along with promises of investigation of corruption and evaluation of the results by disinterested persons. But, in the end, the bulldozers arrived and ground was broken for the houses. Long before they were sold for the then none too shabby price of $17,000 to $25,000 each, the self-proclaimed representative of the people had a ten-foot-high iron fence built around his Foundation. The Cret buildings continued to house only his collection, but Barnes did not abandon his interest in African-American life and culture. In March of 1928, the month Johnson formally committed himself to joining the Fisk faculty, the collector turned to the new medium, radio, to educate a far-flung audience about the influence on Western civilization of primitive sculpture. The address he made over WABC Radio in New York was published two months later in *Opportunity*. The lead article in the May issue of the magazine implored enlightened investors to buy up dilapidated houses in West Philadelphia and convert them into "homes of comfort and respectability" for "all unfortunate peoples who . . . inhabit . . . 'slum' districts," but that was not a challenge of interest to Barnes.[56] He saw his role as an apostle to people of both races who were unaware of "the great art achievements of the Negro." He would tell it on the mountain, and with the good news "generally diffused,"[57] there would be every reason to expect whites to accord blacks the respect they merited and blacks to seize the future sketched by Langston Hughes:

> . . . Bright before us
> Like a flame. . . .
> Broad arch above the road we came. . . .[58]

9

Muse, *Models*, Museum

Barnes's own future would be intimately, but always somewhat inscrutably, intertwined with the translator of the African folktale that had appeared in the May 1926 issue of *Opportunity*. Violette de Mazia probably entered the collector's life several years before she was publicly identified with the Foundation in the magazine's note on contributors. Her given name was a present to herself because she liked the flower violet. Originally she had been Yetta.[1] Her father, Jules Sonny de Mazia, was a Russian Jew. The French government granted him the honorific "de" for commercial services to the republic in 1887-88. His family name may have been Portuguese. Jules was trained as an engineer and had interests in cigar manufacturing as well as the arts. He married a French woman, Fanny Frenkel. Their daughter was born in Paris on August 30, 1899, five years after her only sibling, Georges. Surviving photographs of the de Mazias taken in the first decade of the last century show a handsome, well-dressed family; in one of them the children are on holiday with their parents at the Black Forest spa of Baden-Baden. For some years they lived in Belgium. In her Brussels secondary school, Yetta excelled in mathematics. She also was a gymnast, a competitive swimmer, and an aspiring actress. When the family moved to London about the time of the First World War, she studied at St. John's Wood Priory House School and the Camden School of Art. As a French citizen, she could have returned to France after the Armistice, and it is not clear whether she met Barnes in Paris, London, or elsewhere. Or even precisely when.

The collector undoubtedly provided the editors of *Opportunity* with the affiliation information about the Foundation contributors, and he must have been anticipating her employment as an "instructor." De Mazia had visited the United States in 1925, but it was not until September 1926, four months after the publication of the African arts issue of the Urban League journal, that she arrived on the *SS Carmania* seeking permanent residence. The ship's manifest of alien passengers indicates that her destination was the North Broad Street home of her cousin, Samuel Bayuk, a cigar manufacturer who was part of

151

Philadelphia's Russian Jewish community. The twenty-seven-year-old immigrant was soon employed as a French teacher at Miss Sayward's School for Girls, a few blocks from Barnes's former home on Drexel Road in Overbrook, and also gave French lessons to the Mullen sisters. But according to the collector's preface to the first trade edition of *The Art in Painting*, written in January 1926, de Mazia, along with Laurence Buermeyer, had provided "fine services in bringing into orderly arrangement [his] scattered notes relating to paintings in the galleries of Europe." Had he employed her abroad and arranged for her passage from Southampton so she could join him in Philadelphia? Or had she become acquainted with Barnes on her earlier visit and then returned to England to tell her parents of her intention to settle in the United States and seek citizenship? Years later, de Mazia indicated in her *Who's Who* entry that she had arrived in 1927, but that was not the case.

The nativism, permeated with anti-Semitism, that was rife in America in the twenties, as well as Barnes's marital status, may have been an element in the seemingly contrived confusion surrounding the timing and circumstances of the initial association between de Mazia and her employer. Fear of communism and labor violence, which swept the country during the Red Scare of 1919 and 1920, combined with reports that millions of war-weary Europeans were clamoring for transportation to America, produced a law, the Johnson-Reed Act of 1924, drastically restricting immigration. At the same time, Henry Ford's *Dearborn Independent* ran an infamous series of articles, amounting to a defamation campaign, about a cabal of Jewish bankers conspiring to rule the world. In what has been called the Anglo-Saxon Decade, prejudice became culturally institutionalized in exclusive colleges, suburbs, and clubs.[2] Barnes, of course, had nothing but contempt for the old stock upper class, which led and supported the postwar surge of nativism, and it is entirely credible, therefore, that he would have gone to considerable lengths, and thoroughly enjoyed the game, of slipping de Mazia into Philadelphia under their stuffy noses. He counted among his friends such established German Jews as the rare book dealer A. S. Rosenbach and Eastern European Jews like the artist Arthur Carles whose sister he employed as a teacher. He had facilitated, if not promoted, Dewey's romance with Yezierska. But a break, and one of the few imaginable, upon any blatant affair with de Mazia was the collector's quarter-century marriage to a woman whose family money had enabled him to launch his immensely lucrative Argyrol business.

Barnes had previously mentioned another woman in his life in letters to Dewey. During the autumn of 1920, he described a "Mrs. Skemp," an unpublished poet and occasional art student, whom he had met on Cape Cod several years earlier. She was "a marvelous person," he said, "with a mind that t[ook] in with one reading all the Santayana aesthetics [he had] put in her hands." But more than a "fine intelligence," she was "a stunning woman physically. Helen of Troy and Venus were cross-eyed cronies compared to her," he exuded. "Old

Jonathan Edwards or Timothy Dwight would have foresworn monogamy if she had been in their presence very much," Barnes said. He promised to introduce his philosopher friend, but warned him: "Don't make her cry because that's my job and I do it every time she comes to see me. I've had Leo Stein, Glackens and Prendergast meet her and she put them all up on their toes. Leo fell hard for her, but she chucked him and came back to me after she got his number and told it to him in a very penetrating insight expressed exquisitely. It came just on top of one of my rows with him, and I was tickled at his ruffled comb."[3] Philadelphians who loved to gossip about Barnes, even in the early days, whispered about what one Penn alumnus, disgruntled at the apparent alliance between his alma mater and the collector, called "Barnes's flagrancies."[4] The collector may have associated extramarital dalliance with modernism. Carl E. Schorske has noted that "the pioneers of this change explicitly challenged the validity of traditional morality" even as they assailed traditional art.[5] But more than likely, he did not need to intellectualize any assignations. Though Barnes was generally a man of his word, vows, and much else, would always be weighed against the primacy of personal psychological experience.

Even in the raucous 1920s, the psychological and the material forces militating against emigration of a single woman from Europe to the United States were considerable. De Mazia must have had strong hopes, if not promises, that her new life in a new country would provide opportunities for intellectual, financial, or emotional rewards far greater than those to which she could aspire in England or France. But she also may have been escaping the sadness of losing a fiancé in World War I. Or did she leave him to join Barnes in America? A photograph of a handsome young man in a Royal Air Force uniform found in her personal effects seems to be dated after the Armistice. Whatever the various magnets and propellants, de Mazia arrived in Philadelphia as a young woman with a fine command of English, research skills, and a graceful writing style. She was soon enrolled in Tom Munro's Barnes Foundation course in modern art. It would be his last year in Merion, and in responding to a letter from Dewey advising him to find a strong replacement, the collector wrote: "You're right about our need for a good man to take charge. Society demands that it be male and not a female—otherwise, we have at least two people that could handle it. Until we get such a man, I'll do the best I can with my own powers."[6] Mary Mullen was, of course, one of the women to whom Barnes was referring; the other could have been Sara Carles, but was more likely de Mazia.

De Mazia studied directly with Barnes after Munro's departure, and the collector officially appointed her an instructor in the fall of 1927, according to court testimony she gave several years later.[7] The scholarly inclinations of the new teacher, almost certainly encouraged by her mentor, are reflected in an article she wrote on the continuity of traditions in paintings for *Les Arts à Paris*. Published in the October 1927 issue, it reveals a thorough grasp of the Barnesian approach. "An intelligent appreciation and a just understanding of

Titian or Michelangelo," she wrote, "are not restricted to these artists' work but expands into and is enriched by the recognition of their forms as they are modified by men like Renoir and Cézanne on the one hand, and as they were originated in Bellini, Masaccio or Leonardo on the other. 'Enjoying' or 'liking' either the moderns or the old masters without the ability to see them as they stand in the scale of values, in relation to followers and predecessors, is to practice self-deception," she continued. "The comparative-study method questions old and modern masters according to the same criterion of plastic form and directs our judgment toward the thread that links them together."[8] The article, which went on to sketch how Utrillo, Modigliani, de Chirico, and Soutine, in particular, made use of the early Florentine and Venetian traditions, was anthologized in Barnes's 1929 collection of previously published essays entitled *Art and Education*. Barnes sent a copy inscribed "with compliments of Albert C. Barnes" to de Mazia's mother. Fanny de Mazia reciprocated with a book of French poetry.

At about the same time the immigrant teacher made her literary debut as an essayist, she and Barnes began working together on a book that would be published by the Foundation in 1931 as *The French Primitives and Their Forms: From Their Origin to the End of the Fifteenth Century*. Their research involved six trips to Europe over the course of three years with an entourage of three or four other colleagues, including the Mullens and Laura Geiger, an Argyrol plant employee whom Barnes made a teacher. When he wasn't incapacitated by drink or depression, Buermeyer joined them. The group would take over a suite of hotel rooms as offices and spend their days at museums and churches where Barnes would dictate his reaction to frescoes and paintings on panels, glass, and parchment. When one "stenographer falls over, we get another one," he later explained in an attempt to convey the intensity of their efforts. Gathering material for a book was for Barnes "like science." Data must be correlated, analyzed, impressions tested and retested. *French Primitives and Their Forms* was "not," he said, lest anyone doubt it, "something you can write out of your head."[9]

The collector and de Mazia pursued their investigation from Amiens in the north to Avignon in the south, from St. Savin near the Atlantic Coast to Sospel on the Italian border. To show the influence of other traditions, they hunted down fifteenth-century art in Germany, Belgium, Holland, and Italy. Their research, conducted mainly in the summer, took them to Barcelona and Madrid, to Basel, Vienna, and Prague, to London and Glasgow, as well as New York and Chicago. It is little wonder that Laura Barnes, middle aged and childless, deeply resented de Mazia's role. After World War I, she had initially accompanied her husband on many of his buying expeditions to Europe. Now, if she went along on foreign journeys, she would be left to explore gardens and arboreta on her own while Barnes and his research team stalked art. Her sense of loss and injury never abated during the collector's life; her attitude toward de Mazia hardened over the years into a hatred that she did not attempt to hide from her friends. One of them described it as a "blight," which, had she detected it on her beloved plants and shrubs, she would have gone to any length to eradicate, because she knew the insidious damage that could be done.[10]

Unaware or heedless of his wife's pain, or perhaps emotionally unable to provide the obvious remedy, sacking his young assistant, Barnes, instead, gave de Mazia increasing responsibility. He had promoted Geiger from factory to classroom in the fall of 1928 and hired another instructor, Herbert Jennings, but neither they, Nelle Mullen, nor even Mary Mullen ever had the same sustained intellectual engagement with their employer that the immigrant teacher had come to enjoy rather quickly and would maintain for several decades—indeed, in terms of an unwavering commitment to the collector's educational principles, until her own death some sixty years later. In addition to her class in Aesthetic Appreciation, de Mazia had a hand in designing the Foundation curriculum. She shared an interest in music with Barnes (there had been a piano and a reed organ in her parents' home), and it was perhaps she who encouraged him to offer a course on the relation between music and art. They appeared nearly inseparable, and in 1931, as the published co-author of *The French Primitives and Their Forms*, de Mazia filed a declaration of her intention to apply for American citizenship.

The photograph attached to the declaration form shows a young woman with fine, straight hair, parted on the left and styled in a short pageboy. A penciled note on the top of the document tells us that it is light brown and that the applicant's eyes, set far apart and always hidden in later years by tinted glasses, are gray-blue. Her nose is long; her thin lips are not quite smiling. She gives her height as five feet, five inches, her weight as one hundred thirty-two pounds, her nationality as French, her race, in an era when race was defined by ethnicity, as "Russian." The young instructor lists her address as 5711 Thomas Avenue, the three-story twin house where the Mullen sisters lived in West Philadelphia. By 1933 when she files a petition for citizenship, de Mazia is residing in an elegant apartment complex with an indoor swimming pool a few blocks from the Penn campus. Nelle and Mary serve as witnesses, and in May 1934 the petition is granted. The new citizen is made a trustee of the Barnes Foundation a year later. By then she and her employer have written books on the art of Matisse and of Renoir, and before the end of the decade, they will bring out their fourth collaborative volume, a study of *The Art of Cézanne*. Literary collaboration requires an extraordinary intimacy. Whether or not they were lovers, and some of the people closest to de Mazia assume they were, Barnes and his young assistant were soul mates.

The only individual work of art that de Mazia cited in her 1927 debut essay for *Les Arts à Paris* was Seurat's *Models*. Barnes had acquired the monumental painting, an interior showing three nude or partially nude female figures, the year before while it was on exhibit in London. The artist, who invented the divisionist technique known as pointillism, had an interest in psychology that rivaled the collector's own. Heavily influenced by Ogden Rood's *Modern Chromatics*, he set out to evoke the colors of the natural world in the eye of the viewer by manipulating the effects of thousands of juxtaposed, very minute dabs of pigment.[11] Seurat had produced a painterly statement about the modern world of atoms where continuity was an illusion and discontinuity a newly discovered, fundamental law of physics. Working feverishly, it took him at least the whole year of 1887 to complete *Models.* When van Gogh saw the painting in 1888, he hailed his fellow artist as "the master of the *Petit-Boulevard* [the avant-garde]."[12] But *Models* did not sell when first exhibited in Brussels in 1889, and it passed through several hands during the next quarter century. When Roger Fry saw it in the London show, he called it "a wonderfully strange and original composition."[13] Barnes's purchase of the masterwork through the Paris dealer L. C. Hodebert was a coup. His rival, John Quinn, had bought the artist's *Circus* four years earlier, and when Quinn died of cancer in 1924, *Circus* was the only picture he specified should be given to a museum, the Louvre.

Barnes added a Renoir's *The Promenade* to his collection the same year he bought *Models.*[14] In February 1927, he bought another of the painter's works, *The Artist's Family*, which he had first tried to buy twelve years earlier.[15] Toward the end of 1927, however, it was a small book, Leo Stein's long-awaited *The A. B. C. of Aesthetics,* that riveted the collector's attention more than any picture. Writing it had taken all the energy and concentration and courage Leo could summon given his abiding fear that when the book was done, people "would say, surprised like: Is that all?"[16] In fact, their reaction was as much puzzlement as disappointment. In the *Dial*, Dewey's Columbia colleague Horace Kallen declared that "on the whole," Stein's "meaning seems obscure," and commentators in other journals, even when charmed, grappled with what Mortimer Adler called "an almost profound . . . unintelligibility."[17] Barnes, still simmering over Leo's review of the first edition of *The Art in Painting*, told Dewey he found the work "amusing as a biography of the self I saw first in its split-up state" and was purportedly then confronting as a more conscientiously integrated persona. "I saw not a single idea in it on aesthetics that I can't point to in books I read years ago," the collector declared. "It is a record of all his iconoclastic demolitions of everything everybody else has said in philosophy, thinking, education and art."[18]

Stein had cited, in particular, a recent essay Dewey had published in the *Journal of the Barnes Foundation*. He found it an exaggerated and undocumented claim for the psychological and even physiological effects of a viewer's intelligent response to pictures.[19] In calling the criticism to the philosopher's notice, Barnes ridiculed the author as an ineffectual carper. "You better commit suicide," he told Dewey, "but if you decide not to and choose to furnish the evidence he asks for . . . I can give it to you in pretty nearly legal form." Barnes allowed that what Leo had to say "on pictorial qualities is really good because he has experience in that line." But he summed up the slender volume as "valuable chiefly as a record of . . . the compensatory pains of a misspent life."[20] Dewey interpreted Stein's reference to him as a payback for his favorable review of *The Art in Painting* in the *New Republic*, which answered Leo's criticisms of the work in the same journal. When the philosopher's essay had appeared, Leo had told Dewey that the collector's tome was "to him, and to every real connoisseur, simply a cause of laughter."[21] But even Barnes, happily preoccupied with his new research and his new assistant, could not keep the fight going at full throttle for much longer, and he concluded, rather mildly for him, that Leo "is . . . sore that I wrote a book on an objective approach that he should have written if he had the ability."[22]

It wasn't, of course, that the collector was foreswearing slugfests. But, on the whole and with several notable exceptions, he derived more satisfaction from taking on institutions than individuals. There were none he engaged with greater relish than the Pennsylvania (now Philadelphia) Museum of Art. Since 1919, Barnes had been watching the Greek temple, which would be its new home, arise slowly and at public expense on the acropolis overlooking what is now Benjamin Franklin Parkway. By the fall of 1927, artisans were adding ornamental details in multicolored terra cotta high above the ground—in the capitals, just below the roofline, and in the eaves themselves. The neoclassical revival building was a tribute to the civic leadership of lawyer Eli K. Price, vice president of the Fairmount Park Commission, whose persistence over many years was almost singularly responsible for the opening of the museum in March of 1928. The vision realized in tawny limestone was originally that of Peter A. B. Widener, the streetcar magnate and art collector who had begun life, like Barnes's father, as a butcher. Twenty-one years earlier, Widener had made the mayor of Philadelphia an irresistible offer. He said that if the city would provide a site on the flat top of a hill at the edge of Fairmount Park, where a reservoir had recently been closed, and realign a planned boulevard radiating northwest from city hall on the Fairmount axis, he would pay for a museum building and fill it with his pictures.

Widener's enthusiasm for the project went even further back—to 1893 when a collection of rather unexceptional paintings assembled by W. P. Wilstach, a local leather manufacturer, became, by terms of Wilstach's bequest, the property of the city, along with a generous $500,000 endowment for further acquisitions. They joined a hodgepodge of holdings, pictures, plaster casts, and examples of the decorative arts, in Memorial Hall, the cavernous iron-and-glass dome built to house the fine arts exhibit of the Centennial Exhibition of 1876. The world's fair gave birth to the Pennsylvania Museum, essentially as a repository for study materials of its allied school of industrial and applied art. But in 1915, before any ground was broken for a more appropriate structure, Widener died and his promise was buried with him. The collector John G.

Johnson, who survived Widener by two years, did leave his paintings to the city, together with his house on his South Broad Street house, where he directed that they remain. When construction of the parkway building began, the only bequest the museum had in hand was that of George W. Elkins, son-in-law of P. A. B. Widener, and those of his father, William L. Elkins, Widener's business partner. The small but notable collection of British art was joined in 1921 by more fine English paintings from the estate of John Howard McFadden. When Price and his fellow museum board members hired Fiske Kimball as the new director of the Pennsylvania Museum in 1925, they instructed him to seek out other potential donors. John D. McIlhenny, whom Price would soon succeed as president of the Pennsylvania Museum, told Kimball bluntly: "I want you particularly to make friends with influential people in Philadelphia. We will have to have money, and I want you to get in touch with those who have money to give, as well as objects of art to bequeath."[23]

Even before Kimball came on board, the acting director of the museum, Samuel W. Woodhouse, Jr., had made an overture to Albert Barnes. In the spring of 1925, when he learned that the collector had visited the Memorial Hall gallery with a group of students, Woodhouse sent him a gracious note expressing his pleasure that Barnes had found the museum's collections "useful to [his] educational purposes" and offering to provide any assistance that might be helpful on a return visit.[24] Although Woodhouse, like Barnes, was a physician by training, the acting director's antiquarian focus was far a field from the collector's; it was the brilliant and flamboyant Kimball with whom he shared intellectual interests that might have been a basis for friendship. After graduating from the architectural school at Harvard, Kimball had taught at the University of Illinois, earned a Ph.D. in art history at the University of Michigan, and then gone on to the University of Virginia as founding chair of the new architectural school in Charlottesville. As the university's supervising architect, he designed the faculty apartments, a theater, and a gymnasium. His scholarly reputation was secured with the publication of several important architectural histories, and he was named chairman of the restoration committee for Thomas Jefferson's Monticello in 1923, just before he was appointed the first head of the fine arts program that New York University was establishing in collaboration with the Metropolitan Museum.

It took John McIlhenny and Eli Price more than a year to lure Kimball to Philadelphia. The new director of the Pennsylvania Museum received a polite letter from Barnes soon after he took office. The collector was interested in opening the Foundation's classes to students in the museum's art school, and even before he wrote to Kimball, he had sent Sara Carles to talk with him about expanding the art appreciation class she had conducted in Merion for Pennsylvania Academy of the Fine Arts students the previous spring. Barnes's letter mentioned that Carles had told him that the new director would like to see his pictures, and the collector extended a cordial invitation to come as early as the next Sunday. Although Kimball was not free to accept Barnes's offer right away, he invited the collector to call on him in Memorial Hall. Mindful of his fund-raising mandate and genuinely enthusiastic about modern painters, especially Cézanne, Kimball was eager to cultivate Barnes as a potential donor. The collector sought acceptance of his ideas about art education. When they met in early October of 1925, the two men must have carefully appraised one another through their rimless glasses.

Kimball remembered that Barnes acknowledged his "reputation as a wild man" right off the bat and complained, somewhat plaintively, that no one would listen to him.[25] Within a few days, moreover, Kimball received a letter from Barnes suggesting that Tom Munro offer one of the museum's series of public lectures and observing that "his personality has none of the sharp edges which have cut into the art luminaries of this city as mine have done, so he would be able to give the good of the Foundation minus the bad."[26] Kimball replied that while the lectures up to Christmas had been arranged before his arrival, he hoped to fit Munro into the spring schedule and would be happy to talk over the matter with him. The director, only thirty-seven himself, received the younger scholar courteously, but stressed the difficulties of altering preemptively a preexisting program. Although in the end Kimball was not able or willing to secure a lecture slot for Munro, Barnes did not withdraw a verbal invitation he had given to the museum director to visit the Foundation once he had won over his trustees and was ready to discuss his plans for the future. A few months later, in the spring of 1926, Kimball again received, and was this time able to accept, a formal invitation to come to Merion on yet another Sunday afternoon to hear Barnes talk about his pictures. The audience also included Munro's class of Penn students, and the collector's lecture was followed by appreciative comments from Edgar Singer and Louis Flaccus, the university philosophy professors who were then still in Barnes's good graces. The host's precisely measured cocktails and an opportunity for guests to wander at leisure through the gallery followed a round of spirituals sung by the collector's African-American employees. Kimball was awed by the collection and looked forward to more such visits.

Given what he perceived to be an increasingly cordial relationship with the collector, he subsequently telephoned the Foundation seeking admittance to the gallery for visiting friends and professional colleagues. Despite his growing distaste for the casual museum visitor and his disdain for experts, Barnes initially gave his permission. But finally on October 27, 1926, he dictated a letter, much like one he had sent almost exactly two years earlier to Warren Laird, which made his position crystal clear. Barnes told Kimball:

> Repeated applications, similar to that which you made this morning, seem to indicate that you share a very prevalent idea that the Foundation is a place for more or less conspicuous Philadelphians to entertain their friends. When you assumed your present

position more than a year ago, I told you that the Foundation would cooperate with you as an official in any move that could be intelligently interpreted as educational. Also, one of our staff called on you with a plan to help those students of painting at the Institution of which you are head, by a systematic course of study in our gallery. Not a thing intelligent came of these proposals; what did happen was a series of requests to have your friends and acquaintances use the Foundation as a diversion. . . . It would make you or your Institution a passport to the Foundation—which is about the limit in exploitative absurdity.

The Foundation has a charter as an educational institution and it intends to live up to its stated purposes. It provides for all classes of people who show sufficient interest to enroll in and attend . . . classes organized for systematic study. If you have any persons that meet that description, we can take care of them. But for casual visitors . . . . there is absolutely nothing doing. I am writing you frankly so that we shall be spared the nuisance of further "phone calls, pleadings and arguments."[27]

Kimball replied at once with a note that was more defensive, even arrogant, than it was contrite. He protested that he had "taken pains never to pass on anyone . . . unless they [had] a properly sympathetic attitude with the Barnes Foundation and with modern art. I am delighted to be rid of the nuisance of people trying to involve me when they ought to apply directly to you," he wrote. He added that he was sorry Barnes hadn't told him sooner of his annoyance. "Rather than have that, and especially rather than injure our . . . friendly relation, all those people can go to the dickens," the director said. "I do want to give effective cooperation," he concluded. "Why can't you and I talk about it sometime at your convenience?"[28]

Barnes didn't answer. He was preoccupied with a deeper disappointment than the presumptive behavior of the museum's new director—the rapid unraveling of his alliance with the University of Pennsylvania and, given his increasingly closer ties to Violette de Mazia, greater solace than might be his through an arms-length relationship with an institution he considered a local cultural upstart. But the new home of the Pennsylvania Museum was surely going to be grand, and Kimball's stated goal was to make it an institution "of which any city, any nation, might be proud—a source of delight and inner enrichment to every citizen."[29] His immediate problem was that, as the building's chief architect Charles Boire observed, "the City owned damned little art!"[30] With the long-delayed opening planned for March 26, 1928, Kimball not only had to oversee the completion of the first phase of construction but somehow borrow enough art to fill the museum's sixteen finished galleries. Although he had not spoken with Barnes for several months, he sent him a letter in December of 1926 requesting an appointment to discuss the possibility of a loan for the opening exhibition.

His timing couldn't have been worse. The collector had just suspended Penn from further participation in Foundation classes. He was getting ready to sail to Europe and coming down with a viral infection that would delay his journey. Nelle Mullen wrote to Kimball that he should send her a written statement of the essentials of his proposition. The director replied that he had permission from the museum trustees to exhibit modern paintings along with the art of other periods and he wanted "to give these modern masters the very finest representation possible. We could easily secure loans of certain fine pictures elsewhere," he boasted, "but I should prefer to recognize here the commanding position of the Barnes Collection in this field." The director then suggested that the loan he sought might be just "the first step in a cooperation which could go much further when the museum had "additional gallery space and the floor specifically devoted to active education work [wa]s finished and put into operation." Barnes's response through Mullen was that the proposition "would make a horse laugh." It "would be offensive to the intelligence," he said, were it not "so provincial and embedded in the matrix of the stereotyped blah which comes . . . from performers who would like to annex us as a sideshow to their circuses."[31]

The dedication of the museum's new building proceeded, of course, without Barnes or his pictures. Kimball borrowed seventy Renaissance paintings from the Johnson Collection and Impressionist and early modern works from the Carroll Tysons and other collectors. Six hundred prospective donors roamed the galleries during a glittering evening party in early March. By the end of the second day after the official opening, nearly 10,000 visitors had looked at the art and ten innovative period rooms created by the director to display British and American furniture. In Merion, a ten-minute drive from the Fairmount temple, small classes of students studied Barnes's treasury of modern masterpieces. The crusty collector had refused to lend any artwork to Fiske Kimball because he was convinced the Foundation teachers couldn't do without any one of his pictures. The newly created Museum of Modern Art had no better luck than the Pennsylvania Museum when it sought loans for its 1929 opening. But Henri Marceau, the young curator of fine arts at the Pennsylvania Museum, was intrepid.

Marceau also served as curator of the Johnson Collection, and in that capacity, he arranged for Barnes and de Mazia to study at their leisure the fine primitives assembled by the late lawyer-collector. In appreciation of the opportunity, which undoubtedly facilitated their book project, Barnes invited Marceau and his wife to Merion on two occasions. Hopeful that a request to borrow just two paintings might be viewed favorably, the curator sent Barnes a letter asking him to loan the museum El Greco's *Annunciation* and *Vision of St. Hyacinth* for an exhibition of the Spanish painter's work. It would be only for a month, Marceau said, and he would personally oversee the hanging. Barnes retorted that the museum obviously didn't get it. His insulting response began: "You ask me to deprive an educational project, which is in daily operation, of pictures, which are indispensable to that plan, in order to further what would be essentially a grotesque parody on art and education." The collector went on to characterize the proposed exhibition as an event "to entertain an uninformed public and continue to discredit the intelligence of Philadelphia by the pretentious parade of 'society' people and *fonctionnaires*." He criticized an article Marceau had written on El Greco, claiming he had eulogized two pictures known to be fakes. It provided "psychological proof" of his lack of experience, Barnes said. Then having made his customary bow to Freud, the collector concluded with a predictable challenge: "If what I have written seems incorrect, the authorities of your museum may publish their objections, and members of our staff will publish analyses of your pictures as well as your objections."[32] No one bothered.

The collector's bristle was by now well known. In 1928, Barnes was profiled in a sophisticated new magazine, founded just three years earlier, which had quickly caught the fancy of highbrow readers across the country. The *New Yorker* entitled the article by A. H. Shaw "De Medici in Merion." The author described Barnes as an "eccentric, forceful Philadelphia physician" who had "made himself one of the most feared and important figures in the art world." He was "ostentatiously aggressive," Shaw wrote, and he had assembled "the finest collection of modern paintings in the world with the one possible exception of a rich museum in Moscow." The reference was to the pictures acquired by the fabled Russian collectors Sergey Shchukin and Ivan Morozov. Shaw quoted poet Ezra Pound as saying *The Art in Painting* was "the most intelligent book on painting that has ever appeared in America." His article was the source of the oft-repeated story that Barnes once donned "overalls and moved among the visitors at his gallery in the guise of a workman" in order to hear their opinions of his paintings. It also took note of the departure of Buermeyer and Munro and the discontinuation of the university-level courses that had linked the Foundation to Penn and Columbia. "The lectures are now given by Dr. Barnes or by his two lady assistants," Shaw wrote. "The audience usually consists of his employees and a few of their friends who report at the Foundation in the late afternoon after work or on Sunday mornings."[33] The picture of decline painted by the magazine was gloomier than warranted by the facts. There were four teachers and from fifty to seventy-five students taking Foundation classes. But few of the latter were simultaneously enrolled in colleges and universities, and Barnes's attitude toward the Philadelphia-area educational establishment was largely responsible for frustrating his own programmatic objectives.

No school would have seemed a more likely source of students than nearby Bryn Mawr College. A leader in women's education since its founding in 1880, Bryn Mawr began offering history of art courses in 1893 and twenty years later established an art history department under the direction of Georgiana Goddard King, a friend of Leo Stein's and a widely respected specialist in medieval Spanish art. By the early 1920s, Dr. King and another faculty member offered a dozen undergraduate and graduate courses, including one on modern painting. While courses were illustrated with lantern slides and photographs were available for review, students were expected to make trips to Philadelphia and, according to the 1924 catalogue, "the neighborhood to study pictures." But a letter Barnes wrote to a Bryn Mawr faculty member seeking admission to the Foundation in 1929 hints at the difficulty young women encountered who attempted to study the paintings in Merion. The collector's disdain for the elite college, which was located just five miles from the Foundation, had its roots in President Carey Thomas's refusal to allow Bertrand Russell to lecture there in 1921. The philosopher, whom Barnes much admired, had caused a scandal in Britain when after a series of lovers, he lived openly in an adulterous relationship with the woman who carried his child and would become his second wife. But what the collector is not likely to have known is that the animosity harbored by Thomas, a cousin of Russell's first wife, stemmed from the newly married Russell's first visit to Bryn Mawr in 1896 when he flirted conspicuously with the president's younger sister while Alys Smith Russell, a Bryn Mawr graduate, endorsed free love. Barnes told Dewey that Thomas vetoed Russell's appearance on campus "because of his matrimonial mix-up." But "I've got in several good licks for him," the collector assured his friend. "Their art department can't get their classes into my house—so I tell them when they ask permission—until Thomas apologizes to Russell and sends him a special invitation to lecture. Also, I tell their workers when they hunt me up on various causes, that Bryn Mawr is a scholastic mummy that should be prohibited by law from existing above the surface of the earth."[34]

The collector's sardonic language would become acrimonious and vulgar. In early 1924, shortly after Marion Edwards Park succeeded Carey Thomas as president, she asked Barnes to list Bryn Mawr as a participant in the proposed Foundation classes. In support of her request, Park apparently cited the prestige of the college, and when Barnes demanded evidence that Bryn Mawr "courses in art showed that their students had had preliminary training according to . . . principles" the collector considered the essence of "modern educational science," she was angered by his effrontery.[35] According to Barnes, Park responded to a letter of refusal from Nelle Mullen that cited the students' lack of the requisite preparation with an indignant note that asked if she might herself qualify for the Foundation's first-year class.[36] As Barnes explained to the hapless Bryn Mawr faculty member who wrote to him in 1929, "your president, instead of arranging her educational wardrobe to suit an obvious social need, flaunted the silk gown of unanalyzed prestige as the mark of educational rightness. The ensuing correspondence lifted that garment and exposed her soiled and worn out intellectual panties."[37]

Defending his action in denying admission to Bryn Mawr students to Dewey a year after the incident, Barnes said of the college, "they deserve all they get. . . . I acted fairly, justly, in not letting them annex our baby with their tottering, moribund [sic] old lady."[38] Oddly, he had become convinced that Bryn Mawr was spreading the word about his refusal to allow its students to visit his collection, and he was so incensed that he had Mary Mullen mention the college disparagingly in an article she had prepared for the *Journal of the Barnes Foundation* about the problems the Foundation encountered in trying to educate students who had "dabbled in art in college courses."[39] But since an essay by Dewey was to appear in the same issue, he sent the philosopher a copy of Mullen's article with the request that Dewey tell him if he would prefer to have his piece run in a later issue. "I don't think you like to knock just for the sake of knocking," Dewey responded. "I think you have a sensitive constitution and on that account the relative importance of things sometimes get temporarily out of focus—tho not with pictures. So my own judgment is that you are making too much of the Bryn Mawr matter; supposing they have the disposition you attribute to them I can't see how the article remedies the situation. On the contrary they will point to the article as additional evidence that you have it in for them." The philosopher went on to mention that when President Park had lived in Colorado some years earlier, she had cared for his daughter Evelyn who had been sent to the mountains for her health. "I think that if you met her without knowing who she was and independent of this controversy, you would find her a sensible, straightforward woman free from pretence," he said.[40]

The letter had the effect Dewey intended, as Barnes wrote him at once: "I 'see' the rightness of your argument; hence, all reference to Bryn Mawr has disappeared from the article. If Miss Park did what you relate for you and yours, I'm her friend, even though she embarrasses us mightily by rumor that reverberates to us from as far west as California." He added that he had heard that Bryn Mawr students used his book "unofficially."[41] Dewey was grateful for the collector's editorial decision. "I hated to mix the merits of the question with a personal embarrassment like that but I was embarrassed," he wrote. "My guess is that with Miss King out of the scene you could settle matters with Miss Park in half an hour."[42] Barnes took his friend's advice and invited Bryn Mawr's president to visit him at the Foundation, but apparently a rapprochement was not in the cards. A year later he sent off a note to a new lecturer in art history at the college that would have made Dewey blush and remains deeply offensive.

Barnes quoted a note from a Bryn Mawr student who told him that the young teacher had told her he was eager to see Barnes's pictures but had been assured by Dr. King "that everyone who is allowed to even enter the gallery must first pass an examination in art and be subject to a psycho-analytic test." The collector then suggested that the chair of the art history department "should have been more specific in stating what tests we apply and that we apply them only to members of the Bryn Mawr Faculty. Let me," he wrote, "supply Miss King's omissions:

Miss King, being a highly educated, accurately thinking person, means, of course, by "psycho-analytic test" the accepted sex connotations of that term. She should have told you that the "psycho-analytic test," as we apply it to the Bryn Mawr Faculty who come to us depends upon the sex of the applicant. If the faculty applicant is a woman, we test the sensitivity of her clitoris by titillation with the finger. If the faculty applicant is a man, we make an examination of the man's scrotum to determine the presence or absence of testicles.

The reason we make these tests is that it is commonly believed that women candidates for professorship[s] at Bryn Mawr must be sexually dead and the men candidates lacking in testicles. As Miss King can tell you, the vital relations between sex and art have been so definitely established by Freud that no well-informed person would question them.[43]

Using his medical knowledge to craft an obscene insult was Barnes at his worst. He intended to shock and derived some strange pleasure from constructing the current. But the clinical language imperfectly masks the atavistic punch of the gutter fighter.

Barnes would soon have a new public arena in which to indulge his taste for sparring. In the spring of 1929, he started negotiating with Zonite Products Corporation for the sale of the A. C. Barnes Company. Profits from the sale of Argyrol were at an all-time high. The French Army had adopted the antiseptic during World War I to try to control the spread of venereal diseases, and throughout the 1920s, it remained hugely popular for treating conjunctivitis, including a form afflicting soldiers exposed to poison gas, as well as nasal congestion and discomfort. Zonite paid $6 million for the collector's business some fifteen years before the advent of antibiotics, a class of drugs that would reduce the market for Argyrol but never entirely eliminate it. Barnes's attorney Owen J. Roberts took care of the details of the lucrative deal while the collector was in Europe. It was concluded in July of 1929 when, on behalf of the Barnes Foundation to which he had previously given the extant shares in his company, Barnes accepted and promptly sold shares of Zonite stock equivalent to the agreed-upon price. Three months later the equities market collapsed, causing many banks to go under, but the Foundation's endowment was safely invested in tax-exempt bonds. Barnes had unlimited time and plenty of money. "I can buy pictures and I don't have to work," he told Edith Glackens. "Except to get drunk every night."[44] The previous March, Barnes had purchased Renoir's large canvas, *Leaving the Conservatoire*, for $57,500 from the Berlin dealer Paul Cassirer, an acquisition that necessitated rearranging a number of the Foundation rooms to accommodate the studied arrangement of figures grouped outside a building.[45] But while he continued, even accelerated, his quest for art, he didn't become a tipsy reveler, and his brawls moved to the courtroom as he took on the City of Philadelphia in an easy if protracted fight.

Two months after Zonite acquired the Argyrol factory, Barnes bought a three-story brick house at 4525 Spruce Street to use as the Foundation's administrative headquarters. He paid $50,000 for the handsome gated structure, which was situated on a corner lot in a neighborhood of substantial dwellings not far from the Penn campus. In late March of 1930, while he was recovering from surgery on a trip to California and New Mexico with Dewey, the city sent him a dunning note for a $756 bill for school and property taxes. Barnes had previously applied for an exemption, and with his claim disallowed, he took the case to court. He was represented by a new lawyer, a rising star in the Philadelphia legal community named Robert T. McCracken, since his former attorney, Owen Roberts, had recently been appointed to the United States Supreme Court by President Herbert Hoover. Barnes had remodeled the West Philadelphia house to suit his office needs, and he considered it an annex of the Foundation that had been chartered as an educational institution and exempted from taxation since its founding eight years earlier. The city's implausible claim was that the Spruce Street property, with its hardwood floors, kitchen, and bathroom containing an "electric cabinet," looked more like a residence than a place of business and was not contiguous to the Foundation's main property in Montgomery County.

In the suit in equity that he brought against the Receiver of Taxes and the Board of Revision of Taxes, Barnes declared that the building in dispute was the publication center of the Foundation. He set forth the use of each floor: the basement was for storing books and packing them for shipment to schools, colleges, and art galleries; the first floor provided a reception area, a workroom in which clerks sorted mail and answered letters, and a kitchenette where employee lunches were prepared and eaten; the second floor contained offices for Nelle and Mary Mullen, Laura Geiger, and Violette de Mazia; and on the third floor, the president of the Foundation had a suite that included the bathroom with its electric cabinet where he gave himself heat treatments prescribed by his doctor for some internal disturbance—the condition, perhaps related to kidney function, that had hospitalized him in early 1930. Barnes marshaled practical and aesthetic arguments why the literary work of the Foundation needed to be carried out in West Philadelphia. A city location was an easier commute for his staff and nearer the places of business and educational institutions with which the Foundation had dealings. The buildings in Merion could not accommodate his publishing activities without interfering with classes, and no additional structures could be erected without spoiling the grounds that were laid out and planted at great expense and maintained as an arboretum.

A parade of witnesses testified in support of Barnes's contentions. The court was duly impressed when John Dewey rose to declare that the Foundation's classes represented a new departure in the field of art education. Nelle Mullen reinforced her boss's claim that his enterprise was a non-profit entity by producing figures that showed the income from the sale of Foundation books had failed to cover the cost of publication to say nothing of expenses associated with advertising and promotion. Buermeyer came down from NYU to describe the research, writing, and teaching he had formerly done under Foundation auspices and to proclaim the intellectual significance and educational value of the Foundation's most recent offering on French primitives. Herbert Jennings and Laura Geiger told about their classes and the use they made of texts written by authors associated with the Foundation. Violette de Mazia testified that aside from her Tuesday class on aesthetic appreciation, she spent almost all the rest of her time at 4525 Spruce Street. Laura Barnes said she devoted herself exclusively to the Merion property as director of the arboretum and general manager of the building. A construction engineer spoke about the physical modification of the West Philadelphia house for office use, and an accountant declared that his examination of the books of the Board of Revision of Taxes showed that Pennsylvania Academy of the Fine Arts and Curtis Institute of Music, institutions that might be considered analogous to the Barnes Foundation, were exempted from any tax payments.

Shortly before his case was heard in the Court of Common Pleas, Barnes told Dewey he suspected Philadelphia public school officials were behind the attempted assessment. "I want to lick those bastards and lick them right," he said.[46] To him, a tax exemption was a kind of legitimization. It would be a public acknowledgment of the educational character of his experiment. In his lengthy testimony, Barnes stressed that he brought his suit as a matter of principle. From the start, he had offered to contribute the disputed $756 to any charity designated by the attorney for the Board of Education, and when his gesture was ignored, he said he would give it to the police pension fund. His statements before the court about his early interest in art and the laboratory school he created in his Argyrol plant to test his ideas about art education, the letters he introduced into the record in praise of his work, the list he presented of colleges and universities that had ordered Foundation books, his description of his research methods, his revelations about his contributions of some $10 million to the Foundation's endowment and his expenditure of more than $5 million to acquire his collection, all these declarations were verses in a Psalter, a litany produced in his search for validation.

But the loquacious Barnes risked bolstering the tax collectors' weak case when, in answer to a follow-up question about the extent of his financial investment, he said: "But don't forget that there is a string on that. If people do not behave around here I pull that string back and it all drops in my lap. I don't expect to pull it unless they hit me too hard."[47] His lawyer quickly interjected that his client spoke in jest, and Judge Harry S. McDevitt recognized that, however inconsiderate Barnes's statement, under Pennsylvania law, he could not take the Foundation's assets back. The deed of trust made his conveyance to the Foundation irrevocable. True, an apparent escape clause read that "if at any period during the lifetime of the donor, the Board of Trustees decide that the experiment is a failure, they may, by appropriate resolution, dispose of the paintings, by gift or otherwise, to any individual, institution, museum, school or college, specified by the Board of Trustees." But not the real estate on which the exemption from taxation was claimed. Dissolution of the Barnes Foundation would require the court to dispose of land and buildings to another charitable organization, and the transfer and sale of the pictures would be subject to court control, as would disposition of the purchase price.

In a ruling handed down in February of 1931, Judge McDevitt rejected the defendants' arguments that the use to which the building at 4525 Spruce Street was put did not fall under the legal definition of a public charity and, therefore, the property was not exempt from taxation. He accepted Barnes's contention that the West Philadelphia premises were necessary for the discharge of the purposes of the Foundation inasmuch as it was through the Foundation's books, which were written and published there, that educational institutions became acquainted with the work carried out in Merion and, on the basis of such knowledge, might decide to send their teachers to the Foundation's classes for further training. But the city and the school district pressed on with an appeal to the Superior Court of Pennsylvania. They hoped, no doubt, that their chances of winning a reversal might be strengthened by such injudicious remarks as the collector's courtroom aside that his gallery was "no place for the rabble," despite his quick correction: "I have nothing to say against the rabble, only that it is a rabble. I come from the rabble, as I think most of our people did—what was once the rabble. The only thing is, we have risen."[48] The higher court, however, agreed with the chancellor of the Court of Common Pleas, and the tax collectors' appeal to the Commonwealth's Supreme Court was also to no avail, though the case was argued twice—first before a panel of four judges and then before the full court of six. In January of 1934, in a four to two decision, the Supreme Court held that "the limitation that the general public may not use the gallery at will is in accord with the practices of leading colleges and universities, which are tax free. As stated by the President Judge of the court below: 'It must be borne in mind that the gallery is used not as an art gallery as that term is ordinarily understood, but that it is an integral part of a new educational experiment, and the unrestricted admission of the public would be detrimental to the work of the Barnes Foundation as it would be to the work carried on in the laboratories and clinics of the University of Pennsylvania.'"[49] The judges' words must have resonated sweetly in the ears of the proud Penn alumnus, though he had long been confident his case was won. On October 1, 1930, after his day in court, Barnes wrote Dewey that comments reaching him "from all sides indicate that I got away with what I started out to do, namely, to put the defendants on trial as stupid obstructionists instead of being tried ourselves for a paltry sum of money. Beginning this morning, I resume my normal life of exercise and freedom from inordinate emotional strain and excessive work."[50]

As the Great Depression deepened, the collector's ability to avoid psychological stress was a product in no small part of wealth invested in bonds that retained much of their former value despite the bear market. The insulation from the country's economic woes that he enjoyed was not shared by many artists or dealers. Their distress surely enhanced his chances of finding bargains. Without a business to manage, he could devote more time than ever before to his experiments—not only in teaching his method of art appreciation but also in fitting pictures he hunted down into his growing collection. The "normal life" Barnes took up, however, was not altogether placid. Shortly after making his arguments before Judge McDevitt, he confronted the genuinely painful necessity of telling one of the few women painters whose work he ever owned that her paintings had failed to find a permanent home in Merion. The obligation he felt to explain the situation was complicated by his friendly feelings toward her and the financial burden she would bear in taking back the pictures. Barnes met Georgia O'Keeffe in the late1920s. On the occasion of a visit to his gallery in early March of 1930 by her friend, the English artist Dorothy Eugenie Brett, he sent off an invitation to O'Keeffe that included "bed, board & booze. . . . Come on," he said, "to hell with everything else!" Brett added a postscript: "Beautiful pictures & lovely music & the lion is eating out of my hand."[51]

Twenty-seven O'Keeffe paintings had gone on exhibit early the month before at An American Place, the small and enchanting Manhattan gallery that her husband, Alfred Stieglitz, had opened in December in a new skyscraper at Fifty-third Street and Madison Avenue. His wife's work had become the economic anchor of his operations, and meager output on her part or difficulty in attracting buyers in the worsening economy was always a looming threat. He worried that "her things are a bit too daring this year," although the New York critics mostly praised the show.[52] Their accolades, however, did little to offset O'Keeffe's own unhappiness in what was a particularly stressful period in her long life. She had been married to Stieglitz for six years, and two years earlier he had begun an affair with the beautiful young photographer Dorothy Norman, who had studied at the Barnes Foundation in 1924 when she was a Penn student. Given the insult inherent in her sixty-six-year-old husband's increasingly open romantic relationship with a woman of twenty-five, O'Keeffe must have welcomed a weekend escape to a treasure house of art. In addition to talking about pictures, they undoubtedly spoke of New Mexico, the southwestern state Barnes would visit within the month and the landscape that had long occupied a prominent place in O'Keeffe's interior life.

The previous summer she had joined Brett in the red hills outside of Santa Fe, the spare and vivid countryside she had first visited in 1917, as a guest of the high priestess of Taos, Mabel Dodge Luhan. O'Keeffe's 1930 exhibition included nineteen paintings she had made in New Mexico. The new pictures, of trees, landscapes, one of Luhan's porcelain roosters, a Taos headdress, an Indian kachina doll, a "lady santo," several sculptural fragments of a church, and a series of powerful stark crosses, revealed an experimental manipulation of space and were infused with religious feeling.[53] Barnes had been looking at O'Keeffe's work for eight or ten years before he stopped by the show at An American Place a few days after the artist's visit to Merion. As he told O'Keeffe later, he criticized her work in a discussion with the colleagues who accompanied him, but bought two paintings, an earlier still life and the Indian santo, he considered "authentic expression" of the painter. "Just what they are in the hierarchy of the artists they will live with," he wrote, "time alone will tell. Like every other new arrival in our gallery, they will survive or die on what they have in themselves."[54] Initially, Barnes replaced the paintings' silver frames with gold ones, but finding the change unsatisfactory, he put the original frames back. It "is stacking the cards in your favor," he told O'Keeffe. "I let you maintain the identity which you yourself have established and did not insist on you meeting your hanging companions on . . . equal terms. . . . I hope to learn to like the pictures as much as I like you."[55]

But he did not. After a half-year trial, Barnes put the O'Keeffe pictures in the basement. When the artist wrote to him mentioning his purchase of her work, the collector decided he could not avoid answering her. The "difficulty," he wrote to Stieglitz, was to do so "without hurting the sensitivity which is an inseparable part of herself. I like and respect her too much to even cast a shadow on her sunshine," he said. "But she refers to the pictures; and if I don't tell her the truth, which she is sure to find out when somebody else tells her the pictures are not hanging, I am put in a false position. It is because of the dilemma that I send the letter to you and ask you to read it and decide whether or not she should receive the letter."[56] O'Keeffe, of course, read Barnes's carefully worded missive. He began by saying that reading the poetry and contemplating the "wonderings of your letter . . . was like listening to you and enjoying the flavor and color of your picturesque and vivid self." He explained that upon meeting O'Keeffe, he "felt the charm and force" of her art in the self she presented to him. "It made me wonder," he continued, "if I had been blind in not seeing in your paintings the expressions of the qualities I felt were integral parts of your personality." Barnes went on to say that when he had visited the exhibition of her work in New York, he was "still unmoved" by what he saw but decided to make the "experiment" of acquiring some of her pictures so he "could see them day after day." He said he had explained to Stieglitz that

> If after a fair trial, your pictures sang in tune with the paintings in the rest of our collection, they would have a permanent home. I told him also that if they did not fit in, I would put them in the cellar. To that remark Stieglitz replied: "Don't put them in the discard—return them to me and I'll return your money."
>
> . . . I tried [the paintings] in every conceivable kind of company and I continued to do so for a period of six months. It did not turn out as I had hoped and I took the pictures down in early September.
>
> I am deeply and sincerely sorry not only that I couldn't fit the pictures in the collection but that I should have to tell you about it. . . . What it means when an experiment turns out this way is, of course, simply a record of personal reaction—not

a universal law that should bother the artist thus involved. It means merely that I did not see in your work what your words and demeanor convey to me; nor did the objective qualities of your work excite in me feelings which the objective factors of other pictures, painted by persons whom I never met, stir in me. I have had the same experience with other artists whom the world has recognized as important. It may perfectly well be that there are phases of art that I miss because of my own deficiencies.

You like to come over here and you've never been [here] without giving me a great pleasure and quite on par with what the best of our pictures give me. I hope you will not let the [failure of the] experiment bar you from what I know great pictures mean to you and what your visits have meant to me.[57]

Stieglitz wrote to Barnes that while he and O'Keeffe would be glad enough to take the two paintings back, the refund of the purchase price of $2,400 posed a problem. His reference to another artist's comment on O'Keeffe's work prompted Barnes to proffer some husbandly advice before turning to financial matters. Paintings the artist had made earlier in the spring near the home Stieglitz owned on Lake George included a series of six jack-in-the-pulpit pictures. Because of the phallic shape of the forest flower, the abstract compositions were viewed in some quarters as overtly erotic. In his reply to Stiegltiz, Barnes wrote that while American critics had been saying for years that "O'Keeffe's paintings owe their appeal to the revelations of her intimate sexual life," he "never saw that in her work." But the collector couldn't leave it at that. He went on to say, "I imagine that an artist of O'Keeffe's stature and the intelligent, refined and sensitive woman that she is, would be offended by the reiteration that she is telling the world that she has to resort to phallic or other kindred symbolism to obtain the satisfaction which a normal woman secures in the orthodox physiological manner. If the critics keep on repeating that kind of stuff, you as her husband would be justified in killing the ignorant sons-of-bitches."[58]

Commenting on the substance of Stieglitz's letter, Barnes said, "I am sorry that you are both hard up and I appreciate the chagrin that you must have in confessing it to an outsider." He insisted that he was not worried about the money, but it was clear he had no intention of returning O'Keeffe's paintings without reimbursement. He pointed out that it was "good for neither her pictures nor her reputation that the two paintings remain in [his] cellar." They "should be put in circulation," he said, "and somebody given an opportunity to buy them and hang them. There are a number of galleries in New York to which I could offer them" he continued, "but I should hate to peddle them almost as much as I dislike having them accumulate dust."[59] O'Keeffe replied to Barnes in a letter that made plain her continuing distress over her husband's infidelity and the weight put upon her spirits by economic hard times. "Your check for the pictures was made out to me," she wrote. "Stieglitz has never had an interest in them or any other pictures placed through him. . . . If a refund were possible it would naturally be I who would refund what you paid me. I would probably always feel that I would rather refund money and have my paintings back . . . than have them where they mean nothing, but unfortunately as things have gone for me, like for so many others, in the past six months, the luxury of affording such a feeling is beyond me so I have to let the paintings go and accept the fact that you do with them as you wish. . . . My feeling for life seems to be different than most people feel it. So my painting is different. If the one does not support the other in every way they must both go."[60]

Barnes wrote at once to insist that the matter of reimbursement was strictly between her husband and himself. He probably knew that Dorothy Norman's personal wealth represented a cash reserve on which Stieglitz could draw, nevertheless, his reply to O'Keeffe showed a callousness at odds with his earlier concern for her feelings. "Whether Stieglitz was a benefactor or not is irrelevant to the fact that he was a guarantor," Barnes declared. "But don't worry about the matter of the refund. It is not as if Stieglitz has repudiated his obligation and you wanted to save the honor of the family by paying the debt yourself. I'll see what I can do to solve the problem while waiting for Stieglitz to tell me what he thinks is the best plan to pursue in order to avoid reflections upon you, him or myself. In short, it is the ethical question, not the financial one, that interests me."[61] The denouement was that Stieglitz wrote that he would refund the check Barnes had made out to O'Keeffe if the paintings were returned in perfect condition. A dispute ensued about a damaged frame, which Nelle Mullen was left to handle as Barnes made plans to receive a visitor from abroad and then take a winter holiday in the West. Stieglitz returned his money in January, and O'Keeffe and Barnes eventually resumed their friendship, which lasted until the end of the collector's life.

Albert Coombs Barnes, consulting chemist
to the H. K. Mulford Company, in 1896
Courtesy of a friend of the author

Albert and Laura Barnes, circa 1915, on an outing in fine weather
Courtesy of a friend of the author

Albert Barnes and William Glackens, circa 1925, at rest in a woodland
Museum of Art, Fort Lauderdale, FL; Ira Glackens Bequest

Albert Barnes and Violette de Mazia, 1932, strolling in Paris during
a summer of research for their study of *The Art of Henri Matisse*
Courtesy of a friend of the author

Laura Geiger (far left), Nelle Mullen, Albert Barnes,
and Violette de Mazia, on a transatlantic crossing
Courtesy of a friend of the author

The Barnes Foundation in Merion
Urban Archives, Temple University, Philadelphia, PA

John Dewey, "America's philosopher," and
Albert Barnes, holding his dog Fidèle, in the Merion gallery
Special Collections, Morris Library, Southern Illinois University, Carbondale, IL

Albert Barnes and Horace Pippin, 1944, in front of
Domino Players (1943), an award-winning painting by
the artist owned by the Phillips Collection in Washington, DC
*Photo by John W. Mosley in the Charles L. Blockson Afro-American Collection, Temple
University, Philadelphia, PA*

Albert Barnes and Bertrand Russell, 1941,
after the British philosopher's first class at the Barnes Foundation
Urban Archives, Temple University, Philadelphia, PA

Horace Mann Bond, 1949, departing for a visit
to West Africa on which Barnes longed to accompany him
Urban Archives, Temple University, Philadelphia, PA

Remains of Barnes's Packard convertible
after the collector's fatal accident on July 24, 1951
Urban Archives, Temple University, Philadelphia, PA

Richard H. Glanton, president of the Barnes Foundation, 1990-1999
Courtesy of Richard H. Glanton

Bernard C. Watson, president of the Barnes Foundation since 1999
Courtesy of Bernard C. Watson

10

The Dance

At the request of Albert Barnes, John Dewey met Henri Matisse at the dock when the ocean liner on which he sailed from France arrived in New York harbor in mid-December of 1930.[1] It was the third time the celebrated painter had visited the United States that year. Then sixty, he had made the first trip, and his first trans-Atlantic voyage, the previous March when he stopped off in New York for two weeks before taking a train across the country and embarking from San Francisco for Tahiti. Returning to his studio in Nice after two and a half months in the South Pacific, he accepted an invitation to serve on the 1930 Carnegie International Exhibition jury and was back in New York in September in the company of Homer Saint-Gaudens, the director of the Carnegie Institute in Pittsburgh. Matisse had never met the man who at that time owned the largest private collection of his paintings in the world. He cabled Barnes about visiting the Foundation, and the collector responded with delight that he should come the following weekend.[2] Barnes had acquired his first paintings by the artist from Gertrude Stein in 1912, and he would later tell her brother Leo that he was "mighty glad . . . she would sell the two Matisses but not one."[3] He bought the painter's work consistently over the next thirty years and always found in it something uniquely "his own" yet "in line with the traditions."[4] No wonder he was thrilled to receive Matisse's request. Work on the testimony he planned to give in his suit against the tax collectors would be set aside. Matisse was to come to Merion on Saturday morning, the 27th of September.

As it happened, the artist was in the throes of self-doubt despite his fame. Twenty-one years earlier, after two decades of extreme poverty, he had attained a degree of financial security when the Russian textile merchant Sergei Shchukin commissioned two major canvases, *Dance II* and *Music*. He signed a contract with the Galeries Bernheim-Jeune, and towards the end of World War I, he began to take winter sojourns in Nice that soon extended to all but the warmest months of summer. Temporarily abandoning the monumental scale and modern methods of construction that had distinguished his great decorative compositions in favor of a more naturalistic style, he concentrated on the female form. From 1920 to 1927, his favorite model was also his domestic companion. She was the subject of some of his most sensual paintings, the languid *Odalisques*, before she left to establish a life of her own. His ailing wife, from whom he had lived apart for more than a decade, joined him on the Riviera. A new model became her night nurse, and Matisse grew increasingly restless. By 1929 he had virtually stopped painting and was devoting himself to printmaking and sculpture. A friendly critic wrote of his constant struggle "to maintain the vigor of his legendary flexibility, the youth of his line, the vitality of his color."[5] Matisse had traveled west in search of new light. He found it not, at least not immediately, in Papeete but in Philadelphia. His meeting with Barnes marked a critical turning point in the artistic career of the painter then widely acknowledged as France's greatest living artist.

It took place while other foreign members of the Carnegie jury were visiting the Pennsylvania Museum of Art. Saint-Gaudens had arranged the tour for his guests after they finished their deliberations, and he engaged John F. L. Raschen, head of the University of Pittsburgh's modern languages department, to act as their interpreter. As Matisse spoke no English, it was agreed that Raschen should accompany him to Merion. But Barnes could call upon de Mazia to provide whatever translation might be necessary, and on opening the great front doors of the Foundation at ten o'clock to his visitor, he told Raschen to take a long walk. The professor could return for Matisse at noon. The jury members were to lunch with Mrs. John F. Braun, wife of the president of the Philadelphia Art Alliance, and then visit the Widener Collection in Elkins Park before going on to New York. The painter and the collector spent more than two hours looking at pictures and talking about the display and teaching of art. "The only sane place," Matisse wrote in his pocket diary that day.[6] Several weeks later he told an interviewer: "This collection presents the paintings in complete frankness."[7] His host was also forthright. To the painter's complete surprise, Barnes proposed that he paint a mural for the three lunettes, set between the tops of the tall French windows and the roof of the Foundation's main gallery, where his *Seated Riffian* was already hanging. Having purchased more than forty Matisse paintings along with nearly 250 works by Renoir and 100 by Cézanne, the modern artists Matisse most admired, Barnes, who then owned about a thousand pictures, aspired to the new role of patron.

Matisse was intrigued by the formidable challenge inherent in the unanticipated request. But he had recently accepted a commission from a French publisher to illustrate the poems of Stéphane Mallarmé with original etchings, so he hesitated to accept another from Barnes. Perhaps the collector was intent on making his case as forcefully as possible when Raschen came back to the Foundation to fetch the painter. Or perhaps he was listening to Matisse talk of his frequent visits with Renoir in the years just before Renoir's death. Or he and de Mazia might have been telling their guest about the definitive study they had already made plans to write about him. In any case, Barnes ignored the doorbell, and the professor gained entrance through a coal chute in order to whisk the painter to lunch. But the two Chevaliers of the Legion of Honor (Matisse had been awarded his laurel in 1925, Barnes in 1926) had more to say to one another, and upon reaching New York, Matisse arranged to delay his departure for France for several days. On the first of October, he was back in Merion for a second visit.

In the creamy limestone building, filled with masterworks, he studied the irregular space Barnes had selected for a mural. The three lunettes were created by the window cornices and the arches of the three minor vaults above them. Matisse found the arches "very oppressive" and said they "gave a crushing feeling."[8] Their pendentives, triangular pieces of vaulting, separated the lunettes, but stopped short of the tops of the wall panels between the glass-paneled doors. From the gallery floor, the viewing angle of anything painted in the odd space would be extremely acute because the room was high and narrow. A second-floor loggia directly opposite the lunettes would be a better vantage point, but one partly obstructed, nevertheless, by hanging electric light fixtures. Matisse returned to New York and boarded a ship to Le Havre, mulling the difficulties inherent in the proffered commission. But the day after he reached Paris, he wrote to Barnes of his continuing interest in the mural project and his willingness to meet with him in France on the collector's upcoming visit.[9] When interviewed about his trip to the United States by a French journalist, he said: "One of the most striking things in America is the Barnes collection, which is exhibited in a spirit very beneficial to the training of American artists. There old master paintings are put beside the modern ones, a Douanier Rousseau next to a primitive, and this bringing together helps students understand a lot of things that the academies don't teach."[10]

The article appeared in *L'Intransigeant* just as Barnes arrived in Paris. He undoubtedly had in mind the fee he was willing to pay Matisse for his work, but the painter's appreciative remarks about his educational efforts must surely have contributed to the speedy and mutually agreeable conclusion of their negotiations. Matisse returned to the United States on December 15 and, met by Dewey, went with him directly to Merion. No doubt Barnes served them his fine pre-war Scotch and fed them well. The ocean-hopping painter arose early the next day to study the mural space before students arrived for their afternoon class. He then traveled to Baltimore to visit Etta Cone, who, with her late sister, Claribel Cone, had begun collecting his work in 1906 and owned several dozen of his pictures along with important pieces of his sculpture. After agreeing to Etta's request that he make a posthumous portrait drawing of Claribel, Matisse returned to Merion on December 19 from the camp of Barnes's most serious American rival in the acquisition of his work. The next day Barnes gave him a check for $10,000 and a written contract. It called for a subsequent payment of another $10,000 "when the work [wa]s half done," and a third and final payment of $10,000 upon the installation of the mural.[11] Speculation about the fee titillated the art world. "He seems to be getting well paid," Henry McBride wrote to Gertrude Stein, and, indeed, Matisse was initially well pleased with the financial arrangement.[12]

But the painter was forced to conclude that the fifty-two square meters of surface designated for the mural was "not . . . very favorable."[13] In addition to the problems associated with the architecture itself was the double competition he faced from nature, foliage visible through the vast expanse of window-panes, and from the masterworks of men, some of the best pictures in the Barnes collection, hung throughout the gallery. Matisse made some composition sketches as he pondered the possibilities over the course of three more days. In the meantime, Barnes persuaded Dewey to sit for the artist at the Plaza when Matisse went back to New York. From the hotel at the edge of Central Park, Matisse wrote to his wife that his visit to Merion had gone well. "I'm full of strength and enthusiasm," he said. "Barnes is very nice. We have several points in common, but I am less brutal."[14] After drawing several charcoal portraits of the philosopher, he returned once again to Merion and supervised the construction of a template directly from the awkward lunette spaces. It was to guide him in making the canvas on which he would create his architectural painting, but getting the pattern right was difficult because of the curvature of the gallery wall and ceiling. He dined simply with the Barneses on Christmas Day, and then went back to work. On the 26th of December, he wrote to Madame Matisse that he "was full of hope and zeal."[15] Barnes had left him free to choose his own subject. "Paint whatever you like just as if you were painting for yourself," he told Matisse, according to an interview the artist gave several years later.[16] And as Matisse studied the empty mural space in the pale winter light, "a plan of the figures" and even "the colors" came to him.[17] He sailed for France believing that the prestigious commission might not prove too difficult after all. For his part, the collector was riding high. He told Dewey that his time with the painter had been "a great experience."[18]

After bidding his visitor farewell, Barnes boarded a train for Chicago where he caught the Super Chief to Phoenix for a winter holiday in the sun. His letters to Dewey during the next several weeks indicate that Matisse was very much on his mind. A fellow Philadelphian deeply involved in the cultural life of the city had been thinking about the painter, too, and when he sought Barnes's advice, a curious misunderstanding further soured the collector's relationships with the Philadelphia establishment. Upon his return from Arizona, he found a telegram from R. Sturgis Ingersoll, a trustee of the Pennsylvania Museum of Art, asking him to lunch at the Midday Club. Barnes readily accepted the invitation, for this was the young admirer who had written him that *The Art in Painting* "comes so close to being the only intelligent book on the subject that it should have a wide and useful scope."[19] Ingersoll, a prominent attorney from an old Philadelphia family, chaired the museum's Committee on Modern

Art and his ostensible objective was to consult Barnes on the purchase of a Matisse painting he had seen at the Valentine (Dudensing) Gallery in New York on a recent visit with Fiske Kimball. It was the center panel on a triptych, *Three Sisters: Grey Background*, and it is not clear whether Ingersoll knew that Barnes owned the other two, *Three Sisters with "Pink Marble Table,"* which he had purchased from Guillaume in 1922, and *Three Sisters with Negro Sculpture*, which he bought from the Paris dealer the next year.[20] But Ingersoll recognized Barnes as an expert on Matisse, and he may certainly have harbored a small hope that the collector would help the museum buy the picture.

He had no idea that Barnes had been giving a great deal of thought to acquiring *Three Sisters: Grey Background* for himself since the painter's December visit. The two outside "sister" panels were not hanging together in Merion when Matisse was there. The artist told Barnes that he had intended the multi-figure compositions as companion pieces, and he made a rough pencil sketch of the triptych for the collector. At first he got the order wrong, but from the Plaza he sent Barnes a second sketch of the panels he had painted in the spring and summer of 1917 and, using a deft sales pitch, told him: "I will be happy if you are able to reunite these three things which work badly when separated. I am almost reluctant to say how well suited to your ensemble they are. That however is the goal I wanted to attain when I made them." Matisse then added parenthetically, "Dudensing knows that the price he gave me is for you."[21] But Barnes had made no move to acquire the picture when Ingersoll consulted him on whether it would be a wise investment for the new Pennsylvania Museum of Art. The young trustee's request for advice presented him with a moral dilemma even as it spurred his highly competitive spirit.

Ingersoll expressed great enthusiasm for what he hoped would be the museum's first Matisse. Barnes told his host that the painter had been urging him to buy it. Whether or not he conveyed his ambivalence is uncertain, but he did agree to look at the painting again and let Ingersoll know his reconsidered opinion. Several days later, he went to New York and took an option to purchase *Three Sisters: Grey Background* for $15,000, which was more than three times as much as he had paid for the panel he had acquired six years earlier. He then told Ingersoll that he would give the museum his option, but warned him that he only had a few days to raise the money. Since the board of trustees would not meet for some time, Ingersoll had to try to secure the funds himself. On February 25, he informed Barnes that he hadn't been able to get them and asked if Dudensing would agree to hold the picture for another week. When Barnes inquired, the dealer said he needed money at once to buy a villa in France. If Barnes didn't take the Matisse by the 26th, he would offer it to another client. The collector sent his check. Meanwhile, Ingersoll persuaded Kimball and Carroll Tyson, a fellow trustee and collector, to co-sign a note with him at the Provident Trust Company. He and the museum director walked back to his law office from the bank, and after instructing a secretary to get hold of Dudensing, the excited attorney telephoned Barnes at a private number the collector had given him. Kimball had picked up another phone to listen in on the call to Merion and wrote down the conversation on an envelope.

The dialogue recorded on the opposite side of a flap engraved "R. Sturgis Ingersoll / Penlyn, Pennsylvania" reads:

Ingersoll: We take the picture.

Barnes (after a silence): You're just too late. Dudensing said he had to have cash at once and I have paid for it.

Ingersoll: But Dr. Barnes . . .

Barnes: I have the picture.

Ingersoll: You're going to let us have it?

Barnes: The hell I will.

Ingersoll: I am very much disappointed.

Barnes: It is a peach of a picture. I told you I could not obligate myself. Yesterday you told me you couldn't get the money.

Ingersoll: You say the door is closed?

Barnes: Yes.

Ingersoll: I have the check for $15,000 to your order on my desk.

Barnes: There is nothing I can do about it.[22]

When Ingersoll reached Dudensing, the picture dealer confirmed that the Matisse was on its way to Merion. The Philadelphia lawyer felt duped—and he had been but by whom remains less than certain. Gossip around New York at the time was that Dudensing had marked him as a cat's-paw. But Barnes revealed his red tooth and claw when he followed up Ingersoll's phone call about the bank loan with a note: "The situation called for cash and quick action and you lost because you offered the substitutes of hope and delay. I met the situation and the picture is already hanging where Matisse said it should hang. It's going to stay there and money would not buy it."[23] No more than Dudensing did he expect, in the deepening depression, that the Pennsylvania Museum of Art would raise cash in a timely fashion. The day before Ingersoll had telephoned him about his lack of success, Barnes had written to Dewey quite offhandedly, "I bought a good Matisse in New York the other day, along with an extraordinary Rouault at a local gallery."[24]

The next week Kimball sent the cancelled Provident note on to Tyson with a brief letter thanking him for his "kind help in the matter, which was defeated through no fault of ours. We always knew Barnes was a son of a bitch," he added, "and now we can prove it."[25] Two years later, the museum officials' casting of the incident was still rankling Barnes. When Kimball, once again asked him for the loan of some pictures, this time sixteen Cézannes, the collector did not simply refuse but wrote a blustery note with which he enclosed a copy of the telegram Ingersoll had sent him requesting a meeting about the Matisse and a letter he had at that time just procured from Dudensing setting out the sequence of his dealings with the collector on the matter of *Three Sisters: Grey Background*. Referring to the "rumor" that he "double-crossed Mr. Ingersoll," Barnes told Kimball that "the enclosed letter . . . proves the rumor is a lie, and the telegram indicates that the story could have originated only in the imagination . . . of an ignoramus or an ungrateful son-of-a-bitch. It is the accumulation of [such] incidents . . . which go far to explain why the Pennsylvania Museum of art is so often referred to as a 'house of artistic and educational prostitution' that is exploited by self-seeking persons who prey upon the ignorance and confidence of the public."[26] Following his customary saturation strategy, he sent the little "proof" packet around to artists and editors throughout the area.

Contretemps with institutions rarely distracted Barnes for so long, although he also never forgot them. Unfortunately for the Pennsylvania Museum's nascent acquisitions program, he had come to regard completing the triptych as an important goal.[27] The artist, of course, was pleased to hear about the reunion of his three versions of the *Three Sisters*. Barnes wrote him in March of 1931 that the wall on which he had hung the pictures was "as fine a wall" as he had "ever seen in any gallery."[28] The compliment was especially sweet because Matisse was then beginning the exacting process of creating the Barnes Foundation mural. He had rented a huge vacant garage in Nice, often referred to as an abandoned film studio, to have space enough to work on the large project. He repainted the walls to resemble those at the Foundation and added a skylight to duplicate the natural illumination afforded by the French windows. After becoming frustrated in his initial attempt to work out his ideas for the monumental composition on small canvases, he hung three colossal ones at one end of the improvised studio. Although the building was not high enough for them to hang at the same level as the finished panels would hang in Merion, Matisse could stand at the opposite end of the garage and view the canvases from approximately the same level as the mural would be seen from the balcony in the Foundation's main gallery. Alfred Barr believed that Matisse conceived his design primarily from this perspective, despite making studies of the mural as it would be seen from the ground floor.[29]

The artist took his theme from *Dance II*, one of the panels he painted for Shchukin's Moscow home in 1909-10—and which he had first used in the *Joy of Life*, his 1905-06 picture that Barnes had owned for nearly a decade. But he did not treat his commission as another painting. "My aim," he told an

American journalist when the mural was done, "has been to translate paint into architecture, to make of the fresco the equivalent of stone or cement."[30] Standing on a bench, he drew with a stick of charcoal attached to a six-foot bamboo pole. Barnes wrote to ask how the project was coming along and could barely contain his excitement: "How I would like to see you at work on these canvases, and how much I want to have them in our gallery! I am certain you will accomplish a work worthy of your great talent and of the Foundation."[31] Matisse provided progress reports, and in April sent two series of photographs of his charcoal drawings to Merion. "I am searching for the colors," he told his patron.[32] To find them, he had to rearrange all his forms.

The technique he devised was to draw his dancers on large sheets of colored paper then have them cut out and pinned to the canvases. Over and over, thirty different designs, until the arrangement satisfied him completely. His method recalls the practice of the textile weavers in his native Bohain-en-Vermandois, an industrial town in northeastern France. The mature Matisse described the process as "rather like moving counters in a game of checkers."[33] Convinced that the surface to be decorated in the Foundation gallery was insufficiently deep "to crown the three glass doors," Matisse defined the problem to be solved with his paints as creating a "decoration" that did not "oppress the room," but rather gave "more air and space to the pictures to be seen there." By means of "lines . . . colors . . . energetic directions," he would provide the "spectator the sensation of flight, of elevation," which would make "him forget the actual proportions." He would create "the sky for the garden" to be glimpsed outside.[34]

Barnes worried about the developing mural like an expectant father. In May, he wrote to Matisse expressing his concern that it wouldn't fit the allotted space. The plan was to fold the borders of the completed canvas back over wooden stretchers constructed to fill the lunettes, and the collector said that from the photographs, it didn't seem as if there was enough canvas to attach to the stretchers. Matisse immediately dispatched sketches to reassure his patron that he had allowed sufficient excess. Barnes went to Paris the next month to continue his researches for the book he and de Mazia were writing on Matisse, and though he didn't go on to Nice, he apparently was pleased with the painter's progress. He sent him a second $10,000 payment after visiting a retrospective of his work at the Galeries Georges Petit. It was the first to have been held in Paris since 1910, and a show at which Barnes dictated what became "1,000 typewritten pages of analytic notes" as he walked back and forth in front of nearly 150 pictures.[35] But the collector continued to fret about his mural. In August, he dispatched a former Barnes student, who was soon to be named a Foundation instructor, to call on Matisse and report back to him about the size of the border. Writing from the Riviera, Edward Dreibelbies assured Barnes that "a generous width of canvas has been allowed on all four sides," although a scale drawing he made of the work in progress might have enabled someone adept at reading blueprints to see that there was a problem with the over-all dimensions.[36]

The barrage of inquiries and interruptions did not sit well with Matisse. He wanted nothing more than to be left alone to carry on his work. Immersed in experiments with color, he went to Italy in the early fall and drew inspiration from Giotto's great frescoes in Padua. He then requested additional sketches of the space where the mural would be installed in Merion, and the Pinto brothers, three Philadelphia artists whose studies in Europe had been funded by Barnes, made them with help from Pierre Matisse. The painter's son, an art dealer in New York, found the collector "happy as a king."[37] Barnes was planning a trip to France in December and hoped to view the unfinished canvases. But Matisse put him off. He wrote that he must reserve for himself "the possibility of changing things until the last day" if he felt "the possibility of giving the decoration greater fullness or expression."[38] In January 1932, however, painter and patron conferred in Paris. Barnes had agreed that the mural should be exhibited at the Galeries Georges Petit before it was packed for the sea voyage to Philadelphia, and they needed to compare dimensions, so the completed canvases could be mounted on a temporary stretcher.

On returning to Nice, Matisse was appalled to discover that there was a discrepancy between the spaces he had allowed for the pendentives and the measurements Barnes had mentioned during their meeting. A year earlier, the artist had sent for the architect's plans of the gallery to check them against the dimensions on his paper tracing. They differed slightly from the template, and he had apparently followed them in sizing the mural. The tracing had been returned to Merion to aid in the construction of the stretchers, and now Matisse cabled Barnes to confess his fears and request the template be sent back to him. The collector replied that it was in use for another two weeks, but that whatever the blueprints might indicate, the tracing had to be correct since it had been made, under the painter's watchful eye, by Barnes's trusted jack-of-all trades Albert Nulty. When he had a chance, moreover, to compare the template with the measurements Matisse reported using, Barnes realized that the pendentives were twice as wide as the space Matisse had left for them. The horizontal dimension of the overall mural was too short. The painter had made "an enormous mistake. . . . Should I come to Paris immediately with the template?" the collector asked in a cable.[39] In shock, but accepting full responsibility for the error, Matisse cabled his "deepest apologies." He said to send the tracing, but insisted there was no need for anyone to accompany it as an entirely "new composition [wa]s necessary."[40]

Given his trigger temper, Barnes's response to the mishap was remarkably measured, though Pierre Matisse told his father that the collector was reported to have called it "the greatest tragedy of his life."[41] Barnes informed Georges Keller, a Swiss art dealer based in Paris who was helping him locate pictures, about the situation, but asked him to say nothing. Thereafter, Barnes himself rarely mentioned the painter's error. But initially Pierre Matisse had been concerned that "he might adopt a somewhat brutal attitude in the exercise of what he w[ould] judge to be his rights," and he warned his father that the collector would "not put up with the existence of another decoration similar to his own."[42] Barnes's respect for the creative process was too great, however, to ask the artist to destroy a canvas. Matisse told him he intended to finish the panels on which he had worked for a year before starting over.

In March, the two men met in Paris. Matisse gave Barnes a gouache copy of the still unfinished first mural, and in July he began work on a replacement. He took time out the next month, however, to meet again with Barnes. After joining the collector and his wife for a drink in their Paris hotel, Matisse told Pierre his patron was in high spirits as he had just acquired a big Cézanne still life at a bargain price from Bignou. But Barnes declined the painter's suggestion that he consider his *Guitarist* since he was about to buy another Cézanne—*Red Earth*. Back in his studio, Matisse had no time for regrets. He worked furiously, and the new version of the mural was completed in ten months. The artist used the same method as in the first one, but both the composition and feeling were different. He conceived the mural in terms of eight, rather than the original six, dancers. Instead of designing them to convey a lateral movement across the surface of the canvases, he now centered pairs of leaping figures within each of the three panels and placed one reclining figure at the base of each pendentive. He gave the thrusting architectural members, twice the width he had thought them to be, a more active role in the composition thus reinforcing an erotic interpretation of the violent tumbling of the couples. In November, Matisse wrote to his son that the new decoration was "going very well" as he had "greatly profited from the 1st one."[43]

Barnes, too, was "well satisfied" with his work. The primary purpose of his long summer stay in Europe had been to work with de Mazia on their monograph of the painter. "It was real research," he told Dewey, "which determined not only the characteristics of Matisse's form, but also the many traditions" from which he derived it.[44] Only when the manuscript was in the hands of the publisher, however, did he see the mural, which he had once hoped would be finished in time to be analyzed and discussed in the text and reproduced as the frontispiece of the book. In January of 1933, Laura Barnes joined him on a trip to the Mediterranean. While they were in Majorca, the collector persuaded Matisse to meet him in Palma. Reluctantly, the painter took a ferry from Marseilles. He became seasick during the long voyage, and arrived on the Spanish island exhausted and filled with anxiety to await Barnes, who had taken his wife to Gibraltar. The next day they met briefly and the, by then, very ill Matisse returned immediately to France. As growing unrest in Spain had caused the Barneses to change their plans about visiting Madrid, the collector had told the artist that they would come to Nice a week later.

Barnes had waited two years to see the mural and when he looked at it, even though he had not known about the paper cutouts beforehand, he bestowed an enthusiastic imprimatur. Matisse had overheard him say to Mrs. Barnes before they entered the studio, "If I don't like it, I'll just put it aside," but now he declared the panels ready to be shipped to America.[45] The painter, however, did not consider his work done. Pleased, of course, with his patron's reaction, he was beginning to dislike Barnes intensely. Matisse had been offended by probing questions about financial matters he considered personal and thought the collector drank too much and stayed too late when invited to dinner.[46] The challenge posed by the Barnes mural, however, continue to enthrall him. For the next two months he worked intensely. "Despite everything that it is costing me," he told his son, "I cannot . . . help but go right to the end of my idea."[47] He hired a house painter to apply colors to the canvases. In early March, he told a friend "the end is near—win or lose," but still he couldn't let go.[48] He added accents in charcoal to underline certain forms and repainted the shadow-like bands that surrounded each gray figure in darker tints of the background colors. The object was to humanize the dancers, which had been created, as art historian Pierre Schneider has pointed out, by "a mechanical technique using 'prefabricated' materials."[49] In the Merion *Dance*, Matisse took an irreversible step into the modern world by introducing quantitative concepts into the art of painting. He finally laid down his brushes at the end of April. There was no time for an exhibition in Paris. The canvases were packed in crates under his supervision, and he cabled Barnes that he had booked passage on the *Rex* and would reach New York on the 11th of May.

Pierre Matisse met his father at the dock and drove him straight to Merion as the crates went by truck on a less direct route, which was planned to avoid trolley wires and low bridges. When they arrived later that same evening, Barnes had the crates unpacked and the canvases laid out on the gallery floor so they would be ready for attaching to stretchers in the morning. The collector wanted Nulty to do the work, but Matisse insisted on nailing the first canvas himself. It was not their only disagreement. Matisse wanted Barnes to move *Seated Ruffian* and Picasso's *Composition*, which were hung directly underneath the two inside pendentives separating the central lunette from the outer ones. The collector rebuffed the suggestion. He also would not hear of removing a sculptured frieze just below the murals or replacing the frosted glass at the top of the French windows with clear panes. It was then that the strain of the past months and the palpable tension in Merion appear to have brought on what Barnes told Pierre Matisse was his father's "slight heart attack." According to the former physician's report to the painter's son, he administered whiskey and called in a heart specialist, a "great admirer" of Matisse's work, who examined the patient and advised "absolute rest for a long period."[50]

Nevertheless, Matisse felt well enough to oversee the stretching and mounting of the other two canvases several days later. He wrote to his wife that when the mural was in place "the whole ceiling came alive and the radiation from the canvas goes right down to the bottom of the wall. . . . You would believe," he added, "that you were in a cathedral."[51] Barnes apparently thought so, too.

He called the wondrous painted panels a "rose window"—and lectured about them to his students for three hours in lieu of any formal ceremony of unveiling![52] While Henry Hart has said Barnes was "never completely satisfied" with the mural,[53] the collector wrote to the artist eight months after the installation that his appreciation was "growing day by day because I see in it more and more of your artistic personality."[54] For his part, Matisse did not expect Barnes, whose connoisseurship he apparently could not square with what he considered his boorish behavior, to immediately embrace the work. Just before returning to France, he told a reporter for *Art News:* "When a painting is finished, it's like a new born child, and the artist himself must have time for understanding. How then, do you expect an amateur to understand that which the artist does not yet comprehend?"[55] But the collector, of course, did not view himself as an amateur.

Barnes had purchased nine Matisse paintings while the artist was executing the Foundation commission. Over a two-and-a-half year period, he studied hundreds of them. In the late winter of 1930, Barnes and de Mazia had begun research for their book on Matisse at a major retrospective of his work assembled by the dealer Justin Thannhauser for his galleries in Berlin. Following the huge Paris show in June of 1931, they had a chance to see more Matisses in November at the Museum of Modern Art's first large European one-man exhibition, to which Barnes lent nothing. The authors worked like demons. The manuscript was finished in September of 1932 and handed over to Maxwell Perkins at Charles Scribner's, where Henry Hart had recently become an editor. With its 151 black-and-white illustrations, the book was published in January of 1933. Barnes and de Mazia had provided a fine-comb examination of 114 major works. "Intensely alive and adventurous," Matisse is "the foremost painter of the day," they wrote. "The sum and substance of his offending comes to this: that by centering his interest upon decoration he misses the supreme values of painting."[56]

The year the collector died, Alfred Barr wrote in his own monograph, *Matisse,* that in *The Art of Henri Matisse,* a reader could find "formal analyses of particular paintings more through and objective than any ever bestowed upon a living painter before or since."[57] But one of the first reviews, by Thomas Craven in the *New York Herald Tribune,* put Barnes in a royal snit. The critic he had once tried to hire as a collaborator dismissed Matisse's work by saying that "it is difficult to cut very deep into an art that is all on the surface" and disparaged Barnes's "clinical" method of "dismembering an object into its technical components" in analyses that made of "art a dead thing."[58] Other reviewers were more appreciative of the authors' efforts. Writing for the *Saturday Review of Literature,* Frank Jewett Mather, the Princeton art historian who distrusted modernists, congratulated Barnes and de Mazia "upon their sureness of touch and selection."[59] The man to whom the book was dedicated, Leo Stein, found their "treatment . . . very fair."[60]

As Leo told Mable Dodge Luhan, the two "had been for years on unspeaking terms" when they "happened to meet in a gallery in Paris . . . and . . . had a pleasant conversation." Then nothing until, a year or so later, Stein, to his utter astonishment, heard from a friend in New York about the dedication of *The Art of Henri Matisse*. "Who could have done this except Barnes?" he asked Luhan.[61] When the collector finally sent him a copy of the published volume, Leo told Barnes, "It seems to me much better written than your first book—the style is more elastic and agreeable." He went on to say that he hadn't seen Matisse in twenty years, and the Fauve painter he knew "was not yet sure of his road. . . . For that reason 'your' Matisse is more lucid and coherent than 'mine' is, as mine is rather the formative than the completed Matisse," Stein added.[62] But the package from Merion presented the ex-patriot connoisseur with a less agreeable duty than thanking Barnes for a book he genuinely if somewhat grudgingly admired. The collector also had sent him a copy of a new book by John Dewey, which Leo found "perfectly honest, reliable twaddle . . . and oh! so dull." He couldn't get through it. But what should he say to Barnes? They had, after all, "become the greatest chums that ever was," as he told Luhan. The dilemma disturbed his sleep until one morning he "woke up with an inspiration." He decided he would "tell Barnes that Dewey's book is sound though not very lively (sound without fury)."[63] By his own account, he wrote "a very tactful letter" about the latest effort of a man he considered "important for what he said" rather "than for the way in which he said it."[64]

From Stein's point of view, the trouble was that the philosopher had tried to write about something he wasn't steeped in. Indeed, Dewey had included philosophy of art in his general philosophy for the first time in his 1925 book *Experience and Nature*. But under Barnes's always respectful tutelage, and in response to his relentless if affectionate nagging, Dewey turned the William James Memorial Lectures he inaugurated at Harvard into *Art as Experience*, a book, that whatever Leo might think of its style, was hailed upon its publication as "the most important contribution to aesthetics that America has yet produced."[65] The philosopher and the collector had corresponded about the series of ten talks on aesthetics over a period of several months. "I see by the outline in your letter . . . that you've got your teeth in the subject and that's all that is needed to make the presentation worthy of you," Barnes wrote. But "what I'm hoping is that after the lectures you will camp here long enough and frequently enough to convert every single philosophic point into a real, vivid, personal psychological experience." He was confident Dewey could "begin [and he underlined the verb] to make practicable an approach to art appreciation and link it with intelligent educational methods. It would be your monument," he told his friend, "because it would remove both elements from books and pretentious unreality and tie them right up with the every-day living of many people." Dewey had said he wanted to dedicate the James Lectures to Barnes, and the collector, uncharacteristically humbled, admonished him not to "joke like that."[66] But upon the philosopher's return from Cambridge to Manhattan, Barnes persuaded him to make frequent pilgrimages to Merion in order to re-examine his theoretical musings, which Dewey admitted "smelled too much of the lamp," in front of "actual object[s]. . . . If you do that, your book will be done right, and will be worthy of the subject and of you," Barnes inveighed his friend on one such occasion. "Tell your family to hold your mail . . . that you are making a novena that will last two weeks and that nothing is to come between your Jesus and yourself."[67]

Barnes had some spectacular new paintings to show his friend. He was collecting intensely during the period in which Dewey was writing *Art as Experience* in part because of the seriously depressed world art market. "I have been . . . getting the cream for less than the price of skim milk in flush times," he boasted.[68] Barnes always paid cash, and the purchases made in Europe during the summer of 1931 alone included five Matisses, a Renoir, seven early Chinese paintings, a Japanese and a Korean work from the sixteenth century, forty Japanese prints, and, as Barnes shamelessly announced, "a marvelous early Corot portrait" he had bought from the artist's "hard-up granddaughter."[69] A few months later, he had added another Cézanne and Renoir's *Reclining Nude* to his collection. His trip in the summer of 1932 produced three more Matisses and four Cézannes, two of which, he told Dewey, were "equal to the best of ours and put our collection of that painter superior to anything else in the world."[70] In two decades of acquiring pictures, he had refined his tastes, trained his eye, and absorbed vast amounts of information to aid him in his thoughtful aesthetic analyses while also honing the hard-edged, street-tested bargain-hunting skills of a manufacturer of over-the-counter medicine. Dewey stood in awe of his connoisseurship even as he recognized the intractable insecurity and pugnaciousness that coexisted with an awesome talent.

The philosopher proposed that the inscription of Henry Hart's first novel, *The Great One*, which Hart planned to dedicate to Barnes, should read: "To Albert C. Barnes a genius . . . who often makes himself God damned uncomfortable by the way in which he expresses and suppresses it."[71] But he reminded the collector, who had sought his opinion of the young author's intention, that the idea of a dedication had first been his even if his book would not be published for several months. "If you still feel that way," Barnes said, "please use my full name . . . and make the sentiment very modest, something that won't make me blush—for instance: 'To Albert C. Barnes to whose precept and example I owe accuracy and good judgment.'"[72] But Dewey had something else in mind. He had refined his theory of aesthetics as he reflected upon his own responses to his friend's collection of painting and sculpture. Some of his earliest writing on the subject was for the *Journal of the Barnes Foundation*. In acknowledgment of the role Barnes played in the creation of a work, which remains even today among the most significant and original theoretical texts on art, Dewey dedicated *Art and Experience* to "Albert C. Barnes In Gratitude" and wrote in the preface:

> The chapters have been gone over one by one with him, and yet what I owe to his comments and suggestions on this account is but a small measure of my debt. I have had the benefit of conversations with him over a period of years, many of which occurred in the presence of his . . . pictures. . . . The influence of these conversations, together with that of his books, has been a chief factor in shaping my own thinking about the philosophy of esthetics. Whatever is sound in this volume is due more than I can say to the great educational work carried on in the Barnes Foundation. That work is of pioneer quality comparable to the best that has been done in any field during the present generation, that of science not excepted. I should be glad to think of this volume as one phase of the widespread influence the Foundation is exercising.[73]

In sending the collector a copy of the book, Dewey said, "I hope it isn't all unworthy of what I've learned from you."[74] Barnes was overwhelmed. He told Dewey:

> Your dedication and preface make me too drunk to adequately express my appreciation of your friendship, kindness and charity. The dedication tickles my vanity but what you say in the preface gets down deeper and touches something more organic that represents everything I ever had and did. I had hoped that after my death somebody would say something like that but that a man of your stamp would say it during my life seemed to me beyond the realm of possibility. I am so used to knocks, criticisms and abuse that I often wonder if I really deserve anything else. Your preface lifts that from my shoulders and compensates for the difficulties encountered in the process of getting where we are.
>
> The one thing sure about the Foundation is that if I had not had the kind of people around me that I have had, the ship would never have sailed because I recognize my limitations. The Foundation has been to me, not as many people think, a release from life, but a struggle to attain the satisfactions that a normal man gets out of what he should have in the everyday course of events. In other words, it is a case of an obsession that was driven hard enough and intelligently enough to have social value. One of the nicest things you say is the very last sentence that you are glad to have your book as one of the parts of our program of work. We welcome the infant with joy.[75]

Barnes's reading of Dewey's philosophy of art between hard covers led him to engage his friend in a probing conversation about the psychological and aesthetic components of the visible and tangible world of nature. Much of the discussion in *Art as Experience* focused on the artist's creation of a work of art. Laying hold of its "full import," Dewey wrote, is possible "only as we go through in our own vital processes the processes the artist went through in producing the work."[76] Barnes said that even when he encountered a "freak of nature," he went "through the [same] series of coordinated, organic activities as the human artist" whom he "thought produced the object." He might even "make the abortive movements of the brush. . . . Now if I suddenly learn that no human being ever went through those processes in producing the 'curiosity,' does that nullify all these organic activities that I went through in my appreciation?" he asked Dewey.[77] Dewey replied that for him, such freaks assumed "a different quality" the moment he found them to be "accidental product[s] of physical forces." The "psychology of just what we go through in esthetic appreciation of natural scenes" was not addressed in his book, he acknowledged, and went on to suggest that "the organic processes are more diffused, less centered" than those associated with responses to "human productions."[78] Barnes then recalled the "vivid experience, deeply organic" that he had had a decade earlier when, he told Dewey, "the best Picasso I ever saw was lying on an inclined roof opposite my office. The reason it is not in our gallery," he explained, "is that it was made of snow and the sun ate it."[79]

Dewey's response was to refer to an aspect of the collector's past that Barnes must have once described to him. "There is one point," the philosopher said, "which may have made the difference between us seem bigger than it is—in fact it may not exist at all. You have been a painter and anyway have much greater experience with pictures than I have. Consequently your reconstructive processes in perception of either a natural object or a picture are much more pronounced than mine. You would make an art product out of a natural object much more completely than I would. I doubt for instance whether I would have seen the Picasso in the snow picture tho I might have seen a picture....The whole problem ... is a very interesting one and I think new."[80] Was it in high school, where Barnes had shown Glackens his sketches, that he had first tried his hand with a brush? While he was searching for a career after medical school, did he continue the struggle to illuminate the qualities of things on a canvas? The attempts had been abandoned long ago, but perhaps they did shape his response to "that Picasso in the snow." Gazing at it, he told Dewey, "I was conscious of the organic processes that I have when I analyze my reactions to a genuine Picasso. Then I said to myself in going through the same reactions in the genuine Picasso and the one made by God, what difference does it make which artist produced that—that is, whether it was an artist of flesh and blood or the combination of the forces of nature. . . . I was conscious of no difference in the essence of the aesthetic response in the two cases."[81]

Within two days of the publication of *Art as Experience*, Barnes was discussing it in his Foundation talks to students. Gleefully, he reported to the author that he had sold fifty copies. But quizzing students several weeks later about their understanding of the tome led him to suggest to Dewey that he consider engaging someone to simplify and condense its arguments in a textbook version that would be more accessible to general readers. Barnes thought it could be a "best seller," and Dewey said that when he had gotten over his "mild nausea about the volume," perhaps, he could, with Barnes's help, take on the revision himself.[82] At the time, the collector was nurturing the hope of a renewed association between the Barnes Foundation and an established academic institution that might produce classes eager to study his friend's philosophy of art in the presence of his collection of modern masterpieces.

He had admitted to Dewey, within several years of his 1926 "suspension" of his alma mater, that "the first necessity" for making "the Foundation function properly" was "to make an alliance with an organized university, whose Art Department is in the charge of a man . . . who has [the] intelligence and energy to pick from his material those students who show special interest and ability. If we can do that," he predicted, "I believe that the battle from now on will be easy and that the antiquated courses at Princeton, Harvard and Columbia . . . will . . . gradually disappear."[83] But Barnes didn't act on his conviction until the fall of 1933 when he initiated contact with Penn's new president, Thomas Sovereign Gates, a lawyer, banker, and businessman who had previously chaired the university's board of trustees. He asked him to Merion, and Gates, unlike his predecessor, readily accepted the invitation. The collector had several agendas. One was to help a German art historian and dealer of Jewish descent, Grete Ring, find an academic post in the United States.[84] The other was to explore, however tentatively, the possibility of linking the Foundation once again to Penn. The collector sent Gates his 1927 analysis of the University's fine arts program, as well as a copy of the May 1926 issue *Opportunity* to illustrate what he described as his "contributions . . . to the place of the Negro in our social life."[85] In his prompt and gracious letter of response, Gates did not indicate that Penn could find an opening for Ring, but he expressed interest in the Foundation's educational aims and gratitude for the chance to have seen not only the Barnes collection of pictures but also the arboretum.

In the early spring of 1934, the new dean of the School of Fine Arts, George Simpson Koyl, one of the first graduates of Paul Cret's architecture program and Laird's successor, called on Barnes in Merion. As the Depression deepened, he saw his immediate task as assuring the survival of the School. At the same time, Koyl believed that students in the architecture, music, fine arts, and landscape architecture programs should be exposed to a greater number of cultural courses, and he shared his vision with the collector while diplomatically seeking his suggestions on how best to achieve it. Barnes told Koyl that the way to "start" was to undertake "a series of experiments to find the man best qualified by endowment and training to give courses that would lead toward [his] goal. As a start in that direction," he proposed the appointment of the Russian-born composer Nicholas Nabokov as a professor of music and offered to pay his salary for the first year. "The problem of finding a suitable man to teach appreciation of art is more difficult," Barnes said. But he suggested that "Dr. Julius Held, formerly assistant at the Kaiser Friedrich Museum in Berlin might be the right" choice. He recommended that Koyl give Held a trial and said he would make his "paintings available" to the professor's students. "The Hitler tactics is the only reason for Dr. Held's services being available in America," he stressed.[86]

Encouraged by Barnes's letter, Koyl proceeded boldly and, given the collector's sensitivities, recklessly with a direct solicitation. He had a file copy of Barnes's earlier plan for the reorganization of the fine arts curriculum, and he now asked Barnes to fund a lectureship in fine arts and offered to revamp the program along the lines suggested by the collector. But he couldn't promise to bring Nabokov on board. Since Barnes had arranged for the composer's passage to America and was paying him to give a yearlong series of lectures on the traditions of European music at the Foundation, he had both a financial and an emotional investment in finding him a prestigious university position. He had invited Koyl to join him in an experiment. Nabokov was an essential variable, and the dean couldn't dispense with him and hope to keep Barnes's interest. Koyl had said the School "must go very slowly with any appointment to the Department of Music" because it was "not in a position to carry on financially" after the first year.[87] But would Barnes fund a professorship in fine arts bearing his name? "The principal offence of your letter," the collector wrote, "is in asking me to be the sucker you were looking for when, in honest response to the face value of the request, I suggested a tentative practical working plan to relieve the death and desolation at the very core of your Department. Your response is the moral equivalent of a man who after having asked to be invited to dinner attempts to steal the host's spoons. . . .This letter concludes my efforts to make our resources available to the University of Pennsylvania," he declared. "In fact, steps already have been taken to make sure that, after my death, the University will have no finger in our pie."[88]

But they hadn't. Barnes's will remained unchanged for more than a decade. Perhaps he still harbored some hope for reconciliation. In any case, he had little time to brood over the breakdown of his second brief round of discussions with Penn. Ten days after he had handed in the Matisse study to Scribner's, he and de Mazia had begun research for a big book on Renoir. On the same Mediterranean holiday during which he had first laid eyes on the Merion *Dance*, he had tracked down some early Renoir pictures in Paris and five German cities—Berlin, Cologne, Dresden, Essen, and Hamburg. In July of 1933, he wrote Dewey from the French spa, Brides-les-Bains that he was looking forward to accumulating more data at the major exhibition of Renoir's work at the Musée de l'Orangerie in Paris. "You can imagine the job we will have . . . there to check, verify and add to the material we already have," he said in the letter, which he closed with the assurance that he drank to his friend's health every night with "good Cutty Sark" he had brought from home.[89] On receiving the typescript of a portion of the work in progress, Dewey responded that "your brand of American spirits as contained in the chapter sent me is excellent; I enjoyed my drink very much. The percentage of spirit is much higher than 3.2. . . . I learned a lot that was new to me."[90]

Barnes and de Mazia continued their research in Europe during most of the summer of 1934. Despite long days visiting museums and galleries and evenings writing up notes, they occasionally took time out to entertain a dozen Barnes students who were spending four months studying art abroad courtesy of the collector. Barnes not only covered the cost of their transportation but also provided the students with $100 a month each for living expenses. As one young woman later wrote: "For the first time in my young and miserable life, I had PLENTY of everything."[91] But her benefactor didn't have enough pictures, especially at bargain prices. His summer purchases included "three of the best Seurats in the world, two important Cézanne landscapes, the rarest of Renoirs and three other very good Renoirs," according to a year-end report he made to Dewey.[92] Barnes was especially pleased to have bought a Renoir for $67,000 from a private collector who had "paid Durand-Ruel $74,000" for it a few years earlier.[93] By the time he and de Mazia finished *The Art of Renoir*, Barnes had acquired an astonishing 175 of the painter's pictures, including the twin pendants, *Caryatids*. He purchased the lovely coupled nudes in niches in December of 1933 from Jean Renoir for $4,200 each, using as his dealer Etienne Bignou from whom he also then bought Cézanne's early, powerful *Bathers at Rest*.[94]

The major problem with which the authors had to contend in their research was the sheer volume of work that Renoir had produced over the course of his long life. They attempted to solve it by undertaking detailed studies of his paintings during all stages in his career, from the mid-1860s until the artist's death in 1919. Their contribution to an understanding and appreciation of Renoir's so-called "red period," the purified style of his maturity, was groundbreaking. When the monograph was published in 1935 by Minton, Balch and Company, it was the first study of Renoir available in English. Barnes told Dewey it was "chock-full of entirely new objectively verifiable facts never even hinted at by anybody else."[95] Indeed, critics again applauded the exhaustive analyses of individual paintings. In the *New York Herald Tribune*, art historian James Johnson Sweeney, a former Barnes student, called it "a milestone in the appreciation of Renoir."[96] Eliseo Vivas wrote in the *Nation* that the "authors react more sensitively, more fully, and in a better-integrated manner to aesthetic values in painting than any other contemporary writer[s]" with whom she was acquainted. "Even if one should disagree with the high estimate of Renoir at which the authors arrive," Vivas said, "the central value of the book would remain unimpaired." It lies, the reviewer added, in providing a method that "compel[s] the reader to carry on a personal inspection of Renoir and the artists to whom he is related."[97]

The collector recognized that not all the painter's work was fully or successfully realized, but he saw the trajectory of the only Impressionist from a working-class background as relentlessly upward. "To every great tradition upon which he has drawn Renoir has added something new, personal, and of distinguished value," Barnes and de Mazia wrote. "He has achieved a union of expressive force and decorative richness unprecedented in plastic art."[98] In an odd last chapter, they attacked what they perceived as a "Cézanne fetishism," whose existence they held "responsible for a widespread blindness to the excellence of every other painter, and inevitably also to the most distinctive and important qualities in Cézanne himself." Both Renoir and Cézanne, they said, were "so deeply grounded in human nature that to avow an unqualified preference for either is to confess to an essential shortcoming in one's own personality."[99] But they didn't say what it might be.

The authors dedicated their book to Nelle Mullen in recognition of her role in handling all the correspondence connected with its production and in securing copies of more than 150 photographs that were used to illustrate the volume. Four of the 306 Renoir works referenced in the text belonged to Nelle and her sister Mary; 135 were owned by Barnes. The book carried a forward by Dewey in which he said somewhat wistfully: "Since my educational ideas have been criticized for undue emphasis upon intelligence and the use of the method of thinking that has its best exemplification in science, I take profound, if somewhat melancholy, ironic, satisfaction in the fact that the most thoroughgoing embodiment of what I have tried to say about education, is, as far as I am aware, found in an educational institution that is concerned with art."[100]

Upon publication of *The Art of Renoir*, Barnes almost immediately acquired two major portraits by the painter. From the newly opened Bignou Gallery in New York, he bought *The Henriot Family*, which he described to a friend, the writer and photographer Carl Van Vechten, as "a peach of a picture. . . I have been flirting with it for a number of years."[101] He also purchased *Portrait of Mademoiselle Jeanne Durand-Ruel*, a masterpiece of the genre, for $50,000 from Durand-Ruel.[102] Similar in format to *Girl with Jumping Rope*, one of his first Renoir purchases, it, too, was a painting Barnes had coveted for some time, and he came to view it as the artist's most successful work. Securing the long-sought treasures increased the sense of accomplishment he felt as a result of completing his Renoir study. Dewey proposed a celebration in the form of a two-week vacation in the Blue Ridge Mountains of western North Carolina. Barnes gladly agreed to join him. The two friends visited the new, experimental Black Mountain College, where there were no required courses, no examinations, no grades but a great stress on art as a means of teaching students the discipline and value of struggle against their own clumsiness and ignorance.

The collector brought a case of his rare, aged whiskey, which he shared with Dewey and Black Mountain's rector, John Rice, each evening before dinner. He spent his days observing classes taught by the recently arrived Josef Albers, a refugee from Nazi Germany who had taught at the famed Bauhaus in Berlin. The innovative and iconoclastic Rice, a fallen-away Methodist and former Rhodes Scholar, found the collector an engaging visitor who "questioned every man's right to be alive and usually found against the plaintiff."[103] Barnes, in turn, responded sympathetically to the spirit of Black Mountain, but he

took away a poor opinion of the teaching ability of Alpers, who at the time
spoke very little English. The ideal teacher, in Barnes's view, was one whose
"intellectual and emotional capacities enter[ed] into a respectable balance."[104]
Had he described de Mazia? She had proven to be not only an invaluable
research partner but also an instructor of great promise. He believed her capable of carrying on the method of training students that Mary Mullen had
developed in her Argyrol factory classroom. What other qualities and talents
he may have valued in his vibrant associate we will never know for sure.
Toward the end of 1935, Barnes contributed, in part if not wholly, to the thirty-
six-year-old immigrant's purchase of a large brick house on a corner lot in
suburban Penn Valley, not far from Latch's Lane, for the then considerable sum
of $28,500. De Mazia lived in the imposing dwelling, with its circular drive
and tall white pillars, until her death more than half a century later. She kept
there the gouache study Matisse had made for his first version of the Merion
Dance.

11

Varieties of Aesthetic Experience

The public persona of a scold that Albert Barnes had crafted for himself, whether deliberately or not, largely freed him from the civic demands that might otherwise have been made of a rich and prominent collector. He was rarely asked to join boards or address organizations, and his exclusion from the cultural and educational power structure of Philadelphia may have heightened the importance he accorded to an invitation from Central High School to deliver its distinguished Barnwell Lecture in 1936. Over the years, his alma mater had attracted many well-known speakers. They included eminent scholars, artists, and scientists, and Barnes was proud to have been invited to deliver the fifty-fourth in the historic series of addresses. The subject he chose was one that had fascinated and engaged him for most of his life. Before an audience of 1,600 people gathered at the Penn Athletic Club, the collector best known for his modern masterpieces talked about "The Art of the American Negro." To illustrate his lecture, he brought the Bordertown School Glee Club, eleven girls in white middy blouses and fourteen boys in khaki uniforms, to sing spirituals. Their performance moved one reporter to describe the African-American chorus as "a great musical instrument." Speaking from his heart, Barnes, who was so often garrulous, said the singing "did something to you emotionally that was impossible to put into words."[1]

The man long accustomed to "knocks" and long adept at giving them used his public platform to share the deepest part of himself so people would know who he was. The blame he bore for their continuing puzzlement should not detract from the courage Barnes exhibited that April evening. He began by telling the audience of his childhood encounter with black men and women at the camp meeting in Merchantville, New Jersey, and how his desire to recapture the aesthetic phase of the experience led him to study and collect paintings. Any Methodists in the crowd would have understood the importance of seeking experience. In the Wesleyan tradition, a personal experience of regeneration was a requirement for church membership and as sure a confirmation of salvation as it is possible to obtain in this world. Barnes was providing a clue to his motivation for undertaking the great adventure that became the consuming passion of his life. The way in which he defined "genuine experience" on that occasion, moreover, is a key to his concept of art education. He said it results "only when the individual brings to the field in which he is occupied an active interest, alert senses, an open mind, a store of knowledge, and systematic reflection. . . . Experience," he explained, "is a duplex process, involving both the individual and the environment." It occurs "when the individual does something to the environment and the environment does something to him."[2]

Barnes attempted to demonstrate his point by describing the reactions of a painter and a fire marshal to the clangor of fire engines. Sharing common emotions of excitement, curiosity, and concern, the painter might be stimulated by the colors, shapes, and movement associated with the fire to produce a painting while the marshal would draw upon his experience to shape a campaign to extinguish the conflagration with the least possible property damage and human injury. If the marshal succeeds in converting his emotion into a practical and efficient plan to put out the fire, "he is just as much an artist" as "the painter who expressed himself in a picture," Barnes said. Observers who have "kept their senses alive and their perceptions acute to note the significance of each step of the leader's activity" will "have had as authentic an esthetic experience as the most gifted connoisseur of painting gets from his study of pictures," he told the crowd. Calling the common tendency "to look upon art as a thing of the museums, something which belongs to the past, something which only a few especially endowed people are capable of appreciating" unfortunate, Barnes made headlines with his declaration that "the greatest artist Philadelphia has ever produced is Connie Mack," the manager of the Athletics, the city's beloved baseball team. Revealing himself to be a devoted fan, he said that when Mack was successful, the Athletics possessed "the indispensable requisites of great art—unity, variety, individuality, and the production of esthetic pleasure in others. Every baseball lover," he continued, "is alive to the meaning of each play and he experiences vicariously the skill, the hopes, the struggles, defeat, or triumph of the team."[3]

Turning to a description of his first camp meeting, Barnes told his white listeners about witnessing "the vivid, colorful drama performed in a quite individual manner." He said he now knew that he was then having his "first religious experience. . . . I was switched suddenly from my everyday world to the realm of mysticism—a realm where nothing else counts excepts the ineffable joy of the immediate moment," he recounted. Afterwards as he sought out the company of black people, he said he discovered that the men and women he came to know "carried out in their daily lives the poetry, music, dance and drama which, when exercised by a group, g[a]ve the camp meeting its . . . charm." Barnes described African-American religious rituals, which he first observed as a shy, wide-eyed boy standing at the backs of churches. The ceremonies were "characterized by a rhythmic coordination," he said, that gave "to the whole performance a unity and harmony which are the attributes of great art." He went on to paint a romantic albeit appreciative picture of African life before the abduction of vast numbers of blacks on slave ships bound for America. He praised the Africans' "uniquely rich folklore" and "primitive Negro sculpture which compares in artistic values to the finest sculpture of ancient Egypt and Greece." He discussed with keen insight the harsh transition to plantation culture and the role of Christianity in the lives of those held in human bondage, including its promise "to the disinherited and the outcast" of "a happier existence in another world." Reiterating his previously expressed view that spirituals were "the greatest art America has produced," he compared them to "the greatest artistic achievements of the Middle Ages—the cathedrals" on the grounds that "they are an outgrowth of community life inspired by religion. Like the Homeric poems, these spirituals are a work of generations of singers," he said, "so that they represent the collective griefs and aspirations of the race. Their appeal," he argued, "is universal, and they embody the soul of a whole people."[4]

Calling then upon the Bordertown chorus, Barnes became part of the audience that listened to the youngsters present a medley of songs under the able direction of Frederick Work. After the performance, he asked his fellow listeners to examine the emotions they experienced as the music "took possession" of them and "banished all concern." He noted that many had kept time with their feet. "You may have smiled at the homely and picturesque similes in which the Negro embodied his ideas about the particular subject-matter of the song," Barnes suggested. But "'Devil can't do me no harm' is . . . as authentic poetry as that written by Keats or Shelley. The Negro is a poet by nature. . . . His mind instinctively runs to rich, luxuriant images which he organizes rhythmically to meet the requirements of his emotion and temperament." All of us, black and white alike, he stressed, "seek relief from the forces of evil which militate against happiness, and we seek an eternal life-insurance when we sincerely worship." Barnes pointed out that Work had made no attempt to adapt the spirituals "to the spirit of jazz or to the structure of the European musical form. He has kept them in their original and pure state," the collector added, and he encourages individual improvisation.[5]

There was no time to speak of the "poetry of Angelina Grimke, Langston Hughes, Claude MacKay and others," he said. Nor the fiction of Jean Toomer in whose novels "the connoisseur recognizes an equality with the work of the best writers in America and Europe." But he wished to leave his audience with one message, the truth of which he hoped he had demonstrated with the evidence he had presented in his lecture: "Great art . . . is to be found in the activities of every person who puts that flavor of individuality into any work well done, which both satisfies the doer and communicates esthetic pleasure to others. . . . The art of the Negro is great primarily because he is exceptionally endowed with emotion, imagination, and a gift for rhythmic, picturesque, vivid and dramatic expression." If we understand that the "poetry and drama" that the African American lives "every day" is what is "needed to give interest and color to our prosaic civilization," he concluded, "it is incredible that we should not consent to form a working alliance with him for the development of a richer life, to which he will contribute his full part."[6]

Barnes's speech was a formidable challenge in the best tradition of civil rights advocacy. But while his Barnwell Lecture was politely received and the letter the committee in charge of the event wrote to thank him commented upon the liveliness of the evening, his remarks were soon forgotten. The collector himself failed to follow up his address with any immediate, practical initiative that might have benefited African Americans. From the easy perspective of hindsight, we can lament a lost opportunity to build momentum. But what a man so little given to working with others toward a common goal could have accomplished in the midst of the Great Depression is problematic. It is not, moreover, only a matter of his plea falling on ears long deaf to his fulminations. There was the matter of Barnes's own priorities. His impassioned celebration of the gifts of black people was trumped by his obsession with art.

In June, he and de Mazia went to Europe for three months of intensive research on their new project—a book about Cézanne. A huge retrospective of the painter's work at l'Orangerie in Paris provided them with a wealth of source material. To Barnes's immense satisfaction, the French government invited him to give a series of talks on Cézanne at the exhibition, and on July 22, President Albert Lebrun awarded him the title of Officer of the Legion of Honor. But in addition to studying paintings, the collector was buying them. By his own account, he spent $500,000 during the summer of 1936 on art. From a private collection in Switzerland, he acquired Cézanne's *The Drinker* and *The Woodchopper*. He bought four of Matisse's latest paintings, and told a reporter on his return to the United States: "Everyone thought he had shot his bolt. . . . He . . . hadn't shown anything for two years. But this year he had a show in Paris that would knock your eye out! The man has an absolutely new approach to color." Barnes also picked up two works by Raoul Dufy and, a picture that made headlines when he announced his purchases to the press-- Manet's *The Linen*, one of the artist's largest and most acclaimed paintings, which had been famously rejected by the French Salon sixty years earlier. In addition to works on canvas, Barnes added three sculptures to his collection. A figure in calciferous stone, which he described as an "Egyptian piece [that] turned up in Paris very mysteriously," particularly captivated him. "I was thunderstruck when I saw it," he said. "The chap who had it had been over to London with it, but the British Museum couldn't raise the money."[7] Two rare Greek sculptures, dating from the fifth to the seventh centuries B.C., completed his haul. In triumph, he disembarked on August 31 from the French liner *Normandie*. The *New York Times* reported that he was accompanied by "Miss

Violette de Mazia," but the Philadelphia papers tactfully omitted any reference to his collaborator.[8]

In his statements to reporters, Barnes mentioned that French poet and essayist Paul Valéry had agreed to lecture at the Foundation during the coming winter if his health permitted a trip. He also said he had persuaded the picture dealer and author Ambroise Vollard to visit the United States, and while Valéry never came, Vollard's journey was a fitting finale to Barnes's spectacular summer season. It was planned to coincide with a Cézanne exhibit at Bignou's and Keller's New York gallery that included the artist's portrait of the legendary merchant. Barnes arranged for Dewey to speak at the opening, and he seized the opportunity to address the guests himself before introducing Vollard. A few days later the Frenchman traveled to Merion to give a lecture at the Foundation. Upon the advice of Bignou, Barnes had invited the leading New York art critics, many of whom he had previously refused to admit to the gallery, to be present as his guests on the occasion.

The jovial group nearly filled a Pullman coming down by train from New York, and their host sent a fleet of cars to take them from the railroad station to Latch's Lane. After Vollard's talk, which Bignou translated into English, Barnes dismissed the students and gave his guests the opportunity to view his collection while he liberally dispensed his precisely measured highballs until dinner. Henry McBride described the evening as "admirable in every way, good food . . . fabulous whiskey . . . and the sense borne upon all of us that we were participating in a really exceptional occasion. If there had been the faintest touch of eccentricity anywhere in this entertainment," he wrote fifteen years later, "I failed to notice it."[9] But the critic hadn't overheard a conversation between Barnes and Vollard when the guest of honor tumbled on the front steps of the Foundation. As the picture dealer related the incident in his memoirs, his host helped him up and exclaimed: "Ah! Vollard . . . if you had killed yourself, I would have buried you in the middle of the Foundation." Two other guests who had been listening approached the Frenchman later and told him they had discussed the spot he might have chosen if he had been interred there. One thought the dealer, who introduced Cézanne's work to collectors at a time when it was known only to a few artists, would certainly have chosen to be at the foot of the painter's *Bathers*. The second thought his *Card Players* a more likely selection for a grave marker. "I responded," Vollard wrote, "that, for the moment, I didn't feel any disposition to choose."[10]

The day after the festivities in Merion, Barnes went to New York to see the picture dealer off for Paris. A radio address over WINS was arranged for the eve of his departure. The collector introduced Vollard with grandiloquence "as the most important figure in the art history of the nineteenth and twentieth centuries." He saluted his "penetrating foresight, wise judgment, and independence of thought and action" in recognizing the talents of a galaxy of artists whom he brought to public attention.[11] Vollard expressed his "astonishment, even stupefaction" at having found in both private collections and museums "such a great number of masterpieces of artists from old Europe. I can foresee that the coming generations on my side of the Atlantic will have to cross the ocean to really study the art of their respective countries," he said. Paying tribute to the Metropolitan's Havemeyer Collection for which Mary Cassatt bought the first Cézanne he had ever sold, Vollard observed that he was "still under the spell" of his visit to the Barnes Foundation, where he had seen, for the first time in years, many paintings he had long "kn[own], defended and loved." He declared that his visit to Merion had been "the great experience" of his short trip to America. "I assure you," he said, "that there does not exist and will never exist in the world another collection of masterpieces of the two greatest painters of the nineteenth century, Cézanne and Renoir, comparable to the one assembled . . . by Dr. Barnes."[12]

The English art historian Kenneth Clark already knew that the United States was the place to see modern French painting. On his first visit, in the late fall of 1936, he inspected the "glorious higgledy-piggledy" of the Chester Dale Collection, the rather fewer but impressively exhibited pictures assembled by Adolph Lewisohn, and, thanks to careful planning, Barnes's treasures. Invited to Merion a week after the request he made by telegram, Clark spent the night before his appointment with Joseph Widener and took the wise precaution of leaving Widener's car, which he had borrowed, a quarter of a mile from the Foundation. When Clark and his wife, Jane, arrived at the gates, they were scrutinized by a "roughneck" before being admitted to the gallery. Once inside, they found Barnes sitting on a kitchen chair in the great main hall listening to a tape recording of his radio talk about Vollard. Keeping wide of the collector, the Clarks walked quickly through the other rooms. "After about twenty minutes he confronted us, with beetling brows," the art historian recounted years later. "He was dressed in St. Tropez style, and Jane was inspired to say 'What a beautiful shirt you have on, Dr. Barnes.' 'Yes,' he said, 'it's a good one. And I wear red pants on Sundays.'" Clark came to recognize the collector's penchant for "spoof" as he was welcomed back to Merion on a number of occasions during the next several years. But assuming a goodly measure of truth in Barnes's tales of extracting Cézanne and Renoirs from hard-up owners, he bridled at what he considered his host's rapaciousness even as he accepted his hospitality. Cézanne was the nineteenth-century painter who meant the most to Clark, so he did not let his distaste for what he considered a tasteless boast interfere with the "stunning experience" of being able "to see ninety-two" of the artist's pictures in one gallery.[13]

Barnes received with evident pleasure a number of other visitors associated with the arts during the late 1930s and even sought out at least two who never made it to Merion. The multi-talented novelist, music critic, and photographer Carl Van Vechten, a tall, homosexual dandy with corn-silk hair who served as press agent for the Harlem Renaissance, was invited to Merion while the scaffolding for the Matisse mural was still in place on the condition that he come without any of his journalist pals whom, Barnes wrote, "we bury in the manure pit" after "our dogs are finished with them."[14] During his visit, Van Vechten photographed Barnes and soon afterwards began sending him prints of artists who had sat for him, including Matisse, Ethel Waters, and Paul Robeson. "I used to think that Stieglitz was talking through his hat when he claimed that photography, when done by a man who has the internal rumblings which come out as personal expression, is itself art of high grade," Barnes told his new friend. "Your photographs have done more to bring me around to Stieglitz's viewpoint than any others I have ever seen."[15] But it was Van Vechten's appreciation and understanding of black music even more than his artistic talent that recommended him to the collector. Barnes frequently asked the celebrated liaison between New York's black and white cultural elites to come to Merion for performances of the Bordertown singers and beseeched him, without success, to persuade Waters and Marian Anderson to accompany him.

To his guests' surprise, the collector occasionally sought to engage them on the spot as teachers. After returning from Europe in January of 1937 "with a wealth of new things for the Foundation," he welcomed a young, Russian-born dealer, Vitale Bloch, from whose Berlin gallery he had once bought a painting of an angel by an anonymous fifteenth-century Florentine artist.[16] Bloch brought with him a panel by Hieronymus Bosch in which he hoped to interest the collector. As a class was in session, the dealer sat down to listen to the teacher's lecture. When it was over, Barnes suddenly announced that "Mr. Vitale Bloch from Europe . . . would give a talk on Bosch." The panel, a small replica of *The Temptation of Saint Anthony*—a famous triptych, was put on an easel, and the bewildered dealer, who had never before been in the United States, did his best, in his limited English, to talk about the works of the Dutch painter. The collector interrupted with questions about the affinity between Bosch and Matisse, and before the class was dismissed, he had the replica hung in the gallery. Barnes then asked Bloch to his office, invited him to name his price, and handed him a check for the full amount along with an inscribed copy of *The Art of Renoir*. "The whole visit took on for me the colors of a fairy tale," the dealer later told a writer.[17]

If Bloch perceived Barnes as something of a wizard, Pennsylvania Museum of Art officials were inclined to see him as a goblin. A fantastic force, surely, but mischievous and sometimes malicious from their point of view. Out of the blue, in November of 1936, John S. Jenks, the museum's vice president, received a letter from Barnes offering to arrange for an exhibit of tapestries based on the paintings of artists then working in France. They were produced in the factories of Beauvais and Aubusson through the efforts of Marie Cuttoli, the wife of a member of the French Senate, who feared that the enforced idleness of hundreds of skilled workers threatened the extinction of an industry linked to one of the great traditions of art. As the worldwide economic depression approached its nadir, she persuaded the French government to sponsor the tapestry reproduction of contemporary painters' work. Etienne Bignou and Georges Keller had shown a selection from the first series of the modern tapestries at their New York gallery the previous spring, and Barnes had bought two for the Foundation. Now he suggested the museum could host an exhibition of a new series early in 1937.

Jenks was the one Pennsylvania Museum of Art trustee with whom the collector continued to maintain relatively cordial relations. He had visited Merion within the past year, and the new Officer of the Legion of Honor felt comfortable turning to him as he sought to promote French culture in the United States. As the museum was just completing seven new galleries intended for temporary exhibitions, Jenks thought that three of them with good northern light would be an ideal place to show the tapestries. But he was concerned about the expense of an exhibition. Barnes assured him they would "put their heads together and get the money somehow."[18] So Jenks brought the proposal to his fellow trustees and was able to report to Barnes that the idea of the show had been greeted with enthusiastic approval. He said the museum could devote $100 toward an exhibition, and Barnes replied that since two other venues would share the cost, the dedicated funds would be sufficient. He added that he was arranging for the American tour as a favor to Mme. Cuttoli, so he did not want his name used in connection with the exhibit.

Jenks assured the collector his wishes would be respected and suggested the museum's new assistant in decorative arts, Henry S. McIlhenny, as just the person to "look after the tapestries and arrange their hanging."[19] McIlhenny's late father, a former museum trustee, had been a passionate collector of Oriental carpets, but what Barnes undoubtedly found even more intriguing was that the young Harvard graduate had himself begun to collect modern art, including several works by Renoir, Cézanne, and Matisse. As it happened, Mme. Cuttoli found it necessary to postpone the release of the tapestries until the fall of 1937, but when he was in France early that year, Barnes arranged for the exhibition to open in Philadelphia. McIlhenny was solicitous, sending the collector a blueprint of the new galleries so he could see the space allotted for the event now planned for November, and Jenks wrote a gracious letter thanking Barnes for his efforts. But quite as suddenly as the offer of the tapestries had appeared, it was withdrawn—the victim of what Barnes took as a new trespass against him.

The miscreant was the new chief of the museum's education division, Emanuel Mervyn Benson, who had been hired by Kimball with a grant from the Carnegie Corporation, to organize a series of exhibitions. After six years of drastic cutbacks in city appropriations, the director was thrilled to have him on board. Benson had studied art history at Dartmouth and Columbia and, from a base in New York, written about art for some of the country's leading magazines. His inaugural curatorial effort, "Forms of Art," opened at the end of

April. It was advertised as "a fresh approach to the understanding of the art of the past and the present" that demonstrated "how time and place become secondary to the creative character of the works themselves." Benson divided the paintings, drawings, sculpture, and decorative objects he had assembled into three categories, formal and humanized values, social comment and satire, and phases of fantasy. He claimed "unanimity of purpose" united the work of the artists displayed within each section of the show.[20] In fact, his arbitrary divisions seemed to have more to do with subject matter than anything else, and when Barnes visited the exhibition, he erupted—his anger flowing like lava upon an institution and a community he said Benson had disgraced. His complaint echoed the allegation he had made against Penn's Louis Flaccus a decade earlier. The heart of the matter was that the collector believed that the hapless curator had stolen his ideas from *The Art in Painting*. Almost as egregiously, he had corrupted them beyond recognition.

The incident revealed a pattern of response to what Barnes perceived as thefts of his intellectual property and abuses of his good will. The collector initially marshaled evidence that he considered scientific, in this case "thirty-four specific proofs," in support of his charge of plagiarism.[21] He presented them to J. Stogdell Stokes, the president of the Pennsylvania Museum of Art, in a letter demanding the immediate close of the exhibition. In a reply seeking to defuse Barnes's ire, Stokes mentioned that Benson had studied with Dewey, and he then instructed the curator to explain the theoretical basis of his exhibit directly to the collector. Benson wrote that he had, indeed, read *The Art in Painting* and been stimulated by it as he had by the works of other writers who "arrived at analogous conclusions, each through his own experience." All had "undoubtedly left their mark" on the development of his ideas, but "nothing could or would have come of it," Benson said, "if fresh personal experience with art and life over a period of many years had not confirmed a point of view."[22] Unconvinced and unappeased, Barnes likened the curator's audacity to that of "a citizen of another city who came to Philadelphia and tried to sell to the local residents the rights, titles and interests in and to City Hall."[23] He roused the recently organized Artists Union to file a protest with the museum and, as he almost invariably had in the past, Barnes turned to Dewey for emotional support and public commendation of his actions. In the terms of an older psychology than that of William James, he sought the assurance of sanctification on the basis of his aims and aspirations and the earnestness of his effort.

In April of 1937, the seventy-eight year old Dewey had gone to Mexico as chair of a subcommittee of the Commission of Inquiry that took testimony from Leon Trotsky. While Joseph Stalin, former ally of the exiled Bolshevik, was trying him in absentia for treason, Trotsky had sought an opportunity to present his case before an impartial international tribunal. Dewey had conducted an exhausting week of hearings at the villa of the painter Diego Rivera.

Resting afterwards at the Missouri ranch of his daughter, Evelyn, he wrote to Barnes about his disillusion with the Soviet Communist regime and sought his help in publicizing the fraudulent nature of the Moscow Trials. Displaying a parochialism that contrasted starkly with the global concern he had exhibited nearly two decades earlier when he sought to expose the activities of Polish monarchists, the collector replied that he was "head over heels in a fight" that he saw as "a crucial test" over whether or not the philosopher's ideas were "to be allowed to be perverted as instruments of educational chaos." He beseeched Dewey to come to Philadelphia to view the Benson exhibit. "You tell me," he said, "whether or not I sh[ould] proceed with the public show-down. . . . I won't do anything without your approval; and if you do approve, I'll give a public demonstration of what ideas can do when they are fused, integrated, part and parcel of red-hot emotion. For Christ's sake, let's do something—the door has never been left so wide open as it is at this moment, the culprits know it, and they are trembling in their shoes. We can't lose," Barnes assured his friend, "and in winning we make the way much easier for others who believe in education as you've defined it."[24] Dewey, who had signed his earlier letter to Barnes "love and kisses" in playful affection, could not resist the appeal.[25] He would once again act as circuit judge.

The philosopher stopped in Philadelphia in mid-May on his way back to New York. After viewing "Forms of Art," he issued a public statement. The exhibit, he said, was "even more confused, both intellectually and esthetically," than he had been led to believe. "It was bad enough to call it, in the accompanying circular, a 'fresh approach' when the leading idea . . . [wa]s obviously borrowed from *The Art in Painting* without referring to that book. The exhibition itself not only fails to carry out the borrowed idea . . . , but so completely contradicts it as to show that Mr. Benson never got the idea, but only some verbal expressions of it. . . .That Mr. Benson should be thus confused personally is no great matter," the philosopher continued. "That a great public institution should lend itself to propagating the confusion is serious."[26] Dewey's conclusion gave Barnes the license he sought to exact recompense from the museum. Four days after the philosopher issued his report, the collector wrote to McIlhenny that he intended to tell the French officials that he was canceling his request to have the modern tapestries exhibited in Philadelphia. The reason he cited for his decision was "recent factual corroboration" of his "previous statement that the Pennsylvania Museum of Art is an house of artistic and intellectual prostitution."[27]

The language was becoming as familiar as the tactics. Barnes's reaction to "Forms of Art" may well have been intensified, however, by the impending publication of the third edition of *The Art in Painting*. Even as the collector and de Mazia were working on their Cézanne monograph, they collaborated in producing an expanded version of Barnes's first book, which was enlarged to include the fruits of their past twelve years of study. It came out in the fall to generally favorable reviews. In the *New York Times*, Edward Tinker wrote that while some critics might find the book "over ponderous and didactic, the industrious delver into the esthetics of painting [would] find much of interest and profit."[28] The emotional high the collector must have experienced at winning even modest praise from a critic noted for savaging shoddy work was soon obliterated by a darker mood. On Armistice Day he read the local papers with a surge of rage. In announcing a major new purchase for the Pennsylvania Museum of Art, Cézanne's *Bathers* from the private collection of the Pellerin family in Paris, Joe Widener, who negotiated the deal, was quoted as saying that "the acquisition . . . gave to Philadelphia and its neighborhood, the distinction of owning the two best known versions of the painter's favorite subject. The second version, a slightly smaller picture, is in the collection of the Barnes Foundation."[29]

The money for the painting, $110,000, came from the Wilstach Fund, which was administered by the Fairmount Park Commission through a committee chaired by Widener. Usually the sportsman and collector, heir to his father's magnificent Old Masters, had little sympathy for modern art, but Fiske Kimball was keen to own a large Cézanne and easily obtained the enthusiastic support of museum trustee Carroll Tyson. It was Tyson who persuaded Widener to go to Paris to meet with agents for the Pellerin family. Both he and Kimball harbored the fond hope that the Widener Collection, which by terms of old Peter's will his son was empowered to give to any museum in Philadelphia, Washington, or New York, might one day come to the Pennsylvania Museum. They were concerned that Joe's attention had been focused more on horse racing than pictures for a decade and sought opportunities to involve him in the art world and honor him for his place in it. When he returned with Pellerin *Bathers*, Kimball asked him to hang it and crafted his press release to emphasize Widener's role in acquiring what headline writers called "a gem" for the city.[30]

Barnes read the announcement as an attempt to belittle his own proud possession. Dashing off a letter to Stogdell Stokes, he said "the reference to me in this morning's newspapers, by some of the officials of the Pennsylvania Museum of Art, had the reporters on my track before noon with a request for a statement. I dictated something," the collector informed him, "but instead of giving it to the reporters at this time, I am sending it to you, with the suggestion that you use the matter to correct, in a public statement, the stupid assertions of the Museum officials in reference to our picture, and tell them never again to use my name as a stalking horse in their circus."[31] Barnes warned that if the president of the museum did not act, he would issue his own press release. But Stokes made no move, and the collector must have enjoyed the next day's *Philadelphia Record*, the city's sole Democratic paper, which expressed editorial discomfort over the "ready availability of $110,000 for 'The Bathers' and the seeming lack of any funds for all 'The Non-Bathers'" by which it meant the occupants of "no less than 41,000 of this city's dwellings .

. . without bathtubs. . . . Why is it that no such funds are available to give this community the elementary cleanliness in its backyard which would seem to be an essential modern counterpart of the luxury of its front yard?" the editors asked. "The 'Non-Bathers'," they concluded, "can go look at this painting. But they can't wash themselves with clean water in their own homes."[32] Even Barnes's least favorite art critic, Dorothy Grafly, questioned the generous expenditure of city funds on a Cézanne when the Pennsylvania Museum had used none of its own monies or any portion of the Wilstach income to buy paintings by American artists in the past year. When museum officials replied that they had used gifts solicited on the museum's behalf to buy paintings by three Philadelphians, she wrote: "A beggar's tin cup for America; $110,000 for Europe."[33] But the collector's complaint, which he issued publicly four days after writing to Stokes, was in a class by itself.

During the intervening period, he had honed remarks that he then wielded like a scalpel to puncture the museum's balloon. His characterization of the institution's *Bathers* as an "unfinished sketch" in the statement he shared with Stokes became, in his public pronouncement, a painting "of about fifth-rate quality for a Cézanne" that "went begging for a buyer for more than five years." Declaring that "its former owner, in the presence of witnesses, offered to sell the picture to [him] for $80,000" and that shortly afterward a Paris dealer advised him "to offer $50,000 for it," Barnes said, "the city had been 'stung' with an inferior painting and that officials ha[d] propagated . . . transparent ballyhoo and misrepresentation." He described the picture's color as "monotonous, dry, and lusterless, the composition [as] disorganized and mechanically executed, its drawing and modeling [as] inadequate." He said, "the extensive areas of bare canvas serve chiefly as reminders of the general lack of substance in the picture as a whole." The museum's purchase, Barnes grandly proclaimed, "misses fire completely as an example of either Cézanne's perfected technique or of his high status as an artist." His *Bathers*, on the other hand, was "a fully completed painting with a richly-varied color scheme of deep, juicy, sparkling, lustrous colors so well integrated with the skillful drawing, modeling and use of space that the tightly-knit, rhythmic, composition expresses strength, power and satisfying fullness in a characteristic Cézanne form." But the collector was not content to try to make his case on the basis of analysis alone. In a vitriolic coda, he asserted that "the presence in Philadelphia" of the painting that Widener acquired for the museum illustrated what was wrong with "having an absentee dictator of the official art situation, who functions principally at the race tracks of Miami, Saratoga and Deauville."[34]

The "Battle of the Bathers" took place two years before the commercial debut of electronic television. But even with graphics limited to still photographs of a stocky man in a fedora and the two Cézanne canvases of nudes, the print media had a field day. Well aware of the costs of exchanging verbal brickbats with Barnes, museum officials mostly kept their individual and collective mouths shut. Besides, visitors, curious about the painting over which the controversy had arisen, flocked to see it. The papers reported that local artists hoped the row would lead the collector to open his galleries to a greater number of students—and seized the occasion to observe tartly that most of the public would have to accept hearsay evidence as to the relative merits of Barnes's *Bathers*. Notably unsympathetic to Widener, Kimball, et al., the Philadelphia Artists' Union observed that "if museums had the progressive policy of purchasing worthwhile works of contemporary artists while they are living, they would have no need of paying such astronomical ransoms for paintings."[35]

Rallying to the defense of a colleague, the director of the Metropolitan Museum of Art told an inquiring reporter that the Pennsylvania Museum's *Bathers* was "a very fine painting," and painter/collector Tyson, the only museum trustee to respond to journalists' questions, declared it "certainly the greatest Cézanne in the country."[36] The local cultural establishment also received anonymous support from a letter writer to the *Evening Bulletin* who signed himself or herself "Syndic." In an effort to counter Barnes's charge that the Pellerin *Bathers* was unfinished, the writer argued that Cézanne sometimes left parts of a canvas bare intentionally and under painted his pictures, particularly his later ones, so they had a thin, dry appearance that far from being a weakness was a "synthesis and profound summing up of all his experience." "Syndic" congratulated the museum for the purchase of a "superb canvas," ridiculed Barnes's analysis of it ("It is irreverent to seek to find the germ of a man's genius under the glass of a microscope as though it were some sort of patent medicine microbe."), and described *The Art in Painting* as "a masterpiece of dull and pedestrian writing."[37]

The anonymous criticism, which Barnes assumed was the work of someone associated with the museum, gave the collector all the excuse he needed to fan the flames of the fire he had started when he lobbed his first grenade toward Fairmount. In a new letter to Stokes, he called Widener an "ignoramus" and claimed Tyson had admitted "he was half drunk when he talked to a reporter about the museum's Cézanne *Bathers*." Barnes described his rival collector as a "pot-bellied" dispenser of "lecherous looks" whom "many respectable women consider . . . the most disgusting man in the city."[38] When Frank Crowninshield, an art collector and the editor of *Vanity Fair*, came to lecture at the University of Pennsylvania Museum in early December, he found that the table talk at the luncheon in his honor focused largely on Barnes—and so reported to the man who had graciously allowed him to wander at leisure among his paintings earlier in the day. But the squire of Merion was undeterred by wagging tongues. The next month he issued a pamphlet that was designed to keep them in motion. "A Disgrace to Philadelphia," which he tried and failed to persuade the *Nation* to run as an essay, castigated the art museum trustees as exemplifying "the oft-told story of how institutions supported by taxpayers' money are exploited to serve the ends of individuals ambitious for power and social distinction." Displaying his literary tastes as well as the chip on his shoulder, Barnes said:

> The Board represents primarily money inherited from ancestors or accumulated in banking, commerce or manufacturing; not one of its members has ever contributed an idea of his own to the intellectual, artistic or cultural development of the community. It is true that the Board members are well-intentioned citizens of unimpeachable character; it is equally true that the present disgrace brought upon the city is due largely to the fact that a main function of the Museum has been to serve as a pedestal upon which a clique of socialites pose as patrons of art and culture: they are perfect examples of the characters in Edith Wharton's famous story Xingu, "who pursue culture in crowds, as though it were dangerous to meet alone."[39]

Never one to limit attack upon perceived enemies to a single weapon, Barnes moved adeptly from firing sophisticated epistolary missiles to stirring up as much agitation as he could among underemployed artists with the time and inclination to express their grievances in picket lines. In late January, on the occasion of the unveiling of an anti-Fascist mural at Philadelphia's New Theater, the collector rallied some sixty people, including a number of Barnes students, to protest the museum's new exhibition of artwork produced under the aegis of a Depression-era relief program administered by the Works Progress Administration (WPA). It was insufficiently representative of the city's artistic talent, Barnes claimed, and told a crowd of 200 gathered to see the mural that the museum had thrown away "$24,000 in another 'sucker deal.'" As he described the conduct of Fiske Kimball and Mary Curran, regional director for Pennsylvania of the Federal Arts Project, as a "picture of Fascism," pickets marched in front on the museum's entrances.[40] They kept it up for three days, and at one point Barnes urged reporters to join them.

His quarrel with Curran appeared to have stemmed from an investigation he had conducted on the basis of a student's complaint. The young artist told the collector that he would have to withdraw from his Foundation class because of a WPA rule requiring him to work each day in his studio in return for a weekly subsistence wage. No exceptions were allowed by the regional director. When Barnes looked into the matter, he discovered that Curran, the owner of a small gallery, had been expelled from a Barnes course more than a decade earlier and subsequently supported for her WPA post by Kimball, who chaired the Federal Arts Project advisory committee. Promptly organizing Friends of Art and Education, an action committee to which he persuaded Dewey to lend his name as its honorary chairman, Barnes, as president of the Friends, wrote to the head of the Commonwealth's Emergency Relief Board to warn of "bread riots" if there was not a public inquiry into Curran's administration. He employed Hart to write a pamphlet entitled "Philadelphia's Shame" that excoriated the regional director for a catalogue of sins—favoritism, discrimination, anti-unionism, lethargy, and ineptness—and quoted Barnes as saying: "Miss Curran is not only profoundly ignorant of what constitutes a work of art but is so handicapped mentally that she is incapable of obtaining the experience that would enable her either to form an intelligent opinion of art values, or to direct any project participated in by normal human beings."[41] Kimball dismissed the collector's tirade as "rubbish."[42]

Titillated by Leopold Stokowski's romance with film star Greta Garbo and increasingly concerned about the Japanese blitzkrieg across China and German aggression in Europe, the media and the public began to tire of the predictable explosions in Merion. But the collector's little band of self-righteous warriors fired one more broadside. On March 17, 1938, an eighteen-page denunciation of Kimball, his staff, and his board, conceived by Barnes but written by a young attorney, Harry Fuiman, was issued under the title "The Progressive Decay of the Pennsylvania Museum of Art." The director and his assistants were charged with "incompetence and malfeasance" and the trustees with complacency. Echoing the tone of remarks Barnes had made a month earlier when he suggested that ordinary citizens could take their museum back, the new pamphlet observed that "art loving Pennsylvania Museum members," those who "paid their $10 and more annually," had been "disfranchised and their money used by the insiders, mostly social climbers, to exploit the Museum for their own aggrandizement." Voting rights, which all members held prior to 1929, had been subsequently reserved for contributors of $1,000 or more, the Friends of Art and Education noted, and the public had witnessed "its art museum converted into a somnolent rendezvous for the idle rich."[43]

The little booklet found a metaphor for the institution's deterioration in the excrement of birds on its steps and cited as evidence of intellectual rot all Barnes's bugaboos: the "Forms of Art" exhibit, the purchase of the Pellerin *Bathers*, and Kimball's support of Curran. Pronouncing the museum's educational efforts "chaos," the Friends described the mustard limestone building as "a place for aimless wandering and . . . day-dreaming" on the part of a "sentimental class who worship art as something high and holy, without understanding what it is all about." The remedy proposed was an educational program remarkably similar to that conducted in Merion, the dismissal of Fiske Kimball and Henri Marceau, and the abolition of "the anomaly of having as a virtual dictator of city art matters an absentee, Joseph E. Widener, whose principal occupation is the promotion of race-track activities."[44] On his way to France later that spring, the sportsman found himself assigned to a deck chair on the *Normandie* next to one occupied by a familiar-looking man in a soft felt hat with the low crown creased lengthwise, his powerful build not entirely concealed by his blanket, eyes behind his rimless glasses focused on a book. There was no talk of the track at Deauville, art, or anything else. Too proud and stubborn to move or to exchange a word, according to Barnes, they "sat there, side by side, a couple of millionaires on [a] luxury liner" ignoring one another for the entire crossing.[45]

Barnes reached his hotel in Paris, the St. Regis, on the third of June. He had come to France to continue research on the book he and de Mazia were writing about Cézanne. Although he could not know it then, it would be the last summer he would spend in Europe for a decade. The start of his visit was as ominous as the gathering political storm. A letter awaiting the collector on his arrival informed him of the sudden death of William Glackens. The day the *Normandie* steamed out of New York harbor, Butts and Edith had gone to Westport, Connecticut to spend the weekend with Charles Prendergast and his wife. After breakfast on May 22, 1938, the two men were talking in the living room. Glackens suddenly lost consciousness and a half hour later was dead from a cerebral hemorrhage. Barnes later told Henry Hart: "Butts never knew what hit him. That's the best death."[46] But the collector was shocked and grief stricken when he first learned that his friend was gone. He wrote at once to his widow: "I feel a deep sorrow because I loved Butts as I never loved but half a dozen people in my lifetime. He was so real, and so gentle and of a character that I would have given millions to possess. And as an artist, I don't need to tell you I esteemed him: only Maurice [Prendergast], among all other painters I knew, was in his class. He will live forever in the Foundation collection among the great painters of the past who, could they speak, would say he was of the elect."[47]

Concerned for some time that her husband's best canvases were "locked up" in Merion where few could see them, Edith Glackens had written to Barnes a year earlier in an attempt to buy back one of Glackens's most powerful works, *American Girl*. Barnes replied that he would sell the picture to her for $85,000 cash, which was "cheap for its intrinsic value. Don't worry that Willie is not yet appreciated," he told her. "A hundred years from now I'll let you peek down to earth with me, and you'll be satisfied with the position he holds with the stars."[48] Clearly, Barnes didn't want to give up the painting. But Edith's plea had a delayed effect. Barnes loaned *American Girl* to the Whitney for a retrospective of Glackens's work that opened in December of 1938 and moved on two months later to the Carnegie Institute in Pittsburgh. It was one of the very few times, following the 1923 exhibition of his pictures at the Pennsylvania Academy of the Fine Arts, that he let one of his paintings go. Another was for a retrospective of Maurice Prendergast's works. He had hoped to write a book about these two friends, but he never managed to produce the monograph.[49] Perhaps he could never attain sufficient emotional distance to undertake the task.

But he did attend to an obligation he felt to another cherished friend. Soon after Glackens died, Barnes made arrangement for a lifetime stipend for Dewey. At the insistence of Columbia's President Nicholas Murray Butler, the philosopher continued to draw his $12,000 a year salary when he retired in 1930. But in 1938, the university was forced to retrench, and Dewey had to rely on his pension. Adjusting to reduced circumstances with his usual composure, he was stunned to receive a letter from Merion stating that if he didn't mind, the Foundation would begin paying him $5,000 a year. According to his friend and fellow philosopher Max Eastman, the unexpected and generous gesture so overwhelmed him that "he 'acted funny' for two days and wouldn't tell [his] family why."[50] Barnes had, of course, often picked up the tab when Dewey traveled with him, and his friendship with the philosopher was the most important relationship of his life. The loss of Butts, however, reminded him that his Argyrol fortune could no more buy time than it could affection. The man he had known well for twelve years before he called him "Jack," and now occasionally addressed as "Old Potato," was seventy-nine years old. The annuity Barnes chose was modest enough that Dewey would accept it yet sufficient to make the difference between a strained and comfortable old age: summers in a cottage in Nova Scotia and winters in Key West.

Dewey was in Florida when Barnes sent him one of the first copies of *The Art of Cézanne* that he received from his publisher. Harcourt, Brace and Company had released the book early in 1939, which was the centenary of the painter's birth. Barnes and de Mazia had finished writing it in Port Manech, a fishing village in Brittany to which the collector had been introduced by the art dealer Georges Keller in the early thirties and where he subsequently retreated to walk by the sea and put his thoughts on paper at the end of each summer visit to Europe. In 1938, the experience was particularly exhilarating. As his ideas matured about the artist who so fascinated and challenged him, Barnes said he woke in the night with new insights. "The meaning of Cézanne unfolded to me with a fullness I had never suspected," he wrote to Dewey.[51]

The philosopher read his copy of the new book straight through, "let the first reading soak in," then reread certain chapters. He told Barnes: "There is no doubt you have 'got something.' Indeed, it is so fundamental that now it is pointed out, it seems strange it hadn't been seen and said before. It will be axiomatic, I think."[52] Dewey was referring to the authors' treatment of romanticism and realism in the painter's work. They believed that Cézanne was a romantic by which they meant one who "lives partly in the real world we all share," but whose real interests are in the world of the imagination "from which boredom, defeat and disillusionment have been banished." But Barnes and de Mazia stressed that the value, indeed, the only justification of romanticism lies in its capacity to compel an artist to see more clearly and with greater understanding things in the real world. They portrayed not realism but conventionality as the opposite of romanticism. "The art of the romanticist," they wrote, "becomes analogous to the art of the scientist, a process of exploring the environment and bringing to light in it things to which the conventionally minded are permanently blind."[53]

Reviews of *The Art of Cézanne* were more mixed, that is, the praise was greater and the dismissal crueler, than for any of the previous collaborations by Barnes and de Mazia. *Time* declared that "occasionally, in each field, progress in interpretation is marked by a commentary so learned as to become classic. Published last week was a serious book which may well become a sort of Blackstone on Coke to future art students."[54] The *New Yorker* called the monograph "a judicious, penetrating estimate of the artist, his work, and its influence."[55] Paul Rosenfeld described it for readers of the *Nation* as an "excellent study . . . not only of the origins of Cézanne's form and technique in the traditions; of his characteristic explorations of color and light, line and space . . . but also of . . . [his art's] total and profound influence on contemporary painting."[56] In the *New York Times*, Edward Jewel wrote that the book "seems superior in some respects to the earlier studies. The introductory pages reflect a more cogent 'thinking through,' and in them ideas are expressed, often, with greater clearness and economy. There appears less that is redundant and turgid." Although Jewel found the authors "somewhat prone, as usual, to overelaborateness" in tracing the origins of artistic influence, he was intrigued by their suggestion that Cézanne "appears to be inventing a language of his own" comparable to the language invented by James Joyce.[57] In London, the *Times Literary Supplement* commented wryly on the authors' "hopeful industry and aggressive certainty" and noted that their "judgment of values is curious" since "a high proportion of the works which receive the most praise . . . are in the possession of the Barnes Foundation."[58] Most dismissive of all was Milton W. Browne in the *Saturday Review of Literature*. He observed that "the Barnes Foundation with laudable perseverance is still attempting to introduce the scientific method into art history. . . . However, the concept of the scientific in art is highly debatable." Browne could find in the monograph "no new contributions to the interpretation of Cézanne's art," though he said Cézanne scholars "must be thankful" for Barnes's and de Mazia's codification of all the technical means by which Cézanne achieved his goal. But "it should be stated," he concluded, that the authors "have made no concessions to the general public, either in readability or argument."[59]

Barnes had told Dewey that he hoped he had produced a book that would not be "hard sledding for people who don't pay much attention to abstract principles."[60] But if his written words didn't speak to the masses, there were still the class lectures through which he hoped to change the way Americans looked at art. His impulse was, on one level, profoundly democratic. On another level, however, there can be no doubt that Barnes cherished the good opinion of those whose intelligence he held in high regard. It was a matter of enormous personal satisfaction that barely three months after the publication of his last book, he entertained two Nobel laureates, Albert Einstein and Thomas Mann, for lunch at Merion. The great theoretical physicist was a professor at the six-year-old Institute for Advanced Study in Princeton, New Jersey, and the acclaimed author had just completed lectures on *The Magic Mountain* at Princeton University. The "chauffeur" who drove them across the Delaware was the German art historian Erwin Panofsky, who was then teaching at

Princeton, too. Apparently never guessing his identity, the collector provided the three refugees from Nazi Germany with a leisurely guided tour of his collection and the next best thing he had to offer—"a full dose of spirituals" courtesy of the Bordertown chorus, as he later told Carl Van Vechten.[61] Dewey, who had not been able to join his friend on the festive occasion, commented that he must have discovered that Einstein was "a charming human being."[62] Barnes said his guests "were almost garrulous in their expression of appreciation and asked to come again."[63]

Another source of pride and pleasure that spring was a letter from Horace Meyer Kallen, a colleague of Dewey's then teaching at The New School for Social Research. It asked him to join a small, select group that was organizing a celebration of the philosopher's eightieth birthday. "Your relation with him has been so intimate and fruitful," Kallen wrote, "that the committee would not be complete without you."[64] Barnes accepted with enthusiasm as he had in 1929 on the occasion of Dewey's seventieth birthday. Then the secretary of a national committee, which was seeking a hundred members, had written to "Alfred C. Barnes" and the collector had to inform him that he was "Albert." But a decade later Dewey's academic colleagues got his name right. Barnes was one of thirteen people, the rest leading figures in philosophy and education, who spoke at a two-day event held in late October at the Hotel Pennsylvania in New York. Although Dewey elected to sit out the affair at Evelyn's Missouri ranch, the birthday party attracted a thousand well-wishers and widespread media attention. Barnes talked about the application of scientific method to aesthetics, and in lauding Dewey's theory of art as experience, he provided a capsule restatement of his own core belief in the possibility of "verifiable objectivity" in judging pictures.[65] Dewey's comments on the occasion were delivered by Kallen and intended as a guide in troubled times. Less than a month after Germany and Russia had overrun Poland and less than a week after a German U-boat sank a British battleship at anchor in the Scapa Flow near Scotland, America's philosopher wrote that "intolerance, abuse, calling of names because of differences of opinion about religion or politics or business, as well as because of differences of race, color, wealth or degree of culture are treason to the democratic way of life."[66]

Early in 1940, Barnes, who could rarely resist name-calling in the heat of argument with those he judged his cultural inferiors, sought to honor another significant, if far less famous, contributor to the nation's life. He was a black composer who because of his race had been nearly forgotten even by those who sang his songs. When the collector was a student singing spirituals for his supper in German beer gardens, James A. Bland was the brightest star of minstrelsy in Europe, as well as in his native land. The son of a Wilberforce University graduate, who became the first African-American examiner in the U. S. Patent Office, Bland had come to know and appreciate spirituals when he was a student at Howard University. In the 1870s, he joined a minstrel troupe and was an immediate success. For twenty years, he made his home in London and toured music halls throughout Britain and the Continent as a singer-banjoist. Bland wrote some seven hundred ballads, including "In the Evening by the Moonlight," "Oh, Dem Golden Slippers," the theme song for the annual Mummers' Parade in Philadelphia, and one of the collector's favorites, "Carry Me Back to Old Virginny," which expressed the lament of a transplanted slave once again separated from his homeland. Because the music world was not disposed to attribute to blacks compositions of their own creation, Barnes did not know the composer was an African American until Van Vechten told him on hearing the song performed by the Bordertown chorus on a visit to Merion. The writer-photographer also mentioned that Bland had spent his last years in Philadelphia, the city where he had lived as a boy and where he had first become interested in music. Barnes wanted to know where he was buried, and upon investigation, Van Vechten telephoned him to report an extraordinary coincidence. The composer, who had died in 1911, lay in a pauper's grave in Merion!

His resting place had recently been located by James Francis Cook, the editor of the music magazine, the *Étude*, as the result of research undertaken by an emeritus professor at Howard whom Cook had commissioned to write an article on Bland.[67] When Van Vechten conveyed the news to Barnes, the collector felt a rush of excitement and responded with a characteristically detailed plan of action. "I begin immediately to see if I can get the best of the local Negroes to push the matter," he wrote. "One object of this would be to see that the race gets the main share of the glory, instead of, as usual, having it fall in the lap[s] of go-getting whites."[68] But Barnes soon discovered that a committee already had been organized by Cook with the intention of marking Bland's grave with a headstone. He adamantly opposed the idea on the grounds that the cemetery was a "dilapidated, ramshackle affair . . . pretty sure to be ordered removed by the township officials" because of the recent development of "substantial homes" in the vicinity. As he told Van Vechten, however, he would accept an anticipated invitation to join the committee in order to advance his own plan. Barnes's idea was to persuade all the area black organizations, "including churches, to endorse the project and contribute, even if only five cents a person, to the cost of the memorial."[69] To spearhead the drive for funds in the African-American community, he turned to Dr. DeHaven Hinkson, a physician for whom he had made it possible to obtain a year of post-graduate training in Paris when black doctors found it extremely difficult to secure residencies in American hospitals. Barnes suggested to a friend in local government that a small park near the cemetery would be an appropriate place for a memorial. He persuaded the editor of a township weekly to champion the cause in his newspaper and, ever the imaginative publicist, hoped to find a syndicated columnist to write a story on Bland that would spread the news of his plans to pay the composer homage far and wide. A black artist then studying at the Foundation might be engaged, the collector thought, to create a sculpture.

Barnes's shrewd grasp of group psychology and the irascible personality that prevented him from taking full advantage of his knowledge is illustrated by the unfolding of his plans for the Bland memorial. He urged Van Vechten to use his contacts among black artists to secure high-profile subscribers. He was prepared to speak in as many black churches as might be induced by Hinkson to invite him, and he wanted to be able to tell the potential contributors there that Paul Robeson, Marian Anderson, and Ethel Waters headed the donor list. Meanwhile, he sent Van Vechten his own check for $100 as a contribution for a memorial for James Weldon Johnson, the black composer/poet/ novelist and first African-American head of the NAACP who had died in 1938 and whom he had known for fifteen years. Barnes packed the original Bland memorial committee with like-minded acquaintances, including another prominent African-American physician, Dr. Charles A. Lewis, and the blues composer W. C. Handy. Dewey once again lent his name as president of the group. Permission from Bland's surviving sisters to have the body removed would be necessary to carry out the collector's plan. "I'll see to it that the Negroes get the glory for the achievement," Barnes once again assured Van Vechten.[70] He also spoke of establishing two annual James A. Bland Fellowships, with stipends of $1,000 each, for black artists studying at the Foundation once a memorial was in place.

Despite meeting personally with one of Bland's sisters in the spring of 1940, however, Barnes found that a formal document from the composer's kin authorizing the reburial of his body was not readily forthcoming. After a month, he grew impatient and told Van Vechten that his feet were "rapidly getting cold."[71] He warned his ally: "If they don't come across immediately, we're finished and unrekindlable."[72] The sisters then gave their oral permission, but Barnes said he needed a power of attorney. He worried that township officials had begun "to look on the affair more or less as a joke."[73] In desperation, he secured the necessary affidavits from his own lawyer and sent them to the attorney representing Bland's sisters. He soon had them back with proper signatures. Barnes immediately met with Lower Merion Township commissioners, and they agreed to act swiftly. "It's in the lap of the gods," he wrote to Van Vechten.[74] A week later, the local deities said no. Barnes had wanted about twenty square feet in a one-and-one-half-acre park, but the commissioners said they were unwilling to depart from their policy of restricting public lands to the purposes for which they were originally designated when acquired by the township. When a granite headstone was finally erected in the summer of 1946, it was due to the Lions Club of Virginia, the state that six years earlier had made "Carry Me Back to Old Virginny" its official song. The governor of Virginia attended the dedication of the memorial, but Barnes was nowhere in sight.

When the Lower Merion commissioners turned down his plan, he gave up on the project. His unwillingness to challenge township officials may have been related to his decision to expand his footprint in the local community. In October of 1940, the collector paid $45,000 for a grand stone dwelling, which was located less than a mile from the Foundation and around the corner from de Mazia's house. Though he would never write another book, he moved the Foundation's publishing operations, along with its administrative offices, into the handsome eight-bedroom house with a sweeping stairway, fireplaces in nearly every room, and a dozen French windows. He told a reporter that it would eventually house additions to his collection.[75] The quiet, tree-lined area was indisputably a tony residential neighborhood, but no objection was raised to the institutional use of the property. Barnes, de Mazia, the Mullen sisters, and assorted secretaries had offices on the second floor. The ground floor was furnished with American antiques and served as an elegant if intimidating place to interview prospective students. With Europe at war, Barnes could no longer travel abroad in search of pictures, and he concentrated his prodigious energy on overseeing the Foundation's classes.

12

Students and Teachers

Among the students studying at the Foundation in 1940 was an exceptionally talented black artist named Horace Pippin. It was he that Barnes had thought might create a memorial sculpture for Bland, though Pippin was a painter. He lived on a government pension in a cottage in the small country town of West Chester, Pennsylvania, and had to use his left hand to support his right wrist when he held a brush or palette knife. A gunshot wound, which Pippin suffered during World War I as a member of an African-American infantry regiment fighting in the Argonne Forest under French command, left him with a paralyzed arm. The art critic and collector Christian Brinton had seen two of Pippin's canvases in a shoemaker's window and called his work to the attention of the discerning and savvy Philadelphia dealer Robert Carlen. The ebullient Carlen was so taken with the black artist's burnt-wood panels and paintings that he made plans to hold an exhibition of his work. Barnes and de Mazia visited Carlen's gallery a few days before the opening in mid-January of 1940. Pippin's pictures were on the floor facing the walls, but the homemade canvas that he had used was so porous that the paints bled through, and the visitors, intrigued by the images on the back, asked Carlen to turn the pictures around for their inspection. Barnes was instantly captivated by the untrained artist's vision. He purchased one painting on the spot, de Mazia bought another, and the collector asked that a third be reserved for a friend.

Inquiring about a catalogue, Barnes learned that Carlen had prepared one illustrating and describing works for sale but without a foreword. Though the copy and half tones were even then at the printer, the collector insisted that there must be a short introductory essay—and as the presses were stopped, he wrote it himself. Barnes saw the country painter's pictures as the artistic "counterparts" to "the Spirituals of the American Negro. . . . One feels in Pippin's paintings a purpose, possibly not a conscious purpose, to attain a particular end, set by himself and pursued without learning, or even drawing upon, the resources of previous painters," he said. "This explains why his work has the simplicity, directness, sincerity, naïveté, and vivid drama of a story told by an unspoiled Negro in his own words. It is probably not too much to say that he is the first important Negro painter to appear on the American scene." Barnes declared the artist's work among the "most individual and unadulterated painting authentically expressive of the American spirit that has been produced in our generation. To hold against Pippin his present inability to make pigment express his ideas and feelings with refinement and finesse," Barnes concluded, "is equivalent to finding fault with Andrew Jackson because he never went to college."[1]

At the collector's invitation, however, Pippin soon enrolled in de Mazia's advanced class. The train fare from West Chester to Merion was a dollar, and Barnes provided it. When the artist dropped out after five or six months, Barnes did not take offense and continued to act as his patron and champion. Perhaps he was moved by the valor of a man who triumphed over a handicap similar in cause and kind, if not degree, to his own father's; perhaps he understood, as Pippin did instinctively, that an analytical method had the potential to spoil a folk painter; perhaps he grasped the discomfort an African-American war veteran must have felt in a lecture room filled mostly with much younger white students. Pippin, however, was not the only student of color. The artist Claude Clark, who single-handedly developed one of the first college art curriculums with an emphasis on the black experience, also studied at the Foundation in the early 1940s, as did the African-American musician, Kenneth Goodman. When Clark's alma mater, local and largely white Roxborough High School, held an exhibition of his paintings, Barnes, de Mazia, and the Mullen sisters attended as a body to demonstrate their enthusiasm for his work. It was Goodman, a fellow Central alumnus, who took Barnes to hear an African-American singing and praying band at Tindley Temple, one of Philadelphia's largest black Methodist churches, where the collector took off his coat, loosened his collar, and joined in the congregational dancing.[2] But both Clark and Goodman were in their twenties, while Pippin was fifty-one when he was introduced to Barnes. The self-taught artist had been painting for twelve years, and the show Carlen arranged was his first in Philadelphia, although Brinton, at the urging of the artist and illustrator N. C. Wyeth, had previously mounted a one-man show for him at the West Chester Community Center. When Barnes's favorite New York dealer, Etienne Bignou, gave Pippin his third solo exhibition in the fall, it was the first time the exclusive gallery had shown the work of an American.

Carlen showed Pippin's paintings and burnt-wood panels again in March of 1941, and again Barnes wrote a foreword to the catalogue. The Philadelphia dealer sent it to museums, and nine days after the opening of the show, the Whitney Museum of American Art bought a painting. Barnes himself acquired two from the exhibition, permitted his essay to be used in the catalogue for a Pippin show at the Arts Club of Chicago in May and June, and was instrumental in arranging for another solo exhibition of the painter's pictures at the San Francisco Museum of Art (later the San Francisco Museum of Modern Art), which was held in the spring of 1942. He requested that Carlen, who had appointed himself Pippin's agent, show him all the artist's work before it was put on the market. But the wily dealer realized that granting such a right of first refusal to the shrewd collector could cut sharply into his own commissions. To Barnes's dismay, Carlen was soon offering Pippin's pictures to other buyers. When he obtained an assignment for him to create a painting for a 1944 issue of *Vogue* featuring cotton dresses, Barnes accused him of exploiting the black artist. Mixed with the pride the collector took in the growing success of de Mazia's former student was an instinctive feeling that in making art to entertain white society, the black artist was losing his spiritual center. More than his sophisticated design and his bold use of color, what the patron admired most in his protégé was his celebration of the life of black Americans.

The friend for whom Barnes reserved the picture from among the first Pippins he saw was the actor Charles Laughton. They had known one another since 1935, and under Barnes's guidance, the British-born star of stage and screen, who had loved art since his youth, added Renoir's *Judgment of Paris* to his then small but carefully-assembled collection. The outbreak of the war in Europe found Laughton in Hollywood, and after his wife joined him there, they moved from a hotel into a rented house with bare walls. Facing tax problems in the United States and prohibited from bringing his savings out of England under defense-of-the-realm regulations, he jokingly appealed to Barnes to loan him some pictures. Barnes responded by shipping a crate of twenty paintings and drawings, including Utrillo's *Castle in Snow*, Kisling's *Girl in a Tree*, a Vlaminck still life, and a landscape by Soutine. Laughton was overjoyed by his generosity. When the actor visited Merion, where he was always welcome to spend time looking at Barnes's collection as long as classes weren't in session, the two pals indulged their taste for good whiskey and shared jaunts to the local movie theater. But the picture loan was above and beyond any ordinary requirement of friendship. "I am not only fond of Barnes as a person . . . he is a genius," Laughton told a reporter. "Or rather, you might say, he has genius. His talent for collecting the great art of the world and then knowing how to put it together is extremely rare. Dr. Barnes is a national possession. In 100 years the country will realize that. There have only been half a dozen such men in the world."[3]

The caprice with which the collector embraced or turned away the rich and famous is part of the Barnes legend that became firmly rooted in the course of his lifetime. Love of art was a necessary but insufficient criterion for admission to his gallery. Supplicants had to strike his fancy. Though it was not, strictly speaking, true, he relished the widespread suspicion that his policy turned the world upside down by ignoring top dogs and opening his iron gates to the lowly. Those of whatever rank that he detested above all were casual visitors, whom he always regarded as a threat to the Foundation's educational mission. He was usually sympathetic to the pleas of the young, and while a student at

Harvard, journalist and author Joseph Alsop won entry to the gallery by a combination of persistence and flattery and never forgot either the paintings or the words of the imposing man in carpet slippers who opened the door and told him: "Just remember, young man, these pictures you're going to see are the old masters of the future, *the old masters of the future!*"[4]

Barnes also courteously received a number of artists, art historians, and critics who were willing to arrange their visits at his convenience, including Henri-Pierre Roché and Julius Meier-Graefe, but their visits never caught anyone's attention. The stories people enjoyed retelling were how Columbia's Millard Meiss, like Panofsky, got in only by disguising himself as an attendant to an invited guest, and that Meyer Shapiro, who once regretted in print the absence from the 1931 MOMA Matisse exhibition of the artist's pictures owned by Barnes and Sergey Shchukin, was barred in perpetuum. They took note that despite writing a favorable review of *The Art of Painting* before he became MOMA's first director, Alfred H. Barr, Jr. never gained admittance, nor did the Whitney's Lloyd Goodrich. And who could resist repeating the answer provided by a factitious secretary, Peter Kelly, to the letter written by automotive heir and collector Walter P. Chrysler, Jr. seeking permission to visit the Foundation. It was impossible to pass along Chrysler's request to Barnes, "Kelly" said, because he was not allowed to interrupt his boss's "present efforts to break the world's record for goldfish swallowing."[5]

Most recipients of Barnes's rejection letters did not find them as amusing as the writer, but one who shared his stiletto sense of humor was the drama critic-turned-actor Alexander Woollcott. On a national tour of the long-running play, *The Man Who Came to Dinner*, in the spring of 1941, Woollcott, a native of Philadelphia who had also graduated from Central High School, sent his fellow alumnus a collect telegram asking to see an "assorted dozen" of his pictures the very next week. Barnes replied through another supposititious scribe, "Fidèle-de-Port-Manech," which was the name of his dog. Mademoiselle Fidèle explained that she had been alone in the house when Western Union called and declined to accept the telegram due to the household "financial condition." When the operator "explained that it was from such an important man that I should call Dr. Barnes to the phone to take the message," she wrote, "my reply was that Dr. Barnes was out on the lawn singing to the birds and that it would cost me my job if I should disturb him at his regular Sunday-morning nature worship."[6] The cllector couldn't resist passing along his funny retort to the newspapers, and a mock battle ensued in the press between the two wits. At one point, Barnes sent a note to the actor in which he congratulated himself on "trimming the fringe of your intellectual trousers, carried so high that your mental bottom was exposed to the public at large."[7] But he seems to have missed a larger point. As Woollcott and his press agents had calculated all along, the exchange generated invaluable publicity for the Kaufman and Hart play at the Forrest Theater.

The collector's failure to grasp how effectively he was being used may be laid to his preoccupation in March of 1941 with problems he was beginning to have with a new and highly valued Foundation teacher. Three months earlier, the English philosopher Bertrand Russell had embarked on a five-year course of lectures in Merion. The grandson of an iceman had hired the grandson of a prime minister with whom he shared a fundamental belief—that the scientific view of the world is largely the correct one. The circumstances of Russell's coming reveal Barnes at his best; the circumstances of his leaving are another illustration of the collector's quirks of personality that frustrated his noblest visions. From the perspective of the twenty-first century, engaging Russell, whom Barnes had read and admired for three decades, appears to have been a coup, but it also was an act of courage and generosity.

The outbreak of World War II in Europe found the sixty-seven-year-old logician, who had made revolutionary contributions to technical philosophy before he was forty, teaching at the University of California at Los Angeles. He was legally proscribed from taking money out of England, and the deadly stealth of German submarines made it dangerous for him to return home with his twenty-eight-year-old third wife, Patricia Spence, and their infant son. Russell was also responsible for the support of a teenage son and daughter, children from his second marriage, who had joined their father in California during their summer holiday from school in 1939 and now had no choice but to stay in America. He enrolled the two youngsters in UCLA, but hoped to move them, and himself, on to an Eastern campus, since he found the Los Angeles school a spectacularly uncongenial place for anyone with liberal, to say nothing of radical, leanings. Harvard invited him to deliver the William James Lectures in Cambridge in the autumn of 1940, the same prestigious series that Dewey had inaugurated nine years earlier, but it was the "poor man's Harvard," the scrappy City College of New York (now City University), its classes filled with the most gifted sons of immigrants, that offered him an eighteen-month contract early in 1940. With malicious joy, Russell turned in a letter of resignation to the University of California's autocratic president, Robert Sproul, only to learn that there might be problems with his new appointment. When he rushed to withdraw his letter, Sproul, by then tired of dealing with angry citizens who objected to the use of their tax dollars to pay the salary of an infidel, told the English philosopher it was too late. Russell's situation thereafter became rapidly more precarious.

The official announcement of his CCNY appointment on the 26th of February provoked a firestorm. *Marriage and Morals*, the 1929 book specifically cited by the Nobel Committee when it gave Russell the 1950 Nobel award in literature, was touted as proof of his degeneracy. The Protestant Episcopal Bishop of New York William T. Manning, an expatriate Englishman long opposed to Russell's ideas, incited a wave of protest against CCNY's audacity with public charges that Russell was a "recognized propagandist against both religion and morality" who "specifically defends adultery."[8] In a spirit of ecumenism, his Roman Catholic brethren joined in the fray, and newspapers were deluged with letters reflecting the righteous wrath of the American right, the political and social conservatives whom Russell had mocked for years in syndicated columns. For a jittery citizenry, threatened on the far sides of two protective oceans by German and Japanese aggression, it was payback time. They had zero tolerance for perceived menaces from within, a situation Russell, who had condemned the immorality of executing Sacco and Vanzetti, understood before his American defenders. Forced to reconsider its offer, City College, to its great credit, defeated a resolution that called for barring Russell from campus. But a curious lawsuit against the municipality of New York proved the principal vehicle for enforcing the public will against the rights of an individual, albeit not a citizen, to free expression of ideas however contrary to majority opinion.

The day after Russell's appointment had been confirmed, the mother of a CCNY student brought suit to rescind it. She alleged that this "foreign" professor's immoral character made him highly unsuitable as a teacher. In substantial agreement with her view, Justice John E. McGeehan of the New York State Supreme Court ruled that exposure to Russell's ideas would undermine the morals of American students and voided his appointment on the 30th of March. At CCNY, some one thousand undergraduate and graduate students signed a petition in support of the British aristocrat. On other campuses, faculty members awoke to the threat to academic freedom. Convinced that Russell's thought had been grossly distorted and unfairly held up to ridicule, an ever-magnanimous John Dewey, who had long ago detected a disdain for the sensibilities of others in his British colleague that he despised, organized the Committee for Cultural Freedom to defend his fellow teacher. With the support of philosophy departments in ninety-two American colleges and universities, it trained some heavy polemical artillery upon the court's decision. At Dewey's urging, the national officers of the American Association of University Professors beseeched the Board of Higher Education to appeal, and with his help, the American Civil Liberties Union issued a pamphlet challenging the proceedings. But even if the case were accepted by the Court of Appeals, it would not be heard before February of 1941 when Russell had been scheduled to assume his professorship. Besides, the City of New York, which had not been anxious to win the original suit, had no interest in prolonging the controversy. When the Board of Higher Education decided to take the matter to a higher court, its own counsel refused, and Justice McGeehan, in turn, refused the request of another lawyer to have his firm substituted for the board's reluctant attorney.

From Russell's point of view, "a typical American witch hunt" had been instituted against him. A lecture tour he had hoped to undertake became impossible when the owners of assembly halls informed his supporters that they would not rent their facilities. Newspapers and magazines refused to publish his articles. "I was suddenly deprived of all means of earning a living," Russell later wrote. "Only one man did anything practical, and that was Dr. Barnes, the inventor of Argyrol."[9] Genuinely outraged at Russell's treatment by the public, the court, and the press, the collector saw in the situation an intriguing opportunity to supplement his courses in the appreciation of art with a systematic course presenting the political, social, and cultural conditions out of which various traditions in art arose. He discussed his ideas with Dewey. At the end of May, Dewey wrote to Russell in Los Angeles about the possibility of teaching at the Foundation at an annual salary of $6,000, even though the CCNY issue had not yet been finally resolved, because, as he said to Barnes, he decided "an anchor to windward" would relieve the stranded philosopher's financial anxieties.[10] Russell responded at once to express his interest in and appreciation of the offer Dewey conveyed—and to request permission to delay for a while a definite answer. Exhibiting rare humility and patience, Barnes told Dewey that if his colleague should "lose out on the college end, we shall be glad to take him on."[11] He sent Russell information about the Foundation's purposes and added, "The sky is the limit—and if you join us, so also will be what you say and do about living rationally."[12]

It was, therefore, with considerable relief that the Russells left for a family holiday in the High Sierras near Lake Tahoe. But the logician was warned that Barnes "always tired of people before long,"[13] so even as he relished salvation from the "bleak prospect" of removing his older children from their university studies and living "as cheaply as possible on the charity of kind friends," he wrote to ask the collector if his appointment, assuming that he was free to accept it, "would be for a definite or indefinite period."[14] Without hesitation, Barnes offered him a five-year contract. After further discussion by mail of the general content of the proposed lecture series, duing which the collector confided that he, too, had been denounced as a "perverter of public morals."[15] Barnes flew to Lake Tahoe in early August. There the man who had the audacity to exhibit the works of modern French painters and the man who had flaunted conventional views of marriage quickly resolved the lingering details about the terms of Russell's engagement.

The letter confirming their agreement, which they both signed in front of witnesses, was dated August 16, 1940. Quite uncharacteristically, Barnes drew it up himself without consulting his attorney, Robert McCracken. For five years, beginning January 1, 1941, Russell was to deliver "one lecture each week during the school year," extending "from October 1st to May 31st inclusive, each lecture to be delivered in the gallery of the Barnes Foundation."[16] The typed salary figure in the document was $8,000 per year, the same amount CCNY had offered him, but the eight was struck through with a pen line, and a notation in the margin changed the figure to six. On returning home, an elated Barnes asked Russell which textbooks should be used for his course and offered his help in locating a house for the new teacher and his family near the Foundation. Russell, politely suppressing his amusement at the question about texts, replied that he would recommend certain original sources, including Plato, Plutarch, and Jean-Jacques Rousseau, and since he knew of no book dealing in general with his subject, proposed his lectures become such a volume. Barnes jubilantly passed on the news to Henry Hart that, at the end of five years, the Foundation would publish a book by Bertrand Russell. His enthusiasm did not seem to be dampened at all by a further observation in Russell's letter that he would need a house in the country "not less than fifty miles from Philadelphia" and, therefore, a considerable distance from Merion.[17]

On the contrary, Barnes went house hunting for the Russells with a glad heart and enormous energy. An interest in American antiques, which he had been actively buying since the late 1930s, had made him well acquainted with the rolling rural landscape stretching west from the Main Line to Lancaster. A month earlier he had told Dewey of a commitment to support and educate twenty refugee children for the duration of the war in the region's "beautiful farming country."[18] Now he would explore it on behalf of a refugee educator. Driving a Packard, with Fidèle at his side, he set off day after day to investigate available properties. He knew Russell was an earl, a title the logician did not use but had inherited from his grandfather, and the collector felt instinctively that some measure of style was essential in a suitable residence. Apparently, it was Barnes's intention to buy a handsome property and lease it to the Russells. But his future employee insisted that it was "much more important to [his] happiness to live within [his] means" than to live in a beautiful house." He must have a dwelling with not only "a low rent" but also low maintenance—one "cheap to run" and requiring "little service." As kindly as he could, Russell pointed out that choosing a house was "a very personal matter" and that neither he nor his wife wanted to decide on one until they had "seen a considerable selection." Russell did not wish to sound ungracious. "You have given to both my wife and me the opportunity for the sort of life we want," he informed the collector. The exile with few prospects suddenly could look forward "to writing long contemplated books." But in order to achieve his goal, he told his patron that he and Mrs. Russell must organize their living "on such a scale" that he would "not have to do a lot of hack work to avoid debt. . . . I think it is impossible to come to a decision until we are in the East," he added. "What you have already done in giving me the post is so much that no more is needed to secure my life-long gratitude.[19]

Although Barnes had invited Patricia Russell, her son, and his nanny to make Merion their base while Russell lectured at Harvard, her husband wrote to a philosopher he had known for years, Lucy Donnelly at Bryn Mawr, to ask if she might put them all up, "as a feeble substitute for the Renoirs."[20] When Russell told the collector that his wife would be staying with old friends, Barnes took no offense. Indeed, he sent her a personal note in which he said straight out: "Bertrand can put us on the intellectual-educational map in a manner I have long wished for . . . . We can give him an opportunity to fulfill his heart's desire; and woe to those who attempt to pull off another stunt like that . . . in New York."[21] In order to relieve Russell of the need to deliver popular lectures, moreover, he wrote a new contract agreeing to increase his annual salary to $8,000.[22] About the same time, he also agreed to underwrite the cost of publishing the proceedings of a symposium that had been planned by the Committee on Cultural Freedom as a means of discussing the implications of the New York ruling against the English philosopher. In mid-October, he proudly issued a public announcement that Russell had been engaged to teach at the Foundation. "There will be no restrictions" on him, he told the press. "I wouldn't dream of telling any of our staff what they should or should not say. We make sure beforehand that they are honest scholars."[23] When one local newspaper, which had recently run an editorial entitled "Russell's Loss Is Public Gain," didn't print the collector's announcement, he wrote a letter to the editor declaring "the crucifixion of Russell, one of the most distinguished scholars of our age, was a wanton act inspired and fostered by bigoted authoritarians."[24]

Time ran the story of "Russell's Roost" in the same issue it reported Philadelphia's loss of the Widener collection to the National Gallery in Washington, then being built with money donated by the late Andrew Mellon.[25] While local museum officials maintained what the magazine called "the shocked silence of the disinherited," Barnes's spirits soared at the response of area students to the news of Russell's engagement.[26] "We're swamped with applications from outsiders," the collector wrote joyfully in a letter he sent off to Cambridge, Massachusetts, where Russell had begun his Harvard lectures. Explaining that the Foundation generally limited classes to twenty, he said he would leave the matter of the number of acceptances entirely in Russell's hands. He also offered to engage a "rapid-fire stenographer" to take down every word of every lecture if that would help Russell "in the later job of the book."[27] Russell expressed no objections to the proposal, and it was further agreed that his class would be open to fifty students, selected from among five hundred applicants, plus ten or so faculty members from the Foundation and other educational institutions. The day he delivered his first lecture in Merion, January 2, 1941, was one of the happiest days of Barnes's life. The collector permitted a reporter from a Philadelphia newspaper to cover it, and he quoted the famous lecturer as saying: "Dr. Barnes is a man of fine intelligence and liberalism, and I am grateful to him for this opportunity. It is nice to be here and to know that I am not under any censorship." The British philosopher's employer carried on "the Shangri La note," according to the reporter, by saying that Russell could "continue at the Foundation as long as he desires," and he hoped it would be "for eternity."[28]

But the glow began to fade all too rapidly. The Russells had decided upon a two hundred year-old stone house, Little Datchet Farm, with an orchard, barn, peach tress, and fields sloping down to a river. It was in the country about twenty miles from Paoli, the last stop on the train line servicing Philadelphia's western suburbs. "Peter," as Russell called his wife, would drive him to the station for the ride to Merion or, sometimes, drive him the entire forty miles to the Foundation and wait for him to finish his lecture—occasionally taking a seat in one of the straight chairs in the back row and knitting as she listened to her husband. Barnes was almost always there ensconced in an armchair. Initially, Russell spoke in the main gallery. He found, however, that the many paintings of nudes were "somewhat incongruous for academic philosophy" and arranged to hold his class in a smaller, second-floor gallery with less distracting artwork on the walls.[29] Soon after he started teaching, Barnes had him meet with the other Foundation instructors. But the collector was disconcerted to discover that Russell showed no interest in their work nor did he make any effort to acquaint them with his own lecture plan. "This was our first intimation of the shape of things to comes," Barnes later wrote, but it was a teapot tempest that Patricia Russell provoked in late February that made the outline clearer.[30]

One Thursday afternoon, having been asked by her husband to call for him no later than quarter to four and take him on to another engagement, she drove up to the Foundation gates and sent word in that she was waiting outside. When an employee gave Barnes the message, he did not inform Russell who was talking, with Barnes's encouragement, to a reporter. "Peter," according to the collector's version of the incident, soon "burst into the hall and, bristling all over," asked Nelle Mullen "in a sharp, commanding tone: 'Where is Mr. Russell?'"[31] Barnes regarded the intrusion as a "disturbance of the peace," and it seems that the intruder already had a record.[32] Barnes complained to Dewey that Mrs. Russell had twice insulted Laura. His wife, he said, would "have nothing to do with her." But his staff didn't have an option. The no-nonsense Mullens resented, as Barnes did himself, Patricia's penchant for styling herself "Lady Russell." Other Foundation teachers who attended Russell's lectures, and perhaps some students, found her knitting a distraction. And what was she doing in the class anyway without the collector's permission?

"The situation has gotten so that something will have to be done about it," Barnes told Dewey, "but the problem was . . . how to put her in her place without bad effect" on his relations with Russell. "He has made a great hit with everyone," the collector said. His "course of lectures with us is simply a knockout."[33] Indeed, he told Russell, in a letter he had mailed the day before he wrote to Dewey, that the lecture he had just given "surpassed anything I have ever heard . . . in clarity, cogency, logic, humanity, penetration, breadth of view, sincerity, compelling conviction. Not once was there a deviation from that perfect fusion of emotion and idea that characterizes great art," Barnes declared. But the collector also recited the "facts" of the recent disturbance that he said was "an infraction of the Foundation's regulation concerning decorum in the gallery. When the matter comes up for official attention, I'll continue as peacemaker," he assured Russell. He was convinced, Barnes said, that "recurrence" of a similar incident was "extremely improbable."[34]

The remaining twelve weeks of the spring term were notably tranquil. Russell confided in a young Foundation teacher, the Italian-born American artist and photographer Angelo Pinto, that he would like to establish closer contact with the students in his class. Pinto, whom Barnes had sent to Europe and to Africa to study painting, reported the conversation to the collector and asked if he had any suggestions for his new colleague. Pleased as punch with this turn of events, Barnes wrote to Russell: "I know of nothing better than what you are doing, but if you would like to try any other plan, you have only to do it without consulting anybody here. One thing I can say in all sincerity is that your lectures are doing more for those students than you think, or what I thought anybody could do. . . . You've endeared yourself to all of them and if I were a Frenchman I'd kiss you on both cheeks for the benefit you've brought to our efforts to do something worthwhile."[35] The collector provided a foreword to *The Bertrand Russell Case*, which Viking published in June, and as Dewey noted in the essay he contributed to the volume, it seemed that Russell's lectureship was "progressing successfully and to the satisfaction of all concerned."[36] Russell wrote to a friend in England: "Life here, with the job I have, would be very pleasant if there were no war. The country is like inland Dorsetshire. . . . My work is interesting, and moderate in amount. But it all seems unreal. Fierceness," he then added, "surges round, and everybody seems doomed to grow fierce sooner or later. It is hard to feel that anything is worthwhile, except actual resistance to Hitler, in which I have no chance to take a part."[37]

The menace that Russell sensed so keenly in the world at large was not absent from Merion. Even then, unbeknownst to him, Barnes was secretly bristling at what he called the "finality" of the lecturer's classroom pronouncements and his unwillingness to engage in a debate with students Barnes had apparently primed to query him.[38] Dewey, in turn, was troubled by what he perceived as reductionist thinking on Russell's part that resulted in a too rigid separation between "facts" and "values." But the primary source of the collector's increasing frustration with the Foundation's illustrious teacher was what he characterized as Russell's lack of independence from his wife. "She's got him round her little finger and he's done nothing about it," he told Henry Hart.[39] So characteristically seizing the initiative, he wrote an icy letter, under Nelle Mullen's signature, to pretty, redheaded "Peter" shortly after the beginning of the fall term. It followed by a day yet another unauthorized visit she made to her husband's class and catalogued Barnes's complaints, which he believed Russell had never shared with her. In the name of the board of trustees, Mullen wrote:

> The Foundation has never been a place where people may drop in occasionally, at their own volition, nor is any person whosoever allowed to do things that interfere with the

rights of others or are harmful to the Foundation's interests. Admission to the gallery is restricted to persons enrolled in the classes. Membership in a class is valid only when approved by the Board of Trustees, is conditioned by regular attendance at the weekly sessions and is terminated by two consecutive absences or by behavior inimical to the common good.[40]

Russell's response to the institutional insult to Patricia was swift and frosty. In a note to the trustees, he declared: "The letter written on your behalf to my wife is astonishing by its incivility. I fail to see why what you wished to convey could not have been said orally without formality and completely unnecessary rudeness. I had not before understood that my wife was not allowed at my lectures; I do not understand why I was not informed of this. I regret that by asking her to be present I infringed, by ignorance or by oversight, the rules of the Foundation."[41] The response the board received from "Peter," which her husband may well have helped craft, was a gem that, according to Hart, evoked the admiration of the master polemicist.[42] After reviewing her version of the spring encounter with Nelle Mullen, she wrote: "If this seems to the Trustees of the Barnes Foundation a disturbance of the peace, may they long continue to enjoy the unreal paradise where such trifles may be so accounted, for I cannot suppose that they would have the fortitude to endorse a true disturbance of the peace: for example bombs tearing through the roof." Patricia explained that as her husband's research assistant, she had, at his insistence, attended his lectures at various colleges and universities and that had he failed to request permission from Barnes, or understood that permission was granted when in fact it was not, the couple could "only apologize for [her] unintentional trespass." As for her knitting, she was distressed if it had disturbed any students. But knitting was "in no sense an indulgence," she said, and she would "not have run the risk of annoying anyone by it, however slightly," but for a purpose that seemed to her "serious, the wish to diminish the number of those who suffer from cold. If I am sometimes a little cold myself in future, when, having no errands, I wait for my husband outside the Barnes Foundation," she concluded, "I will knit with more zest from a nearer realization of what it must mean to be cold and really without shelter; and I will marvel," she said, "that in such a world anyone would be willing, deliberately, to make one fellow-human cold even for an hour. And I will marvel too . . . that anyone should wish, in a world so full of mountains of hostility, to magnify so grandiloquently so petty a molehill."[43]

If Barnes did, indeed, on one level admire Patricia Russell's skillful parry, it also angered him. He later described her reply as "a tirade composed of arrogance, rage and self-pity."[44] His sarcastic retort was conveyed through faithful Nelle Mullen. "Dear Madam," she wrote. "It was sweet . . . of you to tell us so fully and so modestly how important you have been in the preparation of lectures, how foolish we are in basking in an 'unreal paradise,' how polite and deferential you were on February 27th . . . how sorry for yourself you will be while waiting, without shelter, outside the Foundation's grounds on a cold wintry day, how low class the Foundation is compared to Oxford, Harvard, etc.—in short, that a superior, well-bred, learned, charitable, kind-hearted soul should not be informed by barbarians that her presence in their midst is undesirable. How to bear up under the disgrace is our most serious problem at the moment."[45] Mullen informed Russell that in view of his wife's conduct, the board's letter to her was "inordinately courteous. Never in the history of the Foundation," she said, "had a visitor . . . so grossly violated the accepted standards of social decorum."[46] Immediately after the acerbic exchange, and perhaps because Russell well understood its absurdity in the context of an embattled world, he apologized to his class for his wife's knitting. But echoing the contention in her letter to the trustees, he also mentioned that her presence at his lectures elsewhere produced no comparable objections. Listening, as always, in his armchair, Barnes immediately rose and asked, in front of the students, if their esteemed teacher was implying by his comparison that there was something wrong with the Foundation. Russell said no, thereby establishing a momentary truce.

It lasted less than a month. When, with Barnes's permission, Angelo Pinto asked Russell if he and his brothers might take colored photographs during his class, Patricia replied that while her husband had no objections, he had been officially informed that his "class was disturbed by the less obvious distraction of knitting, although most of the class . . . protested they were not in the least disturbed."[47] Under the circumstances, she suggested Pinto should consult the students. The artist-photographer asked Barnes what he ought to do, and the upshot was that permission to take pictures in Russell's class was withdrawn. When the class next met, Barnes ridiculed the analogy between knitting and photography and recapped, less the students have any doubt of the "larger" context, his laundry list of Patricia Russell's offences. After class, he wrote at once to Russell:

> I was never so sad in my life as I was today while administering the beating you had to take because of your wife's ignorance of abnormal psychology. . . . My bounden educational duty was to show . . . special privilege is intolerable in an informed, democratic community. . . . All of us prefer, much prefer, to forget the past, if you will realize the fact that when we engaged you to teach we did not obligate ourselves to endure forever the trouble-making propensities of your wife. . . . We all like you personally, admire the way you do what you do in your lectures and recognize their importance and value in our educational program. The quarrel has never been between you and us.[48]

Russell solemnly informed his employer that while he would continue to do all in his power, including the utilization of Patricia's "valuable help in research," to make his lectures as good as he could make them, Barnes "was mistaken" in supposing that there was no quarrel with him "since whoever quarrels with my wife quarrels with me."[49] The next day Barnes made it abundantly clear that the Foundation had declared war on Patricia. "If your wife ever enters our gallery," the collector wrote to Russell, "the 'white-haired lady' whom she tried to bully . . . has been informed officially how to deal with the situation."[50] The letter, written on December 6, 1941, was hand delivered, an indulgence that spared the sender, as well, perhaps, as the recipient, the irony of having it delivered by post the day after Pearl Harbor. Later that week, Russell sent the Foundation trustees a dignified note in which he said further discussion of his wife's conduct "would seem unnecessary" in view of the fact that she had "not entered the Foundation since she . . . had any reason to believe that her presence was unwanted and w[ould] not enter it in the future."[51] In a reply, presumably meant to prevent his alliance with Britain's eminent man of letters from unraveling further even as their countries bound themselves together to defeat a common foe, Barnes expressed, through Mullen, his hope that the "elimination of 'Lady Russell' from the scene of the trouble will have been the last step necessary to assure the orderly practice of the principles of democracy and education to which our institution is dedicated."[52]

America's entry into World War II did not ever seriously inconvenience the collector. At the end of January 1942, he acquired the largest Renoir in his collection, *Mussel Fishers at Berneval*, for $175,000, then a record price for the painter's work. A day later, he paid 50,000 francs for his *Girl with a Flower Basket*. Both works were purchased from the Durand-Ruel Gallery in New York. He told the press that he had first tried to buy the *Mussel Fishers*, which had been in the personal collection of the Durand-Ruel family for twenty-nine years, in 1914 and had been actively pursuing it since the late 1930s. Grandsons of Pierre Durand-Ruel, who had bought the painting from Renoir, had sent it to New York for safekeeping. Besides considering *Mussel Fishers*, which was six feet high and four feet and three inches wide, "one of the important pictures of the world," Barnes had wanted the enormous canvas because he considered it a significant transitional work in Renoir's development. He described his acquisition as "a tremendous contribution to art education in America."[53]

But for the moment, the universal call-up of young men for military service was affecting education at the Foundation in much the same way as at most other U. S. institutions. It "played hell," as Barnes later told Leo Stein, with the teaching staff and dramatically altered the gender ratio in the student body.[54] Draft boards were unmoved by Barnes's letters explaining the importance to the nation of his educational program in art appreciation, and three young instructors left to serve their country. Yet Barnes still could not back away entirely from his quarrel with the most celebrated teacher at the Foundation. He was all too ready to believe a second-hand account of a conversation between Russell and Julian Huxley in which Russell had supposedly told Huxley that Barnes had returned, unopened, a letter he had written him with an obscenity scrawled across the envelope. When he confronted Russell, the logician explained that he had shared with Huxley an amusing story he had read in a French book that claimed the collector had written *"merde"* on a letter from the author. Furious about Russell's role in circulating the rumor, Barnes made available to a reporter for the *Evening Bulletin* the whole series of letters he had exchanged with the Russells. He described Patricia to him as "high-hatted," said she apparently had "difficulty swallowing the impressive title of Lady Russell" since "she regurgitates it automatically," and accused her of indulging in "grandstand stunts."[55]

The reporter was Carl W. McCardle, the feature writer who had done a story on Russell when he began teaching in Merion. The collector's conversation with him was part of an interview for a long article about Barnes to which McCardle's subject had rather surprisingly agreed on the condition that the writer focus on the Foundation's educational mission and permit him to review the text before it was offered for publication to any magazine. A few years earlier, Barnes had turned down a request from Archibald MacLeish who had wanted to write about him for *Fortune*. But perhaps at seventy, he set his usual wariness aside in seeking a sympathetic and summative account of his creation of an enterprise that he viewed as unique in American life. Having permitted Angelo Pinto and his brother to take colored photographs of his collection, Barnes even volunteered to lend the prints to McCardle. With this promise of the never-before published pictures as evidence of the collector's cooperation, the young writer lost no time in his selling his idea to the *Saturday Evening Post*.

The popular, Philadelphia-based magazine offered him $3,500 for a long, anecdotal feature that would run in four installments. McCardle signed a contract, and while he read, and perhaps showed, versions of his work to Barnes and appeared to take seriously the collector's protests that he was overemphasizing the "sensational elements of events at the expense of their true meaning," he never shared his final draft with the collector.[56] When Barnes threatened to sue him for violating their agreement, McCardle obtained a galley proof of the series a few days before the first installment was to go on press. Barnes read it with growing indignation and alarm. But because McCardle had not told the *Post* editors of his verbal promise to the collector, Bob McCracken advised his client that it would be futile to try to seek an injunction against the magazine. For a moment, Barnes didn't know what to do. Then calling upon de Mazia and the Mullen sisters to assist him, he sat down with a photostatic copy he had had made of the galleys and removed what he considered "the most glaring of the falsifications, distortions and fabrications."[57]

Fiske Kimball was told that the collector then wrote "ok" on each of his copies of the proofs before he had them delivered to the *Post*.[58] In any case, the magazine accepted almost all of his corrections, including a new quotation that purported to cast his conflict with Russell as a question of autocracy versus democracy rather than anything remotely personal. Barnes had hoped it would be substituted for McCardle's account of their quarrel. When he learned that the *Post* would simply add the summary paragraph, Barnes wrote at once to warn Dewey of the impending publication. He blamed Russell for being the first to make their dispute public by his comments to his class, and a few days later, he sent a letter to Russell recapping the ups and, particularly, the downs of their relationship and accusing him not only of frustrating his "efforts to keep the skeleton in the closet" but, more egregiously, of ingratitude.[59] Russell protested that he was far from ungrateful, but Barnes's attention was focused on a more immediate concern: the image the *Post* series would paint of him as soon as the March 21st issue, which contained the first article, hit the newsstands.

Resorting not to his fists this time but to his pen, he quickly wrote and had printed a pamphlet, entitled "How It Happened," in which he gave his version of how the series came to be and what he thought of it. "I emerge from McCardle's articles too much like a warrior-hero with boots licked clean," he protested albeit rather grandly. "To an informed psychologist, this indicates that what the author has subconsciously produced is a phantasy-portrait of himself. . . . It is wishful thinking *autobiography*. . . . Some of the tales and nearly all of the supposedly verbatim reports of my sayings are really whoppers."[60] But, of course, the larger-than-life stories about Barnes were exactly what the *Post* expected would appeal to readers. To every retail outlet that carried the magazine, the Curtis Publishing Company had provided placards, emblazoned with photographs of Barnes and some of his paintings, that promoted the series under a flaming headline: "Main Line's Millionaire Pepperpot 'The Terrible-Tempered Dr. Barnes.'" So the collector drove to newsstands and drugstores from Merion to Paoli to deliver his pamphlet.

He told Dewey that in every case the manager or proprietor listened to his appeal for "fair play" and after reading "How It Happened" not only gave him the posters but also allowed him to insert a copy of the pamphlet in each copy of the *Post* they had for sale. He carted the placards away, acknowledging gleefully that it was "downright theft."[61] An assistant, loyal Albert Nulty, telephoned the Curtis Publishing Company after each heist and Barnes even sent a notarized statement about them to the *Post*. But to his disappointment, no one ever called the cops. Like his feud with Woollcott, the collector's farcical rampage was good for his opponent's business. The magazine's promotion staff counted on newspaper accounts of Barnes's reaction to the series to boost single-copy sales even as the editors of Philadelphia's dailies saw his antics as comic relief to the grim front-page news about the Germans sealing Norway's ports and the Japanese conquest of Burma. A reader, sensitive to the ironic juxtaposition of articles, wrote that while the collector was "out tooting around tearing up posters . . . all kinds of good guys are going to give more than their pound of flesh to preserve . . . [his] sacred right to lock up his pictures."[62] The editorial writer for the *Record* tartly observed that "during adolescence, allowances are made for putting thumb tacks on dining room chairs. In later years, the practice is considered in the same taste Dr. Barnes would regard the chap who stuck a cud of chewing gum on the bare back of a Picasso bather."[63]

A Foundation teacher wrote a letter correcting the misattribution of the famous painting and attempting to counter the implication of a lack of seriousness in Merion. But when Barnes informed Dewey that he and Henry Hart had outlined a second pamphlet, the philosopher gently suggested that further activity on his part would only serve to advertise the series. An offer of free rebuttal time from a Philadelphia radio station, however, was too appealing to forego. Dewey agreed to provide a brief statement of his view of the *Post* articles in which he stressed the uniqueness of the Foundation, and he counseled Barnes: "The more you say along the line of your own work and experience and motives and [the] less [you] say directly about McCardle the better."[64] The collector, who had been prepared to call the reporter a "crook" and a "Judas Iscariot" as a pale substitute for the kind of language he liked best, listened, in his fashion, to Dewey's advice. He called the articles a "series of fairy tales," described the "mutilation of [his] paintings" in the published reproductions "an artistic crime of the first magnitude," complained that he had received "874 requests for loans to hard up readers of the *Post*," attempted to document McCardle's perfidy by reference to stenographic records of their telephone calls, but then went on to tell the story he felt the reporter had missed about the educational experiment in Merion.[65]

Despite the public airing of Barnes's quarrel with the Russells in the April 4th issue of the *Post*, the logician's classes proceeded uneventfully through the end of the spring term. One student was prompted to write her teacher a letter of support, and Russell replied that he had "sensed that the sentiments of the class were friendly" and had been "very glad of it."[66] By the late fall of 1942, however, attendance had fallen off sharply, though it is hard to say whether the cause was, as the collector later claimed, increasingly perfunctory lectures on Russell's part or, what was certainly an important variable, the draft of young men and the involvement of young women in home-front jobs contributing to the war effort. It is true that between October and December, Russell divided his teaching time between the Foundation and two other institutions where he gave a series of lectures—Temple University and the Rand School of Social Science in New York. In Barnes's view, his outside activity breached the contract implicit in the collector's offer and Russell's acceptance of a $2,000 increase in salary, which Barnes had hoped would enable Russell to concentrate on his writing free of the need to accept any such engagements. But during the subsequent two years, quite apart from financial pressures, Russell had felt a need to speak out on a number of political issues, particularly Britain's policy in an India then seeking independence, as his contribution to Anglo-American relations at a moment when so much depended on the two nations' grand alliance.

"I have had a bellyful," Barnes wrote Dewey as he recounted all of Russell's alleged offences, and enclosed in his letter a copy of another that he had had hand delivered to Little Datchet Farm three days after Christmas.[67] It was an official notice from the secretary of the Barnes Foundation of the termination of Russell's original contract as of December 31. "In case you wish to continue your weekly course of lectures," Nelle Mullen wrote, "the emolument would be the sum of five hundred ($500.00) dollars per month," that is, $6,000 a year, and any new agreement could be terminated by either party with thirty days' notice.[68] Russell lost no time in contacting a lawyer. On the last day of the year, Barnes received a letter from the firm of White and Staples informing him that his former employee was willing to continue his lectures at his old salary and unless he could do so, the Foundation's letter would be accepted by the firm as itself a breach of contract. Barnes had wanted a show down, and now he had his wish.

Students returning on January 7, 1943 were told that their teacher had abandoned them. When Russell learned how his absence from the classroom had been described, he indignantly released a statement to the press saying he had not "discontinued his lectures" but had been discharged from his lecture-ship arbitrarily.[69] Barnes countered with his own media alert. "Mr. Russell . . . runs true to his familiar form of presenting himself to the public as a martyr," he said, and proceeded to release not only a copy of the letter of dismissal, but also a letter, purportedly from a student, that castigated Russell for providing "a sort of Cook's tour of the past," turning "questions aside with a laugh," and implicit anti-Semitism: "misinterpreting old Jewish rituals [and] making them sound silly."[70] On reading the criticism, a former student suggested that "it [wa]s the master's voice in pantomime. . . . The real issue," he wrote, "is a battle of conflicting ideas. Barnes may be accused of mental back-seat driving with Russell insisting on shifting gears for himself."[71] Apprised of events, Dewey warned Barnes, just before entering New York Hospital for prostate surgery, that "a public law suit isn't going to help the Foundation . . . even if the case is legally 100% clear."[72]

But the collector wasn't interested in an out-of-court settlement, and on January 18, 1943, Russell brought suit for the $24,000 in salary he was to receive through 1945. Barnes asked McCracken to represent him, and his lawyer filed an affidavit of defense, knowing there was none. Ever optimistic that he would prevail, the collector went happily off to Providence to give a talk at a meeting of the Rhode Island Philosophical Society, which was meeting at Pembroke College. He entitled it "Having a Hell of a Good Time Playing with Art, Education, Science and Philosophy," and, introduced by the chair of Brown's philosophy department, he and his audience had a wonderful evening. In February, he was honored by the Pyramid Club, an association of black artists living in the Philadelphia area, and he delivered an address at the club's Third Annual Exhibition, which included some of Pippin's work. Soon afterwards, he accepted an invitation from a wealthy Chinese art collector to work with Bignou and Keller to select Chinese and modern paintings for an April exhibit at their New York gallery. With de Mazia, he wrote an essay for the catalogue that sought to show similarities in the intrinsic content of the pictures, and he told Dewey that he hoped to entertain Tse-ven Soong, the Chinese financier and statesman, in Merion to discuss the translation of some of the Foundation's books into Chinese. But Dr. Soong seems to have been detained by world events, and before the exhibit opened in late April, a U. S. District Court judge ruled that Russell was entitled to summary damages. It was a verdict for the plaintiff on the grounds that there was no issue as to the material facts. Judge Guy K. Bard held that any oral agreement between the two parties had no legal standing because its provisions were not specified in the subsequent written contract. There would be a trial in the fall, but only to determine how much Barnes owed to his former employee.

Russell sublet Little Datchet Farm and moved his family into a three-room cottage. Eventually, he rented a house near Bryn Mawr College, where he gave a course of lectures and used the excellent library for research. To his considerable satisfaction, he was commissioned to write an article on American-British relations for the *Saturday Evening Post*. In it, he acknowledged that to nineteenth-century Englishmen, like his grandfather who turned down the post of minister to the United States, America seemed "a strange, wild, revolutionary country." He could understand, in some measure, he said, "the covert bitterness and readiness to quarrel and imagine slights" that he had encountered toward himself and his countrymen during his prolonged visit. "Though Americans are generally friendly and kind toward strangers," Russell noted, "and demonstratively affectionate to those they like, they also do not scruple to express dislike when they feel it and often show in the process considerable brutality. In England . . . you may miss the caresses, but you will also miss the blows."[73] The one the logician had most recently sustained was softened in November of 1943 when Judge Bard awarded him $20,000—three year's salary as provided in the unexpired employment contract minus $4,000 that the court estimated the seventy-one year old philosopher might earn over the next two years through writing and lectures.

Barnes, who had dropped Bob McCracken in a fury before the judgment, appealed the verdict using U. S. Attorney Gerald A. Gleeson, acting in the capacity of a private lawyer, as his new counsel. But the collector lost every round. The Third U. S. Circuit Court of Appeals sustained the opinion of the lower court. With Justice Owen J. Roberts recusing himself because the case involved his former client, the Supreme Court refused to take jurisdiction in the contract dispute. Its decision was announced on Election Day 1944. But by then, after months of waiting for ship's passage, Russell and his wife and their son had returned home to England. In his aborted lectures at the Barnes Foundation, he had given some two-thirds of what became *A History of Western*

Philosophy, one of his most important works. Published in the United States by Simon and Schuster in 1945, the dedication read in part: "This book owes its existence to Dr. Albert C. Barnes."[74] Meanwhile, the collector had published a pamphlet, "The Case of Bertrand Russell vs. Democracy and Education," in which he said "Russell contributed little or nothing to the education of his class."[75] Barnes sent a copy to the master and each of the fellows of Trinity College, Cambridge, where Russell had once studied and was returning for a five-year lectureship. With the money Barnes was forced to pay him, the philosopher bought a house in the bustling, postwar university town. Royalties from the big book he had begun in Merion were his main source of income for many years.

But Barnes also gained something of material value from the relationship. During the summer when he had looked for a house for the Russells in the Pennsylvania countryside, he also found one for himself. It was an eight-room eighteenth-century stone farmhouse, which he named "Ker-Feal"—Fidèle's house in the Breton dialect, and made into a museum of folk art. Barnes's collecting of American antiques had become a serious undertaking. He remembered with pride the Windsor chairs that had been present in his boyhood homes until they were sold and replaced with Victoriana, and for some years, as he once wrote a fellow collector, he had "been trying to atone for the crime."[76] He brought to the search for early American pieces the same fine eye and delight in a bargain that characterized his collecting of Impressionist and early modern paintings. The best furniture and ironware were in the gallery; other good pieces were in his adjacent living quarters, the homes of de Mazia and the Mullen sisters, and in the elegant new "office house." But he needed more room for benches and china and hinges, as well as a retreat. Although he could no longer go to Europe, even with gasoline rationing, he could go to Chester County any time he pleased. As de Mazia wrote two years after Barnes bought Ker-Feal, however, it was "not a storage house for sentimental attachments to early American life."[77] In 1941, the Foundation had begun offering a course in the study of antique furniture, and the collector intended to use his new retreat to extend the Foundation's educational programs. First, however, additions must be constructed, and Barnes entrusted the job to three young architects who had studied with Paul Cret at Penn.

He engaged H. Martyn Kneedler, Henry D. Mirick, and C. Clark Zantzinger to supply plans, specifications, and drawings, as well as supervise the construction of two wings in keeping with the spirit and form of the 1775 house. One wing was to serve as living quarters for the caretakers; the other to provide additional living rooms for the exhibition of furniture. The architects found stone from a nearby quarry that matched the original exactly. Pipes for heat, light, and air conditioning were placed in the exterior walls. Barnes was enormously pleased that it was almost impossible to detect where the old house ended and the new parts began. Renovation began in December 1940 and took about a year to complete at a cost of some $20,000. The collector's relationship with the architects was remarkably sunny and coincided with the period in which he was more or less enraptured by Russell if not his wife. The young men accepted with grace his involvement in the nitty-gritty of reconstruction. Barnes was particularly interested in the process of paint removal from the paneled walls and beams of the original rooms and provided detailed instructions for refinishing them with "copious quantities of linseed oil" after they had been thoroughly brushed with kerosene.[78] He was eager for the architects to use as many as possible of the old hinges he had collected in the new construction. When the job was done, he invited them to come with their wives for "a simple peasant lunch—eggs in lard and 'scrapple'—aroused with a bottle of . . . Vosne Romanee 1926."[79]

He also attempted to help them secure defense contracts by writing to Edward Bruce, the supervising architect of the Federal Works Agency in Washington. When Bruce failed to answer and queries from the architects were met initially with evasions, Barnes suggested to Mirick a possible reason for the "brush-off." Bruce "asked me to go on the Board of Directors of the new National Gallery because—but he didn't say so—in that position I would donate some of our pictures to the Washington gallery," the collector confided. "When he hinted strongly that I would be asked to contribute, I ridiculed the whole bunch of fatheads that control such institutions. This incident, I feel, explains your non-success."[80] It was a revelation about the national art establishment's frustrated pursuit of the Merion collector that became lost in the day's more momentous events: the sinking of the American fleet at anchor in Pearl Harbor.

Barnes furnished only one of the rooms at Ker-Feal with pieces by skilled craftsmen working in the Queen Anne, Chippendale, and Hepplewhite traditions. The rest were filled with choice furniture created by early German settlers of Pennsylvania as well as with typical accessories of about the same period from New England and Virginia. The floors were covered with colorful strips of carpeting hand-woven of flax or wool. On the mantel above the ten-foot-wide kitchen fireplace were displayed pewter and pottery plates and examples of the finest toleware, along with candle boxes, cookie cutters, Betty lamps, and a pipe box. Foot warmers, pans, and various other utensils hung from the mantel to offer material for the study of how Americans living in the seventeenth-century reacted to the world around them. The collector bought at auction and from antique dealers. Some became friends; other enemies; at least one an amiable rival who delighted in outbidding him at sales. Surrounding Ker-Feal was about one hundred and forty acres of farm and woodland intersected here and there with brooks. A swimming pool in the shape of a flat iron was created near the house, and, according to Hart, nine feet of earth were bulldozed off a hillock to enhance the view from a porch attached to one of the new wings.[81] The grounds were Laura Barnes's domain, and she had a series of stonewalled terraces built for planting. If their country house were to provide a site for the extension of classes offered by de Mazia and the other Foundation teachers, it would also enable her to expand the Arboretum School she had just begun after years of nurturing Colonel Wilson's exquisite collection of rare flora in Merion.

Free courses, consisting of fifteen lectures each, in botany, landscape architecture, and horticulture, were offered there for the first time in the fall of 1940. Laura had become director of the arboretum upon Wilson's death twelve years earlier, and she subsequently added to the selection of trees, shrubs, ferns, and woody plants that the former owner of the Foundation property had begun planting in 1887. Her husband encouraged her to audit courses in landscape design, which Penn introduced at the same time workmen under Paul Cret's direction were finishing the gallery. Barnes wanted his twelve-acre botanical park to become an extension of his art collection, and his wife undertook practical experiments to observe the effects of exposure and soil variations on species native to the southeastern Pennsylvania region. Students studying landscape architecture and botany at Penn were permitted to visit the arboretum with their professors for the purpose of inspecting the choice specimens.

In the fall of 1933, the Barneses hired Frank K. Schrepfer, a landscape architect on the university's School of Fine Arts faculty, as a consultant. During the next several years, he worked with them to clarify plans for the development of the arboretum, and gardeners, under his supervision, began to extend and revise the collection and rearrange its plants to heighten their aesthetic interest. In an article published in the journal *Landscape Architecture*, Schrepfer made it clear that the ongoing experiment that Barnes conducted inside the Foundation, as he hung and rearranged his pictures, would be extended to its exterior spaces. The plants in Merion have "a dual purpose," he wrote, "as part of the general collection and as parts of the esthetic scheme. The collection will not be fixed in the sense of a permanent display of certain species and varieties." Plants that seemed less worthy from a decorative point of view would be "replaced by others of greater value," he explained. The objective was "a gallery of beautiful living specimens."[82] There were two hundred species and varieties of lilacs along with formal rose and peony gardens. In spring, pale blossoms suggested Renoir's palette; by fall, the deepening colors echoed Matisse's vibrant hues. Winter's snow fell through broad-leafed evergreens as dark as Henri Rousseau's colors.

The Foundation began offering lectures to its students on the aesthetic qualities and characteristics of plants in 1935. Classes met in the gardens as well as the galleries until the opening of the Arboretum School. The new endeavor coincided with the temporary suspension of Penn's courses in landscape architecture,[83] and in the Arboretum School, at Laura's insistence, the starting point was plants not pictures. She turned to Penn botanist John M. Fogg to design the curriculum. When classes were not conducted outside, they met in the small stone house at 57 Lapsley Road that Barnes had built for Colonel Wilson. The new courses in Merion gave area students an opportunity to study with a Penn landscape architecture teacher, Frederick Peck, as well as with Fogg, who was an expert on magnolia. Laura Barnes gave the horticulture lectures in plant materials. When Fogg took on a demanding administrative post at Penn in 1941, the Merion arboretum faculty was expanded to include three other senior Penn naturalists.[84] By the spring of 1942, there were some eighty students enrolled in "Laura's school," as Barnes called it with some measure of genuine pride and also, perhaps, to distinguish it from *his* school—the art appreciation program in which de Mazia began playing an increasingly important role when the war ended research trips to Europe for her and the collector and deprived the Foundation of several of its most experienced male teachers.

Instructors were generally promoted from the ranks of students. Barnes, who observed countless classes as he sat smoking in his armchair, identified the most promising young men and made his selection on the basis of his judgments about their grasp of the Foundation's approach to art. Once de Mazia was firmly ensconced, he chose no more women. Fred Geasland, a young painter, had been teaching in Merion for four years when he attended one of her lectures and questioned what she meant by the word "took" in discussing artistic influences upon Picasso. Barnes interpreted his query as an affront, asked the impertinent instructor's fellow teachers to sign a statement condemning it, and although most of them declined to do so, Geasland's boldness cost him his job. Another instructor, an immigrant from the Ukraine who had studied both at the Pennsylvania Academy of the Fine Arts and the University of Pennsylvania, was fired for heresy. What began as an invitation to public school teachers to embrace the arts ended with a charge of sabotage of art appreciation that not only deprived the Foundation of an especially gifted faculty member but also of an opportunity to extend its influence.

Jacov Bookbinder came to the United States as a boy of eleven the year Barnes was granted a charter for his educational experiment. Quickly becoming "Jack," he learned to paint at the Academy and simultaneously earned a Penn B.A. in education. Bookbinder became a student at the Foundation in 1935 at the same time he was taking Penn graduate courses in psychology and teaching art in an evening program offered by the School District of Philadelphia. He stayed on for three years, but had no personal contact with the collector until one day Barnes spoke to him about a certain psychology book. He recommended it highly, but could neither lay his hands on his own copy nor recall the title or author. When he said it was by a doctor, however, Bookbinder asked if the book was Bernard Hart's *The Psychology of Insanity*. It was, and the collector was delighted to learn that the young man had read one of his favorite works. Within a few weeks, Edward Dreibelbies, a Foundation teacher with whom Bookbinder had studied the year before, asked him if he would be interested in a teaching position. Bookbinder was at once honored and amused to learn that the collector had been observing him sitting on the edge of his chair and thought him the most attentive student in the class. Indeed, he was generally fascinated by the lectures, but given rather poor ventilation in the gallery, he had chosen his uneasy perch to fight off sleep.

As a new instructor, his starting salary was more than competitive, and both employer and employee were initially pleased with their arrangement. The collector voiced no objection to Bookbinder's continuing his nighttime teaching in the public schools, paid for his passage to Europe for two successive summers, and when going abroad to paint and study art was no longer possible, gave his new protégé permission to teach painting in summer workshops for public school teachers initiated in 1942 by the Philadelphia Board of Education. He occasionally visited him in his apartment and sold him, at cost, American antiques from his own collection. Barnes understood that Bookbinder placed a high value on the independence that he had won when his family immigrated to the United States from Soviet Russia, and he was able to put aside his disappointment when the instructor both refused to criticize Geasland and to ask Russell a potentially embarrassing question, which the collector had suggested to him, at one of the British philosopher's outside lectures on India. But when an advance copy of a seventy-four-page pamphlet that Bookbinder had written on the importance of the arts in the public school curriculum reached his desk in July of 1944, Barnes responded in a way that seemed sadly automatic—a self-programmed but no longer controllable overreaction springing from a legitimate complaint.

"An Invitation to the Arts" contained an introduction by the deputy superintendent of schools. In a single sentence, he mentioned that the author of the pamphlet was a lecturer on art appreciation at the Barnes Foundation. Bookbinder had been aware of the reference before publication, but as he told Barnes when he was summoned to his office, he had not thought it necessary to clear it with the collector since his association with the Foundation was hardly a secret. Flanked by de Mazia and Mary Mullen, who sat silently with note pads in front of them, Barnes told him, as he later reiterated, that the "unwarranted and misleading use" of the Foundation's name "in a public document" put him in "a position of co-responsibility" for the author's "mess of indigestible 'tripe.'"[85] Bookbinder was flabbergasted.

But proud of his effort, which he in no way intended as an exposition or even reflection of the Barnesian method, he told the collector the pamphlet was his "baby" born of a love of art and a belief in education. To Barnes's utter astonishment, moreover, he said that a great educator, whom they both honored, had responded appreciatively to his essay on receiving a copy of the pamphlet. John Dewey had even suggested that Bookbinder send a copy to Robert M. Hutchins, the president of the University of Chicago. Barnes couldn't believe it. Bookbinder said he would bring him the philosopher's letter. The collector waived the offer aside and ordered Bookbinder to request the Board of Education to recall the pamphlet and remove the deputy superintendent's reference to the Foundation. When he refused, Bookbinder was told that he would not be engaged for the upcoming fall term, although his salary would be paid through the end of September if he submitted a letter of resignation by the 31st of August. The dismissed instructor rose without a further word, shook hands with de Mazia and Mullen, and walked out of the room. Barnes ran after him and shouted: "You son of a bitch! Somewhere in your pamphlet, you mention a warm handshake. You shook their hands, but you wouldn't shake mine." Bookbinder aimed for the heart: "Doctor, read the pamphlet again. Nowhere does it say to shake the hand of a Hitler."[86]

The name-calling sobered Barnes. He did not want to fight with a former student. He wanted to take on once again the public school bureaucracy and its, to him, unholy alliance with the Philadelphia Museum of Art, which was manifested in some cooperative programs in art education. Bookbinder was a means of engaging his old enemies. The collector failed to see that the respect with which the young instructor was held by the school administration might enable him to take up, instead, his old dream of conveying to large numbers of teachers a scientific understanding of art and its relation to human nature. He wrote to Bookbinder that if he did not take the initiative to have school authorities remove the name of the Barnes Foundation from the pamphlet, he would take the necessary steps to protect his interests. Bookbinder turned to Robert D. Abrahams, a lawyer just a few years older than he who charged $3 for half-hour consultations in his neighborhood law office. A poet and novelist, Abrahams embraced the opportunity not only to represent a needy client to the best of his considerable ability but also to spar with the local Shakespeare of vituperation.

Barnes produced a spate of letters in hopes of being sued for libel so he could, in turn, as he told Hart, take "drastic legal action."[87] School and museum officials ignored them. Bookbinder did resign at the end of August, but when Abrahams asked Barnes to pay the former instructor $450, an amount equal to two-months wages, the collector reminded him that he had withdrawn the option of resigning the day Abrahams had first written to him as Bookbinder's counsel. His suggestion that the lawyer inhabited "an intellectual slum" brought a clever parody of Barnes's own style in the form of a letter from Abrahams's "secretary" setting forth "the rules for entering into an exchange of invectives."[88] Barnes replied, "Tell your boy friend that . . . your letter illustrate[s] once again that when a stuffed shirt realizes that he is thoroughly licked he often shoots from behind a pair of rayon panties."[89] Abrahams answered with a citation: "Hebrews 13:8."[90] It was a funny, profane complaint, adapted from a then current joke about a boardinghouse guest who offered the biblical reference when asked to say grace in the face of re-heated hash: "Jesus Christ the same yesterday, and today, and forever." Barnes's reply included a quote from a letter St. Paul never wrote, Hebrews 14:1: "And verily I say unto you: Abraham begat Isaac; Isaac begat Jacob; and Jacob begat the illegitimate INVITATION TO THE ARTS which got him into such a disgraceful mess that he had to call on his granddad for succor; and Abrahams obligingly made a sucker out of Jacov."[91]

The comic opera had a ten-month run. Abrahams finally brought it to an end in May of 1945 with another letter to Barnes from his "secretary" that said further mail from Merion would be placed in his "file of Unread Abusive Letters."[92] He had as a trophy a white chicken feather that the collector had sent him for "services as counsel for a member of the personnel of the Philadelphia Board of Education." Bookbinder, who later served for eighteen years as director of art education for the Philadelphia public schools, had accepted a post as consultant to the board, and at his request, Abrahams never tried to sue Barnes to collect the un-paid, and perhaps not-owed, summer salary. Barnes said the "decoration of the Knight of the Order of White Feather" was in recognition of his substitution of "smart-aleckisms" for a legal "show-down."[93] Accepting it with thanks, Abrahams said he had heard Barnes was "Past Master" of the society and assumed "the duties of the Knights involve jousting at windmills."[94]

The collector's final thrust, against the advice of both Dewey and Hart, was a pamphlet of his own. In fact, he wrote two. "Sabotage of Public Education in Philadelphia," published in October of 1945, ridiculed Bookbinder's essay as a "rehash of discarded panaceas" and proceeded to present once again his old complaints about the "policy-making authorities" in the public schools and officials of the Philadelphia Museum of Art.[95] The collector sent the little booklet all around town, and it may well have instigated a series of articles in the *Philadelphia Inquirer* applauding the progressive outlook of the Board of Education. To counter them, Barnes produced "WHITEWASH: Board of Education Style" in which he accused the superintendent of schools and "his stooges" of "negligence, incompetence, false pretense and political chicanery," while extolling the "many honest, capable public school teachers" whom their bosses "kept in a permanent state of frustration."[96] They were the key to the "foothold" he sought "in the public schools—where," as he had told Dewey earlier in the year, "there are lots of worthwhile young people hungry for just what we have to offer."[97] But Barnes was seventy-three. His ties with Bookbinder were broken. Who could be his liaison to the larger community? Who would carry on the work of the Foundation?

13

Penn Again

Barnes had informally reestablished his twice-severed ties with the University of Pennsylvania in late 1941 through a friendly correspondence with the former Arboretum School lecturer John Fogg. It began when he asked Fogg if some arrangement might be made for Bertrand Russell to borrow a library copy of the *Cambridge Medieval History* on a long-term basis. Since Penn had two sets of the eight-volume reference work, Fogg made one available to Russell, and he and the collector continued to write to one another off and on throughout the war years. A month after the German surrender, Fogg, who had by then become Penn's vice provost, sent Barnes a small book by a member of the French underground, which had been secretly published in France during the Nazi occupation.[1] Barnes reciprocated by lending Fogg his personal copy of Dewey's *Freedom and Culture*, and so cordial did their relationship become that it is not surprising that the collector eventually broached with the Penn botanist an idea for reviving his old dream of an alliance between the Barnes Foundation and his alma mater.

The spark that lit the remaining coal among the ashes of his once bright hopes was a letter from an American soldier awaiting discharge. In October of 1945, Lieutenant Roderick M. Chisholm wrote to the Foundation requesting a copy of "The Case Against Bertrand Russell." A graduate of Brown University, where he won highest honors in philosophy, Chisholm had gone on to take a Ph.D. at Harvard and serve for four years with the United States Army, first in the infantry and then as a clinical psychologist. Barnes sent him the Russell pamphlet and, after an exchange of several letters, invited him to Merion. The twenty-nine-year-old philosopher, who had never taught before, sat in on art appreciation classes and had a long conversation with the collector. Barnes told him there was an opportunity for "a man well grounded in philosophy to extend the scope of the Foundation's work."[2] When Chisholm expressed a strong interest in the purposes and program of the educational enterprise in Merion, the collector sent him to see Dewey.

Dewey, who had always believed that a creative linkage with another institution was the Foundation's best hope for survival, talked with Chisholm for several hours one afternoon in late November. At Harvard, the young officer had been attracted to the contemporary Cambridge school of philosophy, particularly Russell and G. E. Moore, but his subsequent movement away from them impressed his kindly interrogator that he had a solid grasp of the technical problems inherent in their work and would one day make his own contributions to epistemology and metaphysics. Their conversation also covered a possible role for a philosopher in Merion. Dewey told Barnes that he had been right about Chisholm's enthusiasm, and added: "I don't believe you could find anywhere a man with a better disposition relative to what you would like to have done. For example, you won't find him seeing the students just during the lecture period. . . . He won't put himself ahead of the students except when he can help them by so doing. . . . There is no doubt about him on the . . . professional side—definitely a learning mind—the type that will go on learning—can't help it. . . . I think you and he, after thrashing out things together, can and will work out something significant."[3]

Barnes had described the Foundation to Chisholm as "practically a virgin field" in terms of its future development.[4] He now invited him to take up the plow there as "Bertrand Russell's successor."[5] But the lieutenant hesitated as he considered his future prospects. He had independent means and excellent preparation for a career in academic philosophy. He met again with a sympathetic Dewey, and Barnes continued to try to influence Chisholm's decision through his friend. "He would have an opportunity to do something absolutely unique . . . bring the forces of well-grounded philosophy to bear upon art criticism." His scant knowledge of painting was not a deficit. He could learn what he needed to know about pictures "within two or three years by attending three times weekly classes" at the Foundation.[6] Dewey's "tender-heartedness for sinners," revealed by a ready acknowledgment of the attractions of university life, produced a letter in which the collector laid out for Chisholm the frustrating history of his relationship with Penn.[7] But the young philosopher's desire for an academic base encouraged Barnes to consider again an affiliation between the Foundation and a college or university.

Chisholm was approached by Harvard, the University of Chicago, and the University of Washington after leaving the Army in February of 1946. About the same time, he encountered a member of the Bryn Mawr philosophy faculty who mentioned an opening in his department. The college's proximity to Merion sparked Chisholm's interest, and Barnes's acquaintance, through Dewey, with Bryn Mawr's new president, Katharine McBride, prompted him to try to secure the job for the man he hoped might carry on his educational efforts. The collector wrote to McBride in early March that should Chisholm take a full-time position at Bryn Mawr, "all the resources of the Foundation would be at his disposal" in order to develop "the link between philosophy and art." Bryn

Mawr, he said would have "an opportunity to take part in pioneer work."[8] The new president informed Barnes that the college moved slowly on appointments, but that she would be glad to consider Chisholm among other candidates. In the end, however, the college concluded that his strengths didn't match the needs of its philosophy department. The decision, from Barnes's point of view, put "another skeleton in Bryn Mawr's closet,"[9] and though a post at Swarthmore suddenly loomed as a possibility for Chisholm, Barnes moved quickly to open direct negotiations with John Fogg on behalf of the returning veteran.

He sent him copies of his correspondence with former Penn administrators and invited him to come to the gallery to discuss "an idea which, under certain circumstances, would be of enormous value to the university." As "part of the Foundation's position," he added, Fogg should meet with Chisholm about a possible job.[10] The vice provost quickly accepted Barnes's invitation, and as soon as their conversation was over, the collector wrote to a Philadelphia friend and fellow Central High School alumnus, Pennsylvania Supreme Court Justice Horace Stern, a Penn trustee whom he had taken into his confidence about his new plan. "I told Dr. Fogg that I am not in the position of a supplicant," he said. "I have something definite to offer which can be of benefit to the University and to the advancement of culture and education for all time." Penn, he further noted, could "take it or leave it," but he must have a reply by the 29th of April.[11] The Barnes proposal had a familiar ring. Chisholm should be appointed a full professor in the department of philosophy with his salary paid by the Foundation. He would conduct one class a week in the gallery for Penn students. The purpose of the arrangement was "to begin a plan to effect, by means of scientific educational methods, the wedding of art and philosophy through the medium of actual experience."[12]

Within five days of Fogg's meeting in Merion with the collector, he had interviewed Chisholm and offered to appoint him the Barnes Professor of Philosophy at an annual salary of $5,000. The young philosopher accepted the position, and Barnes wrote joyfully to Fogg that Chisholm's decision "is the first time in twenty years we have been provided with a man who could continue and expand the work which we have been doing on our own."[13] But while the philosophy faculty, as well as the College dean, Glenn Morrow, found their prospective new colleague to be an engaging fellow with superb qualifications, some of them expressed concern about a full professorship, even without tenure, for a young scholar who had never had an academic appointment. To placate the disgruntled faculty, Fogg tried out on Barnes the possibility of changing the title of the chair to Barnes Professor of Aesthetics and locating it in a new department without, at that time, any other members at all. Predictably, he met with a stone wall of resistance, and he quickly retracted his suggestion. The collector expressed relief that the university was no longer "playing with the idea of suicide." He added that one reason against using the word "aesthetics" in an academic title was that "in the popular mind" the term connoted "a sort of softness or effeminacy," which was "shameful because aesthetics, when treated by scientific method, [w]as as definite as physics, as two-balled as a stallion."[14] Through Stern, Barnes's intransigence on name and location of the chair was conveyed to the trustees, and on the next to the last day of April, the collector's deadline, the Executive Committee of the Executive Board voted to accept the proposal of the Barnes Foundation.

Penn President George W. McClelland wrote to Barnes to convey the university's formal approval. He suggested, however, that "Chisholm's appointment be designated the Barnes Foundation Professorship in Philosophy and that it be made for a period of three years subject to renewal at the expiration of that time." He added that the board of trustees realized that the gallery in Merion provided "a unique milieu for the implementation" of the planned course of study and that students selected for Chisholm's class "should regard it as a very rare privilege. . . . Members of the administration," he concluded, "look forward with eagerness to a new era of educational cooperation between the Barnes Foundation and the University of Pennsylvania."[15] A matter about which the president kept his silence was a memorandum that Justice Stern had shared with him about a likely change in the Barnes Indenture. It appeared the collector had agreed that after his death or Laura's, whomever survived the longest, Penn's trustees would be empowered to choose four of the five trustees of the Foundation following the deaths, resignations, or the expiration of the terms of the trustees appointed during either of the Barneses' lifetimes— and, indeed, Stern had suggested to his friend that the Indenture require the remaining trustees to resign their offices two years after the death of the survivor of the donor and his wife. The original Indenture had called for the Pennsylvania Academy of the Fine Arts and Penn to share the power of appointment, and undoubtedly Barnes intended McClelland be made aware of the proposed amendment. The same day he received the president's letter, he agreed to the university's terms and conditions. "We are greatly pleased to have the opportunity to add our resources to yours," the collector wrote, "and we assure you that we shall make every effort to make the venture a unique and outstanding success."[16]

A public announcement of the new course was issued jointly by McClelland and Barnes in early May. Fogg organized a visit to the Foundation for a group of his administrative colleagues, including the president, vice president, provost, and the dean of the law school. The collector told Dewey they were coming "to look the gift horse in the mouth," but with Stern at his side, he received them graciously and talked at length about his ideas for an objective study of the relationship between art and philosophy while his guests, overwhelmed, looked at his wondrous pictures. Chisholm moved his wife and their baby to the Philadelphia area in June and began a four-month period of intensive reading and research in preparation for his new duties. The Harvard-trained philosopher and de Mazia would provide the intellectual resources for a two-tiered curriculum: one designed for Penn students interested in aesthetics, who aspired to museum careers or careers teaching art at the college level, and the other for students of whatever age and background who wanted to learn to appreciate painting.

Barnes was concerned, however, that for the first few years, Chisholm "not be hampered by a lot of teaching" that would interfere with "research in philosophy applied to art."[17] As the summer wore on, moreover, he developed a greater worry: that his new employee's "interest in the subject was not sufficient" to fulfill the role he had envisioned for him.[18] The troubled collector conferred with Dewey and, at his suggestion, sought help from his old tutor Laurence Buermeyer to whom he had provided a lifetime pension. Buermeyer hadn't had a drink in five years. His sobriety counted for a lot to a man who watched his father succumb to alcoholism. Barnes also was impressed with the "enormous amount of reading in the philosophical and cultural fields" that Buermeyer had undertaken and felt "his feet touch[ed] the ground in a way they ha[d] never done in the past."[19] He looked to him to instruct and inspire his successor. When Barnes joyfully reported to Fogg that he had "succeeded in getting [Buermeyer] to join the Foundation staff . . . to work with Chisholm . . . to make the new course . . . something unique," he concluded with a parody of the doxology so familiar to him from his Methodist boyhood: "Praise God for whom all blessings flow. Praise Him all creatures here below. Praise Him above ye Heavenly Host. Bless Bar-ness, too, but Penn the most."[20] They must now concentrate on the search for a third teacher.

At the end of August, Fogg suggested David Robb, the university's professor and chair of fine arts. At Barnes's invitation, Robb came to the Foundation for a visit. The collector discovered that the art historian had earned his Ph.D. at Princeton, where he had studied with Frank Jewett Mather whom Barnes considered "one of the high priests of art teaching that obstructs education."[21] A second strike against him was that he used photographs in his lectures, though Robb was willing to admit that the practice was "as futile as trying to train an auto mechanic by means of blueprints."[22] He never saw the third pitch. Guiding his guest, who was a specialist in medieval art, through the gallery, Barnes drew him into conversation about the collection and found that he could not identify two Matisse still lifes and, his interrogator later claimed, even misidentified some old masters.

Nevertheless, Barnes found Robb "ready and eager to learn." He told him that "if the Foundation was ever to meet Penn's needs in the field of education in art," the university's fine arts faculty must be "born again, and this," he added, "entails the difficult job of getting rid of fixed habits of thought and action."[23] When Robb asked what specific steps might be required of him, the collector said that he would have to obtain relief from some of his campus teaching responsibilities so he could attend de Mazia's class each Tuesday afternoon for a year. If all went well, Barnes suggested that Penn could begin extensive use of the Foundation's resources in the fall of 1947 by having Robb conduct a class of beginners in the gallery. Buermeyer's view was that if Robb turned out "to be teachable, a closer connection with the fine arts department might prove profitable all around."[24] But Barnes continued to have doubts about his suitability, and several weeks later, he ruled Robb out altogether. The collector expected Penn to keep looking "for a young man unspoiled by phony 'education.'"[25]

He also expected the university to fill half the available places in Chisholm's class. In the spring, Barnes had been encouraged when newspaper stories about his renewed alliance with his alma mater brought a flood of inquiries. He informed those Barnes students who had completed two courses at the Foundation within the past year that they should apply directly to the university for admission to the new course on philosophy and art. Initially, he thought enrollment should be twenty-five, and he sent on to Fogg the names of eighteen individuals who had studied in Merion. He indicated that, if they made application and were admitted, the Foundation would pay the tuition for ten of them, four would be covered under the GI Bill of Rights, and four would have to provide their own fees. Chisholm was to have the final say on both applicants recommended by the Foundation, who would receive a Penn credit for his class, and those coming directly from the Penn student body. Morrow sent him a list of twenty-five names in mid-September, but he soon had a complaint from Nelle Mullen that only two of the individuals "represented direct acquisitions by the university."[26] After a quick visit to Dewey in New York, Barnes proposed dropping the enrollment goal to sixteen, and the dean forwarded the names of additional university students. Among his candidates were students enrolled in the School of Fine Arts, whom Barnes considered "as little qualified to attend the Foundation as members of a leper colony to stay at a health resort" and "permanently barred" from classes held in Merion. The collector was furious with Morrow who, he said, failed even to recognize "suitable material on his own doorstep."[27]

It seems a Navy veteran, recently hired as an assistant to the dean, had written to the Foundation to inquire about taking a class. Jon Dasu Longaker, the stepson of a Penn professor of English, had earned a baccalaureate degree at the university in 1941. Elected to Phi Beta Kappa in his junior year, he had been the first student enrolled in the College to major in fine arts. When he was invited to Merion for an interview, he met with de Mazia and Nelle Mullen. They were impressed by his interest and his background. Longaker not only had an excellent academic record, he was an occasional painter who spoke German, Italian, and French. He was born in Davos, Switzerland to a beautiful German girl whose Rumanian husband had died before their son's birth. After first living with his wealthy maternal grandparents in Dresden, he was taken by his mother to Naples. Her marriage to an American scholar brought her then nine-year-old son to Philadelphia.[28] Seventeen years later, Jon Longaker found himself being ushered by de Mazia and Mullen into a small office occupied by Albert Barnes. The collector questioned him about his ambition to teach art history, and then, to his utter astonishment, told him that he would not only be allowed to take de Mazia's course but also an advanced course taught by Angelo Pinto and, if Chisholm agreed, the new Barnes Foundation Professor's course, as well. He would be groomed, Barnes informed him, to teach university students at the Foundation. Recalling the interview, Longaker says he was "completely blown away by the prospect and forgot to get off the train" on his return trip to the city, so ended up miles from the Penn campus in North Philadelphia.[29]

Informing Fogg of his plan, Barnes requested that Morrow's young assistant be released from his university duties for three afternoons each week. "It will be a job that requires everything he can put into it, including time," the collector wrote, and when the vice provost quickly agreed to speak with the dean, Barnes replied, "Let us pray, particularly that Longaker, who was under Penn's nose all the time, will be the lifesaver."[30] It was now late September, two weeks from the start of Chisholm's class, and Barnes seemed increasingly convinced that he or, at the least, the University, needed one. In August, the Barnes Foundation Professor had been requested to submit an outline of the topics he proposed to discuss in his course. The collector found the syllabus unacceptable because it drew from a variety of leading works in aesthetics when it was his intention that the focus should be primarily on two of his own books, *The Art in Painting* and *The Art in Renoir*, in addition to Dewey's *Art as Experience*. Barnes gave the outline to Buermeyer for "correction," and the ruined philosopher, whom Chisholm soon considered a friend, passed along suggestions to his new colleague for bringing his course in line with the collector's expectations. Forty-eight hours before the first lecture, Barnes asked Chisholm to show him the notes for his presentation. The collector returned them the next day with the request that he prepare something entirely different.

Predictably, the Barnes Foundation Professor's debut was a bust. Students found his delivery "uninspired" and lacking conviction.[31] But Barnes had yet another plan. Each Tuesday, Chisholm was to submit, in triplicate, a full outline of the lecture to be delivered the following Thursday. On Tuesday evenings, he would discuss the material with Buermeyer; on Wednesday mornings with de Mazia whom he regarded as a "mystery" then—and ever after.[32] He "was expected to revise the lecture as she proposed and to be ready up to the hour of the lecture to incorporate any new materials or to make any deletions which she or Barnes might suggest."[33] The procedure was demoralizing, and the situation got worse. During each class session for the next five weeks, the collector sat in a chair, tipped against the gallery wall beneath the Matisse mural, with Fidèle on his lap. He seemed inattentive while de Mazia, who was also present, furiously scribbled notes. Within a day or so of his lecture, Chisholm would receive a detailed letter, signed by Barnes, that noted where he had deviated from instructions and from official views of the Foundation and pointed out his distracting nervous mannerisms. Early in November, the collector ordered him to devote his seventh lecture to the principles of scientific method that link it to expressive form. Barnes then invited McClelland, Penn's provost Paul Musser, Fogg, and Morrow to come to the gallery to hear him. Unaware of the set up, Penn's four top academic officials arrived to take choral parts, albeit unwittingly, in a real, if short-lived, tragedy entitled "The Humiliation of Roderick Chisholm."

The author had written a part for himself, and following what he later described as the young professor's "rambling discourse," he stepped in to summarize the lecture series. He restated the principles that he felt his newest faculty member had "misrepresented and then link[ed] them together" to demonstrate the Foundation's core ideas about art and living.[34] But he said nothing to Chisholm who, for the first time in eight weeks, set about preparing a lecture without interference of any kind. When he delivered it on November 21, there were no auditors except de Mazia. The next day Barnes wrote to him that "a delegation of students" had asked him "to bring the pathetic situation to an end." De Mazia had provided him with her usual "accurate, verified record" of the lecturer's remarks, and the collector suggested that if Chisholm were "sensible," he would decide to make his eighth lecture his last.[35] Did the forty-seven-year-old French woman regard the young American as a rival and encourage Barnes in his nitpicking scrutiny of a tyro teacher? When Hart asked Dewey what, specifically, was wrong with his lectures, the philosopher told him he thought "Chisholm and Miss de Mazia did not get on."[36] Fogg didn't know what to think when Barnes called him to say he had asked the man, whom he had delivered to Penn in an endowed chair just seven months earlier, to resign his professorship a quarter of the way through his first term. "Whatever his defects as a teacher, he is a decent fellow and we don't want to handicap his future by anything we do," the collector wrote. "If he resigns from the Penn faculty the problem is solved. I would tell the students that he was doing research that necessitated his giving up the class. If he decides to continue . . . it would be bad for him because I would have to analyze his last lecture, which was really nonsensical, and he would have no comeback for he has not the resources for a stand-up fight."[37]

Chisholm obliged his employer with a telegram of resignation on the 23rd of November. Although he had gone to his family home in North Atelboro, Massachusetts for the Thanksgiving holiday, he returned to Merion to remove his property from the gallery two days later. What Barnes had wanted, he concluded, "was an independent and definitive 'demonstration' from philosophy of the program with which he identified himself." The situation was "hopeless," he told Morrow, and in light of his relationship with the Foundation, he said he would resign his professorship "at the university's earliest convenience."[38] Barnes went out of his way to pass on to Fogg his lawyer's opinion that the university had no contractual obligation with Chisholm and owed him nothing. But Penn thought differently. Morrow accepted his resignation as Barnes Foundation Professor but asked him to remain on the faculty. Chisholm agreed to do so at the rank of assistant professor and told the dean that he considered the $5,000 annual salary guaranteed him by the Foundation higher than his experience or achievements could justify. Although he was willing to accept half that amount, Morrow felt "the university would cheapen itself" by reducing his pay.[39] Upon his recommendation, which was supported by the provost and president, the Penn trustees approved Chisholm's new appointment at his previous level of compensation through June of 1949. Barnes told Morrow he was pleased and, furthermore, confident that the "quality of the teaching of philosophy at Penn" would not be "impaired" by his former employee's "membership in the faculty."[40] Seething, the dean replied that the university would not have appointed Chisholm to a position the previous spring if it "had not believed he possessed considerable competence as a philosopher. . . . I regret very much," he added, "that he was not able to have a longer period of trial at the Foundation."[41]

The implicit rebuke prompted Barnes to write an angry letter to McClelland charging Morrow with "falsification of the records" and enclosing a previously prepared three-page statement about the Foundation's relationship with Chisholm.[42] When the president replied politely that he was sure there were no differences that could not be resolved, the collector wrote that his letter called to mind the "image of a man who was trying to put out a fire with a brush." Ominously, he continued: "The house that was on fire is a valued part of Penn's resources." It "is burning briskly and you can help to put out the fire by writing me a letter dealing justly with the factors of Morrow's infamous charge. . . . If I receive such a letter by ten o'clock tomorrow . . . I'll smother the rest of the flames."[43] McClelland complied with a carefully worded note saying that upon review of the material Barnes had sent him, he and his administrative colleagues were "entirely satisfied that all was done that could have been done . . . to assist Dr. Chisholm to prepare and deliver lectures at the Foundation."[44] Quite apart from the dangled promise of a tantalizing legacy, the president was relieved that Barnes had taken over the young philosopher's class. The collector told Fogg he would continue it through the end of the academic year as he didn't want the students to suffer on account of the rupture in his relationship with Penn. They were treated to what one recalled as "a virtuoso performance."[45] Barnes devoted each session to the work of a single artist and took the class through detailed examinations of the paintings of Renoir, Picasso, Cézanne, Matisse, and Soutine. His lectures were packed with energy and insight, and, to his listeners' delight, occasional digressions about his personal relationships within the art world.

The day before the collector met the students for the second time as their teacher, he and Laura had attended John Dewey's wedding in Manhattan.

They were the only people besides the eighty-seven-year-old philosopher's children, their spouses, and the officiating leader of the Ethical Culture Society of New York to witness his marriage to the widowed daughter of a family friend who was less than half his age—and contributed much to his happiness during the remaining years of his life. Barnes told the class that Dewey was "the only truly original thinker" he had ever known, and he also spoke with affection about Leo Stein as he reminisced about his early collecting experiences.[46] He seemed to enjoy teaching, but the final day of the term in early February turned out to be the last day of the class. Barnes became irritated when two Penn-supplied students asked questions he considered stupid and abruptly concluded "the time and energy devoted to them had been a dead loss."[47] The next day all the members of the class received a two-sentence memorandum from the Foundation that said: "Circumstances beyond our control have made it advisable to abolish the Thursday class as of this date. Inquiries relative to the matter should be addressed to the University."[48] A letter sent to McClelland was somewhat longer. In it Barnes complained that continuation of the class had "involved a total reorganization of the original plan, and also a difficult job to clear up the chaos. . . . Penn's sole contribution had been the act of its dean" that caused a member of the class to violate "the regulation which applies equally to all students."[49] He had no choice but to ring down the final curtain more than three months early!

The president wondered what had stuck in Barnes's claw. When he found out that it was Jon Longaker's skipping of a Foundation class to assist Morrow, he expressed surprise at the collector's decision, which he said would inevitably cause great disappointment to class members who appreciated and valued highly the instruction they had received from Barnes after Chisholm's withdrawal. He went on to explain that Penn undergraduates had been taking final examinations the previous week and also registering for second-semester classes, so Longaker's absence had been as unavoidable as it was unfortunate since his campus duties involved advising students. Barnes replied that Longaker was "the most hopeful factor" in the plan he had proposed "to take Penn's painting department out of the educational cellar."[50] McClelland assured Barnes that "every possible effort" would be made "to avoid any conflict" that would keep the young administrator from the two classes he would still be attending at the Foundation during the university's spring semester.[51] The weary but patient president told Stern, moreover, that given the collector's continuing interest in the talented assistant to the dean, he was hopeful that "the recent difficulty" would "have no lasting effect."[52]

While several months later Barnes grandly declared that "by their torpor, the authorities have forfeited for . . . the last time one of the most valuable gifts, educational and material, ever offered to a university," he did continue to see and advise Longaker.[53] The erstwhile painter proved as eager as he was promising, and although the collector ridiculed the weight that leading institutions gave to credentials as opposed to knowledge and experience, he urged Longaker to spend the summer at the Sorbonne and then return to America for a Ph.D. He provided him with a three-month itinerary for studying art in European galleries and told him that without spending two summers analyzing the best pictures there, he couldn't even think about teaching at the Foundation. The young man followed his advise, and not only went abroad but upon his return to the United States enrolled in the doctoral program in art history at Columbia. He found that most of his professors treated works of art as if they were documents. Examining the details of paintings like detectives searching the site of a crime for clues, the academic historians took enormous satisfaction in finding, for example, some shred of evidence that suggested "a picture had not been commissioned by the Duke of Burgundy, as everyone had thought, but by the Bishop of Ghent."[54] Longaker gleefully shared his experiences with Barnes, and the two maintained a sporadic but warm correspondence.

The collector was in a genial mood. With reconstruction moving ahead in Europe, old men as well as young men could look forward to visiting Paris again. Furthermore, he had just finished reading a little book that made his heart sing. In a charming autobiographical essay, *Appreciation: Painting, Poetry, Prose*, Leo Stein had written that "the degree of accuracy possible when one deals with art does not amount to science in any rigorous sense." But "intelligently discriminated description" is possible, he said, and "there are good examples in the books of A. C. Barnes." In telling his readers what he had found it useful to know, he explained that "art is . . . intimately connected with everything" and that "with practice seeing pictures was possible everywhere."[55] Barnes embraced the words as a legitimization of what he had been trying to say and teach for thirty years. "*Appreciation* is a knockout!" he wrote the author. "I have never read any other exposition so clear, so sensible and accurately descriptive." He found his erstwhile mentor completely agreed with his own reservations about Picasso's cubist paintings, and words adequate to conveying his pleasure almost eluded him. "What I have said above," he concluded, "is but a feeble expression of my enthusiasm for the book and deep admiration for its creator."[56]

The letter was the first one Leo had received upon the publication of his long-awaited volume. He read it while awaiting a hospital bed in Florence where he was to undergo a second round of surgeries for colon cancer. The first operation had been performed the previous winter, and Stein had paid for it by selling one of his last Picasso drawings. The privations he and Nina endured in wartime Italy had taken a heavy toll on both of them. They had had to hide in cellars during the German occupation and were often hungry and as cold as any victims of war in Lady Russell's imagination. When Leo was able to reestablish contact with the collector, Barnes had sent packages of clothing, food, and coffee for which Stein was immensely grateful. Now he wrote to his cousin to tell him of the collector's praise, and added, "Barnes is a competent person and no flatterer."[57] He had already written to Barnes himself to say how pleased he was to receive his letter. "We have had divergences," Leo told him, "but there has always been, I think, a mutual recognition that neither of us liked twaddle about art instead of hard-headed common sense. We have both of us brains enough to know that aspiration is not inspiration, that until one has reached intelligibility one hasn't said anything." He then said in closing, "Well, good luck to us all."[58] But his had run out. Leo died on the July 29, 1947 after the first of two planned operations. He probably never read the collector's last letter. Dated the 22nd, it said: "O. K., I'll tell the shipper to go heavy on coffee and sugar next time. . . . I sent something to Crown Publishers . . . for publicity purposes. . . . I hope there's a lively scrap with the Picasso dopes so that I can put in my oar. But don't worry, they have nothing but spitballs to shoot." His statement for Crown said:

> Leo Stein's *Appreciation* . . . combines exceptionally good writing and sound thinking with simplicity, clarity and common sense. It furnishes convincing evidence of the author's profound scholarship, discerning judgment and unique first-hand experience with paintings. The book is required reading for our students.[59]

At the time Leo first shared with Barnes an outline for what turned out to be his summative work, the collector lamented that in America, "Matisse has taken a back seat and Picasso rides majestically in the forefront of the band-wagon."[60] But unbeknownst to him, the Philadelphia Museum of Art (which had recently set aside the name of the state and taken the name of the city) was planning a huge Matisse retrospective. Barnes found out about it in March of 1948 when he received a letter from Henry Clifford asking to borrow *The Joy of Life*, *Blue Still Life*, and *The Music Lesson*. The curator mentioned that when he had seen Matisse in Paris not long before, the artist had "said he hoped the Barnes Foundation would be disposed to lend to his show."[61] In fact, Matisse had hoped that the first version of the Merion mural could be brought from Paris, and he had written to his son: "Just imagine Barnes's face when he hears about it!"[62] But the collector's reaction to news of the forthcoming show was memorable even without knowing of the original plans.

He told Clifford the painter must have been spoofing and guessed correctly that Matisse would have enjoyed imagining his reaction to the bold request. When he saw the March issue of the *Philadelphia Museum Bulletin* announcing the exhibit, which was to include ninety-three paintings and nineteen sculptures in addition to drawings, prints, and an illustrated book, his dander was up like a rocket. On page thirty-nine, was a photograph of *The Joy of Life*. Barnes fired off an angry, threatening letter to Kimball and distributed copies in rest rooms and telephone booths inside the museum itself. With some justice, he complained that publishing the picture gave the public the false impression that the artist's masterwork would be included the show. To the museum's new president, Sturgis Ingersoll, who had been elected the previous fall upon the death of Stogdell Stokes, he repeated a demand that the offending issue of the periodical be withdrawn from circulation. The letter, addressed "Dear Sturgeon," contained a bit of doggerel and observed that the "seat of the museum's breeches is missing."[63] A few days after the opening, the collector visited the exhibit with a group of students. As they walked about, he lectured on the paintings. Questions were invited, and a plant soon appeared to ask: "How can a man of Matisse's cultural and artistic stature put his 'blessing' upon an institution which has been so frequently named as a place where both art and education are prostituted?" The answer involved the usual "survey of the relevant facts" as Barnes catalogued the museum's sins.[64] He circulated excerpts from his harangue throughout the city, but when the press gave them little attention, his attack grew nastier.

A second letter to Ingersoll recalled their meeting four years earlier in a city trolley. It occurred just after the publication of Ingersoll's book about the painter and Pennsylvania Academy of the Fine Arts teacher Henry McCarter. In the tribute to his late friend, Ingersoll referred to Barnes as a "patent-medicine manufacturer" who "had been accumulating some contemporary paintings under the advice of Mac's friend Glackens."[65] At the time, the collector dispatched a scurrilous message correcting the author 's misstatements (Argyrol was never patented and he didn't buy pictures at the behest of anyone) to all the students at the Academy. Now he reminded Ingersoll of their streetcar encounter: "When I entered, the passengers were sniffing. I soon verified they were trying to locate the odor of bad liquor that came from your breath. You forced your attentions upon one of the passengers to which he immediately reacted by saying, among other things—'You're drunk—if you bother me, I'll sock you in the jaw.' . . . If you've sobered up since then, you should give your attention, as president of the Philadelphia Museum of Art, to certain matters of public welfare."[66] Among other things, Barnes complained of loud, disparaging remarks Kimball had made about him when the director saw the Foundation entourage at the Matisse exhibit. But the collector, of course, needed neither mercenaries nor volunteers to fight his battles, and if, as he believed, Ingersoll's slighting reference to his source of wealth and initial dependence upon Glackens was an act of revenge, he had himself perfected the art of retaliation. On crossing paths with Kimball at the museum three weeks later, Barnes, according to his own account, "paused long enough to look at his projecting belly and say to [a] companion, in a voice still louder than the director's—'I think he is pregnant, don't you?'"[67] Just two days later, a third encounter took place that was far from accidental and subjected Kimball to far greater and more public embarrassment.

In connection with the Matisse exhibit, the museum engaged six art history professors from area colleges and universities to give gallery talks. In mid-April, Barnes learned that David Robb was to lecture on the last day of the month. Having revived, at a Rittenhouse Club dinner with Penn officials, the possibility of further cooperation between the Foundation and the university by proposing a pre-art program, the collector cried foul. He told Fogg that Robb's appearance could be interpreted as support of the museum's "fraud upon the public" in publishing a photograph of *The Joy of Life*, and he threatened to stage an on-site demonstration of the lecturer's lack "of fitness to discuss Matisse."[68] The vice provost met the professor of fine arts and laid out the situation. He told him, as he had made clear to Barnes, that any faculty member was free to accept invitations to lecture off campus as long as doing so did not conflict with teaching commitments, but he also "urged him to give the matter the most serious consideration" in light of the potential consequences of offending so mercurial and so rich an alumnus.[69] The collector had himself communicated to Robb the likely challenges from the floor he could expect by sending him a copy of the excerpts from his carefully staged talk at the museum earlier in the month. "My coat is off and I am going to see it through," Barnes assured Fogg, though he insisted his sole objective in even bringing the matter to the administration's attention "was to prevent the university from, unwittingly, becoming the dupe of the mental and moral cripples that run the Philadelphia Museum of Art."[70] "Cripple" was a word Barnes used frequently to disparage his enemies. Can one read it as a clue to an image that haunted him—his impaired father missing an arm and some measure of self-respect? We may ponder the possibility, but Penn officials lost little time trying to psychoanalyze the university's potential benefactor. On April 28, Vice President William H. DuBarry sent a note by messenger to the collector informing him that Robb, "without consideration of his professional and personal integrity," had withdrawn from his planned engagement "as a free act" and not at Penn's request.[71] He is "a fine fellow" albeit "a square peg in a round hole," Barnes replied—and proceeded to revise ever so slightly his plans for public confrontation.[72]

Fiske Kimball had stepped in as a last-minute replacement for Robb. He was not about to let Barnes force him to cancel a lecture; nor did he wish to disappoint the people who would have been turned away if there were no substitute speaker. But his expertise was architecture not painting, and he had inadequate time to prepare a talk. Kimball could not have been entirely surprised, however, when he strode into the gallery on the afternoon of April 30, 1948 and found Barnes there with a large contingent of current and former students of the Foundation The director began with a gracious acknowledgment that Robb's absence was his audience's loss and stated straight away that he did not pretend to know much about Matisse or modern art. He then went on to talk about art in general terms, stressing with apparent calculation that "truth in art must be different from scientific truth," and to say something about the painter's historical position and his role in helping select works for the show.[73] After about a half hour, a member of the audience began to ask a series of questions intended to discredit the lecturer. The challenger was

Abraham Chanin, a Barnes alumnus who was then on the staff of the Museum of Modern Art in New York. He observed that Kimball had "not made a single statement that would enable a person of average intelligence to learn what makes a painting a work of art, or what makes a painting by Matisse different from the work of any other modern painter."[74] Before long, Kimball found himself toe to toe with the collector himself. He invited him to answer questions from the audience, but Barnes cagily declined and left it to Chanin to deliver a cogent and enthusiastically received analysis of *The Blue Window.* For the director, who attempted and failed to cut him short in an attempt to make a graceful exit, the afternoon was a rout.

Barnes was convinced that for a shining moment the spirit of ancient Athens had invaded the Greek temple on Fairmount. Buermeyer described the afternoon events as a "demonstration that democracy and education, put into practice, provide the means of intelligent living" in a foreword to stenographic notes of Kimball's abasement that the collector sent around the city.[75] But Barnes couldn't stay away from the superb assemblage of pictures. Security guards reported his visits to the show's curator, and Henry Clifford once again dispatched a request. "All joking aside!" he wrote. "You've been to the Philadelphia Museum a number of times to see my selection of Matisse. Will you now let me come out to Merion someday to see your selection?"[76] Barnes howled with laughter. Adopting a new pseudonym, "Bella Donna van Byttsche," he took out his poison pen and sent Clifford a sample of his mail that mocked what he considered the social pretensions of the museum trustees, staff, and members. He claimed it was from a famous leader of the legal profession, transformed now from a ganoid fish to a lady, who was outraged at his antics: "Pish, and Tush, too, on you for suggesting that persons of our position, who have practically created Art by our patronage . . . do not know what is best for the illiterate and unwashed masses. Why I just love all that fellow Matice's works. I simply go all over with goose pimples every time I barely glance at one. Such depth! Such breadth! Such height! Such width! The daring and dash to it all!"[77]

The Rabelaisian response, which Barnes sent along for good measure, was signed by a Foundation "secretary" named "Phallus Leucorrhea," who claimed to have pushed her boss out of a third-story window—a means of disposing of their nemesis that Ingersoll and Kimball could have been forgiven for contemplating. But then they had a better idea. The May issue of the *Bulletin* carried testimonies to the museum's importance to the educational community from the five college and university faculty members who had given gallery talks, as well as the one who didn't. The publication of Robb's statement put an end to any negotiations between Penn and the Foundation for a full year. In "An Open Letter" to Ingersoll, Barnes accused the essayists of applying a "coat of whitewash" to the museum's "unsavory record."[78] The vitriolic document reiterated his charges against museum officials and ridiculed its academic supporters.

He subsequently boasted of sending copies "from Maine to Florida and from coast to coast."[79]

Missing from the lineup of Tom Sawyer's hoodwinked helpers was any representative of the Haverford College faculty. The Quaker school, then male only, had no fine arts department of its own, though it shared a professor with nearby Bryn Mawr, its sister college. In 1948, Haverford's new president, Gilbert White, who was eager to shed the strong anti-aesthetic bias of Haverford founders and early managers, wrote to Barnes for help in finding a man to teach drawing and painting. The thirty-six-year-old geographer met with the collector several times and was soon persuaded to embark upon a kind of trial marriage. Its purpose, according to Barnes, "was to make the total resources of the Foundation available to the present and future students at Haverford."[80] The first step involved two courses, one to be conducted on campus and the other at the Foundation, by teachers trained at Barnes. The collector had two men specifically in mind: Francesco Carbone, a painter who had been a member of Roderick Chisholm's ill-starred class, and the principal supporting actor in the recent Philadelphia Museum of Art drama, Abraham Chanin. White appointed Carbone a part-time instructor in a new non-credit studio art program on an interim one-year basis. Barnes agreed that he could use the Foundation gallery once he reached the stage of wanting to make objective demonstrations. In addition, Barnes brought Chanin to Merion where he was to work out a curricular plan to be followed the next year in teaching art appreciation to Haverford students. During 1948-49, six Haverford men were to have a chance to study with de Mazia.

Aware that the cooperative relationship between Haverford and Bryn Mawr permitted students enrolled in one school to take at least some courses at the other, Barnes insisted that Bryn Mawr art majors were not eligible for membership in Foundation classes. Since the chairman of their department had given a gallery talk at the Philadelphia Museum of Art and contributed an essay to its *Bulletin*, he was doing his best to contain what he considered a highly contagious disease spread by intellectual contact. But not long after the start of the school year, he discovered that the art history professor shared by the two colleges was conducting a fully accredited course at Haverford. The collector felt insulted; since Carbone's students would not receive credit, it sounded to him as if the Foundation was playing "second fiddle."[81] White got an ultimatum: either give academic credit for Carbone's course or bar the Bryn Mawr professor from the campus.

The young president sought Dewey's advice. The philosopher stressed the high quality of the Foundation's work, and on returning from his trip to New York, White told Barnes that the following year, the course being developed by Chanin would be considered as a substitute for the one offered by the Bryn Mawr art historian. But the collector had already decided to abandon his latest experiment. He and his colleagues "quit," he said, because they felt as if they "had been enticed to join in a confidence game being played by phony educators."[82] Just before for Thanksgiving recess, White reported to the faculty that the new course in painting and drawing had been canceled. In a document entitled "Quo Vadis Haverford College?" Barnes said he should also tell them what "Haverford lost for the future."[83] But there was some gain. A brilliant Haverford sophomore, an African-American artist, athlete, and classics major who had graduated from elite Lower Merion High School, was introduced to the Foundation. Paul Moses and his classmates continued their studies as the collector turned his attention yet again to his alma mater.

Horace Stern had never given up trying to bring the two together. A loyal alumnus himself, with degrees from both the undergraduate arts and sciences college and the law school, he maintained personal contact with Barnes after the flap about Robb's essay in the *Museum Bulletin* brought official negotiations to a stand still. He knew his friend had never contributed any money to Penn despite annual appeals and a personal solicitation for the university's Bicentennial Campaign from a medical school classmate. But a new president, with no former ties to the university, had arrived on campus, and Stern persuaded Harold Stassen that it was worth his while to make an effort to reestablish relations with the irascible doctor in Merion. Coming to Penn after an unsuccessful bid for the Republican presidential nomination, Stassen was forty-one years old and had been elected three times as governor of his native Minnesota. Barnes admired his progressive politics, in what seemed like the old Populist tradition, and readily agreed to Stern's suggestion that he have dinner with the president in late June of 1949. The judge was again the host of a small party, which took place at his home on Rittenhouse Square and included DuBarry and Fogg in addition to Stassen and the collector.

It was a sociable evening, and Barnes got on well with the guest of honor. But when Fogg stressed that Stassen had instituted a "new deal" at Penn, his skeptical friend from Merion reminded him that "bricks cannot be made without straw." Still Barnes told Stern that he "was sympathetic to the ideals of a regenerated Penn" and would do anything he could, consistent with his own views on education, "to further Governor Stassen's end."[84] In the spirit of laying his cards on the table, he wrote the president the next day to say that there had been no follow-up to his suggestion of a year ago for a pre-art program at the university. As far as he was concerned, Penn's inaction, not his anger over the Robb affair, was the reason he "passed out of the picture for keeps."[85] He told Fogg that his letter to Stassen, with which he included a memorandum on his relations with the university over the last quarter of a century, "emphatically does not mean that the resources of the Foundation are at this time or in the future available to Penn." The arboretum was a separate matter. Laura's dealings with the five university faculty members teaching plant science were entirely satisfactory, Barnes said, but providing "students with knowledge that would enable them to have gardens of their own and an intelligent appreciation of other gardens" was "a very simple problem" compared with the Foundation's goal in its art appreciation program. When Chisholm didn't "work out," he told the vice provost, he and Penn became parties in an "educational divorce, executed legally."[86]

But for a time there seemed to be some prospect for reconciliation. Stassen left steamy Philadelphia for a summer holiday in New Hampshire with two gifts from the collector: *The Art of Renoir* and *The Philosopher of the Common Man*, a book of essays written in honor of Dewey's eightieth birthday. Barnes had recommended that he take the first four chapters of the former "in small doses . . . to see how down-to-earth and assimilable by people of ordinary intelligence the whole question of art can be made."[87] In the latter, he suggested Walter Hamilton's "A Deweysque Mosaic" as a blueprint for the administration of any complex organization. Perhaps he had in mind the author's observation that "Dewey's task has been . . . to lure the mind from the demonstration of truth to the prosecution of inquiry . . . and . . . all who go his way must take the path of creative endeavor."[88] What was required of Stassen?

A year later, Barnes claimed university officials knew that the terms for securing a bequest included a total makeover of the fine arts program still presided over by George Koyl, who remained dean of the School of Fine Arts, and David Robb, continuing as chair of art history.[89] But it is not clear they grasped how much they would have to give up to accommodate him. Fogg tried to argue that the university was getting more straw into its bricks all the time and that "with a man like Stassen at the head of the institution, there [wa]s a strong possibility of . . . being able to reinforce all the sectors of the wall."[90] But at seventy-seven, Barnes was more impatient than ever with the sluggish ways of large academic institutions. In July, he returned to Europe for the first time since the start of World War II—and the profound change he encountered there was a keen and poignant reminder of time's passage. When he came home at the beginning of September, he found a letter from Fogg expressing his sense of a real commitment at the top to strengthen Penn's weak spots, but no letter from the president. Barnes replied at once that the vice provost's request that he collaborate with Stassen to "raise the educational status" of the university "at a time when high Penn officials who are responsible for much of the educational disorder . . . are still functioning" was a "pipe-dream."[91]

Barnes was addressing Stassen through the botanist, and the next day he had his response. The president sent a simple note of thanks for the collector's contribution to his summer reading, but Barnes judged it enough to justify his spending the early fall of 1946 searching for someone with elite academic credentials and an interest in art whom he could groom to teach courses for university students at the Foundation. At the same time, he pushed hard for reforming fine arts at his alma mater. In late September, the collector met with Fogg and specified his terms. He said he believed Stassen had what it would take to lift "Penn out of the educational dump," but he was annoyed to have discovered that not only were Koyl and Robb still in positions of power, Jack Bookbinder had been appointed a lecturer in the university's School of Education.[92] Increasingly uncomfortable in his role as intermediary, the vice provost urged Barnes to bring his complaints about Penn's deficiencies directly to the president. Barnes conferred with Dewey, who expressed hope that Stassen would be able to break with the past and "do something sound in educational policy."[93] Mulling his friend's opinion, the collector went off to Europe for another three weeks.

During his stay that postwar autumn of 1949, Barnes concluded that the Boy Wonder, the then current sobriquet for the youngest man ever elected a governor in the United States, wasn't as progressive as his reputation. But while he was abroad, Stassen sent him an invitation to lunch. He had read the files and was ready to discuss the recommendations the collector had made for reorganizing the School of Fine Arts fifteen years earlier. Upon returning to Merion, Barnes read the letter and dispatched a response that must have confirmed the president's suspicion about the impossibility of a bequest from the flinty medical school alumnus. "To expect you, a man not trained in educational science and not having around you anybody who has evidenced any such knowledge, to bring about desired results is practically a confession of a belief in miracles," Barnes wrote. "Your problem, I think, is the very old one of how to eat your cake and have it, too, and is, it seems to me, not unlike that of Hercules when he had to clean out the Augean stable."[94] The collector was furious, moreover, that Stassen had endorsed Philadelphia's corrupt Republican machine in upcoming city elections. "The only way to rehabilitate the [university]," he told Stern, "is to have trained educators of unimpeachable character supplant the present delinquents." The efforts of the "earnest, honest educators now teaching at Penn" won't "be fruitful when educational illiterates and politicians run the show. I have written you frankly and with sorrow in my heart," Barnes said, "because it is my Swan Song."[95] But Stern wouldn't quit trying to patch things up, and the collector couldn't resist a curtain call.

His letters to John Fogg were a mixture of wistfulness for what might have been and vulgar bombast. In one, he recalled the dinner at which he had been introduced to Stassen and inveighed by the vice provost to help the new president improve Penn's academic standing. "God knows I would have been eager to help if your request had been on the level," Barnes wrote. A few paragraphs later, he referred to Fogg's petition as "about on par with a man who would ask the Pope to join him in pissing in the holy water font at St. Peter's."[96] Toward the end of March 1950, Barnes found an actual stage, located in the university's turreted, red-brick Irvine Auditorium, for a spring fling in the best tradition of generations of rowdy undergraduates. It all started when a local novelist, who had gained a measure of fame two years earlier when he won a Pulitzer Prize for his *Tales of the South Pacific*, wrote an article about

Philadelphia's Main Line for the April 1950 issue of *Holiday* magazine, Curtis Publishing Company's upscale monthly.

James A. Michener said the region straddling the tracks of the Pennsylvania railroad represented "suburban America at its best"—a place where "the people are decent, the homes friendly, and the beauty of the land is something rare. . . . Even shorn of its old social glory," he wrote, the "community is still one of the most exclusive in the land." With its rolling hills and plunging streams, the choicest part, according to the author, was Lower Merion. He mentioned, almost in passing, the "world-famous collection of modern French art" assembled there by Dr. Albert C. Barnes about which "the Main Line does not seem overly impressed." In two brief paragraphs, he sketched the story of the collector's bravado trashing of the *Saturday Evening Post* and advised readers that the best way to get in to see his pictures was to "devise some alluring trick." It seems an enterprising college student, denied admittance on three occasions, posed as a steel worker in a letter posted from Pittsburgh and received permission to visit by return mail. Michener went on to speak of the educational institutions for which the Main Line was famous, notably Haverford and Bryn Mawr colleges. There was also an excellent public school system, he observed, and when children from the downriver town of West Manayunk finished "ultralovely Bala Cynwyd Junior High" and went on to Lower Merion High School, you couldn't tell them from their classmates.[97]

The collector didn't need to read anymore. His hand-delivered letter began, "Somebody gave me a copy of that menstrual drip, *Holiday*, in which you let the world know that you are on 'call' by a Philadelphia concern that runs a chain of houses of prostitution of literature." It ended: "You glamorize ordinary people, lick their boots ad nauseam, comfort smug complacency of snobs."[98] Thanking Barnes for his "warm and friendly note" and inquiring if he used "barbed wire for toilet paper," the author confessed that he was "the four-flushing swine who pulled that Pittsburgh iron-worker routine" on the collector twenty-five years ago. "I remember the trip to Merion as about the best intellectual part of my years at Swarthmore," Michener said. "You think there's any chance that my wife—who is a damned good artist and not at all like me—might get a chance to see what you're sitting on over there behind the wall?"[99] Barnes's response drew upon his knowledge of chemistry to ascribe to Michener a penchant for producing foul-smelling compounds and, gratuitously and pointlessly, questioned his sexual orientation presumably because one of the photographs accompanying his *Holiday* article was of an art patron who was known to be gay.

An ill-timed letter from Stassen to the collector reiterating his invitation to lunch arrived just as Barnes learned that Michener had accepted an invitation to give a campus talk on components of good literature. Barnes sent Fogg copies of his exchange with the author and suggested that they be read aloud in connection with Michener's lecture. Taunting Stassen with the loss of a $10 million addition to the university's endowment and a chance to get his "hands on a collection of paintings that would sell . . . for at least twice that sum," Barnes said he hoped they could lunch when the "atmosphere cleared." He also mentioned that he had sent the U. S. district attorney a copy of the letter Michener "was stupid enough to send through the mail" and hinted that a federal officer might nap him on the stage of Irvine Auditorium.[100] But the only confrontation was with Barnes himself. When the evening ended without a call for questions from the floor, the collector mounted steps in the front of the assembly hall and handed Michener an envelope. After quickly opening it and glimpsing at the letterhead, the speaker grasped Barnes's hand and pulled him forward onto the raised platform. As they appeared to embrace, Barnes tossed a few hardball verbal challenges overheard by a reporter, but neither then nor subsequently did Michener accept his appeal to "toe the scratch" in a public debate.[101] It would have been futile, the novelist later suggested, since the collector was "so explosive, so profane, so vitriolic that he quite blasted any potential adversary right off the map." He looked back on his "brush with Barnes as a completely hilarious episode in which a very powerful man quite overwhelmed me."[102]

Barnes saw to it that the local press had as much copy on the scuffle as they cared or dared to print, and he sent a packet of clippings to Jon Longaker at Columbia. His young friend had written that he had passed oral examinations for his doctorate and was finishing his dissertation. "If I hadn't had a year at the Foundation first," he said, "I would surely have turned into one of these picture-detectives who are the art scholars of today."[103] He added that he was in the market for a teaching position and asked Barnes for a letter of recommendation. The collector replied that he should wait a couple of weeks as something might turn up in connection with a situation in which he was involved at the moment. Barnes had just responded to another overture from Stassen with a note that began with a discussion of the difficulty of avoiding "bluntness" when pronouncing "a death" and ended with a tasteless story meant to lampoon the president's motives in dispensing luncheon invitations.[104] But now he briefly imagined that the relationship he desired might be resurrected on terms acceptable to him. Barnes proposed that Longaker seek a post in Penn's department of fine arts, where he would teach but a single course on the appreciation of painting and have a free hand in choosing his students who would travel to Merion once a week for laboratory instruction in the gallery. A copy of the letter went to Stassen, and the president told the collector he would be willing to discuss his suggestion with him or with Longaker whenever it was convenient. But it was likely to be a difficult conversation. Penn provost Paul Musser had warned his boss that to permit an instructor to determine who would be or would not be in his class would be wholly contrary to university policy. "There would be nothing but the usual trouble ahead" if the president proceeded with negotiations," Musser predicted.[105]

Barnes took Stassen's letter as a sign that he had "awakened to the seriousness of the situation" and assured Longaker that the "big shots" would "probably offer all sorts of compromises." He also insisted that they were in a position
to "stand firm and resist all the blandishments."[106] Longaker was willing to
drop everything and come to Philadelphia, but Barnes told him: "We hold all
the trump cards and know when to play them. I will send you word when I
think the time is opportune."[107] To emphasize what he perceived as the weakness of Penn's hand, he wrote to Stassen, "What damned fools you've been to
let it come to such a pass!"[108] The meeting between the president and Longaker
was eventually scheduled for May 22, 1950, a day when Robb also was available to interview the applicant. But five days before it took place, the Pennsylvania primary election was held and the machine-backed Republican
candidates publicly supported by Stassen met resounding defeat at the hands
of more liberal party members. Barnes was annoyed by the former governor's
continuing involvement in politics, and he now told Longaker that the election provided "pretty good evidence that the people resented his making the
university a puppet of a body of hidebound reactionary politicians. When
Stassen is gallivanting around the country, dragging the University's name in
the dirt—here, there and everywhere—the institution, which Benjamin Franklin
founded, sinks to lower levels of degradation, educationally, morally and
spiritually," Barnes wrote. "The same old time-servers and yes-men that composed Penn's Politburo when you were a student there, still run the show in the
same old way. . . . The Penn professor, who recently denounced Stassen in the
press as 'the worst president the University has ever had,' voiced the convictions of the best informed members of the alumni, faculty and student body."[109]

With growing doubts that anything would come of it, Longaker kept his
appointment with Stassen. Since Barnes had sent the president a copy of his
post-election analysis, Stassen had few expectations when he received him.
The interview was over in twenty minutes. No job offer was forthcoming, and
Stassen told Longaker there was no point in his meeting with Robb given the
latest developments. The aspiring teacher reported to Barnes that he had "felt
a certain pride" in being able to give the president "a very glowing account"
of what Penn was "missing out on."[110] Stassen wrote to say that he regretted the
collector's backing away from his proposal and was sorry Barnes "was afraid to
go ahead and help [him] improve the fine arts situation at the University of
Pennsylvania."[111] The proposal was "sucker bait," Barnes informed the president.[112] The two went at it for a few more rounds. Barnes wrote that Stassen was
"what psychologists term a 'mental delinquent,' variously known to laymen as
'dumb bunny,' 'false alarm,' 'phony.'" Santayana, he said, diagnosed every
such individual as "the possessor of a liquid brain."[113] But the stress of keeping up a correspondence with the collector might well produce changes in
anyone's neural substrate, and Stassen finally stopped answering his letters.

A solicitor for Penn's medical school placed a note in the development files that the richest member of the Class of 1892 absolutely refused to make a contribution as he had a "feud with the university." Indeed, Barnes's tumultuous relationship with his alma mater had occupied him for more than a quarter of a century. It had taken an extraordinary amount of time and energy on his part and, to a much lesser but still significant degree, on the part of three presidents. Penn officials took some comfort that the university was still specified in the collector's Indenture. They had a reasonably good idea of the market value of his pictures, but no real notion of what they might do with them if Penn should someday have the power to appoint Foundation trustees. From Barnes's perspective, that was the problem; he was waiting for a creative response. Given his temperament, a proactive approach was fraught with danger, but the reactive stance adopted by successive administrations doomed them. Longaker might develop into the man he was looking for to give intellectual ballast to the Foundation in any future link with another educational institution. The search for an academic partner would go on.

For a time, Barnes considered Sarah Lawrence College in Bronxville, New York. He had become increasingly impressed with its president Harold Taylor, a thirty-five-year-old Canadian who had formerly taught social philosophy and aesthetics at the University of Wisconsin. It had been Dewey's idea to get them together. From what the philosopher knew of the art program at the women's college, an institution a year younger than the Barnes Foundation, it was very much in line with his own thinking, and he urged Barnes to meet Taylor and see if they could "do business."[114] As his relations with Penn were rapidly unraveling, the collector sent Taylor, as well as two other admirers of Dewey's—the *New York Times* drama critic Brooks Atkinson and the historian Arthur Schlesinger, Sr., copies of his correspondence with Stassen. His motive was to offer his alma mater as an example of how he felt "prominent colleges and universities" frustrated "Dewey's plans for education" by giving "lip service to his methods while nullifying them by acts."[115] But the young president was probably not alone when he misunderstood Barnes's intention and politely told Barnes that he was "a little puzzled as to what three outsiders could do to rearrange the educational program at the University of Pennsylvania."[116] With his letter, he enclosed a reprint of an article on education he had written for the *Antioch Review*.

The collector read with appreciation Taylor's call for curricular reform in American higher education to reflect the ideas of William James about the validity of individual experience and Dewey's views on the social uses of knowledge. His only previous contact with the president was a letter Taylor sent him several years earlier asking for support for the college philosophy program, which he had ignored, but now he was intrigued and quite pleased when he received an invitation to visit Sarah Lawrence to observe a workshop for college teachers on contemporary culture. At the time, however, Barnes was considering a June trip to France that precluded his acceptance, so instead Taylor offered to call on Barnes for few hours after he delivered the commencement address at Haverford College. "There is a lot to see and just as much to hear," the collector told him, and asked Taylor to bring his wife and spend the night.[117] Dewey was to have joined them, but Barnes, increasingly concerned about the health problems that had plagued his friend for a year, arranged for him to enter Bryn Mawr Hospital for a medical evaluation. The philosopher's condition and, Barnes claimed, his interest in completing the "interment" of Stassen, caused him to forgo his trip abroad.[118] The discussion with Taylor that proceeded despite Dewey's absence, first at the Merion gallery and later at Ker-Feal, was cagey on both sides. In an earlier letter, Barnes had mentioned that Jon Longaker had applied for a teaching job in Sarah Lawrence's art department and felt he had gotten a brush off. Taylor had looked into the situation and reported that the job had gone to a woman. But the collector brought up his young friend's name again as he hinted at his interest in making the resources of the Foundation available to the Bronxville college, and Taylor promised to talk with him.

Barnes found Taylor to be "full of pep" and yet have "both feet on the ground."[119] He urged him to take de Mazia first-year class to better understand the ethos of the Foundation. When Taylor made it clear that was impossible, Barnes suggested that two Sarah Lawrence students, who had not already studied art at the college, enroll the following October. Longaker, too, he decided should continue his studies in Merion for another year under de Mazia and Angelo Pinto rather than pursuing his search for a college post. The young man could try his teaching wings with a small group of Foundation students in preparation for conducing a course for Sarah Lawrence students in the 1951-52 academic year. But when Longaker actually met with Taylor in late July, he found him cool to Barnes's proposal. Art courses at Sarah Lawrence were not required, and the president could not be sure that there would be a contingent of young women interested enough in the Foundation's approach to painting to make the long trip to Philadelphia once a week. He told Longaker frankly that there was little likelihood that even if two particularly eager women started their studies in the fall and completed the full program in Merion, the college would be in a position to hire them. At one point, Taylor even confided that he thought "the old man was off his rocker."[120] When Longaker reported the substance of the discussion to his mentor, the collector was confirmed in an opinion he had shared with his protégé several days earlier. Sarah Lawrence, he said, aimed "to be ultra cultural and . . . to teach girls the parlor tricks that appeal to bond salesmen and advertising executives when they get the urge to find a mate."[121]

Initially, the collector's reaction to his newly failed experiment was almost philosophical. He told Longaker that it was "difficult for any college president to introduce a new idea that runs counter to those prevalent in his institution. . . . Taylor apparently is satisfied with the workshop setup—and this equals 'Oh, go away and let me sleep,'" he said. "Students subject to such training usually become echoes of what their teachers represent. This is far a field from education as a science and teaching as an art."[122] The next day, Barnes began to interpret Taylor's response in psychological terms. "I think it probable that a large part of his reaction to my proposal is due to the 'nerve' of my practically telling him that his education has not yet begun," he told Longaker. "This is certainly a shock because he is very much in the limelight now. . . . All the reasons he gave you against my proposal were typical 'rationalizations': he is sitting on top of the world, his college is attractive to the kind of people who can pay a good price for what passes for education." Barnes then revealed a plan, the grand scheme, he had never spelled out to Taylor. "What I had up my sleeve," he said, "is that after you had conducted a class of Sarah Lawrence students at the Foundation . . . I was going to ask him to make you chairman of the art department; you to conduct a class at Sarah Lawrence, partly at the college but mostly at the Metropolitan and other galleries in New York."[123] But never mind. Finish your dissertation, he advised Longaker, and show up in Merion near the end of September.

True to form, however, Barnes sent copies of his letter to Taylor, and when the president wrote to him in August to ask what was wrong with giving Sarah Lawrence students an opportunity to express themselves in painting, sculpting, design, and composition, he indulged himself in the kind of vulgarity he seemed to reserve for perceived opponents associated with women's colleges. One can only imagine a tight-lipped Nelle Mullen typing the letter that said: "I don't doubt that your art students enjoy your courses—my contention is that you confuse the values of education with those of diversion and entertainment. If those students are healthy, normal girls, they would get more, and keener, enjoyment from titillation of the clitoris than dabbling with paint, clay, etc. . . . This idea is certainly novel. And, since you pride yourself on being up-to-date—why not be super-duper up-to-date and submit this novelty to your board of trustees? Why not keep ahead of the Joneses?"[124]

Two months later, when a magazine published by the intensely conservative Henry Luce ran a photographic essay about Sarah Lawrence and Taylor, coincidentally, sent the collector a new college brochure, Barnes replied: "The participation of your college in the cheap, histrionic exploitation of 'education' . . . savors of apostasy. You know damned well that that bunch of educational illiterates are the most powerful enemy of our mutual friend whose battle for justice you enlisted to fight. To match the degradation of your going over to the enemy, the girl photographed in *LIFE* should have been nude, with a picture of you standing alongside with your *baguette deboutonnée*. This would have been an appropriate symbol of the conjoined prostitution of art, education and journalism." Barnes also took a crack at the just-published *Essays on Teaching*, a volume edited by Taylor that contained the president's musings on colleges as places for nurturing liberal values. The collector claimed that he had taken part in a discussion of the book where he had declared Taylor's contribution was a synthesis of other people's ideas that should be compared to "a parrot repeating the Lord's Prayer."[125]

When Taylor sent the letter on to Dewey, the philosopher wrote that Barnes already had mailed him a carbon. He added: "The letter is an unusually poor example of a technique he developed when engaged in making and marketing Argyrol in dealing with attempted interferences on the part of [the] A[merican] M[edical] A[ssociation]."[126] The origin of Barnes's approach, however, predated his days as an entrepreneur-seeking acceptance of a new product. It was on the rough and tumble streets of Kensington and South Philadelphia that he had learned to overlook nothing and throw everything he had into each punch. An amused Taylor asked the collector why he couldn't just relax and enjoy life. The answer was Barnes's concern for the future of his Foundation and the shadow of the lost Battle of Cold Harbor that would haunt him all his days.

14

The Last Alliance

Albert Barnes appreciated and found delight in music, he was an avid and discerning reader, but he took real pleasure in the company of few people—and the number dwindled as he grew older. With Glackens and Leo Stein gone, there was, always first and foremost, John Dewey, and then Charles Laughton, Henry Hart, Horace Stern, and perhaps a few others, including Albert Nulty and members of Narberth volunteer fire department. He had become a director of the company, faithfully attended its meetings, and footed the bill for yearly banquets. He liked the firefighters' company, and they felt the same about him. Another new acquaintance of his later years whom he thoroughly enjoyed was Horace Mann Bond, the first black president of a Presbyterian college named after the Great Emancipator. They met at a funeral. It was on the 31st of October 1946, and Barnes was standing in line near the entrance of Tindley Temple, the Methodist church in South Philadelphia named after the African-American pastor and composer of "I'll Overcome Some Day," the hymn that became the anthem of the civil rights movement. Barnes was one of five men, and the only white, scheduled to address the large crowd of mourners who had come to celebrate the life of Nathan F. Mossell.

The first black student to attend the University of Pennsylvania, Mossell had graduated from its medical school ten years before Barnes and gone on to found the Frederick Douglass Memorial Hospital, the only medical facility in the city where African-American nurses and interns could receive specialty training in the segregated community of his day. In the course of a long and distinguished career, the physician had co-founded, with W. E. B. Du Bois, the Philadelphia branch of the National Association for the Advancement of Colored People. Barnes had admired Mossell's 1915 protest over the showing of D. W. Griffith's *Birth of a Nation*, with its sympathetic account of the rise of the Klu Klux Klan, and supported his unsuccessful attempt to gain admittance for black orphan boys to Girard College in 1937. But he grew impatient as he waited for the hearse with the dead man's casket. Turning to the short fellow standing behind him in line, the collector asked if he, too, was a eulogist.

When Horace Mann Bond, the new president of Lincoln University, Mossell's undergraduate alma mater, answered "yes," Barnes said, "I hope you won't talk forever." Somewhat miffed at the rude comment from a stranger, Bond told him he had written out and timed his remarks, which would last for exactly three minutes. The collector replied, "I never have known a Negro preacher who could only talk three minute." The irony of the stereotypical depiction of African Americans that Mossell had fought all his life arising at his funeral was not lost on Bond. He replied angrily that he was "not a Negro preacher."[1]

The rebuff silenced Barnes for a while. When members of the platform party finally entered the church and took their places, however, Bond became the recipient of the collector's whispered views about the remarks made by principal eulogist Arthur Huff Fauset, the anthropologist and educator whom he had once hoped to interest in studying at the Foundation. Instinctively a rebel, Fauset sought to identify Mossell with his own left-wing sentiments, and at one point, as Bond later recalled, the eulogist observed that "Dr. Mossell had the greatest admiration for the new strides toward human justice and equality that had been taken in Russia." Without losing a beat, Barnes said: "He's lying! Dr. Mossell was never fooled by those bastards!" When Fauset went on to tell his audience that "Dr. Mossell smiled" at his every mention of the Soviet Union, the indignant collector nearly shouted, or so it seemed to Bond: "He's telling a God-damned lie! If I had a baseball bat, I'd knock him down!"[2]

Somehow the service concluded without any assaults, and Barnes, apparently impressed with Bond's remarks and perhaps to make amends for his initial discourtesy, insisted that the Lincoln president join him for lunch in Merion. He dismissed Bond's initial refusal on the grounds that he had another appointment with the comment that he should tell whoever was awaiting him that he had broken his leg. Blessing his luck at encountering someone he now identified, with the help of the funeral program, as a potential benefactor, Bond accepted and followed in his own car as Barnes drove, with little regard for speed limits, the few miles to the Foundation. Lunch was milk and crackers, but Barnes's guest was treated to richer fare when he sat in on a lecture on the philosophy of aesthetics delivered to a class of students by Roderick Chisholm and embellished by the comments of his host. The collector gave him autographed copies of his books and later telephoned DeHaven Hinkson, the black physician to whom he had once provided a private, post-graduate fellowship for medical study abroad, to tell him how favorably impressed he was with the president of his alma mater. For his part, Bond wrote to Charles Lewis, a Lincoln alumnus with a Penn M.D. who had also spoken at Mossell's funeral, that Barnes was "one of the most remarkable men" he had "met in all his life." He said the collector had been "very cordial," and while he decided to bide his time before requesting a contribution to his struggling college, he extracted a promise from Barnes to give a talk to the senior class.[3]

A transcendent thread in the cord that would link the collector and the Lincoln president emerged from their family histories. Albert Barnes's father had lost his right arm fighting in the war that secured the freedom of the boy who would become Horace Mann Bond's father. The educator's paternal grandmother was a slave; his paternal grandfather, her white master. Their son, James, graduated from Berea College in Kentucky, then went on to study for the Congregational ministry at Oberlin where he met the young woman, also of mixed race, who would become his wife and Bond's mother. The couple was living in Nashville, where James was teaching theology at Fiske University, when the son they named after the American school reformer, Horace Mann, was born in 1904. He soon moved with his parents to Kentucky, then Alabama, Georgia, and, finally, Kentucky again where, at fourteen, he graduated from Lincoln Institute, a school his father had helped to found, and went on to Lincoln University, a small, rural institution in southeastern Pennsylvania just ten miles north of the Mason-Dixon Line.

The oldest historically black college in the United States, Lincoln was founded in 1854, and when Bond entered sixty-five years later, the strict piety of its Scotch Presbyterian founders and the inclusive humanitarianism of its Quaker supporters still pervaded the campus. The student body, shrunken during World War I to little more than two hundred young men of African descent, was drawn mostly from the working class and heavily from southeastern states. Most were enrolled in the collegiate department. Early law and medical departments had long been closed, but there was still a seminary. The faculty, which Nathan Mossell had sought unsuccessfully to integrate as early as 1883, was entirely white; the curriculum was modeled on that of Princeton with an emphasis on classical languages, the humanities, and the natural sciences. Horace Bond's youth and relatively small size made him a kind of campus mascot. His quick mastery of poker won him acceptance by his classmates. Plunging into extracurricular activities, the precocious youngster ignored his studies for two years, then excelled when he finally began to take them seriously.

Graduating in 1923 at the age of eighteen, he was invited to spend an additional year at Lincoln as a part-time teacher in the education department, library assistant, and dormitory perfect while he took additional courses required for the graduate work he hoped to do in history. Then the same age as the freshmen he was to supervise, Bond permitted, perhaps encouraged, the students to gamble and received a cut of all their wagers. When a parent's complaint alerted school authorities to the situation, the young instructor was forced to resign in disgrace. Ashamed and remorseful, he headed for Chicago where he lived with two brothers, took a job washing dishes, and enrolled in the University of Chicago's graduate department in education whose faculty did not demand that students have the same formal prerequisites demanded by the faculty in history. His father provided him with any funds he could spare and continuing encouragement. But money was tight, and in 1924, Bond accepted an offer to teach at Langston University in Oklahoma. He returned to Chicago to take his master's degree in education in 1926 and begin work on his doctorate, which he was awarded a decade later.

During the intervening years, he alternated between short periods of full-time study and various jobs, serving initially as an administrator at Alabama State College in Montgomery and then as an assistant professor at Fiske University in Nashville, where he had an opportunity to work with the former editor of *Opportunity*, the eminent sociologist Charles S. Johnson. Julia Washington, a member of the city's black elite, was one of Bond's students and would become his wife. After their marriage, she, too, did graduate work at the University of Chicago. Bond went on to serve as a researcher for a Rosenwald Fund project that evaluated schools for African Americans in three southern states, and, finally, as an associate professor in a tenure track position at Fiske. The young scholar published articles based on his field research and experiences in leading black magazines and in *Harper's*, as well as in respected academic journals. He managed to publish an important book, *The Education of the Negro in the American Social Order* (1934), even before receiving his Ph.D., and his 1936 dissertation won a prize as the outstanding thesis in the social sciences for the year and was published later as *Negro Education in Alabama: A Study in Cotton and Steel* (1939).

The new black university in New Orleans, Dillard, persuaded a reluctant Bond to become its first academic dean in 1935. Two years later, he returned to Fiske as professor and chair of education and engaged in further research for the Rosenwald Fund. But in 1939 he again took on an administrative post—and fulfilled a dream of his father's—by accepting the presidency of Fort Valley Normal and Industrial School in middle Georgia. His six-year tenure was a success by any measure. He won significant increases in state funding, used it to finance innovative ideas for relating the education students received at Fort Valley to their everyday lives, and raised academic standards. When the opportunity to become the first black president of his alma mater arose, however, he was ready to move on. As a historian of African-American education, he was well aware of the propitiousness of the moment. A year earlier, Gunnar Myrdal had published *An American Dilemma: The Negro Problem and Modern Democracy* (1944), and Bond understood better than most the truth of the Swedish economist's observation that high priority must be given to reconciling deed with creed in the postwar era.

Lincoln had always played an important role in educating the country's black professional class, but survival required increasing its market share in the face of competition from predominantly white colleges, newly reminded of their moral obligation to African Americans, and expanding state universities. The Oxford school had never had much money in the bank, and its board did not hide the school's precarious financial position from the prospective president. But the prestige and challenge inherent in the post attracted him. Besides, with three small children and no private schools for African Americans, such as the university-related institutions he had attended, accessible from Fort Valley, Bond believed his daughter and two sons would have a better start in Pennsylvania public schools than in the cash-starved schools for black children in rural Georgia. He moved his family into the President's House on the Lincoln campus just before the start of the fall 1945 semester. During his first year, university enrollment increased significantly thanks to the G. I. Bill, and Bond raised $83,000 from alumni even as they complained about the university's athletic program. To carry out the board's fund-raising mandate, however, he would have to depend on his skill in cultivating relationships with potential white benefactors. Barnes seemed like a heaven-sent prospect.

Bond had learned about the collector's love of spirituals at their first meeting, and he delayed a thank you note for his lunch of milk and crackers until he could secure a brochure depicting the Fort Valley Folk Music Festival to send on to him. The celebration of black culture, which had taken place two years earlier, brought the composers William C. Handy and John Work, the poet Sterling Brown, poet and playwright Langston Hughes, and many other African-American musicians and writers to the Georgia campus. "How I should have liked to have been there," Barnes told Bond when he read the brochure.[4] He then fixed the date of January 10, 1947 for his talk to the senior class at Lincoln. Because he had given up driving after dark, moreover, Barnes accepted the president's invitation to spend the night on campus. Years later, Julia Bond still remembered his complaints about her noisy little children. But the nineteen students who gathered in her living room—though little more than a third the number her husband had hoped for—appear to have listened to the rich visitor with quiet but quick attention, and as Horace Bond had counted on, Barnes was stimulated by the chance to address them.

While they were together, the president mentioned to his guest the plight of scholarship students from the British colonies who were mostly very poor and, in any case, faced severe restrictions on the amount of money they could take out of Commonwealth countries to cover their living expenses when school was not in session. Within a few days, he received a check from Merion for $1,000. "What you have done is a veritable Godsend for these boys," Bond said in his letter acknowledging Barnes's generosity. He described the young men from British Guiana, Barbados, Jamaica, and elsewhere as representing "the hopes and the future of tribes and communities and churches." Devising a plan for giving each of the students a pro-rated share of the gift, amounting to nearly $59, he explained that the collector's largess would mean an "overcoat for one man and a pair of shoes, perhaps a shirt; for another . . . the margin sufficient to feed him over the summer." Bond added that the "foreign boys" reminded him of his "own father's generation when, just out of slavery, the whole world appeared to them as a place in which to use their powers and education for human good." He was profoundly grateful, he said, for the funds that permitted him "to be the instrument through which these young men w[ould] be helped to fulfill . . . a very precious mission."[5]

Barnes's winter drive to Oxford inaugurated a series of occasional visits between the collector and the president that extended over the next four and a half years. In February, Barnes conducted a personal gallery tour in Merion for Horace and Julia Bond and members of the Lincoln faculty. Bond wrote that his wife agreed with his assessment that Barnes was "at heart and in person a great teacher."[6] Some time thereafter, he dispatched what he later and regretfully called "a begging letter," which Barnes ignored, but it does not seem to have caused any permanent rupture in their relationship. Bond apologized for his "presumption upon [Barnes's] kindness," and in the fall, the collector again agreed to give a lecture to Lincoln students on a date, January 8, 1948, closely marking the one-year anniversary of his first campus visit. Describing himself as "the world's worst college president," Bond shared with the collector how he turned on its head the unspoken rule that required the leaders of collegiate institutions to maintain good relations with the surrounding community. He explained that he had "recently infuriated a large portion of [the university's] local clientele" by attempting to desegregate the Oxford public school, where black children were taught by a black teacher and white children by a white teacher in the first five grades, though in the next three grades, both black and white children were taught by a white teacher. Justice and an expanding school-age population required that the black teacher conduct integrated classes, Bond argued, and initially, the school board acceded to his request, though it soon reversed itself in the face of protests from white parents. The president's response was to become a candidate for the school board and to bring suit against it. "I have taught and counseled patience all my working life," he told Barnes. "I can take the long view for myself, but for my dear children, I just cannot tolerate anything that affects their future." For them, he was willing to risk becoming "a feared and hated 'bad Nigger' in the view of . . . neighbors."[7]

Barnes applauded Bond's action. "You are doing what probably no other president of a small college would do, i.e., coming out flat-footed for democracy as stated in the Federal Constitution and the Bill of Rights," he said, and then added encouragement and advice based on his own experience. Barnes's celebration of black culture in a private home on Latch's Lane was hardly comparable in terms of potential personal peril to Bond's public stand against school segregation, but the collector meant to be supportive when he wrote:

What I like best about it is the simple statement of irrefutable facts of law and common sense, totally uncovered by the Negro['s] supposed overload—emotion. I faced a similar situation some twenty-odd years ago when I had the Bordertown singers give a concert once or twice a year in our gallery. I got anonymous communications branding me 'nigger lover' and all kinds of abuse from the social and intellectual elite of this community. That lasted for about five years, until the Bordertown Glee Club won the hearts and minds of so many of the really best people that we could not accommodate all those who applied for admission to the concerts.

It's a safe bet that if you can stand the present gaff, you will win hands down in the long run. You are undoubtedly taking the first right step in your appeal to the courts and I hope you don't get cold feet in that respect. Your principal trouble will be, I think, to find a lawyer with the proper spirit, good enough mind, and forceful enough personality to put it over. I think that probably you could pave the way for this by giving your story to the big city newspapers, especially the *New York Times*. . . .

I wonder if you haven't overestimated the number of people who denounce you as a 'son of Ham'; of course, there are plenty such, but I believe that a public airing of the question, such as I have suggested, would not only diminish the number of adversaries but get a lot of people on your side.[8]

In the matter of equal justice for African Americans, Barnes and Bond shared a belief in the possibility of change through education and a commitment to working for it. They were optimists who believed their fellow citizens could be taught to see.

But if the teaching resembled in any measure instruction in art appreciation, it would be, from the collector's perspective, a demanding process. During his early 1948 visit to Lincoln, Walter Fales, a professor of philosophy, asked him if he would return in the spring to speak either to the whole student body at a morning assembly or to members of the campus Philosophy Club some evening. When he issued a specific invitation for 10 A.M. on May 6, Barnes responded grumpily that leaving Merion before the mail came and his employees had arrived for work would "disarrange the Foundation's whole program." More significantly, he pointed out that "abstractions not demonstrated by objective facts amount to just talk which, at its best, is either diversion or entertainment."[9] Fales responded in German that if the prophet would not come to the mountain, the mountain must come to the prophet —"*Wenn der Prophet nicht zum Berge kommt, muss der Berg zum Propheten.*" He requested permission to bring his aesthetics class, as he had done once before, to visit the collection. "Those boys are so appreciative of anything offered them in art, particularly if it is first class, that for their sake I ask you to give us this opportunity," Fales concluded.[10]

The collector's response implied that one visit to see his pictures, as well as his several visits to Lincoln to talk informally about them, was a gesture of friendship; two would be a perpetuation of a pedagogic illusion. He recounted his failed attempts to educate Penn and Columbia students. Quoting himself, he told Fales that "the appreciation of works of art requires organized effort and systematic study, on the same principle that it requires effort and study to become a lawyer, an engineer or a physician. Art appreciation can no more be absorbed by aimless wandering in galleries than surgery can be learned by casual visits to a hospital." What schools from Harvard to Bryn Mawr "mistake for appreciation is what we found is daydreaming," he said. Cutting to the chase, he told the Lincoln professor:

> If you want what help we can afford to Lincoln students, the best way would be for you to select three or four, let them apply for admission to the first-year class beginning next October, present themselves for an interview to the teaching staff, and if it is decided they are suitable material, they will be admitted to the first-year class, which meets every Tuesday and lasts from one to five P.M. The principal difficulty with them, as with all our students, is to get through the crust they have accumulated in their contacts with the usual ways of looking at art as it is presented in the academies, colleges and universities.
>
> There is one thing you can bank on, and that is that there would be no discrimination against your candidates because of race or color. On the contrary, we have found that their native endowment usually provides [them] a better chance of entering our classes than the average white student's. The difficulty here is that we have ten times as many applicants as we can take care of and we limit our classes to twenty-five members to insure the personal contact between teacher and pupil, which is one of the fundamentals of our plan of instruction.[11]

Horace Bond, like many others, was the recipient of a carbon copy of excerpts of Barnes's diatribe at the Philadelphia Museum of Art in the spring of 1948. But in contrast to the starched acknowledgment of even the genial John Fogg at Penn, the Lincoln president responded with hearty appreciation. He told Barnes he read the document "at the end of a long day [when] many difficulties had presented themselves" and found it "as stimulating and refreshing . . . as the fine Scotch" the collector had once offered him, but he "was foolish enough not to take."[12] Barnes expressed his pleasure but said Bond's letter did not mitigate his offense of refusing the whiskey. When the collector sent him further accounts of the Museum rumpus, Bond shared with him a controversy in which he had himself been recently involved in "utter disregard of the proprieties that should bind college presidents." Asked to lend his name to a campaign to make black students aware of scholarship opportunities at white colleges, Bond did and gave the matter little thought until he received a pamphlet containing the solicited endorsements along with what purported to be "a complete list of all the interracial colleges in America." Princeton was there, Bond told Barnes, though he said "it had been a matter of pride for many years that no Negroes were admitted;" Lincoln, which had enrolled a handful of white students from the surrounding area as far back as 1868, was left out. The omission enraged him, and he wrote a stinging letter to the organizer of the campaign, which he mimeographed and mailed to members of the campaign advisory committee, including Henry Luce. "It irks me no end to run into these 'integrationists' who apparently assume that the true solution of the Negro problem is to eliminate everything Negro," Bond wrote to Barnes. "I take a wicked pleasure in throwing the barbed hook into the hide of such people by telling them that if they want to eliminate segregated institutions, why not direct the flow of integration from white into black rather than the commonly assumed notion that it inevitably should be from black to white."[13] He could well appreciate, therefore, the harpoons the collector was launching toward the Greek temple on the edge of Fairmount Park. He told Barnes he had read the "Stenographic Notes Taken at a Lecture on Matisse" with "the greatest joy imaginable. I am still laughing," he wrote. "I do hope that you may continue to spare my life from utter monotony and academic dullness as well as ignorance of art by sending me such enlightening materials."[14]

Throughout the fall of 1948, Barnes shared with Bond copies of his exchanges with Haverford's Gilbert White. The Lincoln president tactfully refrained from commenting on the misadventure of a professional colleague, but as the financial problems of his own university worsened in the face of a decline in the enrollment of returning veterans, he must have dreamed about the possibility that his friendship with the rich collector would benefit Lincoln in material ways. A seemingly trifling incident occurring in January of 1949, however, gave him a jolt of reality. Without his knowledge, a Lincoln student from British Guiana wrote to Barnes of his need for $711 to pay his delinquent tuition and board bills for the term and cover those for the spring semester. Apparently unmoved, Barnes sent the letter on to Bond with the observation that the youth's object must have been to have him "pony up" funds to keep in the president's "good graces."[15] He then wished him Happy New Year. Bond replied that the student was likely to go far because of his "aggressiveness and lack of reticence—in other words," he added, quoting his Kentucky grandmother who "was born a slave and grew up with the salty speech of the mountains—'He has the nerve of a brass-assed monkey!'"[16]

But the president refrained from imitating his pupil in the interest of hanging on to his volatile partner as they danced their strange shuffle. He did ask Barnes to a dinner at Philadelphia's Bellevue Stratford Hotel in celebration of the ninety-fifth anniversary of the founding of the university. It would be held on February 9, and Bond described the party as "an effort to steal Lincoln's birthday back from the G.O.P. and an alumni-morale affair all in one."[17] Hoping to entice the collector, he told him an award would be presented to his friend Justice Owen J. Roberts, who had become a Lincoln trustee after resigning from the Supreme Court and returning to Philadelphia to become dean, at age seventy-three, of the University of Pennsylvania Law School. Bond ended his long note with a funny story about a chance encounter with a wealthy dowager mowing the grass of her estate during his summer visit to England. The president had gone there as a member of the faculty of an international vacation school for educators sponsored by the United Nations, and Barnes responded to his letter somewhat wistfully, as he had not then traveled to Europe since 1939, that he envied the president his foreign sojourn. But he was planning a winter trip to the South, so he declined the dinner invitation.

His attention in the early months of 1949 was, in fact, focused on a civil rights matter in Alabama. A former Foundation student, Claude Clark, was then chairman of the art department at Talladega College. His students had been invited to submit work to a statewide collegiate art exhibition at a new art museum at the University of Alabama in Montgomery. But Clark was informed that neither they nor he would be welcome at the white-only dinner to be held in connection with the opening of the exhibit. When the black artist told Barnes, the collector wrote to the one of the scheduled keynoters, who happened to be his former protégé Tom Munro. At Barnes's urging, moreover, Clark informed Dewey and other prominent white friends of African Americans of the situation. They dispatched letters of protest to the university, and Munro cancelled his appearance. A delighted Barnes told him: "Your cancellation to speak at Alabama is a monument on the road to civilization."[18]

Bond shared with Barnes his own small sign of triumph in September of 1949 when he passed along the good news that Lincoln was expecting fifteen new African students. They would come from Nigeria where an organization of coca farmers had raised $17,000 to pay for their expenses over the next two years. An address delivered at the dedication of the first building at Ashmun Institute, as Lincoln was known before the Emancipation, spoke of the new university as an instrument of Divine Providence to educate "missionaries to Africa," and students from West African countries had been attending Lincoln since the early 1870s.[19] Intensely interested in African affairs, Bond wrote that he would be visiting Sierra Leone, Liberia, the Gold Coast, and Nigeria throughout October on his first trip to the continent so intimately linked to the history of his university. "Shall I pick up (or try to) any objects for you?" he asked. "I hope to get our alumni there started on increasing our own collection."[20] A thoroughly delighted Barnes replied: "Your nice juicy letter . . . brightens the day—and Praise the Lord for the seventeen thousand bucks!" He added: "I wish I could go with you to Africa, for it has been one of my dreams." But he also cautioned Bond "about getting Negro sculpture:—the woods in Belgium and France are full of manufacturers of these fetishes, which are shipped to Africa and picked up by the uninformed," he said. "They are uniformly of inferior quality."[21] He told the president that he was expecting a shipment of several fine pieces.

Bond was the first American educator invited to Africa by Africans themselves. During his visit, he met with Oba Akenzua II of Benin, and thinking that Barnes would be interested in hearing from the ruler of the kingdom from which so many of his art objects had come, he gave him the collector's address. The Oba lost no time in writing to Barnes for a capital loan of £5,000 to start up a timber export business. Learning of the letter several months after his return to Lincoln, Bond apologized for doing the collector "an evil turn." He had been preoccupied with faculty and student grumbling about his extended absence from the campus, and now he seized the opportunity to report on his trip in amusing detail. He gave an account of the Oba's palace, which reminded him of an "oriental court," and encouraged Barnes to make the thirty-hour air journey to visit Benin in the fall when the weather was less hot. "I have never seen such wonderful dancing in all my life," the president said. "For some peculiar reason, the pressure of the culture in which American Negroes live has made a great many ashamed of their African background. However, after seeing the Nigerian dancers, I was convinced that just about everything in American dancing worthy of the name stems from Nigeria. I think it would be worth a trip to you to see these dancers."[22] Bond also mentioned meeting an African artist who would be coming to America in the next few months to study under the auspices of the Barnes Foundation.

As the winter of 1950 turned to spring, Barnes was preoccupied with his fight with Michener and the possibility of Jon Longaker securing a faculty post at Penn—a development that would allow his mentor to resume his abandoned experiment involving the education in art appreciation of students at his alma mater. He also began to experience urological problems that led him to consult a specialist, and it may have been concern about his own health, as much as his concern about Dewey's and, by summer, his relish for finishing off Stassen, that kept him home from Europe. But he went on to court Sarah Lawrence, and in mid-August, not long after the collapse of his suit, the collector received another engaging letter from Bond, at once comic and serious, inviting him to join the Lincoln faculty as a lecturer in art for the coming academic year. In explanation of the proffered title, the president recited the hierarchy of academic ranks ending with "full Professor, Adjunct Professor, and Lecturer. Full Professors do a little work," he said. "Adjunct Professors not as much; Lecturers, hardly any. The Lectureship is therefore the highest rank we can offer. It means," Bond continued, "that the incumbent can be fired at any time; he may quit at any time; and he is endowed with complete prerogatives of giving the President and his fellow-faculty members Hell with no restrictions." Bond then added:

> The remuneration for this post would include all of the usual rights and privileges of members of this Faculty, which are so nebulous as to defy description. Specific cash remuneration would be set by the usual process of bargaining according to the great traditions of the Academic fish market. For your information, our usual compensation for regular members of the Faculty works out to about $9.25 an hour, which many regard to be too much.
>
> The duties of this post would include the request that the incumbent deliver from four to six lectures during the year in the general field of Art, the nature, direction, style, and composition of such lectures to be decided by the Lecturer; . . . and, in addition, or to be included in the above, one or two or more lectures on the specific field of African Art, these latter to be offered as part of the program of the Institute on African Affairs now projected by the University for the year 1950-1951.

. . . We have no money with which to do it, but we do have a tradition; a love for Africa; and several people in the Faculty who know something about Africa. We should be honored to be able to list you, both as a member of the Faculty of the University, and as a member of the Faculty of our Institute on African Affairs.

If you can accept this (not-too-generous) offer of employment, please let me know when we may be permitted to schedule your lectures; and, if subjects for specific lectures could be announced, what they are, and whether you would permit members of the general public in addition to our student body to attend.

Now it is my sincere belief that you could greatly benefit the human race if you could find the time to give even the smallest portion of your time to this institution in this way. The African people, from whom I have the honor of claiming descent, are a people generally blessed with loving, affectionate, and grateful soul. I believe that you could help increase that fund of love and affection and arm it with greater intelligence and appreciation. Certainly we should repay your gift of yourself to us with loving affection and gratitude, if with little else.[23]

Barnes was charmed and returned to an idea he had explored to no avail more than two years earlier. He told Bond:

After I read your . . . letter . . . I was so overwhelmed with joy and with admiration at the ease with which you disposed of the work and worry that face me in the future that I danced the cancan. When equilibrium was restored, an idea popped up that could, under proper conditions, develop into an intelligent plan to take the place of your pipe dream. . . . Here's my counter proposal providing I can get for you, as Professor of Art at Lincoln, a former student of ours who has just finished his Ph.D. in the History of Art at Columbia. If he would accept, you select 12 to 15 of your best students to attend a class at our Gallery one whole afternoon each week, conducted by him in accordance with principles of scientific method of education with works of art as instruments. His services would cost Lincoln no money.[24]

The collector told Bond how to get in touch with Jon Longaker, and the president arranged at once to meet him in a hotel in Harlem. The interview was something of a formality. Longaker found Bond to be "a charming gentleman."[25] Bond, appreciative of Barnes's half step back from paternalism and excited about the chance of establishing a formal connection between Lincoln and the Foundation, wrote to his benefactor that he was "eager . . . to go ahead."[26] He asked if he might visit Merion to discuss the class schedule and other details, and Barnes invited him to come for lunch on Labor Day. The collector said Lincoln's acceptance of his proposal would give him a chance "to show to the world two principles," which he had first espoused twenty-four years earlier in the journal *Opportunity*. The first was that when "given the proper opportunity, the Negro demonstrates that his intellectual capacity is at least equal to that of the white man;" and the second was that "his endowment for aesthetic appreciation is even greater than that of the average white man. . . . What we wish to demonstrate," he told Bond, "can be done only if we get from you a group of students selected by you for the quality of their minds and, especially, for their interest in the courses we have to offer. If you do your part in this respect, we promise to give Mr. Longaker all the facilities necessary to accomplish the purpose [of the experiment]." He then added: "I congratulate you on your good sense in taking up the offer . . . particularly because ever since Stassen became the new president of the University of Pennsylvania, they continually ask me to do a similar thing for their art department. I refuse for various reasons, and in spite of kicking Stassen all over the map, the real big shots at the university are still trying to rope me in. To hell with them!"[27]

Bond was not unaware of the risks and problems Lincoln faced in going forward, especially if Barnes should decide that the young men who enrolled in the Foundation class did not develop according to his expectations. There was also the expense of bus transportation and the need to adjust board charges for students who would be taking fewer meals on campus. But at his meeting in Merion on the 4th of September, the president readily agreed to proceed with the cooperative arrangement, and Barnes volunteered to pick up costs related to travel. Within weeks thereafter, Bond had chosen fourteen students from among those who applied for admission to the art appreciation course and, with Barnes's permission, a Lincoln librarian. Before the somewhat reluctant pupils set foot in Merion, Bond instructed them that they must be "unvaryingly present" and not "obstreperously obstructive in questions."[28] A student chairman was chosen through whom the others were to submit any questions to Barnes. The president provided the collector with information on their backgrounds, including, for most, the occupations of their parents: elevator operator, independent fisherman, post office employee, farmer, auto mechanic, dress maker, florist's assistant, railway clerk, janitor, waiter, and owner of a trucking company. Bond intended to accompany the group to its first class, but, in the end, sent the university's dean, J. Newton Hill, who was Lincoln's William E. Dodge Professor of English and its first black faculty member.

Barnes gave a little speech of welcome. His intention was to get the students excited about what they could do "to help realize" the Lincoln president's "dream . . . [of] fit[ing] them to take the place the Negro deserves in American life."[29] He told Bond he embraced the same goal. The collector was glad Hill had come along, and on the professor's second visit, he suggested to him that he attend de Mazia's class and conduct a weekly seminar at Lincoln "to review, criticize and facilitate assimilation by all the students of the ideas put over in the class and set forth in . . . books" published by the Foundation.[30] Barnes was careful, however, to submit his plan to Bond and seek his endorsement. He recognized that what he was asking would be an added burden for a professor with a heavy teaching load, and he told the president he would like to offer Hill a salary of $100 a month for his work. As a further inducement and in anticipation of Bond's approval, he included a check in his letter for Hill's October stipend. The president replied that the extra money would be a boon to a man with two daughters in college. In words that were music as stirring as spirituals to Barnes's ears, he went on to suggest that the arrangement "would help make the . . . course in art the spear-head for reforming the entire institution along intelligent educational lines." Bond said it had not been easy to make changes in an institution "with an old encrusted tradition." The collector's proposal had "come at the . . . precise" moment it was most "needed," he continued. "I hope you won't think me an obscurantist," he concluded, "if I say that situations of this kind lead me to believe in a kind of Providence of God."[31]

And well they might. Although Bond had no way of knowing it at the time, six days after receiving the president's letter, on October 20, 1950, Barnes changed the Indenture of Trust, which would govern the management of the Foundation after his death, to give Lincoln University, rather than the University of Pennsylvania, the eventual power to nominate four of the five trustees of the Barnes Foundation. By his amendment of Section 2 of Article IX of the Foundation bylaws, moreover, the collector specifically and forever excluded any member of the board of trustees or the faculty of his alma mater, or of Temple University, Bryn Mawr, Haverford or Swarthmore colleges, or the Pennsylvania Academy of the Fine Arts, from serving on the Barnes board.[32] The amendment specified that the Foundation trustees were to control both the art gallery and the arboretum, and renewable terms were set at five years. Other changes made at the time gave Laura the lifetime title of president of the Foundation and director of the arboretum, rather than president and director of the Foundation. Nelle Mullen would become the Foundation's administrative executive or general manager and Violette de Mazia was to be the director of education of the art department of the Foundation. Both Mullen sisters, de Mazia, Albert Nulty, and two other men who worked in Merion were guaranteed life-long employment at specified salaries, notwithstanding possible future physical disability. If they were employed at the Foundation at the time of Barnes's death, Angelo Pinto and ten other male employees were also assured of specific levels of compensation and, upon their deaths, annual pensions were provided for their widows.

The collector said nothing to Bond of the extraordinary opportunity and responsibility he had given to the small, impecunious liberal arts institution of some 500 students. He followed, as usual, the progress of the new students with intense interest, and he was no more tolerant of their shortcomings than he had been of those of Penn undergraduates. He complained to Hill about the behavior of one "inveterate show off." Barnes said Longaker thought the rest of the class was "fine" and was convinced he could "get somewhere" with the Lincoln boys if he had "a fair chance."[33] In November, Bond sent the collector a copy of a proposal for an African Institute. It was a curricular innovation that he hoped would bring distinction to the university, and while Barnes cautioned him to "go slowly," he encouraged the president to share his ideas with Dewey and agreed to address a seminar on African art later in the month. "To treat the subject properly," he pointed out, "the members of the seminar should have had at least the first year of our course on general principles [of art]. . . . Such a course would be effective only if demonstrations are made with objects . . . [that are] the best examples of the various regions of Africa, and conducted by a specialist who knows his stuff." He observed that Longaker was not yet qualified to teach about the art of Africa, but looking to the future, he suggested that the course might one day, "if our experiment with Lincoln turns out well, be conducted at the Foundation." Barnes added that he had told Dewey he "thought it would be a success."[34]

In the late fall of 1950, a urinary condition, which had led the collector to consult William Wallace Dyer, a prominent physician on the faculty of the Penn medical school and a clinician at Bryn Mawr Hospital, the previous spring, caused him increasing discomfort. In early January, he was seen by several specialists. He wrote to Bond about being "out of commission" and said what bothered him most was that he "hadn't been in touch with our experiment with the Lincoln group. . . . Trial and error is inevitable," he told the president, "and my determination to get what we're after is unshakable. The goal is a Negro to be the leader. When I get in proper shape," he added, "I want you to come here and read what I have planned for Lincoln for the distant future."[35] Several weeks later, on the 26th of January, he entered Presbyterian Hospital, as a patient of its chief of medicine—the urological surgeon Francis Grillet Harrison, for the removal of his prostate. He was discharged on the 13th of February, and some weeks thereafter, Bond visited him in Merion. Seventeen years later, the president recalled that Barnes had read to him a "proposed amendment to the by-laws" of the Foundation.[36] It may be that the collector described his plans as intentions because his formal relationship with Lincoln was still so new, but there is no doubt that the change that would give the university effective control of the gallery and arboretum had been legally executed when he talked with Bond during his convalescence.

The president moved swiftly to petition Lincoln's board of trustees to approve Barnes for an honorary degree to be awarded at spring commencement ceremonies. In his letter, he cited the collector's "deep interest and affection for the Negro people."[37] Among the distinguished black members of the board was Nobel laureate Ralph J. Bunche, then director of the United Nations' Department of Trusteeship. Barnes was eager to discuss his long-range intentions for Lincoln with Bunche, and Bond tried unsuccessfully to arrange a meeting. Bunche's schedule was too tight on the mid-April evening he was coming to Philadelphia to speak at Penn, and a later trip to attend a meeting of the American Philosophical Society, during which he had hoped to visit Merion, was cancelled. Barnes was sorely disappointed. He had hoped to enlist the cooperation of the high-profile diplomat in plans that he believed would not only "do something for Lincoln," but also for "interracial relations " that had "no precedent in scope or quality."[38] The letter he personally sent to Bunche boasted somewhat of his achievements, but also reflected emotions at the deepest recesses of his being. In asking for a chance to discuss his hopes for expanding the current experiment, Barnes spoke of never recovering from the thrill of the camp meeting he had observed as a child of eight. He linked the experience to the "germ of the idea" that began to form in his mind when Bond asked him to give a course of art at Lincoln.[39] In his mind's eye, the collector saw the university at the center of something entirely new and wonderful involving art and education that would promote respect and harmony between black and white Americans. The statesman who had been honored for negotiating the settlement between Arabs and Jews that led to the 1949 armistice in Palestine promised to get in touch with him on his next trip to Philadelphia. But Barnes, ever impatient and easily offended, thought he felt the bristles of a brush and quoted the famous *New Yorker* cartoon of a little girl eating broccoli when he sent on Bunche's letter from Lake Success to Bond: "I say it is spinach—and I say to hell with it!"[40]

The president's quick response came in two letters. The first was an official notification that Lincoln's board of trustees had approved the recommendation of its committee on honorary degrees that Barnes be awarded an honorary Doctor of Fine Arts on the fifth of June and urged him to honor the university by accepting it. The second mentioned, in confidence, Bunche's serious vascular condition that Bond speculated prompted him to cram his schedule with paid speeches in hopes of building up a financial legacy for his children. The president went on to say that Lincoln alumnus Kwame Nkrumah, "recently rocketed to the top as 'Chief Minister for His Majesty's Government Business' in the Gold Coast"—and soon to be the first prime minister of independent Ghana, would give the commencement address and just three days later be the guest of honor at an official State Department luncheon.[41] Bond related how he had laid the groundwork by writing to Secretary of State Dean Acheson about Nkrumah's visit. He said he had received an invitation to the Washington affair and intended to try to wrangle more invitations. He told Barnes that he would like to nominate him to receive one as a friend of Lincoln.

The collector agreed to accept an honorary degree if Bond would make it a Doctor of Science in recognition, he said, of "my contributions to science, as recorded in German literature in the early part of the century, our program of scientific method in education in art, and the published statement of Dewey—'I know of no statement of the relation of scientific method to intelligent living—the real meaning of science—equal to that found in the early pages of the first chapter of the present volume' (Foreword to *The Art of Renoir*)." He said he would try to go to the luncheon and saw the affair as a chance "to enlighten the fancy pants in the State Department about what the Negro can do in enriching . . . life in America if he ever had the opportunity. I have verifiable evidence that is Q. E. D. [*quod erat demonstrandum*]," he added. But he also observed that his annoyance at Bunche had stemmed in part from his desire to enlist his help in promoting Bond's own plans for an African Institute. He had intended to press him "to ask one of the big organizations, Ford, Carnegie, Rockefeller, Sage, to put up the money. . . .You can't do it without that help," Barnes told Bond. "If you get it, what we can do with our plans will fit like a glove in making Lincoln unique as an educational institution that gets to the root of the problem of human progress with," he repeated, "the Negro as leader."[42]

From the collector's perspective, the key to achieving his goal of creating a viable and enduring alliance with Lincoln was finding someone to head a joint educational effort. After a quarter of a century, he was still looking for "the man" to carry on his ideals. The ever-sympathetic Dewey told him about a newly minted and promising Columbia Ph.D. then teaching at Howard, and when the young philosopher was invited to speak at Lincoln's student awards ceremony in mid-May, a still recuperating Barnes was driven to campus to hear him. "It always seems like home to me," he told Bond in describing "the placid contentment" he felt on passing through the gates of the university. The visit proved to be an intellectually stimulating and, indeed, a most "memorable experience." Although the collector was disappointed with the speaker's delivery, he was mightily impressed by the content of his talk, which extended ideas in Dewey's *Democracy and Education* on the place of thinking in experience. He took Sing-Nan Fen back to Merion to see his pictures, and the next day informed Bond: "Fen is the man you need. . . . Don't let that man get away from you. He could do two things: 1) start the process of training two of your own best students to get ready to carry out your African course; 2) be the head of Lincoln's department of both philosophy and art." Barnes said he had asked Fen, a thirty-three-year-old graduate of the Central University of Political Science in Shanghai, if he was willing to take de Mazia's course and that the young scholar had said "it would be a 'dream come true.'" He was apparently going to try to arrange to come from Washington to Merion every Tuesday, and the collector was ready to work with him and Hill "to plan the venture," as well as with the university students then enrolled in Longaker's class. "Here's your chance," he said. "Get your hooks on Fen and bring him on your campus where I can be in frequent touch with him. Nobody can guarantee the future, but you can do something worthwhile if you have the right material. . . . My hunch is Fen is the first right step."[43]

As Barnes's habit had long been to consult Dewey on all major—and often minor—matters affecting the Foundation, he made arrangements to meet with him in New York at the end of May to discuss plans for making his "resources an integral part of Lincoln's educational program." He wanted the philosopher's ideas about how Fen could "serve as a catalyst to weld Lincoln and the Foundation in an educational enterprise" without "counterpart anywhere."[44] In preparation for his visit, therefore, he requested a copy of Bond's proposal to the Ford Foundation for support of his African Institute. He thought his old friend might be willing to speak in support of it to various foundation heads.

The Lincoln president was seeking $500,000 for a program that would bring four African students studying in the United States to the Chester County university to teach their native languages to African-American students and hire permanent faculty to inaugurate courses in African studies. He said he would like Fen to be the coordinator but hesitated to make any move without talking to Dean Hill who was unavailable because of illness. "This work is enough to give anybody ulcers," he observed. "I suppose I survive because I was raised on Navy beans, buttermilk, corn bread, and gravy." With commencement approaching, Bond said he doubted any decision could be made until the middle of June, pending even then, Hill's recovery. Besides, he didn't have any illusions that "the stuffed shirts" in the world of philanthropy would give him the money. But he told Barnes that after returning from speaking engagements at two black colleges in the South, he looked forward to talking further with him about Fen at Lincoln's own graduation exercises. He reminded the collector that there would be a "harum-scarum luncheon" for trustees and honorary degree recipients after which he should be prepared to "dash madly out, don a gown, and march to the platform."[45]

Before leaving on the hurried journey that took him to Long Island to greet Nkrumah on his arrival in the United States, to Raleigh, North Carolina, and to New Orleans, the Lincoln president got off one more letter. It was to the chairman of the university's trustee Committee on Honorary Degrees, and it included suggested wording for a citation to be read as Barnes was presented with his Doctor of Science degree. In explanation of the citation's several references to Dewey and its quotation of his dedicatory paragraph in *Art As Experience*, Bond observed that "Dr. Barnes is inordinately proud of the fact that he is a student of John Dewey, and that his principles of art instruction at his Gallery are based on John Dewey's principles." He told the Lincoln trustee to use the material he had prepared as he saw fit —"just don't forget John Dewey."[46]

No one did, but Barnes did not, in the end, make it to commencement. Perhaps he did not wish to be upstaged by one of the most powerful men in Africa to whom the mayor of Philadelphia had given the keys to the city. The British Embassy had failed to send him an invitation to the luncheon for Nkrumah in Washington, and he may have been miffed at the snub. Or he may not have been feeling up to all the hoopla—graduation exercises for the largest class in Lincoln's history that filled the campus gymnasium with 1,000 people. Or he may have been annoyed with Bond. The week before the ceremony, he wrote to him that his recent letter detailing plans for the African Institute seemed to reaffirm what his proposal "crie[d] aloud—i.e., that an enterprise dedicated to the welfare of the Negro race and to general social betterment gives wishful thinking precedence over the blueprint for sound educational methods. . . . The four fellowships you mention correspond to the icing on a cake that you have not the recipe to bake," Barnes said, and added:

All this makes me sad because it forecasts things to come that make impossible what I had hoped to do for Lincoln—namely, carry on there, and to your credit, what we have done alone for so many years. Mr. Hill, as a member of the Tuesday class, saw for himself what that was.

I hold no brief for Dr. Fen, but unless a man of his background is in residence at Lincoln to coordinate philosophy and art, beginning next fall, I prefer to pass out of the picture. Our institution has thrived by scientific method. These two subjects were amalgamated and made an instrument of education. Philosophy at Lincoln is a kind of intellectual calisthenics carried out in an ivory tower with all the doors and windows hermetically sealed from contact with the world we live in. That's nuts![47]

But for all his blustery forecast, Barnes expressed concern about Hill's health and offered to send him to a gastroenterologist at Presbyterian Hospital. Lincoln awarded the collector its honorary degree in absentia, and Bond had the diploma, citation, and hood delivered to Merion. In July, he wrote to ask leave to come himself with Mrs. Bond and a visiting faculty couple who had apparently expressed particular interest in seeing the arboretum. Barnes replied at once that it was "O.K" and set the date for Tuesday, the 17th. "If you're all here at noon and look hungry," he said, "we'll decide what to do."[48] With the collector's permission, the Hills and the widow of a Lincoln professor who was the nephew of the university's founder were added to the party. With Laura at his side, Barnes received them courteously. Bond was pleased to see the framed diploma from Lincoln on the wall of the small room he used for an office. In a genial mood, the collector proposed that a Barnes alumnus, the painter Francis McCarthy, give a studio course at the rural university—and that he would pay his salary. The president said later they also discussed plans for the courses Lincoln students would take at the Foundation in the coming year. It was their last conversation. A week later, at about 3 o'clock in the afternoon, Albert Coombs Barnes was killed almost instantly when he drove his old Packard convertible through a stop sign on a rural highway near Ker-Feal and collided with a ten-ton tractor trailer.

An eyewitness told the *Inquirer* that the automobile "catapulted through the air" into a field adjacent to the intersection.[49] The collector's body landed on the macadam road near the overturned truck. The Chester County corner, who arrived on the scene a few minutes after the accident, ordered it taken to an undertaking establishment in nearby Malvern. Barnes's sole passenger, his beloved mongrel Fidèle, was severely injured in the crash, and a state trooper was forced to shoot the small dog who had been riding on the front seat of the open car beside his master. Joanna Reed, a friend and neighbor of the Barneses living a short way up Bodine Road from Ker-Feal, said the day of his death was the first time Barnes had driven his roadster to his country house since his surgery. Laura had gone out in the early morning to tend the gardens and to supervise the packaging of chickens destined for the freezer in Merion. To her surprise, her husband arrived a few hours later. He had come "to settle [his] mind," he told his wife when she asked what brought him, at mid-week, to the country.[50]

The collector had decided not to re-hire Jon Longaker for the 1951-52 academic year since he still had his dissertation to complete at Columbia. But he had recently engaged two Haverford College graduates, Paul Moses and his classmate William Wixon, to teach, respectively, a new first-year class of Lincoln students and the returning Lincoln students who had studied with Longaker. Both young men had completed Angelo Pinto's advanced class, and they were preparing for their positions by studying informally with Barnes. They had asked him some questions about a Claude painting, and he had told them he would discuss it with them that afternoon in Merion. After lunch, he sat on the porch for a while, then headed back to the Foundation to keep his appointment. Reed said the collector was well aware that the intersection of Routes 401 and 29 was a dangerous crossroads. Indeed, he had petitioned the state to put up the stop sign he ignored. Her theory was that he was distracted when a house and barn that his cook, an unschooled painter, had recently rendered in watercolor came into view. The truck driver, who had the right of way when he slammed into the roadster, escaped with bruises.

A short time after the crash, a large sedan heading east on Old Conestoga Road came upon a wrecking crew still trying to remove his heavily loaded tractor-trailer from Phoenixville Pike. Laura had left the house at Rapp's Corner with Tom Miller, her frequent chauffeur, and several other gardeners about an hour after her husband. She was unaware of his accident until she saw the wreckage of the Packard. Informed of Barnes's death, she told Tom to keep on driving. The Narberth fire chief Albert Nulty, long-time Foundation factotum and friend to both the collector and his wife, went to Malvern to identify the body, and in accord with the Barnes's wishes, Laura gave instructions to have it cremated. As Joanna Reed was making supper for her children, a state policeman called and asked her to take Fidèle's remains to Merion. She did, and speaking briefly with her distraught friend, asked if there was anything she could do for her. "There is nothing anyone can do," the new widow replied. "Albert didn't want it, so there won't even be a funeral."[51] Nulty, accompanied by his daughter Jane and the head gardener, buried Barnes's ashes in a heavily wooded part of the arboretum. Fidèle was laid to rest beside his master. The Narberth Fire Company put up black crepe and flew its flag at half-staff. Laura gave her husband's watch to the chief, and it was passed on to his son, Albert Barnes Nulty, and eventually his grandson, who is named after his father.

The fatal accident was front-page news not only in Philadelphia but also in New York and elsewhere in the nation. The *Inquirer* ran a gruesome photograph of the collector's body being carried from the scene of the wreck. The paper's editorial, entitled "Dr. Barnes' Two Secrets," speculated as to whether the formula for Argyrol would ever be revealed and "whether the public, at long last, would be admitted to his famous tax-free institution."[52] A columnist for the *Evening Bulletin*, who had exchanged a series of letters with Barnes in salty Parisian French, acknowledged that the world was "poorer by the disappearance of any flamboyant individualist in this regimented age."[53] Others who had been seared by his scorn were not as generous. Carroll Tyson told Fiske Kimball that after reviewers ridiculed the pictures he lent the Pennsylvania Academy of the Fine Arts in 1923, the collector "just got soured on the . . . world in general and . . . never got over it. I am in hopes that the town of Merion will put a highway directly through [the] Barnes place," he joked, "and his pictures will have to find a custodian, some place, for instance, like the Philadelphia Museum of Art. Why not?"[54]

The eventual fate of the collection was the focus of gossip and the subject of conjecture in executive suites and boardrooms all over town. "No one really knows who are the Trustees," Penn's vice president William H. DuBarry wrote to a colleague. "Upon [Barnes's] death, a general Trust was to succeed him. . . . As later vacancies occurred, [there were to be] alternating representatives from the University of Pennsylvania and the Pennsylvania Academy of the Fine Arts until five were appointed. He told me he had eliminated the Academy. He told me he appointed me. So there you are. Jack Fogg could get the low down from Mrs. Barnes who is devoted to him."[55] But after Fogg talked with Laura in early September, he could only report that the situation with respect to Penn remained "pretty obscure. Dr. Barnes left his widow as president of the Foundation and executrix of his estate, and I gather that it is her intention, at least for the immediate future, to continue all the educational activities at the gallery which were in operation at the time of Dr. Barnes's death," he wrote to a university trustee. "This means that the courses will continue to be given five days a week and that the gallery will not be open to the public. It is apparently, therefore, too soon to say whether the terms of Dr. Barnes's will carry out any of his earlier announced intentions with respect to the University of Pennsylvania or whether he altered these terms, as he was quite capable of doing."[56]

Horace Mann Bond was one of the few people who had reason to believe that the collector had changed the Foundation's bylaws to give Lincoln the power to nominate its trustees after the death of Mrs. Barnes. But though he remained as president until 1957, no one ever told him that the amendment Barnes had shown him one spring afternoon in Merion had been officially adopted by the trustees of the Foundation. He wasn't sure until seventeen years after the collector's death.[57] He was certain that he and his black brothers and sisters had lost a friend and champion. In a statement to the Lincoln community, he said Albert Barnes had "wanted Negroes to be proud of their own abilities, as he was sensible of their great worth. He wanted Negroes to be proud of their great contributions to the world in the plastic arts—in music — in dancing."[58] At the time of Barnes's death, only Egypt and Ethiopia in all of Africa were independent. He had put together a magnificent collection of African art because he found the sculpture beautiful—and he wanted black Americans to know that they were descended from a great people.

Bond told Henry Hart that Barnes was "perhaps the most interesting human being" he had ever known.[59] He wanted to make a gift, an offering of some sort to the Foundation, and finally he found an appropriate token that he sent on to Nelle Mullen on the six-months anniversary of the collector's fatal collision. It was a book published in 1838 entitled *A Plan for Africans*. The frontispiece was an engraving made by the Philadelphia artist John Sartain of his painting of Elliott Cresson, a Quaker supporter of colonization whose bequest to his sister helped support Lincoln in its early years. Incorporated in the portrait were two African spears, a sword, a powder horn, and an ebony statue. Bond thought they must be among the earliest representations of African art objects in a work of European or American art. He was pleased that the first white philanthropist associated with his university had appreciated them. He knew the fine print would have been treasured by the millionaire that had made Lincoln his last alliance.

15

Postmortem

Laura Barnes never expected the hundreds of sympathy notes that were delivered to Latch's Lane after her husband's death. "I thought I'd barely get ten," she told one of the three friends who helped her address the elegant white envelopes in which she sent out formal acknowledgments.[1] She had come to know Jo Bachman, then in her late thirties, when the Main Line mother of two took horticultural classes in Merion. Bachman had learned of Albert Barnes's accident on returning from a family vacation. In the accumulated mail was a note from her friend and teacher, which had been mailed the day before the fatal car crash. Laura was a guest at her former student's garden party the previous weekend, and she wrote to say how much she had enjoyed it, despite a sudden, soaking thunderstorm, and to compliment Jo on the good use she had made of limited lawn space by the skillful planting shrubs and flowers. The younger woman was one of a number of arboretum alumnae who were devoted to the seventy-seven-year-old widow. They wondered how she would handle the sudden change in her life.

Barnes's will, drawn up seven years before his death and witnessed by Nelle Mullen, noted that he had already given almost all of his property to the Foundation. The final disposition added Ker-Feal and its furnishings along with the small house on Lapsley Lane that housed the horticultural school. The rest of his estate was left in trust to Laura. It totaled just over two million dollars. Most of the money was in municipal bonds, and after his widow's death, Barnes directed that the residuary estate also go to the Foundation. It turned out that the collector had not paid a county personal property tax since 1947, so Laura had to write a check for $70,536.62 to cover the principal and penalties. She gave a rare, seventeenth-century Ruggieri violin he had owned to the Philadelphia Orchestra. As president of the Foundation now, she was guaranteed a lifetime salary of not less than $30,000 a year. The board of trustees, which she chaired, included the Mullen sisters, like her trustees from the start, and de Mazia who had served since Joseph Lapsley Wilson's death sixteen years earlier. The bylaws dictated the four-member board's first official act. There must be five trustees, and Albert Nulty was duly elected thus preserving the governing body's familial character. As secretary of the board, Nelle Mullen became its spokesperson, and she responded to press inquiries about a possible change in the gallery's virtually closed-door policy with the announcement that there were no plans to admit visitors in the near future without special permission. She pointed out that the deed of trust gave the trustees the authority to decide when to admit the public.

Penn's David Robb, the art historian rejected by Barnes for any role in the future of the Foundation, speculated in a letter to Fiske Kimball whether "a taxpayer's suit could be brought" to settle "once and for all" if the gallery could be forced open. "I should certainly be willing to take part in such a move if it could be arranged," he told the museum director.[2] But Kimball, recalling how Barnes had routed the city of Philadelphia in its earlier suit to collect real estate and school taxes, thought it unlikely that "any new suit would get anywhere."[3] An editorial published in a Main Line weekly at the time of the collector's death commented upon Barnes's "psychological independence," which the newspaper defined as "freedom from the nagging need to be cuddled and cheered."[4] His wife shared some measure of it. She was aware of the desire of art professionals and others to have easy access to the collection, but she needed time to contemplate her new situation and weigh the costs and benefits of departing from past procedures. She was responsible for thirty-five employees, an annual operating budget of $150,000, real estate valued at more than $600,000, a $6 million endowment, and the priceless pictures. Months before his death, Barnes had purchased several paintings by Paul Klee and, in a complicated deal with Knoedler, exchanged two oils by Degas for Titian's *Endymion* and traded two Cézannes for two Chardins, *The Laundress* and *The Fountain*. But now the collection was closed—nothing could be added, nothing sold. Laura's obligation was to maintain it for her late husband's intended educational purposes. Between the arboretum and art schools, about two hundred students were enrolled in Foundation classes. The Indenture left her in direct charge of the former and de Mazia of the latter. So be it. They need have little to do with one another; the schools would continue as almost wholly separate entities. Paul Moses and William Wixom, the last teachers hired by Barnes, would study with de Mazia and teach their small first- and second-year classes of Lincoln students. De Mazia would teach the large, introductory first-year class and leave to Angelo Pinto the regular second-year class in Traditions of Painting. The arboretum lectures would be delivered, as they had been for some years, by four Penn faculty members, and friends remember that Laura looked forward to giving her own class in horticulture. After two months of meeting with lawyers and bankers, it would be a relief—and a symbol of life going on in ways that were for her entirely pleasant.

A familiar and comforting rhythm of activity was quickly reestablished in Merion. The fall semester went well, and the spring semester of 1952 was off to a promising start when Jo Bachman took Laura the angel food cake she had baked for her friend's seventy-eighth birthday on the 13th of February. Three days later, Mrs. Barnes, along with de Mazia, the Mullen sisters, and Nulty, were named as defendants in a suit brought against the Foundation by the *Philadelphia Inquirer*. It was filed in the name of Harold J. Wiegand, an editorial writer for the newspaper who lived around the corner from the Latch's Lane property, and asked the court to enjoin the trustees from enforcing rules that deprived the public of "reasonable access" to the galleries.[5] The publisher of the *Inquirer*, Walter Annenberg, had not yet begun to collect his own pictures. His aesthetic focus for the moment was on unlocking the wrought iron gates of the Foundation, and he used the power of the press to try to accomplish his goal. Wiegand's suit was announced with a large three-line head running across four columns in the upper-right quadrant of the *Inquirer*'s front-page. An accompanying story reported that the attorney general of Pennsylvania had praised the newspaper for rendering "a great service" and quoted his opinion that there was "no reason why the Barnes Foundation should be allowed to function as a private club."[6]

In its petition to the Court of Common Pleas of Montgomery County and in its columns, the *Inquirer* implied that the trustees practiced racial and religious discrimination in the selection of students and the granting of cards of admission to the gallery. It asserted, moreover, that the Foundation's educational program lacked standing in the eyes of schools and colleges offering modern art courses, and cited as proof of the program's poor educational quality, a failure to produce even one outstanding figure in the world of art. Not surprisingly, a second-day, page-one article told of "a wave of public congratulations" for the newspaper's efforts.[7] It quoted, and pictured in four separate headshots, art experts from the Philadelphia Museum of Art and Temple University who joined in the applause. But there was no public comment from anyone connected with Penn or the Pennsylvania Academy of the Fine Arts, institutions that still harbored hopes of one day having the authority to appoint the trustees of the Foundation. The *Evening Bulletin* initially ignored the story of the suit, and the feisty *Main Line Times* called the *Inquirer*'s initiative a "publicity stunt."[8]

A stinging retort to the paper's charges was released by Horace Mann Bond, though the *Inquirer* declined to publish it. Quoting Samuel Parr on the death of Samuel Johnson, he declared, "'Now that the old lion is dead, every ass thinks he may kick at him.'" Bond pointed his finger at "the degenerate sons" of Tories who continued to nourish "malicious spite." Taking aim directly at Walter Annenberg, he wrote that no one should be surprised that "the nouveau riche sycophants who attach themselves to . . . scions of decadent culture—in the hope of God knows what—should likewise join in their accustomed jackal's revenge; and while assuming the pose of defending the public interest, and the affected stance of liberality . . . seize with ghoulish enthusiasm their chance to kick the memory of the Old Lion." The Lincoln president defended Barnes as "a friend of all the dispossessed of the world" and characterized the postmortem criticism of him by members of the art establishment as "psychopathic resentment against a man who had their own wealth, and every prerequisite of their level of society . . . but . . . gave open defiance to their caste system of pride and prejudice and pettiness." The attorney general was "a super-snide Jackass" whose office had been notably absent from the civil rights crusades of Nathan Mossell, which the collector had supported with money and words of encouragement. Barnes, Bond said, was "more honest, more intelligent, and more courageous" than all the asses who joined together to violate his memory."[9]

The publisher of the *Inquirer* had, however, the blessings and, indeed, behind-the-scenes aid from an influential ally. *ARTNews* helped gather "evidence" for the case and when it reached the court declared at the start of a long, self-congratulatory editorial, "It's about time." The editors wrote that they "had been waiting patiently for almost half a year . . . for the trustees of the Foundation . . . to adjust it to the accepted practices of educational institutions enjoying immunity from taxes and therefore accountable to the public from which this privilege stems." They labeled the argument that the Foundation was an educational institution utilizing its collection for teaching purposes that would be interrupted by visitors as simply more of "the same old nonsense." The heart of the matter, from the magazine's perspective, was that "the most important collection in the world of French nineteenth- and twentieth-century paintings" had been assembled not only with a "flair for quality . . . but also with tax-free money." Letters were solicited from readers who could document incidences of the Foundation's refusal to cooperate on legitimate scholarly or artistic projects in the interest of "running . . . to cover" the "trick" played on the Internal Revenue Service and, more egregiously, the public by "Barnes and his successors."[10]

The director of the Art Institute of Chicago responded that he was refused entrance when working on a book on Henri Rousseau and that his institution and the Metropolitan Museum of Art were not only denied loans but turned away when they sought to study the Cézannes in Merion. The director of the Brooklyn Museum of Art wrote that only "clearly stated and reasonable restrictions governing the proper use for which art is intended and its safekeeping" could be allowed to modify "the principle of free availability of art to those who seek it." The chairman of the fine arts department at New York University noted that "the exile of the masterpieces in the Barnes Foundation" was "only a shade less complete than that of the Cézannes and Matisses in the Moscow Museum of Western Arts, closed many years ago 'for repairs' and never reopened." Writer and critic John Rewald recalled that when the Museum of Modern Art was about to publish his *History of Impressionism*, Barnes "let it be known that he would confiscate the entire edition if a single one of his pictures were reproduced."[11] MOMA's Alfred H. Barr, Jr. said he received a similar retort when he sought permission to reproduce photographs of a dozen Matisse paintings in his book on the artist.

Amid the general hue and cry a number of people tried to point out that the situation was not "quite so clear-cut, so villain-black and hero-white."[12] The logic of the tax argument was dubious since Barnes paid income taxes while accumulating the fortune he used to buy his pictures. No income taxes were due, moreover, on interest earned on municipal bonds and United States Treasury bills. The Foundation's exemption from property taxes as an educational institution had been upheld by the state's highest tribunal in 1934, and on the basis of that decision, it received a $31,000 tax exemption on the Haywood Road property when its administrative offices were moved there from the city in 1941. While previous legal actions had not tested whether the Foundation lived up to its charter and to the standards required by other educational institutions enjoying the status of a public charity, the voices of former students were quickly raised to attest to the incalculable value of their experience in Merion. One of the most outraged of the alumni, a group that *ARTNews* had described as "oddities who happened to escape the censure" of the terrible-tempered collector, wrote: "Your sensational S.O.S. for assistance in your effort to mobilize your readers into a state of revengeful hysteria and vicious hatred against Dr. Barnes and his Foundation is the most shocking thing I have ever known the editor of a respected periodical to do."[13]

Others recalled that they had been poor and the collector generous, providing stipends along with free classes. Abraham L. Chanin had known Barnes at his best and his worst. As a student in the mid-1930s, he was one of several sent off to roam the galleries of Europe one summer with all their expenses paid. Just after revealing the treat he had in store for the young men, their benefactor announced that they would sail on the North German line. Stunned, the American Jew saw a dream evaporate before his eyes. "He would not, could not," as he later wrote: "go under the Swastika." But he didn't have to. "Look at your tickets," Barnes told him. The ship was chartered by the Holland American Company. The price of the journey was acceptable. The collector had been indulging in a little "taunting testing joke."[14] Some seventeen years later, Chanin spoke out forcefully in defense of Barnes's theory and practice of art education. At the same time, he spoke for vast numbers of people of good will when he wrote: "No one can seriously dispute any more that the best art is ultimately the spiritual and material property of society in general, that too many masterpieces enrich only the lives of a small and charmed circle." He said it was "morally indefensible to exclude the people always. For, plainly and simply, the collection is so magnificent that no really adequate idea of Cézanne, Renoir, Matisse, Soutine, Modigliani or Picasso can be formed without seeing it. Many who cannot join classes are entitled to see the splendor."[15]

Chanin suggested that a compromise should be worked out to open the Barnes gallery in the two summer months when classes were not in session.

Indeed, it seems that several influential Philadelphians had been "working for a friendly deal with the Barnes Foundation" and now felt "very much embarrassed" by the turn to the courts just when they felt "they were getting somewhere."[16] Lawyers for Laura Barnes and the other trustees asked that the suit be dismissed because the Court of Common Pleas was being asked, in effect, to change the charter of the Foundation, which it had no power to do. Their client enjoyed no special tax privileges, they said, and, furthermore, Wiegand was not a proper plaintiff in matters concerning the Foundation's corporate affairs. Quoting its bylaws, which specify the days and hours when students and the public may be admitted to the Merion galleries, the lawyers underlined the qualifying clause "only upon cards of admission" issued by order of the trustees. The way the Foundation is run is "legally within the discretion of the board," they asserted, and "any question of the wisdom or propriety of" the collector's wishes is "irrelevant, immaterial and not subject to the supervision of the court."[17] They further asserted that the allegation that leading colleges gave no credit for Foundation courses, as well as the fact that other art institutions have different rules of admission, were irrelevant to the basic question of whether the court could supervise the management of the Foundation. In a telling forecast of concerns expressed by the Foundation's neighbors forty years later, the Merion Civic Association expressed alarm at the possibility of busses and automobiles clogging local streets if the *Inquirer* proved successful in its legal action to open the Barnes gates.

Oral arguments on the Foundation's motion to dismiss the suit were heard in May. The following month Laura embarked on a small experiment. One day, fifty carefully screened visitors were admitted to the gallery. Alas, a small, rare Chinese vase mysteriously disappeared, and the experiment was not continued when the Foundation reopened after the summer holiday. Barnes's widow responded affirmatively, however, to a State Department request to bring a group of visiting journalists from NATO countries, which prompted syndicated columnist Dorothy McCardle to write that "foreigners are one up on us Americans when it comes to seeing some of the most famous treasures of art in the world."[18] Unmoved by the journalistic drumbeat, the Montgomery County Court of Common Pleas dismissed Wiegand's bill of equity in December. The opinion written and delivered by President Judge Harold G. Knight held that the Foundation's charter and bylaws "seem to make it clear that the primary aim of the Foundation, particularly during the lifetime of Dr. Barnes and his wife, is educational, and any public use of the galleries is purely secondary." He added that "neither the plaintiff nor this court may set themselves up as the judges of the proper method of conducting a course in the fine arts." In answer to an argument made by Weigand's counsel that the manner in which the Foundation conducted its affairs defeated its purposes, the opinion said, "there is no evidence that the experiment has failed. Dr. Barnes, the donor, may have been eccentric, and judged by some standards his educational experiment may have been ill-conceived, but history is replete with instances where experiments in the arts and sciences have been condemned as ill-conceived, and yet have proven in the passage of time, to be of great advantage to mankind."[19] An appeal of the lower court's decision, joined by the state attorney general, was heard by the Pennsylvania Supreme Court in April of 1953. Chief Justice Horace Stern disqualified himself on the basis of his lifelong friendship with the collector. In a four-to-two decision handed down in June, the high court upheld the Court of Common Pleas' dismissal of the taxpayer's suit to force the Barnes trustees to open its collection to the public. The majority found that the attorney general's written consent to Weigand's bill of equity was insufficient to provide legal status for suing the Foundation. Only the state government had standing to question its conduct, and the attorney general had no right to delegate control of the case.

Although Justice Michael A. Musmanno, in a separate dissenting opinion, wrote that the public had "a direct interest in this institution and that interest cannot be ignored by the board of trustees," members of the Barnes board were hugely relieved to be left alone by the courts to get on with their work.[20] Laura concentrated on making the arboretum as important in its field as the gallery was in art. But while the Foundation teachers never sought to turn their pupils into painters, her goal for those enrolled in her school was to make gardeners of them all. The three-year course in horticulture and botany attracted a steady stream of serious students—mostly women but occasionally men, notably almost all the nursery owners in the area. The faculty, plant scientists of national standing, were excellent teachers, and the 2,200 rare trees and shrubs provided a unique textbook. Classes met on Mondays and Tuesdays and were limited to thirty-five students. Laura, who sat in the back row of every one for years, made all admissions decisions. Applicants were required to have two recommendations from either currently enrolled students or alumni. The hard-and-fast rules were no tardiness and only two absences a semester. There were no written examinations, but the petite mistress of the lovely grounds would frequently quiz individual class members as they spilled outdoors after lectures in the Lapsley Road schoolhouse to continue their studies among the woody specimens. She was famously insistent upon correct botanical nomenclature. Students would always find rooted cuttings, labeled with their Latin names and wrapped in newspapers, just outside the door, and to this day, many lovely lawns in the Delaware Valley are graced by umbrella magnolia, prickly ash, and grand tulip poplars that grew from them.

The years after her husband's death were in some ways a very joyous time in Laura's life. She was not lonely. Her friendship deepened with a number of women and men who had completed the regular horticultural course and accepted, along with others, her invitation to return for alumni seminars, which were offered once a month at the arboretum. "Laura was like a butterfly emerging from her chrysalis," Jo Bachman said. "She told us that after the fuss about the pictures at the Pennsylvania Academy, she and Dr. Barnes rarely went out. While he was alive, people didn't ask her to parties because they were afraid he wouldn't come and wouldn't let her come without him or if he came with her that he would be disagreeable."[21] She never was. Laura happily accepted the dinner invitations that were now extended by young friends. Soon her former students were taking her with them to try new restaurants and see Broadway shows. She kept up with a few old friends like former Ambassador William C. Bullitt, whom she would visit in Washington, and she periodically had lunch with her spinster sister Edith in New York. Tom Miller would drive her and one friend or another to visit gardens in New England and on the eastern shore of Maryland. One summer she accompanied John Fogg and his wife on a group trip to Europe to visit the International Flower Show in Vienna and arboreta in Germany, Holland, and Belgium. With them she didn't feel at all like a third wheel.

At home, Laura lived rather simply, although she employed a cook and a maid. Her indulgences were one piece of Belgian chocolate in the afternoon and a single Scotch before dinner. Visitors who sometimes came for tea noticed that there were no photographs of her late husband anywhere. Every Friday she would be driven into Philadelphia to do her food shopping at the Reading Terminal Market then deposited at the Barclay Hotel on Rittenhouse Square or nearby Helen Segal Wilson's for lunch while the chauffeur took her purchases back to Merion. She always invited a friend to join her, and the ladies, in hats and gloves, would walk to the Academy of Music for the afternoon symphony. The seats she held for years were just behind the music critic for the *Evening Bulletin*. She never missed a concert and told her companions the music helped her forget her troubles. String players for the Philadelphia Orchestra often performed at the parties she delighted in giving for a number of years after Barnes's death. Typically, thirty or forty people would be invited for a catered dinner, and in the summer she sometimes entertained on the terrace at Ker-Feal. Former students always looked forward to the Thursday between Christmas and New Year's when she would greet them and their spouses just inside the gallery then leave them to spend the afternoon looking at the pictures before coming to the house, adorned in boxwood and holly, for a reception. In 1954 they reciprocated by throwing a sparkling evening party at The Barclay in honor of her eightieth birthday. The next year she was named an honorary member of the American Society of Landscape Architects, and in 1957, St. Joseph's University awarded her an honorary doctor of horticultural science degree. The gestures of affection and acknowledgments of her accomplishments pleased Laura greatly. The years seemed genuinely golden.

In April of 1958, however, the campaign to open the doors of the Barnes Foundation to the general public was taken up by the attorney general of Pennsylvania. From the perspective of its president and trustees, the nightmare was starting all over again. But at least there was some new energy on the board. Laura chose her friend Joseph W. Langran, a landscape architect teaching at the Arboretum School, as the successor of Albert Nulty, who had died in January of 1957. Sidney W. Frick, a patent attorney who had grown up on Latch's Lane and whose father, Benjamin, also a lawyer, represented the Foundation, replaced Mary Mullen, who had died the previous December. With the support of both men, as well as of de Mazia and Nelle Mullen, Laura was determined to resist the state's efforts. While the Foundation could easily pay township property taxes, the board believed it provided educational value in return for its exemption. The first round in the renewed fight went to Attorney General Thomas McBride and his deputy, Lois G. Forer, who was responsible for the supervision and regulation of charities. They had filed their suit as *parens patriae*, on behalf of the people of Pennsylvania. In response to their petition in Montgomery County Orphans' Court, President Judge Alfred I. Taxis issued a citation requiring the Foundation to show cause why it should not be compelled to maintain an art gallery as stipulated by the terms of Barnes's 1922 gift of his collection to the Foundation. When the *Inquirer* had tried to force the board to admit the public six years earlier, the ruling of the State Supreme Court was that Harold Wiegand had no standing as a litigant and had failed, in any case, to show that the trustees were acting improperly. Now there would be no question of the legal status of the plaintiff, and the issue in question was the collector's intention as expressed in the Foundation charter.

In its answer to the citation, the Barnes board objected that the state's petition did not specify in what manner or to what extent the trustees had failed to maintain an art gallery and by what improper acts any member of the public had been denied access to it. There was no cause for judicial interference in the internal management of Foundation, the board's trial attorney Victor J. Roberts said. But the Orphans' Court judge ruled that the trustees must produce lists of all who had been admitted to the gallery and all who had sought admission and been denied since its founder's death, as well as a breakdown of its annual income. They complied, and in May of 1959, he handed down a decision, which echoed, in effect, the earlier decision of the Montgomery County Court of Common Pleas. The Foundation was an educational institution, Judge Taxis ruled, and as such did not have to give the public access, reasonable or otherwise, to its collection. In entering the state's appeal, Deputy Attorney General Forer argued that if the Foundation did not admit members of the public to the gallery, it should not be entitled to a tax exemption. Laura's lawyer pointed out that under the terms of the Indenture of Trust, the public would be admitted on Saturdays after her death. But the rather narrow issue before the Pennsylvania Supreme Court was whether the attorney general's petition contained enough information to warrant a hearing.

Its unanimous decision, written by Justice Musmanno and rendered in March of 1960, reversed Judge Taxis and agreed that the state had the right to inquire how a tax-exempt gallery could bar the public under any circumstances and still retain its privileged status. "If the Barnes . . . is to be open to a selected, restricted few, it is not a public institution, and if it is not a public institution, the Foundation is not entitled to a tax exemption as a public charity," Justice Musmanno said.[22] The high court sent the case back to the trial judge, and nine months later, Judge Taxis issued a sweeping series of directives. The Foundation must produce detailed financial statements, a list of employees and a description of their duties, a list of art works and their appraised value, a floor plan of the gallery, a weekly schedule of art appreciation classes, and the names and addresses of pupils. Judge Taxis also ruled that the board must permit inspection of its art holdings by a committee of three experts—Henri Marceau, Kimball's successor as director of the Philadelphia Museum of Art, Joseph Fraser, Jr., director of the Pennsylvania Academy of the Fine Arts, and Gordon Washburn, director of fine arts at the Carnegie Institute in Pittsburgh—who were to give opinions about how many visitors could be accommodated at any one time if the gallery were open to the public. He directed Forer to produce a list of the names and addresses of persons who claimed they were refused entry to the gallery and the dates of refusal. Following the exchange of data in Benjamin Frick's office, the experts made their inspection and, emerging from the gallery after the allotted three hours, responded to the questions of waiting reporters in a string of non-technical superlatives in praise of the collection: "magnificent . . . remarkable . . . and overwhelming."[23]

The time had come for compromise. Even though the trustees quietly instituted a program of issuing cards of admission to 100 visitors a week (fifty a day in two groups of twenty-five each for two, two-hour periods on Tuesdays and Fridays), their lawyers recognized the futility of continuing to resist public pressure, whatever they might think of the Commonwealth's legal arguments. Joined by Barnes's old friend, retired Justice Horace Stern, Frick and Roberts met with the new state attorney general, Anne X. Alpern, and with Forer. It was a Saturday, December 10, 1960, and they negotiated far into the evening before reaching an out-of-court settlement. Judge Taxis, who was to begin hearing the case for the second time the following Monday, approved the hard-won agreement that allowed a maximum of 200 members of the public to view the Barnes collection on a first-come, first-served basis on each of two days a week. Art students and teachers of art were to be admitted by special arrangement. A telephone for handling inquiries was to be installed for the first time. Half of the visitors on each visiting day were to arrange their visits in advance, while the others simply stood in line. It was stipulated that after the death of Laura Barnes, the gallery would be open an additional afternoon.

Judge Taxis set March 18, 1961 as the firm date for admitting the general public to the Foundation, although the trustees cited problems encountered in installing a fire escape as necessitating a temporary limit of three visitors to the second floor of the gallery at any one time. The *Inquirer* published a floor plan and list of some of the major works in the collection as a guide to the members of the public crossing the threshold of the Foundation. The board hired Pinkerton guards. But as the *Evening Bulletin* described the scene when the gates were swung open, "the public responded in a turnout that was by no means an overwhelming rush."[24] Although it took from 9:30 A.M. until noon that first chilly Saturday to fill the quota of 100 unreserved visitors, Laura surveyed the crowd and was annoyed by the numbers. Nevertheless, she politely answered questions about the pictures. The attorney general, who had arrived in the company of state police, stood near her and responded to comments. The connoisseurs and the curious, who had been required to check coats and handbags in a makeshift cloak room, were at once orderly and enthusiastic. Without labels on the walls much less a catalogue, some became confused; many others experienced the incomparable thrill of discovery among the profusion of masterpieces. No cameras were allowed, but visitors were permitted to bring pencils and notebooks for sketching. Outside "Friends of the Barnes Foundation," a group about fifteen of de Mazia's current and former students, walked about with signs protesting the opening of the gallery and gave out a four-page statement that began: "Destroying Our Educational Facilities Is Not Building Our Culture." Their teacher, on that day only, was not in sight. But among those who passed through the pickets to take in the collection were art critics who had never seen it before. Writing for the *Inquirer*, Dennis Leon said "the initial meeting with this amazing display is at once an uplifting and a humbling moment. . . . One cannot help but stand awed before these paintings and sculptures, the grandeur of their installation and the moving spirit that recognized their genius and assembled them"[25] John Canaday of the *New York Times* declared that "without question, the pictures . . . live up to their legend."[26] Almost alone in her dissent, Emily Genauer of the *New York Herald Tribune* found them "overvalued" and "over-praised."[27] Years earlier, Barnes had slammed the Foundation's great door in her face as punishment for trying to combine a visit to the gallery with a more mundane mission in Philadelphia, and she wasn't about to forget it.

As humiliating for several of the Barnes trustees as Genauer's rough treatment at the hands of the collector was Lois Forer's success in hauling them into the courtroom they had avoided throughout the litigation process leading up to the dramatic change in the Foundation's admissions policy. It happened because in June of 1961, the board voted to impose a $2 entrance charge to help offset the cost of hiring additional guards. The attorney general considered the fee a means of discouraging visitors. Alpern and her deputy obtained a temporary restraining order, and then sued to enforce the consent decree, which they claimed had been violated by de Mazia when she solicited art students not only to picket but also take up "public" places in the weekly quota of visitors. Victor Roberts wrote to Judge Taxis to explain how the modest admissions charge added a minimum of $45,548 or 18.1 percent to the

Foundation's annual budget, but he could not avoid a hearing on the Commonwealth's petition for a permanent injunction. It began in early April of 1962 and dragged on for a year—past Laura's eighty-ninth birthday.

Forer believed she was fighting a good fight in calling the board to account for its stewardship. The deputy attorney general charged that the trustees were "expending funds to the detriment of the Foundation and then trying to charge the public admission."[28] One by one she called on them. Nelle Mullen was challenged on the size of the telephone bill and asked why, if funds were tight, the board didn't consider selling Ker-Feal, the farm in Chester County. Forer elicited the acknowledgment that it was used only three times a year by Arboretum School students, as well as the further admission that the salaries of maintenance workers had been raised above the level set in the Trust Indenture, with permission of the trustees but without permission of the court, when they threatened to quit for higher-paying jobs. She pointed out that Mullen had no special training in business, finance, or the management of an art gallery. Frick was asked if the board had ever thought about reducing the $30,000 a year salary Laura was paid as president. Langran, the next to take the stand, said in response to Forer's prompting that it would be desirable to hire an experienced art director "if we could afford it," whereupon the deputy attorney general read aloud a portion of the Indenture directing the employment of such a person.[29]

The fourth witness was the focal figure in the state's drive to prove mismanagement since, for more than a decade, letters refusing admission to the gallery to scholars seeking access had borne her signature. In her cross examination of the director of art education, Forer established that contrary to her initial claim, de Mazia had not attended the Polytechnic in London, one of the several schools that she initially listed as an alma mater. Forer also drew forth the information that no art students or instructors had visited the gallery on any day other than Friday or Saturday, when it was open to the public, in spite of a requirement in the consent degree that they should be admitted under special arrangements. In the course of de Mazia's reluctant testimony, it also became clear that every morning before classes, she had paintings moved about to catch the right light or for other reasons related to her plan of instruction. Forer was shocked by the revelation, and later incorporated it in an amended petition that claimed the trustees abused their discretion by a practice that endangered the collection. Only Laura Barnes, who testified voluntarily, seemed to gain the deputy attorney general's respect. She said she welcomed visitors to the arboretum and sent specimens to botanists all over the world. Forer stressed that the state had never received complaints that the arboretum denied information or admission to scholars.

The deputy attorney general called on a stable of experts, however, to try to establish that the Foundation had gone overboard in hiring guards and supervising visitors. She also orchestrated a surprise, which proved a momentary sensation but had little relevance to the questions before the court. Penn art historian Frederick J. Hartt caused a visible stir among spectators when he testified that the collection contained a number of "misattributed paintings or forgeries." Roberts objected that "even if every one" of the pictures were fake, "there would be nothing the Barnes Foundation could do about it" since the terms of the Indenture called for the collection to remain intact.[30] Judge Taxis agreed, but the next day's headlines were already being written. Buried in a paragraph on page 12, the *Inquirer* also noted that Roberts elicited from Hartt the fact that the University of Pennsylvania allowed six transfer credits to students who completed the Foundation's introductory and advanced courses. The *Evening Bulletin* quoted a former Foundation student to the effect that Barnes most likely bought the questionable paintings "fully aware that their authenticity was in doubt, but that he acquired them anyway as examples of the art of a particular period."[31] Several days later Hartt issued a statement saying there were at least six forgeries—four pictures that are supposed to be from 14th- and 15th-century Italy and two French works allegedly from the same period, which, in his opinion, were created after 1900. In May, after examining the collection in the company of Sydney J. Freedberg, chairman of the art department at Harvard, he said there were twenty-six fabrications and perhaps others that might be imitations. The scholars provided a list, which included works said to be by Domenico Veneziano, Giorgione, Pintoricchio, El Greco, Bosch, Paolo Veronese, Fouquet, Rubens, Titian, Tintoretto, Claude Gelée, Chardin, and Longhi. "These dogs are a blot on the collection," Hartt told the press. If the Foundation were "under competent direction," he added, they would have been removed long ago.[32]

In an amended petition submitted to Orphans' Court in June, Forer sought the removal of all the trustees except Laura Barnes on the grounds of mismanagement and abuse of discretion.[33] The petition asked that the court order the Foundation to hire a "qualified" art director and that the Girard Trust Corn Exchange Bank be appointed treasurer "in accordance with the Indenture."[34] It demanded that reasonable regulations be established for admission of art students, instructors, and scholars at times when the art gallery was not open to the general public, and it reiterated Forer's request that the trustees be permanently enjoined from imposing any charge of admission. In response, the Foundation declared the state's motion "highly irregular, impertinent, and uncalled for by any of the circumstances of the case."[35] Victor Roberts reiterated the board's position that a nonprofit corporation had the right to charge admission as it deemed necessary. He said any one of the existing staff could fulfill the duties of an art director. After hearing oral arguments, Judge Taxis ruled that the ouster motion would have to be argued separately as an equity action in the Court of Common Pleas, but Forer did not pursue the option. Everyone may have been growing weary. In March of 1963, another cease-fired was called in the ongoing legal battle. In a forty-six page opinion, Judge

Taxis authorized a $1 admission fee, directed the Foundation to manage its money more efficiently by reducing the number of guards and changing its investment policy, and told the board to admit art students and art instructors in addition to the 200 members of the public given access to the gallery under the 1960 decree. The state decided to wait and see what would happen.

Laura told friends she was getting on with her life because she didn't have time to wait on much of anything. Although increasingly frail, she continued to teach through the end of the 1964 spring semester. Former students contributed funds to establish an annual lectureship in her honor at Penn's Morris Arboretum, where John Fogg was still the director. She invited them all to a grand party on Latch's Lane, which she called her "Swan Song." The music that evening was provided by the concertmaster of the Philadelphia Orchestra, who played the Ruggieri violin that had belonged to the collector. A stroke in her ninetieth year confined her to the Merion house and gardens during most of the last two years of her life. Inside she could gaze with satisfaction at the treasured objects she had collected over the past half century—Tiffany glass, miniature bronze animals and birds, Chinese snuff boxes, and "frog mugs," the drinking cups adorned with ceramic amphibians that bartenders once dispensed to patrons to signal that it was time to call it a night. On days when she was well enough to be taken outside, there were her beloved woody plants and flowers. Laura once told a friend that she would have liked to have had six children, but visitors found her content with her life as it dwindled away. Although her husband had often caused her great distress, she never spoke ill of him after his death. For fifteen years, however, she savored a freedom of association she had never known before. Laura Leggett Barnes died in her own bed at ninety-two on April 29, 1966 when her lilacs were in bloom. Her collectibles and her turn-of-the century furniture went to the Brooklyn Museum of Art, along with thirty-six African bronze, wood, and ivory sculptures and twenty-four small pictures, which she had either purchased herself or Barnes had given her.[36] Her estate was valued at just over $2 million, and her major cash bequests went to arboreta, hospitals, the Philadelphia Orchestra, and a number of other charities. She left $100,000 each to Jefferson University and Penn to establish scholarships in their medical schools to be named after Dr. Albert C. Barnes.

Nelle Mullen survived a little over a year longer than Laura. She had inherited her sister's estate, including twenty-two pictures by Chirico, Pascin, Glackens, Lawson, Charles and Maurice Prendergast, Charles Demuth, and several painters who taught at the Foundation—all works that Mary had bought years before. Nelle's estate, which was bequeathed to nieces and nephews, was valued at $1.4 million. Her collection of some seventy-five paintings contained, in addition to works by American artists, eight Renoirs, a Cézanne, a Degas, two Matisses, a Rouault, a Utrillo, and two Soutines. It was sold at auction for nearly $1.1 million. Nelle had served as president of the Barnes

Foundation after Laura's death. A representative of the Girard Trust Bank, John W. Woerner, succeeded Barnes's widow as the fifth trustee, and when Nelle died, Lincoln University, for the first time, was empowered to make a nomination. It chose George D. Cannon, a New York radiologist who was the chairman of its board of trustees. Dr. Cannon, a member of the Lincoln Class of 1924 and an alumnus of the Barnes art program, was elected in December of 1967 at the same time Sidney Frick became president. Fogg had returned to the Foundation as director of the arboretum the previous year. But the dominating presence in Merion was the only survivor of the original group of five trustees, the doyenne of the gallery, Violette de Mazia.

The commonwealth had demanded that visiting hours at the Foundation be extended after Laura Barnes was gone. According to the consent decree approved by Orphans' Court in 1960, the collection was to be open to the public one additional afternoon a week, but it took de Mazia several months to decide that Sunday was the day that would least interfere with educational activities. Judge Taxis signed another order stating that 100 visitors should be admitted then in addition to the 200 allowed on both Friday and Saturday for a total of 500 visitors a week. Although Forer had accused de Mazia of dogging art lovers as they walked from room to room, keeping tabs on so many was beyond her powers. She now left guarding to the guards and focused on her classes with greater intensity than ever. Barnes's legacy was in her hands and those of her fellow teachers. Both Moses and Wixom were drafted at the end of their first year of teaching, so in 1952 she hired Barton Church, a painter who had studied at the Pennsylvania Academy of the Fine Arts and at the Foundation. The next year, she added another Barnes alumnus, painter Harry Sefarbi, to the staff. The Foundation's first-year class would always be hers, but along with Angelo Pinto, the two new teachers conducted second-year classes for the increasing cohort of continuing students. After the mid-1950s, however, very few came from Lincoln.

De Mazia had devoted twenty-five years to the Foundation at the time of Barnes's death, and she would give thirty-seven years more. For the rich, brilliant, crusty American, she had left family and friends and never looked back. She did not see her only brother, who died in 1960, after the start of World War II, nor did she see her mother, who died the same year as Laura and is buried in Uxbridge, on the edge of London, in an unmarked grave. A nephew who lived in Canada for many years visited her on several occasions, and she stayed in touch with her sister-in-law and niece by letter. The notes were short and affectionate and shared little of her life. Her house on Derwin Road was filled with paintings, many of which Barnes had given her, and in her extensive library were the books they had written together. The inscription on the flyleaf of her copy of *The Art of Renoir* attests to her importance to him on an intellectual level. It reads: "To Vio, the balance-wheel whose acute perception of essentials and unique sense of order, make this book what I consider the best achievement of my life." And in *The Art of Cézanne*, he wrote: "To Vio—to whose modesty and generosity I owe the use of my name as co-author." However intimate their relationship—and in a rare confidence to a woman friend years after his death, she said he would call for her at night on their trips abroad even when she shared a room with Nelle Mullen, there is evidence that she was no more able than others to escape entirely his verbal abuse. "Where is that bitch? Tell that bitch to come here," Julia Bond recalled Barnes shouting during one of her visits to the Foundation when he couldn't find de Mazia.[37] He was more dependent upon the French-born teacher than anyone else; she was utterly devoted to the work they had carried on for so long together.

De Mazia was largely responsible for the design of the basic course offered by the Barnes Foundation for half a century. Building on what she had learned from the collector, she launched the introductory class on the foundations of aesthetic judgment and appreciation in the early 1940s. Thereafter she interviewed every student considered seriously for admission. Applicants who made the first cut on the basis of letters of recommendation (two were required) were directed to meet with her at the Heywood Road house, but a notice on the door would often send them on to her nearby personal residence. She always asked if prospective students were able to commit themselves to coming to Merion every Tuesday afternoon, since no absences were allowed, and the final question was invariably why do you want to take our course in art appreciation. De Mazia liked men, and they almost always won a place in the first-year class. She also encouraged couples to take the course together, and more than a few husbands applied at the behest of wives who had been turned down once and sought to improve their chances on a second try as part of a study partnership. In the early 1960s, she began a seminar for Foundation graduates. It was a kind of "post-doc" in which selected students worked, under her guidance, on independent projects that involved class presentations and group discussion.

During the first decade after the collector's death, when de Mazia made a special effort to attract students from the Pennsylvania Academy of the Fine Arts, the size of the first-year class gradually increased from some sixty students to 130, and by the mid-1960s, enrollment reached 150, though it was not unusual for 10 to 20 percent to drop out before the end of the year. The three-hour sessions were very intensive, and they were orchestrated by a teacher whose mastery of her subject was stunning. Former students invariably recall her erudition and her ability to connect concepts in art to literature, music, and popular culture with rare brilliance. But her love of words sometimes betrayed her. Always complex in structure, her lectures could be circuitous and repetitive. The brightest students sometimes chafed at a pace adopted to accommodate a range of abilities. Nevertheless, they almost always found in her talks nuggets of pure gold. She was a consummate actress, understood that a classroom is a stage, and was always up for a performance. Women, in particular, were fascinated by her appearance. She would pin flowers in her shoulder-length, fine-textured auburn hair, drape a silk scarf around her neck, and wear a dress in a color that complimented the picture that was the main focus of her lecture. Her frocks were usually low-cut, tight at the waist, full skirted—and, as the years passed, seemed increasingly old-fashioned. A small-boned but full-bosomed woman, de Mazia created, consciously or not, a certain air of mystery with dark glasses that she wore to protect her eyes, which were extraordinarily sensitive to bright light. Late spring or dead of winter, she wore sandals. Her jewelry was mostly silver pieces, which Barnes had bought for her on a trip they made together to New Mexico. On her thumb, she always wore a large ring with a moonstone. She spoke, through thin lips, precise English with a heavy French accent. Sometimes she seemed to dance her lectures. Her hands were particularly expressive, and she used them gracefully. Leaning on an umbrella stand at the front of the main gallery, a coil of energy, she would extract all manner of materials from cardboard boxes—milk cartons, grape stems, dresser scarves, different shades of construction paper cut into various shapes—to serve as illustrations. With reproductions propped up on benches, she demonstrated how far the color and tonality in copies could be from the original. But always she taught from the masterworks in the collection, and the focal point of a particular lesson would rest on an easel covered with cloth until the time came, with all eyes fastened upon her, for the unveiling.

There is no evidence that de Mazia shared Barnes's abiding interest in African-American culture or in African Americans. But one of her most appreciative students was Edward L. Loper, a self-taught black painter. After graduating from high school, the clergyman's son had had to forego a scholarship to Lincoln University to go to work in a tanning factory in the midst of the Depression. Within three years, he became the first black person to enter the annual Delaware Show, an art exhibit sponsored by the Wilmington Society of Fine Arts, where he won an honorable mention. The Philadelphia dealer Robert Carlen introduced him to Barnes in 1946, but the recently widowed Loper was unable to leave his job and young children to accept a proffered invitation to study in Merion. When he finally wrote a letter seeking admission, he had begun supporting himself by giving private art lessons and teaching painting at both the Delaware Art Museum and Lincoln. Loper found a friend in de Mazia as well as an inspirational teacher. He studied at the Foundation from 1963 to 1968, and more than two decades later he described her class and her lingering influence as follows:

> She would start lecturing about what was going on in a particular picture. . . . [She would talk about] who [the painter's] references were as he worked and how these references . . . were showing up in his painting. . . . She would show . . . how whatever happened before in the history of painting is what the next series of painters use, and the next series . . . so that everything that you do can [be] traced back through the history of painting. . . . It's just evolutionary—handed down—and . . . nobody is a genius all by himself. . . . They teach that you don't paint the place or thing—you paint

the qualities involved. . . . I thought what I learned from her changed my life completely . . . because it gave me an insight into knowing what I'm doing . . . when I'm
painting now. . . . No one knows exactly what a picture is going to look like when they
start it. . . . You must paint in such a way that the picture grows and keeps on growing.
. . . If they're well painted, people who look at the pictures every time they look will see
something different. They will never see the same thing.[38]

For Loper and generations of other students, the Barnes pictures gave the
Foundation, as a school teaching the philosophy and appreciation of art, an
advantage over college classrooms everywhere.

Although the gallery was closed in the summer, de Mazia, who often seemed
to work around the clock, never took vacations. As Laura did, however, she
gained a degree of freedom with the collector's death that allowed her to
experience new pleasures. For the first time in her life, she accepted invitations
to dinner parties given by her students. She was shy around people she didn't
know, including the husbands of the women in her seminar, and she talked to
them as a young girl addressing her father's friends. She would dress elabo-
rately when she went out for the evening, sometimes wearing sequined gowns,
and carry orchids. She drove herself for years in an old Packard clunker. Away
from the world of art, she often appeared hopelessly naive, and friends came to
feel that she existed on very little money. When a group of six or seven young
women took her to lunch one day at restaurant that was then the fanciest on the
Main Line, she insisted on paying the check and drew from her wallet a $10
bill. It became a custom to give her a token purse at the end of the school year
when she feted everyone enrolled in the Foundation art program at Ker-Feal.
Coffee ice cream and cookies were served among yellow lilies and blue forget-
me-nots. Usually someone read a poem especially composed for their teacher.

A core group of women students who felt especially close to her, young
friends with whom she talked frequently on the telephone about their children, parents, spouses, cannot remember her ever speaking about her own
family. They learned there was a once fiancé who fought in the Great War, but
they were convinced by the way she glowed when she talked about him that
Barnes was the great love of her life. She told them a story about his buying a
Picasso for $45 and about the artist giving him two drawings when he paid for
the painting. She said the collector regretted having passed up a Rembrandt
and that his greatest sorrow was never having had an opportunity to buy a
Velázquez. She quoted Barnes frequently, read from his articles and their co-
authored books, and always conveyed the impression that she thought his
opinions were unassailable. She kept a number of photographs of him and
called one of the two of them and the dog Fidèle eating lunch together in the
Heywood Road house her favorite. In tribute to him, she undertook to rekindle
the intellectual life of the Foundation by restarting and continuing for more
than a decade the *Journal of the Barnes Foundation* under the new title *Barnes
Foundation: Journal of the Art Department*. It became a vehicle for her own

work, essentially refined versions of her lectures, and that of other faculty members, advanced seminar students, and alumni.

The first issue, published in the spring of 1970, opened with a black and white reproduction of a Paul Cret architectural drawing of the Foundation and an essay on method in which the editor is at pains to set the work of the Foundation apart from that of art academies and universities where she claimed the traditions in art are taken "out of their historical context" and viewed "as eternally valid apart from any use that may be made of them. Our view," de Mazia wrote, restating the lesson Loper had learned so well, is that the traditions are "immensely valuable, in fact indispensable, as sources of suggestions, of working hypotheses which may be applied to the artist's own individual problems."[39] She left to the next and subsequent issues a discussion of what to look for in art. Students were warned about the lethal nature of imitation. Drawing examples from the dowry chests of Pennsylvania "Dutch" craftsmen and paintings as diverse as those of Tintoretto and Horace Pippin, she showed that the key to value was the ability of the artist to impart to his or her work what she called "universal attributes," properties that have a broad human significance and evoke a response from the viewer because of what they are and mean.[40] In explaining aesthetic quality, she emphasized the role of distortion that is "justified by what it achieves for the point of the picture," and quoted Shakespeare and Longfellow as aptly as she had earlier quoted Santayana and William James.[41] De Mazia wrote about William Glackens with particular enthusiasm, noting that he "was able for his own purposes to make full use of the Impressionist tradition, to which he contributed a new form . . . his own illustrative interpretations of the picturesque incidents of daily life."[42] Accompanying her essay were thirty-four reproductions of Glackens's paintings and drawings, including *The Head of a Girl in Profile* (or *The Russian Peasant*), which bore a striking resemblance to its owner as she looked in a photograph taken in the 1930s, but may have been someone else.

The 1972 issues of the *Journal of the Art Department* commemorated the fiftieth anniversary of the creation of the Foundation and the one hundredth anniversary of the collector's birth. The frontispiece in the spring issue was a photograph of Barnes gazing intently at a small Flemish painting of a woman at prayer, which he holds in both hands and rests on his knee. Only Fidèle is looking at the photographer. Other photographs show the teaching staff at work. The fall issue carried Carl Van Vechten's striking portraits of Dewey, who had died in 1952, and of Barnes on facing pages, and the editors reprinted a talk James Johnson Sweeney had given at the Metropolitan Museum of Art the previous year on his friendship with the collector. It was an affectionate reminiscence in which the art critic repeated the story Barnes had told him about his earliest interest in painting. According to Sweeney, Barnes said that when his high-school chum Glackens had laughed at the pictures he had taken to him for criticism, the collector had been determined to find out why and thenceforth "learned a lot from" his friend. Sweeney said he had never interpreted the autobiographical snippet as indicating "any artistic ambition" on Barnes's part but rather early "evidence of his taste for painting."[43]

Among the Foundation alumni who contributed to the *Journal* was former Lincoln dean J. Newton Hill, who was then on the faculty of New York University where he gave a course called the Humanistic Tradition in African Art that drew heavily on his Barnes experience. Hill's article on African sculpture suggested, however, a degree of self-liberation from a rigidly formalist approach. While acknowledging the importance of looking for objective characteristics in any attempt to assess the merits of unfamiliar traditions, he stressed the need to acquaint students with the sociological context in which the art of Africa was produced lest they never move beyond "the novelty of the illustrative distortions" to grasp the intrinsic meaning of particular works.[44] What a picture says was a subject to which de Mazia herself returned again and again even as she expounded on "how the artist says his say." A painter might depart from the literal facts of a subject or traditions or techniques employed by others in the process of selecting and organizing materials for the "sake of conveying an aesthetically significant statement." She could even be forgiving of technical flaws if they did not significantly impair the creation of a unique expression. But she never hesitated to condemn the artist, however skillful his means, who failed, in her opinion, to convey a qualitative insight. She reproduced photographs of Thomas Hart Benton's *Figure and Boats* and his *Beach Scene* to make her point. In assessing Franklin Watkins's portrait of J. Stogdell Stokes, moreover, she observed that the picture simply replaced Van Gogh's *Dr. Gachet* with the long-time president of the Philadelphia Museum of Art, and since the popular local painter had added nothing new, in her opinion, his product was "not intrinsically worthwhile from the standpoint of art" however good the likeness.[45]

The analysis may have stung the many admirers of Watkins and Stokes (and given Barnes's ghost a belly laugh), but, in general, de Mazia picked no quarrels with the art establishment. Like the collector, she welcomed artists, even writing in the *Journal* about Alexis Gritchenko's 1958 visit, and rebuffed scholars more often than not. She invited William Fagg, one of the world's leading authorities on African art, to visit the Foundation in the early 1970s when he was director of the Museum of Mankind in London. Impressed with the Merion collection of African sculpture, Fagg nevertheless observed that some of the tribal attributions were mistaken. Instead of changing the labels, de Mazia simply had them taped over. In 1984 she turned down a request by the Smithsonian to microfilm the Foundation's records as part of a nationwide project to document the history of American art. Her contributions to the art education of generations of American students, however, were widely acknowledged as impressive. Lincoln University granted de Mazia an honorary degree in 1969, and as the years passed, she was similarly honored by St. Joseph's and Lasalle universities and Moore College of Art and Design. An award she especially cherished was her appointment as Chevalier of the Order of Arts and Letters by the French Ministry of Cultural Affairs in the spring of 1973. De Mazia's students paid their own "Tribute of Love" to their teacher in the late fall at a program held in the grand ballroom of the Academy of Music. They commissioned Bonnee Hoy, who had studied in Paris with the legendary Nadia Boulanger, to compose a chamber work. "The de Mazia Quintet," a composition in four movements, was premiered (and later recorded) by the Amado Quartet with Hoy at the piano before an overflow crowd of well-wishers. For reasons that still elude the planners, only the guest of honor was absent. Several years later, de Mazia did share the spotlight with film star Sylvester Stallone at a gala hailing "Philadelphia Super Achievers" and benefiting a medical charity for children.

One of her most devoted followers from the early 1970s to the mid-1980s was a young man she hired to move paintings named Nicolas King. A painter who liked to garden, he lived in a room on the second floor of the administration building adjacent to the gallery, and she gave him hours of private instruction. It seemed she might be training King to succeed her. As a kind of superintendent of the gallery, he sought to make himself indispensable. When de Mazia became ill for some weeks in the spring of 1983, he took over her classes. But in the end she found something about him profoundly disappointing and had him removed from the Foundation. Few questioned her decisions. The board of directors was easily dominated by her "sheer tenacity and strength of will," according to Richard Ninneman, a former Philadelphia banker and later editor-in-chief of the *Christian Science Monitor*, who represented Girard Trust on the board from 1978 to 1982.[46] Now the only female trustee, she spoke at meetings with the authority of the founder. "To nearly every change that we would propose," Ninneman recalls, she would say, "Dr. Barnes wouldn't have done it."[47] Frick, the cautious president, felt that court permission was necessary to make any substantive policy alteration, and while the board had won approval in 1971 to raise employee salaries above levels set in the Indenture, he opposed seeking relief from other restrictions.

Ninneman got nowhere when he proposed a variety of ideas to increase revenue, such as taking color photographs of pictures in the collection and turning them into postcards or producing a book, acceding to requests for loans or even arranging a tour of some of the paintings, and hiring a development officer to seek annual contributions from alumni. He succeeded, however, in persuading three of his board colleagues to vote in favor of a $100-a-year fee for both art appreciation and horticulture courses, and with de Mazia abstaining, the trustees agreed to institute the first-ever tuition charge in the 1980-81 academic year. Ninneman also was able to increase returns from the Foundation's portfolio within the restraints of the Indenture by investing in high-yield government bonds. By 1983, the last year of his term, an endowment with a market value of $7.4 million was producing $823,960 in interest income. Admission fees added another $23,830 to the revenue stream, tuition produced $20,630, the sale of books and journals, $8,850, a bond premium, $6,900, and other sources, $6,650, for total revenues of $890,820. Expenses were $682,550 for the year. After subtracting a realized loss on a sale of investments, the Foundation ended up $103,000 in the black and an accumulated excess of revenues over expenses of more than $1.7 million, which was reinvested in more high-yield bonds. During the term of Ninneman's successor, trust banker David Rawson, annual revenues climbed to $1 million, and with expenses at about $800,000 a year, the board was able to plough $200,000 back into the endowment, which had grown to $10 million by 1988. Rawson says the board authorized the purchase of a new heating system and spent funds on the restoration of paintings. He and Benjamin Amos, another Lincoln alumnus who succeeded Cannon, again raised the possibility of a book featuring color photographs of the paintings, but they were never able to win the support of Langran, Frick, or, most importantly, de Mazia.

Despite advances in the chemistry of dyestuffs, the director of education in the Foundation's art department remained adamantly opposed to what she considered the "hoodwinking of the public" in the "use of color reproductions of paintings." She used black and white prints frequently in her classes and profusely in the *Journal*, but when the study of original works were precluded, she argued, they, at least, did not "pretend to show what only the work of the artist itself can show." Black and white reproductions were capable of providing information about "the basic compositional conception of the subject" and "general characteristics of the drawing," she pointed out, even if they could give no clue to colors, textures, and surfaces. De Mazia's point was that a color slide/print and a painting simply didn't "belong to the same medium of expression." Whatever place color reproductions might have in people's lives, they had, in her view, "no place . . . in the honest study of the artist's work." Writing in the mid-1980s, she compared their use in the classroom to "studying Debussy's piano pieces by listening to them being played on a tuba or a trombone."[48] Barnes himself, however, had been intrigued by the work of skilled photographers. In 1933 he allowed Willard D. Morgan of New York to make and sell photographs and lantern slides of his collection. Eleven years later, he permitted Arthur W. Colen to do the same. But there would be no coffee table book purporting to present his pictures to a wider public during the lifetime of the last trustee he had personally named to the Foundation board.

Maintaining Sidney Frick's support on matters about which she felt strongly on the basis of intellectual or moral principle required de Mazia to give in occasionally on less central issues. When the cost of producing the *Journal* began to seem onerous to him, she agreed to finance it from her savings. In

1979, *VISTAS* began publication with the same mission, format, and editors as its predecessor. It was sent free to college and university libraries by the Friends of the Barnes Foundation and sold at a modest cost to students and alumni. De Mazia had intended to have two issues a year, but her increasingly poor health made so ambitious a schedule impossible. When she was more than eighty, the board hired an administrator who reported directly to the president, but he had little real power and lasted only a couple of years. No matter the burdens of age, de Mazia was determined to meet her classes and to compose, always in long hand, her essays. In text and in illustrations, she now occasionally referred obliquely to personal experiences in making aesthetic points. Writing about Soutine's incorporation in his paintings of values from Cézanne, particularly "simplifications and distortions that foster the grotesque and the bizarre," she recalled hearing John Dewey remark as he walked past Cézanne's *Bibemus Quarry*: "'If you were to explode a bomb in the middle of it, you would have a Soutine!'"[49] Oddly moving are the photographs she published of Barnes from her private collection: a tall, slim graduate student with pince-nez and a full moustache wearing a wide cravat and a stiff, wing-collared shirt; as drawn by Glackens, a man of early middle years, still with firm features, slouched in a chair reading a book; and an older, stouter man in a beret by the well at Ker David in Port-Manech, the Brittany village where she had painted a charming picture of little boats and worked so intently with the collector on their monographs.

More than forty years later, de Mazia was expending the same fierce energy on staying alive to carry on the mission of the Foundation. She felt compelled to re-state it for a new generation: "The collection [wa]s not simply an adventitious accumulation of works of art," it was, "in both plan and function, a laboratory for investigating the objective method of understanding and its application to the study of the fundamental principles of aesthetic expression. Every item, every display," she wrote, "is there for and necessary to the carrying out of the Foundation's educational program in the same way that the materials in a chemistry laboratory . . . are there for and necessary to a successful, usable educational experience, i.e. one which equips the student with working knowledge of the concepts with which to explore and unravel the meaning of whatever he encounters in his field of interest."[50] Albert Barnes had once envisioned people across the nation "learning to see," and de Mazia would teach his approach to art until she literally could not raise her head. One day she collapsed in the gallery, and several of the seminar leaders laid her on a table until they could summon a doctor. Another time, she fell down a flight of stairs at home, but staggered to class with broken ribs before seeking medical attention. When she was hospitalized for several weeks with viral pneumonia, she checked herself out on Tuesdays to give her lectures before returning to her bed. She had had breast cancer and her heart was not strong. In 1984, she called on Barnes alumnus Richard Segal, a public high school art teacher and a painter, to return to Merion as her understudy. For two years, despite her illness, he never once taught the first-year class. But he did take over the seminars, and in 1986, he lectured to the beginning students on a half dozen occasions. The next year, he became their principal teacher.

Largely confined to her Derwin Road home, filled with lovely American antiques but grown shabby with the passing years, de Mazia had the company of her tortoiseshell, part-Persian cat, La Mikada, which she held by its tail to brush, and a tamed cockatiel. A physician made weekly house calls, which quickly turned into lessons for him in art appreciation. She lived mainly on the second floor in a sitting room filled with paintings, many of them gifts from Barnes and from artists, and in an adjacent bedroom. For some years, she had served as a kind of dealer for Barnes alumnus Irvin Nahan, whom she sent abroad to study in the summer of 1953. De Mazia admired his work and was always delighted to receive his letters and those of other students who kept in touch by mail or in person. Segal brought news from the classroom. Sidney Frick came every Tuesday to discuss Foundation business. A neighbor sent her a basket containing dinner on Friday evenings, which would be picked up by a Foundation employee and returned the next day with a small gift of linen or crystal. Three former students, a German immigrant and two French-born women, provided much of her care during the last several years of her life. It wasn't a formally coordinated effort because de Mazia had always insisted on one-on-one relationships. Acting independently, they brought her foods and beverages she especially liked—pistachio nuts, oysters, little red potatoes, steaks exactly one-inch thick, a special kind of beer. One often cooked for her. Another drove her to the Foundation on days she could go out. In the last issue of *VISTAS* published before her death, de Mazia wrote about two private-duty nurses at Bryn Mawr Hospital who cared for her there over a period of several weeks. In her essay, she used the cold efficiency and rule-obsessed rigidity of one and the insightful, adaptive sensitivity of the other to illustrate the difference between academic and creative personalities.

Practical nurses took turns staying with her now around the clock. By September she stopped seeing friends, but she did not stop her work. She recommended that Frick appoint her long-time research assistant, Barnes alumna Esther Van Sant, as assistant director of education. On the morning of the 20th, she wrote, as always in longhand, a few more lines of an essay. She died of congestive heart failure in the early afternoon. Her body was cremated, and the papers reported that there were no services and no survivors. But there were—students who would be affected by their relationship to de Mazia for the rest of their lives. Her will left those who had been closest to her tokens of her affection: pieces of Native-American jewelry, a folding easel, an antique goblet, a book, a serigraph by the Arcadian painter Jean Hugo, a silver letter opener, a pottery lamp, a French pewter pitcher. She made small bequests to a niece, a grandniece, and a nephew. The bulk of her estate was to be used to create the

Violette de Mazia Trust. It was empowered to make her teaching materials, including her notes and the Dictaphone tapes of her lectures, available to Richard Segal or any instructors trained either by her or by him. Her general assets, principally her home, her antiques, her art works, and some jewelry, were to be sold and the proceeds invested to provide scholarships for students enrolled in the Barnes Foundation art appreciation program and to support the publication of articles on the philosophy and appreciation of art by students, alumni, and faculty of the program.

When the two friends whom she chose as co-executors of her estate and co-trustees of the Trust, Van Sant and Marcelle Pick, decided to auction the personal property, there was a flurry of intense interest.[51] Christie's preview party at the Philadelphia College of Physicians drew more than one thousand invited guests, including prominent collectors and art enthusiasts with ties to museums or to Barnes. The initial estimate was that the 400 items, which were to be offered in a series of sales, would fetch between $5 and $7 million. The furniture, pottery, and memorabilia, including Matisse's paint-encrusted palette, were auctioned on April 26, 1989 and brought $644,160. On May 10th and 11th, the eight Impressionist and modern paintings and drawings were sold for more than $5 million. A record was set for a Matisse gouache when one of the artist's studies for the Merion *Dance* mural went for $1.65 million. An American and a Japanese bidder paid $1.43 million and $715,000, respectively, for two small Renoir landscapes, and a surrealistic de Chirico painting was purchased by a European dealer for $935,000. Later in the month, twenty-two paintings by American artists were sold for $2.38 million. At $495,000, Thomas Hart Benton's *The Beach* , which de Mazia had used to illustrate deficits of sensuous appeal, brought the highest price, while Glackens's profile of the young woman with red hair went for $19,800. Together with the negotiated sale of some minor works and the sale of a Soutine's *Portrait of A Man* in London, the auction added approximately $8 million to the de Mazia Trust and the sale of the Derwin Road property about $200,000 more. If, as one former student observed, "de Mazia couldn't really imagine a future after she was gone," she had nevertheless provided well for it.[52]

16

Lincoln

The strongest living link to the collector was broken with the death of Violette de Mazia. She had been the last of the Foundation trustees appointed by Barnes. Lincoln University was now empowered to appoint a second member of the five-member Barnes board. It nominated the chairman of its own board, lawyer, diplomat, and civil rights activist Franklin H. Williams. A former U.S. ambassador to Ghana, he was a Lincoln alumnus then serving as president of the New York-based Phelps Stokes Fund, a foundation concerned with fostering educational opportunities for black Americans and Africans. Williams was elected in December of 1988 along with Richard Torbert, a trust banker who replaced his former colleague David Rawson. With Washington attorney Ben Amos, the Lincoln appointee who had served for the past five years, they constituted a majority with no previous ties to the Foundation. Williams had never even visited it. But for several years he had been interested in exploring how the connection between the primarily black liberal arts college and the school in Merion, with its treasure trove of paintings and sculpture, could benefit his alma mater.[1] The Chester County university, coeducational since 1952 and affiliated with the state since 1971, had only one full-time faculty member teaching art history. There was private speculation among its trustees that Foundation funds might now be made available to endow a professorship and encourage blacks to enter a field almost wholly dominated by whites. Nevertheless, Williams stressed that Lincoln's power of appointment should not be read as control of the Barnes. He pointed out that the university had "no direct authority or influence" over Foundation "policies and no title to the Foundation's property."[2] Sidney Frick forcefully reminded the *Inquirer* that "once on the board," Lincoln's appointees were "obligated to carry out the objectives of the Barnes Foundation" as they were elaborated in the Indenture.[3]

The seventy-three-year-old Barnes president was whistling in the dark. He persuaded his long-time ally Joe Langran to accept re-election once again, but the aging landscape architect had long wanted to resign since board meetings required him to drive to Merion from the eastern shore of Maryland. He served but six months of his new term. Frick stepped down shortly thereafter. Lincoln was now firmly in the saddle. It had authority to nominate four Barnes trustees in perpetuity. To replace Langran, the university chose its own long-time trustee Julius Rosenwald 2d, grandson and namesake of the mail-order magnate and philanthropist who had supported black education in the rural South through the foundation that had funded Horace Mann Bond's early social science research. Rosenwald's father, a former chairman of Sears, Roebuck & Company, was a noted art collector who had testified about the non-restrictive visitors' policy at his house gallery, Alberthorpe, in the attorney general's suit to increase public access to the Barnes. Another Lincoln trustee, Shirley Ann Jackson, a highly regarded Bell Labs physicist, took Sidney Frick's seat. Williams quietly eased off Amos, who had been reelected by the Frick-led board without consulting Lincoln. The negotiations were handled by the university's general counsel, Richard H. Glanton, a state-appointed trustee of the university whom Williams had named general counsel to the Barnes Foundation and charged with advising the board on what restrictions were imposed by the Trust Indenture and "what current practices [we]re in place solely by custom or usage."[4] Amos's place went to Lincoln President Niara Sudarkasa, an anthropologist who had done extensive fieldwork in West Africa among people whose forbearers had created the exquisite sculpture in the Merion collection. Inaugurated in 1987 as the first woman to head the university in its 133-year history, she had been born Gloria Marshall in Fort Lauderdale, Florida, raised by Bahamian grandparents, entered Fiske University at fifteen, graduated from Oberlin College, taken a Ph.D. at Columbia, and previously taught at the University of Michigan, where she was the first black woman in the arts and sciences to be awarded tenure. With a shared enthusiasm and great expectations, the new Foundation board elected Franklin Williams president.

The savvy diplomat quickly made several significant but unheralded policy changes. The requirement that half the visitors to the gallery make advanced reservations was quietly dropped, and the court-mandated limit of 500 visitors a week on the two-and-a-half public days was ignored if it meant turning away those already in line when there was still time to see the collection before closing. Williams requested that an inventory be taken of the collection, as well as of the furniture and Pennsylvania Dutch ware at Ker-Feal and in the house on Heywood Road. He also asked for an assessment of the gallery's physical condition, including its security system. At the urging of Richard Feigen, a high-profile New York gallery owner who had joined the Lincoln board at Williams's invitation, the new president appointed an art advisory committee of distinguished professionals.[5] When the committee met for the first time with the Barnes board in late April of 1990, the ailing president participated by speakerphone. The former ambassador had lung cancer, and within a month he was dead.

The art experts reviewed collection management issues with the Barnes trustees and offered the services of their institutions. They welcomed the tentative steps toward rapprochement with the museum community Williams had taken, but now they waited to see what would happen. No outsiders would be able to influence the battle going on at Lincoln over who would be the next head of the Barnes Foundation. The choice lay with the Barnes trustees, but who the Lincoln board nominated to take Williams's seat was a crucial decision. In February of 1990, it had selected attorney Cuyler H. Walker, a grandnephew of the late diplomat and one-time New York Governor W. Averell Harriman, to replace Rosenwald, who had resigned after having second thoughts about his financial exposure. Feigen supported David Driskell, the only other Lincoln trustee with strong ties to the art world, to fill the new vacancy. But the Lincoln trustee who most coveted the job, Richard Glanton, a rainmaker with a prominent Philadelphia law firm, garnered the support of a substantial majority of his fellow trustees and was nominated in June. On the steamy day in late July when the Foundation trustees met at Ker-Feal, Glanton's election as a trustee was a given. The real question was who would succeed Williams as president. Torbert initially supported Sudarkasa, but at the behest of her own board, she declined to be a candidate. She urged him to join her in supporting Walker, who was serving as an assistant to the U.S. Attorney General Dick Thornburgh, the former Pennsylvania governor. But Sudarkasa then changed her mind and gave her support to her own general counsel. By a three-to-two vote, Glanton became president and, as it turned out, de facto director of the Barnes Foundation. In forty-three years, he had traveled a long way from his starting point just outside the small town of Villa Rica, Georgia.

The powerfully built, well-tailored lawyer, a member of the Union League and the board of directors of the Greater Philadelphia Chamber of Commerce, was the fourth child, second son in a family of eleven children. His father was a tenant farmer who also did construction work. As a boy, he dug potatoes, picked peanuts and cotton, helped feed the pigs, milk the cows, and weed the vegetable garden on the farm some forty miles west of Atlanta where he grew up. Glanton didn't attend school regularly until the third grade. He was the first black student to graduate from West Georgia College, where he majored in English and embraced Republican politics. After earning a J.D. at the University of Virginia Law School in 1972, he was an associate at an Atlanta firm for a year before becoming special assistant to the chairman of the legal division of the Equal Employment Opportunity Commission. He had met his future wife while he was a law student in Charlottesville, and after they were married, they lived in Chicago for several years, where Glanton worked as an attorney for American Airlines. A job as litigation counsel to Conrail brought him to Philadelphia, and then from 1979 to 1983, he served as deputy counsel to Governor Thornburgh. Glanton re-entered private practice as a partner at Wolf Block Schorr & Solis-Cohen, where he worked for three years before joining Reed Smith Shaw & McClay, in 1987, the year he became general counsel to Lincoln University.

The first move of the new president of the Barnes Foundation was political: negotiation of a replacement for Torbert. Glanton discussed his intentions openly with former trustee Rawson at a lunch in the Union League at which he outlined his intention to build up the Foundation's $10-million endowment four- to five-fold. Girard Trust had been absorbed by the Pittsburgh-based Mellon Bank, and after Glanton met with its CEO Thomas Donovan, Charles A. Frank III, a newcomer to Philadelphia, was named Mellon East's representative. Glanton then broached an idea that might have brought a large infusion of funds, but horrified much of the art world. He proposed selling pictures. Glanton wanted to raise the profile of the Barnes. On the basis of reports commissioned by Williams from the art conservation consultant Paul Himmelstein and the conservation environment-consulting firm of Garrison/Lull, he decided a large chunk of money was needed for upgrading mechanical systems. Despite improvements made in the mid-1980s to the security system, moreover, he felt it was inadequate for a world-renowned collection. Rough estimates for capital improvements to the gallery, administration building, arboretum, Ker-Feal, and the property on Heywood Road totaled $12.7 million. Deaccessioning some "paintings that were not displayed" but used for teaching purposes and perhaps "one or two others" seemed the quickest route to the cash he sought to rejuvenate an institution that had just passed its sixty-fifth birthday.[6]

Only the Indenture stood in his way. When he was general counsel to the Foundation, Glanton had examined what latitude might exist for change, and as president, he quickly acquired a powerful ally in his attempt to undo Barnes's strictures against selling works from the collection. At the suggestion of John C. Whitehead, the former co-chairman of Goldman Sachs and deputy secretary of state who was visiting the Foundation, he sought advice from art collector and former publisher Walter H. Annenberg. The one-time nemesis of the Foundation, who had challenged its tax-exempt status within months of the collector's death, told a reporter from the *Inquirer*, the newspaper he once owned, that while there were "great Matisses" at the Barnes, there were also "some dogs. There are any number of horrible Renoirs and between twenty and thirty Renoirs that are first-class," he added. "To keep hanging all that is ridiculous."[7] The then eighty-three-year-old former ambassador to Britain was highly energized by his new association with the Barnes Foundation. He had once been the kind of power broker its president aspired to be. Glanton still recalls with keen pleasure the day he and his wife, Sheryl, took tea with Annenberg and his wife, Leonore, at "Innwood," their estate in Wynnewood, Pennsylvania. In fact, the philanthropist, chairman of the wealthy Annenberg Foundation, encouraged the young lawyer, who was so briefly his protégé, to pursue a course on which he could not stay without risking instant pariah status. Members of the art advisory committee cautioned him that the standard policy of art museums in the United States is to sell paintings only to raise money to buy other artworks, not to fund capital improvements. Glanton argued that because the Foundation was established as an educational institution, it need not hold itself to the same standards of behavior. He persuaded the Barnes board to appoint Annenberg honorary chairman of the advisory committee even as the other members urged him to explore fund-raising alternatives to deaccession. "They were telling me we could piece together our support with pins and needles," Glanton recalled. "We just said the hell with them."[8]

Twenty days after Annenberg's appointment, the Barnes board passed a resolution authorizing its president to obtain counsel for the purpose of filing a petition in the Orphans' Court Division of the Montgomery County Court of Common Pleas to amend the Trust Indenture and bylaws so as to enlarge the powers of the Foundation's trustees and officers. In particular, the board sought permission to sell pictures from the collection in order to raise up to $200 million of which some $185 million would be used to establish a new perpetual endowment fund and approximately $15 million would be spent on upgrading and modernizing the facilities. The resolution specified, moreover, that the trustees and officers should be granted leave to rearrange paintings to cover any spaces that might be caused by selling artworks. They also sought relief from restrictions on the investment of Foundation assets and the use of facilities for social functions, as well as the ability to increase times when the public would be admitted to the gallery and the right to raise the $1 entrance fee. In a final, sweeping request, they asked permission "to take any other action regarding the collection, art gallery, arboretum, properties or any other interests of the Foundation" that would "benefit and best carry out the purposes and intent of the Trust."[9] When the petition was filed on March 18, 1991, the private distress of advisory committee members ballooned into widespread outrage among art professionals, Barnes alumni and students, journalists, and others. But Glanton had said he and his fellow trustees would not be dissuaded from taking actions they deemed appropriate by "commentaries from would-be philosopher-kings."[10] The Barnes president contacted Sotheby's in New York and made inquiries at the J. Paul Getty Center in Malibu, California. He told the *Inquirer* that he had discussed the petition, which set an upper limit of fifteen on the number of paintings to be deaccessioned, with Pennsylvania Attorney General Ernie Preate, Jr., and while receiving "no official approval," he said he expected no opposition.[11]

The cooperation of a political pal, however, would not necessarily translate into a sympathetic judiciary. Nor could it protect the Barnes board from the rising firestorm. Writing in the *Inquirer* about the trustees' decision to "cannibalize the collection," the paper's art critic pointed out that "for a museum, selling pictures is like burning the furniture to keep warm."[12] The *New York Times* observed that the board risked "casting both Barnes and Lincoln in a poor light." While noting that auction prices for Impressionist and Post-Impressionist paintings had recently been declining, its Philadelphia bureauchief wrote that the absence of the works put up for sale by the Foundation "will automatically diminish the institution—and scar the reputation of a university that is anxious to justify Dr. Barnes's trust."[13] Several members of the advisory committee spoke publicly about their long-held reservations. In May of 1991, alumni who had studied under de Mazia, and subsequently organized themselves as Friends of the Barnes Foundation, petitioned Orphans' Court to block the proposed sale. A visiting French official told Glanton of his qualms. It quickly became too much controversy for Walter Annenberg. He resigned his honorary post in mid-April. Speaking by telephone from his desert home near Palm Springs, California, he told a reporter in Philadelphia: "I don't want to be around when there's a rhubarb going on." But then he added to it by describing the Merion gallery as "a rabbit warren" with "no end of third-rate stuff." Annenberg said the Foundation needed "a brand new building" to properly display its best pictures and reiterated his belief in the appropriateness of raising funds by getting rid of what he termed "inferior material."[14] Ironically, the aging former ambassador had just announced that his own collection would go to the Metropolitan Museum of Art on the condition that none of the paintings would ever be sold or even loaned by the museum.

The swift and strong opposition to deaccessioning gave members of the Barnes board pause. Sudarkasa was upset by Glanton's angry, public characterization of the Friends group as a wealthy elite who had "leisure time in the afternoon to take a leisure course in art appreciation to help fill out their day."[15] In June, the Lincoln president circulated a resolution among the trustees calling for a withdrawal of the petition to sell pictures, and Glanton bowed to the wishes of his colleagues. The Foundation issued a terse announcement of its decision that emphasized the board's intention to go forward with other requests before the court. The statement cited "mounting adverse publicity" as the principal reason behind the sudden move.[16] Members of the board had learned that the Association of Art Museum Directors was planning to file a brief opposing the sale. They became uncertain that they could count on Preate's support. Most of all, they feared that a continuing dispute could damage Lincoln. It was time to explore alternative means of raising revenues.

The trustees were convinced that in the long run, the freedom to invest in growth stocks, as well as government and municipal bonds, would greatly benefit the Foundation, but in changing to a balanced portfolio, they faced the loss of some of the $900,000 a year they received from fixed-income investments. Money provided by the de Mazia Trust had been paying the salaries and benefits of four of the Foundation's teachers in addition to providing funds for repairing the gallery roof, limited conservation, a new security system at Ker-Feal, additional guards in Merion, and carpeting the room used for seminars. Now the trust agreed to pay the start-up costs for a development office, and when Glanton hired a woman with public relations experience but no track record in fund-raising, it picked up the tab to send her to a class in the subject at night school. Paul Blanchard Associates was engaged to map a long-range strategy and conduct a study to test the feasibility of a capital campaign. The board did not recognize its consultant's name, but Blanchard's father, as a student of John Dewey, had long ago participated in a field survey of Philadelphia's Polish immigrants for Albert Barnes. The trustees did recognize that the Foundation had no constituent base, and for that reason, the 1991 canvass, like the one in 1917, was designed to produce data that could be used to change attitudes and behavior. Blanchard did not find anyone willing even to consider a major gift, so it would be an uphill battle.

Glanton, however, was focusing on more immediate opportunities. He resurrected the idea of a book of color photographs dealing with masterpieces of the Barnes Collection and went about obtaining bids from potential publishers. All the major art book houses saw the opportunity Glanton offered as a prize, and members of the art advisory committee were enthusiastic. Richard Feigen suggested to S.I. Newhouse, Jr., the chairman of Advance Publications, that he get in touch with the Barnes president. Advance then owned Random House Inc., parent company of one of the most prestigious firms in the publishing business, Alfred A. Knopf. Negotiations proceeded for months. Several trustees raised questions about the need to seek court approval in light of the Indenture's restriction about copying works of art in the collection, but Glanton felt justified in moving ahead without it in light of the collector's use of reproductions of his paintings, albeit black and white prints, in his own books and his occasionally allowing magazines the right to use them. Upon its president's recommendation, the Barnes board approved Knopf's offer of a $750,000 advance in return for exclusive rights. A draft contract had mentioned payment to Lincoln University Press, but the signed agreement called for the advance to go to the Foundation. Nevertheless, the university benefited in several ways. Its press, which had not in the past published books, though Lincoln had published an alumni magazine as early as 1884, would be listed as co-publisher. Furthermore, once the Barnes trustees okayed the publishing agreement but before a contract was signed, a representative of the Newhouse Foundation contacted Glanton about making a gift to Lincoln. The New York publisher eventually went by helicopter to Merion where he met with Sudarkasa, and in early April, his foundation awarded a $2 million grant to the struggling institution. It was a stunning contribution from a generous benefactor that overshadowed the only other large gift Lincoln had received in recent years—$500,000 from the Annenberg Foundation.

When the *New York Times* got wind of the Knopf coup, the newspaper queried Alberto Vitale, chief executive of Random House Inc., who said that after the first book featuring selected treasures, the publisher would "do a catalogue and, hopefully . . . come up with other books."[17] For the trade edition, the board agreed that the paintings should be taken out of their frames and photographed without being cleaned, although several museums had offered to undertake the delicate task if they could show them. An official catalogue of the collection would be a far more involved project. In general, the pictures were in excellent condition since Barnes, and then de Mazia, had eschewed methods of art preservation common from the 1920s through the 1960s, which conservators subsequently acknowledged were too aggressive. Nevertheless, loose and flaking paint could be found on a number of the canvases, and routine conservation work, ongoing in a minor way, would have to be stepped up, including, in some cases, the removal of old varnish. Furthermore, attributions for many works would have to be checked by reputable scholars. The board would have to face and come to terms publicly with the fact that Barnes's magnificent eye for modern art was less than perfect when it came to the work of earlier painters. A forthright evaluation of the collection would be a necessary and significant step in enhancing the standing of the Foundation's courses in the general art educational community. Glanton would have liked to have seen them accredited by the Middle States Association, and he tentatively explored the possibility of a cooperative venture with nearby St. Joseph's University. The Barnes educational program, however, was "not a priority" for him.[18] Knopf brought out a handsome volume, *Great French Paintings from the Barnes Collection*, with more than one hundred color reproductions of Foundation pictures, in the spring of 1993, but the *catalogue raisonné* called for in the contract never happened. "There were just so many other issues going on at the time," Glanton noted in retrospect, and, indeed, one of them stemmed indirectly from the publication of the long-awaited book of Barnes pictures.[19]

In January of 1992, the de Mazia Trust filed a petition in Montgomery County Orphans' Court in which the trustees charged that the Barnes board used a Foundation asset, the right to grant a contract to publish *Great French Paintings*, to lure a donation to Lincoln that should have gone to the Foundation. The previous summer, one of the co-executors of de Mazia's estate had requested and been granted official "standing," that is, the right to participate in hearings to be held in connection with the attempt of the Foundation's trustees to deviate from the provisions of the collector's Indenture. Now the de Mazia Trust asked the court to remove the entire Barnes board. It said that since four of the Foundation trustees also served on the Lincoln board, they had an "irreconcilable conflict of interest"—and should be ordered to pay $2 million to the Foundation to make amends for "improperly" diverting funds away from the education program in Merion.[20] The week before, Judge Louis Stefan had granted the de Mazia trustees' request to take depositions related to the book contract, and two days later, the Foundation withdrew its petition to overturn restrictions specified in the Indenture, or subsequently by the courts, on gallery visiting hours and admission fees, as well as on investment policy and use of the Merion building for social functions. De Mazia's executors saw the move as an attempt to avoid the discovery process and conceal facts related to the Newhouse contribution, and in a separate action, they protested it. Stefan disallowed withdrawal, and the legal battle intensified under a new Foundation counsel hired by Glanton. Bruce W. Kauffman, a former Pennsylvania Supreme Court justice (and now a federal judge), was one of Philadelphia's top litigator and one of its best-paid lawyers. His ties to Glanton went back a decade.

Kauffman fired a canon at the bow of the de Mazia bark in mid-April. Stunning the executors, he filed a petition charging that much of the $8 million used to create the long-time teacher's Trust may have come the sale of stolen paintings. Although the petition did not make reference to any specific pictures, Kauffman said that the Foundation believed that more than a dozen works of art by eleven different painters sold at Christie's as de Mazia's property were originally in the Barnes Collection. An accompanying affidavit by Nicolas King, a Foundation employee dismissed by a former Barnes board and rehired by Glanton, charged that the woman who had given him a job moving art when he knocked at her door "misappropriated" *The Beach* by Thomas Hart Benton. Ironically, the picture was one de Mazia considered aesthetically insignificant. The attorney for her executors called the charge "a colossal red herring."[21] But in August, the Foundation asked the court to take control of the de Mazia Trust, replace its officers with members of the Barnes board, and return the proceeds of the sale of the paintings in her estate. To the chorus of former students who protested that the collector had given de Mazia the art in her possession, the Foundation replied that he had no legal authority to do so without taking the matter to his board of trustees for formal action. The surreal quarrel continued for three years. Knopf denied that there was any quid pro quo involved in its securing the Barnes contract. The publisher's attorney pointed out that the Newhouse Foundation had previously made gifts to encourage minority education. Glanton contended that the actions of his opponents were racially motivated. He said the de Mazia Trust was using "all its resources to destroy the [Barnes] Foundation."[22] Unquestionably, plenty of money was being spent on legal fees on both sides, but far from intending to ruin the enterprise in Merion, the trust officers were committed to supporting its educational program—and the board's inattention to it was at the heart of their concern.

Their apprehension was shared by current and former students. The Friends of the Barnes Foundation, who had sought standing to join in the case, were a group of more than seven hundred. They were people who had benefited from the Barnes educational program and wanted to ensure that future generations had the same opportunity. Each year, they paid the $200 Foundation tuition fee for six needy students and distributed the books written by Barnes and de Mazia to university libraries. Oddly, the new Barnes Foundation board never sought to cultivate members of the group as patrons. Because of their distrust of the overall intentions of the Foundation leadership, another cohort of about one hundred current students also requested standing even after Glanton gave up his efforts to sell up to fifteen pictures. The students did not oppose expanding public visiting hours but were "concerned that access" not "swallow up the art department classes."[23] Even as the Barnes alumni withdrew their petition to the court on the grounds that they took Glanton at his word, the students stood firm. In late July, Judge Stefan granted their request and appointed three of their members to represent the group. The hot-button issue for the young crowd was the possibility of intrusion on what they considered the sacrosanct four-days-a-week set aside for classes in the Merion gallery.

The repercussions of protest were not long in coming, and some individuals paid a high price for their actions. De Mazia's chosen successor, Richard Segal, was fired in June after he wrote to the Foundation board expressing his opposition to the sale of paintings and other attempted changes to the Indenture. A month later, the Barnes trustees dismissed Richard Feigen, the most outspoken member of the art advisory committee. The New York picture dealer also received a request from the chair of the Lincoln board asking him to step down as a university trustee. He refused, but Nick Tinari, a young engineer who loved art and was leading the student protest group, had no such recourse when he was expelled in mid-January of 1992 for violating rules of conduct expected of those enrolled in Barnes classes. Among Tinari's offenses was digging through the Foundation's trash for evidence to use in his petitions to the court and photographing the Annenbergs and the former ambassador's niece, Metropolitan Museum of Art trustee Cynthia Hazen Polsky, on a visit to the gallery the previous spring. The eventual effect of his expulsion was to take away his legal standing as a critic. Wendy Hartman Samet, the only professional conservator working on the Barnes paintings, was dismissed later in the month after she wrote to Glanton warning against the dangers of untrained personnel handling the paintings.[24] The Barnes president told reporters who questioned him at the time that he no longer had need of her services since personnel of the National Gallery of Art were providing free technical assistance in connection with the forthcoming Knopf publication. Director of education Esther Van Sant thought she saw the writing on the wall. A co-trustee of the de Mazia Trust but not officially a party to its suit against the Foundation board, Van Sant said her position had become "untenable." She resigned with a letter to Glanton accusing him of actions that increasingly lacked "simple honesty and decency." Her complaints, he said, were part of the "guerrilla warfare."[25]

The president of the Barnes Foundation was not about to be distracted by snipers. After her visit to the Foundation, Polsky had suggested to her Uncle Walter a tour of Barnes pictures as an alternative to selling some. Annenberg liked the idea. He discussed it with J. Carter Brown, outgoing director of the National Gallery, then urged Glanton to contact Brown to pursue the details of a touring exhibition. The Indenture expressly prohibited the loan of any part of the collection, but in an age when blockbuster shows had the capacity to draw huge fee-paying crowds, Glanton saw a grand tour as a way both of raising funds for renovations and enhancing the visibility of the Foundation. "All the experts said no one would pay to exhibit pictures," he recalled.[26] Protocol in the museum world was to loan art for purposes of public education and with the expectation, in many cases, that the loan would be reciprocated in kind for some future show conceived by the lending institution. But the Foundation wasn't interested in borrowing anyone else's paintings. Glanton wanted cash up front for the privilege of exhibiting masterpieces from the Barnes Collection, and he spent the next four years negotiating court permissions and institutional agreements. In the process, he generated an enormous amount of excitement about the works on exhibit and, for a time, attracted a searching public spotlight upon the affairs of the Foundation. Critics lambasted him for turning art into a commodity as if he had invented the technique; supporters praised his initiative and persistence. Almost everyone agreed, some ruefully and some with glee, that Albert Barnes would have abhorred the orgy of merchandising and socializing that accompanied what Walter Annenberg called the "bicycling [of] the collection."[27]

Philadelphia's public radio station, WHYY, broke the story of the world tour in late January of 1992. It was six weeks, however, before the Foundation announced its plans. By early March, Kauffman was willing to admit that arrangements were being made for shows in four venues, the National Gallery of Art in Washington, DC, the Musée d'Orsay in Paris, a museum in Tokyo, and the Philadelphia Museum of Art. He said he hoped to secure the support of the Pennsylvania attorney general, but it wasn't quite in hand on the first of April when he petitioned Montgomery County Orphans' Court for permission to send about eighty pictures on tour. He was able to announce that the National Gallery would organize the traveling exhibition and supervise preparation of the accompanying Knopf book, while the Philadelphia Museum of Art would store the remaining one thousand or so works of art during the process of gallery renovation.[28] In early July, Deputy State Attorney General Lawrence Barth finally told Judge Stefan that his office favored the tour, but he stipulated that the National Gallery should provide written confirmation of the suitability of the art for travel. His caveat was a partial response to representatives of the de Mazia Trust, alumni, and students who, throughout hearings in May and early June, expressed concern that the tour could damage both the Foundation's art and its educational program. On the 22nd of July, Stefan announced his decision that the Barnes board could make a "onetime deviation" from the terms of the Indenture for a traveling show containing as many as eighty-two pictures.[29] Any risk to the paintings in transit or on exhibition, he said, was "outweighed by the greater risk to the collection should it remain in the Foundation in its unrenovated condition."[30]

The ruling was as inevitable as it was judicious. The tour, with four scheduled stops between May 1993 and September 1995, could go forward, but the trustees could not, as they had sought to do, amend Barnes's Indenture. They must submit a plan to the court detailing how the art education program would be continued during the renovation of the gallery, and any painting judged by the National Gallery of Art as too fragile to travel must be omitted from the road show. Alone among the designated venues, the Washington museum was free to the public, so Glanton agreed to accept its various services to the Barnes, including the critical details of inspection, restoration, and shipping, in lieu of a borrower's fee. Carter Brown arranged for him to meet officials of the Museum of Western Art in Tokyo, and the result was a $4.5 million deal with the funds provided by several Japanese sponsors. Underwriting the French segment of the exhibition, the National Bank of Paris paid $2.5 million to the Foundation. At home, the Philadelphia Museum of Art's Anne d'Harnoncourt offered to provide space for displaced Foundation classes in addition to storage facilities. Glanton accepted and agreed to a rental fee of half PMA's profits from admissions to the Barnes show, though, in any case, no less than $500,000. He hired a licensing agent to negotiate contracts with vendors for memorabilia, including posters, calendars, and postcards, that would be sold at every venue. Arrangements were made with Polaroid to produce replicas of sixteen paintings from the exhibit, which were to be priced at $600 each and billed as suitable for framing. Behind the scenes, the Barnes president was talking with several other museums eager to plug into the traveling show's itinerary. He would have to return to court to add more stops, but in light of Judge Stefan's ruling, permission seemed within the realm of possibility. Glanton called the decision "a grand slam."[31] But others were not as ebullient.

The question of readying the pictures for exhibition was particularly sensitive. There were just nine months to complete the task as the show at the National Gallery was to open on May 2, 1993. Critics, including the de Mazia trustees, Barnes alumni and students, and ArtWatch International, a group newly founded in 1992 by a Columbia art historian to monitor the treatment and restoration of works of art of world significance, said more time was needed to examine the pictures and prepare them for the stress of travel. Within days of Stefan's rendering his decision, Augustus F. Brown, a retired professor of linguistics and a Barnes alumnus, took out a full-page advertisement in the local *Main Line Times* to attack a 1991 Foundation renovation budget as "clearly based on hearsay."[32] It was the start of what became a newsletter campaign against the actions of the Barnes board that would last six years and cover all manner of alleged transgressions. The broadsides were detailed and dense; the founding editor and his successor utterly convinced of the justice of their cause. They believed the absence of core pictures would undermine the Barnes education program, and at every turn, they protested what they saw as assaults on the collector's Indenture of Trust. But even as students filed a notice of their intent to appeal Judge Stefan's decision, curators from the National Gallery, with the assistance of experts from the Musée d'Orsay and the Philadelphia Museum of Art, walked through the Merion gallery with their checklists and made selections for the tour, which would focus exclusively on French paintings and provide a "series of snapshots", as one critic observed, of a "half-century's development of modernism."[33]

At a swank press luncheon held at the Foundation in December, Glanton announced that among the masterworks in Merion, Cézanne's *Card Players*, Seurat's *Models*, and Matisse's *The Joy of Life* would be part of the traveling exhibition. The affair was a kind of coming out party for the new regime. Like their predecessors, who had been invited to the party Barnes gave for Vollard fifty-six years earlier, the visiting art critics and editors were mesmerized by what they saw on the burlap-covered walls. Students outside held up placards, "BARNES IS A SCHOOL, NOT A MUSEUM," and Glanton talked about the tour. His guests couldn't take their eyes off the pictures. One of them, Hilton Kramer, who had read *The Art of Painting*, recalled what the collector had said about the "'confusion of values' that tended . . . to prevent people from acquiring a proper appreciation of the aesthetic nature of works of art." He wrote later that he had heard many of the luncheon speakers refer to Dr. Barnes's belief in education, but thought that what they meant by "education" had "little or nothing to do with Dr. Barnes's conception of 'the aesthetic interest' that he had placed at its center."[34]

A matter of color—the fact that Richard Glanton's critics were mostly white—led him to seize upon a troubling explanation for their behavior. "I have been subjected to more racism in connection with the Barnes than when I was a poor person in Georgia," he told a writer for an art magazine.[35] But sorting out motives, his own or anyone else's, in so complex a drama as that unfolding in Merion was, at best, difficult. The demonizing of opponents, and the Brown newsletter regularly portrayed the president's actions on behalf of the Foundation as serving his political ambition, only impeded progress toward resolving disputed issues in a case filled with hard legal calls and ethical dilemmas. The question before the Orphans' Court had been what was legally feasible within the terms of the Indenture and what might be morally permissible given an obligation to honor the donor's intent. The Superior Court of Pennsylvania heard the students' appeal in February and in April, a little more than two weeks before the scheduled opening of the exhibition of Barnes paintings at the National Gallery, affirmed Judge Stefan's order. But even as the paintings were being crated—one by one in specially-designed boxes—for trucking to Washington, questions were raised as to whether the Federal Council on the Arts and Humanities had acted unlawfully in approving government insurance for the show and, indeed, whether a domestic exhibition was even eligible for insurance under a 1975 law intended to cover artworks shipped from abroad. Glanton assured the press that since the exhibition was not contingent upon the federal insurance indemnity, it would open on sched-ule. Coverage, in any case, was limited to $300 million, and the value of the paintings was and is incalculable.

The degree of pent-up interest in the Barnes collection was reflected in the seemingly endless line of people outside the National Gallery of Art, stretched down Constitution Avenue toward the Capitol, waiting for the 11 A.M. opening of the extended road show on the first Sunday in May. Four days earlier, on the 28th of April, the rich and glamorous had attended a preview party. Glanton and his wife joined the new director of the National Gallery, Earl A. Powell 3rd, in welcoming Chief Justice of the United States William Rhenquist along with Pamela Harriman, then the United States ambassador-designate to France, the Annenbergs, cosmetics titan Leonard Lauder, the president of New York's Whitney Museum, and his wife, Evelyn Lauder, and Senator John D. Rockefeller 4th and his wife, Sharon Percy Rockefeller, among other guests. But they could not have been more exhilarated by their experience than Barnes's "plain people" who streamed through the East Building in the course of the next fifteen weeks. Visitors' first encounter with the fabled collection was just outside the entrance to the exhibition where the Merion *Dance* mural was installed in a low space. Mounted near it for comparison was Matisse's initial, unfinished effort to fill the three lunettes in Merion—a recently re-stored full-scale sketch, which was discovered only the year before in Paris. Inside the galleries themselves, the pictures were grouped by artist and chro-nology, starting with a Manet, sixteen of the best of the collector's Renoirs, two Monets, twenty Cézannes, two Gauguins, one Van Gogh, two Seurats, two Toulouse-Lautrecs, three Henri Rousseaus, seven Picassos, two Braques, one Roger de La Fresnaye, two Soutines, four Modiglianis, and ending with six-teen Matisses. Writing for *America*, Leo J. O'Donovan, the president of Georgetown University, observed that "rarely can a long-awaited exhibition have so fully satisfied one's every expectation of it."[36] He seemed to be speak-ing for the 521,000 Americans who trekked through the National Gallery exactly seventy years after visitors scoffed at the pictures Albert Barnes loaned to the Pennsylvania Academy of the Fine Arts in Philadelphia.

The Paris show opened with a series of glittering parties the first week in September. The Barnes trustees walked French President Francois Mitterrand through the galleries of the Musée d'Orsay, and Glanton received a green-and-white ribbon designating him an Officer of the Order of Arts and Letters, a version of the Ministry of Culture award once given to de Mazia. Sixty Phila-delphians, including the mayor's wife and the chairman of the board of trust-ees of the Philadelphia Museum of Art, came with him from Philadelphia for the festivities. The exhibition was the toast of the city. It was heralded on French television and in *Le Monde* and *Le Figaro*. Some 13,000 people a day, almost double the average daily attendance at the d'Orsay, lined up to see the pictures. The final count was 1.5 million visitors, including those who had a chance to see all three versions of Matisse's *Dance* at the Musée d'art moderne de la Ville, where they were displayed together for the first time. The Barnes mural had not been on the original list of paintings to go to Paris, and the Musée d'Orsay did not have space large enough to accommodate it. But when space was found in the city's modern art museum for the unique exhibition of the Merion *Dance*, the sketch previously shown in Washington, and the long-known "first" version, which Matisse had abandoned after learning the measurements were incorrect and finished after the installation of the Barnes mural, Glanton returned to court again to ask permission to ship the fragile panels. Concerned for the safety of Merion *Dance* and fearful of the precedent that would be established if Judge Stefan allowed the Foundation's request, the de Mazia Trust and Barnes students once again opposed him. Attorneys representing all sides argued back and forth, Carter Brown testified in favor of allowing the mural to be shipped, and just before the close of the Barnes show at the National Gallery, the judge ruled in the Foundation's favor. Its president had little time to savor the victory.

As if his ongoing tangles with Barnes loyalists were not enough of a legal hassle for Richard Glanton, he was the defendant during the summer of 1993 in a sexual harassment lawsuit brought by a former colleague at Reed Smith. A federal court jury found that he had "engaged in pervasive and regular sexually discriminatory conduct" towards the plaintiff, but declined to award any damages for sexual harassment.[37] Instead, it gave Kathleen Frederick $100,000 in compensatory damages and $25,000 in punitive damages as a consequence of allegedly defaming comments Glanton made to reporters after her lawsuit was filed. Both parties appealed the verdict, Frederick seeking more damages and the Barnes president, who vehemently denied any sexual relationship with her, seeking to clear his name. Seventeen months later, a confidential settlement was reached, and a U.S. district judge signed a motion to dismiss the lawsuit and vacate the verdict of the jury. Even as the appeals process was going forward, however, Glanton was back in Montgomery County Orphans' Court on behalf of the Foundation.

A number of museums besides the four initially chosen as venues for exhibiting the Barnes pictures had clamored to get the show, and he now sought permission to add two additional stops to the world tour of the collection. Letting it go to Fort Worth, Texas and Toronto, he told Judge Stefan, would produce $6.2 million more in revenue for the Foundation, which it "desperately needed" to strengthen a shrinking endowment.[38] In the course of hearings he explained that since expenses had exceeded income for the past several years, the trustees had been dipping into the nest egg left by Barnes to cover the cost of operations. The president also pointed out that restoration of the gallery and the administration building, originally estimated at $7 million, was likely to run $3 million higher. In early February of 1994, the Orphans' Court judge approved the Foundation's request to mount shows at the Kimball

Art Museum in Fort Worth, Texas and the Art Gallery of Ontario (AGO) in Toronto. But he also put Glanton on a short lead by ruling that the fees resulting from the added venues, together with revenue from catalogue and merchandise sales, must go into a fund earmarked for building restorations and placed under the control of the court. On the advice of the National Gallery of Art's chief conservator, moreover, Judge Stefan ordered that Seurat's large masterpiece, *Models*, be returned to the Foundation at the close of the exhibition in Tokyo. His ruling on the fragile painting, which Wendy Samet pointed out had a long-history of flaking, was a relief to the de Mazia trustees, who had opposed extension of the tour, as well as to the students, who opposed the tour altogether, and not so great a blow to the new hosts as Glanton agreed to substitute another Picasso, Van Gogh, and Cézanne.

The Japanese show was inaugurated with a swirl of festivities characteristic of the corporate marketing of a blockbuster and heightened by the long-standing love affair of the Japanese with Impressionist and Post-Impressionist art. It was heralded by posters in subways, street banners, and commercials on television. Glanton attended a gala dinner given by Joan Mondale, the wife of United States ambassador to Japan Walter Mondale, the former vice president, and he was on hand when a princess of the imperial household cut the ribbon launching the exhibition. Nearly 3,000 people had streamed through the National Museum of Western Art by noon on opening day to see the pictures that were forever beyond the reach of Japanese investors. Six weeks later, the number of visitors totaled 1,070,000, closing in on the Paris count. In Fort Worth, where the show opened on April 24, 1994, just twenty days after the close of the Tokyo exhibit, the launch party drew Governor Ann Richards and Senator Kay Bailey Hutchinson in addition to oil and cattle billionaires. The Kimball Art Museum, the last building designed and completed by world-renowned Philadelphia architect Louis Kahn, was the only museum west of the Mississippi to host the Barnes show. Backed by two local foundations, it paid $3 million for the privilege. The pictures from Merion drew as many visitors, 430,000, as residents of the city and broke a Texas record for attendance at museum exhibitions.

The last stop before the return of the paintings to Philadelphia was Toronto, and the negotiations between AGO director Glenn Lowry and Richard Glanton had begun fifteen months before the show opened in mid-September of 1994. The Barnes president made it clear from the start that court approval was necessary to extend the tour, but the determined Northerner was soon rallying powerful business and diplomatic allies to help persuade the skeptical Southerner that the Toronto museum should be at the top of his list of extra venues if the Foundation won permission to add them. To the Canadians, securing the Barnes exhibition was not a matter of civic pride only; they also anticipated real financial benefits. A year earlier, the provincial government had severely reduced its subsidy for AGO operations, a draconian move that forced the museum to lay off staff and close for seven months. Lowry, who is now the director of New York's Museum of Modern Art, saw the "Great French Paintings from the Barnes Collection" as a chance to reposition the recently reopened gallery. He sold the show to his backers as "an investment with a tangible return" in terms of cultural tourism.[39] Moving aggressively, AGO's chairman, the hugely successful investor Joseph Rotman, took Glanton to dinner at Harry's Bar in New York. Ontario Premier Bob Rae invited him to a meeting at The Jefferson, the elegant old hotel in Washington known as a place for cutting deals. He left having signed a commitment to recommend the Toronto museum to the other Foundation trustees if he could persuade them to go back to court. But while the board did agree to seek an extension of the grand tour, it decided that a foreign location would make winning one more difficult. When Glanton faxed Lowry a letter with the bad news, the AGO director mounted a strategic campaign to win a new hearing. The Canadian ambassador to the United States appealed to Pennsylvania's senators and congressional representatives; the former ambassador, who had become acquainted with the Annenbergs when Lee Annenberg was U. S. chief of protocol, arranged for Lowry to call Walter Annenberg and seek his advice. The AGO director sent each of the Barnes trustees a letter making his case and found sympathetic individuals in important positions in business and education to make personal pleas. The Toronto museum's principal competitor was the Los Angeles County Museum of Art, and in August, after learning that its director had resigned, the Barnes board agreed to reconsider their decision. Lowry and Rotman were invited to make a personal presentation to the trustees. The AGO team met with them in the boardroom at Reed Smith and emphasized, among other things, the Canadian city's cultural diversity. Two weeks later, Glanton told them the board had voted to replace Los Angeles with Toronto. Leaving nothing to chance, Lowry and Rotman followed him to Paris when he went to participate in the opening of the exhibition at the Musée d'Orsay, and in a long meeting at the Ritz, they nailed down the terms of the contract. The AGO show cost $3.2 million, attracted 600,000 visitors, and generated enough revenues to help the museum significantly reduce its operating debt.

To the paintings brought home from Toronto, the Philadelphia Museum of Art exhibition added nineteen of Barnes's choice African sculptures. Glanton called the loan, which was requested by PMA director Anne d'Harnoncourt, "clearly appropriate" since the Philadelphia show was intended to be "the centerpiece" of the international tour.[40] The works in wood and bronze, dating from the late nineteenth and early twentieth centuries, were selected by National Museum of African Art director Sylvia Williams, a Barnes alumna and the daughter of former Lincoln dean J. Newton Hill, who had earlier resigned from the now largely moribund art advisory committee. Also on display in Philadelphia, despite Judge Stefan's order that it be returned to the Foundation, was Seurat's *Models*. Glanton based his decision to include it on the opinion of a National Gallery of Art conservator that trucking the painting from the administration building in Merion the few miles to the Philadelphia Museum of Art would not hurt it. Besides, the judge was dead. In an accident eerily reminiscent of the car crash that killed Albert Barnes, Louis Stefan smashed into a tractor-trailer on a New Jersey highway in early September of 1994 as he was driving to his summer home on Long Beach Island. But news reports of the Barnes president's intention to allow exhibition of the famous pointillist picture caught the attention of the deputy attorney general and moved attorneys for the PMA to seek the sanction of Orphans' Court. Eleven days before the official start of the show, Judge Stanley Ott accepted the assurance of the Foundation trustees and museum officials that including the giant painting posed no undue risk to the masterpiece. At the opening on January 31, 1995, it hung as the focal point of the middle gallery of seven especially designed main-floor galleries in the company of Cézanne's *The Card Players* and Renoir's *The Artist's Family*. Another innovation at the PMA was the display of the Barnes version of Cézanne's *Bathers* on a direct horizontal axis with the museum's version at the far end of a gallery across the hall. The irony implicit in the arrangement was unknown to most visitors, but undoubtedly not lost on the curators whose predecessors' trumpeting of the latter acquisition fifty-eight years earlier had brought down the collector's wrath on their heads.

Visitors who stopped at the PMA's five computer stations set up on a second-floor balcony would not have learned the story of that long-ago eruption, but they could have learned much else from viewing a CD-ROM on Albert Barnes and his Foundation produced by Curtis Wong. It was the brainchild of Carter Brown, and the first commercial product of Corbis Corporation, the other software company owned by Bill Gates. Released to coincide with the Philadelphia opening of the Barnes exhibit and entitled "A Passion for Art: Renoir, Cézanne, Matisse and Dr. Barnes," the CD on sale for $49.95 in the museum's special Barnes gift shop presented a brief biography of the collector and offered several pathways through his collection. It is not an overview of the holdings in Merion, but offers a tour of the galleries with PMA's senior curator Joseph Rishel. Viewers have the opportunity to look at any of 340 featured paintings in detail, as well as call up a limited number of items from the Foundation archives, including photographs, letters about purchases—an odd selection that emphasizes the collector's penchant for haggling over prices, invoices, and stubs from Barnes's checkbook. The quality of the reproductions is generally good, although the richness of the color depends on the size and resolution of the viewer's screen. The *New York Times* reviewer hailed the Barnes disk as "perhaps the best art CD-ROM" he had ever seen.[41] It illustrates the considerable potential as well as the current limits of cultivating an interest in art with point-and-click technology—and like other educational CDs never found the market anticipated by its backers.

The Philadelphia exhibition of Barnes pictures, however, lived up to the expectations of its sponsors, Elf Atochem North America, Inc., First Fidelity Bank, and WCAU-TV, along with those of almost everyone else. It was launched at a gala, black-tie party for major donors to the museum, art professionals, and politicians. A trio of can-can dancers performed on the great stairway as 1,200 guests sampled French and Mediterranean delicacies piled high on buffet tables. The Foundation trustees were there, and Glanton and Sudarkasa joined in the receiving line, but none of them were invited to a sit-down dinner for the PMA's corporate partners that followed at the Rittenhouse Hotel. The omission, when highlighted by the *Inquirer*, prompted a gracious public apology from the museum's director. But the incident produced no Barnesian explosion as both the Foundation and the PMA had a huge stake in the success of the local run of the grand touring show. It was promoted heavily through newspaper and magazine advertisements, radio and television spots, a half-hour television special contributed by the exhibition's media sponsor, direct mailings to 50,000 American Express card holders and 80,000 Philadelphia area residents, shop displays, and hotel packages that featured special admission passes. The ten-week exhibition was extended two weeks by unanimous vote of the Foundation trustees, and by its close had attracted more than 477,000 visitors and grossed more than $7 million. The Barnes show was the most popular in the museum's history. It helped boost membership, attracted business donors who held some fifty parties at the PMA during its run, and contributed an estimated $30 million to the city's economy. There were complaints about the crowds encroaching on private time for viewing and reacting so cherished by connoisseurs, but the hugely hyped hometown exhibition of the Merion masterpieces was a phenomenon that brought people together across barriers of race and class. It fostered, albeit briefly, the linkages that Albert Barnes always had in mind for his pictures.

For a few weeks in February of 1995, in the wake of the Philadelphia opening, Glanton considered switching political parties and challenging Democratic Mayor Ed Rendell in the spring primaries. Despite being courted by union leaders, he decided, in the end, against a run. It was not, however, a matter of his losing his taste for combat. The Foundation president had unfinished business in Merion, and before the PMA show closed, he was back in court seeking permission to extend the tour to yet another venue—the Haus der Kunst in Munich. Although the extension would mean an extra $2.5 million for the Barnes, which Glanton hoped to use for operations and replenishing the endowment, it did not have the unanimous support of the board when Bruce Kauffman sent a letter to Judge Ott to ask approval. Cuyler Walker, for one, found the idea of the request problematic. Since the tour already had yielded more than $14 million, a sum sufficient to cover the cost of renovating the gallery, the young attorney thought the Foundation had a "tough legal argument." With the paintings safely back in Philadelphia, Walker felt the board would be hard put "to justify flying them back to Europe."[42] Indeed, while Kauffman had hoped to make his case in a conference with Judge Ott, the jurist told him to file a petition. When he did, Barnes alumni and students were quick to oppose the Foundation's new move. All concerned parties were invited to a hearing, but then a frustrated Christoph Vitali, the director of the German museum, temporarily took back his bid for the Barnes pictures and Glanton withdrew his request "without prejudice," a legal action that gave him the right to reconsider the step. He said there did not appear to be sufficient time to make necessary arrangements. But a few days later, the Foundation filed a new petition. Glanton announced that the venue, which he still did not name publicly, had "agreed to push back the time of the exhibition" provided the board could obtain "approval from the court in time" to allow for advertising of the exhibition and "properly provide for its transfer."[43]

Since the paintings were to be re-installed in Merion in late October and Vitali insisted a four-month run was necessary to recoup the $4- to $5-million cost of mounting the show, Glanton hoped for a hearing as soon as possible. The May 10 date set by Judge Ott was a long two weeks away, so with little regard for legal etiquette, he sent the jurist a letter requesting the matter be addressed "on an emergency basis"—and drew a sharp rebuke for his ex-parte communication.[44] When the hearing took place as scheduled, it was marked by bitter exchanges among the antagonists. A mystified Vitali, who came from Munich to make an appeal for the pictures, promised a dignified exhibition then turned around and flew back the same day. Twenty-four hours later, Judge Ott turned down the Foundation's plea. In a nine-page ruling, he noted that the only reason for which the late Judge Stefan had allowed the tour was renovations and future repairs of the building in Merion. He rejected the argument that increasing the endowment or defraying operating expenses justified an added venue. He also said that he was "not convinced that present time constraints would permit optimal care."[45] Richard Glanton was furious. The judge "abused his discretion," the Foundation president told the press, and his lawyers quickly filed an appeal in the Pennsylvania Superior Court.[46] Six days later, a three-judge panel handed down a stunning reversal that vacated the Orphans' Court decree. Oral arguments were heard via telephone conference call and the ruling was based on the panel members' belief that Judge Ott had deviated from Judge Stefan's analysis and relied upon a technical application of the trust agreement. Though it had Judge Ott's opinion, the Superior Court did not have the written record of the trial, and it issued only a two-page order. The judges said the Munich show could go on, but they also specified that the fee the Foundation received for the loan go into the fund earmarked for present and future renovations. It was a victory for Vitali who had been trying to land the exhibition for two-and-a-half years, and a partial victory for Glanton who, when first approached by the German director, thought a faster renovation schedule than was the case would preclude the added venue. Opening on June

23, the show drew a record 400,000 visitors. The publicly supported institution stayed open all night to accommodate the crowds just before the paintings were to be taken down and shipped back to America. Added together the viewers of the Barnes pictures at the seven stops on the world tour totaled an estimated five million people. The Foundation realized more than $17 million from fees and sales of memorabilia. It was an accomplishment in which Richard Glanton could rightly take considerable satisfaction. But the irony in the disparity between the acclaim he received abroad and the troubles he faced at home was not lost upon the Barnes president.

A settlement he had reached with the de Mazia Trust in January 1995 had been rejected in July by Orphans' Court. The agreement was meant to end three years of financially—and emotionally—draining litigation. It called for the de Mazia trustees to pay the Foundation $1.5 million within sixty days and $1.25 million over the next seven years to be used for the purpose of continuing classes based on Barnes's theories about the philosophy and appreciation of art. The language of the accord limited the application of the monies to "direct expenses" of the art education program, but the Foundation was specifically exempted from having to give an accounting of its stewardship to the Trust.[47] The two sides agreed that the Trust should be allowed to develop its own programs independent of the Foundation to advance Barnes's aesthetic ideas. They also said they would stay all litigation between them and, upon satisfaction of the conditions of the settlement, drop their respective lawsuits. Furthermore, the Trust promised not to oppose the Foundation's attempt to amend the Indenture, thus clearing the way for Glanton to seek judicial relief from restrictions on public gallery hours, admission fees, endowment investments, and social events on the premises without any well-financed opposition. Lawyers for the de Mazia trustees and counsel for the Foundation presented their arguments to Judge Ott in the April hearing at which Glanton first withdrew his request for adding Munich to the international tour of pictures. On July 10, the judge rejected the proposed alterations to the Trust that formed the basis of the settlement. He noted that the collector and his disciple would be "chagrined if not horrified" at the two parties' "desire to go their separate ways" and found "the need to preserve the sanctity of the donors' written intents more compelling then the immediate, but short-sighted benefits of approving the agreement" before him.[48] A year later, a Superior Court panel reversed Judge Ott once again. The justices said that while they "agreed in principle" with his view about the court's obligation to uphold donor intent wherever possible, they were convinced that the benefits of approving the proposed settlement were "preferable to forcing the parties to continue in what has obviously become a bad marriage."[49]

But the Superior Court did uphold Judge Ott's rulings on two of three other issues that Glanton sought to resolve differently than the jurist allowed in the early fall of 1995. The Foundation asked to raise its entrance fee from $1 to

$10, open gallery doors to the public at its discretion, and overturn Barnes's absolute ban on social functions in Merion. Another request, for the freedom to invest in less restrictive ways than purchasing the government and municipal bonds allowed in the Indenture, was non-controversial and was permitted the first day of the September hearing in Orphans' Court. After considering the other matters before him for a week, Judge Ott permitted the Barnes board to raise the price of admission to $5. He refused to lift the prohibition on events of a social nature even if the objective was fund-raising. In a pointed observation that permitting visitors six days a week "would transform the Foundation into a full-time museum, which goes far beyond the donor's intent," he also allowed one, but just one, extra day for public visitation. Glanton characterized the decision as "outrageous" and asserted that the judge "obviously has a problem with the stewardship of Lincoln University."[50] His appeal won reversal of only the continued ban on parties. But the decision was a cliffhanger. On October 10, as the board proceeded with plans for a gala re-opening of the renovated galleries, Glanton asked the Superior Court for an emergency hearing in order to "avoid the ugly public spectacle" that would ensue if Judge Ott held him in contempt of court and removed him as president as he had been "reliably informed" the judge said he would do if the celebration scheduled for November 11 took place.[51] Nine days later, the court rejected his petition and the Foundation's request that it be filed "under seal," that is, made unavailable to the public or the press. With no other alternative, Glanton then asked Judge Ott for a clarification of his earlier ruling. After a conference in his chambers, the judge gave a qualified approval for the festive dinner in a tented area on the gallery grounds. But while accepting the Foundation's argument that Barnes's stipulation against society events in Foundation buildings did not apply to outdoor arboretum spaces, he also decreed that the guests would not be allowed to set foot inside to see the re-hung collection. The Friends group, which had consistently opposed most attempts to deviate from the Indenture, expressed satisfaction. Glanton issued a press release calling "the effect of the judge's ruling . . . a slap in the face." There was no basis for it "except to punish and harm the Foundation," the president declared, and he said he would direct his lawyers "to file an application seeking Judge Ott's removal from the case."[52] He again appealed to the Superior Court on an emergency basis, and this time another three-judge panel issued a one-paragraph order overturning the ruling of Orphans' Court. Guests would be permitted to tour the gallery "for a reasonable period of time" so long as there was adequate security and no drinks or food were served as they looked at the pictures.[53]

Curiosity about the renovated building was intense. Most people thought it would be a sin to lose the character of the place. Architect Robert Venturi was one of them. Like Barnes himself and also Glanton, the superbly gifted team of Venturi and his wife and partner, Denise Scott Brown, were more honored outside of Philadelphia than in their hometown. The son of an immigrant fruit merchant, Venturi had attended the Episcopal Academy, next door to the Foundation, and remembers Laura Barnes talking to the students on Arbor Days, but he had never visited the collection until Glanton summoned him to discuss the renovation project. A theorist and a practitioner, the architect had studied at Princeton, taught both at Yale and in Paul Cret's old department at Penn, and through his articles and books, as well as his buildings, reintroduced history as a valid element within architectural theory. Venturi, Scott Brown & Associates had done highly acclaimed work around the world, including the Seattle Art Museum and the new Sainsbury Wing to the National Gallery in London. Former ambassador to Britain Walter Annenberg admired the addition and recommended Venturi to the Barnes president. "I was overwhelmed by the paintings in the beautifully-lit settings," the architect says of his first visit in July of 1992, "and I was completely sympathetic to the task at hand."[54] He approached the new commission with reverence.

The Foundation under Franklin Williams had previously engaged Cret's successor firm, H2L2, to carry out a conditions assessment of the gallery. Later, the Princeton-based consultants, Garrison/Lull, had been retained to review the existing environmental control systems and set forth conservation environment parameters. They concluded that most of the systems were at or beyond their expected useful life and were incapable of maintaining consistent temperature and humidity within the rooms housing the collection. Venturi, Scott Brown collaborated with H2L2 during the first phase of the project, which involved renovating portions of the administration building to provide temporary, climate-controlled storage rooms for the collection and the northern end of the services building to house new security-systems and guard-staff facilities. Phase two involved renovating the gallery itself, along with various site improvements, and, for all its difficulty, was pushed forward on a fast-track basis. "On the one hand, we had to make real intrusions to bring the building up to environmental, fire, safety, and accessibility standards," Venturi observed. "On the other hand, we were obligated to respect the Foundation's requirement that the gallery remain visually and perceptually the same."[55] He cleverly took advantage of cavities, including those created by slightly outward slanting walls in some of the rooms, to hide ductwork for a new heating, ventilation, and air-conditioning system. The configuration was a brilliant Cret innovation to allow the pictures on the walls to catch the light, and his successor's biggest challenge also concerned lighting.

To reduce long-term damage to the art, it was essential to control the natural light coming through the south-facing windows. During Barnes's lifetime, semi-opaque, flat roman shades had been installed, and Venturi replaced them with matching ones. In addition, he added roller-type blackout blinds that could be used to achieve complete darkness during non-viewing hours. In removing old and ugly exterior, single-glazed storm window sash units, the architects revealed, for the first time in half a century, the well-scaled muntin pattern and decorative cast-iron rope moldings of the original windows. The new, interior-mounted storm windows, which they matched to the original steel windows, contained neutral density glass of varying transmission levels to accord with the sensitivity to light of the work in each room. They had a laminated plastic interlayer to mitigate ultraviolet radiation. UV-filtering, insulating glass also was added to the skylights in the main stairwell and the second-floor loggia. The level of sunlight could be modulated by operable interior louvres, which the architects installed below them. "Most designers have said windows are not appropriate in museums and art galleries," Venturi noted, "but we love them because they say you are in a real place. The paintings at the Barnes were mostly created in studios with natural light from the north. It's a fact that we not only acknowledge and adore but tried to respect in the process of renovation." Nevertheless, the level of illumination in many of the rooms was often too low to accommodate late-twentieth century sensibilities. Improving the electrical lighting called for a solution that would maintain the overall ambiance within the room ensembles composed by the collector. After careful analysis, Venturi and his team rejected the introduction of contemporary spotlighting. "The light should be perceived as emitted from the paintings rather than flashed upon them," he said, "and besides, typical spotlights cast deep shadows under the frames."[56] He chose instead to modify the existing bronze, globe-type pendant fixtures. To supplement the downlight, components were added that beam light upward toward the white vaulted ceilings. The overall effect is appropriate for today's sensibilities but respectful of Cret's system. The idea was to maintain the original quality of the ambient light while subtly increasing it in every room in the gallery.

In the end, nothing much in the refurbished building looked new. Oak parquet flooring on the ground level, which had cracked in many places as a result of periodic re-sanding, was removed and replaced in the original patterns. On the second floor, the existing strip oak flooring was in far better shape and was restored by simple cleaning and re-waxing. The sand-finished plaster ceilings, which had been disrupted for installation of new mechanical systems, were repaired with no visible seam. Jute burlap from the same mill in Burma from which Barnes had purchased his wall coverings replaced the sun-faded originals. Using photographs made of the walls immediately after Barnes's death as a guide, the paintings, along with the iron hinges, locks, key, and other items, were re-hung within one-eighth inch of the last locations selected by the collector. Matisse's *The Joy of Life* went back in the stairwell, but visitors would be able to see it better because a glass smoke partition at the top of the main staircase that had obscured the best views from the loggia was taken down. The partition had been added in 1961 to meet an early iteration of government-mandated fire and life safety codes, and the Pennsylvania Department of Licenses and Inspections granted permission to remove it primarily because the architects added a sprinkler system to the gallery as part of a new fire protection system. A state-required fire stair was added to increase exiting capacity from the second floor by enclosing a portion of the existing porte-cochere. The partial enclosure also hid a wheelchair lift. With the addition of a passenger elevator in space created by displacing a basement storage area, an office off the gallery vestibule, and a small sky-lit room displaying decorative arts, the main Foundation building was accessible to the disabled for the first time. On the lower level, bathrooms were re-configured to accommodate wheelchairs. The architects also added an orientation room, coat check, art conservation studio, and staff office, and while Venturi, Scott Brown were not involved in the interior design of the lower-level gallery shop, the firm recommended its location.

Exterior renovations included re-pointing mortared joints and cleaning the major facades with water and localized poultices to remove copper staining. Portions of the limestone, which had eroded due to accumulations of atmospheric pollutants, were removed and replaced with patches of re-carved salvaged stone. The front steps, which had rotted from underneath, were replaced with new ones made of limestone from the quarry in France that had supplied the original rock—and completed in record time since the deterioration was discovered a little more than two months before the scheduled re-opening. New railings required by accessibility codes were made of wrought iron and subtly shaped in the style of Cret. The exterior doors were rebuilt using panels, ironwork, and pull handles from the originals. Limestone cut away from the porte-cochere side of the gallery in making the new entrance provided wainscoting for a guardhouse constructed near the main entrance to the property to accommodate visitor check-in. The front gates themselves were refurbished and relocated ten-feet further from Latch's Lane to allow pull-off space for vehicles. Two previously decorative post lights flanking the steps were electrified, and lighting was added on the sides of the new asphalt driveway along with uplights to illuminate the building facades. The total cost of the project was $12 million, which was $2 million above the revised estimate Glanton had previously presented to the court. Venturi said he always considers it a compliment "when people ask where has all the money gone."[57]

Since the $5 million difference between tour revenues and renovation expenses was required by the court to be set aside in a special fund for future repairs and refurbishing of the gallery, the reopening celebration at the Barnes on November 11, 1995 was intended as a fund-raiser to support an educational program for school children. A steering committee of socially prominent, Philadelphia area women, who had aided many good causes over the years, was formed to assist with the planning for the reception and dinner. It was chaired by Sun Oil heiress and Lincoln University trustee Ethel Pew Benson Wister. The honorary committee was studded with people associated with the seven tour venues, including ambassadors and museum trustees and directors, as well as with old and new art collectors. Invitations for the gala sought patron contributions at the $1,000 level; others paid $500 each for the privilege of taking part in the festivities. Preparations went forward amid the uncertainty of whether the court would allow the big party to take place at all. The Glantons dined with the Kauffmans and others who were helping with fund-raising at the Wister estate as the Barnes president and his lawyer considered their appeal of Judge Ott's September ruling reasserting the collector's ban on society functions in Merion.

When the Superior Court reversal came three days before the gala, the planners let out their collective breath. A tour for the news media was held on Friday, the 10th, while anxious neighbors, concerned about traffic congestion, took photographs of the constant stream of taxis and cars. Students and other members of the Barnes Watch walked up and down the street with picket signs protesting the party as a violation of the Indenture. A cluster were still there in the cold and rain on Saturday when 575 guests in black-tie toured what one visitor called the "spanking old" gallery then repaired to white canvas tents for cocktails and an elegant dinner featuring a concoction of chicken and lobster followed by grilled lamb chops.[58] As the chestnut tart was being served, fierce winds blew in the glass-paneled doors of the main tent and caused many to think that Albert Barnes was trying to make himself heard above the chatter. Although the evening's program, which had begun with choral renderings of the national anthems of the United States, France, Japan, and Canada, was far from over, Glanton announced that for safety's sake, everyone should go home. Traffic backed up the length of Latch's Lane had caused delays of up to a half-hour as guests tried to reach the Foundation; when they scurried to leave, the wait was three times longer since valet parking stubs on their car windshields had vanished in the storm.

On Sunday morning sun broke through the clouds, and the ribbon-cutting re-dedication of the gallery, with speeches from the Barnes president and venue hosts, took place without incident. Recent alumni and current students along with neighbors toured the refurbished space. Meridian Bank, which had contributed more than $50,000 in cash and services to the Foundation, hosted a tour for 300 customers, community and political leaders, and the heads of regional non-profit institutions the next evening. Tuesday was given over to an open house for area school students, local college and university art students, and members of the general public. Regular gallery admission, now three-and-a-half days a week, began on Thursday. Visitors found new descriptive material on laminated cards in every room, which told them the names of the artists and the titles of the pictures hanging on each wall. Small numbered plaques under some paintings were related to digital audio guides that allowed users to select commentaries with a Barnesian flavor for eighty paintings, listen to explanations of the wall arrangements, or tour the highlights of the collection. Descending to the lower level, where coats and bags were still to be checked, old-timers were confronted with the most visible symbols of the changing character of the Foundation. Here in the small shop, they found the Knopf catalogue, a collection of essays entitled *The Barnes Bond Connection*, which had been recently published by Lincoln, posters and other memorabilia developed for the tour, and—on a shelf at the back—books by the collector and de Mazia. In the new orientation room, wall texts, photographs, computer stations playing the Corbis CD-ROM, and a short film on videotape introduced viewers to the collector, his approach to art, and his collection. The shift was subtle but unmistakable. Richard Glanton viewed the Foundation he had raised the funds to renovate as a museum. Furthermore, he intended it to be a tourist destination.

But what about the art education program? The Barnes president told a Canadian reporter: "There's no curriculum, there's no degree, there's no course syllabus. It doesn't qualify you to do anything. It has no credit. There are no requirements. There are no standards."[59] He was wrong about there not being a set of courses—and the principal texts were on the walls. The collector believed study at his Foundation would enable quite ordinary people to live more fully, more richly, more deeply. He hoped they could develop discriminating insight there. By learning to see, he felt they would become more alive to their environment. But by his own admission, Glanton had only skimmed Barnes's and de Mazia's books. He was a cultivated lawyer, but not an educator. Education was Niara Sudarkasa's trade. At the reopening celebration, she had said that with the renovations done, the Foundation could "turn its attention to its primary mission, which is to continue and expand the education program as envisioned by Dr. Barnes."[60] She wrote in *The Barnes Bond Connection* of one day establishing an art history program at Lincoln that would focus on the "study of the impact and influence of African art on the art of Europe and beyond." She expressed hope of collaborating with the Foundation "by making use of its extraordinary collection of African art" through "photographs and computer-generated images."[61] Meanwhile, the Merion classes, built around encounters with original works, had languished under the new regime. Enrollment had fallen off sharply, from more than three hundred students in 1988 to less than a hundred seven years later. During the tour, the two remaining veteran teachers of the advanced courses, artists Barton Church and Harry Sefarbi, and the first-year instructor, the ubiquitous Nicolas King, named acting director of the art department by Glanton, had made do with selections from the stay-at-home paintings and with transparencies of the traveling masterpieces. They gave their lectures in the administration building, a nearby private home, and the Philadelphia Museum of Art. The de Mazia Trust had offered to finance the transportation of Lincoln students to the Barnes classes, but there was no response. It was not at all clear that a significant number of the young people enrolled in the Chester County university would be any more eager than their predecessors—at Lincoln or Penn—to pursue the serious study of aesthetics and appreciation of art in Merion. They had grown up in a world of virtual reality, and the challenge would be to entice them to risk the distinctive experience of confronting head-on an actual artwork when they had so little basis for anticipating its transforming power.

17

Neighbors

Signs carried by Barnes Watch protesters standing outside in the rain during the Foundation's re-opening celebration were largely ignored by the partygoers who scurried through the entrance portico. Moving quickly past its terra cotta-and-tile adaptations of African sculpture, they missed the irony implicit in the proximity of the collector's tribute to the creativity of black people and the placards that proclaimed "Lincoln University Betrayed Dr. Barnes's Trust."[1] But it was not the effect on the education program of the nearly three-year closing for renovations that concerned the Foundation's Latch's Lane neighbors. On the street lined with luxuriant maple and chestnut trees, residents were worried about what an anticipated influx of "massive numbers of strangers" would do to the ambience of the neighborhood.[2] Taken aback by Judge Ott's September ruling that the Foundation could be open an additional day a week, they were horrified by Glanton's pursuit of permission for a six-day-a-week option and his stated goal of 120,000 visitors a year. Latch's Lane was zoned residential. The zoning code, adopted after the collector had established his school, allowed for three private educational exceptions. Adjacent to the Foundation on the north was a house owned by St. Joseph's University and used as a dormitory for about thirty undergraduates. On the south, the Episcopal Academy brought 1,030 kindergarten through twelfth-grade students to its thirty-five-acre campus each weekday and created a heavy, albeit brief, flow of traffic in the early morning and at mid-afternoon. Property owners were used to the cars and school buses, but the thought of a fleet of diesel-powered, interstate buses idling engines outside the Barnes moved them to bring their concerns about pollution, noise, and safety to township officials. For most, their homes—a row of stately stone dwellings and a cluster of smaller stucco houses at the north end of the street—were their biggest asset. Directly across the street from the Barnes was a rambling, sixteen-room residence built five years before the Foundation itself on property the collector had owned from 1913 to 1916. Walter Herman, a retired cardiologist, and his wife, Nancy, an artist, had purchased it in 1972 from

Sidney Frick, then the president of the Barnes, who had grown up there. The Hermans' neighbors were lawyers and business people. Many like Walter were Jewish—the grandchildren of immigrants from Eastern Europe. They had worked hard for what they had achieved, and they felt threatened, psychologically and financially, by Glanton's plans, trumpeted almost daily in the press, to transform the Foundation into a major tourist attraction.

On a number of occasions, beginning more than a year before the completion of gallery renovations, Lower Merion commissioner James S. Ettelson and the then Episcopal headmaster James L. Crawford, Jr. warned the Barnes president that a "plan for traffic control and parking to protect the tranquility of the neighborhood" was essential.[3] They took him at his word that one would be in place, along with a reservation system to control the flow of visitors. Upon discovering that neither was, they felt let down and angry. Township officials held several tense meetings with Glanton and his staff immediately before the re-opening events. When the Lower Merion police superintendent expressed concern about crowd control and security arrangements, Glanton reluctantly agreed to hire private uniformed security officers to assist with traffic on Latch's Lane and patrol sidewalks and the Episcopal parking area, on short-term loan to the Foundation, on the night of the gala. But what to do afterwards was an even greater bone of contention. The Merion Civic Association asked the Foundation to consider a shuttle service to take visitors from a permanent off-site parking facility to the gallery. But Glanton's first priority was building a parking lot on the grounds of the arboretum. He saw its presence as central to eventually achieving his revenue goal of $120,000 a month. The process of obtaining approval to proceed with construction, however, was complicated and lengthy. It could take six to nine months under any circumstances, and opposition from adjacent landowners could extend the time frame to a year or more. Glanton wanted the requirement for a zoning hearing waived, but township officials insisted they had no authority to grant special exceptions. He grew impatient at what he described as "a maze of red tape." While the Foundation had been one of several, local nonprofit institutions that had agreed to make voluntary contributions to the Lower Merion treasury, the president now said it would withhold payment unless the township was more cooperative. "They are jerking us around," he told the press. "And I'm not going to pay these bureaucrats to jerk me around."[4] The commissioners, however, were doing what they had been elected to do—listening to neighbors who feared spaces for some fifty cars would do little to address the issue of traffic congestion on Latch's Lane. From an aesthetic perspective, moreover, Nancy Herman was saddened by the probability of losing a "lovely lavender path created long ago by Laura Barnes, a large annual garden filled with dahlias and cosmos, and a patch of rare woody ornamentals."[5] Glanton labeled the opposition "thinly disguised racism."[6]

But he soon moved to find some ground for accommodation. Two weeks after the re-opening ceremonies, the Foundation announced preliminary plans to develop a computerized reservation system and said it would look for a place for off-site parking. From Glanton's point of view, however, the lot on Barnes property was non-negotiable. For their part, the neighbors were convinced by belching buses and frequent gridlock that their formerly, if deceptively, bucolic street was on its way to becoming a commercial district. They grew weary of giving directions and objected to motorists pulling into their driveways and, in several instances, visitors picnicking on their lawns. On December 13, 1995, township officials responded to residents' complaints by sending the Foundation a letter that accused the Barnes of transforming its primary use from a private educational institution, which was permissible under the zoning code, to a museum, which was a forbidden use. They ordered the trustees to reduce visiting hours to two-and-a-half days a week and limit the number of weekly visitors to 500. Failure to comply would invite substantial fines. Although he had lost an ally in Harrisburg when Attorney General Ernie Preate was sentenced to fourteen months in prison for mail fraud related to campaign contributions, Glanton said he would appeal the Lower Merion order to Superior Court. Three days after Christmas, a Foundation attorney wrote to the township that its action had been "discriminatory and unjust."[7] The gallery remained open the three-and-a-half days a week allowed by Judge Ott in September, and on January 18, 1996, the Foundation filed a federal civil rights complaint accusing Lower Merion Township, its fourteen commissioners, and seventeen Merion residents of racial discrimination.

The complaint's basis in law was the Ku Klux Klan Act. When the first draft of the document, drawn up for Glanton by lawyers at Philadelphia's Blank Rome Comisky & McCauley after Kauffman refused to take the case, named only the township, the Barnes president ordered it re-drawn to name persons. Filed in federal court, the lawsuit charged that in "concert and conspiracy with the neighbors, the township and the individual commissioners have in arbitrary, capricious and discriminatory fashion imposed parking, police, fire and zoning requirements, rules and regulations in such a way as to injure the Barnes and interfere with [the Foundation's] beneficial use and enjoyment of its property." It said the township did not enforce or even attempt to enforce such strictures against other institutional neighbors. The complaint alleged that the "conspirators had agreed that the township would concoct non-existent zoning violations to harass the Barnes." It asserted that the township had "coerced" the Foundation "into hiring off-duty Lower Merion police officers to work at the re-opening events for a charge in excess of $10,000." Furthermore, the suit cited remarks made at a November 15, 1995 commissioners' meeting as "racially and religiously biased." It pointed to a comment by State Representative Lita I. Cohen that the Barnes was interfering with the religious practices of Orthodox Jews "by opening its doors" on Saturdays when Jewish families walking down Latch's Lane to synagogue might be endangered by drivers looking for the gallery. The complaint also quoted Foundation neighbor Robert Marmon's reference to "Mr. Glanton and his people" as "carpetbaggers" and another neighbor's observation that he would "prefer living across the street" from a mall. It stated that the township had refused to issue the maximum occupancy certificate required under the fire codes and objected to citations issued to the Foundation for cutting down dead trees. The trustees claimed a plan was afoot that "would seriously impair the ability of the Barnes to raise funds needed to carry out the purposes of the Indenture."[8]

The Barnes lawsuit, which sought compensatory and punitive damages, came as a shock and a surprise to the defendants. The commissioners quickly challenged the accuracy of the allegations. They are "certainly not true," James Ettelson told the *New York Times*. "I hope this isn't an attempt by the Barnes Foundation to willfully impede the zoning process of Lower Merion Township."[9] A tenacious litigator, attorney Paul Rosen, was engaged to represent the township officials as individuals, while Lower Merion itself was represented by the equally tough Paul Diamond as outside counsel. The neighbors, who found their names listed in the random order they had signed an agreement to hire a lawyer just weeks earlier, considered themselves an appendage to the Foundation's complaint about the action and inaction of local government and sought counsel from various sources. Called by the press seeking comments about the suit the day before a process server delivered individually addressed copies to their door, Walter and Nancy Herman immediately contacted a noted antitrust litigator, a friend and neighbor whose property abutted their backyard, and were told that they were faced with a so-called "Slapp" (strategic lawsuit against public participation) suit.[10] Attorney David Weinstein tried to assure them that the complaint would almost surely be dismissed, and he agreed to represent the Hermans and several other neighbors. Eventually, Weinstein and Edward Dennis, a prominent Philadelphia lawyer who is an African American and had formerly been the United States attorney in Philadelphia and the assistant attorney general of the United States in charge of the criminal division, acted as lead attorneys for all the Latch's Lane residents sued by the Foundation. Most had homeowners' umbrella policies that paid for their defense against civil actions. Aghast at being branded racists, they were also "mad as hell" and determined to clear their names.[11]

The commissioners reacted with as much anger and steel as the neighbors. Rosen filed suit against Glanton on March 4, 1996 for defaming his clients in the news media. He called the Barnes president a "power-hungry" lawyer who "has engaged in a historical pattern of intimidation and verbal brutality . . . directed at all who stand in the way of his unquenchable desire for fame, fortune, and even sexual favors." He accused him of playing the "race card" against anyone who challenged his authority or goals, and he faulted the other trustees for permitting, approving, and encouraging a "'smear campaign.'"[12] It was tough language, and left many observers wondering how a squabble over visitor volume, operating hours, and parking had escalated into such a nasty fight. Not least among those troubled by the rapid turn of events was one of the Barnes board members.

The four trustees originally named in the commissioners' action included Frank, Jackson, and Sudarkasa in addition to the Barnes president. Cuyler Walker had gone off the board in December of 1995 when his term expired, and Glanton eventually brought on Lincoln alumnus Randolph Kinder, a Connecticut insurance executive, in his place. Neither Walker nor Kinder were serving as trustees at the time of the filing of the civil rights complaint. But seeking the consent of the three remaining trustees to his intended lawsuit, Glanton had faxed a draft of the document, accompanied by a letter dated January 16, 1996, to Frank, Jackson, and Sudarkasa and asked for their comments. He also sent them a copy of a resolution authorizing the legal action and requested they sign and return it to him within two days. Shocked by what he read, the Mellon senior vice president telephoned Glanton to say that he had serious concerns about the accuracy of the charges and thought it inappropriate to proceed with the action. He then reiterated his position in a letter. Frank recalled the Barnes president telling him he had three signatures without his, though, in the end, Glanton had only his own and Sudarkasa's, and he never acted on the banker's suggestion to call a special meeting of the board to discuss the situation. It was Frank's impression that Glanton saw the filing of the complaint as a way to accelerate the settlement of the parking issue. He later testified that at a board meeting on January 29, 1996, when the president gave a post-facto report on the civil rights litigation and mentioned his intent was "to bring intense pressure" on Lower Merion Township, he asked him: "Could this have been done without reference to race?" Frank said both Glanton and Sudarkasa expressed the opinion that the harassment of the Foundation was "racially motivated." The banker said he then told them they should understand that he had "no personal knowledge about the motivation of the neighbors and the [commissioners]."[13] He also voiced his concern about the cost of a protracted lawsuit, and Glanton told him the lawyers' fees would come from the endowment. Frank was worried. He saw no attempt to impose financial discipline nor, he later recalled, any "strategic direction."[14]

The vehement opposition of the Barnes neighbors to a full-fledged museum may have made the Barnes president belatedly reticent to sketch clearly the path down which he seemed headed in a hurry. As the *Philadelphia Inquirer* pointed out, however, "key to resolving the Barnes's future," was "agreeing upon its identity." The newspaper also was correct when it noted that by taking its dispute with the township "out of the local system, where it belonged," the Foundation had "poisoned the conversation." As one astute observer said, Impressionist paintings may "teach us to look at a bottle, or a mountain, or a face in a new and interesting way," but there was now little chance that life would "imitate art."[15] In fact, the sulfurous battle continued on parallel tracks in federal and county courts and before the Lower Merion zoning board for five more years. Although Glanton had originally threatened to appeal the township's order to cut back public hours to the Superior Court of Pennsylvania, the local zoning board was where he had to make his case. In zoning matters, it was the court of record and had awesome powers.

Hearings on the Foundation's appeal began in February of 1996. Both sides were soon brandishing photographic images in attempts to assign blame for traffic congestion. The township showed neighbors' videotapes of the November re-opening and subsequent days when the comings and goings of large numbers of visitors disturbed the peace of Latch's Lane residents. Barnes officials presented a series of snapshots of long lines of cars they said were generated by events at Episcopal, which neighbors took in stride. Glanton publicly declared that "if the parking lot is granted, and the township agrees to discontinue its unfair treatment, all legal disputes and controversy could be amicably resolved."[16] It was late March, however, before he reactivated his request to start construction. Meanwhile, the hearings continued on the issue of use. The Foundation had to persuade zoning officials that it continued to be predominately an educational institution, in accordance with zoning regulations, or accept the township's view that it was a museum and appeal for an exception to the code, which it could not count on securing without, at the very least, stringent conditions. Lower Merion officials sought to show that the pre-renovation character of the property as a school, with an accessory gallery, had been turned inside out. Glanton testified rather archly that he did not intend to de-emphasize art appreciation classes, but he admitted that enrollment had dropped from 157 students prior to closing the gallery to just ninety-six—a period during which tuition had doubled, from $100 to $ 200. He reiterated his desire to make Barnes courses part of the art history program at a recognized university without giving evidence of even exploratory conversation. He also acknowledged that groups of art lovers were paying $500 or more to hear brief lectures at the Foundation and that they, along with school groups, were welcomed on days other than those set aside for public visitations. Final arguments on the question of whether or not the Barnes had changed its principal function were set for mid-June.

Meanwhile, attorneys for the Lower Merion commissioners filed a motion to dismiss the civil rights discrimination suit on the grounds that the case was a local zoning matter. The Foundation characterized the defamation suit as retaliation and sought to move it from state to federal court. Lawyers for the neighbors filed a motion to dismiss all seventeen Latch's Lane residents from the federal complaint. The Foundation opposed it just as the township opposed the Barnes's effort to change venues. Glanton wrote to the *Inquirer* that Lower Merion's treatment of the Foundation together with the signs displayed the night of November 11 were "reminiscent of the not-so-distant South."[17] A letter from student leader Nick Tinari made clear that the signs had been carried by alumni protesting the "trustees' betrayal" of the collector's bequest and "the legal system that allowed the changes" in the Indenture. Speaking for the neighbors, attorney David Weinstein responded that no citizen should be subject to charges of racism "merely for asking his or her local government to enforce the law."[18] Oral arguments on the federal suit took place before U. S. District Judge Anita B. Brody in early May. Less than a month later, on June 3, 1996, she threw out the Foundation's claims against the neighbors. Brody ruled that the First Amendment gave them the right to protest against traffic problems they blamed on the Barnes and oppose a parking lot, along with the expansion of visiting hours, regardless of their motives. "It does not matter what factors rule the citizen's desire to petition government," she wrote.[19] A deeply disappointed Glanton, reaching once again for an analogy from his youth, said the judge's First Amendment analysis "sounded like the same arguments that were used to justify racism in the South."[20] Brody's seventeen-page opinion did not, however, prevent the Foundation from proceeding with its suit against the township and the commissioners. The claims could go forward, she said, because the Barnes trustees had provided "enough of a factual basis to survive . . . the motions to dismiss."[21] Nevertheless, with the neighbors out of the case, it was going to be exceedingly difficult to prove conspiracy on the part of the commissioners.

For the moment, though, Glanton was preoccupied with another legal matter. Barnes attorney Bruce Kauffman asked the Superior Court to clarify whether the Foundation could remain open in July and August. Glanton wanted to read Judge Ott's ruling on a three-and-a-half day a week public-visitation schedule, which the Foundation had appealed as too restrictive, as at least authorizing three-and-a-half days year round. At the end of May, a Cézanne retrospective opened at the Philadelphia Museum of Art. The exhibition was to run until mid-September, and Philadelphia was its only American venue. City tourism boosters knew the economic value of a blockbuster, in part, as the result of the Barnes show at the PMA the year before, and they, along with museum officials, were promoting group package tours of both the 200-work traveling show and the permanent exhibition of sixty-nine Cézannes in Merion. Documenting worsening traffic on Latch's Lane, neighbors wrote to Pennsylvania Deputy Attorney General Lawrence Barth asking him to enforce their reading of the Ott decision. Since the judge had said that all other aspects of the Indenture would remain unchanged except for the additional day he added to the gallery schedule for public viewing, they believed his decree upheld the collector's intent to keep the doors closed during the hottest months of the year. But on July 2, the Superior Court issued an order suspending the seventy-four-year-old prohibition on summer hours. It said that pending its decision on Ott's denial of the Foundation's request to admit visitors six days a week, twelve months a year, the gallery could remain open in July and August "notwithstanding any contrary language" in the Indenture.[22] Township officials viewed the stopgap measure as lending support to their claim that the Foundation had become a museum.

They had taken Glanton on in federal court two weeks earlier by filing a countersuit against the Foundation in response to its January lawsuit accusing them of conspiring with Latch's Lane residents to shut down the Barnes gallery. Based on the deposition of Barnes trustee Charles Frank,[23] the countersuit claimed that Glanton knew his allegations of racism were false—and that he had filed a civil rights complaint merely to intimidate the township, its commissioners, and the neighbors and obtain speedy approval of a parking lot without going through the normal procedures required of all property owners in Lower Merion. The process was inching forward, but involved delays created by the necessity for a series of public hearings before the zoning board in addition to the hearings on land use. The Foundation had hoped to reach an agreement with St. Joseph's University to route Barnes traffic off bustling City Line Avenue via their shared private byway, Lapsley Lane, so that its impact on Latch's Lane was minimal. But the university was concerned about the safety of students walking down the short, curving street, and the accord the Foundation finally came to with its neighbor called for traffic to enter the Barnes property from Latch's Lane, for buses to unload passengers within the premises, and for both cars and buses to turn left onto Lapsley and then right onto Latch's to exit the area. A planted, landscape buffer was to be provided and maintained between the parking lot and the adjacent street. Some neighbors expressed disappointment with the new plan, but by the third hearing, Foundation representatives offered to have a shuttle service from an off-site parking area in place by January of 1997. Township solicitor Gilbert H. High, Jr. predicted publicly that Lower Merion would give the Barnes permission to build its lot. As summer visitors lined up to visit the gallery, moreover, Glanton extended an olive branch.

"There is not going to be any more name calling," he told a local newspaper. "I think there is a way for us to peacefully co-exist."[24] His lawyers telephoned the attorneys for the neighbors and the township, seeking to open discussion of a possible settlement among all parties. Although the residents of Latch's Lane had been dismissed from the case, a motion seeking reconsideration of a request for final judgment, which had been made by the defendants but not acted upon by Judge Brody in her initial order, was pending before the court. The neighbors' objective was to preclude the Foundation from ever reinserting them into its complaint—a lingering possibility that continued to worry the Latch's Lane families, especially after the judge denied their request.[25] Since the commissioners were heading toward a trial in federal court, they, as well as the neighbors, had reasons to want to resolve their differences with Glanton and his fellow board members. But from the point of view of both the neighbors and the commissioners, reconciliation required a public retraction of the charge that they had acted in a discriminatory manner. Above time and treasure, they valued their good names. Nancy and Walter Herman were prepared to wait as long as it would take for an apology. They had read in the papers about another suit against the Barnes and its president, and they wondered: On how many fronts can Glanton continue to fight?

The legal imbroglio enmeshing him had become further complicated in July when the city of Rome and three additional plaintiffs sued the Foundation's trustees for breach of contract and fraudulent misrepresentation. The action, filed in Federal District Court for the Eastern District of Pennsylvania, contended that Glanton had promised orally and in writing to send the traveling exhibition from the Barnes Collection to the Museo Capitolino in Rome, subject to Orphans' Court approval, but instead made arrangements for its final stop to be at the Haus der Kunst in Munich. Joining the city of Rome in the suit were Muse, an Italian business promoting artistic and cultural affairs, Antonio Guizzetti, the Washington-based consultant who handled negotiations, and Marsilio Editore, an Italian publisher planning a catalogue. The plaintiffs said Rome had agreed to pay $3 million for the exhibition as opposed to the $2.25 million paid by the German museum. They also accused Glanton of using his position as president of the Barnes to gain business for his law firm during the more than two years of discussion. Glanton called the suit a "form of legal terrorism."[26] He said there had been no formal agreement and told a *New York Times* reporter that he had been concerned about security at the Museo Capitolino, Guizzetti's role in the deal, and the form of payment—$1.5 million cash and the rest through a line of credit, whereas the Haus der Kunst had been willing to put cash up front.[27] When the *Philadelphia Inquirer* had broken the story about the Italians' discontent the previous fall, the Barnes president accused the newspaper of wanting "to damage the reputation of a black person."[28] Now a new Foundation attorney, fiercely idealistic, solo litigator Robert J. Sugarman,[29] asked that the Rome complaint be dismissed on the grounds that no contract had been signed and, in any event, the city had not authorized the lawsuit. In early September, a federal judge denied his petition.

While Sugarman and his client were awaiting the decision, Lower Merion solicitor High once again asked the Foundation to apply for a variance to change its use from a school to a museum. When Glanton did not respond to his letter, the township issued a new notice of zoning violation. It instructed the Barnes both to return the use of its gallery to the original, ancillary function as a laboratory for students studying art appreciation and keep it closed to visitors in July and August.[30] Failure to abide by the second cease-and-desist order could cost the Foundation up to $500 a day in fines, and at the last possible moment to do so, Barnes attorneys appealed to the zoning board—an action triggering another round of land use hearings. But two days earlier, Glanton had had a glimpse of the light at the end of the tunnel. On September 3, 1996, the dispute over the parking lot was settled when Lower Merion zoning officials approved the Barnes's compromise plan. Although acknowledging the neighbors' concerns about the adverse effects of increased public access to the collection, they ruled that "if there is to be any significant public access," the public interest would be "enhanced rather than injured" by the proposal before them.[31] "This is a first step toward a fair resolution," Glanton said.[32] But it was not a big enough stride to bring him to the peace table. Acrimony remained in the air even as legal fees on both sides were mounting.

Glanton won relief on one front on September 8 when the Superior Court decided to let the Foundation and the de Mazia Trust go their separate ways. The de Mazia trustees' agreement to stop opposing changes at the Barnes meant he could re-deploy some resources. But the financial ones were not likely to grow as fast as Glanton and his fellow trustees had hoped. On September 12, the same Superior Court upheld Judge Ott's decision permitting public access three-and-a-half days a week, but not six, and capping the entrance fee at $5. At the same time, it reversed a third part of his ruling that would have maintained the collector's ban on "receptions, tea parties, dinners, banquets, dances, [and] musicals" in the gallery on the condition that any such events have as their "sole purpose" the raising of funds for the Foundation.[33] Within two weeks, the Barnes doors were open to patrons of the Pennsylvania Ballet. Invitations to sip wine and tour the gallery as a prelude to the ballet's opening-night gala had been issued in the spring. The ballet's corporate benefactors, such as Comcast and Independence Blue Cross, were entitled to bring ten guests for their $5,000 donations and individual benefactors contributed $500 to enjoy the evening in Merion in addition to attending the first performance of the season in mid-October. In answer to a reporter's question, Glanton explained that the ballet trustee who had arranged the event was a supporter of the Foundation. "The way the world works is that one hand washes the other," he said. "She helped us. Now we're helping her."[34]

As he gave a speech to guests inside the gallery, Barnes alumni stood outside again with protest signs. The neighbors weren't thrilled by the large party either. But unaware of a provision of the Indenture that required the Foundation to pay all legal expenses of any Pennsylvania resident who might legitimately suspect that prohibited "society functions" were being held in the gallery and went to court to try to prove his or her claim, Bob Marmon wrote a letter himself asking Judge Ott to find the Barnes trustees in contempt of Orphans' Court. Although Ott ruled that Marmon had no standing, he ordered Assistant Attorney General Barth to investigate his allegations. A year later, Barth filed a report in which he said the reception for ballet patrons "clearly violated" the wishes of the collector and recent court rulings.[35] He stopped short of concluding that the reception or, indeed, gallery visits by groups such as Saks Fifth Avenue employees or members of the New Covenant Church on days when the Foundation was closed to the public added up to contempt. But after hearings, Ott took a different view. He wrote that "the group admissions policy now in place brings to mind the 'hall for rent' concept . . . already rejected" by both Orphans' Court and the Superior Court. He refused to buy the idea that a high priced lecture to any group that could afford it was honoring the collector's intention, saying it "flies in the face of Dr. Barnes's expressions that the purpose of his gift was 'democratic' and 'without special privilege.'" The Orphans' Court judge ordered the Foundation trustees to stop conducting group tours on class days "except for groups consisting of 'students and instructors of institutions which conduct courses in art and art appreciation.'"[36] He also told them to develop a plan for fund raising and adopt it after obtaining approval of the Office of the Attorney General.

The Superior Court's earlier affirmation of Ott's decision that the Barnes could be open an additional day a week beyond the two-and-a-half days allowed in the Indenture did not alter the contention of Lower Merion officials that the Foundation was operating in violation of the zoning code and must request and receive a special exception permit from the township. Zoning hearings on land use were held in October, and despite the fact that Glanton had approval to build a parking lot on a portion of the arboretum and the neighbors had a pledge from the Barnes to keep interstate tour buses off Latch's Lane, the long knives came out again. A new contingent of about twenty neighbors from the condominium at the end of the street showed up to voice their concerns. Videotapes were produced of people leaving the gallery who said they had enjoyed a private visit on a day when it was supposed to be closed except for classes. A Barnes employee responded that they had received a lecture on the collector's aesthetic theories. Lawyers for both sides agreed that the case probably hinged on attendance figures. Neighbors counting heads testified that on some days the previous summer, the number of visitors was more than 1,000. A land planner, appearing as an expert witness for the township, said average daily attendance had climbed from just under 200 in 1985 to over 400 in 1996, while the hours students spent in the gallery fell by about half.

Another number of concern was the amount being spent on lawyers' fees. Lower Merion's costs, which were offset to some extent by insurers, approached $450,000 by the fall of 1996, even though Paul Rosen had agreed to work, in part, on contingency. The Foundation's legal bills were coming out of its dwindling endowment. More than $9 million dollars in 1990, it had dropped to just under $5 million five years later. Attorneys' fees had more than doubled from 1995 to 1996, from nearly $360,000 to more than $830,000. The pressure exerted by other trustees upon Glanton to stop the drain may have been reflected in a letter he wrote to the Lower Merion Board of Commissioners in late October suggesting a summit meeting on outstanding issues. Township solicitor Gil High responded that the best way to end what Glanton called "this unpleasantness"[37] was for the Foundation to drop its lawsuit charging the township and its commissioners with racial conspiracy. The Barnes president's habit of sending copies of his letters to the press annoyed township officials, and when Glanton wrote to High in November that he was prepared to recommend to the Foundation board "that the Barnes discontinue the litigation against the township if the township will discontinue the litigation against me and the other trustees," Lower Merion officials interpreted it as grandstanding.[38] The township solicitor suggested it would be better to conduct private business through lawyers, and Rosen sought to make his clients position clear in a letter to Sugarman: the commissioners would not be willing to settle the defamation case "without a public apology and payment of damages."[39]

The aura of mistrust was intensified by several recent motions the Foundation had made in federal court to amend its civil rights complaint. The township objected to its attempt to add Glanton as an individual plaintiff, who would then become eligible for damages if he won the lawsuit, and to its attempt to reinsert the neighbors, who had been previously dismissed, back into the case. The Barnes president replied that Rosen's contingency fee was the major obstacle to an out-of-court settlement. In early December, Judge Brody offered to set up settlement negotiations under Senior U. S. District Judge Louis C. Bechtle, an experienced arbitrator. Lower Merion and its commissioners agreed; the Foundation declined, but indicated its willingness to participate if the chief U. S. District judge, rather than the trial judge, selected the mediator. Brody took her offer off the table. The tumultuous year ended with a ruling by the zoning board that the Barnes Foundation had broken township zoning laws by turning itself from a school into a museum.[40] The long-awaited decision upheld the notice that Lower Merion had issued in the wake of the Foundation's re-opening. The Barnes had been told to limit public visitation to 500 people over two and a half days a week, and it could now face hundreds of dollars in daily fines if it did not sharply reduce admissions to the gallery. But the zoning board also stressed that the Foundation could apply for a special exception for accessory use of its property, a procedure that would allow zoning officials to set conditions under which the gallery could operate without violating residential zoning laws. "Negotiate the numbers," an *Inquirer* editorial pleaded, but the Barnes trustees decided to press on with litigation.[41] In January 1997, Glanton appealed the zoning board ruling to the Montgomery County Court of Common Pleas. Within the hour, the township filed a civil complaint asking that the Foundation be forced to abide by the zoning board's restrictions.

The chances of compromise between the warring parties appeared as bleak as the winter weather. But the working of the judicial process lifted the Hermans' spirits. In early February, Judge Brody denied the Foundation's request to add Glanton as a plaintiff to its civil rights complaint and to reinstate the neighbors as defendants. Furthermore, she refused its plea to dismiss Lower Merion's counterclaim that Glanton fabricated charges of racism and used charitable funds to file a baseless lawsuit. The Foundation also suffered a crucial setback on another front. U.S. Magistrate Judge Diane M. Welsh narrowed its ability to explore racial problems in Lower Merion Township by ruling that only racial issues directly involving the gallery were relevant. Sugarman appealed; he also protested efforts of township lawyers to probe the Barnes's financial records and described their filing of a memorandum in federal court, which included the sworn deposition of the Barnes business manager that Glanton, who took no salary from the Barnes, charged his parking space in his law firm's office building to the Foundation, as "pure retaliation."[42] Glanton, however, remained calm and gracious when he met with the Foundation's Latch's Lane neighbors in early April for the first time since the filing of his civil right complaint. He outlined his plans for traffic control and listened to their suggestions. The next day the Lower Merion Planning Commission gave its preliminary approval for his parking lot plan, which had already won the support of the zoning hearing board, after he agreed to all its conditions, including a ban on tour buses on Latch's Lane and a shuttle-bus system to bring visitors from an off-site parking location. Within the week, members of the Board of Commissioners voted unanimously to send the plan on to the next stage in the drawn-out process that a cascade of lawsuits had not shortened by a millimeter.

The Foundation also had something to celebrate in its dispute with the city of Rome. Glanton's bid for dismissal of the breach of contract lawsuit had failed the previous fall. The Barnes president had fired back with counter-claims ranging from abuse of process and defamation to civil racketeering. On April 15, U.S. District Judge Marvin Katz ruled that there was no binding contract between the parties, and therefore "no contract to breach." Rome could not prove that there was ever a "meeting of the minds" on "an essential term," the issue of advanced payment, the federal judge said, adding: "Not all betrayal is a tort."[43] As Barnes watchers pondered the phrase, Lower Merion officials filed a motion in Judge Brody's courtroom for a summary judgment in the Foundation's civil rights complaint against them. Producing a letter written in October 1995 by a land-development consultant to a Barnes administrator that warned of the thicket of regulations the Foundation would have to navigate to win township approval of a parking lot, they said it proved, along with boxes full of other documents, that Glanton knew all along that racism was not involved in Lower Merion's treatment of the Foundation. There wasn't enough evidence to go to trial, the commissioners' lawyers argued. Glanton said he had "reams of proof" and immediately filed a motion asking Brody to find that the township lacked evidence for its counterclaim, which contended that the Foundation had filed its lawsuit with an ulterior motive. Backstage, Sugarman gave High a letter saying the Barnes would consider payment of "a nominal contribution" to settle matters. The Lower Merion solicitor viewed it as a "crack in the door," but answered that any settlement must be based on a court judgment in the township's favor and the Foundation's willingness to assume all the township's legal costs.[44]

A repeat of the 1996 summer crowds and revenues was not in the cards for 1997. Although Glanton had petitioned Orphans' Court to remain open in July and August, he withdrew the petition when the court could not schedule a hearing until mid-July—too late, he said, to justify the time, effort, and cost of pursuing the issue. Had he persisted, Ott might well have acceded to his request. Glanton had recently discovered in the Barnes Archives the collector's 1946 letter to Justice Stern describing his frustration with primitive air conditioning systems whose inefficiencies led him to close the gallery to prevent damage to his paintings. Presenting the document, he could then have pointed to the state-of-the-art air conditioning and humidity control systems installed during the gallery's renovation. Lawyers for the neighbors suggested that Glanton's unusual willingness to back down was tied to court support for their request for financial documents. Whatever the reason for his decision, their clients greeted the news with relief. But the Foundation was hardly in retreat. In a Montgomery County Court of Common Pleas, it argued for the right to remain open to the public three and a half days a week while it appealed the township's order to resume a two-and-a-half-day schedule. In early August, Judge Bernard Moore denied the Foundation's request and granted Lower Merion's petition for a preliminary injunction while the appeal was pending. The Barnes trustees received another setback when the township commissioners voted to ban parking on one side of Latch's Lane. Glanton had asked them to wait until after he had his parking lot. He now appealed Moore's injunction, and in another Montgomery County court room argued against the township's claim that the Foundation had changed its primary use. When the gallery's doors opened in September, however, the Foundation had little choice but to abide by the 500 visitors-a-week cap. The Montgomery County Court had denied the request of its lawyers for a stay preventing enforcement of the township limit, so now they asked the Superior Court for one and, in yet another legal maneuver, filed suit to block enforcement of the no-parking ordinance.

The *Inquirer* provided readers trying to follow the increasingly serpentine twists of the Barnes saga with some comic relief later in the month when it reported on a challenge Solicitor High had made in August to the tax-exempt status of the Barnes property the collector bought in 1940 to use for his publishing operations and administrative offices. Glanton had discontinued the former and moved the latter into the collector's residence, so the large stone house located several miles from Latch's Lane on another pretty township street was mostly used for storage. It seems, however, a neighbor had called police about a boisterous party there in the fall of 1996. The complaint caught the township's attention, and in the course of a discovery process related to its various legal tangles with the Foundation, the Barnes business manager was questioned about the property. Her revelation that two female acquaintances of her boss had lived in the house for several months without paying rent prompted High to go to the Montgomery County Board of Assessment and ask for the repeal of the property's tax-exemption. The Foundation appealed his challenge, but failed to prove to the board's satisfaction that the property's principal use was for art-related purposes. The Barnes trustees then put the house on the market and sold it for $850,000.

But it was another September newspaper story that would have a far more lasting impact on the Foundation. The *Inquirer* ran a short feature, with a head shot in color, about the Barnes's new manager of administration. It said Linda Z. Marston had been hired in August to run day-to-day operations. Marston, who had held several responsible administrative posts in federal departments, was described as having a "broad mandate to coordinate Barnes functions."[45] The article also noted that she was the wife of one of Glanton's law partners. But the writer initially missed a salient point: her appointment was a complete surprise to Niara Sudarkasa. The Lincoln president was furious. She fired off a memorandum chastising Glanton for hiring Marston "without informing, much less consulting, the board of trustees." She also wrote: "The [Barnes] president will no longer assume the role of de facto director, and therefore, we need to discuss the role, responsibilities, and tenure of the president as we look to the future."[46]

The relationship between Sudarkasa and Glanton must have been exceedingly complex. He was nimble and suave. She was authoritative with an imposing presence. Though he reported directly to Lincoln's board of trustees, he worked closely with her as the university's general counsel; she was almost, if not quite, his peer as vice president of the Barnes board. They had both achieved a great deal by dint of wit and will, and they shared the certain knowledge that there was not yet equal justice in America. It was Sudarkasa's support that allowed Glanton to fly high as president of the Barnes, but there were limits to her indulgence. Alone among the Foundation trustees, "she could intimidate him," Walker recalls. "'Richard, what is this?' she'd ask, and he'd try to appease her. If she backed him, he had carte blanche. If she stood up to him, he would back down."[47] At Lincoln, he often ran interference for her at the board level, but his politicking, especially his alleged attempt to prevent the re-election of Kenneth Sadler as trustee chairman in the spring of 1997, could be counter productive. She became convinced, moreover, that the Barnes needed full-time, professional direction, and board members agreed to conduct a national search for a paid executive. From her perspective, Glanton's hiring of a personal friend with no background in education or the arts to fill the most senior management position in the Foundation was backpedaling. She saw it as one more example of the unilateral management style of a president who routinely failed to consult with his fellow trustees.

More than the feathers of the Barnes board were ruffled later in the month. If the trustees' confidence in the judgment of their president was shaken by a personnel decision they deemed unauthorized and unwise, it was close to shattered on September 26, 1997 when Judge Brody threw out the Foundation's civil rights lawsuit against Lower Merion Township. She ruled that there was "no evidence whatsoever" to show that the township or its elected commissioners purposely singled out the Barnes for harsh treatment or enforced regulations in a discriminatory manner because of the race of its trustees. "Indeed, the vast majority of the Barnes's evidence has nothing to do with race," Brody said, "but merely details various stages in a run of the mill zoning dispute."[48] Finding nothing to support the claim of a constitutional violation even if all the admissible evidence were true, she concluded a trial was unnecessary and the defendants entitled to summary judgment as a matter of law. Paul Rosen immediately announced his intention to file a petition seeking at least $1.5 million from the Foundation under the "prevailing party statute" of the Civil Rights Act. Ten days later, moreover, Glanton took another hit when the United States Supreme Court denied without comment his request to move from a Montgomery County court to federal court the defamation lawsuit filed by the Lower Merion officials against the Barnes trustees. But that evening, the clouds lifted momentarily. Confirming the vote it had taken six months earlier, the Lower Merion Planning Commission gave final approval for the Foundation's plans for a parking lot. Two days later, on October 8, the building and planning committee, which consisted of the entire Board of Commissioners, gave its unanimous consent. Agreement had been reached when Glanton agreed to adopt and publicize a good-neighbor policy suggested by one of the commissioners. Drafted to reassure the residents of Latch's Lane, it was in the form of a notice to visitors to the gallery that read: "Unless you have called in advance and received a confirmed reservation for the day required, you will not have vehicular access to the Barnes except by shuttle bus from established off-site locations." Bob Marmon called the wording "perfect."[49] Richard Glanton and Walter Herman shook hands.

But the issue of use remained. Later in the month, two judges of the Montgomery County Court of Common Pleas upheld a 1996 zoning board ruling that the Foundation had illegally transformed itself into a museum. In responding to their request for clarification of its decree, however, the zoning board had assured the court that it had no objection to the addition of an extra day for public visits nor was it wedded to the 200-person-per-full-day cap. One appropriate way to determine an acceptable number of visitors, it told the judges, as it had once told Glanton, was for the Barnes to apply for a special exception to operate a museum, in addition to a school, and thereby trigger new zoning hearings that focused on admissions figures. A few weeks earlier, the Commonwealth Court had granted a stay allowing an unlimited number of visitors until it ruled on the appeal of a summer injunction by Judge Moore requiring the Foundation to abide by the lower limits. In November, Judge Brody issued her own directive. She ordered the Foundation and Lower Merion Township to sit down with Senior U.S. District Judge Bechtle and try to reconcile their differences. When she had offered to arrange such settlement talks with Bechtle as mediator eleven months before, the Barnes board had turned down the proposal. Now Sugarman said his clients would comply with her command.

But before Bechtle could even set up a timetable for negotiations, Lower Merion, its commissioners, and the neighbors filed six separate motions for recovery of attorneys' fees. Sensing, perhaps for the first time, the real possibility of financial ruin, the Foundation trustees acquired a new lead attorney. They hired retired federal appeals court judge A. Leon Higginbotham, Jr., then of counsel at the top drawer New York law firm of Paul, Weiss, Rifkind, Wharton & Garrison. On the day before the first of the requests for the awarding of fees and costs were made to the U.S. District Court for the Eastern District of Pennsylvania, he wrote to all counsel proposing a ninety-day stay of all proceedings and expressing the hope that within that time, they would be able to reach a "responsible and fair" settlement. He also said he believed that Brody's decision gave him "a very persuasive case for appeal."[50] A week later, with events rushing forward, he formally asked for time to complete a thorough analysis of the factual and legal basis of the awards motions before filing a response. The eminent former jurist, a noted civil rights scholar who was the first African American to head a federal regulatory commission and one of the youngest judges ever named to federal district court when he was appointed at thirty-five, had lived in Philadelphia for some forty years when he accepted a faculty appointment at Harvard's Kennedy School in 1993. The local legal community still regarded him as a towering figure, and the Foundation could hardly have chosen a more respected co-counsel. But the case would be among Higginbotham's last, for he was mortally ill and would succumb to complications from heart disease within eleven months. His career in the law had paved the way for younger black attorneys like the Barnes president.

For all his troubles in the fall of 1997, Glanton still cut a dashing figure in the larger community. In September, he had been part of a small delegation of Philadelphia cultural, educational, and economic leaders who visited Shanghai for six days. During his stay, he talked to Chinese art museum officials about a possible future exhibition of Barnes paintings in the teeming port city. With legal fees for the current year alone approaching $1 million, the Foundation was running a huge operating deficit, and the possibility of once again using part of the collection to produce an inflow of revenue must have been seductive however far-fetched in terms of the likely acquiescence of Orphans' Court. But Glanton's problems were not just financial. Since Sudarkasa had challenged his leadership of the Barnes board, he could no longer count on his fellow trustees circling the wagons to protect him from any outsider who wanted his scalp. To replace Shirley Jackson who resigned in 1996, moreover, the Lincoln board had named the man he was alleged to have once tried to unseat, its chairman Kenneth Sadler. Sherman White was Charles Frank's successor as the Mellon

Bank representative. Once before, in December of 1993, Glanton had almost lost the Barnes presidency when, at the annual meeting at which Sudarkasa was absent, Frank and Cuyler Walker momentarily persuaded Jackson to accept the position. Now, after eight years at the helm, it was problematic at best that he could hold on to the post that had crowned his fast-track career. He loved the job. He had done it with verve, and he was not going to smile and bow and hand it back.

Three days before the February 1998 meeting of the Barnes board, Glanton sent a memorandum to the Lincoln trustees warning them of looming legal problems. As counsel to the university, he said he thought "it prudent and obligatory to point out that criminal penalties do exist and can be imposed if there is a determination that the university spent funds appropriated by the state without board approval."[51] The issue was $530,000 paid out over a ten-year period to renovate the president's on-campus house. Glanton noted that state legislators were looking at the expenditure, and he suggested that it could come under the scrutiny of the Pennsylvania attorney general. As an addendum, he enclosed a copy of a recent *Inquirer* article reporting that State Senator Vincent J. Fumo, the ranking Democrat on the Senate Appropriations Committee, was investigating the piecemeal project overseen by Sudarkasa's husband, John L. Clark, a contractor who had served as Lincoln's director of physical plant until his retirement a year or so earlier. Glanton wrote that he was sending the memo at the request of Sadler, but the Lincoln chairman told the press he had asked him to say nothing about the matter for the time being and had retained special counsel to review it. Whether the timing was coincidental or the startling communication was a red herring or, as Sudarkasa came to believe, retaliation, the immediate result was that Glanton lost the support of almost the entire Lincoln board. Out of desperation, he had badly overplayed his hand. On February 9th, the Barnes Foundation trustees elected Sadler president, Randolph Kinder vice president, and Sudarkasa, secretary. Although Glanton kept his seat on the board, he authorized the release of a self-serving statement that reflected nothing so much as his raw hurt: "If you know Richard Glanton, he doesn't give up anything without a fight. He has fought hard since 1990 to get the Barnes the recognition that it deserves. . . . You can go to the Foundation and ask the people who work there. They love Richard Glanton, they applaud his efforts, and they praise his dedication."[52]

The next day, Sadler, a Lincoln alumnus and a dentist practicing in Winston-Salem, North Carolina, announced that Earle L. Bradford, Jr., a former Arco Chemical Company executive and the chair of the business affairs committee of the Lincoln board, would serve as interim chief administrative officer of the Foundation. A spokesperson for the Barnes declared that the institution was "now going to focus on improving relationships with the community."[53] Sadler said there would be a national search for a permanent executive director. A few days later, Linda Marston resigned as manager of administration, saying she was shocked to discover that Bradford was being paid $1,000 a day. Sadler ordered an internal audit to assess the Foundation's debt, and he continued to talk at every opportunity about his desire to mend fences. Meanwhile, Higginbotham filed a response to the request by the township, its commissioners, and the Latch's Lane neighbors that the Barnes pay their legal fees and expenses. In an exhaustive brief that recounted heartbreaking episodes of racially motivated murder and other atrocities that had taken place in America earlier in the century, he argued that given the nation's dark history of discrimination, the Foundation trustees were justified in bringing suit on the basis of a perception of racial animosity, even though they did not prevail in court. But if the remaining lawsuits had a life of their own—attorneys for the plaintiffs accused the Barnes of the "shameful exploitation of passions" in an attempt to persuade the court to undo a "dispassionate" decision[54]—Lower Merion officials nevertheless proclaimed their eagerness to work with the new Foundation leadership to find solutions to lingering problems.

For their part, Sadler and Bradford really did seem keen to repair relationships and move on. At the end of April, the acting chief administrative officer issued a news release crafted to present "the new face" of the Barnes. It announced that a visitor management system, designed to control the timing of visits to the gallery by requiring the purchase of reserved tickets for staggered hours throughout the day, would begin the next month. Callers seeking reservations would also be able to purchase tickets for on-site parking. Bradford said that ground would be broken in June for the lot, which he expected to be operational by summer's end. In conjunction with the announcement of the system to handle gallery access in a way, Sadler emphasized, that considered "the needs of the neighborhood," the Foundation applied to the zoning board for permission to increase the number of visitors from 500 to 1,500 during a three-and-a-half day week.[55] Some residents of Latch's Lane were skeptical. "It remains to be seen if they will do what they say," Walter Herman told a reporter.[56] Part of the legacy of perceived bad faith was tied to such alleged evasions of the law as the arrival of senior citizens in Blue Bird school buses on days when the gallery was closed to the public. To drive home the point, the neighbors, joined by the township, filed a petition in the Court of Common Pleas in early May citing at least eight violations since mid-November of 1997 and asking that the Barnes be held in contempt of a court order prohibiting any non-student visitors Mondays through Thursdays. Wearily, the Foundation filed a request to dismiss the petition. On the same day, Anita Brody sent a memorandum to the lawyers involved in the civil rights case to say that she and Lower Merion Township had become litigants in an appeal of her property tax-assessment. She told them to notify the court if they felt she should step down, and when Sugarman, who continued as Glanton's personal attorney, quickly obliged, the case was reassigned to Judge Ronald L. Buckwalter.

More zoning hearings were held in June and July of 1998. Barnes representatives argued that the Foundation should be allowed to admit an additional 1,000 visitors a week fifty-two weeks a year. A planner, who was hired by the Foundation, attributed problems observing regulations the previous summer to demand created by the Cézanne exhibition at the Philadelphia Museum of Art. Underlying all the testimony was the question of how many visitors does it take before the Barnes becomes a museum. Appearing as witnesses for the Foundation, PMA director Anne d'Harnoncourt and Jeremy Sabloff, director of the University of Pennsylvania Museum of Anthropology and Archaeology, said they did not see how the requested increase would affect in any adverse way the Barnes educational program. In Orphans' Court, as part of their petition for summer hours, Foundation lawyers finally presented Albert Barnes's 1946 letter about his failed struggles to control heat and humidity. In a much-anticipated decision, Judge Ott ruled early the following month that the Foundation could remain open in July and August. "Dr. Barnes would have embraced the modern technology which has eliminated the dangers" to his pictures, Ott said.[57] But Barnes trustees made no immediate move to take advantage of the ruling, as they faced a continuation of hearings before the zoning board whose approval was still crucial to further opening the gallery doors.

Sadler did, however, make an important decision relevant to the future of the Foundation. After Pennsylvania Assistant Attorney General Lawrence Barth asked the Barnes for a detailed accounting of spending over the past decade, he hired Louis R. Pichini, a Deloitte & Touche investigator who was former head of the criminal division of the U.S. Attorney's Office in Philadelphia, to conduct a forensic audit of the Foundation's finances between 1992 and 1998. When Glanton learned of the new president's move, he fired off an angry letter accusing his fellow trustee of "a shocking abuse" of his authority.[58] He also wrote to Bradford charging that under the interim chief administrative officer, the endowment had been depleted by more than $4 million. Glanton said that Bradford and Sadler, with the support of White and Sudarkasa, were "attempting to spend the Foundation into insolvency."[59] But it was the former president's civil rights complaint and his public characterization of his opponents' motives that had triggered a large portion of the legal bills now being paid out of principal. In a letter dated August 28, 1998 and filed in Montgomery County Court on the 8th of September, the president of Lincoln University apologized for the remarks of her onetime friend and ally to the Lower Merion commissioners. "Please accept my sincere apology for any discomfort or emotional distress any of your clients may have felt as a result of the published statements of Richard Glanton," she wrote to their attorneys. If he accused the commissioners of "being racially biased against the Barnes," she continued, "he did not seek my authorization or approval, nor, to my knowledge, did he seek the authorization or approval of the other Barnes trustees. . . . To the extent that Mr. Glanton's personal views were attributed to the Barnes trustees, please be advised that such attribution was, and is, wholly inaccurate."[60]

The letter prompted the commissioners to drop Sudarkasa from their defamation suit, along with Shirley Jackson, by then president of Rensselaer Polytechnic Institute in Troy, New York. Their action was a huge relief and may have been the first good thing that had happened to the Lincoln president in months. Sudarkasa's significant accomplishments, including increasing enrollment from 1,200 to 2,000 students, growing the endowment by 366 percent to nearly $14 million, raising faculty salaries, and building a new classroom facility as well as a dormitory while balancing the budget, were being overshadowed by the growing furor about university spending practices. Ironically, her administration was in the midst of a study, funded by the Ford Foundation, of the possibility of establishing a collaborative program in art history and museum studies between the university and the Barnes.[61] But, sadly, as the new academic year began, the focus of much of the Lincoln community was not on the future but the past. An extensive audit, undertaken in February at the board's request, found "questionable transactions," including alleged conflicts of interest involving Glanton, who had resigned as university counsel in March, and Eugene Cliett, Lincoln's vice president of fiscal affairs.[62] According to a university statement, Cliett, who had also resigned his post, was approving checks for legal fees to Glanton's law firm at roughly the same time Glanton, as the Barnes president, was directing computer and printing business to a consulting firm owned by Cliett.[63] The audit also found problems ranging from poor record keeping and failure to follow spending guidelines to questionable bidding on construction contracts. When it was forwarded to state government officials, the Pennsylvania Senate voted to withhold two-thirds of the university's annual subsidy until Lincoln submitted to a second audit by the state Auditor General's Office of Special Investigations and took any required corrective actions. The state House of Representatives voted to undo what the Senate had done, but funds were delayed anyway when the Senate adjourned for the summer without acting on Lincoln's appropriation.

Glanton's feud with Sudarkasa grew as sizzling as the weather. The former Lincoln general counsel wrote to Auditor General Robert Casey, Jr. that the Lincoln president ordered the Peat Marwick audit for the sake of "vengeance" and to deflect attention from unauthorized spending on her home. He leveled new charges against her husband related to the alleged burial of "hazardous waste" on school property and alleged efforts to hide leaking underground fuel tanks. He said Lincoln officials had entered into several contracts with a company owned by Sudarkasa's son without disclosing the relationship to the board or to him.[64] Copies of the blast, which called on Casey to freeze payments to the auditors hired by the university, turned up in Lincoln dormitories and on windshields of cars parked on campus. As state examiners combed through the financial records of the Chester County school, two anonymous letters—one signed by "Allied Friends of Lincoln"—also circulated around the university calling for the president's resignation. Forced to defend herself at an emergency meeting of the Lincoln trustees, Sudarkasa said the accusations against her and her husband were either "totally and completely untrue or a gross misrepresentation of the facts."[65] After she spoke, board members learned that a resolution to end her tenure would be introduced at the regularly scheduled September meeting. In one of his irate missives to Barnes president Kenneth Sadler, which he released to the press, Glanton implied that as chairman of the Lincoln board's business committee, Earle Bradford would be handling Sudarkasa's severance negotiations. He demanded that the Foundation's interim chief administrator be "terminated" upon receipt of his letter.[66]

The board's search for a permanent executive director was, in fact, nearing completion. But during his brief tenure Bradford had made measurable progress on one issue that vexed the neighbors above all others. He reached agreement with the Adam's Mark Hotel on nearby City Line Avenue to use its large parking lot as a staging area for tour buses to drop off and pick up passengers. When the Foundation opened on September 4, 1998, groups visiting the Barnes were taken from the remote site to Latch's Lane by a shuttle service. The neighbors cheered, and cheered again six days later when the contempt citation, which they had requested in the Montgomery County Court of Common Pleas the previous spring, was issued against the Barnes for violations of the visitor limits set in 1996 by the zoning hearing board. Although he did not impose a fine, Judge Bernard Moore told the Foundation, in effect, to stop allowing high school classes, church groups, and Elderhostel tours in excess of the 500 person-a-week cap and on days reserved for matriculated Barnes students. An appeal was filed as Foundation officials prepared for their final presentation before the zoning board. In documents submitted by their lawyers, they argued that 78,000 visitors a year could be admitted to the gallery without turning it into a museum. They requested a special exemption to permit 1,500 visitors a week fifty-two weeks a year, while the township proposed a weekly limit of 1,050 visitors or more than double the then current level. Neighbors and Lower Merion officials were concerned about the proportion of visitors to students. They wanted to prohibit the Foundation from counting as students those not enrolled in Barnes classes. The lawyers for the Foundation trustees said men and women enrolled in the gallery docent program should be counted as enrolled students and a maximum of 275 non-Barnes students, affiliated with accredited or certified educational institutions, should be admitted each week in addition to 1,487 other visitors. They proposed limiting the student population to a weekly maximum of 500 and educational programming to thirty weeks a year. They suggested that during the summer, the gallery be open a half-day on Tuesdays and a full-day Wednesdays through Fridays, leaving the gates closed on weekends—a concession that delighted the neighbors. But doing the arithmetic, the Latch's Lane residents also protested that 136,676 people a year going in and out of the Foundation were too many.

The bitter civil rights lawsuit that had arisen out of the dispute over zoning came to an end even as the wrangling over numbers continued before the hearing board. On September 24, the Barnes Foundation and Lower Merion Township reached a settlement. Leon Higginbotham agreed not to challenge Judge Brody's decision dismissing the Foundation's suit for lack of evidence. The Barnes withdrew with prejudice all claims in the case. Brody's 1997 summary judgment became the final judgment of record. The Barnes also agreed to contribute $100,000 to Lower Merion—a sum earmarked not for legal fees but for charitable purposes or civic causes. In return, the township agreed to drop its countersuit accusing the Foundation of abusing the legal process by filing a bogus complaint. The two sides also said that they would "consult and work with" Judge Bechtle to effect the settlement's goals and intents.[67] The agreement did not, however, dispose of the defamation suit that the commissioners, acting as individuals, had brought against the Barnes trustees, although only Glanton remained as a defendant.

The former Barnes president was now facing another lawsuit as well. It was brought against him by Niara Sudarkasa who contended that he had divulged confidential lawyer-client information in a "campaign of destruction" to discredit her and drive her from office. Eugene Cliett also was named and accused of providing Glanton with financial documents. The Lincoln president asked for more than $5 million in damages from her onetime friend and still fellow Barnes trustee, $1 million from Cliett, and $1 million from Glanton's law firm. Her suit said that she had undertaken to oust Glanton as the Barnes president because he was acting like a "dictator" and running the Foundation like a "private slush fund and patronage haven."[68] She claimed that a spate of letters he wrote criticizing her conduct as the president of Lincoln was an attempt to get even. If it was, he did, although a Common Pleas Court judge eventually dismissed all her claims against him, ruling that their disagreement was a public dispute between public figures.

While Sudarkasa's lawsuit was pending, the Auditor General's Office issued a report that described a "pattern of mismanagement" at Lincoln where, it said, "internal controls were absent or ignored." Sudarkasa both accepted responsibility and issued a detailed rebuttal. But Casey's findings were like gasoline thrown upon coals of discontent that burned slowly on a campus where there was never enough money to make life entirely comfortable for students and faculty. Four days before Lincoln's board of trustees was to vote on whether to fire her, the embattled president told a campus convocation that she would resign effective December 31, 1998. A supportive former trustee who took the podium after she concluded her remarks said the controversy swirling around

Sudarkasa was "about the Barnes."[69] State Senator Fumo let it be known that he would move to withhold Lincoln's already delayed appropriation of $11 million if the outgoing president was given severance. After several meetings, the board relieved her of all her duties on October 3 and replaced her with its own vice president, a Lincoln alumnus and mathematics professor at Howard University named James Donaldson, while saying she could keep her title and her house until the end of the year. Late in November, the legislature finally approved the school's 1998-99 appropriation.

Earlier in the month, Earle Bradford had handed over his responsibilities as chief administrator to a permanent executive director. Kimberly Camp is a native of Camden, the New Jersey city across the Delaware River from Philadelphia, who headed the Charles H. Wright Museum of African American History in Detroit for four years before she was recruited by the Barnes trustees. A painter and doll maker, she had gained national attention for her Kimkins, small figures with hand-painted clay faces and soft hand-dyed muslin bodies dressed in traditional African garments. Camp had majored in fine arts and art history at the University of Pittsburgh and, after working as a professional illustrator, earned a master's degree in arts administration at Drexel University in 1986. She subsequently held several national fellowships and served as a staff member of the Pennsylvania Council on the Arts in Harrisburg before going to Washington as director of the Experimental Gallery at the Smithsonian Institution in 1989. When she accepted the presidency of the Wright Museum five years later, her task was to oversee the growth of its collections and coordinate the institution's move from 28,000-square-foot building to a new 120,000-square-foot facility for which construction had just begun when she came on board. Under her leadership, the Wright's staff, paid attendance, and operating budget were quadrupled, but turbulence marked her tenure. A strong-willed management style alienated staff, volunteers, and former supporters even as she succeeded in presenting several highly regarded touring exhibitions and a staff-produced show on black neighborhoods destroyed in the name of urban renewal. The Barnes board agreed to pay Camp, who was forty-two at the time of her appointment, $150,000 a year. The trustees wanted the roller-coaster ride to end. They were counting on her to stabilize the Foundation.

A little more than two weeks after she started her new job, the Lower Merion zoning board ruled that the Barnes could double the number of visitors it had previously been allowed to admit in a year without the gallery losing its "accessory" use status—and the Foundation trustees decided not to appeal the decision even though the total was significantly below their request. The public admissions cap was raised by the township from 26,000 to 62,400. It was more people than the neighbors wanted on Latch's Lane but a number they could live with. The zoning board said the gallery could be open three days a week all year round, although it must be closed weekends in July and

August, and that on each day the doors were open, it could admit 400 visitors. On days when the collection is technically closed to the public, the zoning board was willing to allow up to 100 visitors but they would have to count against a weekly maximum of 1,200. It exempted Barnes students from the caps and made no ruling on the number of students the Foundation could enroll in its art appreciation and horticultural classes. Walter Herman said he thought the decision was "a good compromise."[70] But implementation of the critical ruling was delayed for ten months until Camp was able to assure the zoning board that the reservation system was fully operational, the parking lot was finished and met all the conditions imposed by the township, and that Latch's Lane was free of tour buses. Nevertheless, when the Barnes trustees met on December 2, they could reflect on a tumultuous year in which they had made significant progress toward putting the demons of the past behind them. It was time for the annual election of officers, and Sadler was asked again to serve as president. Kinder was re-elected vice president and White, treasurer. No vote was taken on secretary, the office held by Sudarkasa. Glanton remained a trustee. The troubles linked with his tenure as head of the Foundation were not over, but Judge Higginbotham had helped resolve issues between Lower Merion and the Barnes in a way that allowed the start of a healing process. For his own ailing heart, there would be no mending; he died on the 14th of December.

Five months later, the end game in the Lower Merion commissioners' defamation suit against Glanton seemed about to begin with pre-trial arguments, followed by jury selection, scheduled for May 10, 1999. In a last-ditch effort to move the case out of the Montgomery County Court of Common Pleas, Sugarman appealed to the state Supreme Court to use its "king's bench power" to take jurisdiction on the grounds that the issues revolved around the "denial of basic First Amendment rights of freedom of speech." He was turned down on Friday, the 7th of May. Later that afternoon, he met with Rosen, insurance company attorneys, and Harris T. Bock, director of Philadelphia's Dispute Resolution Institute, in Rosen's office. The lawyers negotiated into the evening. Neither side wanted a trial, but without an apology, the commissioners were ready to press ahead. A courier took papers to Richard Glanton in his office on the twenty-fifth floor of a nearby building. Close to midnight, with rain falling outside, the former Barnes president took the elevator to the lobby and there signed a letter that Sugarman called a "conditional retraction." It read in full:

This letter confirms my previous statements that the quotations attributed to me in the articles in question referring to racism did not refer to nor were they intended to include the commissioners or the staff of Lower Merion Township.

I cannot accept responsibility for any interpretation or misrepresentation of my comments. However, to the extent that a reader would consider any of my statements relating to racism to refer to the commissioners, you may consider this letter a retraction of such statements. I regret any discomfort this may have caused the commissioners.[71]

Glanton agreed to pay $400,000 in legal fees, and Rosen said he would accept the payment as his fee in full. The commissioners considered themselves "totally vindicated—totally."[72] Jim Ettelson, the Merion representative on the board, had been following developments by telephone from his own office—seventeen floors above the suite occupied by Reed Smith. After four years of sometimes bitter argument, he felt more drained than elated as he looked out a window and, in the light of a street lamp, caught sight of Glanton driving off in his black Mercedes.

The impresario of the touring exhibition, who could take credit for beautifully restored gallery spaces and must accept blame for squandering precious endowment monies on lawsuits and alienating so many natural allies, had served on the Barnes board for nine years. But neither he nor Sudarkasa was ever formally re-nominated by Lincoln for second five-year terms. In May of 1999, Sudarkasa, who had by then left the Philadelphia area, resigned as a Barnes trustee. After struggling unsuccessfully to regain the Foundation presidency, Glanton was eased off the board, under the same convenient circumstances that had allowed him to arrange for Benjamin Amos's departure a decade earlier. The university trustees chose the highly regarded former, and first African American, president of the William Penn Foundation, Bernard C. Watson, along with Jeff R. Donaldson, an artist and former dean of the College of Fine Arts at Howard University, as replacements for Sudarkasa and Glanton. In June, both educators were elected to the Barnes board. Watson, who came to Philadelphia from Chicago in 1967 as associate and then deputy superintendent of the city's school district and was later professor and chair of urban education and then academic vice president at Temple University, was elected president of the Foundation the following December.

Watson and Camp inherited an institution whose finances were in shambles. The paintings and sculpture purchased by Albert Barnes and installed in his Merion laboratory had survived him by nearly half a century, but the future of the collection and that of the educational program it serves was not at all certain. The Foundation's endowment was essentially gone. In November of 1998, the board asked permission of Orphans' Court to withdraw $2,747,272 from the restricted capital account, which had been created with the tour revenues not previously spent on renovations and then totaled nearly $5.8 million. Having already incurred expenses, largely apart from legal fees, of more than $500,000 to comply with Lower Merion zoning board conditions that would allow them to admit more visitors, the Barnes wanted to use $1.1 million to pay bills associated with the construction of the parking lot—the project finally completed, some fifteen months after ground was broken, in October of 1999—along with walkways and curb cuts, new restroom facilities in three former garages, bus loading and unloading "sleeves" and glass enclosed shelters, and a storm-water management system. The Foundation also said it needed to spend some $480,000 on the arboretum, approximately

$376,00 for security improvements, including construction of a rear guard and gate house, more than $250,000 for exterior restoration of the administration building, some $177,000 to inspect and patch the gallery roof and clean, restore, and repoint the gallery's south facade, $250,000 for associated professional services, and $75,000 for draws on a letter of credit. Although Judge Ott allowed the withdrawal of more than $1.6 million for project expenditures as costs might be incurred, he refused to allow any of the escrow funds to be used for the lot, professional services, and several other items objected to by Pennsylvania's deputy attorney general. At that point, the trustees cashed in the remaining bonds and other investments in the endowment and created an account to use for operations.

The Foundation's annual expenses, which reached a high of $5.1 million in 1998 when it paid out $1.9 million in legal fees, were down to about $3 million two years later. Camp called the 2000 budget "woefully inadequate," and it subsequently climbed to $4.2 million. "At the current level of admissions," she said then, "the cost of operating the gallery is about $60 a head."[73] Despite the renovation completed in 1995 and the spending approved from the court-monitored renovation account, the executive director cited a long list of other physical needs—a new roof for the gallery, repair of crumbling stone on the gallery's rear exterior wall, upgraded climate control for the administration building where many pictures hang that are never seen by the public, and renovation of the arboretum school house and of the carriage house, to say nothing of essential investments in new telephone and computer technology and the ongoing restoration of pictures—for which there was no money. Plagued by annual deficits, she has been unable to balance the budget, but she reduced losses to $834,000 in 1999-2000 thanks, in large measure, to a $760,000 grant from the Violette de Mazia Trust. The gift reflected the de Mazia trustees' conviction that Camp, who describes the art assembled in Merion as a "teaching collection," intended to put "significant focus on the Barnesian educational program."[74]

Enrollment in the art department had sunk to a low of sixty students in 1997-98.[75] Reportedly, it tumbled even further over the next several years, but the goal of the executive director has been to build it up to previous levels—and in the 2002-2003 academic year, there were 102 students. Camp also has inaugurated an outreach program that brings elementary and secondary school students to the gallery. After Nicolas King suddenly resigned in the summer of 1999, a young woman who had studied at the Barnes in the mid-1990s took over the first-year class along with the seminar. But John Gatti, a local artist new to the Foundation and its pedagogy, soon replaced her, although veteran instructors Harry Sefarbi and Barton Church continue to teach their second-year classes. Tuition for the art department had risen to $650 by the 2002-2003 academic year, and for arboretum classes, it was $800. The annual fees are presently $1,000 for each program. But there are other classes, begun in the fall of 1998, that are free, as the Foundation's educational program once was, and represent the de Mazia Trust's most important single investment in carrying on the work of Dr. Barnes and his principal disciple.

They were initially taught in Merion by Frederick Osborne, a former dean at the Pennsylvania Academy of the Fine Arts when he was still a professor there, on two evenings a week from October through March. When Osborne, who studied with de Mazia in 1962-63, moved on to the presidency of Lyme Academy College of Fine Arts in 2002, the foundational class, Learning to See, was continued by Marilyn Bauman, another teacher trained by de Mazia, who works under his supervision. Two of Osborne's former students took over his practicum on Traditions in Art. The de Mazia Trust compensates the Foundation for opening the gallery, pays the three teachers' salaries, and provides scholarships to the more than thirty students enrolled in the two-year program. It is specifically designed for educators in the field of art, the audience that was always of most interest to the collector, with the thought that "they will disseminate the pedagogy throughout the educational profession." Recalling that de Mazia conveyed to her students "an ability to get at the heart of what a painter was trying to say from the evidence the painter presented to the viewer" despite the intellectual "boundaries"—the "rigid sense of beginnings and ends, rights and wrongs"—implicit in her approach, Osborne says the challenge faced by her successors is "to establish the relevancy of the philosophy de Mazia passed on to them to contemporary aesthetics." The long-time educator says his objective and that of his colleagues is to enable twenty-first century art teachers to apply the method of art appreciation developed by Barnes in their own classrooms and studios, and to do so he employs pedagogical concepts that transcend those of the collector. At the same time, he finds the core of Barnes's writing "absolutely timely."[76] Students in the de Mazia Trust courses use *The Art in Painting*, several essays written by the book's author between 1915 and 1925, and Dewey's *Art and Experience* along with many of de Mazia's articles as their main texts. The first-year course is offered through the Academy's continuing education program and carries with it four PAFA credits, a feature that is of significance to teachers seeking advanced certification or degrees. It is wholly independent from the classes offered by the Foundation, but the model of collaboration with another institution, which was followed off and on by Barnes himself, is one Camp hopes to emulate and, several years ago, she held preliminary talks about the possibility with Temple. Because "Lincoln doesn't have a strong art department," she said the university to which Barnes gave the power to appoint Foundation trustees is not presently ready to be part of such a conversation.[77] But in 2002, Lincoln did begin sending some biology majors to the Arboretum School, and a few of its students attended a short series of lectures on ceramics.

In an effort to bring professional management to the Barnes, Camp has increased the staff to twenty-six persons. She hired new directors of education and of the arboretum, both positions specified in the Indenture, along with directors of two positions, development and finance, which are not mentioned in the governing document. Recently added were a registrar and a conservator, and the executive director also has created an eight-member Curatorial Advisory Committee, which is chaired by Joseph Rishel, curator of European painting at the Philadelphia Museum of Art. The first phase of a project to digitize documents in the Foundation archives, initiated by Richard Glanton and paid for out of operating funds, has been completed but funds are needed to evaluate another 300,000 items. Scholars may one day be able to access some archival materials—most likely at a price—on the Barnes Web site, which was created for the Foundation by students at West Chester University and opened in July of 2000. Camp has established a docent program of volunteers to provide guided tours to groups. But as one measure of how strapped the Foundation is for cash, docents, who must have taken Barnes courses along with a special training program, were initially required to pay for their own parking. The trustees and the executive director recognize that effective fund raising is the key to the Foundation's survival. A fledgling corporate partners program is in place, and Camp has created a separate not-for-profit organization, known as The Barnes Society, as a means of recognizing donors. Handicapped by out-of-date records of names and addresses and a legacy of distrust, she wants to reach out to alumni, who dissolved the long-active Friends of the Barnes group in 1996 after six-years of fighting with Glanton over proposed changes they perceived as contrary to the collector's intent. A two-person development staff had written numerous grant proposals with so little initial success that as the 2000-2001 academic year began, Camp faced a mounting operating deficit and announced that without further donations, she would be unable to met the payroll or other basic expenses in six to twelve months. The executive director said she needed $15 million over the next five years just to keep the doors open and sought $70 million in new endowment to build long-term stability. Was Camp crying wolf? In conversations conducted behind closed doors, members of the philanthropic community, who had previously turned down Barnes requests, discussed the Foundation's plight and concluded that the wolf was approaching the door.

In November of 2000, the J. Paul Getty Trust made a $500,000 grant for broadly defined planning expenses, and its president, Barry Munitz, said he hoped that others would follow suit. The Getty also provided experts to assess the archives on Latch's Lane and security at Ker-Feal. Before the end of the year, the Pew Charitable Trusts matched Getty's contribution with $500,000 of its own, which was restricted to assessment of the collection and given with the understanding that the funds would be administered by the Los Angeles foundation for the Barnes's benefit. Pew subsequently added another half million dollars. The Wilmington Trust Company also made a $500,000 grant, and in the spring of 2001, the Henry Luce Foundation contributed yet another

$500,000 and the Andrew W. Mellon Foundation made a $250,000 award, which it increased to $300,000 in 2002 and $500,000 in 2003, for inventory and cataloging of the collection.[78] Meanwhile, letters mailed from Merion to thousands of potential donors asked them to join a "Campaign to Save the Barnes." It said nothing specifically about objectives or aspirations, but Bernard Watson knew from the start that a strategic plan was essential if the Barnes was to be taken seriously by the foundation world. He made the creation of one a priority for the board. "Our first goal is financial stability," he told an interviewer six months after taking office. "But the trustees have no intention of running the Foundation. We will hold the executive director accountable."[79]

Besides his philanthropic experience, the greatest asset that the new president brings to his position is a reputation for straight dealing. While he cannot escape the past, neither is he responsible for it, and his focus is on the present and the future. Under his leadership, the board of trustees approved a road map developed for the Foundation by Deloitte & Touche. The plan endorsed in December of 2000 called for operating Ker-Feal as a living history museum, converting the former Barnes residence into a space for rotating interpretive exhibits, and moving the administrative offices off-site. The estimated capital costs were then $5.6 million. Another $3 million would be needed to complete a full-scale assessment of the Barnes holdings, including the continuation of efforts to organize and digitize historic documents. A bigger development office and an image-burnishing offensive were also part of the new initiative, as was an expansion of the Foundation's art education and arboretum programs. In the spring of 2001, the Foundation won permission of Montgomery County Orphans' Court to proceed with another component of the plan—lending or sending on tour some 150 paintings as well as works on paper, pottery, textiles, and other artifacts in the current administrative offices and in storage. Among what Camp likes to call "hidden treasures" are pictures by Courbet, Glackens, Pascin, and Soutine, but no one expects them to evoke the same degree of public interest as the first road show of masterpieces from the core of the collection.

Aggravating the Foundation's financial woes ten years after Lincoln University gained control of the board was the failure of the new administration to quickly put to rest a lingering issue between the Foundation and its neighbors. As the prevailing defendants in the civil rights lawsuit brought against them by the Barnes under Glanton's leadership, the neighbors were entitled to attorneys' fees and expenses upon a finding that the action of the Foundation trustees was "frivolous, unreasonable, or groundless." Represented by Paul, Weiss, Rifkin, the Barnes board opposed the efforts of six of them to secure a fee award amounting to several hundred thousand dollars. Largely ignoring previous court decisions, U.S. District Court Justice Ronald L. Buckwalter ruled in November of 1999 that the claim filed by the Foundation was neither frivolous nor unreasonable, that is, legally insufficient since he said the plaintiffs could in good faith have argued that the *Noerr-Pennington* doctrine was not applicable to the case. But "it does come close to being groundless" for lack of "direct evidence of racial hostility," he conceded. Nevertheless, Buckwalter decided that given what another federal judge called the persistence of the "reality of discriminatory behavior" in mainstream American life, albeit often "masked in more subtle forms," the "inferences drawn were reasonable, at least, for the purposes of establishing a complaint."[80] Lawyers for the Latch's Lane residents appealed his ruling, which came after the judge failed to persuade the Foundation to make a discounted payment. David Weinstein maintained that if "left undisturbed," the district court's denial of attorneys' fees and costs would "have a substantial and long-lasting chilling effect on the exercise of First Amendment rights by private citizens."[81] The resistance of the Barnes to a figure the neighbors' lawyers agreed to accept in subsequent non-binding arbitration meant that both sides were forced to mount oral arguments in the United States Court of Appeals for the Third Circuit. On March 5, 2001 a panel of three judges reversed the 1999 order of the district court denying the award of Weinstein's fees. The next month the full court denied the Foundation's petition for a rehearing, thereby letting stand the judges' determination that there was no factual basis on which the Barnes could have relied in bringing suit for racial discrimination against the five neighbors other than Bob Marmon. While well satisfied that the Foundation will have to pay their lawyer as well as its own, the families living across the narrow, tree-lined street from the most important collection of modern art in the world remaining in private hands are still looking for an apology.

However stressful the Barnes War may have been for them and whatever adverse effect the attention it called to the institutional character of the east side of Latch's Lane may yet have on their property values, the effect of nearly six years of controversy was far worse for the Foundation. Legal skirmishes depleted financial reserves and siphoned creative energy. But if the Barnes trustees have their way, the future will be vastly different. The Foundation wants to find itself a more congenial neighborhood. Bernard Watson knows the area philanthropic landscape well, and facing up to the Barnes's potentially fatal financial problems, he sought the help of local philanthropists. A Deloitte & Touche audit would confirm his worst fears: losses of $1.36 million in 2000-2001, which had to be covered by funds released from the Foundation's pension plan, and the expected exhaustion of cash reserves by the end of 2002. Working adroitly behind the scenes, Watson shopped for a deal. In December 2001, he arranged a meeting at the offices of The Pew Charitable Trust with Pew's president, Rebecca W. Rimel, and Harold F. "Gerry" Lenfest, a cable-TV pioneer who serves as chairman of the Philadelphia Museum of Art. They discussed the hand he had been dealt: priceless assets, no money in the till, and little prospect of any without radical structural changes. He told them what they needed to hear: he was considering proposing to his board that the Barnes collection be moved to the Benjamin Franklin Parkway in center city Philadelphia.

Pew had watched his predecessor's campaign to circumvent the complex zoning procedures of a powerful local government, which appears foolish in retrospect, with concern about its wastefulness. As a major supporter of local cultural organizations, and one committed to helping boost the regional tourist economy, however, it had a keen interest in the Barnes's survival. Lenfest had seen the Barnes pictures for the first time just the previous month and was "overwhelmed" by the collection.[82] But the inherent conflict between the values of a suburban community and the values of an institution that considered attracting more visitors essential to increasing its revenue stream seemed irresolvable. Both Rimel and Lenfest also knew that to raise substantial funds for any charity it takes a board large enough to give significant numbers of major donors an opportunity to play a meaningful role in overseeing the institution's governance. Talk of relocating the Foundation, by Richard Glanton and others, had never seemed more than the kind of daydreaming ridiculed by Albert Barnes as a common substitute for stepping up to the challenge of "learning to see" with discipline and rigor. The collector had built his limestone gallery for the sole purpose of displaying the paintings and sculpture that were the textbooks of his school. It had been brilliantly restored in the mid-1990s. Now Watson was asking what assistance Pew and the Lenfest Foundation might provide if the Barnes board agreed to go to court to try to overturn the Barnes Indenture.

Rimel and Lenfest responded with imaginative generosity to the Barnes president. In partnership with the Annenberg Foundation, they would provide $3.1 million in operating funds to the Barnes for at least two years. Of far greater long-term significance, they promised to help the beleaguered Foundation raise $50 million for an endowment and $100 million to build a new home on or near the Benjamin Franklin Parkway, the grand boulevard crowned by the Greco-Roman Philadelphia Museum of Art, which is the chosen site of a planned museum to house works of the American sculptor Alexander Calder and on which already is located the Rodin Museum, a Paul Cret gem filled with casts of Auguste Rodin's statuary along with his watercolors and drawings. The philanthropists' offer was contingent, first, upon the move; second, on the expansion of the Barnes board to fifteen members of which Pew and the Lenfest Foundation would initially, but only once, have the right to approve seven members; and third, on the Barnes's securing modification or elimination of other "restrictive conditions" in its bylaws that were seen as inhibiting "its ability to raise funds." [83]

Watson took the offer back to Merion. Over the next few months, the Barnes board considered several options. [84] Watson described them as including the filing of a petition for reorganization under the United States Bankruptcy Code. He also said the trustees looked at the possibility of merging the Foundation into another entity, "such as an existing and well-established arts or educational institution,"—a move sacrificing its independence and specifically forbidden by the language of the Indenture short of failure to preserve the Foundation by any other means. Another option reviewed by the board was entering into a management agreement with "one or more arts or philanthropic institutions" that would run the Barnes in exchange for, among other things, loans from the collection. And finally the trustees talked again, as Glanton had done when he assumed the presidency a dozen years earlier, about the possibility of selling pictures. Neither of the latter options seemed to them to assure "long-term financial stability," Watson said.[85] So the Barnes board voted to accept the offer Rimel and Lenfest had put on the table.

Its new philanthropic partners had pledged to cover the legal costs of a court petition, and one of Philadelphia's most respected lawyers, retired federal judge Arlin M. Adams, a former president of the American Philosophical Society and an emeritus trustee of the University of Pennsylvania, agreed to serve as lead counsel. His firm, Schnader, Harrison Segal & Lewis, filed a petition on behalf of the Barnes in Montgomery County Orphans' Court on September 24, 2002 to amend the Foundation's charter and bylaws. The trustees' simultaneous public announcement of their efforts, complete with a statement by Philadelphia Mayor John F. Street saying the city would be honored to host the Foundation, was greeted with unbounded editorial enthusiasm by the *Philadelphia Inquirer* ("a masterpiece of an idea") and even Lower Merion's own weekly newspaper acknowledged that "Philadelphia's gain" wasn't necessarily the suburban township's "loss."[86] Within the week, it was reported that quiet fund-raising, spearheaded by Rimel and Lenfest and underway for many months, had netted pledges of at least $80 million of the $150 million the two philanthropists had promised to help secure for the Barnes. Most of the potential donors were said to have firmly linked their gifts to court approval of the requested changes to the collector's Indenture. But with a lead corporate donation of an unconditional $2 million from Comcast, the huge cable company on whose board Bernard Watson serves, the campaign to move the Barnes was well underway by the end of 2002 despite the sluggish stock market and weak economy.

Not everyone, however, was happy about the prospect. It was only a few hours before the public announcement of the sweeping changes the Barnes sought in the trust governing Foundation operations that Watson informed Lincoln University officials of the plans that had been seriously discussed in select philanthropic circles for nearly a year. The rural, largely African-American institution, to which the collector had given the power to nominate four of five trustees, would have a vastly diminished role under the proposal before the court. The petition called for the extant Barnes board to elect three additional trustees, and then the eight-member board would chose seven more trustees who would be approved jointly by Pew and the Lenfest Foundation. Lincoln would continue to have the right to nominate trustees to the expanded board, but its share would shrink from 80 percent to 26.6 percent—and the nominating committee of the Barnes board would have the right to decide not to advance a Lincoln nomination. Lincoln vice president Grant D. Venerable 2nd told the *New York Times* that the surprise move called to mind Reconstruction schemes to disenfranchise newly freed slaves.[87] Eight days after the university learned of it, the executive committee of the Lincoln board voted to oppose the Barnes petition. Its resolution noted that the proposal before the Montgomery County Orphans' Court left open the possibility that the Foundation could one day eliminate any role whatsoever for Lincoln. Efforts by Barnes attorneys to reassure the university and resolve differences failed to forestall Lincoln's filling of a formal challenge to the Foundation's attempt to expand its board. The move pitted Lincoln trustees against their own nominees, and the irony became more excruciating when the Barnes legal team filed its own court papers attacking the legitimacy of Lincoln's stewardship on the basis of the collector's displeasure over Horace Mann Bond's failure to quickly engage a young Howard University philosopher, Sing-Nan Fen, to chair the university's philosophy and art departments in 1951 (see chapter 14) and on the status Lincoln subsequently acquired as a state-related rather than a wholly private institution. The first reason was feeble at best, and the second was linked to a curious concern about Lincoln's "dependence on government funding that enables politicians to interfere with its educational decisions."[88]

It is true that between them, Pennsylvania's legislature and its executive branch appoint fourteen of Lincoln's thirty-nine trustees, and in January 2002, the state Senate named Richard Glanton. The former Barnes president resigned sixteen months later when he accepted the position of senior vice president for corporate development in charge of mergers and acquisitions at Chicago-based Exelon Corp., a client of his law firm and one of the largest utilities in the nation. Before heading west, Glanton called upon his fellow university trustees to replace the Barnes board, an action beyond their power, until the expiration of terms, despite their displeasure. But Lincoln was serious about its challenge. It had the public support of Julian Bond, the chair of the National Association for the Advancement of Colored People and the son of the university's former president. He questioned whether "race [was] an issue" in the Foundation's petition to expand its board in a manner that significantly reduces Lincoln's historic role in nominating board members.[89] The then chair of the university's board of trustees, Adrienne G. Rhone, said Lincoln sought to intervene "as a point of integrity to honor Dr. Barnes's wishes."[90] Days before Orphans' Court Judge Stanley Ott heard oral arguments addressing the issue of who should be allowed to participate in the case, the then governor-elect, and now governor, of Pennsylvania, former Philadelphia mayor Ed Rendell, offered to help broker a solution. Though his move highlighted the importance of the stakes, it produced no immediate results.

In addition to Lincoln, three students enrolled in Foundation courses also had filed a legal challenge to the Barnes petition expressing concern that the changes sought by the trustees would endanger the Foundation's educational purposes and might result in the "reduction or elimination of existing classes and seminars."[91] Even though the Barnes trustees said they intended to maintain the collector's wall ensembles and hold classes in the new gallery, the students, and also the trustees of the de Mazia Trust, none of whom are opposed to relocation per se, wanted an ironclad guarantee that the Barnes administration would not neglect the educational core of the Foundation as it courts visitors to a dazzling new concession on Philadelphia's museum midway. Both groups argued that the request of the Barnes board to allow future trustees to amend the institution's bylaws without seeking judicial sanction put a great deal, potentially, at risk. Judge Ott, however, denied them standing at the same time he ruled that Lincoln could participate fully in all aspects of the formal hearing to determine the future of the Barnes Foundation. Pennsylvania Attorney General Mike Fisher subsequently announced that he had no objection to a move from Lower Merion into the city. At his request and as a result of an agreement reached with the de Mazia Trust, however, the Foundation trustees amended their petition to stipulate that art from the "gallery collection" will never be loaned or sold, that the "composition and arrangement of works exhibited in the gallery" will be preserved, and that a "Barnesian art education program" will be maintained "on a permanent basis."[92] The new document also adds Lincoln to the list of institutions whose trustees and faculty may not serve on the Barnes board,[93] reflecting a policy adopted by the university itself in 1998, and it provides that this prohibition in addition to sections of the bylaws related to the Foundation's educational purpose and board size may not be amended without court approval. These revisions in the Barnes proposal, together with a review of its financial situation, prompted Attorney General Fisher to file a formal response strongly supporting the Foundation's bid to change its locale and limit Lincoln's rolie in its affairs.

But governance issues remained a major stumbling block to a flight to the city. When Barnes attorney Arlin Adams told Judge Ott on September 2, 2003 that the petition to move the collection was close to being withdrawn, he was signaling the rapidly waning patience of the Pew, Lenfest, and Annenberg foundations. The late Walter Annenberg was fond of quoting the aphorism, "No good deed goes unpunished," and as it became less than certain that negotiators for Lincoln and for the Barnes could find a number between four (the 80 percent of the historic Barnes board Lincoln had the right to nominate) and twelve (80 percent of the proposed board) that was acceptable to both the university and the Foundation's financial backers, the latter were tempted to think the former ambassador was right. Adams's comment to the court prompted the new chair of Lincoln's board, Frank Gihan, to declare publicly that the university was not insisting on nominating a majority of an expanded Barnes board. Local and state politicians, eager to add a stellar cultural attraction to center city Philadelphia, redoubled their backstage efforts to keep the curtain from ringing down on a play in progress. On September 12, the one-year anniversary of the filing of the original petition to move the Barnes collection, Bernard Watson announced an agreement whereby the Foundation would again amend its request, now proposing that Lincoln nominate five trustees— a third of an expanded board. The university, in turn, pledged to drop its opposition to the changes sought in the Indenture.

For their part, the neighbors, their concerns about traffic now largely addressed, would be sorry to lose the gallery. Though the Foundation's administrative offices and the arboretum would remain on Latch's Lane under the proposal before Orphans' Court, they wonder for how long—and if the Barnes trustees should eventually move the former and abandon the latter what would happen to the property? The future not only of a lovely botanical garden but also of a unique educational experience and magnificent art collection is in the hands of a judicial system that has historically given great weight to proprietary claims and, while sensitive to the imperative to find solutions, in any particular case, that will most benefit society as a whole, seeks assiduously to fathom donor intent.

Epilogue

Interpreting intent for a new time is never easy. Nevertheless, under United States law, the doctrine of *cy pres* (from the Norman French *cy pres comme possible*) calls for following the donor's wishes as closely as possible even when his or her specific mandates cannot be carried out. Deviation from the administrative terms of a trust may be permitted when changed circumstances make adherence to them impractical, but as a *University of Pennsylvania Law Review* article critical of past Barnes trustees has pointed out, the intended use of deviation is "to perpetuate the viability of the donor's specific intentions."[1] The moral and legal presumption in favor of the gift giver is rooted in the high value Americans place on the right to property. Through will, testament, or trust, individuals can do what they want with what they own as long as their writ shall run. In England, Parliament has sought to limit dead hand control by giving national collections the right to alter terms of bequests after fifty years. In Scotland, the time period is only twenty-five years, and in 1997, a special parliamentary commission allowed the city of Glasgow to send the bulk of an eclectic collection of more than 8,000 works of art it had been given by Sir William Burrell outside the United Kingdom against the late shipping magnate's wishes.[2] The trustees of the Burrell Fund and others who opposed the city's efforts to obtain an export license for the art argued that would-be benefactors might have second thoughts about making bequests if they believed their provisions for managing them would be overturned after their deaths. The sanctity of charitable trusts and indentures is particularly important issue at the end of an era that has seen the creation of vast new wealth. Although art is part of the world's cultural heritage, those now beginning to assemble collections and collectors of the future may be reluctant to donate their masterpieces for public enjoyment if today's guardians of what had been freely given by past benefactors are faithless.

Judge Stanley Ott must be convinced by the Barnes attorneys that the best way to continue to carry out the collector's mission for his Foundation is to load the artwork on a truck and unload it in a new gallery. They must demonstrate to him that evolving needs of the institution justify shredding core elements of Barnes's elaborate operating restrictions while honoring his prohibitions against loans, sales, and new acquisitions. Quite apart from the expansion of the Barnes board, which is impracticably small by the standards of today's educational and cultural institutions that find it necessary to supplement their endowments, the breadth of the current trustees' initial request for change was staggering. It was narrowed by the necessity of placating opponents. Indeed, the Barnes board appeared to have seriously underestimated Lincoln's pride in the trust that Albert Barnes bestowed on the institution as a direct result of his friendship with its first African-American president. Approaching the 150th anniversary of its founding, in 2004, the university, which learned of the collector's decision giving it power to nominate trustees seventeen years after his death, was angered to learn so late in the game about the newest plans affecting its relationship to the Foundation. It fought hard not to lose substantially more of its limited influence on Barnes affairs. Yet the prospective donors were unwilling to tolerate anything less than a self-perpetuating board independent of any other institution. As the autumn of 2003 begins, the three sets of players in the ongoing drama have reached a compromise that they hope will sway Orphans' Court. The stakes involved in the petition before Judge Ott are high. Barnes dictated that if the "collection . . . should . . . for any . . . reason become impossible to administer the trust hereby created . . . shall be applied to an object as nearly within the scope herein indicated and laid down as shall be possible . . . in connection with an existing and operating institution then in being and functioning in Philadelphia . . . or its suburbs."[3] Parsing those instructions is not a task anyone wants to undertake. The alternative, in the view of the Foundation board, is to move the collection to the Parkway with the blessings of a philanthropic community committed to assisting with the transition. Barnes meant for his art to be used by students and enjoyed by a wider public. He wanted more than anything else to convince people of the merit of looking hard at individual paintings and sculptures. The odds of their doing so are at least as great in a Philadelphia gallery as in the one in Merion.

Traveling to Europe on a number of occasions while writing about Albert Barnes and his Foundation, I re-visited some favorite collections. In Paris, at the Musée de l'Orangerie, which houses paintings collected by Paul Guillaume and donated to the French government by his widow, Soutine's *The Little Pastry Cook* recalled the version of the artist's portrait owned by the Foundation. Among the Impressionist works from the Jeu de Paume and the Post-Impressionist paintings from the Musée National d'Art Moderne, now displayed at the Musée d'Orsay, I found in an upper-floor gallery Renoir's late *Bathers*, which Barnes had wanted to buy when the French government momentarily hesitated to accept the painting offered as a gift from the artist's family. A highly finished study for the central figure in Seurat's *Models* is there, as is one of the series of four portraits Cézanne painted of *The Card Players*, a picture smaller than the Barnes masterpiece. Another painting in the magnificent series is in London's Courtauld Gallery at Somerset House.[4] An integral part of the oldest institute for teaching the history of art in Britain, the gallery houses the fine Impressionist and Post-Impressionist collection of the textile manufacturer Samuel Courtauld. Among the pictures he bequeathed for public display, Van Gogh's *Self-Portrait with a Bandaged Ear*, Cézanne's *La Montagne Saint-Victorie*, and Modigliani's *Female Nude* bring immediately to mind Barnes's version of Cézanne's mountain, his van Gogh *Self-Portrait with Grey Hat*, and his voluptuous Modigliani, *Reclining Nude from the Back*. Across the Thames at the National Gallery, *Tiger in a Tropical Storm*, a Henri Rousseau jungle picture reminiscent of the Foundation's *Scout Attacked by a Tiger*, hangs in the East Wing in a room dominated by the third of Cézanne's three large canvases of bathers. Its label notes that the other two are in the United States at the Philadelphia Museum of Art and the Barnes Foundation.

It would have been pleasant, but proved impracticable, to recapture other long-ago experiences—viewing the collections of the Russian industrialists, Sergey Shchukin and Ivan Morozov, now divided between the State Hermitage Museum in St. Petersburg and the Pushkin Museum of Fine Arts in Moscow, as well as seeing the numerous fine paintings of the late nineteenth and early twentieth centuries purchased from private troves and residing in the Museum of Western Art in Tokyo. Nor did I make my way, as I had hoped, to two other collections that I have never seen—the pictures assembled by the Dutch patron Helene Kröller-Müller in the Rijksmuseum Kröller-Müller near Otterlo in The Netherlands and those assembled by the art critic Karl Ernst Osthaus in the Museum Folkwang in Germany's Ruhr Valley. Reflecting on my foreign journeys—and the excursions in search of paintings I made and failed to make, I find myself embracing, without apology, a populist view that great art belongs, where it is most accessible, in cities.

The Barnes Impressionist, Post-Impressionist, and early modern paintings compare admirably with any assemblage in the world. No American collected them with more enthusiasm, in greater numbers, or, overall, more discrimination than the irascible doctor. But he also left us art from Africa of astonishing stylistic breadth. Neither in his acquisition nor display did he make invidious distinctions between the aesthetic achievements of different cultures. The collector provided us with a kind of metaphor for his acuity when he told John Dewey that he had seen a Picasso in the snow. His legacy can be judged, in part, bitter if it is measured by the controversy that he courted and that his Indenture has provoked since his death. But Albert Barnes deserves more honor than he has received for the moral sensibility that informed his appreciation of the talent and capacities of men and women of African decent, for the intellectual discernment that permitted him to grasp how their art enriched the larger Western aesthetic tradition, and for the liberal spirit that guided his creation of a school to teach generations of students his method of analyzing the structure of the painted canvas by focusing on the expressive ordering of form and colors. As for the pictures, wherever they will hang in the future, for these, we can all be grateful. They speak for themselves—and provide a lesson worth learning about the difficult and imprecise science of philanthropy.

Notes

Introduction

1. Albert C. Barnes, "The Art of the American Negro," in *The Barnwell Addresses*, vol. II (Philadelphia: The Central High School, 1937), p. 379. Barnes delivered the fifty-fourth Barnwell Address at his alma mater on April 27, 1936.
2. See Samuel A. Floyd, Jr., *The Power of Black Music: Interpreting Its History from Africa to the United States* (New York: Oxford University Press, 1995), p. 40.
3. Barnes, "The Art of the American Negro," p. 376.
4. Ibid., p. 380.
5. John Dewey, "Dedication Address," *Journal of the Barnes Foundation*, May 1925, p. 5f.
6. Albert C. Barnes, "Negro Art and America," *Survey Graphic*, March 1925, p. 669.

Chapter 1: The Early Years

1. Robert W. Todd, *Methodism of The Peninsula* (Philadelphia: Methodist Episcopal Book Rooms, 1886), p. 181.
2. Ibid.
3. See Nancy L. Stein, Elizabeth Wade, and Maria D. Liwag, "A Theoretical Approach to Understanding and Remembering Emotional Events," in *Memory for Everyday and Emotional Events*, edited by Nancy L. Stein, Peter A. Ornstein, Barbara Tversky, and Charles Brainerd (Mahwah, NJ: Lawrence Erlbaum Associates, Inc., 1997), pp. 15-47.
4. "A Clever Town Built By Quakers," *Harper's New Monthly Magazine*, February 1882, p. 325.
5. Ibid.
6. See Theodore Hershberg, "Free Blacks in Antebellum Philadelphia," in *The People of Philadelphia*, edited by Allen F. Davis and Mark H. Haller (Philadelphia: Temple University Press, 1973), p. 111.
7. See *Philadelphia: A 300-Year History* (New York: W. W. Norton & Company, 1982), p. 385f.
8. *Douglas's Monthly*, February 1862. Quoted in Philip S. Foner, "The Battle to End Discrimination Against Negroes in Philadelphia Streetcars: (Part I) Background and Beginning of the Battle," *Pennsylvania History* 40 (July 1973), p. 266 and in *Philadelphia: A 300-Year History*, p. 386.
9. See W. E. B. Du Bois, *The Philadelphia Negro* (1899), reprint edition (Philadelphia: University of Pennsylvania Press, 1996), pp. 200 and 208. Statistics are for 1880. During the generation between the American Revolution and the War of 1812, itinerant Methodist preachers reached out to black slaves and lower-class whites alike in a still unparalleled effort to create an interracial society. Methodist circuit riders preached against the evils of slavery. They believed freedmen and women

could be educated to accept the responsibilities of citizenship and called for the removal of legal obstructions from their forward path. No race was cursed; no individual was predestined to damnation. All who embraced Jesus as their Savior would be raised to a common height. Evangelicals did not distinguish among people on the basis of color but on whether or not they had experienced a rebirth in the Lord. Although, as the nineteenth century wore on, many white Methodists made shameful compromises with the slave system, Methodism was, at its core, integrationist. In the antebellum South, its churches were biracial; in the North, black Methodist preachers were invited to address white Methodist congregations and, in Philadelphia, two of them, Black Harry, who accompanied Bishop Francis Asbury on his missionary journeys, and Richard Allen, founder of the independent African-Methodist Episcopal Church, were among the most popular speakers of their day. Before and after the Civil War, camp meetings, which were almost always organized by Methodist ministers, welcomed both black and white worshippers. In addition to Todd, see Carter G. Woodson, *The History of the Negro Church* (1921), Second Edition (Washington, DC: The Associated Publishers, 1945) and John B. Boles, editor, *Master & Slaves In the House of the Lord: Race and Religion in the American South 1740-1870* (Lexington: The University of Kentucky Press, 1988).

10. The marriage record for Barnes's parents, filed in the Philadelphia City Archives, gives Lydia's last name as "Schafer," but the 1880 U.S. Census, a Bureau of Pensions form, which was completed by or for John Barnes on May 4, 1898, and the inscription on family tombstones in the Odd Fellows Cemetery in Burlington, New Jersey indicate that the correct spelling is "Schaffer."

11. Albert C. Barnes to Alice Dewey, September 10, 1920. Barnes Foundation Archives. Quoted in a Foundation document entitled "The Barnes Foundation Historic References."

12. The friend's daughter was Jane Nulty. Her father, Albert Nulty, worked for Barnes for more than forty years, and Nulty's children regarded Albert and Laura Barnes almost as grandparents. In the Minutes of the Abington Monthly Meeting, I found a reference to a Sarah Fuller Barnes who may have sailed with the Proprietor on the *Welcome*. Her husband, John, a tailor from the village of West Chiltington in Sussex on England's southern coast, arrived on an unknown ship in the summer of 1683. He built a house in Penn's "greene country towne," but he also purchased land in rural Abington Township. John Barnes lived in Abington for twelve years. After his wife's death and a second marriage, he returned to Philadelphia but not before deeding a 120-acre tract to the Friends on which to build a school and meetinghouse. When he died in 1710, he left an estate of 700 pounds—a handsome sum for a tradesman—but no surviving issue. His will does mention his kinsman, "John Barnes," so it may be he who was Albert Barnes's first paternal ancestor to settle in America. See Mary Sullivan Patterson, "John Barnes—the Man who Owned Jenkintown," *Old York Road Historical Society Bulletin*, March 1960, pp. 13-29.

13. Quoted in Richard M. Ketchum, *The American Heritage Picture History of the Civil War* (New York: Doubleday & Company, 1960), p. 462.

14. Albert C. Barnes to John Dewey, November 3, 1944. *John Dewey Papers*. Special Collections Research Center, Morris Library, Southern Illinois University, Carbondale.

15. See Eileen Southern, *The Music of Black Americans: A History* (New York: W.W. Norton & Company, 1971), p. 96f.

16. W. E. B. Du Bois, *The Souls of Black Folk* (1903), reprint edition (New York: Alfred A. Knopf, 1993), p. 198.

17. Barnes, "The Art of the American Negro," p. 330.

18. See *Philadelphia Inquirer*, August 7, 1883. Reprinted in Andrew Manship, *History of Gospel Tents and Experience* (Philadelphia: published by the author, 1884), p. 41.

19. See *Philadelphia Inquirer*, August 31, 1883. Reprinted in Manship, p. 69. Quotation, p. 46.

20. Manship, p. 40. The author contrasts the humble congregants described in the passage I quoted to congregants of higher social status, e.g., "an honorable gentleman that I had seen sitting as a judge of the court in this city" and "a military gentleman," to illustrate the breadth of the revival's appeal.

21. Barnes, "The Art of the American Negro," p. 380.

22. See Henry Louis Gates and Nellie V. McKay, general editors, *The Norton Anthology of African American Literature* (New York: W. W. Norton & Company, 1997), p. 5.

23. See account of "Having a Hell of a Good Time Playing with Art, Education, Science and Philosophy," a speech Barnes gave to the Rhode Island Philosophical Society, reported by G. Y. Loveridge, *Providence Journal*, January 15, 1943.

24. Albert C. Barnes to Horace Stern, April 11, 1949. *George W. McClelland Administration Records*. University of Pennsylvania Archives (UPA). As an adult, William Scott Vare built a huge contracting company on city business and established a political power base among Philadelphia's ethnically defined wards and the rowhouse neighborhoods below South Street. Elected to the U.S. Senate in 1926, thanks to a well-oiled GOP machine, he was denied his seat when it was established that he had violated the law by spending too much money, at least $800,000, during his campaign!

25. Albert C. Barnes to Horace Mann Bond, September 22, 1949. Archives of Lincoln University and *Horace Mann Bond Papers*, Special Collections and Archives, W.E.B. Du Bois Library, University of Massachusetts, Amherst. Quoted by Julian Bond in "One Memory of Dr. Bond," *The Barnes Bond Connection* (Lincoln University, PA: The Lincoln University Press, 1995) p. 68.

26. See "Having a Hell of a Good Time Playing with Art, Education, Science and Philosophy."

27. Among living alumni, Central could claim one of Philadelphia's richest men, streetcar magnate Peter A. B. Widener, who would later use his fortune to build up a fabulous art collection, the city's most respected lawyer, John G. Johnson, already a discerning collector of paintings, and its most famous painter, Thomas Eakins.

28. Alexander Dallas Bache, *Report to the Controllers of the Public Schools on the Reorganization of Central High School of Philadelphia*, December 10, 1839 (Philadelphia: Board of Controllers, 1839), p. 16. Quoted by David Fleming Labaree, "The People's College: A Sociological Analysis of the Central High School of Philadelphia, 1838-1939," University of Pennsylvania dissertation, 1983, p. 40. Bache, the grandson of Benjamin Franklin, was the second president of Central.

29. Albert C. Barnes to Alice Dewey, September 10, 1920. Barnes Foundation Archives. Quoted in a Foundation document entitled "The Barnes Foundation Historic References."

30. See Ira Glackens, *William Glackens and The Eight* (New York: Horizon Press, 1957), p. 161.

31. Barnes studied English composition, elocution, rhetoric, and logic along with mathematics through the calculus, Latin and German, history, political economy, mental sciences (psychology), geography, natural history, chemistry, physics, astronomy, anatomy and physiology, two years of bookkeeping, and, by the time he graduated, he would take eight semesters of art. He stood nineteenth in his class at the end of his freshman year and won a "meritorious" notice, an honor he also achieved at the end of each the following three semesters. Inexplicably, however, Barnes's grades begun

to slip as he entered his senior year, and with an average of 77.2, he stood twenty-fourth among the remaining twenty-six students in his graduating class.

32. Glackens and Sloan both entered Central the year before Barnes. Glackens must have dropped out for several terms, since he did not graduate until February of 1890. Sloan left without graduating in April of 1888.

33. Albert C. Barnes to Alice Dewey, September 10, 1920. Barnes Foundation Archives. Quoted in a Foundation document entitled "The Barnes Foundation Historic References."

34. Central's original classical elective was abandoned in 1839, three years after its founding, and only reinstated in 1889, the year of Barnes's graduation, when the school adopted a new curriculum that was self-consciously college preparatory.

35. See Henry Hart, *Dr. Barnes of Merion: An Appreciation* (New York: Farrar, Straus and Company, 1963), p. 33. Barnes's widow, Laura, cooperated in the book's publication.

36. See "Having a Hell of a Good Time Playing with Art, Education, Science and Philosophy."

37. His three-year medical school average was a solid 84.5 on the basis of seventeen graded examinations. His best marks were in general pathology (96), medical chemistry (95), and general chemistry (94); his worst, aside from a failing grade in histology his first year, were in obstetrics (76) and clinical surgery (70).

38. See Ira Leo Schamberg, "A. C. Barnes, M.D., vs. J. F. Schamberg, M.D.: A Chemotherapeutic Confrontation," *Transactions and Studies of The College of Physicians of Philadelphia*, fourth series, p. 289.

39. Albert C. Barnes to John Dewey, December 31, 1919. *John Dewey Papers.*

40. See Richard J. Wattenmaker, "Dr. Albert C. Barnes and The Barnes Foundation," in *Great French Paintings from The Barnes Foundation* (New York: Alfred A. Knopf, 1993), p. 4. Wattenmaker gives no sources for his statements that Barnes served as an intern at Polyclinic or Mercy hospitals, but as a former teacher at the Barnes Foundation would have had access to documents in the Foundation's still largely uncataloged archives.

41. See Hart, p.34.

42. Ibid.

43. *Medical Class of 1892 Decennial Book* (Philadelphia: University of Pennsylvania, 1902), p. 16. UPA. Humboldt University (known as the University of Friedrich-Wilhelm in the 1890s and later as the University of Berlin) has no record of Barnes as either a regularly enrolled or special student and the Technical University of Berlin lost its record of matriculated foreign students during World War II.

44. See "Having a Hell of a Good Time Playing with Art, Education, Science and Philosophy."

45. See Hart, p. 35.

46. See A. H. Shaw, "De Medici in Merion," *New Yorker*, September 22, 1928, p. 29 and Carl W. McCardle, "The Terrible Tempered Dr. Barnes," Part I, *Saturday Evening Post*, March 21, 1942, p. 96.

47. See Jonathan Michael Liebenau, "Medical Science and Medical Industry, 1890-1929: A Study of Pharmaceutical Manufacturing in Philadelphia," Ph.D. dissertation, University of Pennsylvania, 1981, for a brief history of H. K. Mulford and Company.

48. See Albert C. Barnes to John Dewey, May 15, 1918 and October 15, 1945. *John Dewey Papers.*

49. Albert C. Barnes to Horace Mann Bond, May 28, 1951. *Horace Mann Bond Papers.*

50. See *Medical Class of 1892 Decennial Book*, p. 16, UPA, and letter from Albert C. Barnes to Ralph Bunche, March 12, 1951, *Horace Mann Bond Papers*. In his biography of his father, Ira Glackens also refers to Barnes's study of medicine in Germany. See Glackens, p. 164. But in response to a query from the author, the archivist at Ruprechts-Karls-Universität Heidelberg could find no record of a degree being conferred upon Barnes in 1900. McCardle's report (ibid., p. 97) that Barnes did not receive a Heidelberg Ph.D. because he refused to pay a $50 fee cannot be substantiated and is unlikely since his dissertation would hardly qualify for a research degree even if he had been able and willing to pay the required fee. But Barnes did hold an A.M. from Central High School. His alma mater customarily awarded a master's degree upon request to its alumni who had earned university degrees, and the credential-conscious physician asked for and received his second Central degree in 1894.

51. An account of Barnes meeting with Hermann Hille is given in a letter Hermann Hille wrote to William Schack, July 13, 1961, after the publication of *Art and Argyrol* (New York: Thomas Yoseloff, 1960) in which Schack repeated the erroneous rumor that Hille had committed suicide. See *William Schack Papers*. Archives of American Art, Smithsonian Institution.

52. Barnes to Bunche, March 12, 1951. *Horace Mann Bond Papers*.

53. See Albert C. Barnes and Hermann Hille, "A New Substitute for Silver Nitrate," *Medical Record* (now the *New York Medical Journal*), May 24, 1902. Reprinted in *Materia Medica*, vol. 175, pp. 3-8.

54. Albert C. Barnes to John Dewey, December 8, 1925. *John Dewey Papers*.

55. See Albert C. Barnes and H. Hille, "The Pharmacology of Iron; With Especial Reference To A New Compound of Iron," *Therapeutic Monthly*, June 1901, p. 56f.

56. See Albert C. Barnes and H. Hille, "A New Method of Making Tannin Available As An Intestinal Astringent," *Philadelphia Medical Journal*, July 1901, p. 111f.

57. Wallace was a self-taught chemist who was first employed by the University of Pennsylvania in 1880 to manage the chemical storeroom. In 1888, he began assisting the eminent chemist Edgar Fahs Smith with his lectures and, in 1891, was appointed an assistant and, later, an instructor in chemistry. He published a number of papers with Smith and was elected to the honorary scientific fraternity, Sigma Xi. In 1916, Penn awarded him an honorary doctorate in chemistry, and from 1920 until his retirement in 1931, he held a full professorship in inorganic chemistry.

58. Barnes and Hille, "A New Substitute for Silver Nitrate," p. 5.

59. Ibid., p. 8 and "About Silver," a promotional pamphlet distributed by Barnes and Hille and preserved in the Archives of the Philadelphia College of Physicians.

60. See *Annual Report of the Commissioner of Patents for the Year 1902* (Washington, DC: Government Printing Office, 1903), p. 937.

61. See notes made by William Schack after a conversation with Hermann Hille, which followed the publication of *Art and Argyrol*. *William Schack Papers*.

62. Ibid., p. 40. As both earlier and subsequent biographers did, Hart may have taken the $1,600 figure from Carl W. McCardle's account of Barnes's life in the *Saturday Evening Post*. See "The Terrible Tempered Dr. Barnes," Part II, March 28, 1942, p. 21. McCardle interviewed Barnes at length for the article to which Barnes objected strongly upon its publication. But since Hart had many conversations with Barnes over the course of several decades and wrote his memoir with the cooperation of Laura Barnes, I accept the figure, which is not otherwise verifiable, as accurate. The point is that Barnes and Hille got their business going with remarkably little capital.

63. See Albert C. Barnes, "The Barnes Foundation," *New Republic*, March 14, 1923, p. 65.

64. Information about the partnership agreement between Barnes and Hille is found in the Bill in Equity brought by Barnes against Hill in the Court of Common Pleas of Philadelphia County, No. 4, March Term 1907, No. 5686.
65. Albert C. Barnes to John Dewey, December 8, 1925. *John Dewey Papers*.
66. Albert C. Barnes to J.F. Schamberg, May 7, 1917. Reprinted in Schamberg, p. 291.
67. See notes made by William Schack after a conversation with Hermann Hille's daughter, which took place following the publication of *Art and Argyrol*. *William Schack Papers*.
68. Albert C. Barnes to John Dewey, April 18, 1925. *John Dewey Papers*.
69. See *Barnes et al. v. Pierce* (Circuit Court, S.D. New York, September 23, 1908), *Federal Reporter*, vol. 64., pp. 213f.
70. See McCardle, Part II, p. 21 and Hart, p. 40.
71. See Frank Jewett Mather, "John G. Johnson," *Nation*, April 19, 1917, p. 467 and Aline B. Saarinen, *The Proud Possessors* (New York: Random House, 1958), pp. 92-117.
72. *Albert C. Barnes v. Hermann Hille*, Court of Common Pleas of Philadelphia County, No. 4, March Term 1907, No. 5686.
73. Hart, p. 43. See also McCardle, II, p. 78. A note written by William Schack, based on a conversation with members of the Hille family, states the purchase price was $350,000. See *William Schack Papers*.
74. See Hermann Hille to David M. Fell, April 10, 1942. *William Schack Papers*.
75. See *Philadelphia: A 300-Year History*, p. 492.
76. See Carol Golab, "The Immigrant and the City: Poles, Italians, and Jews in Philadelphia, 1870-1920," in *The People of Philadelphia*, edited by Allen F. Davis and Mark H. Haller (Philadelphia: Temple University Press, 1973), p. 224.

Chapter 2: Experiments in Education and Living

1. Barnes, "The Barnes Foundation," p. 65.
2. See Stuart D. Brandes, *American Welfare Capitalism: 1880-1940* (Chicago: The University of Chicago Press, 1976), p. 59.
3. Barnes, "The Barnes Foundation," p. 66.
4. Albert C. Barnes to John Dewey, April 5, 1942. *John Dewey Papers*.
5. George Santayana, *Reason in Common Sense* (New York: Charles Scribner's Sons, 1905), p. 291.
6. George Santayana, *Reason in Art* (New York: Charles Scribner's Sons, 1905), p. 222.
7. Mary Mullen, "An Experiment in Adult Negro Education," *Opportunity*, May 1926, p. 160.
8. Barnes, "The Barnes Foundation," p. 65.
9. Mullen, p. 160.
10. Albert C. Barnes to John Dewey, October 20, 1920. See also Barnes to Dewey, June 30, 1920. *John Dewey Papers*.
11. Mullen, p. 161.
12. Albert C. Barnes to John Dewey, September 2, 1920. *John Dewey Papers*.
13. Barnes, "The Barnes Foundation," p. 66.
14. Mullen, p. 161.
15. Barnes, "The Barnes Foundation," p. 66. See also Hart, p. 45 and Schack, p. 58f.
16. Mullen, p. 161.
17. Barnes, "The Barnes Foundation," p. 66.
18. I have used the original spelling, "Latch's," with an apostrophe throughout the book. The street eventually came to be known as "Latches" Lane.

19. At the south end of Rose Hill was "Greystone," the large estate of Joseph B. Townsend, a prominent attorney and a director of Pennsylvania Hospital. Across the way was "Corkerhill," the home of Frank Thomson, the former president of the Pennsylvania Railroad Company, and at the north end was property that had been owned by the Latch family for generations. "York Lynne," the nineteen-acre estate of banker John Odgers Gilmore, president of the Colonial Trust Company, surrounded the Barnes's property on two sides. Samuel Croft, founder and president of a large confectionery and chocolate company, owned "Villa Zorayda" on the west side of the road.

20. In 1912, when the six-acre Marston property across the street from "Lauraston" became available, Barnes paid $18,750 for the parcel. The next year he acquired another two-acre tract for $25,000 from the estate of John W. Lodge and six and a half acres, at a cost of nearly $60,000, from the estate of Edward B. Latch. After renovating the Marston house, he sold it to Ella Longstreth Supplee. He sold the Lodge property to Arthur M. Lewis, and he had built and then sold four substantial houses on the former Latch land.

Chapter 3: The Collector and His Tutors

1. Saarinen, p. 94.
2. Albert C. Barnes, "How To Judge A Painting," *Arts and Decoration*, April 1915, p. 246.
3. See John Sloan, *Gist of Art* (New York: American Artist Group, 1944), p. 25. Sloan quotes Glackens on Barnes's nascent collection.
4. Ibid.
5. Ibid.
6. Ibid., p. 248.
7. Guy Pène DuBois, *William J. Glackens* (New York: The Whitney Museum of American Art, 1931), p. 12. For contemporary assessments of the painter, see Richard J. Wattenmaker, "The Art of William Glackens," University Art Gallery Bulletin, (Rutgers University, New Brunswick, NJ), vol. 1, no. 1 (1967), pp. 1-11, and William H. Gerdts, *William Glackens* (Ft. Lauderdale, FL: The Museum of Art and New York: Abbeville Press, 1996).
8. See Ira Glackens, *William Glackens and The Eight* (New York: Horizon Press, 1957), p. 155. Glackens's story of his father's relationships with his friends devotes a chapter to his ties with Barnes based on letters and family stories as well as his own memories.
9. Forbes Watson, "William Glackens," *Arts*, April 1923, p. 248.
10. Albert C. Barnes, *The Art in Painting* (1925), third edition (New York: Harcourt, Brace & World, 1928), p. 289.
11. Albert C. Barnes, "L'Art de William Glackens," *Les à Arts Paris* (November 1924), p. 3.
12. See Glackens, p. 156.
13. Helen Farr Sloan to William Schack, April 25, 1957. *William Schack Papers.*
14. See Robert Henri to Albert C. Barnes, January 1, 1914, *Robert Henri Papers*, Yale Collection of American Literature, Beinecke Rare Book and Manuscript Library, Yale University, "L'Art de William Glackens," p. 3, and Barnes, *The Art in Painting*, p. 494f.
15. William Glackens to Edith Glackens, February 16, 1912. Quoted in Glackens, p. 158.
16. A detailed account of Glackens's purchases, checked against gallery records, was provided by Anne Distel, "Dr. Barnes in Paris," in *Great French Paintings from The*

Barnes Foundation, p. 34. See also John Rewald, "Dr. Albert C. Barnes and Cézanne," *Gazette Des Beaux-Arts*, Janvier-Fevrier 1988, pp. 173-181 and John Rewald, *Cézanne and America: Dealers, Collectors, Artists and Critics, 1891-1921* (Princeton, NJ: Princeton University Press, 1989), passim.

17. William Glackens to Edith Glackens, February 21, 1912. Quoted in Glackens, p. 159.
18. Ibid., p. 160.
19. Barnes, "How To Judge A Painting," pp. 217 and 246.
20. Leo Stein to Albert Barnes, July 8, 1947. Quoted in Leo Stein, *Journey Into Self* (New York: Crown Publishers, 1950), p. 294.
21. See Brenda Wineapple, *Sister Brother: Gertrude and Leo Stein* (New York: G. P. Putnam's Sons, 1996), p. 204f.
22. Glackens, p. 216.
23. Leo Stein to Trigant Burrow, June 30, 1934. Quoted in *Journey Into Self*, p. 140.
24. Albert C. Barnes to John Dewey, October 12, 1927. *John Dewey Papers.*
25. See Albert C. Barnes to Leo Stein, March 30, 1913. *Leo Stein Papers.* Yale Collection of American Literature, Beinecke Rare Book and Manuscript Library, Yale University.
26. See François Daulté, *Auguste Renoir: Catalogue Raisonné de l'Oeuvre*, vol. I (Lausanne, Switzerland: Durand-Ruel, 1971), no. 144 and no. 180. According to Daulté, Barnes paid 11,500 francs for *Girl with Jumping Rope.*
27. See Distel, pp. 34 and 297
28. See Distel, p. 301. With Durand-Ruel acting as agent, Barnes eventually bought *Women in Striped Dress* in 1915 for 40,000 francs, which was 5,000 francs more than Vollard's 1912 asking price.
29. "Art in France," *Burlington Magazine*, January 1913, p. 240.
30. See Rewald, *Cézanne and America*, p. 162. The paintings were *Still Life*, *Peach and Grape on a Plate* and *Still Life, Three Apples.*
31. Ibid., p. 263. Distel gives the date of the sale of the portrait of Mme Cézanne as 9 December and the price as 40,000 francs. She says it was on 11 December that Vollard sold the other Cézannes, which she identifies as *Bathers* and *Still Life*. See Distel, pp. 30f.
32. See "Art in France," p. 242 and Distel, p. 31. Distel gives the price for *Women with Bouquet* as 24,000 francs and *Women Crocheting* as 17,000 francs. See p. 297.
33. Albert C. Barnes to Arthur B. Davies, February 4, 1913. Barnes Foundation Archives. Quoted in a document entitled "The Barnes Foundation Historic References."
34. See Saarinen, p. 216.
35. See Rewald, *Cézanne and America*, p. 263.
36. Albert C. Barnes to Leo Stein, March 30, 1913. *Leo Stein Papers.*
37. Barnes, "How To Judge A Painting," p. 219. See also Hart, p. 53.
38. See Rewald, *Cézanne and America*, p. 264.
39. See Distel, p. 35f, 54, and 297.
40. See Rewald, *Cézanne and America*, p. 265ff.
41. See Distel, pp. 35 and 297.
42. Quoted by Rewald, "Dr. Albert C. Barnes and Cézanne," p. 175 and *Cézanne and America*, p. 266.
43. Albert C. Barnes to Leo Stein, February 9, 1914. *Leo Stein Papers.*
44. Barnes gave Stein a standing offer of 15,000 francs for the Renoir nude to induce him to withdraw his promise to the rival buyer, but Stein honored his commitment. See Albert C. Barnes to Leo Stein, February 27, 1914 and Leo Stein to Nina Auzias, spring 1914. *Leo Stein Papers.*

45. Albert C. Barnes to Leo Stein, February 27, 1914. *Leo Stein Papers.*
46. See Rewald, *Cézanne and America*, p. 256; Albert C. Barnes to Leo Stein, March 30, 1913, *Leo Stein Papers*; and Wineapple, p. 378. Rewald puts the date of the Cézanne sale in 1913, but Wineapple, more reliably in this case, in the spring of 1914.
47. See John Richardson, *A Life of Picasso*, vol. II (New York: Random House, 1996), pp. 311 and 467 and Rewald, Rewald, *Cézanne and America*, p. 267.
48. See Distel, p. 297f and Rewald, *Cézanne and America*, pp. 267 and 279. Rewald stated that Barnes bought four Renoirs on April 29, but with the assistance of Caroline Godfroy-Durand-Ruel and others, Distel has identified seven works, which the Durand-Ruel account books record as purchased on May 14. They are: *Seated Women*, 1875; *Women Fixing Her Hair*, 1887; *View of Cagnes*, 1908; *Landscape with Figure*, 1894: two works with identical titles, *Study of a Head of a Girl*; *Study, Woman Torso*; and *Bather Reflected in Water*. The Cézanne was designated *Le Moulin*, according to Rewald, who believed it might have been the landscape with a single house known as *Mill*, 1888-90.
49. Quoted by Rewald, *Cézanne and America*, p. 267.
50. Albert C. Barnes to Leo Stein, February 9, 1914. *Leo Stein Papers.*
51. Guy Pène DuBois, "A Modern American Collection," *Arts and Decoration*, June 1914, p. 305.
52. Barnes, "How to Judge A Painting," p. 248.
53. Glackens, p. 162.
54. Recounted in William Glackens to Edith Glackens, October 25, 1914 and October [n.d.], 1914. See Glackens, p. 162f.
55. See Distel, p. 299.
56. See Rewald, *Cézanne and America*, p. 268. The painting was not a self-portrait but *The Artist's Family*. According to Christopher Riopelle, Barnes finally acquired it through the dealer L. C. Hodebert on February 18, 1927. See *Great French Paintings from The Barnes Foundation*, p. 79.
57. See Rewald, *Cézanne and America*, p. 268.
58. Albert C. Barnes to Leo Stein, July 17, 1914. Barnes Foundation Archives. Quoted in a document entitled "The Barnes Foundation Historic References."
59. Albert C. Barnes to John G. Johnson, January 21, 1915. Barnes Foundation Archives. Quoted in a document entitled "The Barnes Foundation Historic References."
60. Albert C. Barnes to Josiah Penniman, January 27, 1924. *Josiah H. Penniman Administration Records*, University of Pennsylvania Archives.
61. See Albert C. Barnes to Durand-Ruel, June 9, 1914. Cited by Rewald, *Cézanne and America*, p. 267.
62. Albert C. Barnes to John Dewey, October 12, 1921. *John Dewey Papers.*
63. Albert C. Barnes to John Dewey, July 19, 1920. *John Dewey Papers.*
64. Barnes, "How To Judge A Painting," p. 217.
65. See Michael Stein to Gertrude Stein, June 3, 1916. *Gertrude Stein and Alice B. Toklas Papers.* MSS 76. Yale Collection of American Literature, Beinecke Rare Book and Manuscript Library, Yale University. Cited by Rewald, *Cézanne and America*, p. 249. See also Wineapple, pp. 128 and 130.
66. Leo Stein, "Cézanne," *New Republic*, January 22, 1916, p. 297f.
67. Albert C. Barnes, "What Causes Aesthetic Feeling," *New Republic*, February 19, 1916, p 75.
68. Stein, "Cézanne," p. 297.
69. Leo Stein, "Supports His Psychology," *New Republic*, February 26, 1916, p. 105.
70. Albert C. Barnes, "That Psychology Again," *New Republic*, March 18, 1916, p. 188.
71. Michael Stein to Gertrude Stein, June 3, 1913. *Gertrude Stein/Alice B. Toklas Papers.*

Chapter 4: Mr. Dewey

1.   See Edward Burns, ed., *Gertrude Stein on Picasso* (New York: Liveright, 1970), p. 14.
2.   Leo Stein, *Appreciation: Painting, Poetry and Prose* (New York: Crown Publishers, 1947), p. 175.
3.   Albert C. Barnes, "Cubism: Requiescat In Pace," *Arts and Decoration*, January 1916, p. 121f.
4.   Albert C. Barnes to Leo Stein, July 17, 1914. Barnes Foundation Archives. Quoted in a document entitled "The Barnes Foundation Historic References."
5.   See Distel, pp. 69, 86, and 299f.
6.   See Thomas P. Beyer, "What Is Education?" *Dial*, vol. 61 (August 15, 1916), p.103. Cited by George Dykhuizen, *The Life and Mind of John Dewey* (Carbondale: Southern Illinois University Press, 1973), p. 180.
7.   John Dewey, "Theories of Knowledge" in *Democracy and Education* (1916). Reprinted in Louis Menand, ed., *Pragmatism* (New York: Vintage Books, 1997). Quotation, p. 211.
8.   Albert C. Barnes to John Dewey, July 19, 1929. *John Dewey Papers*.
9.   Irwin Edman, *Philosopher's Holiday* (New York: The Viking Press, 1938), p. 141.
10.   Ibid., p. 142.
11.   See Hart, p. 64.
12.   See Corliss Lamont, ed., *Dialogue on John Dewey* (New York: Horizon Press, 1959), p. 47.
13.   Shana Alexander, *Happy Days: My Mother, My Father, My Sister and Me* (New York: Doubleday, 1995), p. 128.
14.   Ibid., p. 129.
15.   Evidence of Dewey's poignant restraint is found in the love poems he wrote to and about Yezierska. The suggestion of emotional immaturity on her part, which matched his emotional reserve, is found in Yezierska's fictionalized accounts of their relationship, particularly *All I Could Never Be* (New York: Brewer, Warren & Putnam, 1932), and her more openly autobiographical *Red Ribbon on a White Horse* (New York: Scribner's, 1950). A careful and extensive study of the relationship between Dewey and Yezierska was made by Jo Ann Boydston and, with her assistance, Louise Levitas Henriksen prepared a detailed and fascinating account of her mother's life. See *The Poems of John Dewey*, edited with an Introduction by Jo Ann Boydston (Carbondale: Southern Illinois University Press, 1977) and Louise Levitas Henriksen, *Anzia Yezierska: A Writer's Life* (New Brunswick, NJ: Rutgers University Press, 1988).
16.   Albert C. Barnes to John Dewey, November 7, 1917. *John Dewey Papers*.
17.   John Dewey to Albert C. Barnes, November 8, 1917. *John Dewey Papers*.
18.   Albert C. Barnes to John Dewey, January 10, 1918. *John Dewey Papers*.
19.   John Dewey to Albert C. Barnes, January 22, 1918. *John Dewey Papers*.
20.   Albert C. Barnes to John Dewey, January 21, 1918. *John Dewey Papers*.
21.   See John Dewey to Albert C. Barnes, January 24, 1918, and Alice Dewey to Albert C. Barnes, March 15, 1918. *John Dewey Papers*.
22.   See Albert C. Barnes, November 16, 1929. *John Dewey Papers*.
23.   Albert C. Barnes to John Dewey, January 24, 1918. *John Dewey Papers*.
24.   See Alice Dewey to Albert C. Barnes, March 15, 1918. *John Dewey Papers*.
25.   See Albert C. Barnes to Alice Dewey, March 14, 1918, Alice Dewey to Albert C. Barnes, March 15, 1918, and Albert C. Barnes to Alice Dewey, April 27, 1918. *John Dewey Papers*.

26. See Lamont, p. 27 and Steven C. Rockefeller, *John Dewey: Religious Faith and Democratic Humanism* (New York: Columbia University Press, 1991), p. 334f

27. See John Dewey, "Introduction," in F.M. Alexander, *The Use of the Self*, in *Late Works*, vol. 6, p. 317. Quoted by Rockefeller, p. 461.

28. See Albert C. Barnes to John Dewey, April 5, 1918. *John Dewey Papers.*

29. Frances Bradshaw replaced Sterling Lamprecht, a student of Dewey's about whom Barnes had some doubts and persuaded Dewey to ease off the team on the grounds that he was soon to begin Army service.

30. Albert C. Barnes to John Dewey, April 20, 1918. *John Dewey Papers.*

31. Albert C. Barnes to John Dewey, May 15, 1918. *John Dewey Papers.*

32. John Dewey to Albert C. Barnes, May 16, 1918. *John Dewey Papers.*

33. Albert C. Barnes to John Dewey, April 26, 1918. *John Dewey Papers.*

34. Albert C. Barnes to Alice Dewey, April 27, 1918. *John Dewey Papers.*

35. Albert C. Barnes to John Dewey, May 24, 1918. See also Barnes to Dewey, May 16, 1918. *John Dewey Papers.*

36. Albert C. Barnes to John Dewey, May 24, 1918. *John Dewey Papers.*

37. Anzia Yezierska, *All I Could Never Be* (New York: Brewer, Warren and Putnam, 1932), pp. 58-60. Quoted by Henriksen, p. 96. Yezierska and Boydston believe that the letters quoted in *All I Could Never Be* and in *Red Ribbon on a White Horse* (New York: Charles Scribner's Sons, 1950), were part of Dewey and Yezierska's actual correspondence. See Henriksen, p. 309, footnote 99.

38. Albert C. Barnes to John Dewey, June 28, 1918. *John Dewey Papers.*

39. Albert C. Barnes to John Dewey, June 12, 1918. *John Dewey Papers.*

40. See Hart, p. 66.

41. Albert C. Barnes to John Dewey, June 28, 1918. *John Dewey Papers.*

42. John Dewey to Albert C. Barnes, July 12, 1918. *John Dewey Papers.*

43. Irwin Edman, "The Fourth Part of Poland," *Nation*, vol. 107 (September 28, 1918), p. 342.

44. See Jay Martin, *The Education of John Dewey: A Biography* (New York: Columbia University Press, 2002), p. 297.

45. Dewey identified three major obstacles to the complete and successful integration of the Poles into American society: the attempt of older Americans "to impose external habits upon . . . immigrant[s]" instead of associating with them as "equals" who contribute "value" to the nation's life; the vanity and personal ambition of the political and religious leaders of the foreign-born; and "the plunge en masse into congested industrial centers" of a peasant people whose lack of formal education together with their "emotional knowledge of the glories of historic Poland" combined "to make them readier material for subjection [by] . . . a self-constituted circle of men . . . who. . . [we]re playing Providence to the destinies of nations." He said that Paderewski and his co-conspirators had hoodwinked an American press that was as susceptible as ordinary Poles to "the glamour of a great name and personality" and little interested in the affairs of "foreigners." Not at all sanguine about the outcome of the convention, he warned that what was at stake might well be the "future of Poland." See John Dewey, "Autocracy Under Cover," *New Republic*, vol. 16 (August 24, 1918), pp. 103-106.

46. Albert C. Barnes to John Dewey, August 15, 1918. *John Dewey Papers.*

47. On the basis, in part, of his attendance at the Detroit convention, Irwin Edman developed his data into an article for the *Nation* in which he accused the head of the Paris-based reactionaries of "pronounced anti-Semitism." Despite "murmurings" against its financial mismanagement, the monarchist faction had easily secured passage of a resolution recognizing its members "as controlling Polish affairs in this

country and abroad," Edman reported. He depicted the vote as a "definite stand . . . against Americanization" and "the principle of self-determination reversed in our midst." See Edman, "The Fourth Part of Poland," p. 342f.

48. See John Dewey to Albert C. Barnes, August 22, 1918 and August 29, 1918. *John Dewey Papers.*
49. See John Dewey to Louis D. Brandeis, August 29, 1918. *John Dewey Papers.*
50. Albert C. Barnes to John Dewey, August 30, 1918. *John Dewey Papers.*
51. Albert C. Barnes to John Dewey, September 7, 1918. *John Dewey Papers.*
52. See Albert C. Barnes to John Dewey, December 9, 1918. *John Dewey Papers.*
53. Yezierska, *Red Ribbon on a White Horse*, p. 113.
54. Anzia Yezierska, "Wild Winter Love," *Century*, vol. 113 (February 1927), p. 490. See discussion by Henriksen, p. 113.
55. John Dewey, #6, *The Poems of John Dewey*, p. 6.
56. Yezierska, *Red Ribbon on a White Horse*, p. 116.
57. See John Dewey to Albert C. Barnes, September 17, 1918. *John Dewey Papers.* Also Henriksen, p. 115.
58. John Dewey to Albert C. Barnes, September 16, 1918. *John Dewey Papers.*
59. John Dewey to Albert C. Barnes September 17, 1918 and October 10, 1918. *John Dewey Papers.*
60. John Dewey to Albert C. Barnes, n.d. *John Dewey Papers.*
61. Albert C. Barnes to John Dewey, November 19, 1918. *John Dewey Papers.*
62. Albert C. Barnes to G.M. Hitchcock quoted in Albert C. Barnes to John Dewey, November 25, 1918. *John Dewey Papers.* See also *Dial*, vol. 65 (December 28, 1918), p. 597.
63. Albert C. Barnes to John Dewey, December 9, 1918. *John Dewey Papers.*
64. Albert C. Barnes, "Democracy, Watch Your Step!" *Dial*, vol. 65 (December 28, 1918), pp. 595-597.
65. Ibid., p. 597
66. Albert C. Barnes to John Dewey, December 21, 1918. *John Dewey Papers.*
67. Albert C. Barnes to John Dewey, December 9, 1918. *John Dewey Papers.*
68. Albert C. Barnes to Jay Frank Schamberg, May 7, 1917 and May 11, 1917. Reprinted in Ira Leo Schamberg, p. 291.
69. Albert C. Barnes to Jay Frank Schamberg, May 11, 1917. Reprinted in Schamberg, p. 291.
70. Albert C. Barnes to Jay Frank Schamberg, May 26, 1917. Reprinted in Schamberg, p. 292.
71. Albert C. Barnes to Jay Frank Schamberg, February 14, 1919. Reprinted in Schamberg, p. 292.
72. Jay Frank Schamberg to Albert C. Barnes, February 25, 1919. Reprinted in Schamberg, p. 292f.
73. Albert C. Barnes to Jay Frank Schamberg, February 26, 1919. Reprinted in Schamberg, p. 293.
74. Albert C. Barnes to Jay Frank Schamberg, March 1, 1919. Reprinted in Schamberg, p. 294.
75. John Dewey to Albert C. Barnes, January 9, 1919. *John Dewey Papers.*
76. John Dewey to Albert C. Barnes, April 16, 1925. *John Dewey Papers.*

Chapter 5: "The Temple in Merion"

1. Jean Renoir, *Renoir, My Father* (Boston: Little, Brown and Company, 1962), p. 456.
2. See Distel, p. 299.

3. See Albert C. Barnes and Violette De Mazia, *The Art of Renoir* (Merion, PA: The Barnes Foundation, 1935), p. 78.
4. Albert C. Barnes to John Dewey, February 17, 1920. *John Dewey Papers.*
5. Leo Stein was detained as the son of an enemy alien, although his German-born father was, in fact, long dead and had been a naturalized American citizen.
6. Leo Stein, "Practice—Nirvana," miscellaneous papers, undated. *Leo Stein Papers.* Quoted by Wineapple, p. 167.
7. Hart, p. 72.
8. Leo Stein to Albert C. Barnes, December 29, 1920. *Leo Stein Papers.* Quoted in Stein, *Journey Into Self*, p. 83f.
9. Albert C. Barnes to John Dewey, February 17, 1920. *John Dewey Papers.*
10. Leo Stein to Albert C. Barnes, March 8, 1921. *Leo Stein Papers.* Reprinted in *Journey Into Self*, p. 86f.
11. Albert C. Barnes to John Dewey, May 14, 1921. *John Dewey Papers.*
12. Rewald, *Cézanne in America*, p. 271f. In addition to *Sainte-Victorie* (V.457), Rewald lists Barnes's purchases as: *La Chaumière* (V.451), *Cruche, pommes et rideau* (V.499), *Nature morte* (V. 745), *Petite Estaque, vue de la mer* (V.293), *Pommes, rideau, cruche, serviette* (V.601), *Pommes et poire dans une assiette* (V.740), *Chrysanthèmes* (V.755), *Rosiers, cafetière, bouteille et rideau* (V.602), *Fruits et tête de morte* (V.758), *Pot vanné, fruit et serviette* (V.737), *Fruits et rideau bleu* (V.611), and *Fruits dans une assiette et pot de confitures* (V.363).
13. Albert C. Barnes to John Dewey, June 30, 1920. *John Dewey Papers.*
14. Albert C. Barnes to John Dewey, January 4, 1921. *John Dewey Papers.*
15. See Rewald, *Cézanne in America* p. 271.
16. Albert C. Barnes to John Dewey, June 30, 1920. *John Dewey Papers.*
17. Helen Farr Sloan to William Schack, April 25, 1957. *William Schack Papers.*
18. Barnes paid Alfred Stieglitz $175 for the four paintings. See Alfred Stieglitz to Albert C. Barnes, May 18, 1921, and Albert C. Barnes to Marsden Hartley, June 2, 1921, *Alfred Stieglitz/Georgia O'Keeffe Archive*, MSS 85, Yale Collection of American Literature, Beinecke Rare Book and Manuscript Library, Yale University.
19. See Alice Dewey to Albert C. Barnes, May 30, 1920 and Albert C. Barnes to Alice Dewey, July 1, 1920. *John Dewey Papers.*
20. Albert C. Barnes to Alice Dewey, Ibid.
21. Albert C. Barnes, "Renoir: An Appreciation," *Dial*, vol. 68 (February 1920), p. 167.
22. Albert C, Barnes, "Cézanne," *Arts & Decoration*, November 1920, p. 44B.
23. Albert C. Barnes to John Dewey, January 29, 1921. *John Dewey Papers.*
24. See Dorothy Grafly to William Schack, June 6, 1957, *William Schack Papers*, and Aileen Saarinen's notes on a conversation with R. Sturgis Ingersoll, Roll 5-1560, *Aileen Saarinen Papers*, Archives of American Art.
25. Among the other artists represented in the show were Louis Bouche, James A. Daugherty, Bernard Gussow, and Maurice Stern. See Record of the Purchases from "Later Tendencies." Archives of the Pennsylvania Academy of the Fine Arts.
26. "Expert Praises Modern Show," *Philadelphia Inquirer*, May 1, 1921. Clipping in Archives of the Pennsylvania Academy of the Fine Arts.
27. Henry James, *The American Scene* (New York: Charles Scribner's Sons, 1946), p. 277. Originally published 1907.
28. "Modernists Insane, Say These Medics," *American Art News*, June 4, 1921, p. 3.
29. "Comment on the Arts," *Arts*, June-July 1921, pp. 36 and 38. Barnes's remarks, made in response to a writer's request for his views, were originally published in Hamilton Easter Field, "Dr. Barnes Says Modern Artists Not Insane," *Brooklyn Eagle*, May 22, 1921, p. 22.

30. "Counter Attack In Fight On Modernists," *American Art News*, October 15, 1921, p 1.
31. Albert C. Barnes, "The Temple," *Opportunity*, May 1924, p. 138f.
32. Ibid., p. 139.
33. Ibid.
34. Ibid., p. 140.
35. See Albert C. Barnes to Arthur Carles, April 18, 1921. Archives of the Pennsylvania Academy of the Fine Arts.
36. Alice Dewey to Albert C. Barnes, August 19, 1920. *John Dewey Papers*.
37. Leo Stein, "Notebook, August 1929 to August 1930." Reprinted in *Journey Into Self*, p. 115.
38. Paul Cret, "The Building for The Barnes Foundation," *Arts*, January 1923, p. 8.
39. John Dewey to Albert C. Barnes, January 15, 1920. *John Dewey Papers*.
40. John Dewey to Albert C. Barnes, March 5, 1922. *John Dewey Papers*.
41. Albert C. Barnes to John Dewey, March 7, 1922. *John Dewey Papers*.
42. Albert C. Barnes to Horace Mann Bond, May 21, 1951. *Horace Bond Papers*.
43. "Dr. Barnes Gives $6,000,000 for Art Museum in Merion," *Public Ledger*, January 13, 1923, p. 1. Cf. "Merion to House Art of 'Radicals'," *Evening Bulletin*, January 13, 1923. p. 3.
44. See Distel, p. 298.
45. See Christopher Riopelle, *Great French Paintings from The Barnes Foundation*, p. 64 and Jack Flam, *Great French Paintings from The Barnes Foundation*, p. 306. *The Joy of Life* is knows as both *La joie de vivre* and *Le bonheur de vivre*. The French title, *La joie de vivre*, was preferred by Dr. Barnes.
46. Albert C. Barnes to William Glackens, January 22, 1923. Quoted in Glackens, p. 167f.
47. See Irene Patai, *Encounters: The Life of Jacques Lipchitz* (New York: Funk & Wagnalls, 1961), pp. 201-216.
48. In *Soutine* (New York: Crown Publishers, 1973), Raymond Cognait says Barnes purchased seventy-five paintings; Robert Carlen, the Philadelphia art dealer, told William Schack, the number was sixty. See Cognait, p. 65 and Schack, p. 121.
49. See Biddle, pp. 235f.
50. Forbes Watson, "The Barnes Foundation," *Arts*, January 1923, pp. 9 and 13.
51. "Merion to House Art of 'Radicals.'"
52. Watson, p. 16.
53. See "Merion to House Art of 'Radicals'" and "Dr. Barnes Gives $6,000,000 for Art Museum in Merion."
54. "African Art Work for Merion Museum Is Most Comprehensive in the World," *Public Ledger*, February 5, 1923, p. 3.
55. Barnes had urged Dewey to help Buermeyer find a post at Columbia, and while Dewey was willing to recommend Buermeyer's philosophical articles to his colleagues there, he could promise nothing in terms of an academic appointment for the author. Quotation Albert C. Barnes to John Dewey, January 17, 1921. *John Dewey Papers*.
56. See "African Art Work For Merion Museum Is Most Comprehensive in the World."
57. Paul Guillaume, "Le Medici de le Monde Nouveau," *Les Arts à Paris*, January 1923, p. 2.
58. Albert C. Barnes to John Frederick Lewis, May 21, 1923. Archives of the Pennsylvania Academy of the Fine Arts.
59. Albert C. Barnes to Arthur B. Carles, April 5, 1923. Archives of the Pennsylvania Academy of the Fine Arts.

60. Albert C. Barnes to John A. Myers, April 10, 1923. Archives of the Pennsylvania Academy of the Fine Arts.

61. Albert C. Barnes, Introduction to *Catalogue of an Exhibition of Contemporary European Paintings and Sculpture, April 11, 1923 - May 9, 1923*, pp. 3 and 5-7. Archives of the Pennsylvania Academy of the Fine Arts.

62. C.H. Bronte, "Simple Artistry Versus Chaotic," *Philadelphia Inquirer*, April 15, 1923, p. 7.

63. Edith Powell, "Peale Portraits—Ultra-Modern French Art," *Public Ledger*, April 15, 1923, p. 11.

64. Francis J. Ziegler, "Many Paintings of Many Different Kinds," *Record*, April 15, 1923, p. 4.

65. Dorothy Grafly, "Old Portraiture Praised, Modernists' Art Decried," *North American*, April 15, 1923. p. 6.

66. Albert C. Barnes to Henry Clifford, March 22, 1948. Archives of the Philadelphia Museum of Art.

67. See Dorothy Grafly to William Schack, June 6, 1957. *William Schack Papers*. Cf. Schack, p. 131.

68. Albert C. Barnes to John Dewey, April 20, 1925. *John Dewey Papers*.

69. Albert C. Barnes, "The Barnes Foundation," *New Republic*, March 14, 1923, p. 65ff.

70. Estimate is a projection based on E. Baldwin Smith, *A Study of the History of Art in the Colleges and Universities of the United States* (Princeton, NJ: Princeton University Press, 1912), p vi.

71. Albert C. Barnes to Josiah H. Penniman, January 27, 1924. *Josiah H. Penniman Administration Records*.

72. Warren P. Laird, "Confidential Report to the President On the Proposition by Albert C. Barnes," February 11, 1924. *Josiah H. Penniman Administration Records*.

73. Josiah H. Penniman to Albert C. Barnes, March 18, 1924. *Josiah H. Penniman Administration Records*.

74. Albert C. Barnes to Josiah H. Penniman, March 20, 1924. *Josiah H. Penniman Administration Records*. The other two "heirs" to the Barnes Foundation, according to the Indenture of Trust of December 6, 1922, would be the Pennsylvania Academy of the Fine Arts and whatever trust company or financial institution should be treasurer of the corporation at the time of the death of the survivor of Barnes and his wife.

75. See Warren P. Laird to Josiah H. Penniman, March 24, 1924. *Josiah H. Penniman Administration Records*.

76. Josiah H. Penniman to Albert C. Barnes, April 4, 1924. *Josiah H. Penniman Administration Records*.

77. Albert C. Barnes to Josiah H. Penniman, April 10, 1924. *Josiah H. Penniman Administration Records*.

78. Josiah H. Penniman to Albert C. Barnes, April 10, 1924. *Josiah H. Penniman Administration Records*.

79. Albert C. Barnes to Josiah H. Penniman, April 14, 1924. *Josiah H. Penniman Administration Records*.

80. Mark Van Doren, "The College of the Few," *New Republic*, April 16, 1924, p. 205.

81. Albert C. Barnes to Josiah H. Penniman, April 14, 1924. *Josiah H. Penniman Administration Records*.

82. Albert C. Barnes to Josiah H. Penniman, April 21, 1924. *Josiah H. Penniman Administration Records*.

83. See Josiah H. Penniman to Albert C. Barnes, May 2, 1924. *Josiah H. Penniman Administration Records*.

84. Albert C. Barnes to Josiah H. Penniman, May 3, 1924. *Josiah H. Penniman Administration Records.*

85. See Josiah H. Penniman to Albert C. Barnes, May 9, 1924. *Josiah H. Penniman Administration Records.*

86. "Art Critics Flay Barnes Foundation," *North American*, May 20, 1924 and "U. of P.'s Fostering of Modernist Art Scored by Grafly," *North American*, May 18, 1924, p. 1.

87. The course was to be an elective open to BFA candidates, who had taken Everett's general history of painting and sculpture, and to graduate students of approved preparation. When Barnes objected to the idea of a prerequisite, however, Laird diplomatically backed down. He persuaded the Fine Arts Faculty to agree to one of several history courses as a suitable prerequisite to Modern Art and assured the collector that the College Faculty would be asked to admit the course, without prerequisite, to its roster of electives, beginning with the second term, and that provision would be made for non-degree candidates to enroll in it.

88. Albert C. Barnes to Warren P. Laird, October 22, 1924. *Josiah H. Penniman Administration Records.*

89. Warren P. Laird to Albert C. Barnes, October 27, 1924. *Josiah H. Penniman Administration Records.*

90. "Dr. Barnes' Charge Stuns Art Faculty," *Evening Bulletin*, May 26, 1924.

91. See Albert C. Barnes to Hugh H. Breckenridge, April 29, 1925. *R. Sturgis Ingersoll Papers.* Archives of American Art, Smithsonian Institution.

92. Albert C. Barnes to John Dewey, February 6, 1925, *John Dewey Papers.*

93. See Distel, p. 298 and Wattenmaker, p. 12.

94. See Albert C. Barnes to Josiah H. Penniman, January 20, 1925. *Josiah H. Penniman Administration Records.*

95. Albert C. Barnes to Edgar A. Singer, January 25, 1925. *Josiah H. Penniman Administration Records.*

96. See Albert C. Barnes to John Dewey, February 11, 1925. *John Dewey Papers.*

97. Albert C. Barnes to Edgar A. Singer, February 16, 1925. *Josiah H. Penniman Administrative Records.*

98. Albert C. Barnes to Josiah H. Penniman, February 16, 1925. *Josiah H. Penniman Administration Records.*

99. Josiah H. Penniman to Albert C. Barnes, February 17, 1925. *Josiah H. Penniman Administration Records.*

100. Albert C. Barnes to John Dewey, February 11, 1925. *John Dewey Papers.*

101. Albert C. Barnes to Edgar A. Singer, March 7, 1925. *Josiah H. Penniman Administration Records.*

102. Albert C. Barnes to John Dewey, March 14, 1925. *John Dewey Papers.*

103. John Dewey, "Dedication Address," March 19, 1925. Ms. in the *John Dewey Papers.* Reprinted in the *Journal of the Barnes Foundation*, May 1925, pp. 3-6.

104. "Madame Jonnesco Predicts America Will Lead in Art," *Public Ledger*, March 20, 1925, p. 2.

Chapter 6: The Art in Painting

1. Alvin Johnson to William Schack, October 13, 1955. *William Schack Papers.*

2. Albert C. Barnes to John Dewey, December 31, 1919. *John Dewey Papers.*

3. Albert C. Barnes to John Dewey, June 30, 1920. *John Dewey Papers.*

4. Alvin Johnson to William Schack, October 5, 1955. *William Schack Papers.*

5. Albert C. Barnes to John Dewey, February 17, 1920. *John Dewey Papers.*

6.   See Thomas Craven, "The Progress of Painting," *Dial*, April 1923, pp. 357-367 and June 1923, pp. 581 to 593. Quotations p. 365. Within a few years, Craven repudiated modernism as an imported ideology in his polemic *Modern Art* (New York: Simon & Schuster, 1934).

7.   Thomas Hart Benton to William Schack, June 28, 1955. *William Schack Papers*. Cf. Thomas Hart Benton, "Form and the Subject," *Arts*, June 1924, pp. 301-308 and *An American in Art* (Lawrence: University of Kansas Press, 1969), p. 57.

8.   Thomas Hart Benton to William Schack, December 24, 1957. *William Schack Papers*.

9.   Thomas Hart Benton to William Schack, August 18, 1955. *William Schack Papers*.

10.   Thomas Hart Benton to William Schack, June 28, 1955. *William Schack Papers*.

11.   Albert C. Barnes to John Dewey, September 17, 1920. *John Dewey Papers*.

12.   Albert C. Barnes to John Dewey, November 3, 1921. *John Dewey Papers*.

13.   Alice Dewey to Albert C. Barnes, March 13, 1920. *John Dewey Papers*.

14.   Alice Dewey to Albert C. Barnes, May 30, 1920. *John Dewey Papers*.

15.   Ed. Note to "Some Remarks on Appreciation," *Arts*, January 1923, p. 25.

16.   Mary Mullen, *An Approach to Art* (Merion, PA: Barnes Foundation, 1923), p. 11f.

17.   See Laurence Buermeyer, *The Aesthetic Experience* (Merion, PA: Barnes Foundation, 1924).

18.   See McCardle, Part III, April 4, 1942, p. 34.

19.   Albert C. Barnes, *The Art in Painting* (1925), Second Edition (New York: Harcourt and Brace, 1928), p. 26f.

20.   "Renoir: An Appreciation," p. 166.

21.   George Santayana, *The Sense of Beauty* (New York: Charles Scribner's Sons, 1896), p. 193.

22.   *The Art in Painting*, p. 72.

23.   Clive Bell, *Art* (New York: Frederick A. Stokes Company, 1914), pp. 8, 12, and 16.

24.   Ibid., p. 25.

25.   *The Art in Painting*, p. 49f.

26.   Sarah Boxer, "Vivid Color in a World of Black and White," *New York Times*, Section B, p. 11, April 28, 2001.

27.   *The Art in Painting*, p. 109.

28.   Ibid., pp. 110f, 188, and 117.

29.   Ibid., pp. 120, 129f, and 140. Though formerly attributed to Giotto, the authorship of the fresco cycle in the upper church of S. Francesco, Assisi is now in doubt.

30.   Ibid., pp. 65 and 67-69.

31.   Ibid., p. 26.

32.   Ibid., pp. 165, 150, 153f, 156f, and 159f.

33.   Ibid., pp. 179f and 172f.

34.   Ibid., pp. 174-178.

35.   Ibid., p. 190ff.

36.   Ibid., pp. 192-195.

37.   Ibid., pp. 254-256.

38.   Ibid., p. 261. Barnes referred to *Street in Delft* as *The Little Street*.

39.   Ibid., p. 280f.

40.   Ibid., pp. 284-288.

41.   Ibid., pp. 297-300 and 305f.

42.   Ibid., pp. 309 and 312f.

43.   Ibid., pp. 316 and 318f.

44.   Ibid., p. 327.

45.   Ibid., p. 335ff.

46.   Ibid., pp. 329, 339, 345, and 330-332.

47. Ibid., pp. 340 and 345-348.
48. Ibid., pp. 349 and 351f.
49. Ibid., p. 357ff.
50. Ibid., p. 359ff.
51. Ibid., p. 362f. Quotation comparing Glackens to Renoir is from the first edition, p. 289.
52. Ibid., p. 373ff.
53. Arthur C. Danto, "Every Straw Was the Last," *New York Times Book Review*, November 22, 1987, p. 13.
54. *The Art in Painting*, pp. 380-384.
55. Ibid., pp. 390-393.
56. Ibid., p. 394ff.
57. Ibid., pp. 397-404.
58. By the second (1928) edition, the number of artists had grown to 122 and the number of paintings to 325. In the third (1937) edition, more than 200 artists were mentioned and some 340 paintings.
59. *The Art in Painting*, pp. 412f, 415, and 417.
60. Ibid., p. 419f.
61. Raymond Weaver, "Inductive Criticism of Art," *New York Herald Tribune*, January 31, 1926, p. 14.
62. Joseph Wood Krutch, "Plastic Form," *Nation*, March 10, 1926, p. 259.
63. Alfred H. Barr, Jr., "Plastic Values," *Saturday Review of Literature*, July 24, 1926, p. 948.
64. H. I. Brock, "How to Detect the Presence of True Art," *New York Times Book Review*, June 20, 1926, p. 16.
65. Robert Cortes Holliday, "First Aid in Art," *Bookman*, September 1926, p. 97.
66. *Times Literary Supplement*, June 30, 1927, p. 450.
67. Albert C. Barnes to Leo Stein, March 6, 1925. *Leo Stein Papers*.
68. Leo Stein, "The Art in Painting," *New Republic*, December 2, 1925, p. 56f.
69. Albert C. Barnes to John Dewey, November 27, 1925. *John Dewey Papers*.
70. Albert C. Barnes to John Dewey, November 30, 1925. *John Dewey Papers*.
71. Albert C. Barnes to John Dewey, December 2, 1925. *John Dewey Papers*.
72. John Dewey, "Art in Education—and Education in Art," *New Republic*, February 24, 1926, p. 12.
73. Albert C. Barnes to John Dewey, November 27, 1925. *John Dewey Papers*.
74. Thomas Munro, *Toward Science in Aesthetics* (New York: The Liberal Arts Press, 1956), p. 92.

Chapter 7: The Art of Polemics

1. Albert C. Barnes to Paul Guillaume, August 16, 1926. Archives of the Barnes Foundation. Quotation formerly displayed in the now closed Orientation Room.
2. Albert C. Barnes to John Dewey, May 6, 1942. *John Dewey Papers*.
3. *Nation*, May 13, 1925, vol. 120, p. 553.
4. Albert C. Barnes to John Dewey, January 7, 1921. *John Dewey Papers*.
5. Albert C. Barnes, "Day-Dreaming in Art Education," *Journal of the Barnes Foundation*, April 1926, pp. 44-48.
6. Albert C. Barnes to Edgar A. Singer, March 17, 1925. *John M. Fogg Papers*. Special Collections of the University of Pennsylvania Library.
7. Josiah H. Penniman to Edgar A. Singer, March 19, 1925. *Josiah H. Penniman Administration Records*
8. Albert C. Barnes to John Dewey, March 21, 1925. *John Dewey Papers*.

9. See N. E. Mullen to Edwin G. Broome, February 26, 1925. *Josiah H. Penniman Administration Records*. Barnes occasionally had Nelle Mullen sign his letters to people with whom he had an adversarial relationship.

10. Albert C. Barnes, "The Shame in the Public Schools of Philadelphia," *Journal of the Barnes Foundation*, April 1925, pp. 13-17.

11. Laurence Buermeyer, "The Graphic Sketch Club and Art Education," *Journal of the Barnes Foundation*, April 1925, pp. 22, 20, 21, and 24.

12. The award was established by the highly respected former editor of the *Ladies Home Journal*, Edward Bok, whose rise to a position of power and prominence was a rags to riches story, not unlike Barnes's own, in that it was linked to the Dutch immigrant's intelligence and ingenuity. The collector, however, dismissed him as an "ignoramus." See Albert C. Barnes to John Dewey, March 9, 1922. *John Dewey Papers*.

13. Albert C. Barnes to John Dewey, April 1, 1925. *John Dewey Papers*.

14. Alon Bement to Josiah H. Penniman, March 27, 1925. *Josiah H. Penniman Administration Records*. Penniman expressed regret to his fellow educator that any guest should have given offence, while pointing out that Penn could not be held responsible for the actions of individuals who were not University employees. See Josiah H. Penniman to Alon Bement, March 31, 1925. *Josiah H. Penniman Administration Records*.

15. Alon Bement to Thomas Munro, March 28, 1925. *Josiah H. Penniman Administration Records*. Munro's answer was a smart-alecky note of thanks for the 'lecture on deportment." See Thomas Munro to Alon Bement, March 30, 1925. *Josiah H. Penniman Administration Records*.

16. See Edwin G. Broome to John Dewey, March 30, 1925. *Josiah H. Penniman Administration Records*.

17. John Dewey to Edwin G. Broome, March 31, 1925. *Josiah H. Penniman Administration Records*.

18. See Theodore M. Dillaway to Warren P. Laird, March 31, 1925. *Josiah H. Penniman Administration Records*.

19. Albert C. Barnes to Edgar A. Singer, April 4, 1925. *Josiah H. Penniman Administration Records*.

20. Albert C. Barnes to Edgar A. Singer, April 6, 1925. *Josiah H. Administration Penniman Records*.

21. Edgar A. Singer to Albert C. Barnes, April 10, 1925. *Josiah H. Penniman Administration Records*.

22. Albert C. Barnes to Edgar A. Singer, April 15, 1925. *Josiah H. Penniman Administration Records*.

23. Albert C. Barnes to Edgar A. Singer, April 20, 1925. *Josiah H. Penniman Administration Records*.

24. Albert C. Barnes to John Dewey, April 8, 1925. *John Dewey Papers*.

25. Louis Menand, *The Metaphysical Club* (New York: Farrar, Straus and Giroux, 2001), p. 373.

26. John Dewey to Albert C. Barnes, April 25, 1925. *John Dewey Papers*.

27. John Dewey to Albert C. Barnes, April 16, 1925. *John Dewey Papers*.

28. John Dewey to Albert C. Barnes, April 16, 1925. *John Dewey Papers*.

29. Albert C. Barnes to John Dewey, April 16, 1925. *John Dewey Papers*.

30. Albert C. Barnes to John Dewey, April 20, 1925. *John Dewey Papers*.

31. Louis W. Flaccus to Albert C. Barnes, April 8, 1925. See also Albert C. Barnes to Edgar A. Singer, April 9, 1925. *Josiah H. Penniman Administration Records*.

32. "Construction and Controversy," *Journal of the Barnes Foundation*, October 1925, pp. 1-3. The unsigned editorial was composed by Laurence Buermeyer according to a letter from Barnes to John Dewey, September 26, 1925. *John Dewey Papers.*

33. Albert C. Barnes to Warren P. Laird, October 13, 1925. *Josiah H. Penniman Administration Records.*

34. Albert C. Barnes to Louis W. Flaccus, February 23, 1916. *Josiah H. Penniman Administration Records.*

35. John Dewey, "Art in Education—and Education in Art, *New Republic*, February 24, 1926, p. 11f. Delighted with the article, Barnes told his friend: "It overwhelms me with shame that what I tried to do in my book, and am trying to do with the Foundation, seem a series of isolated ejaculations compared with the smooth, unified harmony that you make of those two objects in your article." Albert C. Barnes to John Dewey, December 2, 1925. *John Dewey Papers.*

36. Albert C. Barnes to Louis W. Flaccus, February 23, 1926. *Josiah H. Penniman Administration Records.*

37. Josiah H. Penniman to Albert C. Barnes, March 2, 1926. *Josiah H. Penniman Administration Records.*

38. Albert C. Barnes to Josiah H. Penniman, March 3, 1926. *Josiah H. Penniman Administration Records.*

39. Josiah H. Penniman to Albert C. Barnes, March 4, 1926. *Josiah H. Penniman Administration Records.*

40. Memo from Warren P. Laird to eight University colleagues, March 24, 1926. See also Thomas Munro to Warren P. Laird, March 22, 1926. *Josiah H. Penniman Administration Records.*

41. Josiah H. Penniman to Albert C. Barnes, May 20, 1926. *Josiah H. Penniman Administration Records.*

42. Albert C. Barnes to Josiah H. Penniman, May 21, 1926. *Josiah H. Penniman Administration Records.*

43. Warren P. Laird to Josiah H. Penniman, October 27, 1926. *Josiah H. Penniman Administration Records.*

44. Albert C. Barnes to Edgar A. Singer, November 2, 1926. *Josiah H. Penniman Administration Records.*

45. Louis W. Flaccus, *The Spirit and Substance of Art* (New York: F.S. Croft & Co., 1926), p. vi.

46. Albert C. Barnes to Louis W. Flaccus, November 23, 1926. *Josiah H. Penniman Administration Records.*

47. Edgar A. Singer to Albert C. Barnes, November 25, 1926. *Josiah H. Penniman Administration Records.*

48. Albert C. Barnes to Edgar A. Singer, November 27, 1926. *Josiah H. Penniman Administration Records.*

49. Nelle E. Mullen to Edward W. Mumford, November 27, 1926. *Josiah H. Penniman Administration Records.*

50. Albert C. Barnes, "The Barnes Foundation and the University of Pennsylvania," November 27, 1926. *Josiah H. Penniman Administration Records.*

51. Louis W. Flaccus, "Preliminary Statement," November 30, 1926. *Josiah H. Penniman Administration Records.*

52. John Dewey to Edgar A. Singer, December 1, 1926. See also John Dewey to Edgar A. Singer, December 11, 1926. *Josiah H. Penniman Administration Records.*

53. Edgar A. Singer, Memorandum, November 30, 1926. *Josiah H. Penniman Administration Records.*

54. Warren P. Laird to Albert C. Barnes, December 4, 1926. *Josiah H. Penniman Administration Records.*
55. See Josiah H. Penniman to Albert C. Barnes, December 7, 1926. *Josiah H. Penniman Administration Records.*
56. A. Reilly to Warren P. Laird, December 8, 1926. *Josiah H. Penniman Administration Records.*
57. Nelle E. Mullen to Edward W. Mumford, December 10, 1926. *Josiah H. Penniman Administration Records.*
58. Albert C. Barnes to Edgar A. Singer, December 10, 1925. *Josiah H. Penniman Administration Records.*
59. Edgar A. Singer to Albert C. Barnes, December 21, 1926. *Josiah H. Penniman Administration Records.*
60. Albert C. Barnes to Edgar A. Singer, December 23, 1926. *Josiah H. Penniman Administration Records.*
61. Albert C. Barnes, "Resume: Obstacles at U. of P.," December 24, 1926. *John M. Fogg Papers.*
62. Charles W. Burr to Lewis F. Pilcher, December 19, 1926. *Josiah H. Penniman Administration Records.*

Chapter 8: A New Valuation of Black Art

1. Sadie Tanner Mossell, "The Standard of Living Among One Hundred Negro Migrant Families in Philadelphia," Ph.D. dissertation, University of Pennsylvania, 1921, p. 9.
2. Paul Guillaume and Thomas Munro, *Primitive Negro Sculpture* (London: Jonathan Cape, Ltd., 1926), p. i. Originally issued by the Barnes Foundation in the spring of 1926, the trade edition was released later the same year by Harcourt Brace in New York and Cape Ltd. in London.
3. Albert C. Barnes to Paul Guillaume, March 1, 1923. Archives of the Barnes Foundation. The quotation was formerly displayed in the Foundation's new closed Orientation Room.
4. See Alois Riegl, *Stilfragen* (Berlin: George Siemens, 1893). Cited by Robert Goldwater in his compelling study, *Primitivism in Modern Art* (Cambridge, MA: The Belknap Press of Harvard University, 1986), p. 26f.
5. See Wilhelm Worringer, *Formprobleme der Gotik* (Munich: R. Piper, 1912). Translated as *Form in Gothic* (London: Putnam, 1927). Cited by Goldwater, p. 28f.
6. See Emile Durkheim, *The Elementary Forms of the Religious Life*, 1915 (New York: The Free Press, 1965), p. 148f.
7. See Maurice de Vlaminck, *Portraits avant décès* (Paris: Flammarion, 1943), p. 107. Cited by Goldwater, p. 87.
8. The date was probably the late summer or early fall of 1906. See Gertrude Stein, *The Autobiography of Alice B. Toklas* (New York: Harcourt Brace, 1933), p. 63. Also Gertrude Stein, *Picasso* (Paris: Floury, 1938), p. 22. Cited by Goldwater, p. 145.
9. Paul Guillaume, "The Triumph of Ancient Negro Art," *Opportunity*, May 1926, p. 146. The recent discovery in the Picasso archives of about forty photographs of African women, which were taken at the turn of the last century by Edmond Fortier in Senegal, reinforce the theories of Barnes, his colleagues, and subsequent art historians about the artist's use of African models for inspiration. See Michael Kimmelman, "Photographs That Fed Picasso's Vision," *New York Times*, January 11, 1998, Arts & Leisure Section, p. 45.
10. Guillaume and Munro, p. 134.
11. *Saturday Review of Literature*, December 4, 1926, p. 391.

12. See Carl Einstein, *Negerplastik*, 2nd edition (Munich: Kurt Wolff, 1920), pp. ix-xii. Discussed by Goldwater, p. 35f and Guillaume and Munro, p. 4.
13. Roger Fry, "Negro Sculpture" in *Vision and Design*, 1920 (London: Chatto & Windus, 1928) p. 100.
14. Guillaume and Munro, pp. 33, 49, 51, and 57.
15. Lewis Mumford, "Art, Modern and Primitive," *New Republic*, December 1, 1926, p. 49.
16. Albert C. Barnes, "Negro Art and America," *Survey Graphic*, March 1925, p. 668f.
17. Langston Hughes, quoted by Arna Bontemps in his Introduction to Langston Hughes, *Not Without Laughter* (New York: Collier Books Edition, 1969). Cited by Patrick J. Gilpin, "Charles S. Johnson: Entrepreneur of the Harlem Renaissance" in Arna Bontemps, ed., *The Harlem Renaissance Remembered* (New York: Dodd, Mead & Company, 1972), p. 237.
18. Albert C. Barnes to Alain Locke, March 11, 1924. *Alain Locke Papers*. Moreland-Spingarn Research Center, Howard University.
19. Quoted in "The Debut of the Younger School of Negro Writers," *Opportunity*, May 1924, p. 143.
20. Carl Van Doren, "The Younger Generation of Negro Writers," *Opportunity*, May 1924, p. 144f.
21. Alain Locke, "Harlem," *Survey Graphic*, March 1925, p. 630.
22. Albert C. Barnes to Alain Locke, February 8, 1925. *Alain Locke Papers*. Quoted by Mark Helbling, "African Art: Albert C. Barnes and Alain Locke," *Phylon*, March 1982, p. 57.
23. Albert C. Barnes to Alain Locke, March 3, 1924 and March 28, 1924. *Alain Locke Papers*.
24. See Albert C. Barnes to Alain Locke, March 3, 1924. *Alain Locke Papers*.
25. Albert C. Barnes to Charles S. Johnson, March 22, 1924. *Alain Locke Papers*.
26. Charles S. Johnson to Albert C. Barnes, March 26, 1924. *Alain Locke Papers*.
27. "Dr. Barnes," *Opportunity*, May 1924, p. 133.
28. Paul Guillaume, "African Art at the Barnes Foundation," *Opportunity*, May 1924, pp. 140 and 142. Reprinted from *Les Arts à Paris*, October 1923.
29. Barnes, "The Temple," p. 139 and Alain Locke, "A Note on African Art," *Opportunity*, May 1924, pp. 134 and 138. Barnes's essay is reprinted from *Les Arts à Paris*, November 1924.
30. Langston Hughes, *The Big Sea* (New York: Hill and Wang, 1940), p. 185.
31. Langston Hughes, "My Early Days in Harlem," April 7, 1963. James Weldon Johnson/Langston Hughes Ms. 730. *James Weldon Johnson Papers*. Beinecke Rare Book and Manuscript Library. Yale University. Quoted in Cary D. Wintz, ed., *Remembering the Harlem Renaissance* (New York: Garland Publishing, Inc., 1996), p. 396.
32. Alain Locke, "Enter the New Negro," *Survey Graphic*, March 1925, p. 632.
33. Alain Locke, "Race Contacts and Interracial Relations," in Jeffrey C. Stewart, ed., *Race Contacts and Interracial Relations: Lectures in the Theory and Practice of Race* (Washington, DC: Howard University Press, 1992), p. 91. Quoted by Menand, p. 397. The lectures were delivered in 1915 in Washington, DC and repeated the next year.
34. Alain Locke, "The Art of the Ancestors," *Survey Graphic*, March 1925, p. 673.
35. Barnes, "Negro Art and America," p. 668f.
36. Alain Locke, "Too Certain of Our Philistines," *Opportunity*, May 1925, p. 155.
37. "Harlem Types," *Survey Graphic*, March 1925, p. 653.
38. Alain Locke to Carl Van Vechten, May 24, 1925. See also Locke to Van Vechten, June 1, 1925 and October 6, 1925. *Van Vechten Papers*. Yale Collection of American

Literature, Beinecke Rare Book and Manuscript Library, Yale University. Cited by Helbling, p. 63.

39. Aaron Douglas, "Harlem Renaissance," p. 14. *Aaron Douglas Papers*. Special Collections, Fisk University. Quoted by Amy Helene Kirschke in *Aaron Douglas: Art, Race, and the Harlem Renaissance* (Jackson, Mississippi: University Press of Mississippi, 1995), p. 110.

40. See Interview of Aaron Douglas by Ann Allen Shockley, November 19, 1975. Black Oral Histories (BOH). Special Collections, Fisk University. Incident cited by Kirschke, p. 37.

41. Ibid.

42. *Crisis*, January 1928, p. 15.

43. See Douglas Interview, BOH. Cited by Kirschke, p. 109.

44. "Negro Art," *Opportunity*, May 1926, p. 142.

45. Guillaume, "The Triumph of Ancient Negro Art," p. 146.

46. Laurence Buermeyer, "The Negro Spirituals and American Art," *Opportunity*, May 1926, p. 158ff.

47. Albert C. Barnes, "Negro Art, Past and Present," *Opportunity*, May 1926, p. 148f.

48. Ibid., pp. 149, 168, and 169.

49. See Laura V. Geiger to Alain Locke, April 15, 1924. *Alain Locke Papers*.

50. Laurence Buermeyer, "An Experiment in Education," *Nation,* April 15, 1925, vol. 120, p. 443.

51. "Dr. Barnes' School Plan Stirs Merion," *Evening Bulletin,* April 14, 1927. Clipping in Barnes File, Free Library of Philadelphia.

52. The headmaster of Episcopal Academy said he would welcome the prospective center; others declared Barnes's proposal "outrageous" and promised to fight it "with every ounce of energy." Reactions quoted in "Merion Grids To Fight Negro School Plan," *Philadelphia Inquirer*, April 14, 1927, p. 11.

53. Paul B. Hogans, *A New Plan for Negro Education* (Merion, PA: The Barnes Foundation, n.d.), p. 8f.

54. Myra H. Colson to Charles S. Johnson, May 11, 1924. *Alain Locke Papers*.

55. Quoted in "Dr. Barnes' School Plan Stirs Merion."

56. A.L. Manley, "Where Negroes Live in Philadelphia, " *Opportunity*, May 1923, p. 14.

57. Albert C. Barnes, "Primitive Negro Sculpture and Its Influence on Civilization," *Opportunity*, May 1928, p. 147.

58. Langston Hughes, "Youth," *The New Negro*, 1925, (New York: Arno Press and the New York Times, 1968), p. 5.

Chapter 9: Muse, *Models*, Museums

1. See *Barnes Foundation vs. Harry W. Keely*, Philadelphia Common Pleas Court No. 1, December Term 1929, No. 6368, p. 40a. For other information about de Mazia's family, the author is indebted to her niece, Celeste de Mazia, who graciously shared family letters and mementos, and to her nephew, Anthony de Mazia, who shared his memories of the aunt he visited in Merion on several occasions.

2. See E. Digby Baltzell, *The Protestant Establishment* (New York: Random House, 1964), pp. 197-225.

3. Albert C. Barnes to John Dewey, November 2, 1920. *John Dewey Papers*. See also Barnes to Dewey, November 3, 1921. *John Dewey Papers*.

4. Harry M. Watts to Warren P. Laird, April 28, 1925. *Josiah H. Penniman Administration Records*.

5. Carl E. Schorske, *Thinking With History: Explorations in the Passage to Modernism* (Princeton, NJ: Princeton University Press, 1998), p. 49.

6. Albert C. Barnes to John Dewey, May 2, 1927. *John Dewey Papers.*
7 . See *Barnes Foundation vs. Harry W. Keely*, p. 40a.
8. Violette de Mazia, "Continuity of Traditions in Painting," in Albert C. Barnes, ed., *Art and Education* (Merion, PA: The Barnes Foundation, 1929), p.105f. The original French version of the essay was entitled, somewhat misleadingly, "*L'Art Ancien a la Foundation Barnes.*"
9. Quoted by Schack. p. 218. See also *Philadelphia Record*, "Barnes Foundation Contests Tax Levy," October 1, 1930, p. 4.
10. Joanna Reed in a conversation with the author, April 24, 1997.
11. The French translation of *Modern Chromatics* was published in 1881. See Everdell's discussion of Rood's influence on Seurat, p. 71f.
12. Vincent van Gogh to Theo van Gogh, 553 F, *Correspondence*, p. 246. Quoted by Robert L. Herbert, *Georges Seurat* (New York: Museum of Modern Art, distributed by Henry Abrams, 1991), p. 279.
13. Roger Fry, *Dial*, September 1926, p. 228.
14. In January 1926, he had paid $28,000 to the Galerie Barbazanges in Paris for the picture of Adrienne, a Renoir family maid and the artist's model, walking with a small girl in a wood. See *Great French Paintings*, p. 300.
15. In 1915, Joseph Durand-Ruel told him he thought Renoir intended to leave the painting to the Louvre, but Barnes never gave up wanting it, and when the painting descended to Renoir's youngest son, Claude, he made another offer through Hodebert that was accepted in February 1927.
16. Leo Stein to Ettie Stettheimer, September 8, 1924. *Leo Stein Papers.* Quoted in Wineapple, p. 311.
17. H. M. Kallen, *Dial*, February 1928, p. 147 and M. J. Adler, *New York Evening Post*, October 15, 1927, p. 15.
18. Albert C. Barnes to John Dewey, October 12, 1927. *John Dewey Papers.*
19. See Leo Stein, *The A. B. C. of Aesthetics* (New York: Boni & Liveright, 1927), p. 29f and John Dewey, "Affective Thought in Logic and Painting," *Journal of The Barnes Foundation*, April 1926, pp. 3-9.
20. Albert C. Barnes to John Dewey, October 12, 1927. *John Dewey Papers.*
21. Recalled in John Dewey to Albert C. Barnes, October 17, 1927. *John Dewey Papers.*
22. Albert C. Barnes to John Dewey, October 19, 1927. *John Dewey Papers.*
23. Quoted by George and Mary Roberts, *Triumph on Fairmount: Fiske Kimball and the Philadelphia Museum of Art* (Philadelphia: J. B. Lippincott Company, 1959), p. 53.
24. Samuel W. Woodhouse, Jr. to Albert C. Barnes, May 4, 1925. WDH-Series 1 B. Philadelphia Museum of Art Archives (PMAA).
25. Quoted by the Roberts, p. 79.
26. Albert C. Barnes to Fiske Kimball, October 5, 1925. *Fiske Kimball Records.* Series 1 B. PMAA.
27. Albert C. Barnes to Fiske Kimball, October 27, 1925. *Fiske Kimball Papers.* Series 16. PMAA.
28. Fiske K. Kimball to Albert C. Barnes, October 28, 1926. *Fiske Kimball Papers.* Series 16.
29. Fiske Kimball, "A Message From the New Director," September 1, 1925. Published in *Pennsylvania Museum Bulletin*, vol. 21, no. 96 (October 1925), p. 3.
30. Quoted in R. Sturgis Ingersoll, "The Creation of Fairmount," *Philadelphia Museum of Art Bulletin*, vol. 61, nos. 287-66 (Fall 1965-Winter 1966), p. 25.

31. Quoted by Roberts, p. 80, Schack, p. 173, and Hart, p. 113. Both Kimball's letter and Barnes's response is missing from the collection of Kimball's records and papers in the Archives of the Philadelphia Museum of Art.
32. Albert C. Barnes to Henry Marceau, December 19, 1929. *Henry Marceau Papers.* PMAA.
33. A. H. Shaw, "De Medici in Merion," *New Yorker*, September 22, 1928, pp. 29-34.
34. Albert C. Barnes to John Dewey, January 4, 1921. *John Dewey Papers.*
35. Mary Mullen, "Learning To See," *Journal of the Barnes Foundation*, January 1926, p. 14. See also Mary Mullen, "Problems Encountered in Art Education," an adaptation of the earlier article in *Art and Education* (Merion, Pennsylvania: The Barnes Foundation Press, 1929), Third Edition, p. 260 and Lawrence Buermeyer, *The Aesthetic Experience*, p. 165. Barnes quoted Buermeyer's observations in *The Art in Painting*, p. 425.
36. See Albert C. Barnes to Walter Fales, March 24, 1948. Copy provided the author by Jon D. Longaker.
37. Albert C. Barnes to Hornell Hart, November 20, 1929. *Marion Edwards Park Papers.* Bryn Mawr College Archives.
38. Albert C. Barnes to John Dewey, November 12, 1925. *John Dewey Papers.*
39. "Learning To See," p. 8.
40. John Dewey to Albert C. Barnes, November 13, 1925. *John Dewey Papers.*
41. Albert C. Barnes to John Dewey, November 14, 1925. *John Dewey Papers.*
42. John Dewey to Albert C. Barnes, November 16, 1925. *John Dewey Papers.*
43. Albert C. Barnes to Edward S. King, March 3, 1930. *Marion Edwards Park Papers.*
44. Quoted by Glackens, p. 169.
45. See *Great French Paintings from The Barnes Foundation*, pp. 52 and 299 and Albert C. Barnes to John Dewey, March 5, 1919. *John Dewey Papers.*
46. Albert C. Barnes to John Dewey, September 19, 1930. *John Dewey Papers.*
47. *Barnes Foundation vs. Keely, Receiver of Taxes, et al.*, 164 A, 117, Superior Court of Pennsylvania, January 25, 1934, p. 3.
48. Quoted by Lois G. Forer in "No Place For the Rabble," *Horizon*, spring 1964, p. 7. Ms Forer was the Deputy Attorney General of Pennsylvania, assigned to the supervision and regulation of charities, when the Attorney General of Pennsylvania brought an action against the Barnes Foundation in 1958 on behalf of the Commonwealth as *parens patria.*
49. *Barnes Foundation vs. Keely, Receiver of Taxes, et al.*, 314 Pa. 112, 171 A, 267, Supreme Court of Pennsylvania, January 30, 1934, p. 3.
50. Albert C. Barnes to John Dewey, October 1, 1930. *John Dewey Papers.*
51. Albert C. Barnes to Georgia O'Keeffe, March 11, 1930. *Alfred Stieglitz\Georgia O'Keeffe Archive*, MSS 85, YCAL.
52. Quoted by Roxana Robinson, *O'Keeffe: A Life* (New York: Harper & Row, 1989), p. 348.
53. For an insightful discussion of the work in O'Keeffe's 1930 exhibition, see Robinson, p. 349f.
54. Albert C. Barnes to Georgia O'Keeffe, March 21, 1930. *Alfred Stieglitz\Georgia O'Keeffe Archive.*
55. Ibid.
56. Albert C. Barnes to Alfred Stieglitz, December 19, 1930. *Alfred Stieglitz\Georgia O'Keeffe Archive.*
57. Albert C. Barnes to Georgia O'Keeffe, December 19, 1930. *Alfred Stieglitz\Georgia O'Keeffe Archive.*

58. Albert C. Barnes to Alfred Stieglitz, December 24, 1930. *Alfred Stieglitz\Georgia O'Keeffe Archive*.

59. Ibid.

60. Georgia O'Keeffe to Albert C. Barnes, ca December 28, 1930. *Alfred Stieglitz\Georgia O'Keeffe Archive*.

61. Albert C. Barnes to Georgia O'Keeffe, December 30, 1930. *Alfred Stieglitz\Georgia O'Keeffe Archive*.

Chapter 10: The Dance

1. See Albert C. Barnes to John Dewey, December 10, 1930. *John Dewey Papers*.

2. See Albert C. Barnes to Henri Matisse, September (n.d.), 1930. Barnes Foundation Archives. Cited by Jack D. Flam, *Matisse: The Dance* (Washington, DC: The National Gallery of Art, 1993), p. 16.

3. Albert C. Barnes to Leo Stein, March 30, 1931. *Gertrude Stein and Alice B. Toklas Papers*.

4. Albert C. Barnes to Leo Stein, April 16, 1946. *Gertrude Stein and Alice B. Toklas Papers*

5. E. Tériade, "L'actualité de Matisse," *Cahiers d'art* 4 (7) (1929), p. 286. Translated and quoted by Flam, p. 14.

6. Matisse pocket diary, September 27, 1930. Matisse Archives. Translated and quoted by Flam, *Matisse: The Dance*, p. 19.

7. E. Teriadé, "Entretien avec Teriadé," *L'Intransigeant*, October 20 and 27, 1930. Translated and quoted by Flam, p. 19.

8. Henri Matisse to Alexandre Romm, February 14, 1934. Reprinted in Jack D. Flam, *Matisse on Art* (London: Phaidon Press, 1973), p. 69.

9. Flam found a notation in Matisse's diary about his sending the letter. See Jack D. Flam, *Matisse: The Dance*, p. 19 and p. 79, note 26.

10. E. Teriadé, "Entretien avec Teriadé," translated and quoted by Flam in *Matisse: The Dance*, p. 19.

11. The French text of the letter of agreement is quoted by Flam in *Matisse: The Dance*, p. 80, note 34.

12. Henry McBride to Gertrude Stein, June (n.d.), 1931. Reprinted in Donald Gallup, ed., *Letters Written to Gertrude Stein* (New York: Alfred A. Knopf, 1953), p. 252.

13. Henri Matisse, "Repertoire 6," 1946. The phrase in one of Matisse's notebooks, written and then crossed out, is translated and quoted by Flam in *Matisse: The Dance*, p. 18.

14. Henri Matisse to Amélie Matisse, December 22, 1930. Matisse Archives. Translated and quoted by Flam in *Matisse: The Dance*, p. 22.

15. Henri Matisse to Amélie Matisse, December 26, 1930. Matisse Archives. Translated and quoted by Flam, *Matisse: The Dance*, p. 22.

16. Dorothy Dudley, "The Matisse Fresco in Merion, Pennsylvania," *Hound & Horn*, January-March 1934, p. 301.

17. Henri Matisse to Amélie Matisse, December 26, 1930. Matisse Archives. Translated and quoted by Flam in *Matisse: The Dance*, p. 22.

18. Albert C. Barnes to John Dewey, January 2, 1931. Barnes Foundation Archives. Quoted by Flam in *Matisse: The Dance*, p. 22

19. Quoted in Nathaniel Burt, *Palaces for the People: A Social History of the American Art Museum* (Boston: Little, Brown, 1977), p. 281.

20. See *Great French Paintings from The Barnes Foundation*, p. 309f. Barnes paid 22,500 francs for his first Sister panel and 80,000 francs for the second, which had belonged to Tetzen-Lund.

21. Henri Matisse to Albert C. Barnes, January 1, 1931. Barnes Foundation Archives. Translated and quoted by Flam in "Henri Matisse," *Great French Paintings from The Barnes Foundation*, pp. 253 and 310.

22. "Conversation Between R. Sturgis Ingersoll and Dr. A.C. Barnes February 26, 1931 Regarding Matisse & Three Sisters." *Fiske Kimball Records*. Series 1. PMAA.

23. Albert C. Barnes to R. Sturgis Ingersoll, February 26 (?), 1931. Quoted by Schack, p. 231.

24. Albert C. Barnes to John Dewey, February 24, 1931. *John Dewey Papers*.

25. Fiske Kimball to Carroll Tyson, March 2, 1931, *Fiske Kimball Records*. Series 1.

26. Albert C. Barnes to Fiske Kimball, April 26, 1934. *Fiske Kimball Records*. Series 1.

27. Part of the appeal of the paintings lay in their transitional nature. Although displaying the severe verticalism of Matisse's earlier work, they anticipated the more fluid decorative style of the next decade,

28. Albert C. Barnes to Henri Matisse, March 20, 1921. Quoted by Flam in note 9 to "Henri Matisse" in *Great French Paintings from The Barnes Foundation*, p. 310.

29. See Alfred H. Barr, Jr., *Matisse: His Art and His Public* (New York: Museum of Modern Art, 1951.). p. 241. See also Flam, *Matisse: The Dance*, p. 23. Flam quotes a letter a Barnes teacher, Edward Dreibelbies, wrote to the collector upon visiting Matisse's studio that seems to confirm Barr's interpretation.

30. Dudley, p. 299.

31. Albert C, Barnes to Henri Matisse, February 10, 1931. Barnes Foundation Archives. Quoted by Flam in *Matisse: the Dance*, p. 82, note 67.

32. Henri Matisse to Albert C. Barnes, April 24, 1931. Barnes Foundation Archives. Translated and quoted by Flam in *Matisse: The Dance*, p. 33.

33. Henri Matisse, "Repertoire 6," 1946. Translated and quoted by Pierre Schneider, *Matisse* (New York: Rizzoli, 1984), p. 619.

34. Dudley, p. 300.

35. Albert C. Barnes to John Dewey, November 6, 1931. *John Dewey Papers*.

36. Edward Dreibelbies to Albert C. Barnes, August 2, 1930. Barnes Foundation Archives. Quoted by Flam, *Matisse: The Dance*, p. 35.

37. Pierre Matisse to Henri Matisse, November 29, 1931. Pierre Matisse Gallery Archives (PMGA) at The Pierpont Morgan Library, New York. Quoted by John Russell in *Matisse: Father & Son* (New York: Harry N. Abrams, Inc., 1999), p. 64.

38. Henri Matisse to Albert C. Barnes, November 6, 1931. Barnes Foundation Archives. Translated and quoted by Flam, *Matisse: The Dance*, p. 45.

39. Albert C. Barnes to Henri Matisse, February 22, 1933. Matisse Archives. Translated and quoted by Flam, *Matisse: The Dance*, p. 46. In addition to relying on the misleading blueprints, Matisse had apparently compounded his error by overlooking two strips of paper that were suppose to have been attached to the bases of the template pendentives and had been included in the original package sent from Merion.

40. Henri Matisse to Albert C. Barnes. Quoted by Hart, p. 120. Hart, who was probably shown the cable by Laura Barnes, gives no date, and Flam could not locate the cable in the Barnes Archives.

41. Pierre Matisse to Henri Matisse, February 26, 1932. PMGA. Translated and quoted by Flam, *Matisse: The Dance*, p. 48.

42. Ibid.

43. Henri Matisse to Pierre Matisse, November 5, 1932. PMGA. Translated and quoted by Flam, *Matisse: The Dance*, p. 52.

44. Albert C. Barnes to John Dewey, November 16, 1932. *John Dewey Papers*.

45. Henri Matisse to Pierre Matisse, April 23, 1933. PMGA. Quoted by Flam, *Matisse: The Dance*, p. 59.

46. See Henri Matisse to Pierre Matisse, February 2, 1933. PMGA. Cited by Flam, *Matisse: The Dance*, p. 57.
47. Henri Matisse to Pierre Matisse, February 27, 1933. PMGA. Translated and quoted by Flam, *Matisse: The Dance*, p. 58.
48. Henri Matisse to Simon Bussy, March 7, 1933. Matisse Archives. Translated and quoted by Flam, *Matisse: The Dance*, p. 58.
49. Schneider, p. 623.
50. Albert C. Barnes to Pierre Matisse, May 15, 1933. PMGA. In quoting the letter (*Matisse: The Dance*, p. 61), Flan writes "mild heart attack," but Barnes actually wrote "slight hear attack." The collector quotes the diagnosis of the specialist he called in to examine Matisse as "a disturbance of the heart and circulation." He assured Pierre Matisse that "there was no immediate cause for alarm," but added that "when a man reaches your father's age, it is necessary for him to readjust his life to changed conditions which advancing years bring on."
51. Henri Matisse to Amélie Matisse, May 17, 1933. Matisse Archives. Translated and quoted by Flam, *Matisse: The Dance*, p. 62.
52. Dudley, p. 303.
53. Hart, p. 120.
54. Albert C. Barnes to Henri Matisse, January 17, 1934. Matisse Archives. Quoted by Flam, *Matisse: The Dance*, p. 64.
55. "Matisse Speaks," *Art News*, June 3, 1933, p. 8.
56. Albert C. Barnes and Violette de Mazia, *The Art of Henri Matisse* (New York: Charles Scribner's Sons, 1933), p. 210f.
57. Barr, p. 222.
58. Thomas Craven, "Matisse in the Laboratory," *New York Herald Tribune*, February 26, 1933, p. 6.
59. Frank Jewett Mather, "Matisse," *Saturday Review of Literature*, March 25, 1933, p. 503.
60. Leo Stein to Albert C. Barnes, October 20, 1934. Quoted in *Journey Into Self*, p. 147.
61. Leo Stein to Mabel Dodge Luhan, February 6, 1934. Quoted in *Journey Into Self*, p. 136.
62. Leo Stein to Albert C. Barnes, October 20, 1934. Quoted in *Journey Into Self*, p. 147.
63. Leo Stein to Mabel Dodge Luhan, November 17, 1934. Quoted in *Journey Into Self*, p. 150f.
64. Leo Stein to Mabel Dodge Luhan, December 2, 1934. Quoted in *Journey Into Self*, p. 152.
65. Ernest J. Bates, "John Dewey's Aesthetics," *American Mercury*, vol. 33 (1934), p. 253.
66. Albert C. Barnes to John Dewey, February 24, 1931. *John Dewey Papers*.
67. John Dewey to Albert C. Barnes, March 3, 1931 and Albert C. Barnes to John Dewey, February 17, 1933. *John Dewey Papers*.
68. Albert C. Barnes to John Dewey, December 6, 1934. *John Dewey Papers*.
69. Albert C. Barnes to John Dewey, November 6, 1931. *John Dewey Papers*.
70. Albert C. Barnes to John Dewey, November 16, 1932. *John Dewey Papers*.
71. John Dewey to Albert C. Barnes, November 18, 1933. *John Dewey Papers*. The actual dedication of Hart's novel, *The Great One: A Novel of American Life* (New York: The John Day Company, 1934), read: "To Albert C. Barnes with appreciation of the influence he has been in my life." The main character, however, is not an art collector but a politician modeled on the Republican senator from Pennsylvania, Boies Penrose.
72. Albert C. Barnes to John Dewey, January 15, 1934. *John Dewey Papers*.

73. John Dewey, *Art as Experience*, 1934, (New York: Perigee Books, 1980), p. viii.
74. John Dewey to Albert C. Barnes, March 21, 1934. *John Dewey Papers.*
75. Albert C. Barnes to John Dewey, March 24, 1934. *John Dewey Papers.*
76. *Art as Experience*, p. 325.
77. Albert C. Barnes to John Dewey, March 28, 1934. *John Dewey Papers.*
78. John Dewey to Albert C. Barnes, March 28, 1934. *John Dewey Papers.*
79. Albert C. Barnes to John Dewey, March 29, 1934. *John Dewey Papers.*
80. John Dewey to Albert C. Barnes, March 30, 1934. *John Dewey Papers.*
81. Albert C. Barnes to John Dewey, March 30, 1934. *John Dewey Papers.*
82. Albert C. Barnes to John Dewey, April 18, 1934 and John Dewey to Albert C. Barnes, April 20, 1934. *John Dewey Papers.*
83. Albert C. Barnes to John Dewey, February 14, 1929. *John Dewey Papers.*
84. The previous spring the Nazi boycott of Jewish enterprises had demonstrated both to Germans and to the outside world that German Jews were effectively hostages, and as the year progressed, the brown shirt shock troops of the new regime systematically removed them from German civic and cultural life. Dr. Grete Ring "has occupied exalted positions in the University and the Kaiser Friedrich Museum and the Pinakothek of Munich," Barnes wrote the Penn president. But "having had a Jewish grandfather who was the most highly esteemed jurist in Germany, Dr. Ring is an outcast." See Albert C. Barnes to Thomas S. Gates, September 23, 1933. *Thomas S. Gates Administration Records.* University of Pennsylvania Archives.
85. Ibid.
86. Albert C. Barnes to George S. Koyl, March 10, 1934. *Thomas S. Gates Administration Records.*
87. George S. Koyl to Albert C. Barnes, March 16, 1934. *Thomas S. Gates Administration Records.*
88. Albert C. Barnes to George S. Koyl, March 17, 1934. *Thomas S. Gates Administration Records.*
89. Albert C. Barnes to John Dewey, July 3, 1933. *John Dewey Papers.*
90. John Dewey to Albert C. Barnes, September 18, 1933. *John Dewey Papers.*
91. Ann Eshner to William Schack, March 22, n.d. *William Schack Papers.*
92. Albert C. Barnes to John Dewey, December 1, 1934. *John Dewey Papers.*
93. Albert C. Barnes to John Dewey, December 6, 1934. *John Dewey Papers.*
94. See *Great French Paintings from The Barnes Foundation*, p. 300. Probably painted around 1910, the *Caryatids* were found in Renoir's studio at the time of his death nine years later. Barnes had owned a version of the lithograph Cézanne made of *Bathers at Rest* since Ira Glackens purchased it for him in 1912.
95. Albert C. Barnes to John Dewey, December 14, 1934. *John Dewey Papers.*
96. James Johnson Sweeney, "Analytical Study of the Work of Renoir," *New York Herald Tribune*, June 9, 1935, p. 5.
97. Eliseo Vivas, "Analysis of Renoir's Art," *Nation*, August 28, 1935, p. 250.
98. Albert C. Barnes and Violette de Mazia, *The Art of Renoir* (New York: Minton, Balch and Company, 1935), p. 160.
99. Ibid., pp. 220 and 216f.
100. John Dewey, Forward to *The Art of Renoir*, p. x.
101. Albert C. Barnes to Carl Van Vechten, April 8, 1935. *Van Vechten Papers.*
102. See *Great French Paintings from The Barnes Foundation*, p. 299.
103. John A. Rice, *I Came Out of the Eighteenth Century* (New York: Harper & Brothers, 1942), p. 332.
104. Albert C. Barnes to John Dewey, March 25, 1936. *John Dewey Papers.*

Chapter 11: Varieties of Aesthetic Experience

1. Laura Lee, "Calls Negro Art Best in America," *Evening Bulletin*, April 29, 1936, p. 13.
2. Barnes, "The Art of the American Negro," p. 376.
3. Ibid., p. 377ff.
4. Ibid., p. 379ff.
5. Ibid., p. 382f.
6. Ibid., p. 385f.
7. "Dr. Barnes Acquires $500,000 Art Gems," *Philadelphia Inquirer*, September 1, 1936, p. 1.
8. "Barnes Acquires $500,000 In Art," *New York Times*, September 1, 1936, p. 21.
9. Henry McBride, "Dr. Barnes R.I.P.," *Art News*, September 1951, p. 51.
10. Ambroise Vollard, *Souvenirs d'un Marchand de Tableaux* (Paris: Albin Michel, 1937), p. 414.
11. Albert C. Barnes, "America Welcomes One of Its Great Benefactors," Radio Speech, November 9, 1936. *Van Vechten Papers*.
12. Ambroise Vollard, Radio Speech, November 9, 1936. *Van Vechten Papers*.
13. Kenneth Clark, *Another Part of the Wood: A Self Portrait* (New York: Harper & Row, 1974), p. 243f.
14. Albert C. Barnes to Carl Van Vechten, September 14, 1933. *Van Vechten Papers*.
15. Albert C. Barnes to Carl Van Vechten, September 28, 1933. *Van Vechten Papers*.
16. Albert C. Barnes to Carl Van Vechten, January 22, 1937. *Van Vechten Papers*.
17. Vitale Bloch to William Schack, January 26, 1957. *William Schack Papers*.
18. Albert C. Barnes to John S. Jenks, November 19, 1936. *Fiske Kimball Records*. Series 1.
19. John S. Jenks to Albert C. Barnes. November 25, 1936. *Fiske Kimball Records*. Series 1.
20. "Forms of Art Exhibition," cover of brochure and p. 2. Exhibition Files. PMAA.
21. Albert C. Barnes to J. Stogdell Stokes, May 18, 1937. Quoted by Schack, p. 263. The copy of this letter and several others exchanged between Barnes and Pennsylvania Museum of Art trustees and administrators in the eight-month period between May and December 1937, which were originally held in the Archives of the Philadelphia Museum of Art, have been displaced and were not available to the author.
22. E. M. Benson to Albert C. Barnes, May 1, 1937. Quoted by Schack, p. 263f. See note 21.
23. Albert C. Barnes to E. M. Benson, May ?, 1937. Quoted by Greenfeld, p. 188f. See note 21.
24. Albert C. Barnes to John Dewey, May 10, 1937. *John Dewey Papers*.
25. John Dewey to Albert C. Barnes, May 2, 1937. *John Dewey Papers*.
26. John Dewey, "Comments on the 'Forms of Art' Exhibition at the Pennsylvania Museum of Art," May 14, 1937. *John Dewey Papers*.
27. Albert C. Barnes to Henry P. McIlhenny, May 18, 1937. Quoted by Schack, p. 264. See note 21.
28. Edward LaRocque Tinker, "New Editions, Fine and Otherwise," *New York Times*, December 12, 1927, p. 31.
29. "Cézanne 'Bathers' Bought by Museum; $110,000 Painting On Exhibition Today," *Philadelphia Record*, November 11, 1937, p. 2.
30. "Cézanne Art Gem Acquired by City," *Philadelphia Inquirer*, November 11, 1937, p. 6.

31. Albert C. Barnes to J. Stogdell Stokes, November 11, 1937. *Fiske Kimball Records.* Series 1.
32. "'The Bathers'—And the Non-Bathers," *Philadelphia Record*, November 12, 1937, p. 12.
33. Dorothy Grafly, "Pennies for America," *Philadelphia Record*, November 14, 1937, Metropolitan Section, p. 14.
34. Albert C. Barnes to J. Stogdell Stokes, November 11, 1937 and "City 'Stung' on Cézanne Art Collector Barnes Declares," *Philadelphia Inquirer*, November 16, 1937, p. 1. See also "Was City Stung by Bathers?," *Philadelphia Record*, November 16, 1937, p. 5, "Widener Is Chided For Art Purchase," New York Times, November 16, 1937, p. 21, "The Old Swimming Hole," *Evening Bulletin*, November 17, 1937, p. 12, and "Cézanne, Cézanne," *Time*, November 29, 1937, p. 22.
35. "Why Confuse the Poor Artist," *Twelve Twelve*, December 1937, p. 19. *Fiske Kimball Records*. Series 4.
36. "'Bathers' Rescued By New Experts," *Evening Bulletin*, November 17, 1937, p 3.
37. Syndic, "Letter to the Editor," *Evening Bulletin*, December 3, 1937, p. 32.
38. Albert C. Barnes to J. Stogdell Stokes, December ?, 1937. Quoted by Schack, p. 269. See note 21.
39. "A Disgrace to Philadelphia," January 3, 1938, p. 3. *Fiske Kimball Records*. Series 6.
40. "Another Museum 'Swindle' Is Charged by Barnes," *Philadelphia Inquirer*, January 24, 1938, p. 1. Once again this Philadelphia story was reported in the *New York Times* ("WPA Artists Picket Show To Arouse Interest In It," January 24, 1938, p. 1) and *Time* ("In Philadelphia," February 14, 1938, p. 43). The "sucker deal" apparently involved the purchase, out of the Elkins Trust, of one of Cézanne's paintings of Mount Ste. Victoria for $36,000, which Barnes said was offered to several buyers for $12,000 just before the sale. The picketers' complaint was that local WPA shows were held much too infrequently.
41. Henry Hart, "Philadelphia's Shame: An Analysis of the Un-American Administration of the Federal Arts Project in Philadelphia," p. 11. *Fiske Kimball Records*. Series 6.
42. "Museum and Barnes At It Again," *Philadelphia Inquirer*, January 25, 1938, p. 17.
43. Harry Fuiman, "The Progressive Decay of the Pennsylvania Museum of Art," pp. 18and 4. *Fiske Kimball Records*. Series 6.
44. Ibid., p. 14ff. Neither the city father nor the museum trustees took up Barnes's suggestions, though Mary Curran was eventually relieved of her position by the director of the Federal Arts Project.
45. Quoted by Carl W. McCardle, "The Terrible Tempered Dr. Barnes," *Saturday Evening Post*, March 21, 1942, p. 96.
46. Hart, p. 175.
47. Albert C. Barnes to Edith Glackens, June 3, 1938. Quoted in Glackens, p. 259f.
48. Albert C. Barnes to Edith Glackens, May 14, 1937. Quoted in Glackens, p. 257.
49. Barnes wrote a short article about Glackens when his friend received the Temple Gold Medal from the Pennsylvania Academy of the Fine Arts for his painting *Nude*. See Albert C. Barnes, "L'Art de William Glackens," *Les Arts è Paris*, November 1924, p. 257f.
50. Max Eastman, "John Dewey," *Atlantic Monthly*, December 1941, p. 685.
51. Albert C. Barnes to John Dewey, February 13, 1939. *John Dewey Papers.*
52. John Dewey to Albert C. Barnes, February 9, 1939. *John Dewey Papers.*
53. Albert C. Barnes, *The Art of Cézanne* (New York: Harcourt, Brace and Company, 1939), p. 103f.
54. "Barnes on Cézanne," *Time*, February 20, 1939, p. 53.
55. "The Art of Cézanne," *New Yorker*, March 4, 1939, p. 72.

56. Paul Rosenfeld, "The Permanence of a Painter," *Nation*, February 25, 1939, p. 240.
57. Edward Alden Jewel, "An Interpretive Criticism of the Art of Cézanne," *New York Times*, April 9, 1939, p. 10.
58. "Analysis of Cézanne," *Times Literary Supplement*, May 20, 1939, p. 298.
59. Milton W. Browne, "Science and Cézanne," *Saturday Review of Literature*, March 25, 1939, p. 11.
60. Albert C. Barnes to John Dewey, February 13, 1939. *John Dewey Papers*.
61. Albert C. Barnes to Carl Van Vechten, January 26, 1940. *Van Vechten Papers*.
62. John Dewey to Albert C. Barnes, May 29, 1939. *John Dewey Papers*.
63. Albert C. Barnes to Carl Van Vechten, January 26, 1940. *Van Vechten Papers*.
64. H. M. Kallen to Albert C. Barnes, May 15, 1939, *John Dewey Papers*.
65. Albert C. Barnes, "Methods in Aesthetics," *The Philosopher of the Common Man: Essays in Honor of John Dewey to Celebrate His Eightieth Birthday* (New York: G. P. Putnam's Sons, 1940), p. 103.
66. Quoted in a news article, "Dr. Dewey Is Hailed On 80th Birthday," in the *New York Times*, October 21, 1939, p. 19.
67. See Kelly Miller, "The Negro Stephen Foster," *Étude*, July 1939, pp. 431f and 472.
68. Albert C. Barnes to Carl Van Vechten, February 6, 1940. *Van Vechten Papers*.
69. Albert C. Barnes to Carl Van Vechten, February 20, 1940. *Van Vechten Papers*.
70. Albert C. Barnes to Carl Van Vechten, February 22, 1940. *Van Vechten Papers*.
71. Albert C. Barnes to Carl Van Vechten, April 1, 1940. *Van Vechten Papers*.
72. Albert C. Barnes to Carl Van Vechten, April 3, 1940. *Van Vechten Papers*.
73. Albert C. Barnes to Carl Van Vechten, April 15, 1940. *Van Vechten Papers*.
74. Albert C. Barnes to Carl Van Vechten, April 17, 1940. *Van Vechten Papers*.
75. See "Barnes Says U. of P. Won't Get Collection," *Philadelphia Inquirer*, October 11, 1940, p. 25.

Chapter 12: Students nd Teachers

1. Albert C. Barnes, Foreword to the Catalogue for the Horace Pippin Exhibition, Carlen Galleries, January 19 - February 18, 1940. Pierre Matisse Gallery Archive (PMGA) at The Pierpont Morgan Library, New York. The catalogue listed the painting Barnes had bought for himself, *Abraham Lincoln and His Father Building Their Cabin on Pigeon Creek*, de Mazia's purchase, *Birmingham Meeting-House*, and the picture the collector had reserved for Charles Laughton, *Cabin in the Cotton*, as loans for the exhibit.
2. Barnes was so impressed with the music and the preacher that, for a time, he regularly took his staff to Sunday services at Tindley Temple. See Violette de Mazia, "Transferred Values," *The Barnes Foundation Journal of the Art Department*, Autumn 1978, p. 12.
3. Laura Lee, "Dr. Barnes Likes Laughton But oh, that 'Only Suit'," *Evening Bulletin*, October 17, 1940, p. ?. Clipping in Temple University Urban Archives.
4. Joseph Alsop, *The Rare Art Traditions: The History of Art Collecting and Its Linked Phenomena Whenever These Have Appeared* (Princeton, NJ: Princeton University Press, 1982), p. 97.
5. Peter Kelly to Walter P. Chrysler, Jr., April 4, 1939. PMGA.
6. Albert C. Barnes to Alexander Woollcott, March 23, 1941. *Henry D. Mirick Papers*. Special Collections of the Van Pelt-Dietrich Library at the University of Pennsylvania. See also "All Woollcott and a Yard Wider," *Philadelphia Record*, March 26, 1941, p. 14.
7. Quoted in Samuel Hopkins Adams, *A. Woollcott: His Life and His World* (New York: Reynal & Hitchcock, 1945), p. 224.

8. Quoted by Paul Edwards in the Appendix to Bertrand Russell's *Why I Am Not A Christian* (New York: Simon and Schuster, 1957), p. 209.
9. Bertrand Russell, *Autobiography* (London: Allen and Unwin, 1967), vol. II, p. 219f.
10. John Dewey to Albert C. Barnes, May 30, 1940. *John Dewey Papers*.
11. Albert C. Barnes to John Dewey, June 3, 1940. *John Dewey Papers*.
12. Albert C. Barnes to Bertrand Russell, June 3, 1940. *Bryn Mawr College Archives*.
13. Russell, *Autobiography*, vol. II, p. 221.
14. Bertrand Russell to Albert C. Barnes, June 18, 1940. Quoted by Schack, p. 320.
15. Albert C. Barnes to Bertrand Russell, June 24, 1940. Quoted in Barry Feinberg and Ronald Kasrils, *Bertrand Russell's America: 1896-1945* (New York: The Viking Press, 1974), p. 181.
16. Albert C. Barnes to Bertrand Russell, August 16, 1940. Bryn Mawr College Archives.
17. Bertrand Russell to Albert Barnes, August 17, 1940. Quoted by Schack, p. 325.
18. Albert C. Barnes to John Dewey, July 11, 1940. *John Dewey Papers*.
19. Bertrand Russell to Albert Barnes, August 24, 1940. Quoted by Schack, p. 326 and Howard Greenfeld, *The Devil and Dr. Barnes: Portrait of an American Art Collector* (New York: Viking Penguin, 1987; reprint, New York: Penguin Books, 1989) p. 205 (reprint edition).
20. Russell, *Autobiography*, vol. III, p. 39.
21. Albert C. Barnes to Patricia Russell, August 28, 1940. Quoted by Greenfeld, p. 206.
22. When the *New York Times* published a story a few days later that suggested, based on a reporter's conversation with Barnes, that Russell's contract with the Foundation forbad him to give public lectures, Barnes whipped off a denial. He assured Russell that he had emphasized that "the cessation of popular lectures was decided by yourself alone and had nothing to do with our contract." See Albert C. Barnes to Bertrand Russell, October 22, 1940. Bryn Mawr College Archives.
23. "Russel [sic] To Teach At Foundation," *Evening Bulletin*, October 15, 1940, p. ?. Clipping in the *George W. McClelland Administrative Records*. UPA.
24. Abert C. Barnes, Letter to the Editor, *Philadelphia Inquirer*, October 18, 1940, p. 12. The offending editorial had been published six days earlier.
25. See "Russell's Roost," *Time*, October 28, 1940, p. 48.
26. "Widener to Washington, *Time*, October 28, 1940, p. 32.
27. Albert C. Barnes to Bertrand Russell, November 1, 1940. Quoted by Schack, p. 327.
28. Carl W. McCardle, "Russell Predicts World Air Force," *Evening Bulletin*, January 3, 1941, p. 3.
29. Russell, *Autobiography*, vol. II, p. 221.
30. Albert C. Barnes, "The Case of Bertrand Russell vs. Democracy in Education," (Merion, PA.: The Barnes Foundation, 1945), p. 4.
31. Albert C. Barnes to Bertrand Russell, March 3, 1941. *John Dewey Papers*.
32. Albert C. Barnes to Patricia Russell, October 21, 1941. *John Dewey Papers*.
33. Albert C. Barnes to John Dewey, March 4, 1941. *John Dewey Papers*.
34. Albert C. Barnes to Bertrand Russell, March 3, 1941. *John Dewey Papers*.
35. Albert C. Barnes to Bertrand Russell, March 13, 1941. Bryn Mawr College Archives.
36. John Dewey and Horace Kallen, *The Bertrand Russell Case* (New York: Viking Press, 1941), p. 7.
37. Bertrand Russell to Gilbert Murray, June 18, 1941. Quoted in Russell, *Autobiography*, vol. II, p. 250.
38. Albert C. Barnes to John Dewey, June 30, 1941. *John Dewey Papers*.
39. Hart, p. 198.
40. Nelle E. Mullen to Patricia Russell, October 31, 1941. *John Dewey Papers*.

41. Bertrand Russell to the Trustees of the Barnes Foundation, November 1, 1941. Bryn Mawr College Archives.
42. See Hart, p. 198.
43. Patricia Russell to Albert C. Barnes, November 1, 1940. *John Dewey Papers.*
44. "The Case of Bertrand Russell vs. Democracy in Education," p. 6.
45. Nelle E. Mullen to Patricia Russell, November 5, 1941. Bryn Mawr College Archives.
46. Nelle E. Mullen to Bertrand Russell, November 3, 1941. Bryn Mawr College Archives.
47. Patricia Russell to Angelo Pinto, December 1, 1941. *John Dewey Papers.*
48. Albert C. Barnes to Bertrand Russell, December 4, 1941. Bryn Mawr College Archives.
49. Bertrand Russell to Albert C. Barnes, December 5, 1941. Bryn Mawr College Archives.
50. Albert C. Barnes to Bertrand Russell, December 6, 1941. Bryn Mawr College Archives.
51. Bertrand Russell to Albert C. Barnes, December 11, 1941. Bryn Mawr College Archives.
52. Nelle E. Mullen to Bertrand Russell, December 15, 1941. Bryn Mawr College Archives.
53. "Renoir Picture That Knocks You Cold is Dr. Barnes' for $175000," *Evening Bulletin*, January 27, 1941, pp. 1 and 7.
54. Albert C. Barnes to Leo Stein, April 16, 1946. *Leo Stein Papers.*
55. Carl W. McCardle, "The Terrible-Tempered Dr. Barnes, *Saturday Evening Post*, April 4, 1942, p. 35.
56. Albert C. Barnes, "How It Happened," p. 3. *Fiske Kimball Papers.* Series 6.
57. Ibid., p. 5.
58. Marginal notation made by Fiske Kimball in his copy of "How it Happened."
59. Albert C. Barnes to Bertrand Russell, March 26, 1942. Bryn College Archives.
60. "How It Happened," p. 6f.
61. Albert C. Barnes to John Dewey, March 20, 1942. *John Dewey Papers.*
62. "'Pennsylvania Station' Toots at Dr. Barnes," a letter to the editor from "Pennsylvania Station," *Philadelphia Record*, March 31, 1942, p. 12.
63. "Strip Tease in Merion," *Philadelphia Record*, March 21, 1942, p. 6.
64. John Dewey to Albert C. Barnes, April 8, 1942. *John Dewey Papers.*
65. "Dr. Barnes Tells His Story," typescript of WCAU radio address delivered April 9, 1942. *John M. Fogg Papers.*
66. Bertrand Russell to Carolyn Lewis Lovett, April 16, 1942. Rosenbach Museum Archives.
67. Albert C. Barnes to John Dewey, December 28, 1942. *John Dewey Papers.*
68. Nelle E. Mullen to Bertrand Russell, December 28, 1942. *John Dewey Papers.*
69. "Russell Tussle," *Time*, February 1, 1943, p. 56.
70. Statement of Dr. Albert C. Barnes, January 16, 1943, a typescript, which includes a letter from R. D. Bulley to Albert C. Barnes, January 12, 1943. *Langston Hughes Papers.* Yale Collection of American Literature, Beinecke Rare Book and Manuscript Library, Yale University.
71. "New Echo of Barnes-Russell Spat," a letter to the editor from "A Former Student," *Philadelphia Record*, February 15, 1943, p. 8.
72. John Dewey to Albert C. Barnes, January 16, 1943. *John Dewey Papers.*
73. Bertrand Russell, "Can Americans and Britons Be Friends?" *Saturday Evening Post*, June 3, 1944, p. 57.

74. Bertrand Russell, *A History of Western Philosophy* (New York: Simon and Schuster, 1945), p. xi.

75. "The Case of Bertrand Russell vs. Democracy and Education," p. 12.

76. Albert C. Barnes to J. Stogdell Stokes, March 26, 1937. *Fiske Kimball Records.* Series 1.

77. Violette de Mazia, "The Barnes Foundation." *House & Garden*, December 1942, p. 40.

78. Albert C. Barnes to H. Martyn Kneedler, Henry D. Mirick, and C. Clark Zantzinger, July 22, 1941. *Henry D. Mirick Papers.*

79. Albert C. Barnes to H. Martyn Kneedler, Henry D. Mirick, and C. Clark Zantzinger, November 10, 1941. *Henry D. Mirick Papers.*

80. Albert C. Barnes to Henry D. Mirick, December 7, 1941. *Henry D. Mirick Papers Papers.*

81. See Hart, p. 187. Descriptions of the furnishings are derived from Albert C. Barnes, "What Ker-Feal Represents," *House & Garden*, December 1942, pp. 47 and 92f.

82. Frank A. Schrepfer, "The Arboretum of the Barnes Foundation," *Landscape Architecture*, October 1935, p. 24.

83. Despite the addition of a one-year master's program in 1939, enrollment in Penn's landscape architecture program plunged in the last years of the Depression. A cash-strapped university made its decision to suspend courses knowing that if the United States became involved in the war, there was little chance of turning the situation around in the face of a draft.

84. The new teachers were the widely respected Edgar T. Wherry, a professor of botany, D. Walter Steckbeck, an associate professor of botany, and Henry T. Skinner, the director of the Morris Arboretum, the large botanical garden in the Chestnut Hill section of Philadelphia that Penn acquired in 1932 upon the death of Lydia Morris.

85. Albert C. Barnes to Jack Bookbinder, July 28, 1944 and September 1, 1944. Correspondence and other materials related to Barnes's quarrel with Bookbinder were graciously made available to the author by Roger D. Abrahams, son of the late Robert D. Abrahams.

86. An account of the July 27, 1944 exchange was given by Bookbinder to William Schack. See Schack, p. 364. The incident was confirmed by implication in a letter Barnes wrote to Bookbinder the following day in which he refers to Bookbinder's "word-bandying and name-calling." See Albert C. Barnes to Jack Bookbinder, July 28, 1944.

87. Hart, p. 219.

88. Albert C. Barnes to Robert D. Abrahams, December 7, 1944 and Robert D. Abrahams's "Secretary" to Albert C. Barnes, December 12, 1944.

89. Albert C. Barnes to "Evelyn," December 13, 1944.

90. Robert D. Abrahams to Albert C. Barnes, December 14, 1944.

91. Albert C. Barnes to Robert D. Abrahams, December 15, 1944.

92. Robert D. Abrahams's "Secretary" to Albert C. Barnes, May 17, 1945.

93. Albert C. Barnes to Robert D. Abrahams, May 9, 1945.

94. Robert D. Abrahams to Albert C. Barnes, May 10, 1945.

95. Albert C. Barnes, "Sabotage of Public Education in Philadelphia," October 1945, p. 5f. Barnes recalled the pamphlet, perhaps on the advice of his attorney, because the final one-sentence paragraph, following a paragraph on the failings of the superintendent of schools, could be read as saying the superintendent had had a "long career of educational sabotage" when, in fact, the collector had meant the Board of Education. See Albert C. Barnes to John Dewey, October 8, 1945. *John Dewey Papers.*

96. Albert C. Barnes, "WHITEWASH: Board of Education Style," November 1945, p. 4.

97. Albert C. Barnes to John Dewey, January 24, 1945. *John Dewey Papers.*

Chapter 13: Penn Again

1. The book was Vercors's *Les Silences de la Mer*. Barnes has mastered French sufficiently well to read it, and he pronounced the story a work of "sheer beauty." See Albert C. Barnes to John M. Fogg, July 6, 1945. *John M. Fogg Papers*. Special Collections of the Van Pelt-Dietrich Library at the University of Pennsylvania.
2. Albert C. Barnes, "Chisholm and the Foundation," a typescript dated November 21, 1946, p. 1. *John M. Fogg Papers*.
3. John Dewey to Albert C. Barnes, November 24, 1945. *John Dewey Papers*.
4. "Chisholm and the Foundation," p. 1.
5. Quoted in Roderick M. Chisum to William Schack, April 16, 1958. *William Schack Papers*.
6. Albert C. Barnes to John Dewey, December 6, 1945. *John Dewey Papers*.
7. Albert C. Barnes to Roderick M. Chisholm, December 19, 1945. *William Schack Papers*.
8. Albert C. Barnes to Katharine E. McBride, March 5, 1945. Bryn Mawr College Archives.
9. Albert C. Barnes to Katharine E. McBride, March 29, 1945. Bryn Mawr College Archives.
10. Albert C. Barnes to John M. Fogg, April 17, 1946. *John M. Fogg Papers*.
11. Albert C. Barnes to Horace Stern, April 19, 1946. *John M. Fogg Papers*.
12. Nelle E. Mullen to John M. Fogg, April 20, 1946. *John M. Fogg Papers*.
13. Albert C. Barnes to John M. Fogg, April 24, 1946. *John M. Fogg Papers*.
14. Albert C. Barnes to John M. Fogg, April 27, 1946. *John M. Fogg Papers*.
15. George W. McClelland to Albert C. Barnes, April 29, 1946. *John M. Fogg Papers*.
16. Albert C. Barnes to George W. McClelland, April 29, 1946. *John M. Fogg Papers*.
17. Albert C. Barnes to John M. Fogg, May 25, 1946. *John M. Fogg Papers*.
18. Albert C. Barnes, "Chisholm and the Foundation," p. 1.
19. Albert C. Barnes to John Dewey, July 29, 1946. *John Dewey Papers*.
20. Albert C. Barnes to John M. Fogg, August 9, 1946. *John M. Fogg Papers*.
21. Albert C. Barnes, "Report on the University of Pennsylvania—Barnes Foundation Experiment," a typescript dated April 10, 1947, p. 3. *George W. McClelland Administration Records*. University of Pennsylvania Archives.
22. Quoted in Albert C. Barnes to John M. Fogg, August 28, 1946. *John M. Fogg Papers*.
23. Quoted in Albert C. Barnes to John M. Fogg, August 28, 1946. *John M. Fogg Papers*.
24. Laurence Buermeyer to Albert C. Barnes, August 28, 1946. Quoted in Albert C. Barnes to John M. Fogg, August 29, 1946. *John M. Fogg Papers*.
25. Albert C. Barnes to John Dewey, September 11, 1946. *John M. Fogg Papers*.
26. Nelle E. Mullen to Glenn R. Morrow, September 16, 1946. *John M. Fogg Papers*.
27. "Report on the University of Pennsylvania—Barnes Foundation Experiment," p. 4f.
28. What de Mazia and Mullen are not likely to have learned is that Longaker's mother was the centerpiece of an international scandal when she met her future husband aboard the yacht of English friends on a holiday in the Mediterranean and, when he left her in Capri to return to his classes at Penn, pursued him to America as a stowaway. In the glare of publicity, she was promptly deported, and he followed her to Rome where she married him.
29. Jon D. Longaker to the author, May 6, 1997.
30. Albert C. Barnes to John M. Fogg, September 20, 1946 and September 23, 1946. *John M. Fogg Papers*.

31. Anthony R. Heffron, "A Gentler Dr. Barnes," *Pennsylvania Gazette*, June 1993, p. 47.
32. Roderick M. Chisholm to the author, July 5, 1997. Professor Chisholm died in 1999.
33. Roderick M. Chisholm, "Statement," a typescript dated January 30, 1947, p. 1. *John M. Fogg Papers*.
34. "Report on the University of Pennsylvania—Barnes Foundation Experiment," p.7 and "Chisholm and the Foundation." p. 3.
35. Albert C. Barnes to Roderick M. Chisholm, November 22, 1946. *John M. Fogg Papers*.
36. Hart, p. 234.
37. Albert C. Barnes to John M. Fogg, November 23, 1946. *John M. Fogg Papers*.
38. "Statement," p. 3 and Roderick M. Chisholm to Glenn R. Morrow, November 25, 1946. *John M. Fogg Papers*.
39. Glenn R. Morrow to Paul H. Musser, December 6, 1946. *George W. McClelland Administration Records*.
40. Albert C. Barnes to Glenn R. Morrow, December 5, 1946. *John M. Fogg Papers*.
41. Glenn R. Morrow to Albert C. Barnes, December 9, 1946. *George W. McClelland Administration Records*.
42. Albert C. Barnes to George W. McClelland, December 11, 1946. *John M. Fogg Papers*.
43. Albert C. Barnes to George W. McClelland, December 16, 1946. *John M. Fogg Papers*.
44. George W. McClelland to Albert C. Barnes, December 16, 1946. *John M. Fogg Papers*.
45. Heffron, p. 47.
46. Ibid., p. 48.
47. "Report on the University of Pennsylvania—Barnes Foundation Experiment," p. 8.
48. Memorandum "To All Members of the Thursday Class," February 7, 1947. The document was provided to the author by Jon D. Longaker.
49. Albert C. Barnes to George W. McClelland, February 7, 1947. *George W. McClelland Administration Records*.
50. Albert C. Barnes to George W. McClelland, February 11, 1947. *George W. McClelland Administration Records*.
51. George W. McClelland to Albert C. Barnes, February 15, 1947. *George W. McClelland Administration Records*.
52. George W. McClelland to Horace Stern, February 21, 1947. *George W. McClelland Administration Records*.
53. "Report on the University of Pennsylvania—Barnes Foundation Experiment," p. 9.
54. Jon D. Longaker in conversation with the author, June 10, 1997.
55. Leo Stein, *Appreciation: Painting, Poetry, Prose* (New York: Crown Publishers, 1947), pp. 44, 8, and 104.
56. Albert C. Barnes to Leo Stein, July 3, 1947. *Gertrude Stein and Alice B. Toklas Papers*.
57. Leo Stein to Fred Stein, July 13, 1947. *Reprinted in Journey Into Self*, p. 295.
58. Leo Stein to Albert C. Barnes, July 8, 1947. *Reprinted in Journey Into Self*, p. 294.
59. Albert C. Barnes to Leo Stein, July 22, 1947. *Gertrude Stein and Alice B. Toklas Papers*.
60. Albert C. Barnes to Leo Stein, April 16, 1946. *Gertrude Stein and Alice B. Toklas Papers*.

61. Henry Clifford to Albert C. Barnes, February 23, 1948. *Fiske Kimball Records.* Series I.
62. Henri Matisse to Pierre Matisse, ?,?, 1947. Quoted by John Russell in *Matisse: Father & Son* (New York: Harry N. Abrams, 1999), p. 299.
63. Albert C. Barnes to R. Sturgis Ingersoll, April 5, 1948. *John M. Fogg Papers.*
64. Albert C. Barnes, "Excerpts from Dr. Barnes' [sic] Talk at the Philadelphia Museum of Art on April 7, 1948," a typescript. *John M. Fogg Papers.*
65. R. Sturgis Ingersoll, *Henry McCarter* (Cambridge: The Riverside Press, 1944), p. 72.
66. Albert C. Barnes to R. Sturgis Ingersoll, April 26, 1948. *George W. McClelland Administration Records.*
67. Albert C. Barnes to R. Sturgis Ingersoll, April 29, 1948. *George W. McClelland Administration Records.*
68. Albert C. Barnes to John M. Fogg, April 16, 1948. *John M. Fogg Papers.*
69. John M. Fogg to Albert C. Barnes, April 22, 1948. *John M. Fogg Papers.*
70. Albert C. Barnes to John M. Fogg, April 23, 1948, *John M. Fogg Papers*, and Albert C. Barnes to William H. DuBarry, April 24, 1948, *George W. McClelland Administration Records.*
71. William H. DuBarry to Albert C. Barnes, April 28, 1948. *John M. Fogg Papers.*
72. Albert C. Barnes to William H. DuBarry, April 28, 1948. *John M. Fogg Papers.*
73. Notes Fiske Kimball made for his April 30, 1948 talk are quoted by Roberts and Roberts, p. 252.
74. "Excerpts from Stenographic Notes Taken at a Lecture on Matisse by Fiske Kimball," a typescript, provided to the author by Jon D. Longaker.
75. Ibid.
76. Henry Clifford to Albert C. Barnes, May 16, 1948. *John M. Fogg Papers.*
77. "Bella Donna van Byttsche" to Albert C. Barnes, May 21, 1948. *John M. Fogg Papers.*
78. Albert C. Barnes to R. Sturgis Ingersoll, June 16, 1948. *George W. McClelland Administration Records.*
79. Albert C. Barnes to Horace Stern, April 11, 1949. *Harold E. Stassen Administration Records.* University of Pennsylvania Archives.
80. "Summary of Dr. Barnes' Talk to a Class of Art Students," a typescript dated January 7, 1949. *Harold E. Stassen Administration Records.*
81. Albert C. Barnes to Gilbert F. White, October 23, 1948. Lincoln University Archives.
82. "Summary of Dr. Barnes' Talk to a Class of Art Students."
83. Albert C. Barnes, "Quo Vadis Haverford College?," a typescript dated December 1, 1948. Lincoln University Archives.
84. Quoted in Albert C. Barnes to John M. Fogg, June 28, 1949. *John M. Fogg Papers.*
85. Albert C. Barnes to Harold E. Stassen, June 24, 1949. *Harold E. Stassen Administration Records.*
86. Albert C. Barnes to John M. Fogg, June 28, 1949. *John M. Fogg Papers.*
87. Albert C. Barnes to Harold E. Stassen, July 1, 1949. *Harold E. Stassen Administration Records.*
88. Walter Hamilton, "A Deweyesque Mosaic," in The Philosopher and the Common Man (New York: G.P. Putnam's Sons. 1940), p. 170.
89. See "Barnes Replies," *Main Line Times*, April 20, 1950, p. 2.
90. John M. Fogg to Albert C. Barnes, July 26, 1949. *John M. Fogg Papers.*
91. Albert C. Barnes to John M. Fogg, September 6, 1949. *Harold E. Stassen Administration Records.*
92. Albert C. Barnes to John M. Fogg, September 29, 1949. *Harold E. Stassen Administration Records.*

93. Quoted in Albert C. Barnes to Harold E. Stassen, November 3, 1949. *John M. Fogg Papers.*

94. Ibid.

95. Albert C. Barnes to Horace Stern, November 25, 1949. *Horace Mann Bond Papers.*

96. Albert C. Barnes to John M. Fogg, March 8, 1950. *John M. Fogg Papers.*

97. James A. Michener, "The Main Line," *Holiday*, April 1950, pp. 35, 40, 48, and 52.

98. Albert C. Barnes to James A. Michener, March 16, 1950. *John M. Fogg Papers.*

99. James A. Michener to Albert C. Barnes, March 28, 1950. *John M. Fogg Papers.*

100. Albert C. Barnes to Harold E. Stassen, March 30, 1950. *Harold E. Stassen Administration Records.*

101. Albert C. Barnes to James A. Michener, March 31, 1950. *John M. Fogg Papers.*

102. James A. Michener to William Schack, June 14, 1957. *William Schack Papers.*

103. Jon D. Longaker to Albert C. Barnes, March 31, 1950. Harold E. *Stassen Administration Records.*

104. Albert C. Barnes to Harold E. Stassen, April 3, 1950. *John M. Fogg Papers.*

105. Paul W. Musser, "Memorandum," a typescript dated April 21, 1950. *Harold E. Stassen Administration Records.*

106. Albert C. Barnes to Jon D. Longaker, April 22, 1950. Courtesy of Jon D. Longaker.

107. Albert C. Barnes to Jon D. Longaker, April 26, 1950. Courtesy of Jon D. Longaker.

108. Albert C. Barnes to Harold E. Stassen, April 22, 1950. *Harold E. Stassen Administration Records.*

109. Albert C. Barnes to Jon D. Longaker, May 18, 1950. Courtesy of Jon D. Longaker.

110. Jon D. Longaker to Albert C. Barnes, May 24, 1950 Courtesy of Jon D. Longaker.

111. Harold E. Stassen to Albert C. Barnes, June 12, 1950. *John M. Fogg Papers.*

112. Albert C. Barnes to Harold E. Stassen, June 14, 1950. *John M. Fogg Papers.*

113. Albert C. Barnes to Harold E. Stassen, June 26, 1950. *John M. Fogg Papers.*

114. John Dewey to Albert C. Barnes, n.d. Quoted by Harold Taylor in *Dialogue on John Dewey*, p. 45.

115. Albert C. Barnes to Jon D. Longaker, August 1, 1950. Courtesy of Jon D. Longaker.

116. Harold Taylor to Albert C. Barnes, May 4, 1950. Sarah Lawrence College Archives.

117. Albert C. Barnes to Harold Taylor, June 2, 1950. Sarah Lawrence College Archives.

118. Albert C. Barnes to Jon D. Longaker, July 7, 1950. Courtesy of Jon D. Longaker.

119. Ibid.

120. Jon D. Longaker to the author, summer 1997.

121. Albert C. Barnes to Jon D. Longaker, July 27, 1950. Courtesy of Jon D. Longaker.

122. Albert C. Barnes to Jon D. Longaker, August 1, 1950. Courtesy of Jon D. Longaker.

123. Albert C. Barnes to Jon D. Longaker, August 2, 1950. Courtesy of Jon D. Longaker.

124. Albert C. Barnes to Harold Taylor, September 5, 1950. Sarah Lawrence Archives.

125. Albert C. Barnes to Harold Taylor, November 2, 1950. Sarah Lawrence Archives.

126. John Dewey to Harold Taylor, November 17, 1950. Sarah Lawrence Archives.

Chapter 14: The Last Alliance

1. Conversation recalled and quoted in a letter Horace Mann Bond wrote to Raymond Pace Alexander, March 9, 1968. *Horace Mann Bond Papers.*

2. Horace Mann Bond, "Albert C. Barnes, The Barnes Foundation, and Lincoln University," a typescript of an unfinished autobiography, p. 3. *Horace Mann Bond Papers.*

3. Horace Mann Bond to Charles A. Lewis, November 2, 1946. Lincoln University Archives.

4. Albert C. Barnes to Horace Mann Bond, December 2, 1946. Lincoln University Archives.

5. Horace Mann Bond to Albert C. Barnes, January 19, 1947. Lincoln University Archives.
6. Horace Mann Bond to Albert C. Barnes, February 13, 1947. Lincoln University Archives.
7. Horace Mann Bond to Albert C. Barnes, October 11, 1947. Lincoln University Archives.
8 . Albert C. Barnes to Horace Mann Bond, October 13, 1947. Courtesy of Jon D. Longaker.
9. Albert C. Barnes to Walter Fales, March 18, 1948. Courtesy of Jon D. Longaker.
10. Walter Fales to Albert C. Barnes, March 20, 1948. Courtesy of Jon D. Longaker.
11. Albert C. Barnes to Walter Fales, March 24, 1948. Courtesy of Jon D. Longaker.
12. Horace Mann Bond to Albert C. Barnes, April 22, 1948. Lincoln University Archives.
13. Horace Mann Bond to Albert C. Barnes, April 28, 1948. Lincoln University Archives.
14. Horace Mann Bond to Albert C. Barnes, May 19, 1948. Lincoln University Archives.
15. Albert C. Barnes to Horace Mann Bond, January 11, 1949. Lincoln University Archives.
16. Horace Mann Bond to Albert C. Barnes, January 19, 1949. Lincoln University Archives.
17. Ibid.
18. Quoted by Gilbert M. Cantor, *The Barnes Foundation: Reality vs. Myth* (Philadelphia: Chilton Books, 1963), p. 80. See also Vincent Jubilee, "The Barnes Foundation: Pioneer Patron of Black Artists" in the *Journal of Negro Education*, vol. 51, no. 1 (Winter 1982), p. 47. Jubilee cites a letter to him from Clark, dated January 19, 1978, as the source of his information.
19. Cortlandt Van Rensslear, "God Glorified By Africa," 1856. Quoted by Horace Mann Bond in *Education for Freedom: A History of Lincoln University, Pennsylvania* (Lincoln University, PA: Lincoln University, 1976), p. 249.
20. Horace Mann Bond to Albert C. Barnes, September 17, 1949. Lincoln University Archives.
21. Albert C. Barnes to Horace Mann Bond, September 22, 1949. Lincoln University Archives.
22. Horace Mann Bond to Albert C. Barnes, February 9, 1950. Lincoln University Archives.
23. Horace Mann Bond to Albert C. Barnes, August 18, 1950. Courtesy of Jon D. Longaker.
24. Albert C. Barnes to Horace Mann Bond, August 21, 1950. Courtesy of Jon D. Longaker.
25. Jon D. Longaker to the author, summer 1997.
26. Horace Mann Bond to Albert C. Barnes, August 30, 1950. Courtesy of Jon D. Longaker.
27. Albert C. Barnes to Horace Mann Bond, August 31, 1950. Courtesy of Jon D. Longaker.
28. Horace Mann Bond to Albert C. Barnes, October 3, 1950. Lincoln University Archives.
29. Albert C. Barnes to Horace Mann Bond, October 7, 1950. Courtesy of Jon D. Longaker.
30. Albert C. Barnes to Horace Mann Bond, October 12, 1950. Courtesy of Jon D. Longaker.
31. Horace Mann Bond to Albert C. Barnes, October 14, 1950. Lincoln University Archives.

32. Article IX, Section 2 incorporates into the bylaws the Indenture of Trust of December 6, 1922, whereby Dr. Barnes established the Foundation.
33. Albert C. Barnes to J. Newton Hill, October 27, 1950. Courtesy of Jon D. Longaker.
34. Albert C. Barnes to Horace Mann Bond, November 6, 1950. Lincoln University Archives.
35. Albert C. Barnes to Horace Mann Bond, January 9, 1951. *Horace Mann Bond Papers.*
36. Horace Mann Bond to Mayme B. Rothenberger, March 22, 1968. *Horace Mann Bond Papers.* Mrs. Rothenberger was the Register of Wills for Montgomery County, Pennsylvania.
37. Horace Mann Bond to Walter G. Alexander, March 7, 1951. *Horace Mann Bond Papers.*
38. Albert C. Barnes to Horace Mann Bond, March 8, 1951. *Horace Mann Bond Papers.*
39. Albert C. Barnes to Ralph J. Bunche, March 12, 1951. *Horace Mann Bond Papers.*
40. Albert C. Barnes to Horace Mann Bond, April 26, 1951. *Horace Mann Bond Papers.*
41. Horace Mann Bond to Walter G. Alexander, April 28, 1951. *Horace Mann Bond Papers.* Kwame Nkrumah took his A.B. at Lincoln in 1939 and earned a Bachelor of Sacred Theology degree in 1942. He also earned two master's degrees and a Ph.D. from the University of Pennsylvania. As Chief Minister for His Majesty's Government Business, Nkrumah was titular head of his country's new reform government. He was given the title of Prime Minister for the Gold Coast in 1953, and in 1957 the Gold Coast became an independent nation known as Ghana.
42. Albert C. Barnes to Horace Mann Bond, May 1, 1951. *Horace Mann Bond Papers.*
43. Albert C. Barnes to Horace Mann Bond, May 17, 1951. *Horace Mann Bond Papers.*
44. Albert C. Barnes to Horace Mann Bond, May 21, 1951. *Horace Mann Bond Papers.*
45. Horace Mann Bond to Albert C. Barnes, May 24, 1951. *Horace Mann Bond Papers.*
46. Horace Mann Bond to Walter C. Alexander, May 27, 1951. *Horace Mann Bond Papers.*
47. Albert C. Barnes to Horace Mann Bond, May 28, 1951. *Horace Mann Bond Papers.*
48. Albert C. Barnes to Horace Mann Bond, July 11, 1951. *Horace Mann Bond Papers.*
49. "Dr. Barnes Is Killed in Collision; His Art Collection to Stay Intact," *Philadelphia Inquirer*, July 25, 1951, p. 1.
50. Quoted by Hart, p. 242.
51. Quoted from memory by Joanna Reed in a conversation with the author, April 24, 1997.
52. "Dr. Barnes' Two Secrets," *Philadelphia Inquirer*, July 26, 1951, p. 16.
53. Paul Jones, "Dr. Barnes and His Pictures," *Evening Bulletin*, July 26, 1951, p. 18.
54. Carroll S. Tyson to Fiske Kimball, August 24, 1951. *Fiske Kimball Papers.*
55. William H. DuBarry to a colleague he addressed as Jack, August 15, 1951. *Harold E. Stassen Administration Records.*
56. John M. Fogg to George A. Sagendorph, September 10, 1951. *Harold E. Stassen Administration Records.*
57. Bond wrote to Henry Hart in 1964 after reading his memoir of Barnes to ask if he knew whether Lincoln's trustees would have the right eventually to nominate the trustees of the Barnes Foundation. But he still didn't know the answer to the question when he wrote to Judge Raymond Pace Alexander in 1968 to ask the name of the Register of Wills in Montgomery County. See Bond to Hart, August 15, 1964, Bond to Alexander, March 9, 1968, and Alexander to Bond, March 20, 1968. *Horace Mann Bond Papers.*

58. Horace Mann Bond, "Dr. Albert C. Barnes and Lincoln University," an undated typescript. *Horace Mann Bond Papers.*

59. Horace Mann Bond to Henry Hart, August 15, 1964. *Horace Mann Bond Papers.*

Chapter 15: Postmortem

1. Comment recalled by Josephine Bachman in conversation with the author, May 6, 1997.

2. David M. Robb to Fiske Kimball, September 3, 1951. *Fiske Kimball Papers.* Series 6.

3. Fiske Kimball to David M. Robb, September 6, 1951. *Fiske Kimball Papers.* Series 6.

4. "Dr. Barnes and Purpose," *Main Line Times*, August 2, 1951, p. 12.

5. "Inquirer Starts Court Action To Give Public Right To See Art in Barnes Foundation," *Philadelphia Inquirer*, February 7, 1951, p. 2.

6   "Attorney General Praises Move To 'Unlock' Art," *Philadelphia Inquirer*, February 7, 1951, p. 1.

7. "Experts Here Hail Inquirer On Art Suit," *Philadelphia Inquirer*, February 8, 1951, p. 1.

8. "Publicity Suit," *Main Line Times*, February 28, 1952, p. 16.

9. Horace Mann Bond, "Dr. Albert C. Barnes: A Lion Among Asses, one of whom is a Snide Jackass," an undated typescript. *Horace Mann Bond Papers.* Bond's remarks must have been written shortly after February 7, 1952 when the *Inquirer* published its first article about the suit against the Barnes Foundation as Nelle E. Mullen wrote to him at the end of the month to apologize for taking "so long" to thank him for his "very nice tribute to Dr. Barnes" and his "reference to the Attorney General," which she described as "most fitting." See Mullen to Bond, February 26, 1952. *Horace Mann Bond Papers.*

10. "Barnes pro bono publico," *ARTNews*, March 1952, p. 15.

11. "Communications on the Barnes suit," *ARTNews*, May 1952, p. 10.

12. Abraham L. Chanin, "No Dark Villain or Fair Hero In Barnes Foundation Drama," *Compass*, March 16, 1952, p. 24. Clipping in the *Horace Mann Papers.*

13. "Barnes pro bono publico" and "Communications on the Barnes suit," *ARTNews*, May 1952, p. 10.

14. Abraham L. Chanin, "Parnassus in Merion, Pa.," *ARTNews*, February 1961, p. 66.

15. Abraham L. Chanin, "The Battle Over Treasures Of the Barnes Foundation," *Compass*, March 9, 1952, p. 24 (clipping in the *Horace Mann Papers*) and "No Dark Villain or Fair Hero In Barnes Foundation Drama," p. 24.

16. Uncle Ben, "Suit Demands General Access To Barnes Art," *Main Line Times*, February 21, 1952, p. 3.

17. Quoted in "Court to Rule If Trustees Must Open Barnes Galleries, *Evening Bulletin*, March 14, 1952, p. 2. See also "Museum Defends Admission Rules," *New York Times*, March 15, 1952. p. 11. The same day the *Philadelphia Inquirer*'s article about the Foundation's answer was buried among the obits. See "Barnes Reply Contends Court Can't Intervene," p. 18.

18. Dorothy McCardle, "Foreigners View Barnes Art But American Still Barred," *Evening Bulletin*, November 9, 1952, Metropolitan Section, p. 1.

19. Quoted in "Court Dismisses Suit to Open Barnes Art Galleries to Public," *Evening Bulletin*, December 10, 1952, p. 4.

20. Quoted in "High Court Refuse to Open Barnes Foundation to Public," *Evening Bulletin*, June 1, 1953, p. 10.

21. Conversation with the author, May 6, 1997.

22. Quoted in "Suit to Open Barnes Gallery," *Philadelphia Inquirer*, March 23, 1960, p. 5.

23. "Court Test Coming on Closed Door," *Philadelphia Inquirer*, December 10, 1960, p. 1.

24. Henry R. Darling, "Visitors Are Sparse But Enthusiastic At Opening of Barnes Gallery," *Evening Bulletin*, March 19, 1961, p. 1.

25. Dennis Leon, "Public Given First Glimpse of Superb Barnes Collection, *Philadelphia Inquirer*, March 19, 1961, p. 1.

26. John Canaday, "Art Lives Up to Its Fabulous Legend As Unexpected Wonders Are Disclosed," *New York Times*, March 19, 1961, p. 80.

27. Emily Genauer, "The Barnes Myth Exploded," *New York Herald Tribune*, March 26, 1961, p. 19.

28. Quoted in "Barnes Gallery Defies Court On Admissions, State Says," *Philadelphia Inquirer*, April 6, 1962, p. 1.

29. Quoted in "Some Art In Barnes Gallery Called Forgeries," *Philadelphia Inquirer*, April 12, 1962, p. 12.

30. Ibid., p. 1.

31. "Barnes Knew of Forgeries, Some Say of Collection," *Evening Bulletin*, April 8, 1962, p. 3.

32. Quoted in "26 Barnes Paintings Are Fakes, 2 Experts Say," *Evening Bulletin*, May 22, 1962, p. 1.

33. The deputy attorney general cited the trustees for negligence on three main counts: operating the art gallery in ways that deliberately harassed visitors, treating the scholarly world with contempt, and wasting money by employing too many guards; spending more than 80 percent of the Foundation's $305,076 yearly income on purposes other than the gallery, namely the maintenance of the arboretum, conduct of its class, and the maintenance of Ker-Feal; and failing to take steps to increase income, specifically, seeking court approval for a less restrictive investment program that might yield greater returns.

34. Quoted in "State Wants Four Barnes Trustees Fired," *Evening Bulletin*, June 8, 1962, p. 1.

35. Quoted in "Barnes Foundation Defends Trustees in Ouster Attempt," *Philadelphia Inquirer*, November 29, 1962, p. 37.

36. The paintings included three Renoirs, two Matisses, two Henri Rousseaus, a Soutine, a Utrillo, and Delacroix's dramatic *Desdemona Being Killed by Her Father* in addition to six canvases by Glackens, three by Ernest Lawson, and several others. Some years earlier, she had given a maquette of the Merion *Dance* mural to a friend.

37. Quoted in Lucinda Fleeson, "Rebirth of the Barnes," *Philadelphia Inquirer Magazine*, November 11, 1990. p. 28.

38. Edward L. Loper, Interview 21 (May 12, 1989), pp. 70f, 74, 76, and 87. *Oral History Collection of the Archives of American Art.*

39. Violette de Mazia, "Method," *Barnes Foundation Journal of the Art Department*, Spring 1970, pp. 9f.

40. Violette de Mazia, "What to Look for in Art," *Barnes Foundation Journal of the Art Department*, Spring 1971, p. 16.

41. Violette de Mazia, "Aesthetic Quality," *Barnes Foundation Journal of the Art Department*, Spring 1971, p. 20.

42. Violette de Mazia, "The Case of Glackens vs.. Renoir," *Barnes Foundation Journal of the Art Department*, Autumn 1971, p. 24.

43. James Johnson Sweeney, "The Albert C. Barnes Collection," *Barnes Foundation Journal of the Art Department*, Autumn 1972, p. 30.

44. J. Newton Hill, "A Look at African Sculpture," *Barnes Foundation Journal of the Art Department*, Spring 1974, p. 46.

45. Violette de Mazia, "Creative Distortion IV: Portraiture II," *Barnes Foundation Journal of the Art Department*, Spring 1974, pp. 22, 25, and 24.
46. Quoted in Lucinda Fleeson, "Rebirth of the Barnes," p. 11 and confirmed in a conversation with the author, October 1, 1999.
47. Conversation with the author, October 1, 1999.
48. Viloette de Mazia, "The Lure and Trap of Color Slides," *VISTAS*, 1984-86, pp. 30, 31, and 34-36.
49. Viloette de Mazia, "Transferred Values," *VISTAS*, spring-summer 1979, p. 33.
50. Viloette de Mazia, "The Barnes Foundation: The Display of Its Collection," *VISTAS*, 1981-1983, p. 119.
51. The original co-trustees and executors were Van Sant and Gilbert M. Cantor, an attorney and author of *The Barnes Foundation: Reality vs. Myth*. When Cantor died, de Mazia named Pick
52. Marlene Dubin in conversation with the author, November 5, 1997.

Chapter 16: Lincoln

1. See George D. Cannon to Donald L. Mullett, March 2, 1986. Lincoln University Archives. Mullett was then interim president of Lincoln.
2. Quoted in Grace Glueck, "Small University Gains Control of the Barnes Foundation," *New York Times*, October 19, 1989, Section C, p. 19.
3. Quoted in Lucinda Fleeson, "Lincoln University To Control $1 Billion Barnes Art Collection," *Philadelphia Inquirer*, September 27, 1988, Section A, p. 20.
4. Quoted in Glueck, p. 24.
5. The art advisory committee included Mary Schmidt-Campbell, commissioner of the New York City Department of Cultural Affairs, Anne d'Harnoncourt, director (now president) of the Philadelphia Museum of Art, David Driscoll, a professor of art history at the University of Maryland at College Park and a specialist in African-American art who also had come on the Lincoln board at Franklin Williams's urging, Tom Freudenheim, assistant secretary for museums at the Smithsonian Institution, E. Roger Mandle, deputy director of the National Gallery of Art, Gary Tinterow, associate curator of European painting at the Metropolitan Museum of Art, Sylvia Williams, director of the National Museum of African Art, and the late Kirk Varnedoe, then director of the department of painting and sculpture at the Museum of Modern Art, in addition to Feigen himself.
6. Richard C. Glanton in conversation with the author, March 2, 2000.
7. Quoted in Lucinda Fleeson, "Barnes urged by Annenberg to sell some art," *Philadelphia Inquirer*, April 18, 1991, Section A, p. 8.
8. Richard C. Glanton in conversation with the author, March 10, 2000.
9. The resolution was adopted unanimously by the Barnes Foundation Trustees on December 19, 1990. A copy is in the possession of the author. Quotation in Petition by Richard H. Glanton, Esquire, Dr. Niara Sudarkasa, Shirley A. Jackson, Ph.D., Charles A. Frank, III, and Cuyler H. Walker, Esquire, Members of the Board of Trustees of the Barnes Foundation, to Amend the Trust Indenture and Agreement Dated December 6, 1922 and Articles IX and X of the bylaws of the Barnes Foundation, presented to the Court of Common Pleas of Montgomery County, Pennsylvania, Orphans' Court Division, March 18, 1991, p. 4f.
10. Quoted in Michael Kimmelman, "Trying to Open Up the Barnes, and Pay Some of the Bills, Too," *New York Times*, February 7, 1991, Section C, p. 19.
11. Quoted in Lucinda Fleeson, "Museum seeks to sell art," *Philadelphia Inquirer*, March 24, 1991, Section A, p. 7. Glanton's law firm and the political action committees of several companies on whose boards of directors he served had been generous

contributors to Preate's campaign; the ambitious attorney general planned to run for governor.

12. Edward J. Sozanski, "Barnes art sale should be last resort," *Philadelphia Inquirer*, April 14, 1991, Section F, p. 1.

13. Kimmelman, ibid. and his "The Barnes Explores Other Byways," *New York Times*, April 21, 1991, Section 2, p. 35.

14. Quoted in Fleeson, "Barnes urged by Annenberg to sell some art."

15. Quoted in Lucinda Fleeson, "Friends as foes," *Philadelphia Inquirer*, June 18, 1991, Section E, p. 5.

16. Quoted in Stephan Salisbury, "Plan to sell paintings is dropped," *Philadelphia Inuirer*, June 22, 1991, Section A, p. 1.

17. Quoted in Grace Glueck, "Barnes Foundation to Permit Color Reproductions of Its Art," *New York Times*, June 10, 1991, p. 11.

18. Richard C. Glanton in conversation with the author, March 10, 2000.

19. Ibid.

20. Quoted in Julia M. Klein, "Suit aims to oust Barnes' trustees, *Philadelphia Inquirer*, January 17, 1992, Section A, p. 1 and Andrew Decker, "Future Shock at the Barnes, *ARTNews*, September 1992, p. 110.

21. The comment by S. Gordon Elkins is quoted in Julia M. Klein, "Barnes levels new charges; de Mazia Trust stole art, petition says," *Philadelphia Inquirer*, April 16, 1992, Section E, p. 1.

22. Richard H. Glanton, Letter to the Editor, *Philadelphia Inquirer*, January 16, 1994, Section E, p. 4.

23. William Bradbury, attorney for the Concerned Students of the Barnes Foundation, quoted in Leonard W. Boasberg, "Another group sues to block any changes by Barnes trustees," *Philadelphia Inquirer*, June 25, 1991, Section D, p. 4.

24. Samet, a consultant paid by the de Mazia Trust, had requested a list of the pictures to be removed from their frames for photographing for the Knopf book and permission to examine them and make recommendations about their condition. She also offered to organize a training session for handlers, including photographer Robert Owen.

25. Quoted in Julia M. Klein, "Barnes official resigns," *Philadelphia Inquirer*, February 21, 1992, Section C, p. 1.

26. Richard C. Glanton in conversation with the author, March 2, 2000.

27. Quoted in David D'Arcy, "Barnes Storm," *Vanity Fair*, August 1991, p. 166.

28. In the end, the paintings were stored in the Barnes administration building adjacent to the gallery with only the Merion *Dance* going to the Philadelphia Museum of Art after it was exhibited in Paris.

29. Quoted in Edward J. Sozanski, "One judge's decision for dollars and sense," *Philadelphia Inquirer*, August 2, 1992, Section H, p. 1.

30. Quoted in Julia M. Klein, "Judge allows paintings from the Barnes to go on tour," *Philadelphia Inquirer*, July 23, 1992, Section A, p. 1.

31. Ibid.

32. A.F. Brown, "Open Letter to the Citizens of Montgomery County: The Barnes Case," *Main Line Times*, July 26 1992, p. 7.

33. Stephen Salisbury, "Captured on canvas, the modern world dawns." *Philadelphia Inquirer*, January 27, 1995, Section GB, page 5.

34. Hilton Kramer, "Barnes' 'Confused Values' World Tour Ready to Roll," *New York Observer*, December 14, 1992, p. 23.

35. Steven Vincent, "Tour de Force," *Art & Auction*, April 1993, p. 114.

36. Leo J. O'Donovan, S.J., "Idiosyncrasy and Genius," *America*, July 17, 1993, p. 18.

37. Quoted in Joseph A. Shobodzian, "After the Glanton verdict, a legal debate goes on quietly," *Philadelphia Inquirer*, August 15, 1993, Section E, p. 2.
38. Quoted in Julia M. Klein, "Barnes Foundation asks approval from judge to add stops to art tour, *Philadelphia Inquirer*, October 24, 1993, Section B, p. 5.
39. Quoted in Ron Graham, "Barnes or bust," *Toronto Life*, September 1994, p. 65.
40. Quoted in Julia M. Klein, "Museum to show Barnes sculptures," *Philadelphia Inquirer*, January 12, 1995, Section B, p. 3.
41. Stephen Manes, "An Electronic Gallery of Rare Art," *New York Times*, February 14, 1995, Section C, p. 8.
42. Cuyler H. Walker in conversation with the author, March 29, 2000.
43. Quoted in Leonard W. Boasberg, "Barnes Foundation renews request to extend art exhibit's tour," *Philadelphia Inquirer*, April 19, 1995, Section E, p. 5.
44. Quoted in Leonard W. Boasberg, "Munich gallery sweats out Barnes show," *Philadelphia Inquirer*, April 30, 1995, Section K, p. 11.
45. Quoted in Leonard W. Boasberg, "Barnes art won't hang in Munich," *Philadelphia Inquirer*, May 12, 1995, Section B, p. 6.
46. Ibid.
47. Quoted in "The Supervision of Trust," *Barnes Watch* 32, p. 2.
48. Quoted in "Art and Education, The Last Stand?" *Barnes Watch* 35, p. 2.
49. Quoted in Leonard W. Boasberg, "Tie is severed between Barnes, de Mazia trust," *Philadelphia Inquirer*, September 11, 1996, Section B, p. 2.
50. Quoted in Leonard W. Boasberg, "Founder's orders stand, Barnes Foundation told," *Philadelphia Inquirer*, September 22, 1995. Section B, p. 2.
51. Quoted in Leonard W. Boasberg, "Barnes Foundation seeks court action to hold gala," *Philadelphia Inquirer*, October 13, 1995, Section B, p. 5.
52. "The Barnes Foundation Appeals Court Decision," a Barnes Foundation press release dated November 2, 1995.
53. Quoted in Leonard W. Boasberg, "Court allows Barnes' guests at dinner a feast for eyes, too," *Philadelphia Inquirer*, November 9, 1995, Section B, p. 1.
54. Robert Venturi in conversation with the author, March 2, 2000.
55. Ibid.
56. Ibid.
57. Ibid.
58. Michael Kimmelman, "Barnes Foundation, "A Recluse No More," *New York Times*, November 24, 1995, Section C, p. 22.
59. Quoted in Kate Taylor, "Who was Dr. Albert Barnes?" *Globe and Mail*, February 19, 1994, Section C, p.8.
60. Quoted in Edward J. Sozanski, "Can the Barnes continue art education prescribed by the doctor," *Philadelphia Inquirer*, January 7, 1996, Section L. p. 11.
61. Niara Sudarkasa, Introduction to *The Barnes Bond Connection* (Lincoln University, PA: The Lincoln University Press, 1995), p. 23.

Chapter 17: Neighbors

1. See Nicholas M. Tinari, Jr., Letter to the Editor, *Main Line Times*, December 7, 1995, p. 14. Richard Glanton later claimed that the sign read "Lincoln University Go Home," but photographs support Mr. Tinari's memory of the wording. Another placard read "From L.A. to Pa. Money Buys the Law," a slogan reflecting the former students' opinion that the emergency reversal of the Orphans' Court decision on gala guests in the gallery was a class issue, that is, access to funds secured expert legal services that in the Barnes case, like, in their view, the Simpson murder trial, affected

the outcome. It is asking a lot, however, to think that African Americans would read the sign as other than racist.

2. Anonymous neighbor quoted in Kyle York Spenser, "Neighbors aren't cheering art collection's homecoming," *Philadelphia Inquirer*, October 23, 1995, Section W, p. 1.

3. James L. Crawford, Jr. to Richard H. Glanton, November 14, 1995. A copy of the letter is in the possession of the author.

4. Quoted in Kyle York Spenser, "Barnes links no-tax payment to parking lot," *Philadelphia Inquirer*, October 17, 1995, Section W, p. 1.

5. Nancy Herman to Jane Pepper, August 20, 1996.

6. Quoted in Kyle York Spenser, "An enduring tension part of Barnes legacy," *Philadelphia Inquirer*, November 27, 1995, Section N, p. 4.

7. Peter Kelsen's December 28, 1995 letter is quoted in Beth E. Yanofsky, "Barnes attorney says gallery will defend its right to operate," *Main Line Times*, January 4, 1996, p. 1.

8. *The Barnes Foundation vs. the Township of Lower Merion, the Lower Merion Board of Commissioners, Gloria P. Wolek, Frank Lutz, Kenneth E. Davis, Phyllis L. Zemble, Ora R. Pierce, James J. Prendergast, Alan C. Kessler, Brain D. Rosenthal, Joseph M. Manko, Howard L. West, W. Bruce McConnell III, James S. Ettelson, David A. Sonenshein, Regene H. Silver, Steven Asher and Ina Asher, Robert and Toby Marmon, Walter and Nancy Herman, Arthur Gershkoff, Leonard H. and Beth R. Ginsberg, Mark and Marlene Moster, James Nealon, Lester Schaevitz and Diane Schaevitz, Michael Toaff and Anna Levy-Toaff, and Bruce Schainker*, Civil Action No. 96-CV-0372, United States District Court for the Eastern District of Pennsylvania, January 18, 1996, pp. 11, 15ff, 20, and 23.

9. Quoted in "Art Foundation Sues, Claiming Discrimination," *New York Times*, January 19, 1996. Section A, p. 27.

10. Slapp suits were virtually unheard of before 1970. Since then, tens of thousands of Americans have been sued for speaking out at public hearings or contacting their elected representatives about the alleged misdeeds of corporations or governments and an uncounted number have been silenced by threats of legal action. In the Barnes case, all the neighbor defendants filed motions to dismiss the Foundation's claims. The legal ground on which they took their stand was the so-called *Noerr-Pennington* doctrine, which had originated in anti-trust law and holds that parties petitioning governmental agencies or authorities are protected by the First Amendment regardless of their motives. But since the heart of the Barnes's allegation of racial hostility was based on Robert Marmon's resort to what sounded to Glanton like "code words," Marmon went to considerable lengths in his deposition to explain that to him "carpetbagger" was a political term that meant "someone who comes into a jurisdiction," without "any direct relationship" to it, for the purpose of "personal gain." The management consultant also stressed that the phrase "people" was a "term of art in his profession" referring to the "executive team." See *Barnes vs. the Township of Lower Merion et al.*, Reply Memorandum in Support of the Motion by Defendants, Steven Asher, Ina Asher, Walter Herman, Nancy Herman, Robert Marmon and Toby Marmon, for the Award of Attorneys' Fees and Cost, March 31, 1999. Quotation pp. 21 and 24.

11. Walter Herman, April 2, 2000, in conversation with the author.

12. *Kenneth E. Davis, James S. Ettelson, et al. vs. Richard Glanton et al.*, Civil Action 96-03920, Court of Common Pleas of Montgomery County, March 4, 1996, paragraphs 2, 44, and 45. See also Beth E. Yanofsky, "Barnes dispute escalates, commissioners sue," *Main Line Times*, March 7, 1996, p. 7.

13. Charles A. Frank, III, April 17, 1996, deposition in *Davis vs. Glanton*, p. 232f.

14. Charles A. Frank, III, in conversation with the author, April 25, 2000.

15. Jane R. Eisner, "Poles apart in a remarkable setting," *Philadelphia Inquirer*, March 24, 1996, Section E. p. 5.

16. Richard H. Glanton, Letter to the Editor, *Philadelphia Inquirer*, April 7, 1996, Section E, p. 4.

17. Ibid.

18. Nicholas M. Tinari, Jr. and David H. Weinstein, Letters to the Editor, *Philadelphia Inquirer*, April 14, 1996, Section F, p. 6.

19. *The Barnes Foundation vs. Township of Lower Merion et al.*, Memorandum and Order of Judge Anita B. Brody, June 3, 1996, p. 7.

20. Quoted in Anne Barnard and Leonard W. Boasberg, "U.S. judge rejects Barnes' race suit," *Philadelphia Inquirer*, June 6, 1996, Section A, p. 14. Glanton also expressed dismay that Judge Brody had refused to disqualify herself from the case on the grounds that her daughter was under consideration for a position on a Lower Merion advisory committee. The Foundation's attorney had made the request shortly before she rendered her decision, but Brody informed him that her daughter had withdrawn her name for the unsalaried post for unrelated reasons. Nine days after her ruling, the Barnes trustees petitioned the United States Court of Appeals to remove Brody from the lawsuit because she was a participant in Lower Merion civic life. The Third Circuit judges rejected the request the next month. When counsel to the Foundation tried again in 1997 on the grounds that three township commissioners wrote letters of recommendation in support of her daughter's unsuccessful bid to gain a seat on the board of directors of the Southeastern Pennsylvania Transportation Authority, the U.S. Court of Appeals rejected the request without comment.

21. *The Barnes Foundation vs. Township of Lower Merion et al.*, Memorandum and Order of Judge Anita B. Brody, June 3, 1996, p. 3.

22. Quoted in Anne Barnard, "Barnes will remain open for the summer, *Philadelphia Inquirer*, July 3, 1996, Section B, p. 1.

23. Frank gave his deposition on April 17, 1996. See footnote 13 above. He retired from Mellon Bank on May 31, 1996 and subsequently announced his resignation from the Barnes board of trustees. Soon after Frank's testimony, Lower Merion moved to drop its suit against him. Its counterclaim against the Foundation was filed on June 18, 1996.

24. Quoted in Beth E. Yanofsky, "Glanton extends olive branch; officials wary," *Main Line Times*, July 4, 1996. p. 1.

25. Judge Brody denied the request for final judgment on July 22, 1996 on the grounds that the neighbors failed to overcome the presumption against piecemeal appeals and that the certification they sought would most likely delay the termination of the litigation. See *Barnes Foundation vs. Township of Lower Merion et al.*, Memorandum and Order of Judge Anita B. Brody, July 22, 1996.

26. Quoted in Leonard W. Boasberg, "Barnes is sued by Rome over lost exhibit," *Philadelphia Inquirer*, July 30, 1996, Section C, p. 1.

27. See Michael Janofsky, "Italians Sue The Barnes Because Show Didn't Go to Rome," *New York Times*, July 31, 1996, Section C. p. 1.

28. Quoted in Leonard W. Boasberg, "The turmoil over the Barnes art touches another country," *Philadelphia Inquirer*, October 23, 1995, Section C, p. 7.

29. Blank, Rome, Comisky & McCauley, the law firm that had filed the civil rights complaint on behalf of the Foundation trustees, had pulled out of the federal case on June 18, 1996.

30. Since the zoning hearing board had ruled during closing arguments in June that the validity of an enforcement notice must be determined on the facts as they existed at

the time the notice was issued, the new notice, and the subsequent withdrawal of the original notice, meant that activity on Latch's Lane during the Cézanne show could be considered as evidence.

31. Findings, Opinions & Order in Appeal No. 3393 Before the Zoning Hearing Board of Lower Merion Township, Montgomery County, Pennsylvania, September 3, 1996, p. 11.

32. Quoted in Beth E. Yanofsky, "Parking on-site okayed at Barnes," *Main Line Times*, September 5, 1996, p. 1.

33. Appeal from the Decree September 21, 1995 in the Court of Common Pleas of Montgomery County, Orphans' Court Division, No. 58-788, in re *The Barnes Foundation*, Superior Court of Pennsylvania, September 12, 1996, p. 7.

34. Quoted in Anne Barnard, "Fund-raising affair to be hosted by Barnes," *Philadelphia Inquirer*, September 25, 1996, Section B, p. 4.

35. Report of the Office of Attorney General, as Parens Patriae for Charities, in the Court of Common Pleas of Montgomery County, Orphans' Court Division, No. 58-788, in re *The Barnes Foundation*, August 8, 1997, p. 10.

36. Memorandum Opinion and Order Sur Report of the Office of Attorney General, Judge Stanley R. Ott, Montgomery County Court of Common Pleas, Orphans' Court Division, November 5, 1997, pp. 4 and 6.

37. Richard H. Glanton to Gloria Wolek, October 25, 1996. Quoted in Anne Barnard, "Barnes effort at L. Merion truce flops," *Philadelphia Inquirer*, November 7, 1996, Section B, p. 3.

38. Richard H. Glanton to Gilbert P. High, Jr., November 12, 1996. Quoted in Beth E. Yanofsky, "Barnes tries again for settlement; township wary," *Main Line Times*, November 21, 1996, p. 1.

39. Paul Rosen to Robert Sugarman, November 25, 1996. Quoted in Beth E. Yanofsky, "Lower Merion opposes adding Glanton to case," *Main Line Times*, November 28, 1996, p. 1.

40. By permitting public access to the gallery of approximately 100,000 visitors in 1996, the board said that the Barnes could no longer claim to be primarily an educational institution. It further noted that traffic associated with such visits impacted the neighborhood in ways unlike traffic to and from St. Joseph's and Episcopal and created "severe congestion on the road and hazardous conditions for pedestrians in the area." See Beth E. Yanofsky, "It's a museum says the board," *Main Line Times*, January 2, 1997, p. 4.

41. "The art of compromise," *Philadelphia Inquirer*, December 31, 1996, Section A, p. 14.

42. Quoted in Christina Alex, "Lower Merion wants Barnes to open up financial records," *Main Line Life*, April 3, 1997. p. 7.

43. Quoted in Shannon P. Duffy, "Rome v. Glanton Dismissed," *Legal Intelligencer*, April 16, 1997, p. 1.

44. Quoted in Anne Barnard, "Town: Barnes suit short on proof," *Philadelphia Inquirer*, April 26, 1995, Section B, p, 1.

45. Anne Barnard, "Barnes official took job with her eyes open," *Philadelphia Inquirer*, September 24, 1997, Section B, p. 1.

46. Quoted in Anne Barnard, "Glanton steps down as head of the Barnes Foundation," *Philadelphia Inquirer*, February 10, 1998, Section A, p. 10.

47. Quoted by Cuyler H. Walker in conversation with the author, March 29, 2000.

48. *The Barnes Foundation vs. Township of Lower Merion et al.*, Memorandum and Order of Judge Anita B. Brody, September 26, 1997, p. 28f.

49. Quoted in Anne Barnard, "Agreement is reached for Barnes lot," *Philadelphia Inquirer*, October 9, 1997, Section B, p. 1.
50. A. Leon Higginbotham, Jr., Memorandum to all Counsel, November 11, 1997.
51. Quoted in Rick Henson, "Glanton sent memo on Lincoln house to board," *Philadelphia Inquirer*, February 12, 1998, Section A, p. 8.
52. Quoted in Rick Henson and Anne Barnard, "Glanton steps down as head of the Barnes Foundation," *Philadelphia Inquirer*, February 10, 1998, Section A, p. 10.
53. The spokesperson for the Foundation was A. Bruce Crawley. He was quoted in Rick Henson, Stephanie A. Stanley, and Julia M. Klein, "Barnes Foundation appoints an interim manager," *Philadelphia Inquirer*, February 11, 1998, Section B, p. 1.
54. *Barnes Foundation vs. Township of Lower Merion et al.*, Reply Memorandum in Support of the Motion by Defendants, Steven Asher, Ina Asher, Walter Herman, Nancy Herman, Robert Marmon and Toby Marmon, for Award of Attorneys' Fees and Costs, United States District Court for the Eastern District of Pennsylvania, March 31, 1998, p. 35.
55. "The New Face of The Barnes Foundation," a news release issued by the Foundation and dated April 23, 1998.
56. Quoted in Stephanie A. Stanley, "Barnes vows to regulate crowds," *Philadelphia Inquirer*, April 24, 1998, Section B, p. 4.
57. Quoted in Stephanie A. Stanley, "Judge says Barnes can open in summer," *Philadelphia Inquirer*, August 5, 1998, Section B, pp. 1 and 3.
58. Quoted in Bill Marshall, "Barnes bans disobedient tour bus," *Main Line Times*, September 24, 1998, p. 5.
59. Quoted in Bill Marshall, "Barnes can open all year," *Main Line Times*, August 6, 1998, p. 5.
60. Quoted in Rick Henson, "Barnes trustee makes apology," *Philadelphia Inquirer*, September 9, 1998, Section B, p. 6.
61. A group of advisors from the museum and educational communities who had been meeting with Sudarkasa for nearly a year would soon recommend that any such effort begin with a three-step initiative: the hiring of a tenured chair of fine arts at Lincoln, increasing the faculty within the two-person department that employed neither professor full time and offered only a general survey course in art history along with occasional specialized classes in Chinese, African, and African-American art, and the inauguration of a series of activities and events, including field trips and a campus visit by a practicing artist, that would be designed to generate student interest in art and increase awaresess of job opportunities existing in the museum world where there was a dearth of African Americans and other minorities.
62. The finding by KPMG Peat Marwick was quoted in Rick Henson, "Lincoln University audit finds conflicts of interest," *Philadelphia Inquirer*, June 1, 1998, Section A, p. 1.
63. Glanton and Cliett were investment partners in a Philadelphia cable TV station, although Glanton insisted in a letter to Sadler that they were not business associates during the period that Cliett's company was providing services to the Foundation. The forensic audit, commisioned by the Barnes trustees and undertaken by Deloitte & Touche, found that Cliett billed the Foundation $292,455 in 1996 and 1997.
64. Quoted in Rick Henson, "Glanton pens attack on Lincoln U. president and audit," *Philadelphia Inquirer*, June 12, 1998, Section B, p. 1.
65. Quoted in Angela Couloumbis, "Lincoln president: Accusations untrue," *Philadelphia Inquirer*, July 19, 1998, Section B, p. 1.
66. Quoted in Bill Marshall, "Glanton wants Bradford to resign," *Main Line Times*, August 27, 1998, p. 1.

67. *Barnes Foundation vs. Township of Lower Merion et al.*, Settlement Agreement Memorandum of Understanding of Judge Ronald L. Buckwalter, October 1, 1998, p. 4.
68. Quoted in L. Stuart Ditzen, "Besieged Lincoln president sues school's ex-attorney," *Philadelphia Inquirer*, October 2, 1998, Section B, pp. 1 and 3.
69. Quoted in Rick Henson, "Pa. probe assails Lincoln U. practices," *Philadelphia Inquirer*, September 10, 1998, Section A. pp. 1 and 16.
70. Quoted in Andrew Rice, "L. Merion raises visitor cap for Barnes," *Philadelphia Inquirer*, November 20 1998, Section B, p. 1.
71. Richard H. Glanton to Paul R. Rosen, May 7, 1999. Quoted in Stephanie A. Stanley, "Commissioners' lawsuit against Glanton settled," *Philadelphia Inquirer*, May 11, 1999, Section B, p. 2.
72. Ibid., p. 1.
73. Kimberly Camp, June 28, 2000, in conversation with the author. By 2001, expenses were $3 million a year, and still far greater than the Barnes Foundation could bear without going bankrupt.
74. Camp is quoted in Bill Marshall, "CEO turns the page at Barnes," *Main Line Times*, September 30, 1999, p. 1. The statement by Marvin Garfinkel, attorney for the de Mazia trustees, was quoted in Stephanie A. Stanley, "Barnes wins grant from old supporter," *Philadelphia Inquirer*, August 4, 1999, Section B, p. 2.
75. See Nicholas King to Earle Bradford, Memorandum re "Student Report Requested by Peter Kelsen," dated June 30, 1998, in possession of the author. King reported that there were sixty-four students enrolled in arboretum classes for 1997-98. The executive director of the Barnes Foundation refused the author's request for specific enrollment numbers for 1998-99 and 1999-2000.
76. Frederick Osborne, February 16, 2000, in conversation with the author.
77. Kimberly Camp, June 28, 2000, in conversation with the author.
78. The initial phase of the project will take several years and produce a computerized database listing the some 6,500 objects in the collection, as well as providing visual documentation. Emily Croll, director of the effort, puts the total number of objects at closer to 8,000 if household furnishings in Merion and at Ker-Feal are included in the count. See Edward J. Sozanski, "First Barnes inventory begun," *Philadelphia Inquirer*, April 20, 2003, Section H, p. 11.
79. Bernard C. Watson, June 19, 2000, in conversation with the author.
80. *Barnes Foundation vs. Township of Lower Merion et al.*, Memorandum of Justice Ronald L. Buckwalter, United States District Court for the Eastern District of Pennsylvania, November 24, 1999, pp. 1, 9, 6, and 10.
81. *Barnes Foundation vs. Township of Lower Merion et al.*, Brief for Appellants, United States Court for the Third Circuit, June 30, 2000, p. 44.
82. Quoted in Peter Dobrin, Patricia Horn, and Don Steinberg, "Big money lining up to support the Barnes," *Philadelphia Inquirer*, September 29, 2002, Section A, p. 18.
83. Declaration of Bernard C. Watson in the Court of Common Pleas of Montgomery County, Orphans' Court Division, No. 58-788, in re *The Barnes Foundation*, September 12, 2002, paragraphs 16 and 5.
84. In addition to Bernard Watson and Jeff Donaldson, the board now included Stephen J. Harmelin, the managing partner of Dilworth Paxon, Jacqueline F. Allen, a judge on the Philadelphia Court of Common Pleas, and Stephanie Bell-Rose, president of the Goldman Sachs Foundation.
85. Declaration of Bernard C. Watson in the Court of Common Pleas of Montgomery County, Orphans' Court Division, No. 58-788, in re *The Barnes Foundation*, September 12, 2002, paragraphs 9, 8, and 11.

86. "Art of the deal," *Philadelphia Inquirer*, September 26, 2002, Section A, p. 24 and "Why not let Barnes move to Center City?," *Main Line Times*, October 3, 2002, p. 18.

87. See Ralph Blumenthal, "Small University In Battle for Control Of Billions in Art," *New York Times*, October 30 2002, Section E, p. 1.

88. Quoted in Jim McCaffrey, "Barnes works to minimize Lincoln U role," *Main Line Times*, November 28, 2002, p. 7.

89. Quoted in Patricia Horn, "NAACP Chief crusades against Barnes plans," Philadelphia Inquirer, May 27, 2003, Section B, p. 1. Julian Bond had first raised his concerns in a letter to the heads of the Pew, Lenfest, and Annenberg foundations in January 2003.

90. Adrienne G. Rhone, "Founder's desires must be observed," *Philadelphia Inquirer*, December 16, 2002, Section A, p. 19.

91. Quoted in Patricia Horn, "Students: Don't move Barnes art," *Philadelphia Inquirer*, October 11, 2002, Section B, p. 1.

92. Petition of the Barnes Foundation for Leave to File An Amended Petition to Amend Its Charter and Bylaws in the Court of Common Pleas of Montgomery County, Orphans' Court Division, No. 58-788, in re *The Barnes Foundation*, June 5, 2003, Exhibit E (Indentures as Amended), pp. 5 and 16, and Exhibit D (Bylaws), p. 2.

93. The institutions originally specified by Barnes included the University of Pennsylvania, Temple University, Bryn Mawr College, Haverford College, Swarthmore College, and the Pennsylvania Academy of Fine Arts.

Epilogue

1. Chris Abbinante, "Protecting 'Donor Intent' in Charitable Foundations: Wayward Trusteeship and the Barnes Foundation," *University of Pennsylvania Law Review*, vol. 145, no. 3 (January 1997), p. 684.

2. The compromise decision retained Sir William's prohibition in the case of delicate pieces, such as tapestries, and restricted loans to public collections.

3. Bylaws of the Barnes Foundation, Article IX (Indenture of Trust of December 6, 1922), paragraph 11.

4. The fourth version of *The Card Players* is owned by the Metropolitan Museum of Art in New York.

Index

Breinigsville, PA USA
29 March 2010
235140BV00002B/4/P